The way we build now
form, scale and technique

The way we build now
form, scale and technique

Andrew Orton

Illustrated by
Michael L.C. Ong RIBA, APAM

SPON PRESS
Taylor & Francis Group

London and New York

First published by E & FN Spon 1988
Reprinted 1991, 1993, 1994

Reprinted by Spon Press 2001
11 New Fetter Lane, London EC4P 4EE

Spon Press is an imprint of the Taylor & Francis Group

© 1988 Andrew Orton

Printed in Great Britain by St Edmundsbury Press Ltd,
Bury St Edmunds, Suffolk

ISBN 0 419 15780 8

British Library Cataloguing in Publication Data
Orton, Andrew
        The way we build now: form, scale and technique.
        1. Building
        I. Title
        690   TH145
ISBN 0 419 157870 8

Contents

Acknowledgements

A number of people have helped in the task of producing this book and their help is gratefully acknowledged. The drawings in chapter two were done by Barrie Doggett. The drawings in chapters three and four and the axonometric detail drawings in the remaining chapters were done by Peter O'Malley. All other drawings in the book, including the main axonometric drawings, were done by Michael L.C. Ong. Typing was speedily carried out by Josie Murphy and Margaret Sanders. Photo reductions were done by Ian Pope and photographic processing was done by David Buss. The book design is by Theresa Orton.

Neil Taylor, Idris Price and Nigel James of Gifford and Partners read and commented on chapters one and four; Brian Forster of Ove Arup and Partners supplied detailed comments on chapter two as did Roger Davies; Alan Stevens of Gifford Building Services and Roy Owen read and commented on chapter three. Ward Architectural Systems supplied information for chapter three. The help afforded by all these people and by the designers of the buildings included in chapters five to twelve is gratefully acknowledged. With only one exception, the descriptions and drawings of the buildings selected were checked for accuracy by one member and, in most cases, by two members of the original design team. This does not mean that they necessarily concur with the views expressed nor even that a check such as this can guarantee that errors are not still present, although, if errors do exist, they are not expected to be significant ones. A very large number of sources have been consulted and some of these are given in the references. The sources are too numerous to list in their entirety but the assistance provided is duly acknowledged. Finally I should like to record the valuable contributions, on general matters, made by Aled Williams, Professor Paul Snowden, Dr Paul Crichton, Philip Woodfine, Martin Crane, Richard Crane, Clara Williams, Harriet Williams, Noel MacDonald and James MacDonald.

Introduction

In this book, an attempt is made to give a perspective on the practice of building design in the industrial economies. The aim is to see how buildings have been designed, within the context of their time and place, and, in particular, how the scale and type of use, as well as known physical principles and building techniques, affect the final form of the building. The book starts with a review of some of the fundamental ideas in building technology, which are selected on the basis that they are what everyone involved in building design might be expected to know. The book then looks at a panorama of buildings completed over the last twenty-five years, in order to show how constructional materials have been used over the complete range of the building scale, how principles have been applied in practice and what sidelight this throws on the various building types and their methods of design.

In as much as the book is about building design, it is linked to architecture but the book does not consider, except in an incidental way, those aspects of the design to do with history, economics, planning, art or society at large, subjects which can be assumed, in all cases, to have at least a superficial connection with the ideas which form the basis of a contemporary architecture. A major theme of the book concerns the use of building materials. For the building designer, materials are of paramount importance

and, inseparable from the design concept for the building, although this aspect is often rather poorly revealed in drawings. The book limits itself to discussion of structural or semi-structural materials and to the technical properties of these materials rather than to their other more evocative qualities, to do with texture, scale, colour and so on, which are taken for granted.

The first part of the book, chapters one to four, looks at some principles relevant to the selection of materials, to structural design and to cladding of buildings. It also looks at some general principles concerned with the heating, cooling, ventilation, lighting, acoustics and fire safety of buildings. This part of the book is intended to serve as a systematic reference for some of the ideas discussed in the second part of the book, as well as being a short, unified treatment in its own right. The fundamental properties of materials are introduced and the effect these material properties have on the designer's selection and use of materials in building is pointed out. Although there is a continual evolution in the use of building materials, the rate of change is slow and those materials which were important twenty-five years and more ago, for example masonry, concrete, wood, steel, glass and even many plastics, are just as important today. This state of affairs looks set to continue, whatever new combinations of materials may arise, because of the building industry's need for materials in bulk that are cheap, cheap anyway compared to those in manufacturing industries. Nevertheless there continue to be developments in the properties and methods of use of the existing building materials as well as in applications of new materials. Developments in glass, rigid plastics and fabrics over the last twenty-five years have already led to new kinds of architecture, when these materials have met a specific need.

The second part of the book, chapters five to twelve, looks at a selection of buildings designed over the last quarter century in order to illustrate some of the various kinds of building in use and to provide examples of design in practice. These chapters consider respectively houses and community buildings, office buildings, public buildings, residential buildings, highly-serviced buildings, sports and warehouse buildings, space structure buildings and high-rise buildings. The categories are somewhat arbitrary and can overlap. However over the complete range of buildings considered there is a clear evolution in the forms and materials used, corresponding to the different purposes and scale of the buildings. The buildings considered in chapters five to nine are categorized by type of use; in those buildings considered in chapters ten to twelve, structural considerations have a more dominant effect on the overall form, because of an increase in scale, either in the distance spanned or in the height to which the building rises. These buildings are examined in the spirit of an investigation but are intended to throw light on current practice rather than to constitute a history as such. All these buildings have been chosen to make up a balanced range, not only of different types of use, but of different materials and forms, at the various scales. With only one exception, the buildings are all completed buildings, that is buildings that have been both designed and built. An effort has been made to select buildings, well-known or not, which have simple geometries and typical or interesting forms or uses of material. They are not particularly selected for their merits as architecture. The designs are offered as representative examples of good practice, which are interesting in themselves and from which something can be learned, rather than as designs that are satisfactory in all respects. But buildings should not be expected to be without their faults. Perfectionist attitudes in criticism are harmful, in as much as they dismiss the difficulties and thus fail to confront the design problem in its entirety. The description and discussion of the buildings is brief but further published information about the buildings, where available, is given in a list of references at the back of the book.

One thread running through both parts of the book is the idea of scale, which affects the way buildings look, as well as some of the technical solutions adopted. It is hoped that a sufficiently large number of examples are presented in the second part of the book so that the ways in which changes of physical scale fundamentally alter the nature of the design can emerge. Although the size of building continually increases, it still does not match the increase in scale of operations or the increase in scale of most lives lived. As examples might be instanced the increase in speed and distances of travel or the enormous increases in work output made possible by office or industrial machinery and equipment. The resulting increased traffic in operations and services, together with centralisation and rationalisation, seems to lead to requirements for larger facilities, anyway for some important building types. In spite of countercurrents, these new, larger types of building look here to stay. As for the effects of this on building design, a good starting point is the remark by Valéry: 'In the physical world, one cannot increase the size or quantity of anything without changing its quality; similar figures exist only in pure geometry'. Questions about scale crop up in discussion of high-rise buildings, of which there are a number in this book, but also in connection with facilities such as those provided for travel, shopping, health care and housing. Knowing the physical size of things is a discipline imposed by drawing and one common area for everyone engaged in design. But orders of magnitude may also be usefully applied to more abstract quantities, such as amounts of heat, light or force, and, in this book, wherever possible, an attempt has been made to supply these figures too.

In order to maintain an overall view, subject matter in the book has been condensed as far as possible. A small amount of background knowledge about buildings has been assumed. Many of the terms referred to in the second part of the book are introduced in the first part, although such cross-referencing is incomplete. For further reading, reference should be made to some of the standard texts, a selection of which are given in the bibliography at the back of the book.

Notes on Chapters

Chapter one is a survey and comparison of some important technical properties of structural and semi-structural building materials. It includes a brief introduction to some mechanical properties of materials, a survey of the major construction materials and tables, showing properties and uses. The survey of materials splits them into the general categories of masonry, cement and concrete, metals, wood, plastics, fabrics and glass. Within the general categories of cement and concrete, metals, wood and plastics, one basic type is selected for outline examination with notes made of its important properties from the designer's point of view, these basic types being, respectively, normal weight reinforced concrete, construction grades of low carbon steel, common softwoods and glass-reinforced polyesters. Notes about variants on these basic types are provided afterwards. There are two types of table in this chapter. The first type of table gives a list of typical properties of materials within each general category, and includes one table which is used to compare materials from the different categories. All values given are approximate guides only and most useful for purposes of comparison. Note that the strengths of materials given are ultimate breaking strengths not working stresses; working stresses are derived by dividing the ultimate strengths by a factor of safety. The second type of table shows, usually in a very simplified form, some of the common ways in which these materials are used, either as building elements or as complete building structures. These tables give approximate proportions of the elements in typical applications, for example span to depth ratios. Mostly the proportions depend on the scale of the application but as a general and approximate rule, these proportions can be assumed to be valid over the given range of dimensions. In large degree, such proportional rules and range of spans depend on history, economics and recent experience in the use of the materials rather than on simple physical properties such as weight, strength or elasticity, although these also play a part and set limits. Such simple rules-of-thumb leave out many of the factors which would need to be considered in a final analysis, including the loads and the acceptable performance, and may be misleading in some cases. Nevertheless the figures can give useful orders of magnitude and may be used for preliminary design depending on the circumstances and accuracy required. The detailed calculation of structural elements is an analytical check, rather than a part of the preliminary design, which is the concern here. With increasing pressure for more economic use of material, as well as labour and plant, it seems likely that calculations will need to become ever more sophisticated to ensure that a proper factor of safety exists under all conditions with the smaller sizes that economy demands. But in these circumstances the need for first approximations, for iterative refinement, is just as important. Sizing of elements based on proportional rules can be checked against other approximate methods, including those which take the actual loadings into account, for example those methods given in chapter two. Although qualifications are made on the use of these tables, the whole topic of the circumstances in which the figures would be exact has not been broached and, in general, would not be helpful given the many factors involved and the lack of precise information available at preliminary design stage, when they are expected to be used. One column in each of the second type of table gives a list of some factors which may be critical in the sizing of elements. Note that these are factors to do with the structural performance and not with other general considerations. In some tables this same column also contains general remarks.

Chapter two gives an outline account of some topics in the structural design of buildings. Formulae are introduced more as a shorthand way of presenting basic relationships than as a means of achieving accurate numerical answers. However the formulae may be used for preliminary assessments. Reasonably correct answers will depend on a good understanding of the particular problem and an appropriate choice of figures for use in the formulae. The chapter includes tables which give some information about estimating forces and bending moments in elements, floor structures and complete frames under vertical and horizontal loads and ways of sizing common structural elements. The charts may be used for preliminary work using the calculated forces and the given allowable stresses and deflections. Some formulae give exact answers rather than the approximations which are the general rule. However, once again, these tables are primarily intended to demonstrate the action of frames and elements under load and to give orders of magnitude rather than to give good numerical answers. If the tables are used for preliminary design the answers that are given may be checked against the proportional rules and dimensions given in chapter one. Note that calculations are based on the use of working loads, rather than ultimate loads, and, in general, are based on the use of allowable stresses and deflections, rather than ultimate stresses, although figures for ultimate stress are sometimes contained in the formulae.

Chapter three is an outline of some of those topics and physical principles which have a bearing on the type of enclosure selected for the building and the environmental conditions within the building. It includes brief discussion on issues to do with humidity, condensation, heating, cooling, ventilation, lighting and acoustics. Like the rest of the book, this chapter is chiefly concerned with those elements of the building which have an important physical presence, such as windows, cladding elements, suspended ceilings, mechanical ducts and plantrooms. Plumbing, waste disposal, telecommunications, security and alarm systems are not considered. Formulae are included in the chapter but, as before, more for their economy in presenting information than for their value in providing accurate numerical answers. However they can be used for general estimates in combination with appropriate data.

Chapter four concerns a subject which has an important influence on the form and choice of building materials, namely fire and the concepts established to provide fire safety. Some formulae which help to quantify some effects of fire are included, although such work on quantification is still at an early stage. The particular figures given are indicative only.

Both the international system of units, or SI system, and the old imperial or English system of units are used. In fact the imperial system of units is now largely confined to the United States and the use of these units in this book is therefore guided by American practice. The SI system is treated as the principal system, to which most countries are expected to convert in due course, with the eqivalent American unit given alongside. There are exceptions to this: for those topics connected with lighting and acoustics, but not thermodynamics or structural mechanics, only SI units are used as the older units have become obsolete; and in the second part of the book, the buildings looked at have been left in the units that they were originally designed in, be these inches, feet, pounds, tons or millimetres, metres, newtons, tonnes and so on. Metric equivalents of buildings designed in imperial units are given in the descriptions. Strictly speaking pounds, tons and tonnes, because they are used as units of force, should be written as pounds force, tons force or tonnes force but in this book are kept in their simple, colloquial form, without use of the word 'force'. Any reference in the book to tons. refers to the American ton equal to 2000lb and not to the long, English ton which is equal to 2240lb and is slightly greater than the metric tonne. Coversion factors to change from SI to imperial units are given in the right hand column of some tables in chapter one and in the appendix. In other charts in chapter one, both systems of unit are used.

When the dimensions of an element in section are provided, the width is given first, followed by the depth, as in 'two by four' for a piece of timber. The only exception is for rolled steel sections in which, by convention, the depth of the section is given first followed by the width and/or weight of the section in kg per metre run or lb per foot run. This is usually preceded by the shape designation of the section. Unless stated to the contrary, a given width, depth or diameter refers to the overall or outside dimension. Elements or buildings said to be in concrete are assumed to be reinforced in some way, unless stated to the contrary, this being the way concrete is almost invariably used. Algebraic symbols used in the first part of this book, chapters one to four, are, where possible, in standard notation. The definition and units of each symbol are only given once within each chapter, at its first mention in the chapter. In general English rather than American usage and spelling have been adopted in the book, although concessions are made to local usages in the second part of the book. For technical words, either the normal English or American words have been adopted, whichever seems clearer. Where there is a choice, the alternative word is usually given in brackets at its first occurrence in each chapter or building description. A possible source of confusion between normal English and American usage is in the naming of floors. The floor above ground level is known as the first floor in English usage but the second floor in American usage. To avoid the confusion, in this book, the ground floor is taken as level one, that above referred to as level two and so on. Credits for the buildings looked at in the second part of the book are generally only given for the architects and structural engineer as this book is mainly concerned with the ideas that these two professionals bring to the design.

Chapter One

Building Materials

Those properties of matter which are of most interest in materials used for the structure and cladding of buildings are their cost, their mechanical properties, including their weight, their thermal, acoustic and optical properties, their dimensional stability and durability and their resistance to fire. Other important properties connected with the basic properties of the bulk material are the ease of manufacture and ease of working of the material, the corrosion and chemical resistance and the texture and appearance of the material. Materials may be split up into: *metals and their alloys,* which generally are crystalline, that is have atoms which are packed together in space in regular, repeating arrangements; *polymers* or *plastics* which consist of complex 'chain' molecules; *ceramics,* which are inorganic non-metals and which, generally, are crystalline; *glasses,* which generally are non-crystalline, inorganic non-metals but can be metallic too; and *composites,* which consist of a matrix material with strengthening elements to give the composite stiffness and strength; both natural and artificial composites are available. The most important *mechanical properties* of building materials are their weight, tensile strength, yield strength, shear strength, compressive strength, ductility, toughness, impact resistance, fatigue resistance, elasticity and creep under load. Other important mechanical properties are their strain capacity and their resistance to rain and moisture penetration. All quoted properties of materials implicitly refer to those values given by standard tests and, in many cases, the full details of the test need to be known in order to assess the material properly. Some properties, for example the compressive strength of concrete, depend on the way the test is done and may reflect other, more fundamental properties.

PROPERTIES OF MATERIALS

Mechanical Properties

The *tensile strength* of a bar, σ_{TS}, is the stress, calculated as force divided by the original area of the bar, which causes fracture of the bar in tension. The *yield stress,* σ_y, is the stress at the yield point; the yield point is the point at which plastic flow of the material begins to occur. Below the yield point the material is *elastic* and is able to recover its original shape when the load is removed. Above this point the material is said to be *plastic* and undergoes a permanent deformation, which remains after the load is removed. Some materials do not have a properly defined yield point and instead a *proof stress* is used which is equal to the stress when the strain in the material has some fixed value, normally 0.1% or 0.2%. The yield stress and proof stresses are about two-thirds of the tensile strength of the material. If a material is tested in bending then the calculated tensile stress at which fracture of the material occurs is known as the *modulus of rupture*. In general the modulus of rupture is close to but different from the tensile strength of the material. Stress in a material causes strain. The strain in a uniform bar is equal to its change in length over its original length. For many materials in the normal working range of stress, the stress is proportional to the strain and the material is then said to be *linear-elastic*. In practice many materials exhibit plastic behaviour, in which permanent deformations occur, as well as elastic behaviour. The *modulus of elasticity* of a material is the ratio of stress to strain and is low if the material has a large stretch under load. For a linear-elastic material, the modulus of elasticity is constant up to a point just below the yield point but, above this, large deformations or strains may occur with only small or no increases of stress. The modulus of elasticity is needed to calculate deflection, although a slightly different value of the modulus may be used to calculate deflection due to bending to that used to calculate the extension of a bar in tension, for example.

A property of a material which may be bracketed with its modulus of elasticity is its creep. *Creep* is the slow, continuing deformation of a material with time under a constant load and may be contrasted with the instantaneous deflection of the load when it is first applied. For a linear-elastic material in the normal working range of stress, this instantaneous deflection is that calculated using the modulus of elasticity. One simple way of measuring the effects of creep is to use the creep factor which is the ratio of the strain in the material due to creep to that due to the instantaneous elastic strain. The creep rate increases with temperature. At ambient temperatures most metals used in building have insignificant creep deflection. By contrast, concrete and plastics have significant creep deflections at room temperatures which must be taken into account. As well as those movements due to the application of load,

movements in materials may also take place due to curing and stabilisation, loss of volatile elements, changes in moisture content or in temperature. These movements may be split up into *reversible movements*, such as those generally associated with temperature movements, and *irreversible movements*, such as those generally associated with curing of the material, for example shrinkage. A material which experiences only small or negligible movements with time, except those due to an applied load, is said to be *dimensionally stable*.

The *ductility* of a bar in tension is its percentage increase in length at fracture over its original length before loading. Materials with high ductility, such as polythene or mild steel, are said to be *ductile materials*, while materials with low ductility, such as glass, are said to be *brittle materials*. A property of a material associated with brittleness is the *strain capacity* of the material. A material with a low strain capacity, such as glass or concrete, will crack when the strain in the material reaches a relatively low value, while a material with a high strain capacity, such as aluminium, will not crack or fail even when the strain is high. Some materials such as plastics, cement pastes and concrete become more brittle with time and have decreasing strain capacity which may lead to cracking and loss of strength or resistance to rain penetration. Another property which is related to brittleness is toughness. The *toughness* of a material is the energy absorbed in making a unit area of a crack in the material. It is an indication of how easily cracks can spread in that material. For example copper or aluminium have high toughness while glass, in which cracks spread very easily, has low toughness. Closely related to toughness is fracture toughness. The *fracture toughness* of a material gives a direct indication of how likely it is that the material will fail by fast fracture and, more specifically, what sizes of defects may be tolerated in the material when it is in service; high values of fracture toughness indicate good resistance to failure. Fast fracture is a failure of a material in a brittle manner, in which existing but small, perhaps almost invisible, cracks in the material suddenly increase in size, usually causing a complete and sudden failure of the material, in a brittle manner, at stresses well below the yield strength of the material. For example,

glass fails by fast fracture at room temperatures. Materials of high toughness generally have high fracture toughness but note that some materials, such as plastics, although reasonably tough have poor fracture toughness because of the effect of a low modulus of elasticity. As well as glass, some types of steel can fail in a brittle manner, if at a sufficiently low temperature. Small defects are always present in materials but only constitute a hazard if they are able to increase in size. A material with a low fracture toughness can be safe if the defects are small.

One way in which cracks could increase in size is through fatigue. *Fatigue* can occur when a material is given repeated cycles of stress, that is the material undergoes a fluctuating stress, which, for example, may change from tension to compression. In some materials if the working stresses, which fluctuate, are kept below a certain value then fatigue is found not to occur over the normal life time of the material. The *fatigue ratio* is the ratio of this stress to the tensile strength of the material. If fatigue does occur then small cracks in the material will slowly increase in size and may be the cause of failure of the material by a fast fracture when the crack reaches a certain critical size. Whether fast fracture occurs depends on the fracture toughness of the material at that temperature and the stress in the material. In building, only in a few cases are materials likely to be prone to fatigue failure because, in general, the number of cycles of stress which building elements undergo is small. The choice of a building material may involve consideration of a large number of general properties, and other technical properties as well as the mechanical properties of the material. For purposes of comparison Table 1.1 lists some of the relevant properties for one material in each of the main classes of building materials. The values given are indicative only but serve to illustrate some of the fundamental differences in behaviour of the materials in each class.

MASONRY

Introduction

The use of masonry is one of the oldest and most widely used methods of construction. Masonry units may be made from a variety of materials including burned clay, unburned clay or adobe, calcium silicate, gypsum, stone, concrete and glass. Structural masonry is generally made with clay or concrete units. Traditionally masonry has been used in great thicknesses to provide stability and to make up for its lack of tensile strength. However, in modern practice, masonry walls are thinner and therefore require greater tensile strength to achieve stability. Tensile strength can be provided by reinforcement or by prestressing or, to a smaller extent, by strong mortars. Buildings in earthquake areas, and sometimes high rise buildings not in earthquake areas, use reinforced masonry as a general method of construction. The reinforcement is laid in the bed joints or grouted into cavities or other voids. However, in general use, masonry is unreinforced except over small areas where the reinforcement can prevent visible cracking. Table 1.2 gives a comparison of the properties of some common types of masonry. Table 1.8 illustrates some of the forms in which masonry has been built, either as individual elements or as complete structures, and lists typical sizes used.

Characteristics of Masonry

Important general characteristics of masonry and masonry structures compared to other building materials and structures are as follows:

Masonry has very low or non-existent flexural and tensile strength, together with high compressive strength. This explains the use of funicular shapes, that is shapes which will eliminate bending for any particular pattern of loads. Arch, column and surface shapes can be made funicular, the object being to ensure that, as far as possible, any section through any part of the structure is in compression over the whole of the section area, whatever the applied load. Reinforcement can be used to overcome the weakness in tension or, alternatively, prestressing may be used to prevent tension occurring at all.

Because unreinforced masonry lacks flexural strength and is prone to failure by buckling, it requires frequent lateral support from horizontal or vertical elements such as floors, walls or piers. Masonry elements need to have certain proportions, for example maximum proportions of height to thickness, to prevent the occurrence of buckling.

The high compressive strength of masonry and the need for stability explain the use of high multi-storey load bearing masonry with cellular arrangements in plan.

Masonry is brittle and fails in a sudden manner.

Masonry is anisotropic, that is, it has different properties in different directions. The flexural strength of masonry perpendicular to the bed joints is approximately three times that parallel to them, for example, and explains the preference for vertical lateral supports where the masonry is put into bending.

The weight of masonry materials, and other weights on it, generally increase the stability of accurately constructed masonry against lateral or uplift forces. However, the heavier the masonry, the less efficient it is as an insulating material and the slower it is to lay.

Workmanship has a large effect on the strength and stability of the finished masonry building.

Many kinds of masonry units are available. Clay, aggregates, and other materials used for brick and blockwork are widely available in many parts of the world. In addition, the facilities required for the manufacture of masonry units do not necessarily require large investment. Only moderate amounts of energy are required to produce masonry units.

Masonry in general has excellent fire resistance and is non-combustible.

Masonry units can usually be cut and shaped on site without undue difficulty but at some cost.

Masonry in straight lengths is fast to lay and, therefore, can be economic. Internal or external corners need to be built straight and plumb and this requirement increases the time and cost of construction.

Masonry units can give a variety of scale and textures to buildings.

The jointing, or bonding, of masonry units is easily accomplished and this makes for great flexibility in plan and elevation. For the same reason masonry buildings are easy to demolish or adapt for changes in use.

Masonry cannot be laid in cold weather because of possible frost damage to the mortar while it is curing. Strong mortars give greater protection against frost but, in the finished state, are more likely to allow the appearance of visible cracks than a weaker mortar mix.

Masonry units are porous, that is, contain voids. However, the permeability of masonry to fluids is variable depending on how much linking exists between the voids. Most masonry units are porous to some degree, going through cycles of wetting and drying.

Clay Bricks

Clay bricks are usually made in sizes that are convenient to handle on site and to shape and fire at the brickworks. Their size gives a small scale pattern to brickwork elements such as walls and columns. Clay brick is available in an enormous range of colours and textures, may be used with a variety of mortars and has a wide range of compressive strengths. Clay brickwork is extremely durable although the bricks can suffer damage from frost, chemical attack by sulphates and other soluble salts. In all these cases, water is required before damage can occur; in general, brickwork that is not left saturated for any length of time will not deteriorate. Movement in brickwork is caused by changes in temperature and moisture content and, as brickwork is weak in tension, this can cause cracking unless there are sufficient movement joints. Clay bricks expand after firing as they take up moisture from the atmosphere and should not be used until about 15 days after firing. Various types of clay brick are available. Common bricks are for general use, facing bricks are used where the masonry requires a good looking, textured surface. Perforated and hollow clay bricks and blocks are available which save weight and in some cases allow grouting of reinforcement into the voids.

Calcium Silicate Bricks

These bricks are made from lime and silica sand and are often known as sand lime or flint lime bricks. They do not exist in very high strength units. After curing, the bricks shrink slightly and are better used with mortars able to accept this shrinkage. Unlike clay bricks they do not contain harmful salts and thus are not liable to chemical attack in this way.

Concrete Bricks

These bricks are generally made of dense concrete but in the same sizes as clay bricks. These bricks shrink slightly after curing.

Dense Concrete Blocks

These blocks are made of dense concrete but are very much larger than concrete bricks, typically twice as long and twice as high. The greater height of the block gives greater compressive strength to a wall made of block than one of brick. In addition, block walls can be built faster and therefore more cheaply than brick walls. The blocks are made solid or with voids. The voids may be filled with steel and concrete to increase tensile strength or with insulation to save energy.

Aerated Concrete Blocks

These blocks are made of light aerated concrete and provide higher insulation and have lower compressive strength than dense concrete blocks. They are also faster to lay and easier to cut than dense concrete blocks.

Natural Stone

A very large number of natural stones have the durability and strength to be used in masonry walls. However, buying and laying stone tends to be more expensive than is the case with manufactured masonry units.

CEMENT AND CONCRETE

Introduction

An enormous amount is known about cement and concrete as a result of research programmes and its use in buildings and bridges. Hence, in spite of its discontinuous and fissured nature as a hardened material, a reliable finished product can be obtained in concrete with reasonable care in mixing and forming. The basis of modern production of elements in cement and concrete is hydraulic cement powder, one of the most versatile binders known. About 950 million tonnes of cement powder is produced each year worldwide, of which approximately 185 million tonnes is produced in Western Europe and 70 million in the United States. Concretes can vary greatly in their composition but those in general use may be classified either as high strength concrete, normalweight concrete, lightweight concrete, no-fines concrete, aerated concrete, sprayed concrete and fibre reinforced cements and concretes. Other concretes are available for particular purposes. Overwhelmingly use is made of Portland or blended Portland cement but other cements are used in special circumstances. Concrete may be used unreinforced, reinforced with steel or fibres or prestressed. Another important distinction is by method of production between cast-in-place concrete, which is poured into its final position on site, and precast concrete, which is poured and cured under controlled conditions in a factory and must then be transported to site. Concrete elements can also be precast on site for lifting into their final position by crane. Methods are available for continuous casting of concrete, both vertically and horizontally. For example, vertical slipform techniques are commonly used in the building of tower structures.

Normalweight Structural Concrete

The basic components of concrete are coarse and fine aggregate, cement powder and water; admixtures are occasionally added in too. Most often the fine aggregate is a sand. The quantities of aggregates, cements or admixtures used may be varied to suit particular circumstances. A typical hardened and compacted concrete is a two-phase material with between 60% and 75% of coarse and fine aggregate, which should be inert filler material, an important constituent, and between 25% and 40% of hardened cement paste, which is the binder formed from the reaction of water and cement powder known as hydration. Voids of free water and air occupy between one and ten per cent of the volume of the mix and have a major influence on the strength and associated properties of the hardened mix; the number of voids, that is the porosity of the concrete depends greatly on the mix quantities and the compaction of this mix, although the permeability of the concrete depends not only on the porosity but also on the size, distribution and especially the continuity of the pores. A well-compacted mix would contain about 2% of voids.

The type of concrete mix and the properties of the hardened concrete may be altered by varying the proportions of the constituents, by altering the type of cement and aggregates and by the use of admixtures. By contrast, the cost of the mix is substantially dependent only on the amount of cement powder used. The aggregates must be strong and durable materials in order to take the applied loads and must not react chemically with the cement paste. Aggregates help to reduce the volume changes in the concrete due to shrinkage or temperature changes. Aggregates can be selected in order to provide a concrete with properties such as low weight, low shrinkage, high thermal insulation, good fire resistance.

Various kinds of cement are available, for example, those having rapid hardening properties or those giving resistance to chemical attack, such as sulphates in the soil. Blended cements are also available giving low heat output during the curing period of concrete; they are used in large volume pours. The blended cements consist of mixtures of Portland cement and carefully graded waste materials such as ground blastfurnace slag, pozzolanas and pulverised fuel ash. The waste material is either mixed with cement at the cement factory or included when the final concrete mix is made. They may replace up to about 70% of the Portland cement which would have been required.

The mix proportions of the concrete, and admixtures, will generally control the strength, permeability, frost resistance and resistance to chemical attack. In particular, the strength of the hardened concrete is very dependent on the water to cement ratio. A typical value of this ratio is about 0.5 by weight. An increase in the value of this ratio would produce a concrete with more voids giving lower compressive strength. A large number of properties, such as tensile strength, durability, chemical resistance and density, which helps to give impermeability, are related to the compressive strength of concrete so that this property is the one used as a convenient indicator for quality control. The aggregates and mix proportions can be controlled to provide the required workability of the wet concrete during placement. For example, mixes can be made suitable for pumping; a typical pump mix may have a so-called slump value of 75mm (3in). A high slump value indicates good workability. Admixtures are available to produce so-called fluid concrete having a slump value of at least 150 mm (6in). Admixtures are also available to retard the setting of the wet concrete and this can be used in hot weather to prevent a premature set or where an exposed aggregate finish is required and the partially set cement paste on the face of the concrete may be washed off and brushed to expose the aggregate. Table 1.3 gives a comparison of the properties of some typical concretes and hardened cement pastes. Table 1.9 illustrates some of the forms which concrete has taken, either as individual elements or as complete structures, and lists typical sizes used.

Characteristics of Structural Concrete

The important general characteristics of hardened normalweight concrete and concrete structures, made with Portland cement, compared to other building materials and structures are as follows:

Concrete has a high ratio of compressive strength to bulk cost, so that it is particularly suitable for use in walls and columns.

Except as prestressed concrete, concrete has a low strength to weight ratio accounting for a general preference for steel or timber beams when there are long spans, and light applied loads.

In building, the weight of concrete can provide good sound insulation, for example in floors.

Concrete is non-combustible, non-flammable and has good fire resistance. This latter property often gives it a decisive advantage over steel. The fire resistance is slightly decreased by aggregates containing silica which can cause bursting of the outer layers if the temperature exceeds about 580°C (1,100°F). There is no damage to reinforced concrete at temperatures below 300°C (580°F) and a limestone aggregrate can tolerate temperatures up to about 800°C (1,500°F) without significant damage.

Unreinforced concrete is able to accept modest amounts of tension, up to approximately a tenth of its compressive strength. This property is crucial, enabling concrete to accept some shear stress without cracking. In this respect it is usually better than unreinforced masonry. However, in absolute terms, the tensile strength is still low and this is a major disadvantage of the material leading to cracking and deterioration of the surface.

A property particularly associated with concrete is shrinkage, which is the permanent, irreversible contraction of concrete caused by loss of water after hardening; the loss of water is that from the cement paste gel, after water from the voids has evaporated. The rate of shrinkage is rapid in the period immediately following the set of the concrete but slows down with time. Although concrete may swell with absorption of water, the reversible expansion and contraction is much smaller than the initial shrinkage movement. Because of the low tensile strength of concrete, shrinkage when restrained leads to cracking.

Cast-in-place reinforced concrete as a method of construction is able to accommodate itself to non-standard areas and awkward shapes. By its nature it forms heavy, rigid, fireproof construction with relative ease.

Because all the necessary materials are readily available, construction work using cast-in-place concrete may start almost immediately, this sometimes giving faster completion times than if shop fabricated elements are used, such as those in steel or precast concrete.

About 50% of the cost of cast-in-place construction is associated with the formwork. Hence, standard dimensions, enabling constant re-use of shuttering and simple outlines, will significantly reduce the cost of cast-in-place concrete work.

In order to obtain good strength and durability in the long term, concrete must be allowed to mature, or cure, in reasonably controlled conditions of temperature and humidity after the initial set of the concrete. In general moderate temperatures, between 20° and 40° (68°F and 86°) and moist or wet conditions are beneficial. The total curing period is extremely long, that is, there is a steady gain in properties over time. However curing is often assumed to be over after the concrete has gained a reasonable strength, although curing and strength are not related. It is best to specify a minimum curing period, usually of at least seven days.

Concrete may be mixed on site or supplied ready mixed. The wet concrete can be transported to its final position on site by pumping, by the use of a crane and skip, by a belt conveyor or by other simpler methods. Pumping concrete is quicker than any other method and is especially suitable for large pours. A low output pump could supply 25 m³ per hour at a maximum distance of 150 metres horizontally and 20 metres vertically. Bigger pumps can treble these distances. More fluid concrete mixes are required for pumping. More water, more sand and less coarse aggregate, especially rounded coarse aggregate, make the mix more fluid but all these factors tend to make the hardened concrete have more shrinkage and creep, and less durability.

Concrete cannot be placed during very cold weather because freezing water will destroy a partly set concrete. An approximate limit is that no wet concrete, after being placed in its final position, be at a temperature less than 5°C or 40°F. Even then insulation of the concrete will be necessary and the curing period, required to gain strength, will be long. In hot weather the problem during placement is to prevent a premature set and, after placement, to ensure a proper cure. The concrete must be prevented from drying out too fast because this may cause cracking.

One of the principal disadvantages of using cast-in-place concrete is the time required before the removal or striking of the formwork. This period of time is necessary to allow the concrete to gain sufficient strength before it has to support itself; therefore the period before the removal of formwork needs to be longer for horizontal elements, such as beams and slabs, than for vertical elements, such as columns. Because of the cost of the formwork and to allow as rapid re-use as possible, cements which gain strength quickly are preferred by contractors. However, these cements generate such heat after setting that they may cause thermal cracking. In addition, the high temperature at which curing takes place leads to losses in the long-term properties of the concrete. Slag cements and other low heat cements are beneficial in this respect. The formwork to beams and slabs is usually removed after a reasonable period of time, see below, but with the props remaining for a further period.

Typical minimum periods before striking formwork for concrete with a surface temperature of 16°C (60°F) are:

Vertical formwork to columns, walls and large beams   9 hours
Slab soffits (props left under)   4 days
Beam soffits (props left under) 8 days
Props to slabs   11 days
Props to beams   15 days

The quality of concrete as a finished product depends almost entirely on the knowhow, workmanship and organisation of the contractor and supplier.

Portland cement concrete has low resistance to chemical attack, for example, from weak acids or sugar solutions. Often the attack is from sulphates in the soil and, in some circumstances, from dissolved carbon dioxide in rainwater. In most cases with a good concrete, the attack is so slow as to be unimportant. The actual danger of deterioration will depend on the particular circumstances, especially the degree of attack, the materials and the workmanship.

In general, reinforced concrete is a durable material but should not be thought of as maintenance free. The alkalinity of hard concrete generally protects the steel reinforcement against corrosion, assuming the reinforcement is embedded into the concrete by a sufficient amount; this would be at least 25mm (1in) if the concrete were exposed to the outside. Concrete of low permeability is needed to give the concrete greater life against external attack. Low permeability can be obtained by high dosages of cement powder in the mix, also giving higher strength, by good compaction, by long moist cure periods and by paints and other barriers which protect the surface. Paints must be permeable to water vapour to allow the concrete to dry out and so help to prevent frost damage to the concrete and degradation of the paint. Wide cracks must be avoided. Common agents of external attack are soluble sulphates in the ground

or carbon dioxide and chlorides in air or water. These form salts that corrode the steel reinforcement and cause the concrete to spall. The life of concrete may also be reduced by chemical reactions, for example, by the use of aggregates that react with the cement paste.

A technique still under development is impregnation of cement paste or concrete with polymers, or sulphur. Any porous material such as concrete contains voids which, if filled by some such materials, is found to increase both strength and durability.

Concrete is subject to dimensional changes due to temperature variations, initial shrinkage and reversible moisture movements among others. As noted previously, concrete has low tensile strength and the dimensional changes may cause the concrete to crack. Measures to prevent cracking are necessary in the design of concrete structures but may not always be completely successful.

On loading, an elastic material undergoes an instant deformation causing an elastic strain. As noted previously, some materials, including concrete, continue to deform even though there is no increase in load. This deformation causes a further strain, the creep strain, which for concrete, over time, is usually greater than the elastic strain; the creep strain always increases with time and eventually approaches a limit, the limiting strain depending on the level of stress. Creep is higher at higher temperatures being about double at 70°C (158°F) that at 20°C (68°F). Creep may be harmful or beneficial depending on circumstances.

Unreinforced concrete can be thought of as a brittle material, having a low value of fracture toughness and, consequently, must be protected against cracking, for example that due to moisture changes, by reinforcement or by the provision of movement joints. The effects of initial shrinkage can be greatly reduced by allowing a major part of this to take place between construction joints before the structure is completed.

Concrete has a relatively high value of elastic modulus. For example, a concrete column of common proportions has only small elastic deflections under load. Concrete may also be useful as a tie when it is required to limit the extension; the tie would normally be prestressed. Long term loads cause further slow deformations by creep and this effectively reduces the value of the elastic modulus of the concrete.

Compared to steel, concrete has high internal damping. This property would make it a suitable material for a frame carrying vibrating loads or for a chimney subject to wind buffeting, for example.

Reinforced concrete by its weight, rigidity and damping characteristics is a natural choice for high rise frame structures too, although heavily loaded columns can be bulky. However, the physical properties of concrete are not necessarily decisive, the cost of labour and speed of construction also being important factors to consider on such a building project. High strength concrete is increasingly used to limit the size of heavily loaded concrete columns.

Concrete is available in a wide range of strengths. The range of use is extended still further by reinforcement and prestressing. Prestressing is a different concept from reinforcement and allows the efficient use of the complete concrete section. For this reason off-the-shelf precast components requiring high strength are usually supplied as prestressed units.

Concrete is slightly permeable to water but a well-designed, properly compacted mix has such low permeability that it can be said to be waterproof for most practical purposes. It is usual to specify a minimum dosage of cement in order to achieve a low water to cement ratio and a minimum thickness to achieve good compaction. As noted, the permeability of concrete can be greatly reduced by long curing periods in moist conditions. This is particularly important for biended cements using waste material as a partial replacement for Portland cement. It has been found that underwater concrete structures, particularly those under high pressure, are almost self-sealing because of the beneficial effects of a wet cure. Faults in construction can be remedied by pressure grouting. Generally concrete is permeable to gases such as air or water vapour. However, with care, concrete can be made impermeable to air under moderate pressure.

Compared to steel, reinforced and prestressed concrete buildings are awkward and time-consuming to demolish. Similarly, a reinforced concrete building is difficult to alter after completion, although hardened concrete can be drilled and cut through with diamond discs, thermal lances or jack hammers.

Detail drawings for reinforced concrete construction are time-comsuming to produce and to alter, if last minute changes to plans are necessary.

A large number of surface finishes can confidently be produced on cast-in-place or precast concrete. Because of the extra expense of precast work, it is usually limited to elements of structure that are repeated. However, a wider range of finishes is available in precast work and quality control is easier. Therefore, a better product is usually obtained. Stains and streaks from weathering need not be unsightly if the surface is modelled, for example, with vertical ribbing. Flat surfaces will show colour differences after weathering. A variety of textures may be given to the surface. An exposed aggregate finish may be obtained by tooling, abrasive blasting or by washing and brushing soon after casting to remove the cement paste and fine aggregate on the surface. Concrete may also be cast against aggregate or any pattern in the formwork, regular or irregular. A finer textured surface is obtained by rendering or by textured paints, coloured as required. Rendering, and paints with low water vapour permeance, substantially increase the durability of concrete. Colour may be given to concrete surfaces by water or solvent-thinned paints and these can have a life on an outside surface of ten and up to fifteen years. Alternatively, a more subdued colour may be produced by the use of coloured cements, although these significantly affect the cost of the concrete and may lose their colour in time. Common colours are dark grey, white, yellow and terra cotta.

Wet concrete has only very poor adherence to hardened concrete. Where joints are required between wet and hardened concrete, the hard concrete must have been roughened to provide a mechanical key, preferably with reinforcement passing across the joint. In some cases it will be necessary to apply a bonding compound, for example, when applying thin screeds on the top of a concrete floor or for repair work. The bonding compounds are based, mostly, on epoxides and polyvinyl acetate, but other polymers can be suitable too.

Special polymer concrete mixes are used for repair work, based on cement and aggregate mixes containing synthetic polymer resins. For small repairs cement may be omitted from the mix altogether. The long term durability of these repairs will depend on properly cutting out defective concrete and establishing a good bond between new and old work. To prevent detachment of the repair mix, the shrinkage should be minimised and the coefficient of thermal expansion kept similar to that of the concrete under repair. Creep helps to prevent detachment if, as is usually the case, shrinkage and temperature changes set up stresses near the repair surface. The repair mix may be applied by hand or by spray.

Concrete structures will crack and if the cracks become wide, they will need to be filled to prevent further deterioration or to prevent water seepage through the concrete, for example. Special injection mixes, containing polymers, can be pumped into the cracks under pressure to effect a repair. The polymers used are adhesive polymers with low surface tension so that they can penetrate the cracks; they are often based on latex or epoxide resins. The resins have very different properties from the hardened concrete to be repaired, being much more flexible and having higher coefficients of thermal expansion and should be thought of more as adhesive gap fillers than as materials able to properly restore the integrity of a cracked structure. Note that the alkalinity of the concrete helps to prevent corrosion; resins do not provide such protection.

Concrete may be cleaned either by chemicals, water spray or grit blasting. However, some cleaning treatments can dull the surface and remove sharp edges to detail work.

Lightweight Aggregrate Concrete

Lightweight concrete is the name given to concretes having weights less than or equal to about 20 kN/m³. Structural lightweight concretes are produced by the use of lightweight aggregates, which are usually artificial, and are porous when compared to dense aggregates. There are a large number of lightweight aggregate types, some being coated to prevent absorption of water. Structural lightweight concrete compared to dense concrete can save foundation costs by reducing weight, or, alternatively, allow thicker sections, reducing the amount of reinforcement needed and the congestion of bars. Lightweight concrete is easy to fix to and to cut and drill. General costs of handling and transport are

considerably reduced too. In addition lightweight concrete has good impact strength and can have higher frost resistance than dense concrete. However, lightweight aggregates are expensive and, for the same strength, more cement powder is required. They require more care in mixing and handling than dense concrete. In general lightweight concrete has higher shrinkage and creep, and lower tensile strength and modulus of elasticity than dense concrete. However, its creep and modulus of elasticity ensure that overall it is less likely to crack than dense concrete when undergoing dimensional changes, especially when these are due to temperature variations. Lightweight concrete also has better fire resistance and thermal insulation than dense concrete.

No-fines Concrete

No-fines concrete is formed by omitting fine aggregate from the concrete mix so that less cement powder is used and voids are formed within the mix. The concrete, therefore, is light and provides moderately good thermal insulation. Lightweight or dense aggregates may be used, usually of a single size. The concrete is cheaper to produce than dense concrete, but is not normally reinforced. This concrete has been used in house construction where a large number of units are required. The walls are usually rendered on both sides because of their porosity. Another use for no-fines concrete is as precast blocks.

Aerated Concrete

The introduction of gas bubbles into a cement mix can produce a hardened product with a cellular structure known as aerated concrete. The concrete does not usually contain any aggregate, except very fine aggregate. Aerated concrete is light and, therefore, has good thermal insulation. It is also easy to fix to and to cut. It has high water absorption but, nevertheless, a low rate of penetration by water, and reasonable frost resistance and durability. Aerated concrete is used as masonry blocks and, when reinforced, as panel units for floors and roofs.

Polymer and Polymer Cement Concretes

Polymer concretes are concretes in which the aggregates are bound together by a resin instead

of cement powder. The resin subsequently polymerizes and creates a concrete with a continuous polymer phase. Polymer cement concrete is made by adding a polymer or monomer to a normal concrete mix; the polymer is dispersed so that this concrete behaves more like a normal concrete. An intermediate form is polymer impregnated concrete which is made by impregnation of a polymer or monomer into a hardened cement concrete. As a class polymer concretes have higher strength than normal concretes especially in tension and flexure. They are also more flexible, that is, they do not crack as readily as normal concrete and therefore are more watertight than normal concrete. In addition they are quick setting and have good bond to existing hardened concrete and good resistance to freezing and chemical attacks. However, they have a high coefficient of thermal expansion, lose strength at temperatures above about 100°C (212°F) and have significant creep, especially at high temperatures. Nevertheless, these concretes are of great value for repair work or where a more resilient hardened concrete is required.

Sprayed Concrete

Sprayed concrete is distinguished from other concretes not so much by its composition as by its method of formation. A mixture of cement, aggregate and water is projected from a nozzle at high velocity against a backing surface and forms a surface which will harden into a dense concrete. In general, the mix is very rich in cement and sometimes incorporates fibre reinforcement. Sprayed concrete is generally used in thin layers. It is reasonably waterproof and has good crack behaviour. Its interest for designers is that it allows the formation of complex shapes at reasonable cost. It is extensively used in repair work and in areas where access is difficult. Techniques also allow sprayed concrete to be formed on overhead, upside-down surfaces. Sprayed concrete may be formed by a wet or dry technique. The principal difficulty in construction is rebound of sprayed material which can leave voids in the hardened concrete.

Fibre Reinforced Cement and Concrete

Fibres of glass, steel, polymers and other materials may be added to cement and to concrete mixes to improve the tensile and impact strength of the hardened cement or concrete. The practical effect of this is that fibre reinforced cement panels, for example, may be made which are thin and light. Finer detail may be used than in reinforced concrete which, in some circumstances, can crack and break off in pieces on its external layer, outside the cage of steel reinforcement. could crack or break off. Fibre reinforced cement is used in repair work and semi-structural applications. There is a fall off in its impact strength with time. Other long term properties are uncertain so that its use as a structural material is limited at present. However, it still gives the promise of a cheap, composite material that does not necessarily require bar reinforcement. A typical glass fibre reinforced cement product has 5% by weight of glass. It can be made either by spraying or by premixing and casting into a mould. As with other reinforced composite materials, properties depend on the amount of reinforcement present. It has similar weathering properties to ordinary cement and concrete, except that being made in sections which are generally much less than 50mm (2in) thick, it is much more affected by surface phenomena such as carbonation than normal concrete elements and is prone to 'crazing'.

Ferrocement

A Ferrocement is made up of a medium strength cement mortar with very closely spaced steel reinforcement in at least two directions. It is quite distinct from reinforced concrete in its behaviour and types of use. Because of its good tensile and flexural strength, it may be used in very thin sections, down to about 12mm ($\frac{1}{2}$in) in thickness and up to about 75 mm (3in), although it can be made thicker. The steel reinforcement can be provided by expanded metal, welded mesh, woven mesh or steel bars and wire. The spacing of the bar is typically about 12mm ($\frac{1}{2}$in). Ferrocement can be formed into difficult curved shapes by merely plastering onto mesh without the need for any formwork; it gives a higher quality surface than sprayed concrete but usually at higher cost. Hence it is generally more economic where labour costs are low.

Types of Cement

Portland cements:
These cements account for almost all the cement sold worldwide.

Slag cements:
These cements are low heat and made by mixing blast furnace slag with ordinary Portland cements. The slag reacts chemically with products of cement hydration and can replace up to about 60% of the Portland cement that would otherwise be required. Only a small number are made. They can have good resistance to chemical attack. The significance of these low heat cements, and others such as mixtures of Portland cement and pulverised fuel ash, is that they allow very large pours of wet concrete, over 1,000 cubic metres at one time, without excessive heat being generated that would allow the new concrete to develop major cracks on cooling.

Pozzolanic cements:
These cements are made by mixing Portland cement and pozzolanas, such as fuel ash. The pozzolanas can replace up to about 30% of the Portland Cement that would otherwise be required. This is a low heat cement with good chemical resistance providing concretes of good workability.

High Alumina cements:
These cements are very rapid hardening and provide very good chemical resistance. In general, they are not recommended for structural concrete because of their susceptability to convert to a weaker and more porous state.

METAL

Introduction

Construction materials are used in large quantities and it is therefore important that the materials used be cheap. Although bulk costs of metal are high compared to most other building materials, iron and steel, and aluminium to a much lesser extent, are still reasonably priced compared to other metals and have found wide application in building. Several thousand types of steel and aluminium alloys are produced for specific purposes. Of these only a small number are in general use in the construction industry.

Iron has a much longer history as a building material than steel. Cast iron was first in general use as a building material towards the end of the eighteenth century. Development was rapid and within fifty years wrought iron was being produced and within another fifty years steel had been discovered and was being produced in quantity. The rate of production of steel increased markedly over the following years and today about 720 million tons of steel per year is used worldwide of which approximately 120 million tonnes is used in Western Europe and 115 million tonnes in the United States. Of this worldwide total, about 70 million tonnes of steel per year is used in the construction industry. The cost and properties of steel make it a basic material in all industrialised countries. Steel consists of iron alloyed with small amounts of other elements, the most important being carbon. There are various types of steel produced, the cheapest and most popular being 'Carbon Steels' which contain about 0.1% to 1.5% of carbon, and usually some manganese and silicon as well. Of these carbon steels still the most common type is mild steel having about 0.15% to 0.25% of carbon content. Because of the large number of steels available it is likely that a suitable one can be found for any particular application. The principal criteria used in the selection of steel are price, strength, availability, corrosion properties, toughness (to prevent fractures), and weldability (ease with which welding may be done).

Aluminium (aluminum) is almost invariably used as an alloy. It is about one and a half times as expensive as steel per unit volume but can be economic as a construction material in some cases. Aluminium was produced in workable quantities some years before the turn of this century but was only used in large quantities much later, mainly by the aircraft industry. Aluminium has a very high strength to weight ratio and good corrosion resistance. It is also easy to work and form into complex shapes. The principal criteria used in the selection of aluminum alloys are strength, price, forming properties, corrosion properties, weldability and the amount of the loss of strength and toughness after welding.

Structural Carbon Steel

Structural Carbon Steel is easily the most important class of steel for the construction industry, these steels being cheap and convenient to use; the class includes steels having not more than 0.25 % carbon and no alloying elements present in quantity except silicon and manganese. There are several grades of structural carbon steel available, those having higher carbon contents being stronger. However steels having higher carbon contents are, in general, more brittle at low temperatures and harder to weld. A range of so called 'notch ductile' steels are available, at extra cost, to overcome problems of brittleness. Table 1.4 gives a comparison of properties of some typical steel and aluminium alloys used in the construction industry. Table 1.10 illustrates some of the forms in which steel has been used, either as individual elements or as complete structures, and lists typical sizes.

Characteristics of Structural Steel

The important general characterists of structural carbon steels and steel structures compared to other building materials and structures are as follows:

Steel has a high ratio of strength to weight combined with a low ratio of cost to strength, accounting for the widespread use of steel as roof beams and sheeting material especially for medium and long spans for which self-weight is the most significant load.

Steel for construction purposes is produced in the form of straight or curved rolled sections of various cross-sectional shapes, or flat plate. Special shapes may be cast in structural steel but the steel is inferior to rolled steel and more expensive to use.

Although the use of high strength steel will often produce a lighter structure for the same design strength than one in a weaker material, the structure may suffer from excessive deflection or instability. In such cases it may be necessary to use a larger amount of material of a lower quality or a different material altogether, such as wood.

Steel loses strength and stiffness at high temperatures. At 480°C (900°F) steel keeps about two-thirds of its original stiffness and strength. However the fall off in stiffness is rapid above this temperature. Steel may be protected by insulating with concrete, sheet materials or intumescent paint. Alternatively the temperature rise may be limited by the use of large thick steel sections, by placing steelwork outside the building enclosure or by circulating cooling water within hollow steel sections.

Mild steel corrodes faster than most other kinds of steel, although it requires only minimal protection against corrosion when the relative humidity is less than about 70%. Unpolluted atmospheres and low temperatures also slow down or prevent significant corrosion. Hence different considerations apply if the building is in an alpine or industrial area. In moist air at normal temperatures mild steel will rust and in air at high temperatures mild steel oxidises rapidly. In such conditions it may be advisable to change to other materials with better corrosion characteristics such as wrought iron or aluminium alloy. Alternatively a weathering or stainless steel may be used both of which act by forming protective oxides on the surface in the right conditions. If an ordinary mild steel is used it may be protected by galvanising, if the pieces are not too large, or by one of the very large number of paint treatments. The choice of paint and paint system depends on the environment and in particular on the microclimate of the most vulnerable components. Corrosion protection by painting requires surface preparation, usually blast cleaning, followed at once by a priming coat for example red lead or zinc chromate with a thickness of $15\mu m$ to $50\mu m$. Total thickness of primer should be between $40\mu m$ and $80\mu m$, applied in one or two coats; note that $100\mu m = 0.1mm = 0.004in = 4$ 'thou'. Compatible finishing coats are necessary on steelwork with outside exposure and are applied in one or two coats each $30\mu m$ to $50\mu m$ thick. The total thickness of primer and finish is generally between about $100\mu m$ and $300\mu m$, a greater thickness being used in corrosive atmospheres.

Compared to timber and precast concrete, high strength connections are very easily made between steel components. Connections in steel can be made by welding or bolting; they are a significant proportion of the total cost of a steel structure. Normal jointing methods are tolerant of small dimensional errors in fabrication or erection of the steelwork. A cheaper and easier connection may be made if the joint is not required to be a fixed one. The high performance of a steel joint is attributable both to the strength of steel and to its ductility, in effect its ability to transfer load from an overstressed to a less stressed part of the joint.

Most jointing methods are improved by use of a material which has such a combination of strength and 'plasticity' and this accounts for the use of steel for connections in wood and precast concrete and, often, for the initial choice of a steel structure.

In general steelwork is joined by bolting on site and by welding in a workshop; control of quality is more difficult with site welding. However welding is used on site, when the necessary quality can be achieved and when the reduced thickness of metal and the monolithic structural behaviour of the welded joint is advantageous.

Steel may be cut in the workshop by sawing with a circular saw, by shearing in a guillotine or by flame cutting. Holes are usually made by drilling or in some cases by punching.

Convenient connection methods and a high strength to weight ratio make steelwork suitable for prefabrication and fast erection on site. However the size of prefabricated components is limited by the means of transport to site and sometimes the capacity of cranes on site. For road transport, steel components should generally be less than about 3m (10ft) in width and 20m (60ft) in length.

Steel is dimensionally stable although it is subject to temperature movements. In general a conventional single storey building of simple shape with steel columns would require a movement joint at approximately 50m (160ft) intervals.

Steel is a nearly perfect elastic material at normal working loads. In general, this enables its behaviour to be accurately predicted by elastic theory and economic use to be made of the material.

Steel has good ductility. Thus at ultimate loads steel fails in a safe way, giving large deformations before any sudden loss of strength except when this failure is due to instability or due to brittleness from an unsuitable steel or welding procedure having been chosen. Hence, taking account of instability, steelwork structures may also be economically designed by 'plastic' theory based on the behaviour of steel structures at failure.

The weldability of a steel is usually measured by its carbon content, or carbon equivalent value for all steels that are not pure carbon steels. This value should be less than about 0.55% for the normal welding procedures and in most cases should be less than about 0.42% to avoid preheating and other precautions which will increase welding costs. The types and quantities of the alloying elements in most mild steels as compared with high strength steels, make it easy for a sound joint free of cracks to be produced by welding. Mild steel is said to have good weldability and this is an important factor in its popularity.

It is possible for steel to fail in a brittle manner by fast fracture. This is more likely to happen to a steel with, for example, a high carbon content, high strength and thick sections when used at low temperatures. Two properties related to ductility which determine the likelihood of this happening are toughness and fracture toughness. A high value of toughness indicates that it will be difficult for a crack to propagate. A high value of fracture toughness indicates that the material will have to be under high stress and have large cracks within it before fast fracture can occur. Mild steel can have good fracture toughness and this is another factor in its popularity. At extra cost weldable higher strength steels with good fracture toughness are available.

High strength carbon steels generally have high carbon equivalent values, and, as noted, special procedures must be followed in order to weld these steels. The objective is to avoid any significant cracks or any loss of properties which may occur near the weld as a result of the heat generated by the welding process. If steels are to be used at high stresses then the value of fracture toughness must move up in step to ensure that inclusions or flaws in the steel, of a certain maximum size, do not increase the likelihood of a brittle failure. If there is no increase in fracture toughness then only small defects can be allowed in the steel. If the limits are exceeded, the factor of safety against brittle fracture will be eroded.

Because steel structures are easy to erect they are also easy to alter and demolish. Therefore steel is a very suitable material for demountable and temporary buildings or building liable to need minor structural alterations, such as new staircases.

Steel can conveniently be fabricated into components of many shapes, especially from thin plates.

The ductility, lightness and strength of steel make it particularly suitable for use in structures in earthquake areas.

Steel only has a small amount of internal damping. However purpose designed devices can damp steel structures which are subject to vibration, such as bridges, towers and high-rise buildings. Compared to a fully welded structure damping can often be approximately doubled by the use of friction grip bolts, which can absorb the energy from vibrations. However to absorb the energy, there must be slip, which would not be allowable under normal conditions but could be utilised under extreme conditions.

To obtain steel plate or rolled steel sections at the lowest cost, or to obtain any steel to a particular specification, it will generally be necessary to reserve the required tonnage at a steel mill in the next schedule for rolling of steel sections. Hence economic use of steel or special applications require advance planning. In general the minimum quantities of plate or rolled steel ordered in order to benefit from the lower mill price are 20 tonnes for each section size of the same linear weight and metallurgical grade.

The costs of fabricating steelwork in the workshop can be reduced by good production engineering, which would include repetitions of dimensions, section sizes, diameters of bolts, types of joint and so on. One hour of labour is equivalent in cost to about 40kg (85lb) of steel and this means, in practice, that extra material is used if this saves even small amounts of labour. This ratio of costs particularly affects methods of detailing steelwork connections.

High Strength Low Alloy Steels

These steels consist of carbon steels to which additional alloying elements have been added to improve properties. Some of the most useful of these in construction are the weathering steels which do not require corrosion protection because of the formation of a protective oxide coat on their surface. However they require care in selection to ensure they are matched to their atmospheric environment, in detailing to prevent lying water and staining of other materials and in erection to prevent damage and discolouration. For exposed steelwork that does not require fire protection, the extra expense of weathering steel may be offset by the elimination of painting. Some low alloy steels have been specifically designed for construction in low temperatures. Popular types are available as plate, rolled and hollow sections.

Heat Treated Alloy Steels

Alloy steels may be quenched and tempered to produce even higher yield and ultimate strengths than the high strength low alloy steels. They are weldable and have much better corrosion resistance than mild steel for example. They are mostly produced as plate.

Structural Cold Formed Sheet and Strip Steel

This class includes all thin steel sheet and strip which can be formed into shapes cold, that is at room temperatures, for a variety of purposes. Purlins, light trusses, roof and floor panels are commonly made in this way. Cold forming increases the yield strength but decreases the ductility of the original steel. Hence the strength and ductility of a cold-formed section will be altered more at the corners of the section where there is more cold working. Cold formed steel is usually made from structural carbon or high strength low alloy steels with low yield strength and high ductility. It can be protected against corrosion by galvanizing. It is manufactured with a range of finishes. Cold-formed members are usually less than 1½mm (1/16in) thick and can be shaped by equipment, such as press brakes and roll forming machines. Hence difficult shapes can be made economically. The design of thin cold-formed steel elements is more complex than the design of thicker hot rolled elements. Local buckling of a flange, for example, is often a critical factor although the element is not usually considered to have failed because local buckling has taken place. Webs of beams, material strength and connections all need more careful consideration.

Steel Wire

In the construction industry, steel wire refers to high tensile cold-drawn carbon or alloy steel with diameters between about 3mm and 8mm (1/8in and 1/3in). It is generally used as a prestressing wire and, most often, in prestressed, pretensioned elements such as precast concrete beam and floor units. A slightly different wire is used for making up strand. Stainless steel wire is available but is about ten times the price of carbon steel. Bridge wire, used in making up rope cable for bridges is heavily galvanised to prevent corrosion. Wire has high contents of carbon and manganese for high strength. It also has good toughness and fatigue resistance.

High Tensile Alloy Steel Bars

High tensile steel bar is available as solid round bars with diameters between about 20 and 40 mm (¾in and 1½in). It is used as a general purpose tie bar and for prestressing. Thread is added to the bars by rolling on, giving higher strength bars and greater fatigue resistance than bars with cut threads.

Strand and Rope Cable

Strand cable is made up of high strength cold drawn wires which twist round a central wire. Seven wire and nineteen wire strand are typical sizes in use. Typical diameters of strand are between 8mm and 25 mm (1/3in and 1in). Strand is used for prestressing and in bridge and cable structures. Rope cable is made of several strand cables which twist round a central strand or other core material. Rope cable is used in bridges, for which galvanised bridge wire is necessary, and in other cable structures. Strand and rope both have high axial strength, and are without great bending stiffness, so that they may be also used in structures which work by changing shape under load such as cable, net and air-supported structures. Rope cable although more expensive than strand cable has less bending stiffness and higher 'stretch' under tension because of the tightening in the packing of the helically shaped strand within the cable. The greater the number of wires and strands in the rope the greater the stretch due to this tightening and the greater the flexibility of the rope in bending. For example a 6 x 37 rope

(6 strands of 37 wires) is more flexible than a standard 6 x 19 rope of the same area. Rope is normally made with the wires in the strands twisted in the opposite direction to the way the strands are twisted in the rope; in this way the wires on the outside of the rope are approximately parallel with the axis of the rope. In building applications, the wire is preformed to a helical shape so that the wires do not 'spring' in the finished strand. Strand may also be preformed in the same way if it is to be used in rope. The stretch available in rope is very often an advantage in cable structures. Socket and clamp fixing generally grip better on rope than strand.

Steel Castings and Forgings

It is sometimes necessary that steel parts be made as castings or forgings. This may be the case for complicated shapes such as joints which may be very difficult to fabricate by other methods. Casting consists of pouring molten metal into a mould; forging consists of shaping the component between dies while it is still hot. Castings and forgings steels are in general more brittle and more difficult to weld than rolled mild steel and greater care is needed to ensure that they are safely used and made. Nevertheless with modern steels, by following set procedures, castings and forgings can be reliably made and joined together. Forgings generally have better metallurgical properties than castings although casting steels can still be produced with high toughness and resistance to impact by alloying. More complicated shapes should be obtained by casting rather than forging the steel, and for small numbers of components casting is likely to be cheaper than forging. In the construction industry, high quality casting steels allow complicated or shaped joints to be made which can then be conveniently welded to the straight members which are to be joined together. For simpler joints the normal procedure is to weld the members to each other directly but, although this is generally cheaper, it induces stress concentrations and other defects near the weld just where the joint is often highly stressed and this could cause cracks to develop especially in structures subject to fluctuating loads so that in these cases, too, cast joints be preferred.

Cast Iron

Ordinary cast irons have low toughness and very poor resistance to impact and usually fail in a brittle manner. However they have a reasonably high compressive strength, good internal damping which reduces their susceptability to fatigue failure, much better corrosion resistance than mild steel (although they do corrode) and are easy to make and finish into complicated shaped components. Properties of cast irons may be improved by alloying and special treatments. The principal modern types of cast iron are white and grey cast iron, grey cast iron being the more common grade. Malleable cast irons are also available and have better properties than the white or grey irons. Casting substantially reduces the cost of producing elements because of the elimination of machining and may be used even when accurately made items are required. For buildings, a close grained grey cast iron or a malleable cast iron, such as spheroidal graphite cast iron, would be suitable; they may be used for secondary elements or elements, such as columns, which are in compression.

Stainless Steels

Stainless steels describe those steel alloys which have a chromium content of between about 10% and 30%. There are three metallurgical types: martensitic, ferritic and austenitic. The austenitic stainless steels and related steel castings and forgings are the most important, especially the austenitic chromium-nickel-molybdenum types. All the austenitic types are weldable and have good corrosion resistance, high ductility and toughness at low temperatures. There are a very large number of stainless steels available including wrought and cast stainless steels which could both be suitable for connections or structural members. Stainless steel is expensive but is well protected against corrosion by an oxide film on its surface so that it may be used as thin sheet as well as in structural applications such as cladding support brackets.

Structural Aluminium Alloys

Wrought aluminium alloys divide into two main categories: those whose strength is produced by heat treatment, the heat-treatable alloys, and those whose strength is produced by cold working, the non heat-treatable alloys. The non heat-treatable are, in general, not as strong but have better corrosion resistance. Alloy elements used are magnesium, silicon, zinc, and manganese.

The alloying elements increase strength without significantly affecting the good corrosion resistance of pure aluminium. Commercial aluminium alloys are light and strong but have a low modulus of elasticity compared to mild steel. Hence the size of aluminium elements is often determined by consideration of their stiffness. Corrosion resistance is excellent compared to mild steel although some alloys may still require additional protection, for example by painting. Generally, it is more difficult to weld an aluminium alloy than a steel one and bolting is the usual method of joining the elements together. Structural aluminium alloys are normally used in the form of rolled sections but aluminium alloys are available for making more complicated shapes as castings.

WOOD

Introduction

Wood is a natural composite material consisting principally of lignin stiffened with fibres of cellulose. It has a cellular structure which may be likened to a bundle of tubes lying in the direction of the grain, having approximately square cross-sections and weakly glued one to the other. This model can explain why wood is weak across the grain, and why because of the buckling of these cellular tubes, its compressive strength is only about a third of its tensile strength. It also accounts for its high resistance to impact loads and to brittle failure, and for its high strength to weight ratio which is comparable with steels. Wood is by far the most popular construction material worldwide in terms of the amount used and the number of suitable applications. Commercial woods are split into softwoods from coniferous trees such as pines and firs and hardwoods from deciduous, broad leaved trees such as oak, ash and iroko. However the development of reliable wood glues has brought in a range of manufactured products based on wood such as glued laminated timber, plywoods, particle and fibre boards. Table 1.5 gives a comparison of properties of some woods and wood-based products at a moisture content of 12%. Table 1.11 illustrates some of the forms in which wood has been used, either as individual elements or as complete structures, and lists typical sizes.

Characteristics of Softwood

Important general characteristics of softwoods and wood structures compared to other building materials and structures are as follows:

Wood has a high ratio of strength to weight combined with a low ratio of cost to strength, accounting for the widespread use of softwoods as roof and floor beams and as planking and panels in roofs, floors and walls, especially for short and medium spans.

Wood has very high tensile strength although this is often difficult to exploit fully because of the large connections that would be required. Wood is used in compression elements because compression joints are relatively easy to make and because the wooden element is light but bulky enough to prevent buckling.

Because of its structure, wood has different properties along the grain and across the grain. Except for shrinkage, properties in the tangential and radial directions across the grain, differ only slightly. In general quoted properties for wood are those along the grain.

Growing timber consists of a central core of heartwood, which is dead tissue, surrounded by sapwood which is living tissue. Sapwood is more permeable and not as strong as heartwood. However after cutting and seasoning the difference in strength is usually small.

Wood has an extremely wide range of properties, depending both on the type of tree used and the part of the tree from which the wood has been cut.

Wood is sensitive to changes in moisture content, the percentage of water present relative to the dry weight of the wood; seasoning consists in drying timber, usually in kilns, from moisture contents of about 100 per cent to 12 or 20 cent, when it would be suitable for use in a building. Moisture content affects the weight, strength, durability and size of wood. For example fairly dry wood has about twice the strength and stiffness of green wood, and shrinkage of the wood in the tangential direction across the grain even with modest changes in relative humidity can cause warping and splitting of the wood. In practice the dimensional changes are the most serious, sometimes causing an effective failure of floors and roofs even though the strength and stiffness are still adequate. For this reason it is important to build with timber having about the same moisture content as the one it will have in the completed building.

Wood has decreased strength under long-term loads and at high temperatures. Conversely it has good resistance to short term loads and increased strength at low temperatures. For this reason heat, usually as steam, is used to make bending and shaping of wood easier. Temperatures above about 100°C (212°F) should not be held more than a few days or permanent loss of strength ensues.

Wood has good stiffness, that is to say it has a moderately high value of elastic modulus. Nevertheless, deflection is often the critical factor in the design of timber beams. Under long term loads, the further deformations due to creep may cause unsightly sagging, if not taken into account at the design stage.

Wood has good toughness. This indicates that it will not fail in a brittle manner and that the material has good resistance to impact loads. Noises are indications that wood is moving or under stress but are not necessarily signs of incipient failure.

Wood is an excellent material to cut and work and, because of its structure, it is able to accept nails of a reasonable size without this causing splits along the grain. However the weakness of softwood in tension across the grain means that joints must be large and it is these that often determine the sizes of the elements. Common methods of fixing are with nails, screws, bolts, nail plates, bent metal plates, split rings, shear plates and plywood and steel gusset plates. It is difficult to achieve any major degree of rigidity in a timber joint except by the use of glues. However in general glues need to be used under controlled conditions in a factory.

Wood treated with a preservative can be a permanent building material. A number of preservatives are available which may be applied on site by brush or dipping but are most often done in bulk under factory conditions by pressure treatments. In general softwoods, and the sapwood parts in particular, are absorbent and can be impregnated with preservative to a good depth. The decay of wood only occurs when there are food substances for the fungi, a suitable temperature, moisture and some air. Elimination of any one of these things, or sometimes merely good ventilation, will prevent decay without the use of a preservative. Generally preservatives are not necessary for wood at temperatures below about 4°C (40°F) and above 43°C (110°F) or for wood sheltered from the weather and kept in an atmosphere with a low moisture content, that is to say less than about 20 %. In unfavourable conditions, woods vary considerably in their resistance to decay. In some places wood may also be attacked by termites and marine borers.

The surface of wood may be protected against softening, discolouration and embrittlement by the application of paint or stain. Staining is very much easier to renew than painting. However paint gives a wider choice of colours and also restricts

movement of the wood due to moisture changes to a very much greater degree.

Wood has a high value of internal damping and this combined with its lightness makes it a very suitable material for a properly connected structure in an earthquake zone.

The fire safety of timber structures depends on the ignition characteristics of the materials present and on how the flames, heat and smoke will spread. Wood by itself is difficult to ignite at ordinary temperatures although it is possible for wood to ignite even without a flame at temperatures as low as about 120°C (250°F) if enough heat is present over a period of time. Flame spread on wood surfaces is controlled by the use of fire retardants. Some fire retardants are hygroscopic however. The fire resistance of wood members during a fire is good, because the charred layer of wood protects the remaining wood; such members need to have dimensions that allow for the charring and have connections that are properly protected against fire.

Convenient connection methods and a high strength to weight ratio make wood components suitable for prefabrication and fast erection on site. Wood has a particular advantage when made into panel systems and generally components can be manhandled. In addition, wood systems can be erected in almost any temperature or weather except high wind.

Wood is a renewable material and uses only very small amounts of energy in making its finished products. Its strength to cost ratio is likely to remain high.

Wood is almost always supplied in straight lengths and in general with a stress grade. The stress grade of the softwood has associated recommended allowable figures for stiffness and strength. There are usually several stress grades within each species of wood. Common species of softwoods are: Douglas Fir, Pitch Pine, Larch, Western Hemlock, Parana Pine, Redwood, Scots Pine, Whitewood, Canadian Spruce, Sitka Spruce, European Spruce, Western Red Cedar; see below.

Hardwood

Worldwide hardwoods are very little used compared to softwood. Softwoods give a higher yield per acre of ground, are easier to work, fix and to season. However hardwoods are more durable, have better fire resistance, and, in general, have greater stiffness and strength. They can be competitive with steel and concrete beams at longer spans and greater loads, when softwood beams would become too bulky. They are often more durable than softwoods. There is a good choice of hardwoods, although most of them are relatively little known.

Glued Laminated Timber

Glued Laminated Timber refers to layers of sawn wood with their grains parallel which are glued together to make a single element. Usually at least four laminations are used. Glulam is usually produced in straight lengths but at extra cost can be formed into almost any curved shape as long as the radius of the curves is not sharp. The properties of glulam essentially depend on the type of timber used. Any species of wood will be adequate if it can be glued and has suitable properties for its likely uses. Douglas fir, Southern pine, Redwood and Whitewood are common choices.

The great advantage of glulam timber is that, unlike solid natural wood, large members may be produced at reasonable cost. In addition faults in individual laminations are less significant than in solid timber members; the better quality wood is used only in those laminations where it is most necessary, for example at the top and bottom of a beam. Present glues require careful control in use and in hot, moist or polluted atmospheres only certain glues are suitable. Glulam is made up with wood having a moisture content of less than 18% and is therefore dimensionally stable in normal indoor conditions which have similar levels of moisture. However glulam can be used outside if the wood used is durable or able to accept preservative treatment.

Plywood

Plywood is made in sheets and generally has an odd number of layers of wood glued together with their grains at right angles to that in the adjacent layer. In this way plywood overcomes the weakness across the grain of natural timber, although thin plywood should only be spanned in the direction of its face grain. Plywood has a very high strength to weight ratio. Because of its structure it can take high concentrated loads. It has a low coefficient of expansion and moves very little with changes in moisture although there could be swelling at edges. Plywood is made with many species of wood and is made in various grades. Construction plywood is classified as interior or exterior grade, the exterior grade having a completely waterproof glueline. Plywood sheet is very extensiveley used as a panel by itself or in single and double layers as stressed skin panels.

Particle Board

Particle board is made in sheets and generally uses wood chips, and other finer particles which are held together by a binder, normally a resin binder. Although particle board has only a fraction of the strength of plywood it still has adequate stiffness and strength in bending for use as floor panels and sufficient strength in shear and direct tension and compression for use as shear panels or as components in a wall system. However particle boards only have limited resistance to concentrated loads and suffer from creep deflection and loss of strength in the long term. Particle boards made with urea formaldehyde resin can have permanent loss of strength and stiffness in moist conditions. Other resins however allow the particle board to recover its properties after drying out. In moist conditions, high temperatures cause even faster deterioration of the resin binders.

Types of Softwood

Redwood (Europe). A general purpose softwood of moderate strength but with tendency to be knotty. The sapwood will usually require preservative treatment but absorbs preservative well. The heartwood has good resistance to decay. *Californian Redwood* (USA) is similar but more durable.

Scots Pine (Europe). Similar in type and properties to *Redwood* (Europe).

Canadian Spruce (Canada). A wood which is widely available and of moderate strength but poor resistance to decay. It hardly absorbs preservative and therefore is generally only used where conditions make decay unlikely. *Sitka Spruce* (N.America, UK) is similar in type and properties.

Whitewood (Europe), also known as *Deal.* Similar in type and properties to *Canadian Spruce.*

Western Red Cedar (N. America). A low strength wood but with good resistance to decay and low movement when moisture content changes. Easy to work.

Western Hemlock (N. America). A general purpose softwood which is widely available with moderate strength and durability. Absorbs preservative well.

Douglas Fir (N. America) also known as *Columbia* or *Oregon Pine.* A good quality straight grained softwood with moderately high strength and moderate durability. Only has a small amount of sapwood.

Larch (Europe, America). A strong and tough wood having above average movement with moisture content changes. The sapwood generally needs preservative treatment.

True Firs or *Hem-fir* (N. America, Europe). This category represents several types of tree. The firs generally have moderately good strength and moderate durability. It can be difficult to make them absorb preservative.

Parana Pine (S. America). A softwood of moderate strength and durability. Will absorb preservative.

Radiata Pine (Africa, Australasia). Similar in properties to *Parana Pine.* Moderately high moisture movement but absorbs preservative well. *Patula Pine* (Africa, Australasia) is similar in type and properties. It is very fast growing and generally has very little heartwood.

Southern Pine (U.S.A.) This category represents several types of tree. The woods generally have moderate strength with high proportions of sapwood.

Types of Hardwood

Beech (Europe, N. America, Japan). A hard and high strength wood but prone to decay and with high moisture movement.

Ash (N. America, Europe, Japan). A hard and high strength wood with good elasticity and resistance to shock. Decays fairly easily. Fairly easy to work. *Hickory* (N. America) has similar properties.

Maple (N. America). A hard and high strength wood. *Sycamore* and *Plane* (Europe) are similar in type and properties.

Oak (Europe, N. America, Japan). A hard and high strength wood almost always with excellent resistance to decay and hard use. Can be difficult to work.

African Mahogany (W. Africa). A wood of moderately high strength and a good looking interlocking grain. Can be hard to work. Some species are prone to decay. *Spanish Mahogany* (S. America) is related in type and has similar properties.

Afrormosia (W. Africa). A dense, very high strength wood with good durability. Only small moisture movement. Often used as a substitute for *Teak*.

Iroko (Africa). A high strength wood with good resistance to decay and only small moisture movement. Also used as a substitute for *Teak*.

Keruing (S.E. Asia). A high strength wood with only moderately good durability. Suffers from high moisture movement.

Teak (S.E. Asia) A good looking and very high strength wood with excellent resistance to decay and hard use. It has very good fire resistance.

Red Meranti (S.E. Asia), also known as *Seraya*. A uniformly grained wood of moderately high strength with great durability. Reasonably easy to work.

PLASTIC

Introduction

The construction industry worldwide uses over a quarter of all the plastics produced. However of the large number of plastics available, only a small number are suitable for use in the major elements of a building. The principal distinction among plastics is between the thermosetting and thermoplastic materials. The more important class are the thermosetting plastics which harden irreversibly after curing while thermoplastic materials will soften on reheating. Both types may be reinforced by fibres and in the case of thermosetting plastics this is almost always necessary to obtain reasonable mechanical properties. Plastics are in widespread use because of their high strength to weight ratio, their ease of forming, their translucence and their resistance to corrosion.

The most popular thermosetting plastic in use in the construction industry, on grounds of cost, strength, relative hardness and toughness, is fibreglass reinforced polyester, GRP, also known as GFRP, a composite having a polyester resin matrix and glass fibre reinforcement. In a reinforced plastic the matrix binds the fibres together and protects them from damage; the fibres are much stronger than the surrounding matrix material. Resins that have been used as the matrix in structural plastics are polyester, epoxy, silicone resins and phenolic, all thermosetting plastics. Fibre reinforcements that have been used include various types of glass, hessian, asbestos, steel, viscose rayon and aramids, such as Kevlar. The properties of the hardened composite depend on the properties of the matrix and the reinforcement and, especially, on how much reinforcement is added in each direction. Fillers such as glass, mica and sand can also be incorporated to improve properties. Thermoplastic materials in use in the construction industry include polyvinylchloride or pvc, polymethylmethacrylate or acrylic, polycarbonate, nylon and polypropylene. They are generally produced as sheet, partly because they can be easily moulded to different shapes subsequently. As structural plastics have outstandingly high strength to weight ratio, they are commonly used in single and double skin panels, sandwich panels

and pipe. The flexibility of single skin panels can be overcome by shaping them; in this way domes, shells and folded plate structures have been successfully built. Drawbacks to the general use of plastics in construction are their cost, this being dependent for most plastics on the price of crude oil, their durability, fire resistance, low surface hardness and elastic modulus as well as their loss of strength and other properties with time. Much work has been done on long term properties although the durability of plastics is still a matter for debate.

Plastics are more properly referred to as polymers, being made up of long molecules which are linked together. The properties of the plastic depend on the molecular structure and on the way the links between molecules are made. The properties also depend on how close the plastic is to its glass temperature; above this temperature, the plastic is rubbery with a low elastic modulus, and thermoplastics, if heated high enough, become viscous and malleable; below the glass temperature, the plastic is brittle. For many plastics, room temperature is well below their glass temperture, so that normally they behave as brittle materials but plastics with glass temperatures near room temperature are more flexible at this temperature. Only small changes in temperature are needed to make large alterations in the properties of the plastic. For example, unlike most metals, an increase in temperature even of $10°C$ ($18°F$) has a major effect on the strength, creep, elastic modulus and, therefore, the stiffness of the plastic. In general the operating temperature for plastics should be no more than 50% greater than the glass temperature. In addition to temperature, the mechanical properties of a plastic will depend on its conditions of use since fabrication. The factors involved are the operating temperatures and stresses as well as the conditions of exposure, including exposure to any acidity in the atmosphere. It is common practice to talk of the history and remaining life of a plastics product, the life being affected by previous stress and temperature conditions. The basic mechanical requirements for an element are stiffness and strength; failure of these properties is unlikely or would take a long time if the operating temperatures and stress levels are kept low. Table 1.6 shows a failure in tension in GRP would take about 50 years, if the stress level is kept at half of its short term tensile strength. However if kept at high stresses, failure may be rapid; in some cases the quoted short term strength may only be held for a matter of seconds before failure occurs. Thermoplastics are much more affected by loss of properties due to time and temperature than thermosetting plastics, A disadvantage of plastics is their flammability. Almost all plastics will burn, even though most plastics commercially available incorporate fire retardant fillers and additives and could be classified as flame resistant to some degree. Plastics have high calorific values, about twice that for wood, and thus can burn fiercely, releasing large amounts of heat. In addition when burning, most plastics produce thick smoke which is often toxic or corrosive. If a fire does establish itself, additives cannot be expected to significantly alter these properties. Compared to other building materials all plastics, especially thermoplastics, have poor dimensional stability; for example they deform, when heated to temperatures above room temperatures. On further heating some plastics will melt and drip and this may constitute a fire hazard. Table 1.6 gives a comparison of properties of some typical plastics used in the construction industry. Table 1.12 illustrates some typical applications of plastics and fabrics as elements or as complete structures.

Glass Reinforced Polyester

Important general characteristics of GRP (GFRP) elements compared to other building materials and elements are as follows:

GRP has a low weight as well as a high strength to weight ratio.

GRP has moderately good tensile, compressive and shear strength; however, strength is dependent on temperature and at high temperature even moderate stresses can cause failure with time. As the properties of GRP deteriorate with time, high factors of safety are necessary for long-term loads.

The polyester resin used in the production of GRP hardens and cures by polymerization, not by evolution of volatile by-products, and this is responsible for the generally good properties of the hardened resin. However the resin is brittle and needs the strength imparted to it by the glass fibres; generally structural GRP contains between 25% and 60% of glass fibre reinforcement.

GRP is generally anisotropic, that is its properties vary with the direction, depending on how much reinforcement is present in each direction.

GRP has a high but acceptable coefficient of expansion; polyester resin by itself would have excessive movement.

GRP will creep, that is it will continue to deflect, if there is a permanent load on it. This creep will be faster at higher temperatures. GRP does not soften but must be used at temperatures well below that at which there is oxidation leading to deterioration. The maximum operating temperature is about 70°C (160°F). Phenolics and silicone resins have better resistance than polyesters at high temperature.

GRP is an elastic material with a non-linear stress-strain curve at low load. It exhibits only a limited amount of plasticity before failure and this means that stress concentrations in the material can lead to cracking or crushing rather than the slow yield and relief available in more ductile materials such as steel. Because of this, connections are usually made by the embedment of more ductile materials within the plastic at the connection points.

GRP exhibits a limited amount of plasticity at high load, that is it gives some warning of failure when overloaded if the rate of loading is not high. Impact loading, however, can cause a sudden brittle failure.

GRP has a low modulus of elasticity and, because it is used in thin sections, deflection is often a critical factor in design. To overcome this flexibility GRP is often used in the form of shaped or double skin panels in which deflections are easy to control. The modulus of elasticity decreases with increase in temperature and time under load.

The durability of GRP elements are very dependent on the amount of care exercised in manufacture, especially with elements made by hand. The durability is increased by a hard gel surface of low porosity. Some fire retardants and finishes increase porosity and can reduce the life of the surface. Agents of attack include uv light, humid atmospheres, especially with dissolved chemicals, and water, which gets through the surface by capillary action. Additives will reduce damage caused by uv light. Increases in temperature significantly speed up chemical reactions and, therefore, the extent of damage. Surfaces which do deteriorate may be recoated, although the quality of work may not match that of the original.

GRP for construction purposes can be made by a hand lay-up or spray technique or by closed mould systems usually using a hot press. In the hand method a gel coat is applied to the mould and this will give a smooth finish to the GRP as well as protection, particularly against an unacceptably fast deterioration of the bond between the fibre and matrix due to water penetration. Resin and glass fibre is then laid on until the necessary thickness is achieved. The glass fibre can be in the form of sheets of chopped strand mat cr woven fabrics using rovings or yarns. Strand is made up of many small filaments of glass fibre and the strand can be made into thicker bundles called rovings, or yarn if it is twisted. In the spray technique glass rovings are chopped up and fed into a spray of resin. The resin spray mixed with chopped strand is pointed at the mould until enough thickness has been built up. After spraying the glass fibre and resin is rolled to even out and consolidate the mix. In all cases the strength of GRP is dependent on curing at the correct temperature and maintaining this for a suitable curing period.

GRP is combustible and produces toxic smoke when it burns. However retardants against the surface spread of flame can be incorporated and give some degree of flame resistance. However, fire retardants may affect durability and do not necessarily have any beneficial effect, and may even increase the danger from smoke. Although GRP elements cannot be said to have fire resistance, barriers to the spread of flame can be provided by fire resistant boards incorporated within the element or by coating with an intumescent paint.

GRP is not a hard material and its surface will scratch.

GRP can be made translucent.

GRP units are often supplied as shaped units which are usually light and easy to stack and transport.

GRP is impermeable to water and vapour across a reasonable thickness of material.

The production of GRP components requires the use of oil and large inputs of energy. Therefore the price of these items has a significant effect on the price of finished GRP products.

Structural fixings of GRP elements on site are usually accomplished by bolting to the supports. Given its limited plasticity, GRP normally has nylon and metal parts laid into it during manufacture for stiffness and strength, especially around the fixing points.

Sandwich Panels

For large plastic panels, or where, for example, it is convenient to incorporate thermal insulation in the panel, it is usual to use a sandwich construction.

The sandwich consists of a thin, but relatively strong, skin surrounding a low density rigid foam. The sandwich panel is very much stronger and stiffer than a single skin panel would be. In bending, the outer skin of the sandwich may be thought of as taking the tension and compression while the inner rigid foam takes shear. Generally the foam is stuck or bonded to the outer skin. Various thermosetting and thermoplastic resins are available for rigid foam, the most common being phenolic, polyurethane and expanded polystyrene or pvc. The outer skin is usually a reinforced plastic such as GRP. However so called structural foams are also available in which the sandwich panel is made of a single material, which is a foam inside but will form a solid outer skin against a mould surface during its manufacture. Thermoplastic resins such as ABS and polycarbonate have been used as well as thermosetting resins such as polyurethane.

FABRIC

Introduction

Fabric structures have been in use for a very long time as temporary forms of shelter. Modern practice is considerably different however both in the type of fabrics used, which mostly are made of mineral, metal or synthetic fibres often of recent development, and in the type of structures built, which are stressed skins without random creases or wrinkles. Modern stressed skin fabric structures are of three main types: pneumatic structures, which are high pressured gas systems, air-supported structures which are large, low air pressure systems and tents which are fabrics in a relatively high state of stress put into shape by tensioning the fabric against boundary elements and other supports such as cables, beams, arches and columns. The outstanding characteristics of fabric structures are their visual lightness and their flexibility in bending, although the forces generated in supports and foundations by fabric structures can be very large. Fabrics require different methods of design from the vast majority of building structures which are rigid and cannot change shape to any significant extent when the loads change. Fabrics can be used in combination with rigid elements such as beams and columns or

flexible elements such as cables and ropes. Considerable variation in properties is achievable by different weaves, coatings and finishes. An optimum combination of mechanical strength, creep performance, light transmission, ease of jointing, flame performance, weathering and air permeability must be achieved. Usually a compromise is necessary to balance one set of properties against another.

Fabrics may be made of mineral fibres, such as glass, organic fibres such as cotton, metal fibres such as stainless steel, or one of the wide range of synthetic fibres such as polyester. Leaving aside the weaker unwoven fabrics, the two main type of textile are woven fabric and mesh, both made from yarn. The yarn is closely woven for a fabric or coarsely woven for a mesh or fine gauge net; yarn is made by spinning, drawing and then twisting together of long fibres. A film or coating is usually applied to a woven fabric to make it impermeable, to prolong its life and improve other properties. Among the coatings available are polyurethane, silicone, fep, polytetrafluorethylene (ptfe), synthetic rubbers and plasticised polyvinylchloride (pvc). PTFE has been widely used on glass fabric and pvc on polyester fabric; see below. Woven fabrics are anisotropic, that is, have mechanical properties dependent on the direction in which the fabric is stressed. A mesh may be used alone or, in covered areas, as reinforcement to plastic film, which by itself has only moderate strength. In the latter case the mesh is usually sandwiched between two layers of film and is then known as a reinforced film, although these reinforced films do not yet make viable structures. Other alternatives are synthetic rubber which is easy to stretch and put into shape but not very durable or thin metal sheet such as stainless steel which is strong and very stable but hard to get into shape. Most of these membrane materials are isotropic, that is have similar mechanical properties in any direction in which the fabric may be stressed. Rubber is anisotropic however. Table 1.7 gives a comparison of properties of some fabrics used in the construction industry, and the yarns in them. Typical applications of fabrics are given in Table 1.13 .

Woven Fabric

Important general characteristics of fabrics and

fabric structures compared to other building materials and structures are as follows: Fabric has moderate to high tensile strength but no effective compressive strength because buckling, or creasing, takes place. The strength of the fabric depends mainly on the fibre used.

Fabric has a low or zero shear modulus, that is to say the material can be made to shear with little or no effort. A fabric which does possess shear stiffness is less tolerant of errors in the designed shape of a structure made from it and less easily adapts its shape to changes in load and therefore is more liable to crease. The shear modulus depends on the fibre, weave and coatings used.

Fabric has low weight and a very high strength to weight ratio.

Because of the manufacturing process, fabric, in general, is anisotropic exhibiting different properties in the warp and fill (weft) directions. In the fill direction the fabric has lower strength and greater elongation. The properties in the two directions can be made more nearly equal by initially tensioning the fabric in the fill direction.

In general, fabrics extend easily initially as the yarn straightens. This is known as decrimping. After decrimping the yarn is much harder to stretch.

Fabrics made from synthetic materials lose strength when loaded over a period of time. An increase in temperature also causes a loss of strength.

A problem with some fabrics, especially fabrics made from synthetic fibres, is creep, that is the continual increase in length of the fabric, under a constant load. Because of this, fabric structures lose tension with time. Temperature and humidity can increase the creep of some materials.

Fabrics are generally elastic materials with a non-linear stress-strain curve at low load. At high load they exhibit some plasticity, that is they have a permanent extension even after the load is removed. The plasticity is influenced by the rate of loading.

Fabric is generally supplied in rolls and may be cut into any developable shape. Non-developable shapes, which may be synclastic such as domes or anticlastic such as saddle surfaces, are formed by cutting various sizes of flat shapes which are then joined together. Fabric structures, especially tent structures, need accurate fabrication.

Fabrics can be made reasonably tough, that is reasonably resistant to tears. Tears can exist in a stressed fabric for a long period of time, depending on the tear length, the permanent or mean stress field, the fluctuations of stress and the fabric yarn and weave. However in general large tears once started can travel fast. For the same weight of fabric, an open weave with thick threads provides better resistance to tearing than a more uniform weave with closely spaced and thinner threads.

Jointing of fabrics is achieved by heat welding, cementing, sewing and clamping, depending on the characteristics of the coating and substrate material. For example glass fibre fabrics are welded because sewing damages the glass fibre; neoprene is cemented in order to make it waterproof. Clamping is a site joint, which still relies, however, on edges that have been prepared by sewing, welding or cementing.

Fabric structures may be erected in low temperature conditions. They may also be designed for very quick erection.

Fabrics are usually easy to transport even though some fabrics can be damaged by folding.

The dimensional stability of a coated fabric, that is the degree to which it changes its dimensions over time and under different conditions depends mainly on the fibre. By contrast the light transmission, flame performance, permeability, weathering and durability will depend mainly on the coating in use.

Fabrics may be designed to absorb sound. Inner acoustic linings or vertical drapes may be used where it is required to muffle or prevent the reflection of sound waves on the surface of the main fabric.

High temperatures decrease the strength and increase the stretch of fabric. Conversely, low temperatures decrease stretch of the fabric but make it easier for tears to propagate. Most fabrics will not deteriorate to any significant extent in the range of temperatures from at least - 40°C (- 40°F) +60°C (+ 140°F).

Types of Fabric

Organic Fibre Fabrics These fabrics are made from natural materials such as wool, cotton, hemp and silk. They deteriorate under outdoor conditions and have poor elastic properties compared to synthetic fibres.

Mineral Fibre Fabrics These fabrics are made from minerals such as glass and carbon fibres. As fabrics they can have high strength but can be difficult to use because of their high elastic modulus or lack of stretch. This means that accurate cutting patterns and careful handling are required. *Glass* fibre is a mineral fibre that has found application. It is dimensionally stable over a large range of temperature and humidity conditions and has high strength and a high elastic modulus. Present evidence suggests these properties will be maintained in the long term. Despite the high modulus of glass fibre, the glass cloth usually has some initial stretch as the yarns straighten.

Synthetic Fibre Fabrics. A large number of fabrics for building are made from synthetic fibres. Typical fibres used include those from polyamides, polyesters, acrylics, aramids and polyvinyls. Nylon and Perlon fabrics are made from polyamides. *Nylon* has high strength and a low elastic modulus, that is to say a high ability to stretch. However creep extensions take place with an increase in temperature and humidity. Hence at constant load in working conditions where there are likely to be variations in temperature and humidity, nylon will extend in an unpredictable way, so that, in general, the material exhibits poor dimensional stability. A temperature increase also causes a loss of strength. Nylon absorbs moisture and degrades under uv light although both these effects may be controlled by a suitable coating. Fabrics made from polyester include Terylene and Dacron. *Polyester* is the most commonly used fabric yarn. It has high strength and a moderate elastic modulus. Polyester cloths are produced in a not dissimilar range of strengths and stiffnesses to glass cloths, although the strength and stiffness of the polyester fabric decreases faster than glass, when it is under load. The long term strength is as important as the short term strength. In general, polyester has good dimensional stability although an increase in temperature causes creep extension as well as a loss of strength. A fabric made from acrylic is Dralon. The best known fabric made from aramid is Kevlar.

Types of Coating

The most common materials for coatings are polyvinyl chloride (pvc), ptfe, silicone and some of the synthetic rubbers. As a coating, *pvc* is quite cheap, easy to use and stable under normal weather conditions. In addition it is possible to alter the colour and light transmittance of fabrics coated with pvc. Both uv and visible light may be absorbed in varying degrees. It is possible to use pvc in the form of film reinforced with a polyester mesh; it has also been used as a coating on nylon, vinyl and glass fabric. However the most common combination is pvc-coated polyester fabric, which is easy to join and has good stretch, that is it has a low modulus of elasticity; the latter property means that the material does not require tight dimensional tolerances and can be handled without special precautions being necessary. To protect the fabric it is important that uv light be excluded as far as possible and for this reason the light transmission through the fabric is usually limited. The pvc coating tends to pick up dirt but it may be given a metal foil, acrylic or pvf finish to improve durability and the run-off of dirt. The material known as *ptfe* has good resistance to chemical attack and to uv light. Dirt does not adhere to the material and there is no noticeable discolouration with time; it can be made translucent. A common combination is ptfe-coated glass fabric which has good durability but with its high elastic modulus needs accurate fabrication. The glass fibres are brittle and the material requires careful handling to prevent permanent creasing of the fabric. *Silicones* are durable materials and, being largely transparent to uv light, have good resistance to it. They also maintain their flexibility over the long term. The material may be made with a very high degree of translucency, much greater than that of ptfe. A common combination is silicone-coated glass

fabric which has good durability and a high elastic modulus, like ptfe-coated glass fabric. Because of its translucency, the fabric may be used in double layers and still give high light transmission. Synthetic *rubbers* are very flexible, that is to say they will extend without cracking or being damaged. They are often used where large extensions are expected. Their durability, however, is reduced by contact with some gases. Hypalon and neoprene are synthetic rubbers which have been used on nylon fabric, and also on polyester and glass fabric.

GLASS

Introduction

Glass is usually a transparent material made by fusing sand with soda or potash and other materials. In chemical terms it is amorphous, a substance which has cooled to the solid state without crystallizing. Although there are hundreds of types of glass they all share broadly similar properties, the main ones being transparency, high compressive strength, brittleness and good resistance to most corrosive agents. The most important category of glass is soda-lime-silica glass and these glasses are the only ones in general use in the construction industry. Most window glass is used in an annealed condition, that is, after manufacture, the hot glass is slowly cooled in a controlled way to reduce the locked in stresses that result from temperature differences during the cooling process.

Annealed Glass

The important general characteristics of glass and glass assemblies compared to other building materials and structures are as follows:

> Glass is usually made transparent to visible light. However by the inclusion of metal oxides and some other materials the glass can be made to absorb and thus filter out certain colours in visible light, as well as some transmissions of other wavelengths. This can also be done by thin films on the surface of the glass. For example solar radiation transmissions, which may cause excessive heat gain inside a building, can

be reflected on the surface as well as absorbed by the glass, although, as some half of the solar radiation transmissions are contained within visible light, there is a limit to the amount of solar radiation which can be stopped without unduly affecting the transparency of the glass.

Glass is a very durable material. It has a hardness comparable with steel, so that it is difficult to scratch, and has good resistance to almost all acids, including those dilute acids sometimes present in rainwater. Apart from occasional cleaning glass is virtually maintenance free. As well as having good hardness, glass has the advantage over most plastics of not colouring yellow with age.

Glass is an elastic material. However, unlike other elastic materials, such as steel, it cannot yield in a 'plastic' manner under tension so that flaws or scratches on the surface of the glass, cause high stress concentrations there and make the glass fail in a brittle manner.

Glass is a strong material in compression but is only able to realise its full strength in tension with specimens that are free of scratches, such as is approximately true for glass fibre reinforcement in resins and other materials. Therefore the tensile strength of glass depends on the state of the surface and has only an approximate meaning for a working size sample of annealed glass.

Glass can take much higher tensile stresses if these are caused by very short term loads. The allowable tensile stresses for such short term loads are more than double those for long term loads.

Glass has low thermal conductivity. This means that significant temperature differences are likely within any glass in general use, as is the case for plastics which also have low thermal conductivities. However, glass is a more brittle material than most plastics and these temperature differences can lead to cracking. These limitations may often be overcome by using a thin glass or toughened (tempered) glass.

Flat sheets of glass up to about 40mm (1½in) thick may be cut by scoring the surface and then producing a brittle failure along the scores lines by bending or heating. In thicker glass, cuts near the edge of the sheet or the formation of awkward shapes will need to be done by diamond sawing. Glass may also be drilled and this is one way of making a corner. Glass may be ground, for example to remove sharp edges or to produce straight or bevelled edges.

Annealed glass is usually available in flat sheets with thicknesses of between 3mm and 25mm (⅛in and 1in). Because of the way glass is manufactured, particularly if the float glass process is used, it is not usually economic to specify glass except in the form of flat sheets.

Glass windows are usually set into a wood or metal frame and sometimes directly into concrete or masonry. In all these cases flexible compounds are used between the glass and the surround to take up movement of the glass. An alternative construction where larger clear areas of glass are required is to use thick toughened (tempered) glass or thick annealed glass which can be joined together by metal fixing plates or by silicone-type adhesives. Temperature movements must be allowed for; temperatures differences between the edges of window glass, which are shielded by the surround, and the rest of the glass can cause cracking, unless properly detailed.

Toughened Glass

Toughened glass, also known as tempered glass, is about five times stronger in bending than ordinary annealed glass because the surface of the glass is prestressed in compression. No tensile stresses will occur on the surface at all unless the applied stress is greater than this prestress. Toughened glass is made by rapidly cooling the surface of glass when it is at a high temperature. This process not only produces compression on the surface but tension in the middle of the toughened glass and this accounts for the characteristic way toughened glass shatters into small pieces when broken. This is a relatively safe way for failure to take place. The greater safety of toughened glass over annealed glass is an important reason for its selection. Because toughened glass effectively has a significant tensile strength, it is able to accept not only the applied stress due to loads but also stresses due to temperature differentials. In this way it can take thermal shocks without cracking. Disadvantages of toughened glass are its loss of properties above about 300°C (575°F) and the fact that it may not be drilled, cut or shaped in any way after toughening has been carried out. Toughened glass has been widely used in buildings. High glass wall elevations have been constructed using toughened glass, the glass wall being hung from supports to avoid buckling and having glass fins to buttress it against horizontal loads.

Laminated Glass

Laminated consists of a transparent plastic sheet, usually polyvinylbutyl, which, at manufacture, is sandwiched between two practically identical sheets of annealed glass under heat and pressure. The resulting laminate has considerable resistance to impact loads. If the laminate is cracked then the plastic layer, which is relatively strong and flexible, holds the two glass sheets together and keeps the laminate intact except in extreme circumstances. Laminated glass is widely used as 'safety glass'.

Wired Glass

Wired glass consists of ordinary annealed glass which has a light wire mesh incorporated within its thickness. The wire enables the glass to be seen and prevents pieces of glass detaching themselves if the glass cracks. Wired glass is often used in building elements such as doors to provide fire resistance for periods of about half an hour.

Table 1.1 — Comparison of Material Properties

Property	Masonry (Clay Brickwork)	Reinforced Concrete (with 4% reinforcement)	Steel (Mild Steel)	Wood (Whitewood)	Glass Reinforced Plastic (polyester)	Glass (Annealed Soda Glass)	Fabric (Polyester yarn with pvc coating)	Conversion to change from metric to imperial units
Type of Material	Ceramic	Ceramic with metal	Metal	Natural Composite	Synthetic Composite	Glass	Polymer	
Specific Gravity (w)	2.2	2.4	8.0	0.46	1.8	2.4	1.4	
Weight (ρ) kN/mm^3	22	24	78	4.5	18	24	14	x 6.36 lb/ft^3
Tensile Strength (σ_{TS}) N/mm^2	1	18	400	75	250	50 (1500 for unflawed glass)	1000	x 145 lb/in^2 (psi)
Compressive Strength (σ_c) N/mm^2	15	45	400	25	150	200	none	x 145 psi
Flexural Strength - Modulus of Rupture (σ_b) N/mm^2	1.5	18	400	50	300	55	none	x 145 psi
Elastic Modulus (E) KN/mm^2	20	35	210	10	15	74	14	x 145 kips/in^2 (ksi)
Fracture Toughness (K_c) MN/m$^{\frac{3}{2}}$	0.9	(0.6 for unreinforced concrete)	140(low carbon steel) 50(medium carbon steel)	12	20	0.7	Tear strength can be high	x 910 lb/in$^{\frac{3}{2}}$
Toughness (G_c) kJ/m^2	0.02	(0.03 for unreinforced concrete)	100 (low carbon steel) 12 (medium carbon steel)	10	10	0.01	..	x 5.71 lb/in
Impact Strength	negligible	tolerable if reinforced	good	moderately good	moderately good	negligible	good	
Elongation % - ductility	none	5(but cracks develop)	22	..	..	none	14	
Creep Factor - final creep strain to elastic strain at working stresses	2	2	negligible at normal temperatures	1	1-10(high at high temperatures)	negligible at normal temperatures	significant at high stresses	
Fatigue Ratio in reversed bending - working stress as a proportion of flexural strength below which fatigue does not affect life of material (10^7 cs)	..	..	0.42	0.30	0.20	..	..	
Damping -damping ratio	..	high	negligible	moderate	high	negligible	..	
Reversible Moisture Movement %	0.02	0.02	none	1.50	small	none	small	
Initial Expansion (+) or Shrinkage(−) %	+0.05	−0.02	none	..	small	none	..	

Table 1.1 continued   Comparison of Material Properties

Property	Masonry (Clay Brickwork)	Reinforced Concrete (with 4% reinforcement)	Steel (Mild Steel)	Wood (Whitewood)	Glass Reinforced Plastic (polyester)	Glass (Annealed Soda Glass)	Fabric (Polyester yarn with pvc coating)	Conversion to change from metric to imperial units
Coefficient of Thermal Expansion (α) x 10^{-6}/°C	6	12	12	4	14	8	..	x 0.556 x 10^{-6}/°F
Thermal Conductivity at 5% moisture content (λ) W/ m°C	0.70	2.00	45.00	0.13	0.20	1.00	..	x 6.938 btu in/ hr ft² °F
Temperture held 1 hour at which material begins to soften or has lost half its strength °C	..	300-800	480	180	150	500	70 (failure at joints)	x 1.8 then add 32 for °F
Energy required to make material GJ/m³	9	5	260 (320 aluminium)	0.3	100	50	..	1 tonne of oil is energy equivalent of 40 GJ
Strength to Weight Ratio (σ_{TS}/w or σ_b/w) N/mm²	0.5	8	60	150	145	22	780	x 145 psi
Elastic Modulus to Weight Ratio (E/w) kN/mm²	9	15	27	22	8	30	10	x 145 ksi
Efficiency of Material for making light column elements of solid section ($E^{\frac{1}{2}}/w$) KN$^{\frac{1}{2}}$/mm	2	2.5	1.8	7	2.5	..	..	
Efficiency of Material for making light wall panels of solid section ($E^{\frac{1}{3}}/w$) KN$^{\frac{1}{3}}$/mm$^{\frac{2}{3}}$	1.2	1.4	0.8	4.8	1.5	1.8	..	
Bulk Cost	low	low	high	very low	very high	high	very high	
Tensile Strength to Bulk Cost	very low	low	high	high	low	very low	high	
Compressive Strength to Bulk Cost	high	high	high	moderate	very low	low	..	
Elastic Modulus to Bulk Cost	high	high	high	moderate	very low	low	very low	
Fire Resistance of individual elements	very high	high	very low	high	very low	very low	..	
Combustibility of untreated material	non-combustible	non-combustible	non-combustible	combustible	combustible	non-combustible	combustible	
Flame Spread of untreated material	none	none	none	flame spread	flame spread	none	flame spread	
Smoke Generation	none	none	none	toxic fumes	toxic fumes	none	toxic fumes	
Durability of treated material in temperate climate	indefinite	indefinite	> 50 years	variable	< 50 years	indefinite	15 years	

Table 1.2   Properties of Masonry as built

Property	Clay Brickwork	Calcium Silicate Brickwork	Dense Concrete Blockwork	Aerated Concrete Blockwork	Natural Limestone	Conversion to change from metric to imperial units
Specific Gravity	2.2	2.0	2.1	0.9	2.2	
Weight kN/m^3	22	20	21	9	22	x 6.36 lb/ft^3
Compressive Strength N/mm^2	3-24	3-8	3-24	6	10	x 145 lb/in^2 (psi)
Flexural Strength N/mm^2 - parallel to bed joints - perpendicular to bed joints	2.0 0.8	1.2 0.4	1.0 0.4	0.5 0.3	. .	x 145 psi
Elastic Modulus kN/mm^2	5-25	14-18	5-25	2-8	15	x 145 kips/in^2 (ksi)
Creep Factor - final creep strain to elastic strain at working stresses	1.2-4.0	. .	2.0-7.0	2.0	. .	
Reversible Moisture Movement %	0.02	0.01-0.05	0.02-0.04	0.02-0.03	0.01	
Initial Moisture Expansion (+) or Drying Shrinkage (−) %	+0.02 - +0.08	−0.01 - −0.05	−0.02 - −0.06	−0.05 - −0.09	+0.01	
Coefficient of Thermal Expansion x 10^{-6}/°C	5-8	8-14	6-12	8	4	x 0.556 x 10^{-6}/°F
Thermal Conductivity at 5% moisture content W/ m °C	1.3	1.2	1.2	0.3	1.3	x 6.938 btu in/ hr ft^2 °F

Table 1.3   Properties of Concrete

Property	Structural Concrete	Lightweight Concrete	No-fines Concrete	Autoclaved Aerated Concrete	Polymer Concrete (Polyester Mortar)	Glass-fibre Reinforced Cement (5% fibre)	Sprayed Concrete without fibre reinforcement	Conversion to change from metric to imperial units
Specific Gravity	2-4	0.4-2.0	1.5-1.9	0.6-0.9	2.4	2.5	2.3	
Weight kN/m^3	24	4-20	15-19	6-9	24	25	23	x 6.36 lb/ft^3
Long-term Compressive Strength N/mm^2	20-100	5-60	4-9	3-6	50-100	30-100	30-60	x 145 lb/in^2 (psi)
Long-term Flexural Strength - Modulus of Rupture N/mm^2	3	3	1	1	10-40	15-20 (10years)	3	x 145 psi
Elastic Modulus in Compression KN/mm^2	15-40	5-25	15	1.5-9	3-15	20-30 (10years)	20-30	x 145 kips/in^2 (ksi)
Impact Strength	very low	low	very low	very low	high	high but decreases	low	
Tensile Strain Capacity % - elongation before cracking	0.004-0.012	..	..	..	1-5	0.05	..	
Creep Factor - final creep strain to elastic creep strain at working stresses at 20°C (68°F)	1-3	2-4	2-4	1-3	4-7	2-5	2-5	
Reversible Moisture Movement %	0.02-0.10	0.03-0.20	..	0.02-0.03	..	0.15-0.30	0.15-0.30	
Initial Drying Shrinkage %	0.02-0.08	0.03-0.04	0.01-0.03	0.02-0.09	1.00	0.15-0.30	0.15-0.30	
Coefficient of Thermal Expansion x 10^{-6}/°C	7-14	6-12	4-8	8-10	20-40	7-11	7-14	x 0.556 x 10^{-6}/°F
Thermal Conductivity at 5% moisture content W/ m °C	1.6-2.2	0.2-0.9	0.8(dense aggregate)	0.3	..	0.5-1.2	1.6-2.2	x 6.938 btu in/ hr ft^2 °F

Table 1.4   Properties of Steel and Aluminium Alloys

Property	Prestressing Strand	High Strength Low-Alloy Steel	Structural Carbon Steel	Coldformed Steel	Casting Steel	Wrought Iron	Grey Cast Iron	Wrought Aluminium Alloy	Conversion to change from metric to imperial units
Carbon Content %	0.60-0.90	0.10-0.28	0.10-0.25	0.20-0.25	0.15-0.50	0.05	2.50-4.50	..	
Specific Gravity	7.8	7.8	7.8	7.8	7.8	7.6	7.2	2.8	
Weight kN/m³	77	77	77	77	77	75	71	27	x 6.365 lb/ft³
Tensile Strength N/mm²	1200-1800	400-700	400-560	280-600	400-600	300-350 (in r. line)	150-350	200-550	x 145 lb/in² (psi)
Yield Stress or 0.2% Proof Stress N/mm² - stress at or near which permanent deformation starts	1100-1700	340-480	240-300	200-500	200-400	180-200 (in line of rolling)	..	120-500	x 145 psi
Elastic Modulus kN/mm²	165	210	210	210	210	190	210	70	x 145 kips/in² (ksi)
Fracture Toughness at 20°C(68°F) MN/m$^{\frac{3}{2}}$ - resistance to brittle failure	10-150	10-150	50-400	20-400	20-200	100-300	5-20	25-50	x 910 lb/in$^{\frac{3}{2}}$
Temperature at which alloys have Charpy V-notch value > 27J (= 20 ft-lb) °C	..	−15	−50	−15	−30	..	+20	−50	x 1.8 then add 32 for °F
Elongation % - ductility	4	15	15-25	12-25	15-20	8-25	2	8-20	
Fatigue Ratio in reversed tension - working stress as a proportion of tensile strength below which fatigue does not affect life of part (10^7 cycles)	0.3	0.5	0.4	0.4	0.3	0.2-0.5	0.4	0.3	
Weldability	not suitable for welding	good with right alloys	good if low-carbon steel	generally good	moderate	generally poor	poor	good if right alloys	
Coefficient of Thermal Expansion x 10^{-6}/°C	12	12	12	12	12	12	12	24	x 0.556 x 10^{-6}/°F
Thermal Conductivity W/ m °C	45	45	45	45	45	45	45	205	x 6.938 btu in/ hr ft² °F
Temperature at which metal has 50% of room temperature strength °C	350-500	500	500	500	500	500	can crack at high temperatures	190	x 1.8 then add 32 for °F
Corrosion Resistance of untreated metal	poor	moderate to good	poor	poor to moderate	moderate	good	good	very good	

Table 1.5   Properties of Wood

Property at 12% moisture content	Hem-fir Softwood	Kapur Hardwood	Hem-fir Glulam Timber	Douglas Fir Plywood	Wood Chipboard	Conversion to change from metric to imperial units
Specific Gravity	0.40	0.73	0.41	0.56	0.71	
Weight kN/m³	3.9	7.2	4.0	5.5	7.0	x 6.36 lb/ft³
Mean 7-day Tensile Strength of good quality working size sample N/mm²						
- along grain	60	115	75	40	15	x 145 lb/in²
- across grain	2	4	2	..	..	(psi)
Mean 7-day Compressive Strength of good quality working size sample N/mm²						
- along grain	24	45	30	25	..	x 145 psi
- across grain	3	6	3	3	..	
Mean 7-day Flexural Strength of good quality working size sample - Modulus of Rupture N/mm²	42	85	50	60 (face parallel to grain)	15	x 145 psi
Elastic Modulus in bending kn/mm²	9-10	12-20	10	10-12	2-3	x 145 kips/in² (ksi)
Creep Factor - final creep strain to elastic strain at working stresses	0.5-1.5	0.5-1.5	0.5-1.5	0.5-1.5	..	
Reversible Movement for 30% change in relative humidity %						
- along grain	0.05	0.05	0.05	0.25(in plane)	0.25(in plane)	
- across grain	1.0-2.5	1.0-4.0	1.0-2.5	2.00(across plane)	4.50(across plane)	
Coefficient of Thermal Expansion x 10⁻⁶/°C						
- along grain	3.5	4	3.5	..	..	x 0.556
- across grain	34	40	34	..	..	x 10⁻⁶/°F
Thermal Conductivity across grain W/m °C	0.14	0.21	0.14	0.16	0.14	x 6.938 btu in/ hr ft² °F
Variation in Strength with Temperature - % strength compared to 20°C (68°F) strength						
−50°C (−58°F)	150	150	150	150	..	
20°C (68°F)	100	100	100	100	..	
50° C (122°F)	75	75	75	75	..	

Table 1.6   Properties of Structural Plastic

Property	Polyester Resin (thermosett.)	Polyester with Chopped Strand Glass Mat	Polyester with Woven Glass Rovings	Polyester with Unidirectional Glass Rovings	Glass Reinforced Epoxy	Polycarbonate (thermopl.)	Acrylic (thermopl.)	Conversion to change from metric to imperial units
Glass content by weight %	nil	25-50	50	60	60	..	..	
Specific Gravity	1.1 - 1.5	1.4-1.6	1.7-1.8	1.8-1.9	2.1	1.2	1.2	
Weight kN/m^3	12	15	18	19	21	12	12	x 6.36 lb/ft^3
Short Term Tensile Strength at 20°C (68°F) N/mm^2	40-80	80-175	210-250	660	350-550	60	50-70	x 145 lb/in^2
Short Term Flexural Strength at 20°C (68°F)-Modulus of Rupture (N/mm^2)	50-90	125-210	220-300	700	500-825	80	90-100	x 145 lb/in^2
Short Term Elastic Modulus in bending in direction of fibres at 20°C (68°F)	2-5	6-10	15	30	35	2.6	3.2	x 145 kips/in^2
Fracture Toughness at 20°C (68°F) MN/m$^{\frac{3}{2}}$	0.5	10-20	10-30	10-40	40-50	1-2	1-1.5	x 910 lb/in$^{\frac{3}{2}}$
Long Term Tensile Strength (10 years) at 20°C (68°F) put as proportion of short term strength	..	0.5	0.5	0.5	0.5-0.65	0.20	0.25	
Creep Factor - final tensile creep strain (10yr) to short term elastic strain at 20°C (68°F) at stress of 33% of short-term tensile strength	..	1	1	1	1	1.5-2	1.5-2	
Shrinkage %	0.004-0.080	..	..	..	..	..	..	..
Water Adsorption over 24 hours %	0.15-0.60	..	..	..	0.20	0.15	0.30-0.40	
Coefficient of Thermal Expansion x 10^{-6}/°C	100-180	20-30	10-15	10-15	10-15	70	60-70	x 0.556 x 10^{-6}/°F
Thermal Conductivity W/m °C	0.2	0.2	0.2	0.2	0.25	0.2	0.2	x 6.938 btu in/ hr ft^2 °F
Softening Temperature or Maximum Operating Temperature °C	70	70	70	70	110	120	75	x 1.8 then add 32 for °F
Visible Effect of Weathering	yellows	yellows	yellows	yellows	no effect	yellows and becomes brittle	no effect	

Table 1.7   Properties of Fabric

Property	PVC coated Polyester Fabric	PTFE Coated Glass Fabric	Silicone Coated Glass Fabric	Neoprene Coated Nylon Fabric	Conversion to change from metric to imperial units
Specific Gravity of Fabric Yarn	1.38	2.55	2.55	1.14	
Weight of Fabric Yarn kN/m³	13.5	25.0	25.0	11.2	x 6.36 lb/ft³
Short Term Tensile Strength of Fabric Yarn N/mm²	1100	1500-2400	1500-2400	500-960	x 145 lb/in²
Tenacity N/tex - short term strength to linear density in tex of fabric yarn	0.90	1.10	1.10	0.95	note: a tex is the weight in gm of 1 km of yarn and a measure of av. thickness
Elastic Modulus of Fabric Yarn kN/mm²	14	65	65	6	x 145 kips/in²
Elastic Modulus to Linear Density of Fabric N/tex	12	30	30	5	
Weight of a Typical Fabric N/m²	8(0.7mm thick)	15(1mm thick)	11 (0.9mm thick)	7(0.8mm thick)	x 3.01 oz/yd²
Short Term Tensile Strength of Fabric N/50mm width					
- Warp direction	1800(0.7mm thick)	6500(1mm thick)	6500(0.9mm thick)	2000(0.8mm thick)	x 0.114 lb/in
- Weft (Fill) direction	1700	5500	6000	1600	
Long Term Tensile Strength of Coated Fabric (2 years) under continuous load as proportion of short term strength	0.5	0.6	0.6	..	
Tear Strength of Fabric N					
- Warp direction	300(0.7mm thick)	270(1mm thick)	400(0.9mm thick)	500(0.8mm thick)	x 0.225 lb
- Weft (Fill) direction	350	350	450	700	
Elongation of Fabric %					
- Warp direction	14	6	5	25	
- Weft (Fill) direction	20	7	5	30	
Shear Strength of Fabric N/degree	small	450(1mm)	..	small	x 0.225 lb/°
Combustibility of untreated fabric	flammable	hardly flammable	hardly flammable	flammable	
Durability years	10-15	25	25	8-12	

Table 1.8   Vertical Support Elements   Masonry

Element	Horizontal and Vertical Section	Typical Heights (h) (m)	(ft)	h/d between Lateral Supports	Critical Factors for Sizing	Remarks
Masonry column	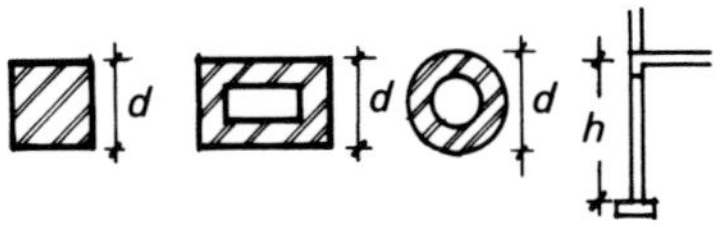	1-4	3-12	15-20	Buckling and crushing ($h/d > 6$) Crushing ($h/d < 6$) Bending	h is vertical distance between lateral supports and d is thickness of column
Masonry wall	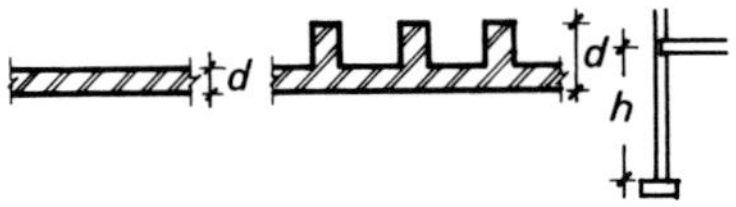	1-5	3-16	18-22	Buckling and crushing ($h/d > 6$) Crushing ($h/d < 6$) Bending	h is vertical distance between horizontal lateral supports; wall may also have vertical lateral supports
Reinforced and prestressed masonry columns and walls	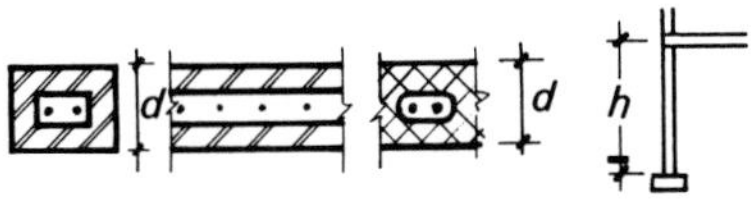	2-7	6-22	20-35	Bending	h is vertical distance between horizontal lateral supports; wall may also have vertical lateral supports

Table 1.8 continued   Horizontal Beam and Slab Elements - Floors   Masonry

Element	Section and Plan	Typical Depths (d) (mm)	(in)	Typical Spans (L) (m)	(ft)	Typical L/d	Critical Factors for Sizing/ Remarks
Masonry arch and fill	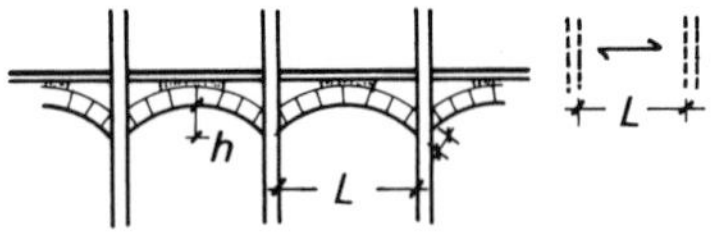	50-225	2-9	2-5	6-18	20-30	Bending or cracking from loads at quarter points. Fill above arch crown helps to prestress arch L/h ratio about 10-20
Reinforced brick beam	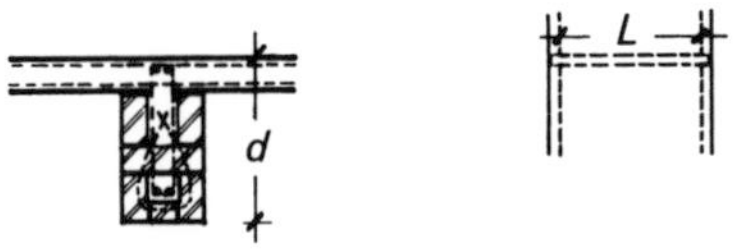	300-600	12-24	4-12	15-40	10-16	Deflection and splitting at brick joints. Bending

Table 1.8 continued   Horizontal Beam and Slab Elements - Roofs   Masonry

Element	Section and Plan	Typical Depths (d) (mm)	(in)	Typical Spans (L) (m)	(ft)	Typical L/d	Critical Factors for Sizing/ Remarks
Masonry shells		75-125	3-5	6-15	20-50	80-120	Bending at edge of shell Shell has funicular shape for major load so as to reduce tension and shear stresses Reinforcement may be necessary for larger spans
Masonry arch		70-600	3-24	8-50	25-160	30-60	Bending or cracking Arch requires funicular shape for load due to self-weight Flat arches cause high sidethrust L/h ratio about 5
Vaults and domes		50-150	2-6	5-40	16-120	30-80	Domes have been built spanning up to 40m and stone vaults up to 20m Vaults built at high level require buttresses

Table 1.8 continued   **Wall and Roof Systems**   **Masonry**

Element	Section and Plan	Typical Heights (H) (storeys)	Typical H/W	Remarks
Multistorey loadbearing walls with concrete slabs	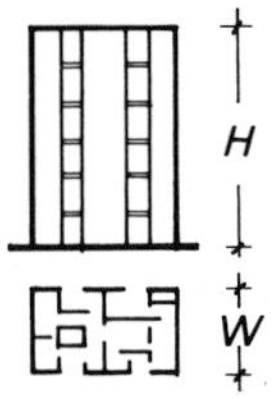	5-25 storeys	1.5-3.5	Most economic for buildings with small room areas Lateral forces resisted by walls in plane of forces
Masonry towers	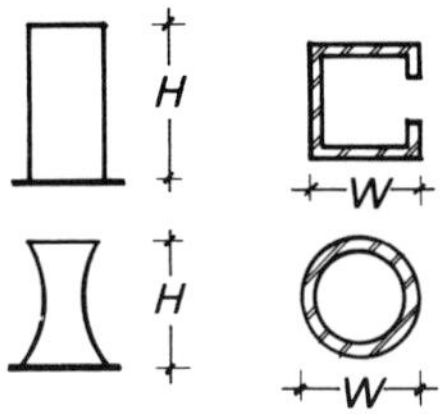	5-25 storeys	3-6	Sections may require stiffening with rings or horizontal slabs at intervals Lower heights permit higher values of L/d Wind forces are lower on towers of circular section

Table 1.8 continued   **Below Ground Elements**   **Masonry**

Element	Section	Typical Heights (H) (m)	(ft)	Typical H/d	Remarks
Reinforced masonry retaining wall	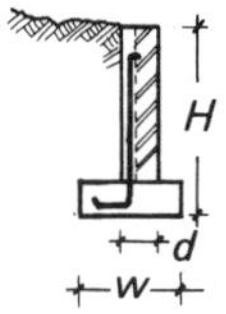	1-6	3-20	10-15	Wall made of reinforced hollow blocks or units with reinforced concrete pockets w about $H/2$ - $2H/3$
Masonry rubble in baskets	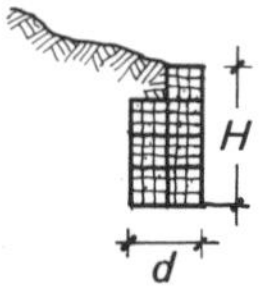	1-3	3-10	1-2	Rubble masonry block walls usually more economic than thick mass concrete retaining wall

Table 1.9   Vertical Support Elements   Concrete

Element	Horizontal and Vertical Section	Typical Heights (h) (m)	(ft)	h/d between Lateral Supports	Critical Factors for Sizing	Remarks
Cast-in-place column - single storey - multistorey	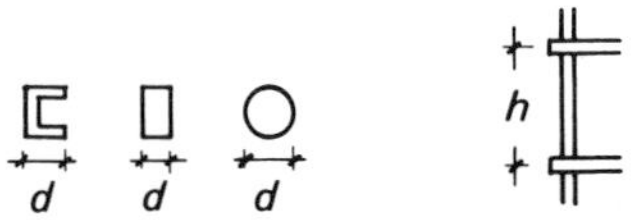	2-8 2-4	8-26 8-12	12-18 6-15	Buckling and crushing($h/d>10$) Crushing($h/d<10$) Bending	Columns rigidly connected to beams form frames which act as a vertical bracing system
Cast-in-place wall	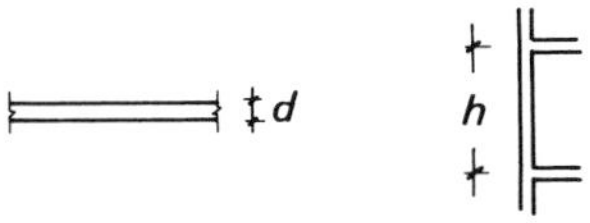	2-4	8-12	18-25	Buckling Construction method	
Cast-in-place no-fines wall	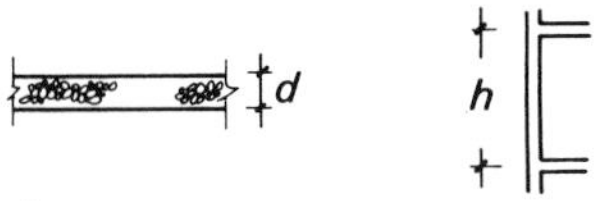	2-3	8-10	10-15	Crushing	Often used for housing Dimension $d>$ 200mm
Precast column - single storey - multistorey	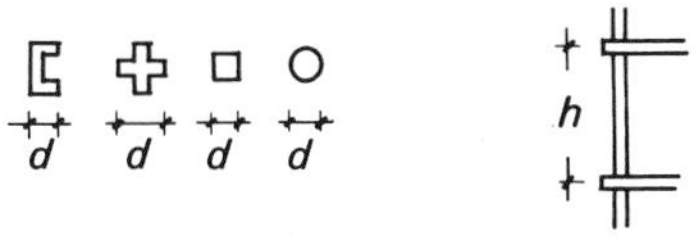	2-8 2-4	8-25 8-12	15-30 6-20	Buckling and crushing($h/d>10$) Crushing($h/d<10$) Bending Connections	Variety of high quality finishes available with precast products
Precast loadbearing panel	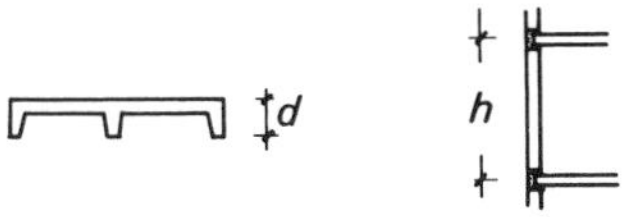	2-3	8-10	20-25	Buckling Connections Handling stresses	
Precast tilt-up panel	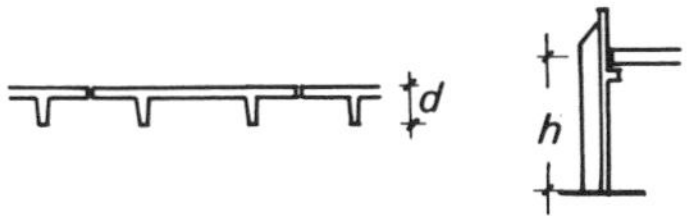	4-8	12-25	15-25	Handling stresses	
Prestressed concrete columns - single storey - multistorey	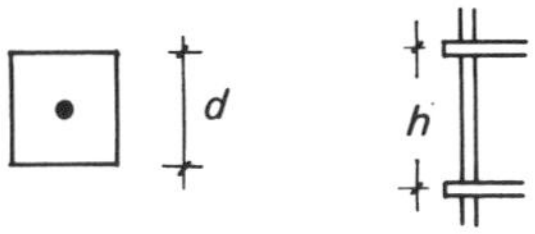	4-8 2-4	12-26 8-12	15-25 10-20	Buckling	Prestressing helps to eliminate tensile stresses due to bending
Prestressed concrete hangers		1-40	3-120	1-150	Variation in load	Stiffer and more resistant to corrosion than the steel tie

Table 1.9 continued Horizontal Beam and Slab Elements - Floors Concrete

Element	Section and Plan	Typical Depths (d) (mm)	(in)	Typical Spans (L) (m)	(ft)	Typical L/d	Critical Factors for Sizing/ Remarks
One-way solid slab - reinforced - prestressed	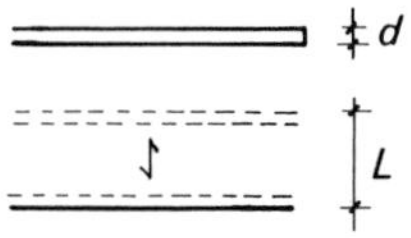	100-250 125-200	4-10 5-8	2-7 5-9	8-22 18-30	22-32 38-45	Deflection Bending Simply supported slabs have the lower values of L/d in given range.
Reinforced two-way slab	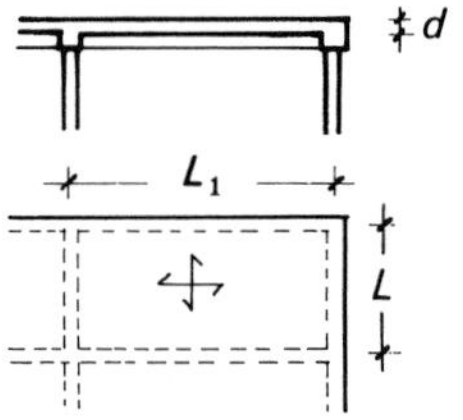	100-250	4-10	6-11	20-35	28-35	Deflection Bending Suitable for heavy loading and concentrated loads $L < L_1 < 1.4L$
One-way ribbed slab (pan joist) - reinforced - prestressed	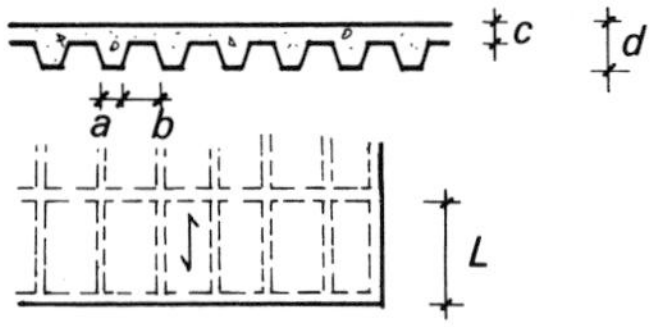	225-600 300-450	9-24 12-18	4-12 10-18	12-40 35-60	18-26 30-38	Deflection Bending Shear Most suitable for long spans with light loads Dimensions a, b and c as below
Two-way waffle slab - reinforced - prestressed	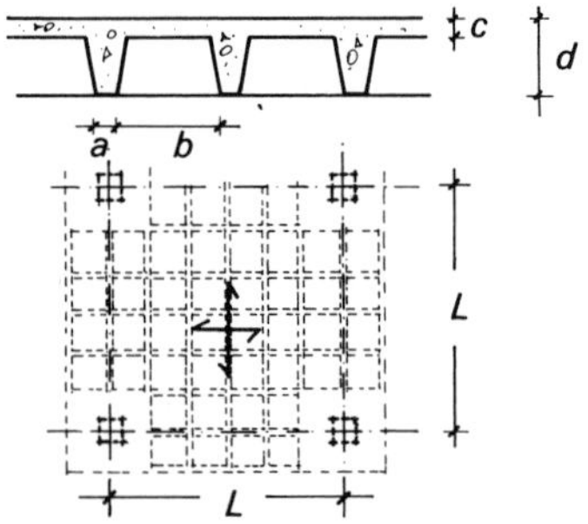	350-650 450-650	14-25 18-25	9-15 10-22	30-50 35-72	18-24 25-32	Deflection Bending Form moulds of standard size available More costly to form than ribbed slab Dimensions for a are 100-200mm, b are 900-1800mm, c are 60-100mm approximately
Reinforced one-way joists with hollow blocks (filler blocks)	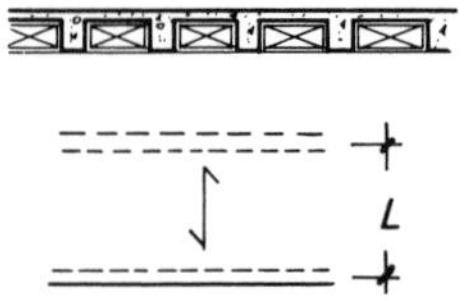	150-300	6-12	3-7	10-22	20-25	Bending Shear Small holes in the floor easily made for services

Table 1.9 continued		Horizontal Beam and Slab Elements - Floors					Concrete

Element	Section and Plan	Typical Depths (*d*) (mm)	(in)	Typical Spans (*L*) (m)	(ft)	Typical *L/d*	Critical Factors for Sizing/ Remarks
Flat slab without drop panels (flat plates) - reinforced - prestressed	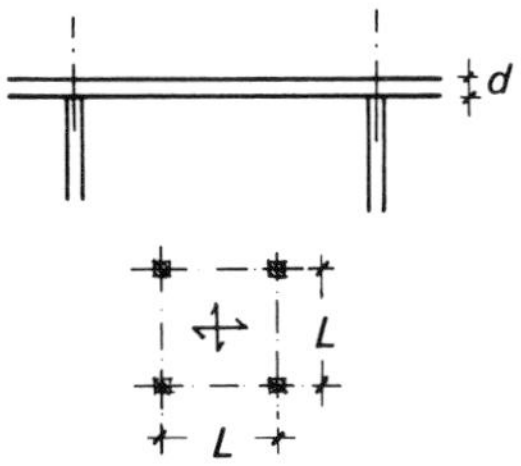	125-200 200-225	5-8 8-9	4-8 9-10	15-25 30-35	28-36 40-48	Shear round columns Deflection Bending Compared to beam and slab, flat slabs save depth and formwork costs but have lower resistance to lateral forces
Flat slab with drop panels - reinforced - prestressed	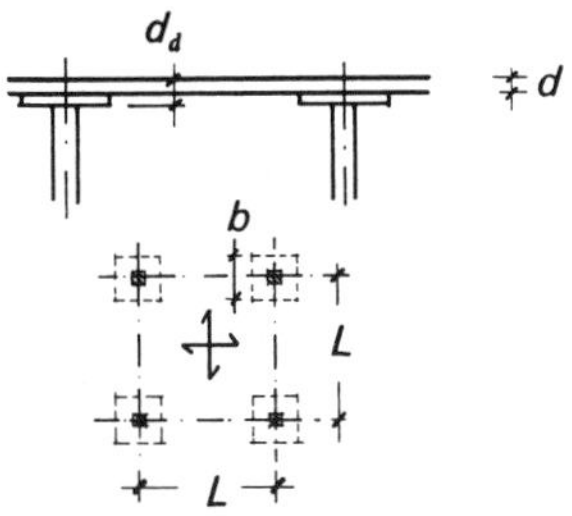	125-300 200-225	5-12 8-9	5-10 12-14	15-35 40-45	28-36 40-48	Shear at drops Deflection Bending Dimension d_d is about 1.25d-1.45d; *b* is about L/3
T or L Beam - reinforced - prestressed	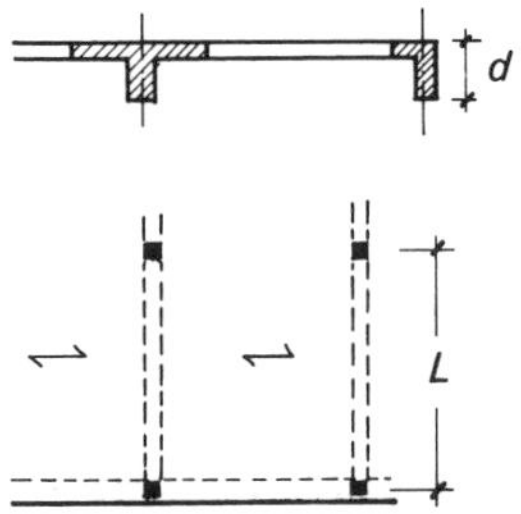	400-700 300-850	15-28 12-32	5-15 9-24	15-50 30-80	14-20 20-30	Beams usually spaced at about 3-7m giving slab depth between 100-175mm Simply supported beams have the lower values of L/d in the given range
Wide beam - reinforced - prestressed	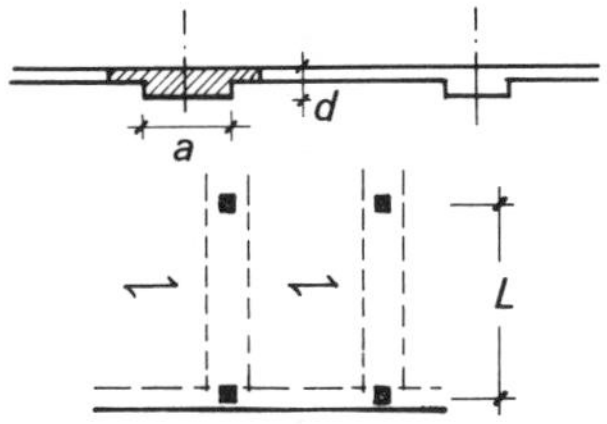	350-650 300-500	14-25 12-20	6-12 9-15	20-40 30-50	16-22 22-32	Deflection Bending Used where height is limited Simply supported beams have the lower values of L/d in the given range Dimension *a* is about 600-1200 mm

Table 1.9 continued | Horizontal Beam and Slab Elements - Floors | Concrete

Element	Section and Plan	Typical Depths (d) (mm)	(in)	Typical Spans (L) (m)	(ft)	Typical L/d	Critical Factors for Sizing/ Remarks
Partially prestressed ribbed floor	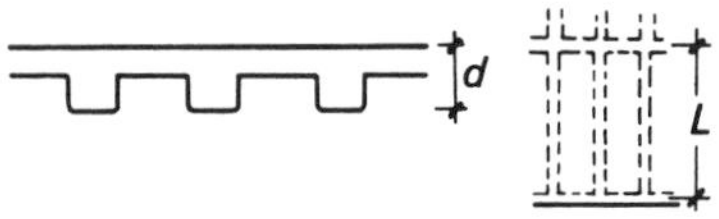	300-500	12-20	10-15	30-50	35-40	Live load Deflection Bending Less creep and upward deflection than fully prestressed floor
Block and joist floor (joists prestressed)	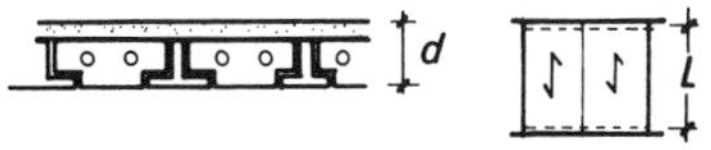	150-200	6-8	3-7	10-22	30-35	Bending Deflection Block and joist are precast but have cast-in-place topping 50-75 mm thick.
Precast prestressed planks	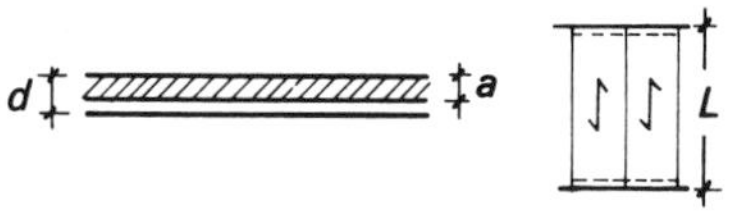	100-200	4-8	6-9	20-30	35-45	Live load deflection Bending Slabs more than 175mm deep often built with voids Topping depth, a, is 50-75mm thick.
Prestressed hollow core slab	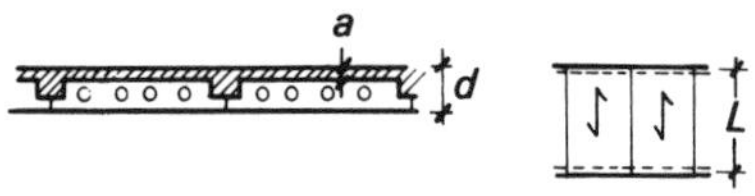	100-350	4-14	6-10	20-32	35-40	Bending Joists are precast but have cast-in-place topping of depth, a, 35-50mm thick.
Widespan slab - reinforced - prestressed	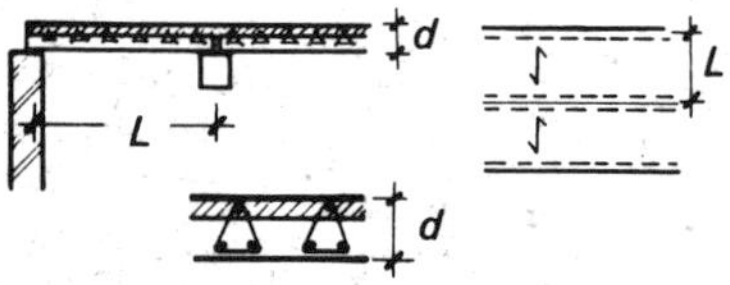	100-300 100-225	4-12 4-9	3-7 4-9	10-22 15-30	26-32 35-45	Bending Deflection Slabs are precast with cast-in-place topping Slab often propped during construction.
Precast prestressed double-T beams	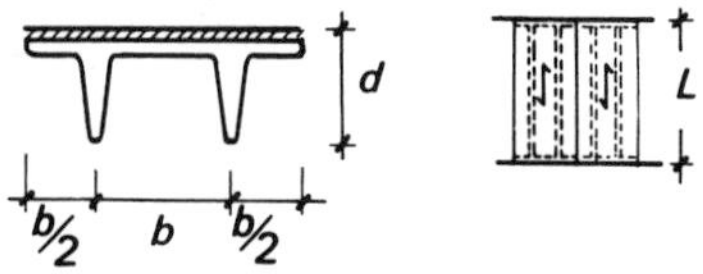	350-800	14-30	9-18	30-60	20-30	Live load Bending Shear Handling stresses Beams have cast-in-place topping 50-75mm thick

Table 1.9 continued — Horizontal Beam and Slab Elements - Roofs — Concrete

Element	Section and Plan	Typical Depths (d) (mm)	(in)	Typical Spans (L) (m)	(ft)	Typical L/d	Critical Factors for Sizing/ Remarks
Reinforced one-way solid slab	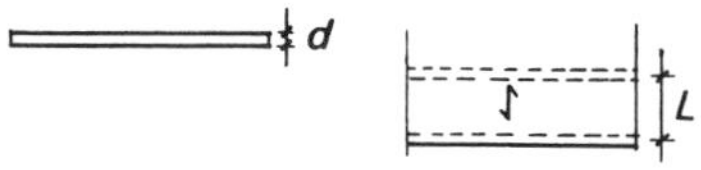	125-500	5-20	3-6	10-20	20-30	Deflection Bending
Reinforced one-way ribbed slab (pan joist)	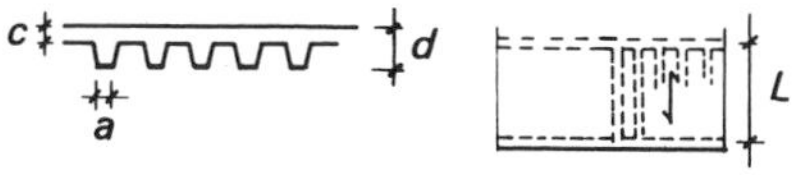	500-1200	20-50	6-14	20-45	25-30	Deflection Shear Bending Dimensions for a are 100-150mm; c are 50-100mm.
Reinforced two-way waffle slab	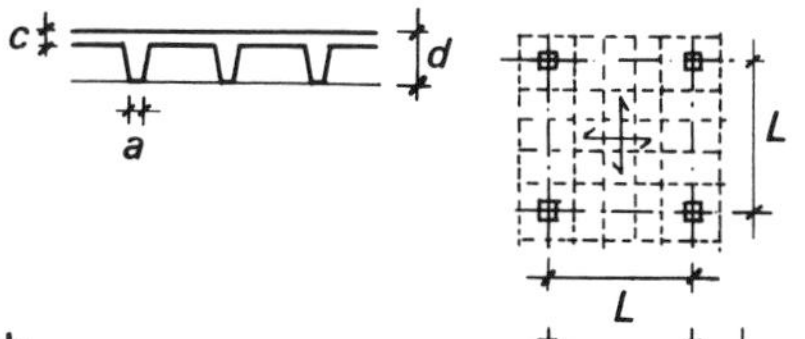	625-1500	25-60	9-16	30-55	20-25	Deflection Bending Dimensions as above
Reinforced flat slab without drop panels	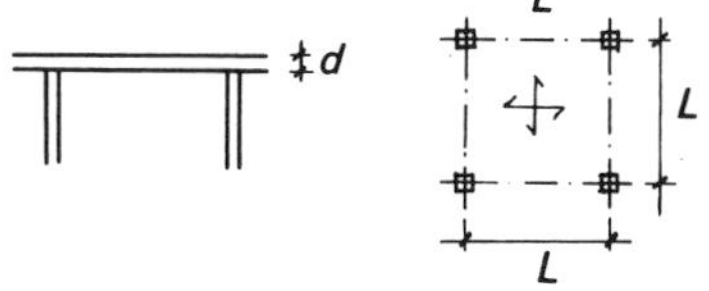	400-900	16-35	4-8	15-25	32	Shear round columns Deflection Bending
Prestressed hollow core slabs	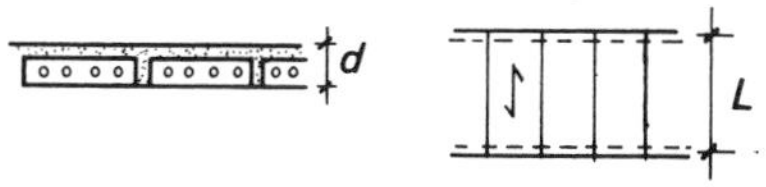	100-200	4-8	6-10	20-35	40-50	Compressive strength of unit Live load variation Slabs are precast but have 50-75mm cast-in-place topping
Prestressed double-T beam	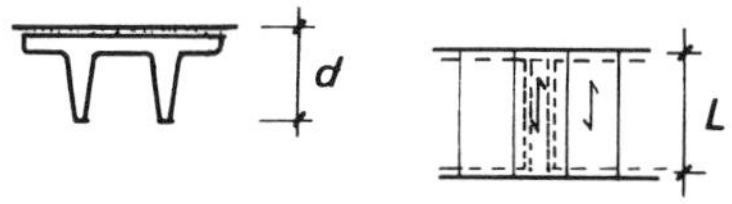	350-800	14-30	12-25	40-80	30-35	Bending Shear Handling stresses
Prestressed single-T beam	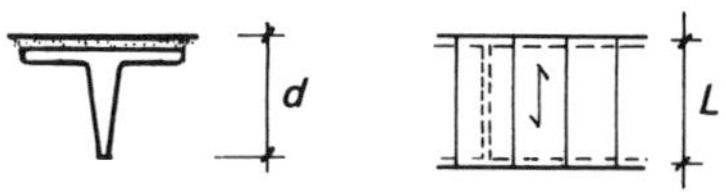	750-2500	30-100	15-25	50-80	30-35	Bending and shear Handling stresses Beams are precast but have 50-75mm cast-in-place topping
Reinforced aerated concrete slabs	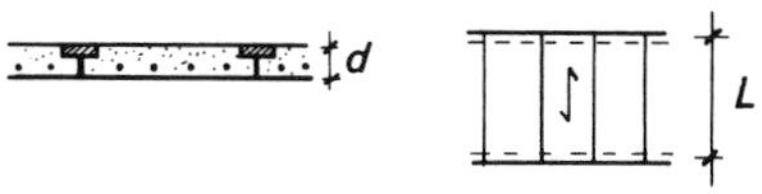	100-200	4-8	2-5	6-16	20-25	Bending Slabs connected by strip of cast-in-place concrete

Table 1.9 continued | Horizontal Beam and Slab Elements - Roofs | Concrete

Element	Section and Plan	Typical Depths (d) (mm)	(in)	Typical Spans (L) (m)	(ft)	Typical L/d	Critical Factors for Sizing/ Remarks
Reinforced inverted hyperbolic paraboloids (umbrellas)	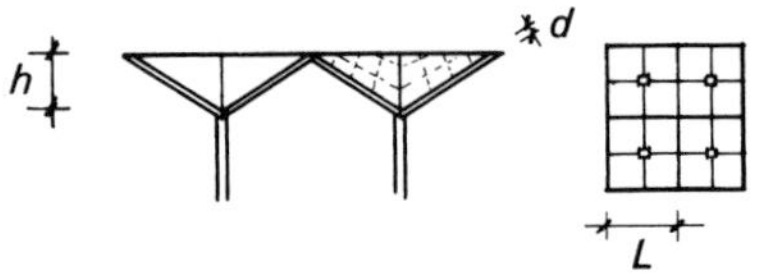	75-100	3-4	9-15	30-50	120-200	Cover to bars Tension reinforcement required at top of umbrella Umbrellas are independent and may be at different heights L/h ratio about 6-12.
Reinforced hyperbolic paraboloid shell	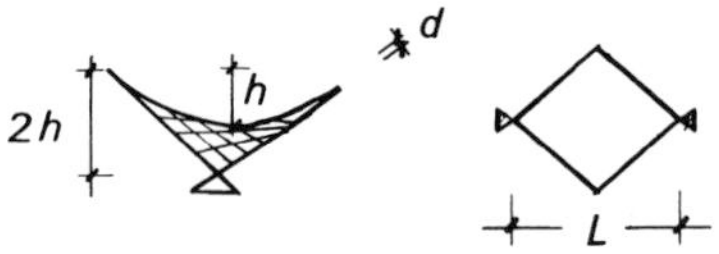	75-100	3-4	15-55	50-180	200-450	Deflection at tips Cover to bars Edge beams may be prestressed to overcome tensile stresses L/h ratio about 4-7
Domes	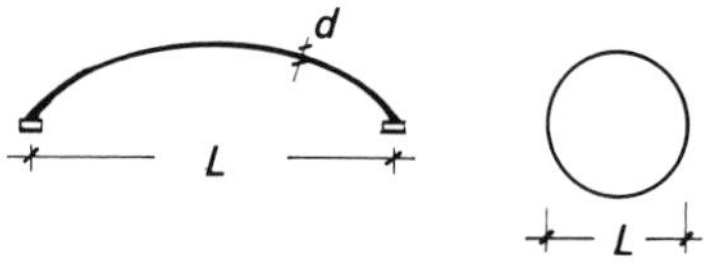	75-300	3-12	15-120	50-400	300-450	Shell buckling Cover to bars Minimum thickness, d, about 60 mm Tension ring at base often prestressed
Reinforced concrete folded plates	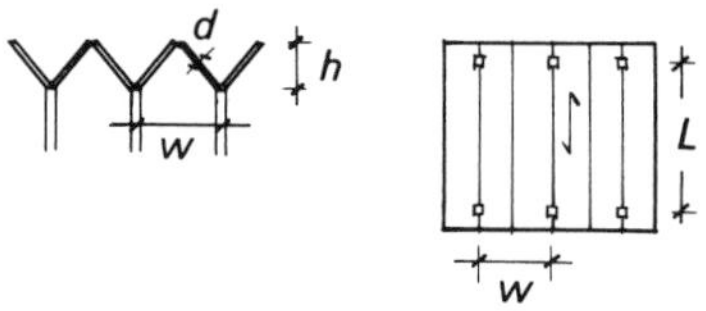	75-125	3-5	9-36	30-120	40-50 (w/d)	Bending in slab Tie force in valley Minimum thickness about 60mm L/h ratio about 8-15
Reinforced long barrel shell	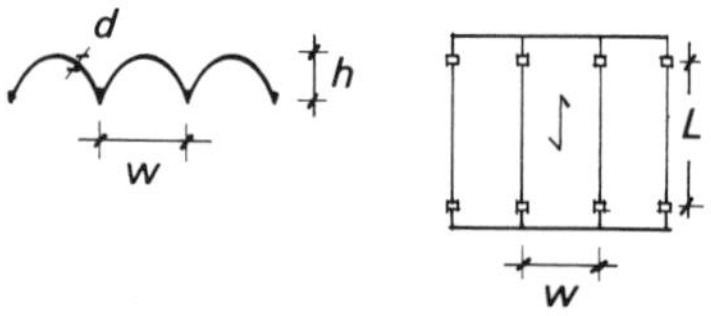	75-100	3-4	25-40	80-120	50-65(w/d)	Cover to bars Minimum thickness about 60mm Shell often prestressed to overcome tensile stresses L/h ratio about 10-15.
Reinforced skew grid	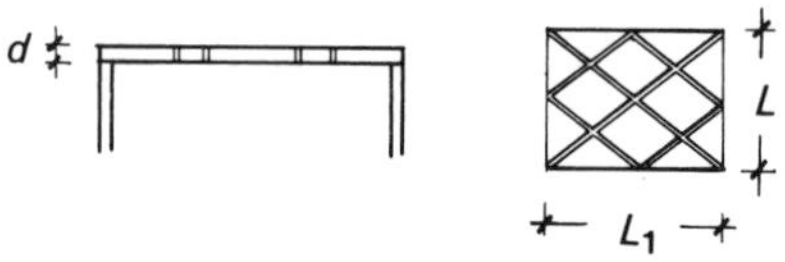	300-700	12-28	10-20	32-65	25-35	Deflection Bending Corners stiffer with skew grid than with grid parallel to sides thus allowing larger spans

Table 1.9 continued — Wall and Frame Systems — Concrete

Element	Section and Plan	Typical Spans (L) (m)	(ft)	Typical L/d	Remarks
Single storey precast frames	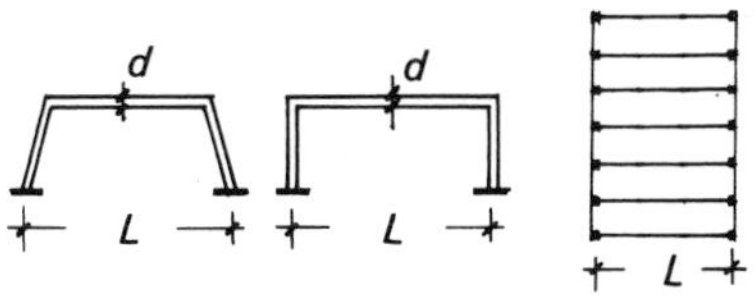	12-24	40-80	22-30	Joints in horizontal member usually at corner or about L/4 from corner if frame is large
Arches	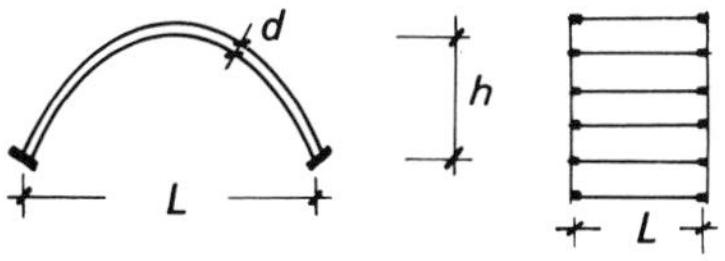	15-60	50-200	28-40	Arches usually continuous and fully rigid between springing points L/h ratio about 4-12
Precast exterior frames with interiors cast-in-place	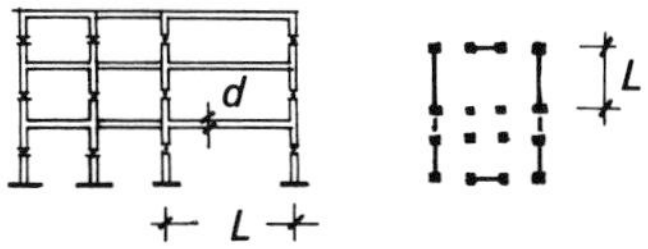	6-12	20-40	22-30	Connections between precast components done with cast-in-place concrete Interior frame may also use precast elements or be cast against precast permanent formwork System used for buildings up to about 20 storeys high Spans given indicative only
Cast-in-place floor and wall panel systems	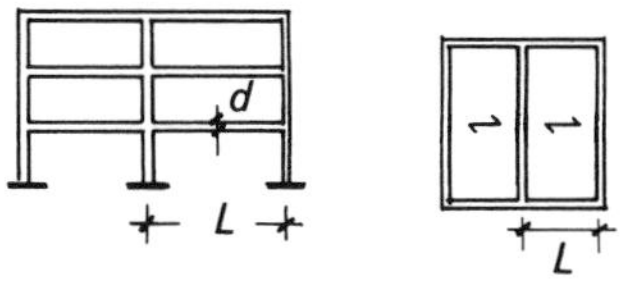	6-12	20-40	25-30	This system usually uses a standard rapid formwork system System is inherently rigid and used for buildings up to about 20 storeys high
Precast floor and wall panel systems	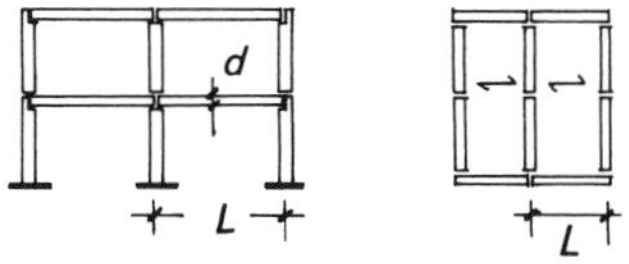	6-12	20-40	22-25	Usually no rigid joint between floor and wall panels; hence system similar in many respects to load bearing masonry with floor slab System economic up to about 15 storeys
Precast beams and columns with precast floor units	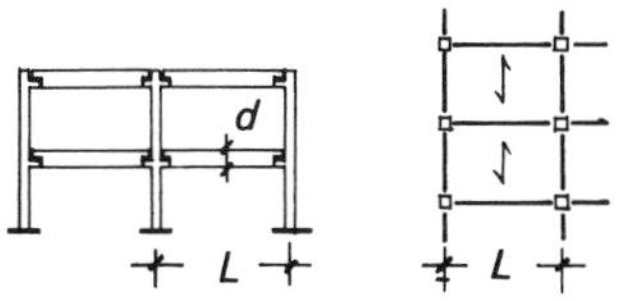	6-12	20-40	14-16	With rigid connections, system can only go up to about 2 storeys without extra vertical bracing

Table 1.9 continued   **Wall and Frame Systems**   Concrete

Element	Section and Plan	Typical Heights (H) (storeys)	Typical H/W	Remarks
Multistorey cast-in-place frames	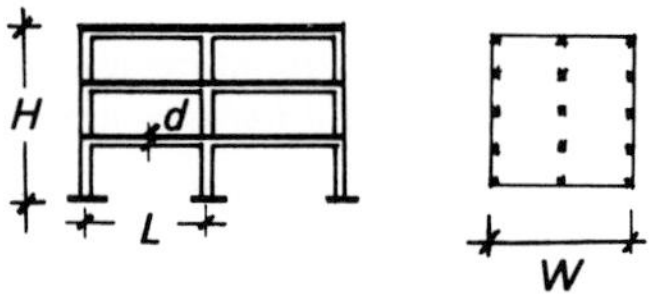	5-15 storeys	1-5	Cast-in-place frames without extra vertical bracing are economic up to about 15 storeys L/d ratio about 20-40
Shear walls or cores with rigid frame	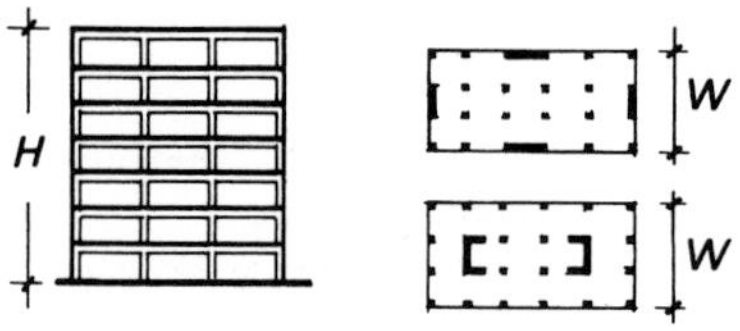	10-55 storeys	4-5	Shear wall or core interacts with rigid frame to provide a vertical bracing system which is stiff over height of building Given values of height ratio (H/W) larger for buildings less than about 20 storeys high
Framed tubes and core		40-65 storeys	6-7	Also known as tube in tube system Framed tube interacts with core
Core structures with suspended floors or semi-rigid frame	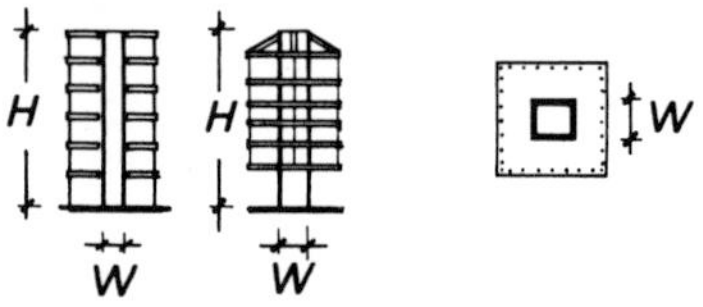	10-30 storeys	8-12	Core provides all lateral stability Only limited plan areas with suspended floors

Table 1.9 continued   **Below Ground Elements**   Concrete

Element	Section	Typical Heights (H) (m)	(ft)	Typical H/d	Remarks
Retaining wall	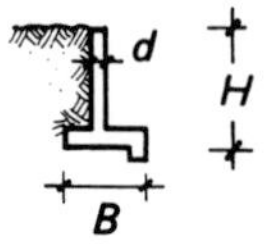	2-6		10-12	Dimension B is about $H/2$-$2H/3$ Toe helps to prevent sliding
Shell and box enclosures	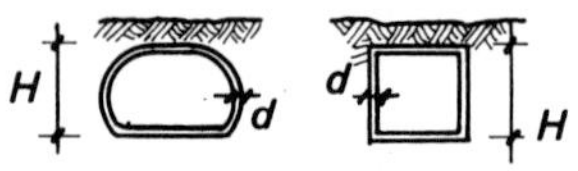	1-4		25-30	Used for subways, culverts etc. Loading depends on soil type and depth

Table 1.10   Vertical Support Elements   Steel

Element	Horizontal and Vertical Section	Typical Heights (h) (m)	(ft)	h/d between Lateral Supports	Critical Factors for Sizing	Remarks
Rolled steel of open section - single storey - multistorey	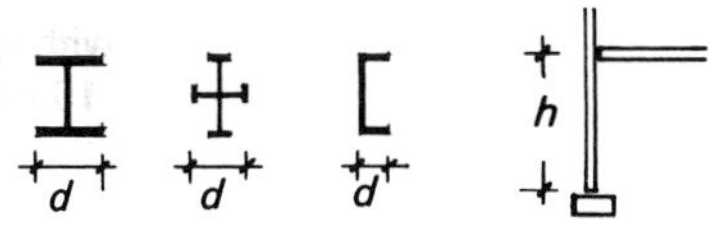	2-8 2-4	8-25 8-12	20-25 7-18	Buckling ($h/d>14$) Buckling and compression ($h/d<14$)	Standard rolled sections usual but special shapes may be made by welding Connections easier with open rather than closed sections
Rolled steel of hollow section - single storey - multistorey		2-8 2-4	8-25 8-12	20-35 7-28	Buckling ($h/d>20$) Buckling and compression ($h/d<20$)	Closed sections have smaller exposed surface and greater torsional stiffness than open sections of same weight.
Lattice column		4-10	12-30	20-25	Buckling	Lattice may be used if large column required
Steel and concrete composite column	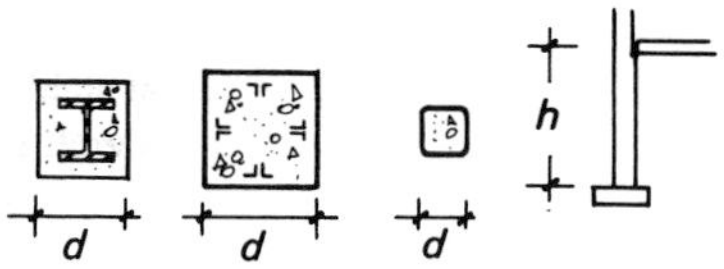	2-4	8-12	6-15	Buckling and crushing ($h/d>10$)	Concrete increases stiffness and fire resistance
Cold-formed steel studs with steel panels	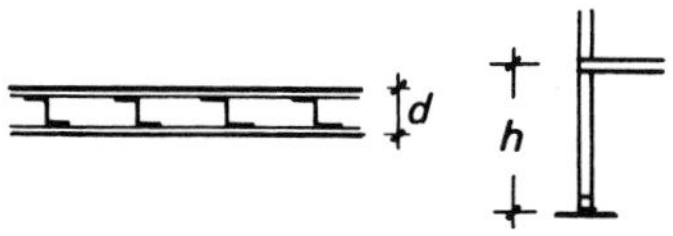	2-8	8-25	15-50	Buckling	Steel studs can also be stiffeners for gypsum, GRC or plywood panels
High strength steel hangers	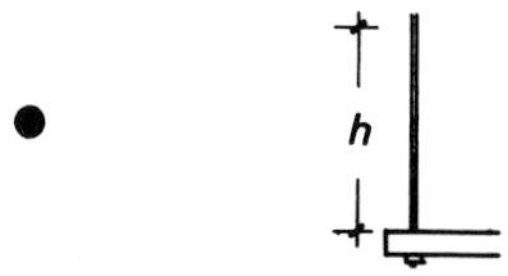	1-40	3-120	..	Axial stiffness	Hangers usually solid rods, strand or rope cables. Rods have less tensile strength but axially stiffer than cable

Table 1.10 continued   Horizontal Beam and Deck Elements - Floors   Steel

Element	Section and Elevation	Typical Depths (d) (mm)	(in)	Typical Spans (L) (m)	(ft)	Typical L/d	Critical Factors for Sizing/ Remarks
Steel decking	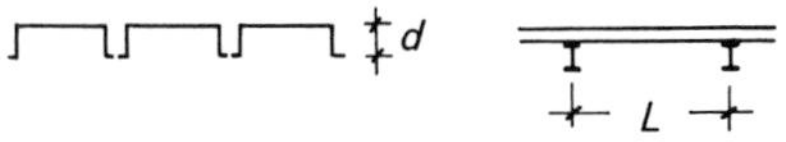	50-75	2-3	2-3	6-10	35-40	Deflection
Cold-formed steel deck with composite concrete topping	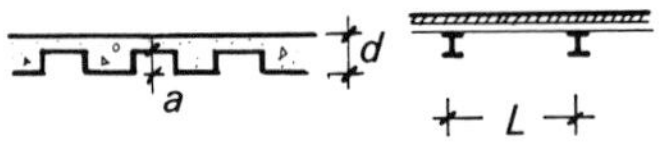	100-150	4-6	2-4	6-15	25-30	Deflection of deck when used as formwork Thickness of concrete for fire protection Dimension $a \approx 40$-80mm
Wide flange rolled steel section	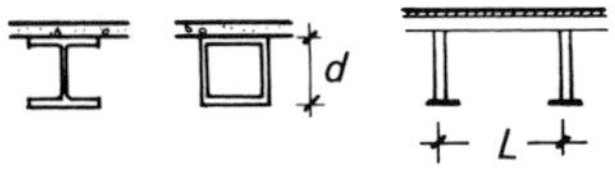	100-500	4-20	4-12	15-40	18-28	Deflection
Deep rolled steel section	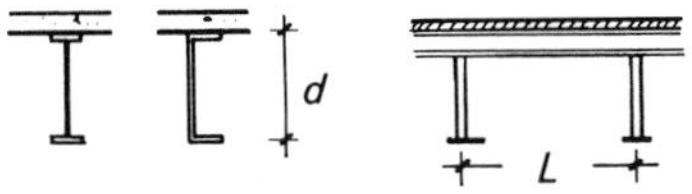	200-500	8-40	6-30	20-100	15-20	Deflection Bending strength
Rolled steel truss	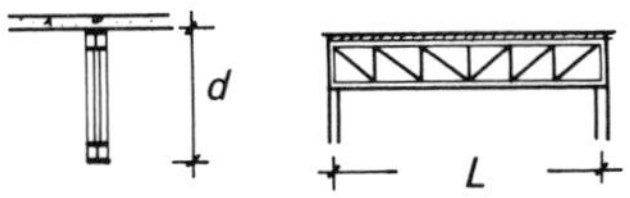	1000-4000	40-160	12-45	40-150	8-15	Axial compression of members Joints Deflection
Vierendeel girder	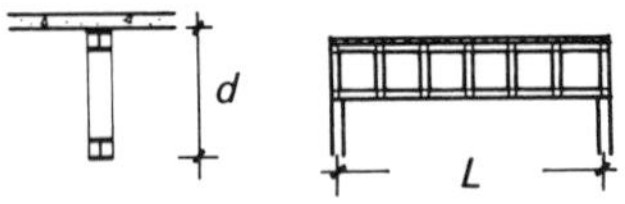	1000-3000	40-120	6-18	20-60	4-12	Bending strength of members near supports Deflection
Composite concrete steel girder	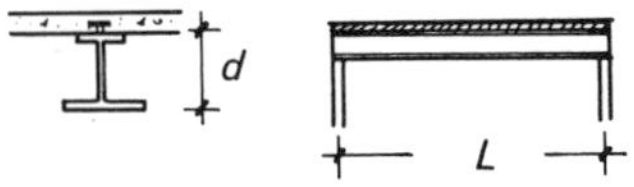	300-1000	12-40	7-15	25-50	20-25	Often used with secondary steel joists between girders Saving of about 25% in steel compared to non-composite section

Table 1.10 continued
Horizontal Beam and Deck Elements - Roofs
Steel

Element	Section and Elevation	Typical Depths (d) (mm)	(in)	Typical Spans (L) (m)	(ft)	Typical L/d	Critical Factors for Sizing/ Remarks
Cold-formed steel deck		25-120	1-5	2-6	8-20	40-70	Deflection
Steel sandwich panel		75	3	2-3	8-10	25-30	Sheet has injected plastic foam insulation Good bond of insulation to steel sheet is important.
Channel reinforced woodwool deck		50-150	2-6	2-4	6-12	20-25	Deflection Strength
Cold-formed steel sections		120-300	5-12	3-12	10-40	25-35	Deflection Often very flexible about minor axis
Cold-formed open web steel joist		300-1000	12-40	5-20	15-65	15-25	Deflection Buckling
Wide flange rolled steel section		100-500	4-20	6-14	20-45	20-30	Deflection
Deep rolled steel section		200-1000	8-40	6-60	20-200	18-26	Deflection Bending strength Buckling of top flange

Table 1.10 continued Horizontal Beam and Surface Elements - Roofs   Steel

Element	Section and Elevation	Typical Spans (L) (m)	(ft)	Typical L/d	Remarks
Rolled steel castellated beam	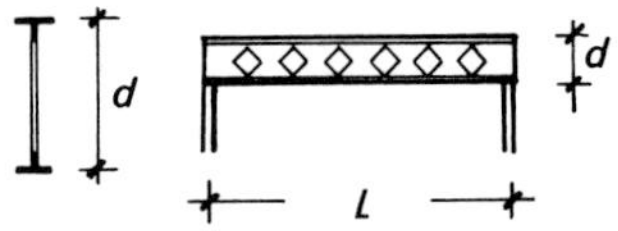	6-18	20-60	10-18	Web buckling Shear
Flat rolled steel truss	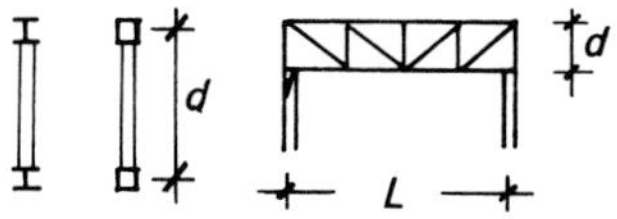	12-75	40-250	10-18	Bending strength Deflection Typical spacings of trusses 6-12m Truss cambered for spans >25m
Sloping rolled steel truss	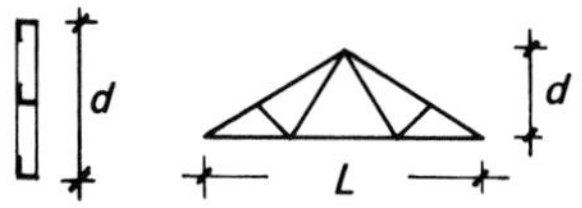	8-20	25-65	5-10	Truss often bolted up from steel angle sections

Table 1.10 continued   Horizontal Beam and Surface Elements - Roofs   Steel

Element	Section and Plan	Typical Spans (L) (m)	(ft)	Typical L/d	Remarks
Two-layer space frame	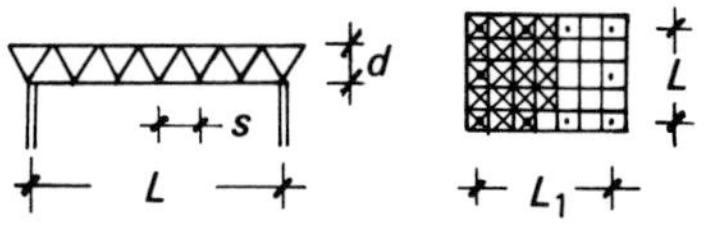	30-150	100-500	15-30	Space frame has pinned or semi-rigid joints and works as 3-dimensional reticulated structure Plan geometry based on rectangular, triangular or hexagonal grids Size of grid, d, about 1.4h and about 5-12% of span, L $L < L_1 < 1.4L$
Braced barrel vault	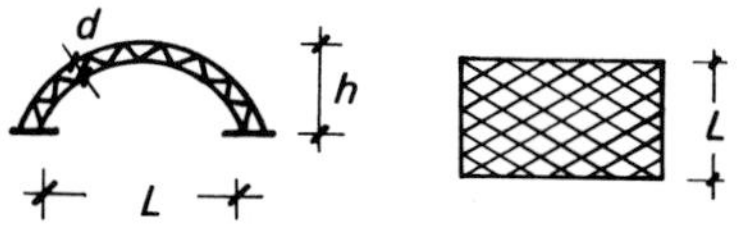	20-100	65-320	55-60	Vaults may have single or double layer of steelwork L/h ratio about 5-6

Table 1.10 continued   Horizontal Beam and Surface Elements - Roofs   Steel

Element	Section and Plan	Typical Spans (L) (m)	(ft)	Typical L/h	Remarks
Corrugated arch	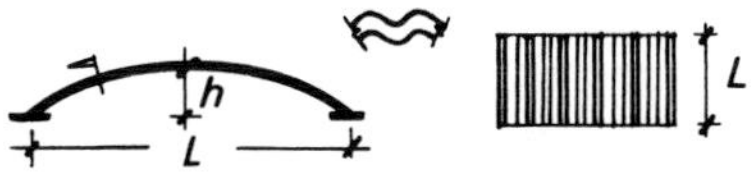	30-45	100-150	4-5	Made with two layers of cold-formed corrugated sheet bolted together with insulation between
Cable-stayed roof beams	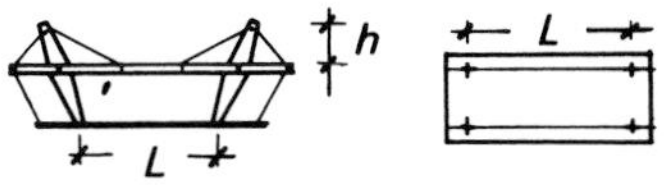	60-150	200-500	5-10	Cables serve to support horizontal beams and increase the span
Hanging cable roof	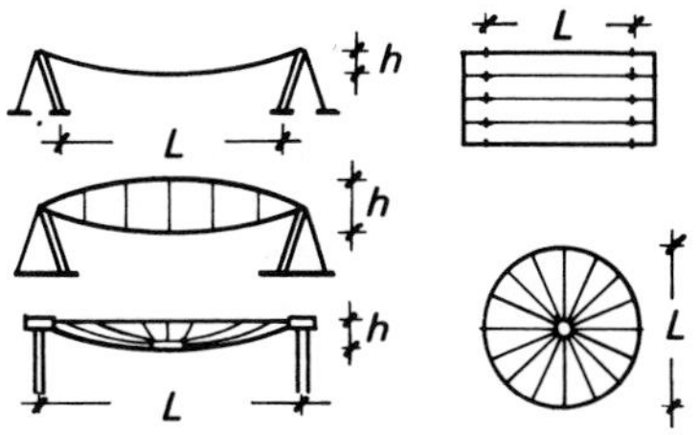	50-180	160-600	8-15	Roofs have single curvature (gutter) shape or synclastic double curvature (saucer) shape
Net roof with rigid covering	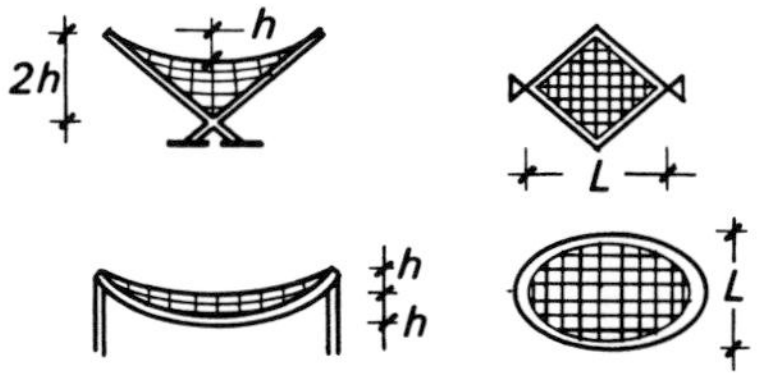	30-180	100-600	6-12	Roofs have anticlastic double curvature (saddle) shape
Single-layer domed grid	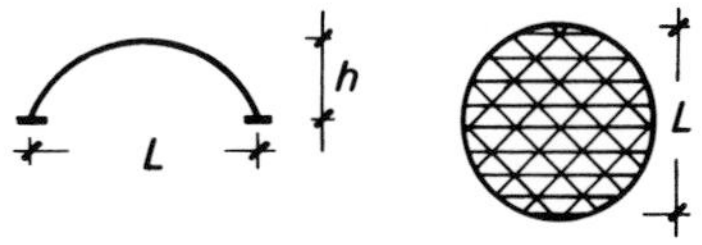	15-100	50-350	5-7	Double-layer domes also constructed spanning up to 200m
Double-layer stressed skin folded plate	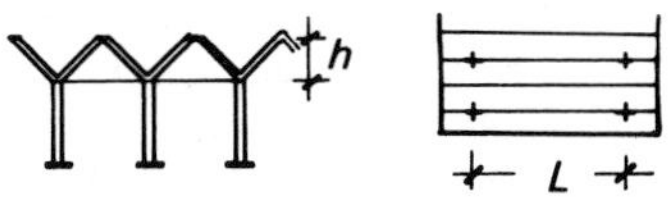	9-30	30-100	10-20	Single-layer skin construction possible spanning up to about 25m. Failure usually caused by connections or buckling
Double-layer stressed skin hyperbolic paraboloid shell		9-30	30-100	6-12	Steel sheets are laid along the straight line generators on the hp surface and slightly twisted across their width
Air supported stainless steel membrane	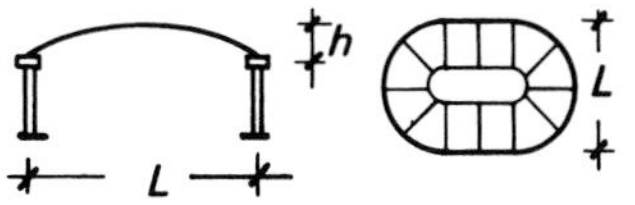	80-300	250-1000	25-30	Low L/h ratio gives roof wind uplift and requires only small change in shape from flat plan shape

Table 1.10 continuedFrame Systems

Element	Section and Plan	Typical Spans (L) (m)	(ft)	Typical L/d	Remarks
Single storey rigid frame		9-60	30-200	35-40	Frame is rigid in its own plane Typical spacing of frames $L/4$-$L/6$
Arch		60-150	200-500	40-50	Buckling often critical Arch usually has pinned connections at base and sometimes at apex too Typical L/h ratio about 5-15
Single storey beam and post		6-40	20-120	12-20	Frame not rigid in its own plane so vertical bracing necessary e.g. with rigid gables connected to roof plane
Multistorey rigid frame		6-20	20-50	20-35	Sidesway at top and between storeys often critical Rigid joints between beams and columns obtained by welding or welding and bolting System economic up to about 25 storeys With moment joints between beams and columns, obtained by bolting, building may go up to about 15 storeys without the use of extra vertical bracing
Shear truss and simple frame		typical height, H 5-20 storeys		H/W 6-8	Frame is not rigidly connected to shear truss Shear truss more efficient as vertical bracing than rigid frame

Table 1.10 continued   Frame Systems   Steel

Element	Section and Plan	Typical Heights (H) (storeys)	Typical H/W	Remarks
Shear truss and rigid frame	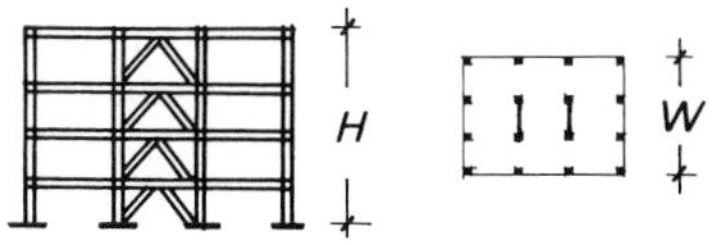	10-40 storeys	3-4	Frame is rigidly connected and interacts with shear truss Frame provides ductile strength in earthquake areas
Shear truss and rigid frame with belt trusses	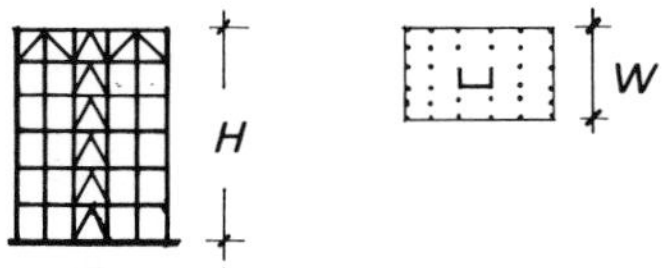	40-60 storeys	5-7	Horizontal belt trusses reduce sidesway
Framed tube	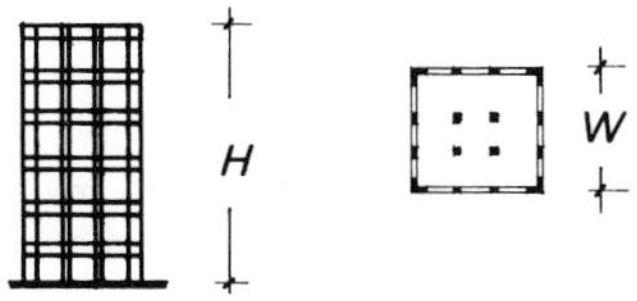	30-80 storeys	5-7	Deep column and beam sections stiffen frame so that it can behave like a perforated tube
Diagonal truss tube	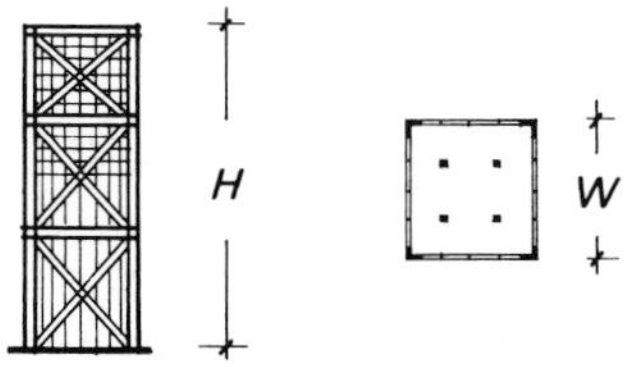	60-110 storeys	5-7	Diagonals take horizontal and vertical loads and stiffen frame

Table 1.10 continued   Below Ground Elements   Steel

Element	Section	Typical Spans (L) (m)	(ft)	Typical L/d	Remarks
Steel corrugated shells	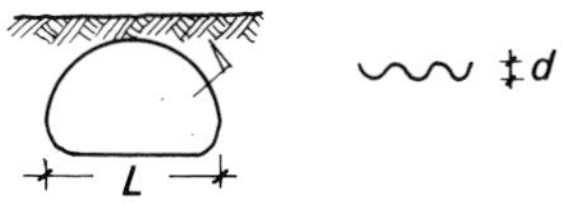	2-8	6-26	30-80	Pipe arches usually made from galvanised cold-formed steel sheets with corrugations about 50-100mm deep and bolted together with high strength bolts Compression in sheet depends on soil and depth of cover

Table 1.11   Vertical Support Elements   Wood

Element	Horizontal and Vertical Section	Typical Heights (h) (m)	(ft)	h/d between Lateral Supports	Critical Factors for Sizing	Remarks
Glued laminated timber column		2-4	8-12	15-30	Splitting and crushing ($h/d < 15$) Crushing and buckling ($h/d > 15$)	Ratio $w/d \approx$ 2-3 Multistorey columns may require lower h/d ratios than those given.
Stud frame wall panel	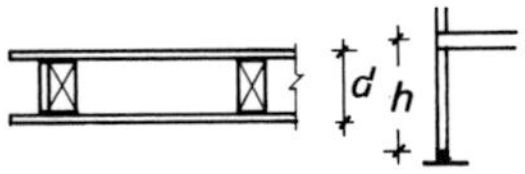	2-4	8-12	20-35	Crushing and buckling Thickness of insulation required	Studs usually at about 400mm centres with plywood or other sheeting nailed to it.
Solid timber column	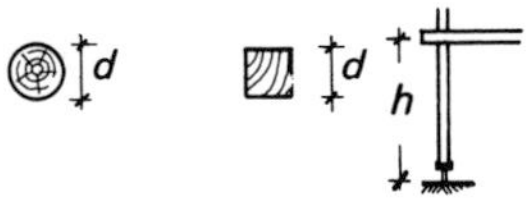	2-4	8-12	15-30	Warping or distortion of timber	Multistorey columns may require lower h/d ratios than those given

Table 1.11 continued   Horizontal Beam and Deck Elements - Floors   Wood

Element	Section and Plan	Typical Depths (d) (mm)	(in)	Typical Spans (L) (m)	(ft)	Typical L/d	Critical Factors for Sizing/ Remarks
Particle boards	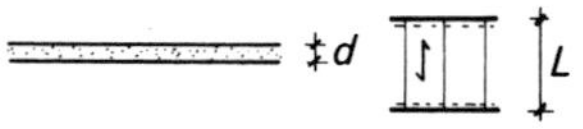	12-30	0.5-1.25	0.3-0.6	1-2	24	Strength Creep deflection
Plywood floor decking	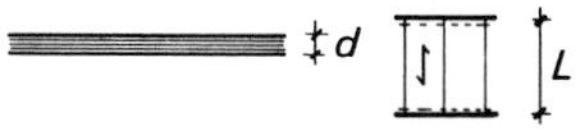	12-30	0.5-1.25	0.3-0.9	1-3	30-40	Deflection Point loads Strength.
Softwood floor boards	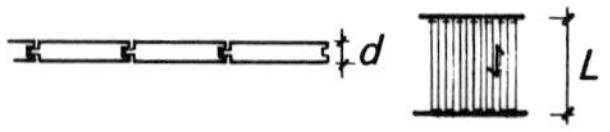	16-25	0.5-1.0	0.6-0.8	2-2.5	25-35	Deflection Strength
Joists with floor board - softwood - hardwood	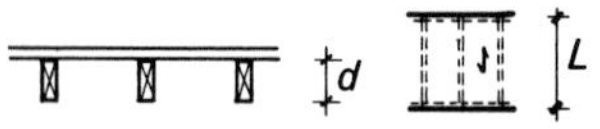	200-300 100-250	8-12 4-10	2-6 2-7	6-20 6-22	12-20 22-28	Deflection Spacing of joists is about 450-600mm.
Glued laminated timber beam	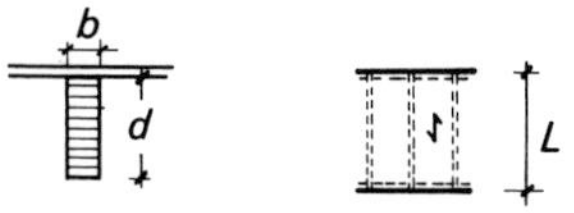	180-1400	7-55	5-12	16-40	14-18	Deflection Ratio d/b about 3-5 to prevent instability of unrestrained section.
Open web joist with wood flanges and steel tube diagonals	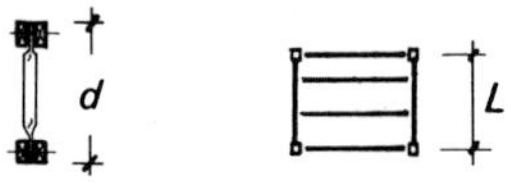	500-2000	20-80	5-18	16-60	8-10	Deflection Vibration

Table 1.11 continued Horizontal Beam and Deck Elements - Roofs **Wood**

Element	Section and Elevation	Typical Depths (d) (mm)	(in)	Typical Spans (L) (m)	(ft)	Typical L/d	Critical Factors for Sizing/ Remarks
Roof planks	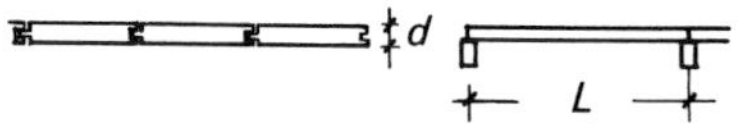	25-75	1-3	2-6	6-20	45-60	Deflection Planks assumed to be simply supported
Plywood roof decking	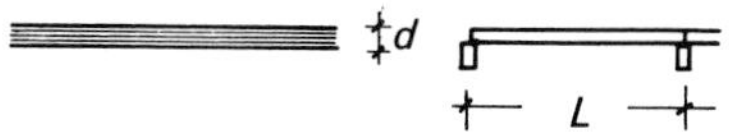	10-20	0.5-0.75	0.3-1.2	1-4	50-70	Deflection Decking assumed to be continuous
Stressed skin plywood roof panels	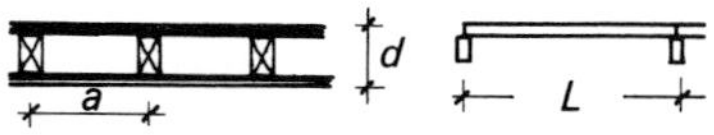	100-450	4-18	3-7	10-24	30-35	Deflection Panel assumed to be simply supported Dimension a is about 300-500mm
Trough decking with plywebs	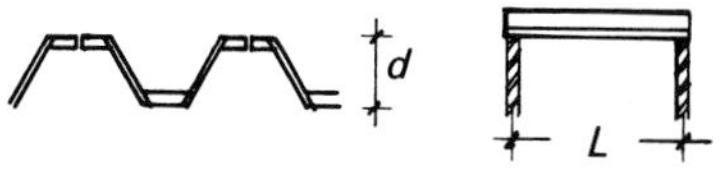	225-400	9-16	5-12	16-40	25-30	Decking assumed to be simply supported
Joists with roof deck - softwood - hardwood	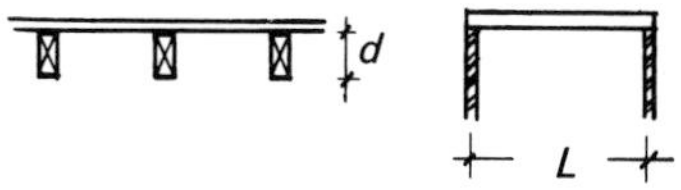	100-225 100-250	4-9 4-10	2-6 3-8	7-20 10-25	20-25 30-35	Deflection Joists assumed to be simply supported and spaced at 600mm
Roof purlins - softwood - hardwood	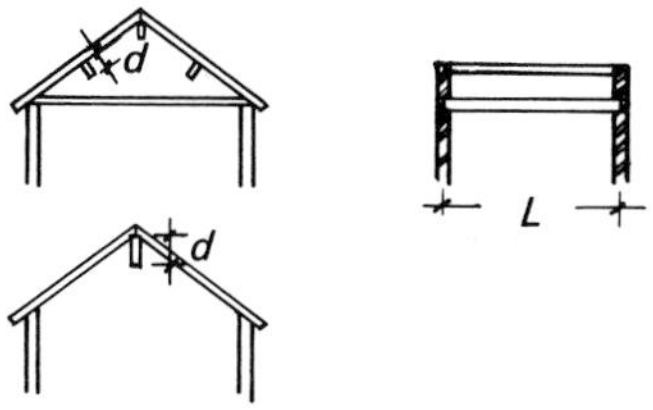	150-300 200-400	6-12 8-16	2-5 3-8	6-16 10-25	10-14 15-20	Available length and depth of wood Bending strength Purlin assumed to be simply supported and carrying about 2m width of roof

Table 1.11 continued | Horizontal Beam and Deck Elements - Roofs | Wood

Element	Section and Elevation	Typical Depths (d) (mm)	(in)	Typical Spans (L) (m)	(ft)	Typical L/d	Critical Factors for Sizing/ Remarks
Glued laminated timber beam with roof deck	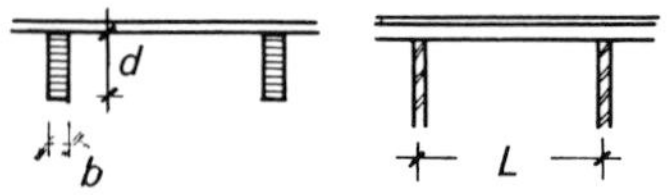	180-1400	7-55	4-30	12-100	15-20	Deflection Beams assumed to be simply supported with spacing L/3-L/5 Ratio d/b about 5-8
Glued plywood box beam	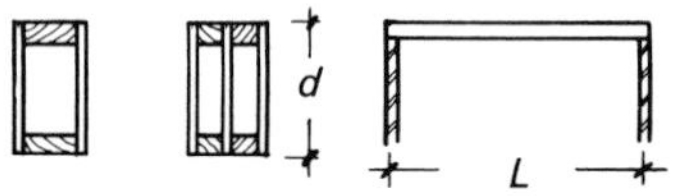	200-2000	8-75	6-20	20-65	10-15	Deflection Bending strength Longitudinal Shear Web buckling Beams assumed to be simply supported
Open web joist with wood flanges and steel tube diagonals	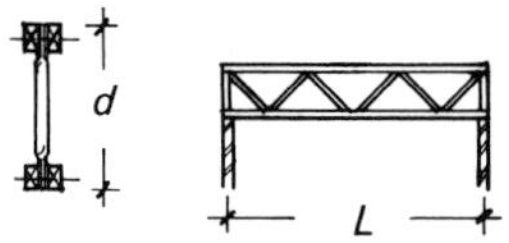	500-2000	20-80	9-30	30-100	10-15	Webs bolted to flanges
Trussed rafter without purlins	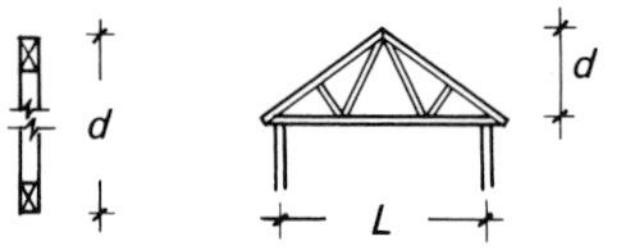	1200-2000	50-80	6-10	20-30	4-6	Strength of joints Bending in rafter Assumed spacing 600mm
Sloping trusses with purlins	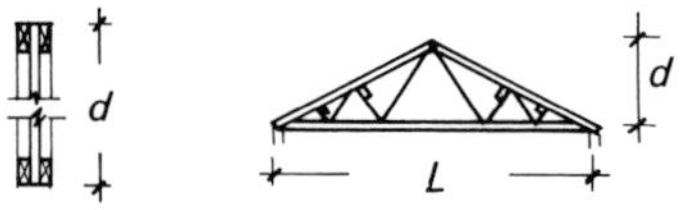	1000-3000	40-120	6-20	20-65	5-7	Strength of joints Assumed spacing is 2-5m
Flat top timber girders	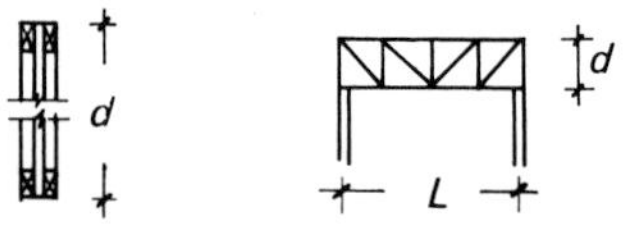	1500-3000	60-120	12-25	40-80	8-10	Strength of joints Assumed spacing is 4-6m

Element	Section and Plan	Typical Spans (L) (m)	(ft)	Typical L/h	Remarks
Stressed skin panel folded plate roof	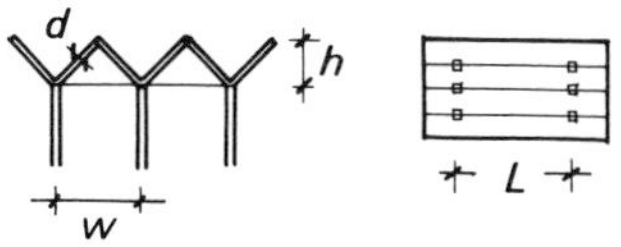	9-20	30-65	8-15	Panel has 2 skins with w/d ratio of 20-30 and thickness of about 75-200mm
Three-layer stressed skin ply hyperbolic paraboloid		12-30	40-100	2-8	Shell has edge beams with L/d ratio of about 60-80
Three-layer stressed skin ply barrel vault	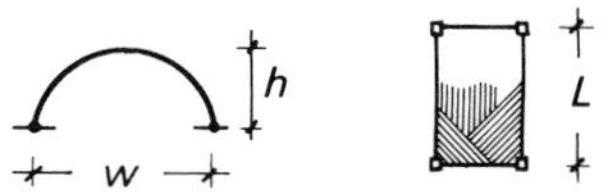	9-30	30-100	4-8	Shell has edge beams Ratio w/h about 2-4
Pyramid roof	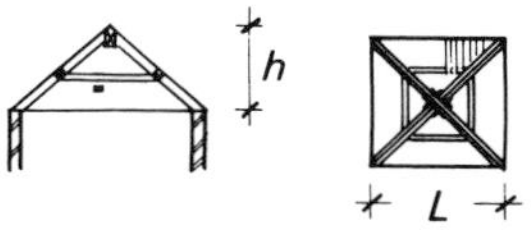	12-35	40-115	2-6	Simple to construct Often used with steel tension members at base
Glued laminated timber dome	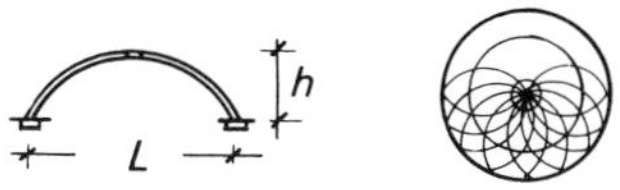	12-100	40-320	5-7	Typically, dome members have 3-way grid, radial lines or lamellar curve patterns when projected on plan Connections semi-rigid or pinned
Lamellar arch roof	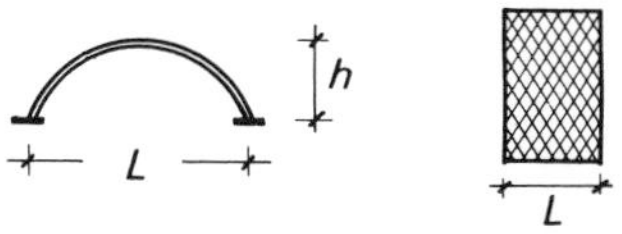	15-25	50-80	5-7	Typically, members on 2 intersecting parallel lamellar lines making diamond shapes when projected on plan
Warped rectangular grid (hyperbolic paraboloid)		12-80	40-260	5-10	Grid covered with ply panels Ratio L/d about 60-80
Domed grid shell	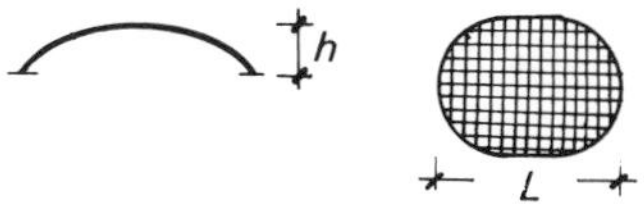	12-30	40-100	5-7	Grid members flexible to allow shaping to curve Shape reasonably close to funicular shape for dead load

Table 1.11 continued　　　　　　　Frame and Wall Systems　　　　　　　Wood

Element	Section and Plan	Typical Spans (L) (m)	(ft)	Typical L/d	Remarks
Rigid glued laminated timber frame	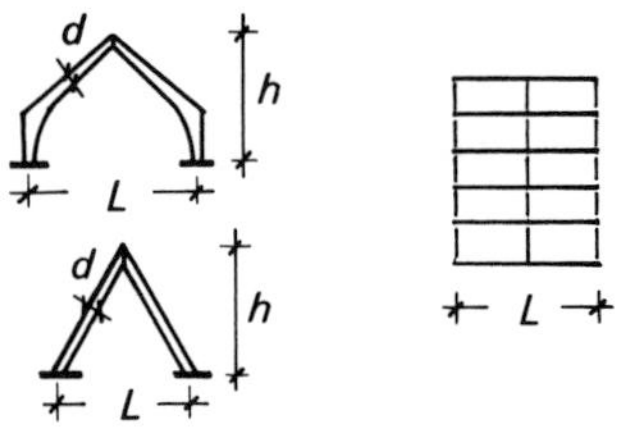	12-35	40-115	30-50	Spacing of frames about 4-6m Laminated frame may be curved and of varying depth but more expensive than uniform straight members Ratio L/h about 5-7
Glued laminated beam and post	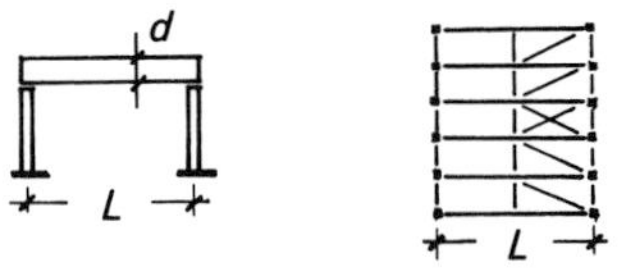	4-30	12-100	18-22	Frame not rigid in its own plane so vertical bracing necessary e.g. with rigid gables connected to roof plane
Plywood box portal frames	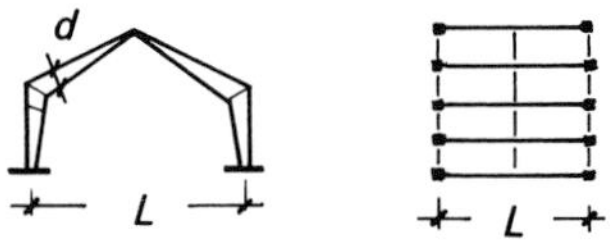	9-45	30-150	20-40	Box beams made of solid section timber flanges, glued and nailed to plywood side pieces, acting as webs Spacing of frames about 4-6m
Glued laminated arch	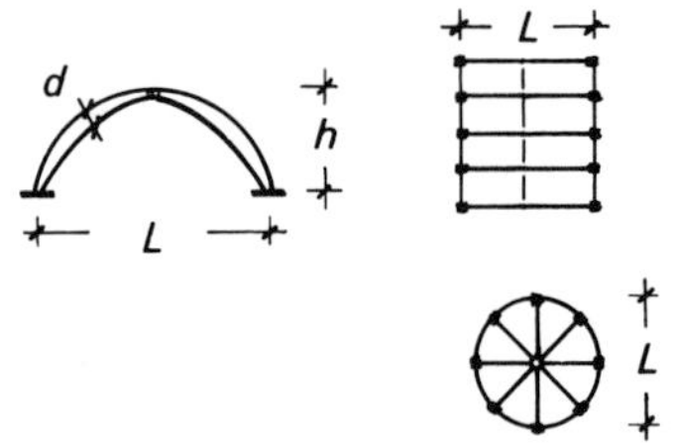	15-100	50-325	30-50	Maximum convenient transportable lengths 15-25m Arch shape is nearly funicular for important load case Arches may have rectangular or circular plan Ratio L/h about 5-7
Plywood floor and wall panels	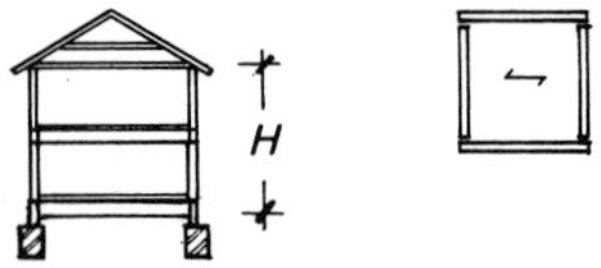	Height, H 2-4 storeys			Enclosures usually built in platform construction in which vertical framing members are not continuous
Braced frame	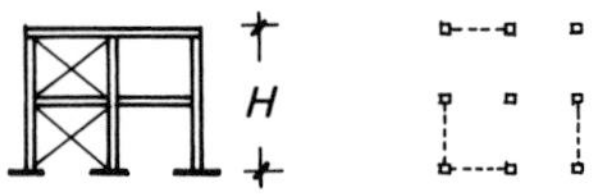	2-4 storeys			Frame may be braced with diagnol steel rods or plywood panels acting as diaphragms

Table 1.12   Surface Elements - Roofs   Plastics

Element	Axonometric	Typical Spans (L) (m)	(ft)	Critical Factors for Sizing	Remarks
Domes using shaped panels	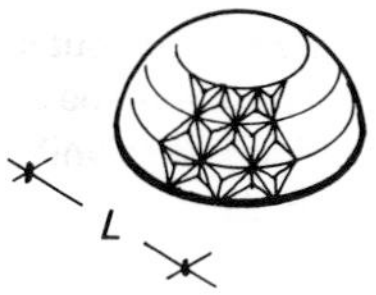	5-20	15-60	Thickness affected by size and shape of panel	Domes may have rectangular or circular base Made by bolting together shaped panels Plastic panels typically 2-6mm thick but thicker than this at edges
Folded plate structures using shaped panels	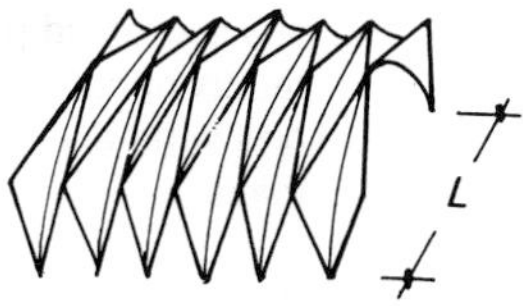	5-20	15-60	Thickness affected by size and shape of panel	Made by bolting together 2 or 3 different types of shaped panel Panels may be double skin with insulation between
Shaped roof panels	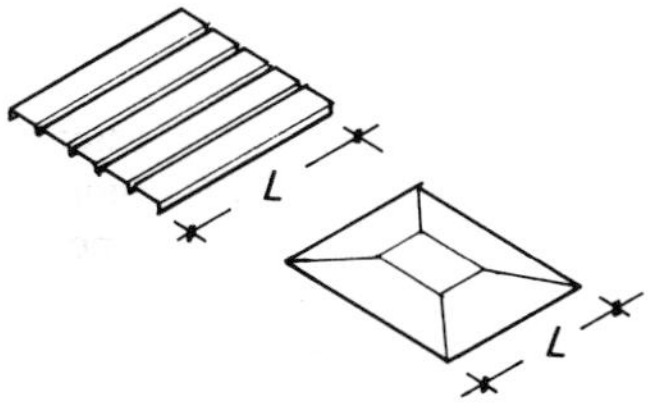	1-5	3-16	Deflection	Panels must be shaped or have stiffeners to overcome flexibility
Laminated panel	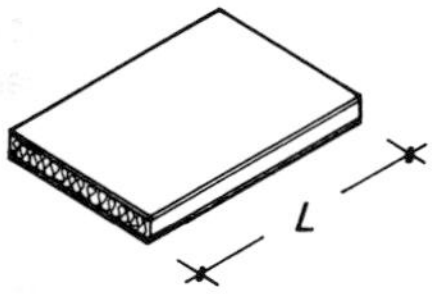	4-6	12-20	Deflection	Made from good quality grp with 40-60mm insulation between skins Used for roofs but also as load-bearing panels and for floors in 2 or 3 storey buildings of small plan area

Table 1.13 | Surface Elements - Roofs | Fabric

Element	Axonometric	Typical Spans (L) (m)	(ft)	Typical Curvatures (m)	(ft)	Critical Factors for sizing	Remarks
Fabric tent	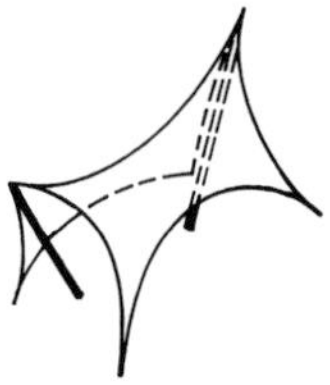 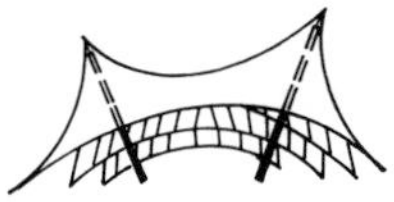	9-18	30-60	25-35	80-120	Radius of curvature Tear strength Wind or snow loads	Surface of tent has anticlastic (saddle) shape at each point and is prestressed Typical prestress in fabric 5-10 kN/m Prestress determined by loads and curvature.
Cable reinforced fabric tent	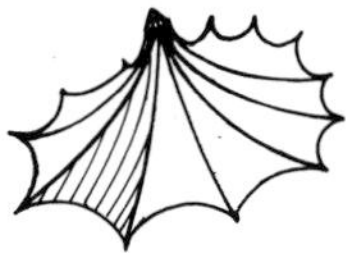 	18-60	60-200	80-100	250-325	Tear strength of fabric, spacing of cables, radius of curvature and wind and snow loads	Surface of tent has anticlastic shape and is prestressed by pulling on cables Prestress in fabric and cables determined by loads and curvature.
Prestressed steel net with fabric covering	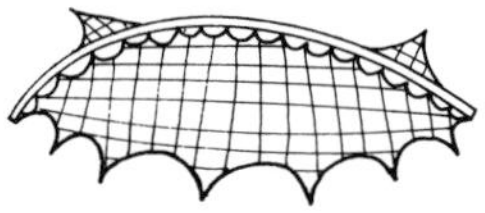 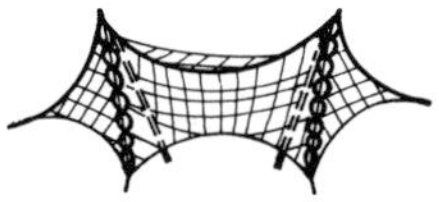	25-100	100-300	..	..	Radius of curvature Wind or snow load	Size of cable mesh about 500x500mm Surface of net has anticlastic shape Typical average stress in net 40-60kN/m High strength of net allows large radius of curvature
Air supported membrane		15-45	50-150	..	..	Radius of curvature Tear strength Wind or snow loads	Inflation pressure low Surface of membrane has synclastic (dome) shape at each point and is prestressed.
Cable stayed air supported membrane		90-180	100-600	80-100	250-325	Tear strength of fabric, spans, spacing of cables and snow loads	Cables anchored to a ring beam that has a funicular shape Low rise of roof gives wind uplift on it
Pneumatic frame (prestressed tube)	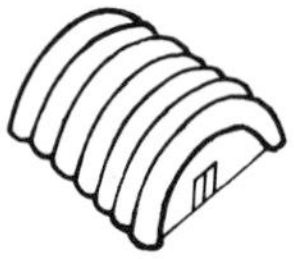	6-45	20-150	..	..	Tear strength Shape and diameter of tube Wind or snow loads	Tubes require large diameters and high pressures to achieve sufficient stiffness

Chapter Two

Building Structures

The principal function of the building structure is to transfer all the loads on it to ground. The loads on the building can usually be split up into gravity loads, which act vertically, and lateral loads, which act in any horizontal direction. All matter on earth is subject to the acceleration of gravity and therefore possesses weight, which acts vertically downwards. As well as these gravity forces, building structures can also be subject to the accelerations due to earthquakes which act principally in horizontal directions and therefore cause horizontal inertial forces on the building. Another horizontal force is that due to wind. The building structure must have sufficient strength to resist these loads and, as important, sufficient stiffness when it resists loads so that the movements and deflections are not excessive. However it is not possible to prevent movement altogether, as the structure takes up the load on it, because all materials deform under load. A material in which the deflection is directly proportional to the load, at normal working loads, is said to be *linear-elastic*. If all the loads, whether vertical or horizontal, that act on the building structure are balanced by forces from the ground then the structure is said to be in *equilibrium*. If there are no dynamic forces on the building such

as those due to earthquakes or wind buffeting then the building will be at rest and is said to be in static equilibrium; a few buildings will also need to be analysed for the dynamic loads on them if these are significant. It is possible to design a structure that satisfactorily withstands loads from one direction, for example vertical loads due to its self-weight, but is unstable and collapses even under a small force from, for example, a horizontal direction. A building is said to be *stable* if it is able to withstand the expected range of forces no matter in which direction they act. Checking stability always entails looking at buildings as three-dimensional structures in which the instability may occur in any direction (*2.1*). The stability of any rigid element in space is only guaranteed if translational movements along the x, y and z axes and rotational movements about these axes are prevented (*2.2*); the axes are normally chosen so that they are at right angles to each other. It follows that at least six forces, or three forces and three moments or any intermediate combination, are needed to keep a rigid element in a stable equilibrium in space (*2.3*). Another but less well-defined objective is that the building be *robust*. A robust building can be said to be one built so that the loadbearing elements are resistant to, or protected from,

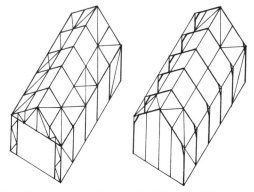

2.1 *Two simple pitched-roof buildings stabilised against horizontal forces from any direction, by trussing, left, or by frame action and trussing, right.*

damage or in which, if damage does occur, it is confined to that part of the building where the damage first occurred and that it is not disproportionate to the cause of the damage. It is usually easy to ensure that, for example, frame buildings, which for any reason sustain damage to their individual beams or columns, are not thereby made unstable overall.

STRESS AND STRAIN

Stress Resultants

As external forces are applied to a building, they engender internal forces in the individual elements

of the building structure. For convenience in analysis the internal forces in each element are split up into component forces which are either rotational forces consisting of *bending moments* and *torsional moments*, or translational forces consisting of *axial forces* and *shear forces*. A translational force is a measurable influence on the element tending to cause translational movement, while a moment is one tending to cause a rotational movement. These component forces and moments are known as *stress resultants*. For an element existing in space six stress resultants will completely describe the forces acting at a cross-section taken through any individual structural member or through a small area element taken from a shell or surface structure. By convention the six stress resultants used are the following: shear force, *S*, acting along the major and minor axes of bending, bending moment, *M*, acting about these two axes, axial force, *P*, acting through the centroid of the section and torsional moment, *T*, acting about the shear centre. In some cases not all these stress resultants exist. For a planar element, loaded in its plane, there is only an axial force, a shear force and a bending moment to consider (*2.4*). In most design work, buildings may be considered as assemblies of planar elements, in which the structure in each individual plane can be analysed separately, ignoring the effects of the forces and structures in the other planes.

Stress and Strain

When a bar is put into tension into undergoes a change in length. The *strain* of the bar at any point, ε, is given by:

$$\varepsilon = \frac{\Delta L}{L}$$

where L is a small length of the bar between two points in mm (in); and

ΔL is the change in length of this small length of bar in mm (in).

For a bar which has a different cross-sectional area along its length, the strain, due to the load, will also vary down the length of the bar (*2.5*). For a bar of uniform section made of the same material the strain due to the load is the same at all points on the bar and can be calculated from the relative movement of the two ends of the bar. The stress, *f*, at any point on a bar made of a linear-elastic

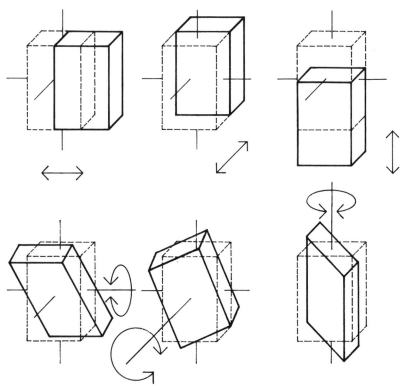

2.2 *Three translational movements, top, and three rotational movements, bottom, are possible independent movements of a rigid body in space and must be assigned values to define the exact position of the body; in a plane two translational movements and one rotational movement are needed to define the position of a rigid body.*

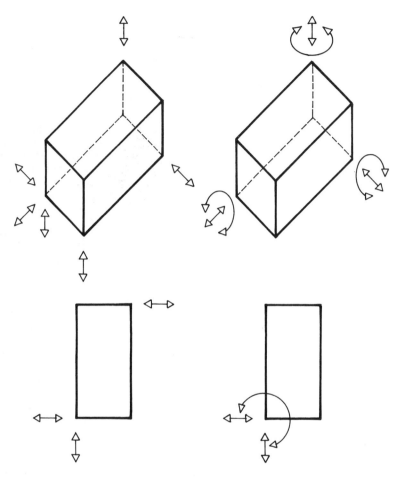

2.3 Two possible combinations of force and moment restraints that are sufficient to fix a rigid body in space, top, or in a plane, bottom.

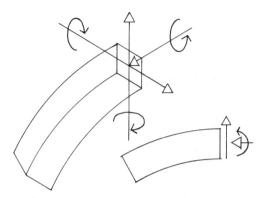

2.4 Stress resultants on element existing in space and in plane.

2.5 Column element with varying cross-sectional area.

material is related to the strain at that point, ε, as follows:

$f = \varepsilon.E$ N/mm² (lb/in²)

where E is the modulus of elasticity of the material in N/mm² (lb/in²).

Elastic Beam

The deflection in a linear-elastic beam, column or tie at normal working loads is proportional to the stress, as the elastic modulus is a constant if the strain is not large. For a column or tie rod (2.32), the shortening or extension under load, e, is therefore given by:

$$e = \frac{P.L}{A.E} = \frac{f.L}{E} \text{ mm (in)}$$

where P is the axial load in the column or tie in N (lb);
L is the length of the column or tie in mm (in);
A is the area of the column or tie in mm² (in²);
E is the modulus of elasticity of the material in N/mm² (lb/in²); and
f is the stress = P/A in N/mm² (lb/in²)

The stress resultants acting at any cross-section through a member, are simply the resultant forces or bending moments due to the summation of all the stresses acting at each point on the cross-section. There are only two types of these stresses, direct stresses and shear stresses. Consider, for example, a very small rectangular area in the web of a steel beam (2.6). A *direct stress* is any tensile or compressive stress which acts across any of the four faces while a *shear stress* is one which acts along any of the four 'cut' faces of the small rectangular area. The direct stresses acting at any cross-section taken through a structural member

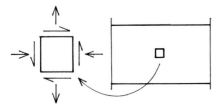

2.6 Small thin rectangular element taken from web of steel beam showing direct and shear stresses on it; when no load acts on the element, the shear stresses on all faces are equal and the direct stresses on opposite faces are equal, if the element is to be in equilibrium.

add up to give the axial force and bending moment acting at that section; the shear stresses add up to give the shear and torsion acting at that section. In some cases the stress resultants are zero: for a tie in tension there is no bending moment however the section through it is taken (*2.32*), the direct stresses all adding up to give a resultant tension force; for an element in simple torsion there is no shear force, the shear stresses all adding up to give a resultant torsional moment (*2.7*); if the section warps when twisted, then the direct stresses will also contribute to the resultant torsional moment (*2.8*). Direct stesses of tension or compression cause any small rectangular element in a member to elongate or to contract in the two directions perpendicular to the two sides, while shear stresses cause the small rectangular element to 'lozenge' (*2.7*). For example in the web of the steel beam each small area in the depth of the web is 'lozenged' by the action of the shear force (*2.9*). The shear stresses acting along the horizontal and vertical faces of each small rectangular area are equal, or very nearly equal, to each other and act so that each small element is always in equilibrium

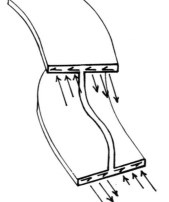

2.8 Shear and direct stresses caused by torsional moment on steel I-section which warps when twisted.

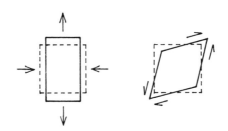

2.9 Action of direct and shear stresses on small element.

(*2.6*). The deflection of a steel beam under load is the result both of such 'lozenging' of these small rectangular elements, due to shear force, as well as the elongation and contraction of the elements due to bending (*2.10*). In a beam of normal proportions, that is when the span length is more

than about five times the depth of the beam, the deflection due to shear is very small compared with that for bending and can be ignored.

JOINTS

Types of Connection

Joints between structural line elements, in one plane, may be classified as simple connections, as sliding connections, as pin or pinned connections and as fixed connections, also known as rigid connections. A *simple connection* allows rotation and movement in any direction except downwards and only transmits shear force that acts downwards at a support. A *sliding connection* allows movement along the line of the element and rotation and only transmits shear force. A *pinned connection* allows rotation but no translational movements; it transmits shear and axial forces but not bending moment. A *fixed connection* does not allow translational movement or rotation and transmits shear, axial forces, bending and torsional moment (*2.11*). In practice it is often difficult to fabricate fixed connections and some rotation may take place between the element on one side of the joint and that on the other. Such a joint is known as a *semi-rigid connection* and, strictly speaking, is the condition of most joints which are described as being fixed or rigid. A *moment connection* could be described as one which although only semi-rigid approaches the behaviour of a fixed connection and transfers a substantial bending moment. Note that connections may be fabricated for particular requirements so that, for example, they may allow rotation in the plane of the elements but prevent twisting about the axis of the element thus allowing torsional moments to be transmitted. This is a common condition at steel beam supports (*2.12*). By contrast the element

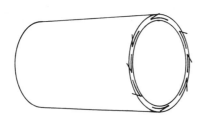

2.7 Shear stresses on tube in simple torsion.

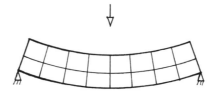   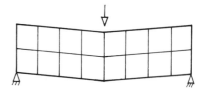

2.10 Schematic diagram showing deflection of beam under point load due mainly to bending, left, and shear, right.

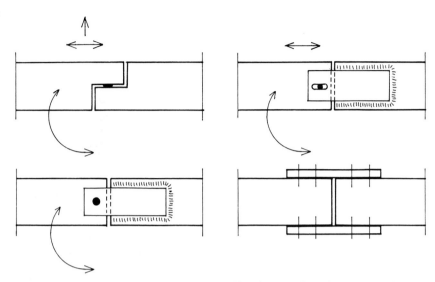

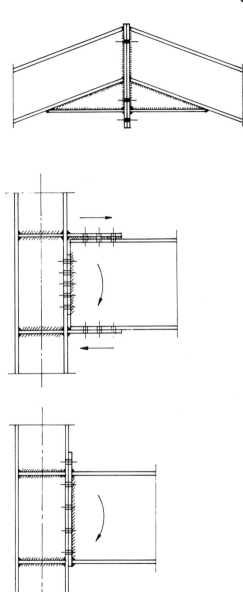

2.11 Simple and sliding connections, top, and pinned and fixed connections, bottom, showing movements allowed by each type.

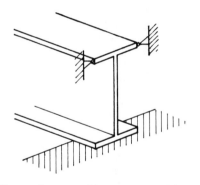

2.12 Connection at steel beam support able to transmit torsional moment but not bending moment in plane of web.

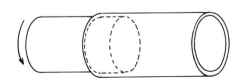

2.13 Connection between steel tubes transmitting bending moment but not torsion.

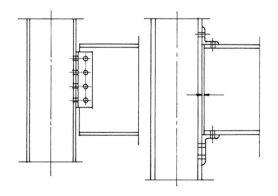

2.14 Simple bolted connections between steel beams and columns.

2.15 Bolted moment connections between steel beams and columns or rafters.

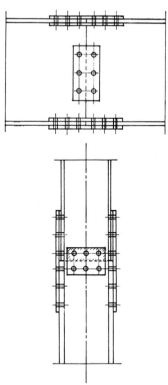

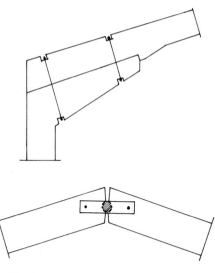

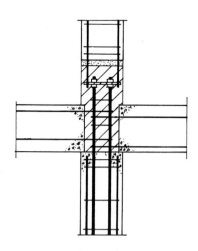

2.16 Connections providing continuity for steel beam and column.

2.18 Fixed and pinned connection at haunch and ridge of precast concrete frame.

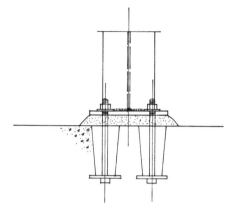

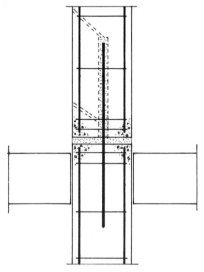

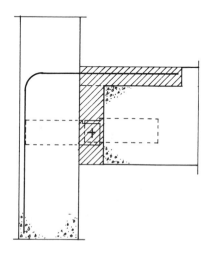

2.17 Detail at base of steel column; a fixed connection requires a large and thick steel baseplate with bolts near the extremities; a pinned connection requires only a small, thin baseplate.

2.19 Pinned connection between precast concrete columns.

2.20 Connections between precast beams and columns with some moment capacity.

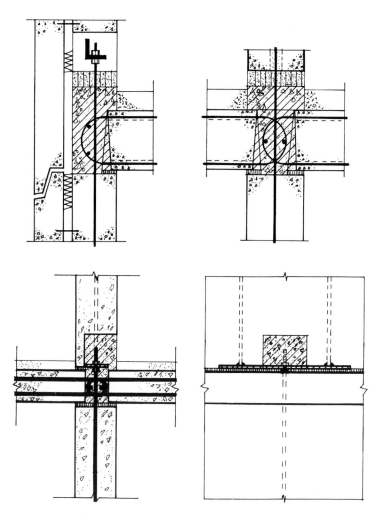

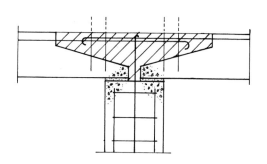

2.22 *Connection providing continuity for precast concrete roof panel but pinned connection with supporting wall below.*

2.21 *Pinned connections between precast concrete floor and wall panels: sections through exterior and interior joints using floor units with nibs, top; section and elevation on interior joint using floor unit with flat ends, bottom.*

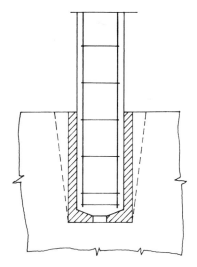

2.23 *Fixed connection between precast concrete column and concrete base.*

may be fixed in its plane to transmit bending but allow rotation about its axis (2.13). Note that if pinned or fixed joints are made between an element and an immovable support then that end of the element may not move translationally or rotate in space, as distinct from a movement which is merely relative to the member on the other side of the joint. Fixed joints, or nearly fixed joints,

between two members are said to provide *continuity* so that there is little or no rotation between the members at the joint and the members behave as if no joint existed. However the joint is not necessarily fixed in space and may rotate about a support for example. A way of characterising the degree of fixity or stiffness

provided by a semi-rigid connection either to a support or another member is to measure the rotation at the joint as the bending moment on the joint is varied. Various types of joints between steel, concrete and wood elements are illustrated, showing what are assumed to be simple, pinned, fixed or moment connections (2.14 to 2.30).

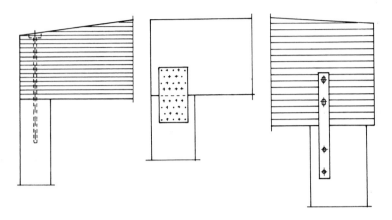

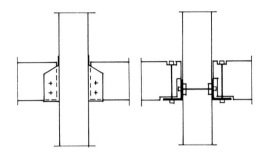

2.27 Simple connection between wood beams and columns.

2.24 Pinned connections between solid or laminated timber beams and columns in post and beam construction.

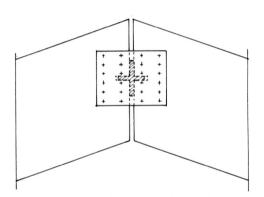

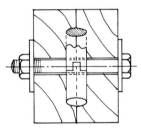

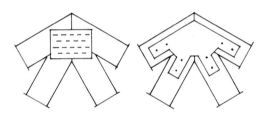

2.29 Pinned connection between wood members in same plane.

2.25 Pinned connection at apex of wood frame.

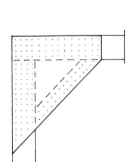

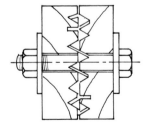

2.26 Moment connection at haunch of timber frame.

2.28 Pinned connection using split ring or toothed plate connection between wood members in different plane.

2.30 Pinned connection at base of wood column.

CLASSIFICATION OF BUILDING STRUCTURES

Beams, Frames and Shells

There are no definitive ways of classifying building structures and a potentially infinite range of types. Whatever way is chosen many building structures will not fall clearly into any one category. However distinctions between the different types of structures are nevertheless useful. A simple classification system, based on the way structural elements are put together and work, is to split up building structures into three types either based on *straight line elements,* such as beams, columns and ties, *shaped line elements,* such as arches, cables and frames, or *surface elements* such as the surface elements that occur in slabs, shells or prestressed membranes. The first type occurs on a line, which is one-dimensional, the second in a plane, which is two-dimensional and the third in space, which is three-dimensional. Elements from the first type may be joined together to create complete structures; for example, beam and column elements can be joined to make a post and beam system; column elements, also known as struts, and tie elements can be joined to make a truss system. The elements are named according to their principal function: columns and ties take axial forces of compression and tension respectively; beams take shear forces and bending moments; arches and cables take axial forces of compression and tension respectively, this time along a curved path; frames take shear, axial forces and bending moments; surface elements take shear and axial

forces acting in the plane of the surface and if they only work in this way are known as *membrane structures.* In practice there may be other stress resultants: elements working principally as beams may take axial forces; those working as columns or arches generally pick up bendings moments and possibly torsion too; those working principally as surface elements, if they have sufficient thickness and rigidity, may pick up bending moments, torsion and shear forces perpendicular to the plane of the surface, as well as the membrane stress resultants that act in the plane of the surface (*2.31*).

Stress Systems

Axial forces in ties can generally be assumed to put the element into a state of *uniaxial stress,* in which there is a uniform direct stress acting across any section taken perpendicular to the axis of the column or tie but no stress across any section taken along the axis (*2.32*). However, as noted previously, in the webs of beams or in thin shells, there is in general a state of *biaxial stress,* in which any small rectangular element in the surface, however it is orientated, has a direct stress acting across all four faces, in the two directions at right angles to each other (*2.6*); as well as these direct stresses, in general, there are also shear stresses acting along all four faces. It is a property of any material in a state of biaxial stress that, at any point, there is one particular orientation of the small rectangular element at which the shear stresses acting along the four sides are zero. Further, the direct stresses acting across the faces in the two

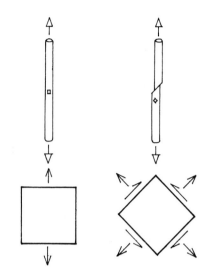

2.32 Rod in tension showing state of stress on elements orientated in line and at 45° to the axis of the rod; a possible mode of failure in shear is indicated on the right hand diagram.

directions at right angles to each other are the maximum and minimum stresses that can exist at that point. Adopting a sign convention in which compressive stresses are positive and tensile stresses are negative, then the maximum stress is a compressive stress and the minimum stress is a tensile stress, in those cases of biaxial stress where both tension and compression are present (*2.33*).

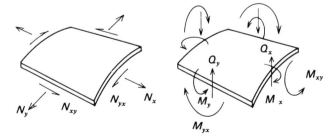

2.31 The membrane forces in a surface element are the stress resultants due to direct and shear stresses acting in the plane of the surface, left; however a surface element of moderate thickness may also contain bending moments, torsional moments and transverse shear forces, right.

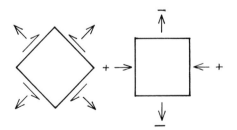

2.33 General state of stress on small, thin rectangular element, left, and principal stresses on element in same position but orientated in the direction of the principal stresses, right.

The maximum and minimum stresses are known as *principal stresses* and the directions in which they occur, the *principal stress directions.* For two-way spanning slabs, and many other elements, a *triaxial stress* exists in which a small rectangular block within the structure has, in general, different direct and shear stresses acting across and along the faces, respectively, in three mutually perpendicular directions. In this case there are three principal directions of stress at any point, and three associated principal stresses, for which, as before, there are no shear stresses along any of the faces of the small block, if the block is orientated in the right direction (*2.34*). Uniaxial or biaxial states of stress can be regarded as special cases of a triaxial state of stress: the state of uniaxial stress in a tie is a special case of triaxial stress for which the principal stress directions are along the axis of the tie and at right angles to it, the principal stresses being zero in the two mutually perpendicular directions at right angles to the tie axis; the state of biaxial stress in a thin plate is a special case of triaxial stress in which the stress at right angles to the plate is considered to be zero because the plate is thin. Because materials undergo both direct and shear stresses, whatever state of stress they are in, even uniaxial tension, failure often occurs as a result of a combination of these two types of stress. A small rectangular piece orientated at 45° to the axis of a tie in uniaxial tension has shear stresses along its faces and these are the maximum shear stresses that exist at that point. The tie may fail in shear, depending on the material, before it fails in direct tension (*2.32*). It is difficult to put a

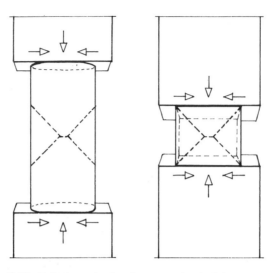

2.35 Cylinder and cube of concrete in triaxial state of stress during compression test showing usual modes of failure.

test cube or test cylinder of concrete into a state of uniaxial compression because the testing machine applies compression at right angles to the test specimen at its ends, as the specimen expands sideways under the load. In general, therefore, a triaxial state of stress exists in concrete cubes or cylinders under test and failure must be explained in these terms. Usually final failure occurs in the same directions, at 45° to axis of loading, the directions in which shearing stresses are greatest (*2.35*). If sideways loads could be applied to the test specimens to give the same compressive stresses in the lateral directions as in the main directions of loading, failure could not occur at all. In practice the lateral stresses in the middle of a

standard test cylinder, it being taller, are less than those in a standard test cube, so that the cylinder fails sooner than a cube made of the same concrete. The cube test gives an apparent compressive strength for the concrete which is about 25% greater than that given by the cylinder test.

SIMPLY SUPPORTED BEAMS

Lines of Principal Stress

Beams are solid elements, usually with the same cross-section down their length, that work in bending and shear. If loads are applied to a beam then they will cause stresses to develop in the beam and these stresses have a pattern depending on what loads are applied. If uniformly distributed load is applied to a rectangular, simply supported beam where the width is small relative to the depth, it may be assumed that there is a biaxial state of stress and the principal compressive stresses act in directions that trace out an arch-shaped pattern and the principal tensile stresses a cable-shaped pattern. Short lines indicating the directions of principal stresses at various points are joined up to make these lines of principal stress and, because principal stresses act at right angles to each other, the two sets of lines are always at right angles to each other at any point. For beams of normal proportions, it can be assumed that there is a linear distribution of direct stress with depth on any vertical section taken through the beam (*2.36*). There is no direct stress in the horizontal plane at mid-depth of the beam, which is therefore known as the *neutral plane* (*2.37*). This can be explained by the fact that lines of principal stress cross the neutral plane at an angle of 45° to the

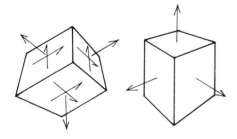

2.34 General state of stress on small cube element, left, and principal stresses on element orientated in the directions of principal stress, right.

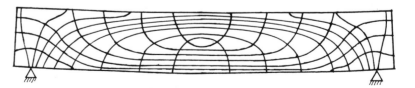

2.36 Diagram showing lines of principal tension and compression in a thin rectangular beam in bending under uniform load, left, with assumed linear variation of bending stress with depth on a typical vertical section, right.

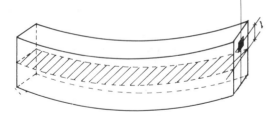

2.37 Beam in bending showing neutral plane shaded and distance, y, of small area from the neutral axis at a typical section through the beam.

horizontal; as the two principal stresses have equal magnitude at this point, when resolved horizontally, in the neutral plane, they cancel out, so that there is no resultant direct stress in the horizontal direction. A small triangular block, at this point, with a vertical edge, therefore has no direct horizontal stress on its vertical face. Resolving vertically, however, shows that, except at midspan, there must be a shear stress acting along the vertical edge in order that the element is in equilibrium. Similar consideration of another triangle with a horizontal edge shows that there is a shear stress, this time acting horizontally, but no direct vertical stress on this horizontal face (*2.38*). The state of stress at this point is known as one of *pure shear* and may be described either by a small rectangular piece orientated at 45° to the axis of the beam, having principal stresses equal in

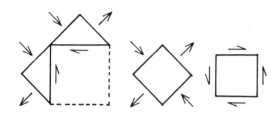

2.38 State of pure shear at mid-depth of a beam on triangular elements, left, and on rectangular elements, at same position but orientated at 45° to or in line with the axis of the beam, right.

magnitude but opposite in direction, or by a small rectangular piece parallel to the axis of the beam on which only shear stresses act, the shear stresses being equal in magnitude to the principal stresses (*2.38*). By contrast, a small rectangular element parallel to the axis of the beam at the very top or bottom of the beam is in a state of uniaxial horizontal stress, as there can be no vertical stress at a horizontal surface. The lines of principal stress show the directions in which the principal stresses act and, as noted previously, have the property that the tension and compression lines always intersect each other at right angles; they are not lines of constant stress but lines of constant 'flow'. If correctly drawn, the spacing of lines indicates the magnitude of stress, lines when closely spaced together indicating high stress at that point. An analogy may be drawn with water flow: if the same volume of water passes between each of the lines of flow, then the water has the greatest speed where the lines are most closely spaced together. Here the flow between lines represents the force in each 'arch' or 'cable', the lines being drawn so that each 'arch' or 'cable' carries an equal force; the speed of flow represents the stress. The diagram of the lines of principal stress indicates that the direct stresses are greatest at the top and bottom of the beam at midspan; this indicates that material could be more efficiently used by the lens-shaped beam, sometimes used in long spans, which are deeper in the middle than at the ends, or by putting more material in the flanges, as is done in the rolling of steel beams with I-shaped cross-sections. For rectangular beams the diagram indicates how tension and compression reinforcement may be efficiently laid out; the reinforcing bars and prestressing cables used in concrete beams to overcome its weakness in tension follow similar paths to the lines of principal tensile stress. More simply the diagram indicates a way of thinking of the beam as a series of arches in compression intersected by a series of cables in tension.

Bending Stress

In any beam which has a linear distribution of direct stress with depth, whatever its cross-sectional shape, the direct stresses of tension or compression, f_y, at any point are given by (*2.37*):

$$f_y = \frac{M.y}{I} \text{ N/mm}^2 \text{ (lb/in}^2)$$

where M is the bending moment, about a principal axis, in N-mm (lb-in);
  y is the distance from the point concerned to the neutral axis in mm (in); and
  I is the moment of inertia of the section about the axis of bending, which is a geometrical property of the section, in mm⁴ (in⁴).

A section has two principal axes of bending which are at right angles to each other; a section which is symmetrical about at least one axis, for example a horizontal or vertical axis, will have at least one principal axis that coincides with an axis of symmetry. For loads in the same plane as one of the principal axes of bending for example a vertically loaded T-section (*2.39*), the stresses of greatest magnitude, f_b, which occur at the points furthest away from the axis of bending on each side, are given by:

$$f_b = \frac{M}{Z_1}$$

and $= \frac{M}{Z_2}$ in N/mm² (lb/in²)

where Z_1 and Z_2 are the section moduli for the beam in mm³ (in³) which are geometrical properties of the section equal to I/y_1 and I/y_2 respectively: if the section is symmetrical about the neutral axis then $Z_1 = Z_2$;
  y_1 and y_2 are the distances from the neutral axis of the beam to the bottom and top of the beam, respectively, in mm (in).

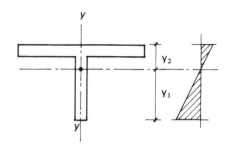

2.39 Section with axis of symmetry about the y axis, showing distances of top and bottom of section from neutral axis, left, and assumed variation of bending stress with depth, right.

Shear Stress

One way of reinforcing a beam, if this is necessary, for example if it is in concrete, is to provide reinforcement along the lines of the principal stresses (2.36). In practice it is usually more convenient to provide reinforcement in horizontal and vertical directions and it is then necessary to find the magnitudes of the direct and shear stresses on small elements orientated in line with the axis of the beam (2.6). The diagram showing the direction of principal stresses in a beam, under uniformly distributed load (2.36) shows a concentration of lines of principal stress intersecting each other in the middle of the beam near the supports indicating, in qualitative terms, that the shear stresses are greater here than elsewhere (2.38). On any vertical section through

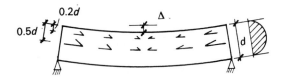

2.40 *Rectangular beam under uniform load showing magnitudes of horizontal shear stress at mid-depth and near top of beam; variation of shear stress with depth on a typical vertical section shown at right.*

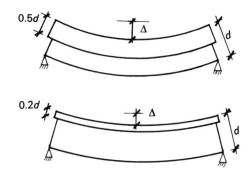

2.41 *Similar rectangular beams cut at middle and near top of section showing different deflections when under the same load.*

a beam, the shear stressess are greatest at the neutral axis (2.37) and decrease to zero at the extremities of the beam section (2.40). The shear stresses are on average greater on a vertical section taken near the supports and, for a uniformly loaded beam, decrease to zero near midspan. If vertical shear stress is present at any point in the beam, then, as noted previously, horizontal shear stress must also be present and must be equal in magnitude (2.6). One way to demonstrate horizontal shear is to consider a rectangular beam cut horizontally first at mid-depth and then near the top of the beam (2.41). If the two pieces are re-attached the strength of the fixings required to prevent horizontal slippage, under a load, along the plane of the cut, is much greater in the former case, the shear stress being higher, than in the latter case (2.40). The average shear stress, f_v, on any horizontal plane cut through the beam, or for rolled steel sections a cut at right angles to the vertical section, at any position in the span, is given by (2.42) :

$$f_v = \frac{V.Q}{I.b} \text{ in N/mm}^2 \text{ (lb/in}^2)$$

where V is the vertical shear force in the span at the vertical section being considered in N (lb);

Q is the moment of that area, beyond the cut taken, about the neutral axis in mm³ (in³); and

b is the width of the beam at the place the cut is taken in mm (in).

Normally, at any given vertical section, all the various factors on the right-hand side of the

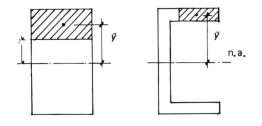

2.42 *Vertical section through rectangular and channel beam showing dimension ȳ used to calculate shear on surface between shaded and unshaded portions.*

equation, except Q, are constant and the expression shows the shear stress to reach a maximum on the neutral axis, decreasing to zero at the extremities of the section. For a rectangular beam this gives a parabolic variation of shear stress with depth (2.40).

Deflection

Ignoring shear deflection, the deflection, Δ, at midspan of any simply-supported linear-elastic beam, with the same section along its length, under uniformly distributed load, is given by:

$$\delta = \frac{5W.L^3}{384E.I} \text{ in mm (in)}$$

where W is the total load on the beam in kN (kips);

L is the span of the beam in mm (in);

E is the elastic modulus of the material in kN/mm² (kips/in²); and

I is the moment of inertia of the beam section in mm⁴ (in⁴).

Alternatively, if the maximum tensile or compressive stress in the beam is f_b, then the midspan deflection is also given by:

$$\delta = \frac{5f_b.L^2}{24E.d} \text{ in mm (in)}$$

where d is the depth of the beam in mm (in).

Beam Design

With *concrete beams* the assumption that there is a linear distribution of direct stress with depth is not realistic. However the beam can be designed by assuming or calculating a lever arm depth (2.43); the *lever arm* depth, l_a is the distance between the resultant of the compression at the top of the beam and the tension at the bottom. There are two conditions to check for bending strength: that the concrete at the top does not fail in compression and that the steel reinforcing bars at the bottom do not fail in tension. A typical procedure is to assume a width of beam, b, which is usually between a third and a half of the depth, d, and then to find a depth which meets the strength condition that the concrete does not fail in compression. The shear condition by the supports is also checked. Additionally cracking and long-term deflection must also be acceptable. In practice this is often the governing condition and, in preliminary design, is catered for by not exceeding given span to depth ratios. The amount of tensile

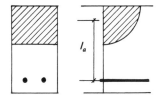

2.43 Section and stress diagram through reinforced concrete beam showing lever arm between steel reinforcement and centre of pressure of concrete in compression.

reinforcement required can then be estimated, by assuming a lever arm depth. The process is iterative and repeated until all aspects seem sufficiently good for the purposes of the exercise. Occasionally, where there is a slender beam which is not laterally stabilised by a floor or roof slab at the top, it is possible for the beam to buckle laterally. This is usually controlled by keeping the ratio, L/b, to be less than about 30 (*2.44*). For *steel beams*, section shapes are devised to minimise the amount of material used so that, by contrast with concrete or wood, lateral buckling is a major consideration. Normally however the compression flange, at the top, where buckling initiates, can be conveniently stabilised by floor or roof slabs and joists. As steel beams, in the way normally used,

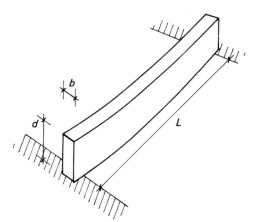

2.44 Simply supported beam showing dimensions d, b and L.

have a linear distribution of direct stress with depth, the elastic formula may be used to calculate a suitable section modulus, Z. Deflection, particularly that connected with live load, can have a determining influence on the moment of inertia selected for the beam, I. Vibration of floor beams may be a problem which is sometimes also solved by increasing the stiffness of the beam, usually by increasing the moment of inertia of the beam. Shear needs to be checked near supports; it can be assumed to be taken by the web only and to have a uniform value over the depth of the web. Usually web buckling and bearing stresses do not need checking in a preliminary design. Beams may also be made of a composite of two materials, combining the best properties of each. For example steel and wood may be bolted together to create a composite beam. The reinforced concrete beam with steel reinforcing bars embedded in concrete is the most common type of composite structure. Another popular type is the *steel and concrete composite beam,* in which a rolled steel beam is used with a concrete slab, either precast or cast-in-place, the tension and shear stresses being mostly taken by the steel and compresssion by the concrete slab (*2.45*). *Shear connectors* are necessary to transfer the longitudinal shear stresses between the steel and concrete, more being needed near supports where shear stresses are greatest. For preliminary design, the steel beam

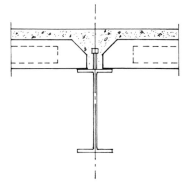

2.45 Composite steel-concrete beam with shear connectors, using precast concrete slabs with cast-in-place topping.

can be quickly sized on the assumption that it carries, alone, three-quarters of the total moment on the composite beam.

For solid rectangular *wood beams*, including laminated timber beams, the elastic formula may be used to calculate the deflection and to find a suitable section modulus, Z. Very often deflection, especially live load deflection controls the sizing and the elastic deflection formula is used to find a section with a suitable moment of inertia, I. However, unlike steel, where there are only a few types in common use, timber has many species each with different allowable stresses; there is a general decrease in these allowable stresses, as well as in the elastic modulus, with time spent under load. The most important structural properties of wood are its strength and elastic modulus. For preliminary design the load considered could be the maximum likely to occur over a period of not more than one week, say, with the allowable stresses and elastic modulus used being those adequate for a loading period of ten years. To prevent lateral instability, the ends of a wood beam should be prevented from twisting at their supports and, if the ratio d/b is greater than five (*2.44*), the top compression edge should be stabilised by floor or roof boards as well. Transverse blocking or bridging should be added if d/b exceeds six. Wood fails in shear horizontally, along the grain, the direction in which it is weaker, rather than across the grain. The bearing stress of the wood beam on its supports may need to be checked, in preliminary design, as wood is weak in compression across the grain. In *prestressed concrete* beams the basic idea is to prestress the beam so that the stresses produced by the prestressing strand largely balances out those due to the applied vertical loads and there is only a uniform axial compressive stress across the depth of the section. Unlike reinforced concrete, the whole of the section is useful in resisting bending moment. In the case of a uniformly loaded and simply supported beam, a prestressing strand could be draped along the length of the beam in a parabolic shape and stressed to cancel out the bending moment due to the long-term load, say, leaving an axial load which gives uniform compressive stress (*2.46*). This is sometimes known as *load balancing*, because the applied loads are balanced by the prestress force. For the

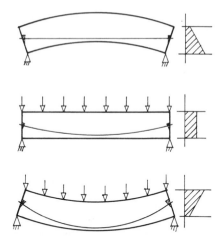

2.46 Schematic diagram of prestressed concrete beam under dead load, top, long-term load, middle, and maximum load, bottom, showing compressive stress on vertical section at midspan in each case, right.

same case, where the live load forms a large proportion of the total load, the prestress force required to balance the applied uniformly distributed loads is determined not by the maximum bending moment but by the difference between the maximum and minimum bending moments at the centre of the span; this is true because both the maximum and minimum loads need to be load balanced as far as this is possible. The idea of prestressing is to give that amount of prestress, no more no less, at a certain distance from the neutral axis of the section so that the concrete everywhere is always in compression and therefore does not crack no matter what the load on it is. In this state prestressed concrete behaves as on elastic material, unlike reinforced concrete, so that all the classic elastic formulae apply. In many other cases the dead load forms a large part of the total load and, in these cases, the prestressing force is fixed by the maximum bending moment at the centre of the span. In practice in both cases, whatever the proportions of dead and live load, a greater prestress force is provided by the prestressing strands than the minimum required to prevent tensile stresses

occurring under dead load. In both cases, too, the section moduli, Z_1 and Z_2 required to prevent overstressing of the concrete depend respectively on the actual prestress force and on the difference between the maximum and minimum bending moments. The stresses in a prestressed concrete beam are due to the addition of the applied bending and the bending and axial force supplied by the cable strand. The maximum bending stresses at any section, f_1 and f_2, at the bottom and top of the beam respectively are given by (*2.47*) :

$$f_1 = \frac{F}{A} - \frac{M - F.e}{Z_1} \text{ and}$$

$$f_2 = \frac{F}{A} - \frac{M + F.e}{Z_2} \text{ in N/mm}^2 \text{ (lb/in}^2\text{)}$$

where F is the prestress force in N (lb);

  M is the applied bending moment in N-mm (lb-ft);

  A is the area of the section in mm^2 (in^2); and

  e is the eccentricity of the prestress force with respect to the neutral axis of the section in mm (in).

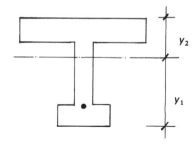

2.47 Prestressed concrete beam section showing distances of top and bottom of section from neutral axis.

Torsion

Many structural elements may be considered, for analysis, to be line or planar elements which receive load only within that one plane. In practice, as structural elements have finite width, the loading may be applied somewhere on the width of the element such that the element may not only be taking bending moment, shear or axial forces but torsional moment too. Torsion occurs in

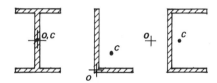

2.48 Vertical sections through members showing positions of centroid (C) and shear centre (O).

an element unless the resultant load on the section passes through the *shear centre* of the section, which is a geometrical property of the section defined by the above statement. For example for an I-shaped steel beam which is symmetrical about the vertical and horizontal axes, the shear centre is at the centroid of the section so that a vertical load that is not applied in the plane of the web, or in general any load that does not pass through the centroid causes torsion. For sections which are not symmetrical about a vertical axis but take vertical load, for example L-beams or channel sections, the position of the shear centre can be found by considering the shear stresses acting on a vertical section through the member; for any L-shaped section it is at the corner and for any channel-shaped section it is completely outside the section on the side of the web furthest from the centroid (*2.48*). The shear centre is coincident with the centre of twist, that is the point about which the member will twist when a torsional moment is applied. In practice torsion in members can be virtually eliminated by suitable bracing to the flanges and webs of the section. If torsion is transmitted to the member then it causes shear stresses and rotations in addition to the stresses and deflections already present. For sections which are not circular the torsion will, in general, cause warping, so that sections through the element are no longer plane and shear and longitudinal stresses are developed. A simple example is that of an I-section steel beam cantilevered and therefore completely restrained at one end but given a twist at its free end (*2.8*). The top and bottom flanges behave somewhat like independent cantilevers in the horizontal direction and therefore give rise to warping of the section and additional longitudinal tensile and compressive stresses and shear stresses. This kind of torsional action may also be developed by buildings which have to resist torsional moments.

Shear Lag

Another phenomenon connected with the bending of beams is shear lag, which is a type of stress concentration. If an I-section steel beam is put into bending then the top and bottom flanges are put into tension or compression and, by the simple theory of bending, sections remain plane; in practice sections which are very deep with wide, thin flanges and thin webs are liable to suffer from *shear lag* in which, because of the flexibility in shear of the webs and flanges, the bending stresses are less in the web and flanges than predicted by the simple theory except at the junction between the web and the flange where they are considerably greater (*2.49*). Shear lag also occurs in complete buildings and is important in high-rise buildings, especially those relying for lateral stability on framed tubes, which are flexible in shear (*2.116*).

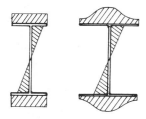

2.49 Vertical sections showing bending stresses in steel beams one of which, with a wide flange, exhibits shear lag in the flange.

CONTINUOUS BEAMS

Determinate and Indeterminate Structures

In a simply-supported beam, if the external loads applied to it are known, then the internal stress resultants, that is bending, shear or axial forces can be worked out by the *equations of statics*. In any planar structure there are three independent equations given by resolving forces, vertically and horizontally and by taking moments about any

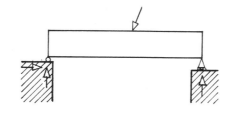

2.50 Simply supported beam with three support reactions taking load applied.

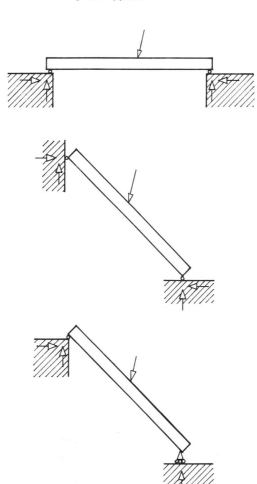

2.51 Level and sloping indeterminate beams, top, and sloping determinate beam, bottom.

point. This is equivalent to saying that the structure does not move vertically or horizontally and does not rotate, so that the forces balance in these three senses. A simply supported beam or truss has no more than three unknown reactions, or forces, on it from the supports. If there is a vertical and horizontal reaction from the support at one end and a vertical reaction from the support at the other end, then there are three unknown quantities which, therefore, may be solved by the three equations of statics (*2.50*). In such a stucture, the internal forces acting on any 'cut' taken through the structure can be found simply by using the equations of statical equilibrium and the structure is said to be *determinate*. In this case there is one unique solution of the equations of equilibrium. Generally speaking a beam which has pinned connections at both ends is not determinate, because there are four unknown support reactions. For example a ladder, which may be idealised as a beam pinned at both ends, is not determinate, whereas a sloping beam with horizontal supports, one of them a sliding support, acts like a simply supported beam and is therefore determinate (*2.51*). An *indeterminate structure* is one in which the three equations of statics do not give one unique solution for the unknown support reactions, but many possible solutions. Unlike a determinate structure, the actual support reactions in an indeterminate structure depend on the material used and the geometrical properties, for example, the length or moment of inertia of the structural member. In a *continuous beam*, unlike a series of simply-supported beams, the spans are joined together and deflect under loads into a continuous curve. Continuous beams are indeterminate structures, but may be analysed in preliminary design by making certain simplifying assumptions to make them determinate (*2.52*).

Design of Continuous Beams

If a deflected shape of the continuous beam is known, for example, by tests on a scaled model, then the bending moments for the load case may be determined exactly. In particular it is sufficient to know the positions of the points of inflection. The *points of inflection* are transition points between the portions of the beam that are bent downwards and the portions that are bent upwards. At the point of inflection itself the beam

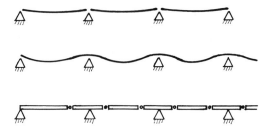

2.52 Deflected shapes of simply supported beams, top, and three-bay continuous beam, middle; model of continuous beam, which is a mechanism and used for preliminary analysis only, shown with pinned joints placed at same positions as points of inflection in continuous beam, bottom.

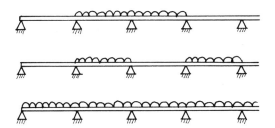

2.53 Loading used to calculate maximum bending at supports and midspan under live load, top and middle, and at any position under dead load, bottom.

is not bent at all and therefore there can be no bending moment there. For the particular load being considered, the beam behaves as if there were a pin connection at each point of inflection (2.52). If, indeed, pin connections are inserted at all the points of inflection then the continuous beam can be made into a determinate structure in which the stress resultants may be rapidly determined using the equations of statics. In general the positions of the points of inflection are not known exactly; however the positions may be guessed at, with sufficient accuracy, by looking at standard cases for which the positions of the points of inflection are known, or by models and even by careful sketching of the deflected shape of the beam. In practice bending moments are often determined by formulae, in some cases using simplifying assumptions. In a simply supported beam the maximum bending moment occurs when the whole beam carries its full design dead and live load. This is not the case for continuous beams of more than two spans where the maximum bending moment at any point always occurs when only some spans are fully loaded. For uniformly distributed load occupying complete spans at a time, the maximum bending moments occur at intermediate beam supports when the span on each side of it is fully loaded; The maximum bending moments occur at midspan of a beam when only that span and the alternate spans are fully loaded (2.53). As dead load is present on all spans, the moment due to this is calculated

separately and added to the moment due to the live load, which is placed so as to maximise, or nearly maximise, the total moment. Where the beam has three or more equal, or nearly equal spans, the interior support and span moments, that is those not part of the two end spans, do not differ significantly between one interior span and the next so that, for preliminary design, all interior spans may be treated as just one case. Tables 2.1 to 2.4 give bending moments and deflections in single span and continuous beams and slabs. The solutions given are approximate except those in Table 2.1 and a few of those in Tables 2.2 and 2.3 for which the answers are exact. Table 2.4 gives ways of approximating loads on various beam and slab systems so that they may be treated, for preliminary design, as one-way spanning elements, using the results in the previous tables.

TIES AND COLUMNS

Ties

Structural members that are subjected to an axial force acting through their centroid can be classified as ties, if in tension, or columns, if in compression. *Ties* must be able to make good tension connections, have sufficient strength and not extend excessively. *Concrete ties* are sometimes used, but invariably will crack under load unless this is small. *Wood ties* are also used, for example, in trusses carrying vertical load but

are limited by the inefficiency of the connection at each end and down the length of the tie. Although ties make good use of material the connections will rapidly increase the overall costs if they are not convenient to make. For this reason *steel ties* are very suitable and are in common use. *Prestressed concrete ties* are also used, being prestressed with a force somewhat greater than the applied tension, so that they do not crack. They have the advantage of having a smaller extension than a steel tie carrying the same force. The tensile stress, f, in the tie is given by:

$$f = \frac{P}{A} \text{ in N/mm}^2 \text{ (lb/in}^2\text{)}$$

where P is the axial tension in N (lb); and
           A is the area of the tie in mm^2 (in^2).
The extension, e, of the tie should be checked and, as noted previously, is given by:

$$e = \frac{P.L}{A.E} \text{ in mm (in)}$$

where L is the length of the tie in mm (in); and
           E is the elastic modulus of the material in N/mm^2 (lb/in^2).

Columns

Line elements which are substantially in compression are known as *columns* or, more generally, as struts. Unlike ties, columns suffer from instability due to buckling. Buckling in columns is potentially dangerous because it occurs suddenly and usually leads to complete loss of loadbearing capacity and, possibly, to substantial damage. Because of the phenomenon of buckling, columns are usually split into two types, *short columns,* which are said to be those which have little or no tendency to buckle, and *slender columns,* which are prone to buckle at loads well below that which would exceed the compressive strength of the material(2.54). A slender column may be thought of as an element, which at high load attempts to relieve itself of the load by buckling in any direction in which it is free to move (2.55). To prevent buckling a slender column must be restrained or a limit placed on the load it is allowed to carry. A useful simplication in the design of columns is that of effective height. The *effective height* of a column with pinned connections to lateral supports at each end is the actual height between the pins (2.56). The

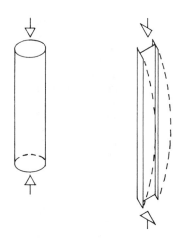

2.54 *Short and slender columns which fail by crushing and buckling respectively.*

effective height of any other column is, in principle, the height of a column pinned at each end which would deflect in a similar way to the column being considered; the effective height depends on the way the column is held at the ends and on whether the column is free to move horizontally at one end. For any particular conditions a factor, *k*, may be derived for design purposes which when multiplied by the actual height of the column between lateral supports gives an effective height (*2.56*). The basic equation which predicts the buckling load, P_{cr} , which is the maximum load a column may carry before it buckles, is given by:

$$P_{cr} = \frac{\pi^2 E.I}{h_{ef}^2} \text{ N (lb)}$$

where   *E* is the elastic modulus of the material in N/mm² (lb/in²);

    I is the moment of inertia of the section about the axis of buckling in mm⁴ (in⁴); and

    h_{ef} is the effective height of the column in the direction of buckling in m (ft).

Note that the buckling load does not depend on the strength of the material but on its stiffness against lateral forces. In short columns the material will reach its yield point before the buckling load is

reached so that, here, the strength of the material is important; in slender columns, the strength of the material is less important. *Concrete columns* are usually said to be 'short' if the ratio of their effective height between lateral supports to width, the so-called slenderness ratio, is less than fifteen; lateral support is usually provided by floors or roofs. In practice almost all concrete columns in buildings can be classified as 'short'. Steel reinforcement is incorporated in the columns and makes them stronger both in compression and in bending; sometimes bending is significant. *Masonry columns* may be unreinforced or reinforced with steel. Reinforced masonry follows similar rules to reinforced concrete. Unreinforced masonry columns could be classified as short if the ratio of effective height to width, the slenderness ratio, is less than about ten, this being the point at which slenderness starts to affect their loadbearing capacity. For unreinforced masonry there is an absolute limit of about 25 on the allowable slenderness ratio because of its relative vulnerability to damage. *Wood columns* could be classified as short if their slenderness ratio is less than ten, there being a rapid decrease in allowable compressive stress above this value. *Steel*

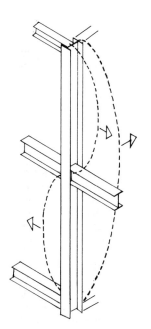

2.55 *Steel column, with a restraint at mid-height in one direction only, showing likely modes of buckling about the major and minor axes of column.*

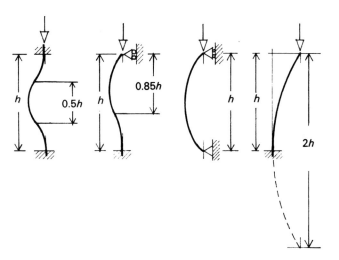

2.56 *Actual and effective height of columns with various end conditions.*

columns are available in a large number of different cross-sectional shapes and the slenderness ratio is defined as the effective height to the radius of gyration. The *radius of gyration* is a geometrical property of the section which may be calculated; for preliminary design, the radius of gyration about the minor or major axis of bending can be approximately related to the least width for some common section shapes (Table 2.7). The radius of gyration, *r*, is defined as:

$$r = \sqrt{\frac{I}{A}} \text{ mm (in)}$$

where   *I* is the moment of inertia about the particular axis of bending concerned in mm⁴ (in⁴); and
   A is the area of the section in mm² (in²).

The slenderness ratio for steel columns, or columns of any other material, should be calculated for that axis about which buckling is most likely to occur, that is the axis for which the slenderness ratio is greatest. The least radius of gyration, r_y, is given by using the value of I appropriate to the minor axis of bending. However the radii of gyration and the slenderness ratio may be required about both the major and minor axes of bending (*2.55*). In steel columns, if the slenderness ratio is below about 20 it has little effect on the allowable stresses in compression but it has an increasing effect above that, and when the slenderness ratio reaches about 100, the strength of the steel, assuming a basic minimum, has practically no effect on the strength of the column in compression. Preliminary design of a column is an iterative process that consists of selecting a section size, usually from standard tables, and with the given effective height and appropriate radius of gyration, finding the allowable stress in compression. This should be greater than the actual working stress in the selected section size.

TRUSSES AND RETICULATED STRUCTURES

Determinate Structures and Mechanisms

Stable assemblages of individual tie and strut elements are known as *reticulated structures*. A triangulated assemblage of tier and struts in two dimensions is known as a *plane truss* and consists, in principle, of elements connected by pin joints working in tension or compression (*2.57*). Trusses

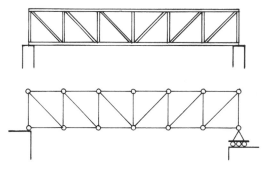

2.57   Plane truss, top, and pinned-jointed model, bottom, which is determinate and used for preliminary analysis.

are often used in place of rolled steel beams; they make better use of material and are more economical for long spans or heavy loads, in spite of the extra costs of their fabrication. An essential point is that the elements are always arranged in triangular configurations which are inherently stable, assuming none of the angles in the triangle is small. Comparing a beam to a rectangular truss, both simply supported, the horizontal top and bottom beam members of the truss carry compression and tension respectively while diagonal and vertical elements serve to carry the shear force which is a maximum near supports (*2.58*). An important aspect of the design of plane trusses is that the top boom be stabilised to prevent buckling in the plane at right angles to the truss (*2.59*). In practice the elements of the truss are not usually connected by pure pin connections so that *secondary bending* is introduced into the members, although the effect is not usually significant (*2.57*). Individual elements will also be subject to local bending if any load is applied at

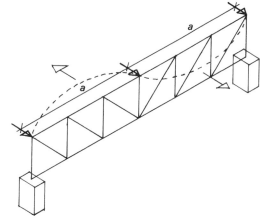

2.59   Top boom of truss restrained at ends and midspan showing likely buckling mode and associated length between lateral supports, a .

right angles anywhere down their length, rather than at the joints of the truss. Trusses are usually determinate structures. Discussion on determinate and indeterminate structures is given later. A feature of determinate structures is their ability to adjust to settlement of the supports or to small changes in length of the members due, for example, to temperature effects without this leading to any change in the forces in the members or to 'locked-in' forces, present even when no load is applied to the structure. The removal of any one member of a statically determinate truss, however, turns the truss into a mechanism and leads to collapse (*2.60*). A simple check for statical determinancy in a planar truss with pinned joints (*2.61*) is given by:

$$n = b + r - 2j$$

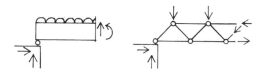

2.58   Load on a beam causes internal forces of shear and bending, while those in an equivalent pin-jointed truss consist only of axial forces in the members.

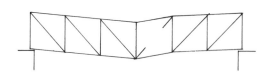

2.60   Removal of member from a determinate truss structure causes bending in members and collapse.

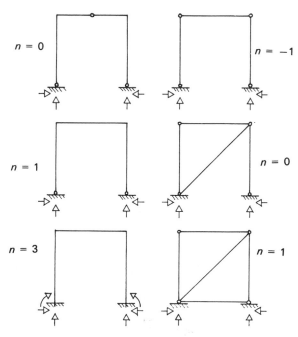

2.61 *Frame structures, left, and truss structures or mechanisms, right, with various values of n.*

two at each joint in a planar structure, from the number of unknown forces in the bars and at supports to give the degree of indeterminacy. For a three-dimensional structure, such as a space truss, where there are three equations of equilibrium at each joint the equation becomes:

$$n = b + r - 3j$$

In general it may be said that the equations of equilibrium for any load either have one solution (determinate) or several possible solutions (indeterminate) or have no solution (mechanism). Note that the bars referred to in the above equation do not have to be straight but could be curved or bent so that this way of checking for determinacy also applies to frames or arches (*2.66*). In these cases however bending moments and shear forces are introduced into the bars as well as the axial forces.

Vierendeel Truss

A *vierendeel truss* is not a truss by the definition given above. It is an assemblage of members that are not triangulated and must therefore work in bending and shear as well as in axial load (*2.63*); It should therefore be classified as a frame structure. It makes inefficient use of material compared to a triangulated truss. The vierendeel 'truss' is often used in place of a triangulated truss when the diagonal members of the truss are an inconvenience.

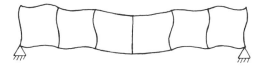

2.63 *Deflected shape of vierendeel truss showing bending.*

Space Frames

A *space truss* is an assemblage of ties and struts in three dimensions connected by pin joints and works in a similar manner to a plane truss. If the truss is composed of polyhedral units which are stable in three dimensions, such as the tetrahedron, which has four triangular faces, then the space truss is also stable in the same way that a plane truss is stable in its own plane if made from

where n is the degree of indeterminacy which is zero for a determinate structure and one or any number above one for an indeterminate structure;

b is the number of bars in the truss structure;

r is the total number of reactive forces, being two for a pinned joint with a horizontal and vertical reaction, three for a fixed support, which also has a moment reaction, and one for a sliding support (*2.61*); and

j is the number of joints including the joints at supports.

If n is one or greater than one then the truss is indeterminate and the forces in it cannot be found out by consideration of equilibrium alone. For statical determinacy n must equal zero, although this is not a sufficient condition; some truss structures may satisfy the condition but because of an improper arrangement of bars, or a particular, special geometry, are unstable; in most frameworks this is not difficult to recognize if it occurs (*2.62*). If the degree of indeterminancy is

less than zero then the arrangement of bars is inherently unstable and known as a *mechanism.* As already noted for the truss (*2.58*), a mechanism can be created by removal of a bar or a support restraint. The equation given simply subtracts the number of equations of equilibrium, there being

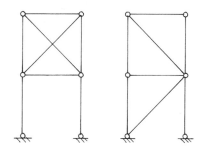

2.62 *Two truss structures with the same number of bars, one being stable, right, one being unstable because of an improper arrangement of bars, left.*

triangular units. In practice most space trusses are mechanisms which however are stable because of the way they are supported in their final position. A *space frame* is similar to a space truss but has fixed or moment connections. However, the term 'space frame' is loosely used to refer to both types. The double-layer space frame has two parallel, or nearly parallel, layers that are connected to each other by diagonal members. The module size may be the same for both layers, or sometimes, the top layer, which, in general, is in compression, may have a smaller module size to prevent buckling (*2.64*). In order to make a regular arrangement, each layer must consist of rectangular, usually square, modules. However triangular and hexagonal modules are alternative geometries that are suitable because, like rectangles, they also fill a plane in a regular way. The efficiency of a space frame which is supported along its edges, rather than by columns at large spacings, can be improved by skewing both layers with respect to

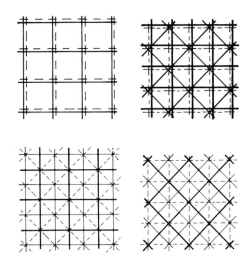

2.64 Various two-layer roof arrangements using square or rectangular grids: gridded trusses, top left; space trusses with equal-sized grids at top and bottom, in line, bottom left, or at 45°, bottom right, to the edge line; space truss with top layer grid smaller and skewed at 45° to bottom layer, top right; thick, medium and dotted lines used for top, bottom and diagonal members respectively.

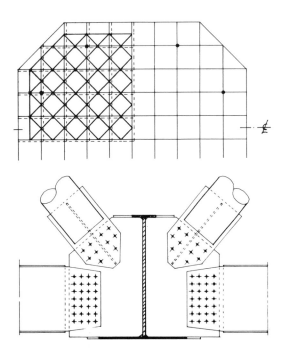

2.65 Half plan and vertical section through bottom joint of space truss with 42ft (12.8m) module and clear span of 336 x 294 ft (102 x 90 m) using tubular members for diagonals and in top layer and I-section in bottom layer; thick, medium and dotted lines used for top, bottom and diagonal members respectively (drawn from material supplied by structural engineer, Geiger Berger).

the edge of the space frame (*2.64*). This allows some members to 'cut the corner' thus effectively reducing the span. The space frame is very much more efficient than a two-way truss system (*2.64*), because the diagonal members are at an angle, whatever vertical section is considered, so that they give the space frame torsional stiffness and the ability to distribute load. The structural action of a space frame is similar to that of a flat slab, especially in the way that the slab action mimics the bending and torsion developed in the space frame. Preliminary analysis for space frames may be done using this slab analogy. The reverse is also true, that is slabs can be modelled as discrete bars which are in a space frame arrangement. In

practice space frames may be uneconomic structures to build, compared to a one-way spanning truss, because of the large numbers of connections required. The number of members and connections necessary quadruples each time the module size is halved, so that, for maximum economy, the module should be as large as possible (*2.65*). As with two-way spanning slabs, space frames become increasingly inefficient as the area spanned departs from a square shape. Tables 2.5 to 2.10 indicate ways of estimating sizes of some common elements in masonry, concrete, steel and wood. The elements are assumed to be under gravity load only, except in the case of the columns in Tables 2.9 and 2.10 for which bending moments may also be due to the effects of lateral forces.

ARCHES AND CABLES

Funicular Shapes

The basic idea behind *arch structures* as well as *cable structures* is that the structures be shaped so that there is no shear or bending moment in them but only axial forces. A structure is said to be *funicular*, when supporting any one particular type of load, if only axial forces exist in it. Cables, being flexible, automatically form into funicular shapes. For example a cable carrying only a uniformly distributed vertical load takes a parabolic shape. Arches with this type of load could take the same shape (*2.66*). Both arches and cables are

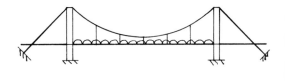

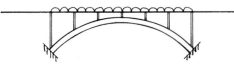

2.66 Cable and arch structures with the same shape carrying the same uniform load.

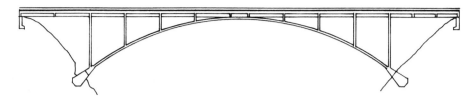

2.67 *Concrete arch bridge structure by Maillart; in this bridge the deck is curved in plan.*

2.68 *Arch and line of thrust, due to two point loads and self-weight of arch; line of thrust is just contained within the thickness of the arch; actual thickness of arch must be greater than this.*

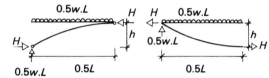

2.69 *Three-pin arch and cable cut at midpoint showing forces acting on one half.*

By altering the weight carried the natural frequencies of the cable may be altered (*2.70*). Cable structures also need to be stabilised in some way to prevent gross deformations as well as flutter. In many cases, cable structures can be stabilised by prestressing the supporting cables in tension such that a disturbing force only has a relatively small effect. *Hanging cable* structures can be stabilised by prestressing the supporting cables with a large dead weight (*2.70*). Three-dimensional surfaces made of hanging cables can take a synclastic, or dish, shape and may be

2.70 *Cable structure with large dead load.*

commonly used in bridge structures (*2.67*). Unreinforced masonry, having little bending strength, unless prestressed, must contain the funicular shape for the load being carried within its thickness (*2.68*). In practice structures are required to take a variety of loads and in order to remain funicular would need to change shape, as a cable does with a load moving across it. This is not possible for a rigid structure, such as a concrete arch, so that some bending and shear is engendered in the structure. Masonry is a special case in which sufficient thickness is given to the masonry to contain all the funicular shapes which exist for known cases of loading. In three-pin arch or cable structures carrying vertical load, the horizontal component of the axial force in the arch or cable, *H*, must be the same at all points along the arch or cable, for horizontal equilibrium (*2.69*), and is given by:

$$H = \frac{w.L^2}{8h} \text{ N (lb)}$$

where   *w* is the uniformly distributed vertical load on the arch or cable in N/mm (lb/in); and
   L, h are the span and rise or sag of the arch or cable in mm (in).

For preliminary analysis a two-pin arch (*2.73*) may be made into a three-pin arch, a pin at the apex making it determinate.

Stability of Cable Structures

A problem with the use of a flexible structure, such as a single cable, is its instability, or *flutter*, when subject to wind forces. The wind gusts and buffeting occur at frequencies which are similar to those of the natural frequencies of the cables used in practical structures. If the frequency of the buffeting coincides with any of the natural frequencies of the cable, particularly the first few natural frequencies, then *resonance* can occur and the flutter or vibration of the cable can increase dramatically. If possible the natural frequency of a cable should differ from that due to the wind. The natural frequency of a cable is given by:

$$\omega = \frac{n.\pi}{L}\sqrt{\frac{T.g}{m}} \quad 1/s$$

where   *T* is the tension in the cable in N (lb);
   g is the acceleration due to gravity in mm/s² (ft/s²);
   L is the length of the cable in mm (ft); and
   m is the weight carried by the cable in N/mm (lb/ft).

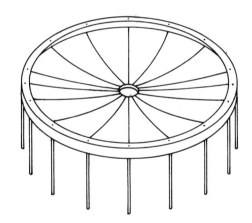

2.71 *Dish structure made by constructing rigid shell on hanging cables.*

2.72 *Hanging cable stabilised by hogging cable.*

stabilised by constructing a rigid shell on top of the cables (*2.71*). In other cable structures, each supporting cable is stabilised by prestressing it against another cable of opposite curvature (*2.72*). Planar structures stabilised in this way are known as *cable truss structures*. Three-dimensional surfaces formed of cables stabilised in this way are known as *prestressed net structures* and must have an anticlastic, or saddle, shape. The prestressed net is stabilised in a similar way to the planar cable truss structure except that the net, being three-dimensional, has each cable stabilised by other cables approximately at right angles to it (*2.73*). *Cable-stayed* structures are those where cables are used to support rigid column or beam elements. Stability is provided by the rigid elements themselves or by additional cables to counteract the forces in the supporting cables(*2.74*).

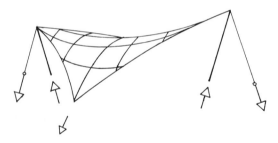

2.73 *Cable net with each cable stabilised by other cables of opposite curvature.*

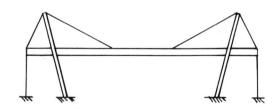

2.74 *Cables used to support roof beams of rigid frame.*

FRAMES

Frame Action

A *frame structure* may be regarded as the simplest system for giving stiffness and strength to a building, while allowing the enclosure and partitioning of the building to be treated separately as non-loadbearing elements. As built, frames are three-dimensional arrangements of linear beam and column elements. However, for structural design, a frame in space may usually be split into several independent planar frames (*2.75*). Such planar frames work principally in bending, like beams. Like beams they also take shear and axial forces but the bending moment usually has the most significant effect on the sizes of members. The structural action depends on there being structural *continuity* between the linear elements of the frame. In this respect they are similar to continuous beams. For example, a three-span continuous beam is similar in action to a single-storey one-bay frame which has been flattened out (*2.76*). Ignoring the effects caused by horizontal deflection of the corner points, the bending moment patterns given by loads at right angles to the elements are identical; one difference is that the two columns of the frame are required to take a compression force due to the gravity load that does not exist in the equivalent continuous beam. Rigid arches may be thought of as a special case of a planar frame that has been shaped so as to reduce as far as is practicable the bending moments present. Single-storey portal frames often have sloping rafter members in order to approximate arch action while not departing from the simplicity of using straight line elements (*2.75*).

The most important structural idea behind the frame is to make all elements work together in bending so transforming, for example, a post and beam construction with pinned feet, from a mechanism to a stable form of construction (*2.61*). If the posts are free-standing columns, with fixed feet, rigid framing transforms them from deflecting like cantilevers under horizontal load, having curvature in one direction only, to deflecting into an S-shaped curve with double curvature and a point of inflection (*2.77*); both the bending moments and deflection of the frame columns are greatly reduced as compared to free-standing columns. Frame action, that is restraint of the columns against rotation, becomes more effective as the stiffness of the beam increases. Frame action is only significant if the beam and column stiffness are comparable and full frame action occurs only when the beam is very stiff compared to the columns (*2.77*). In order to reduce the horizontal deflection of a frame with a beam which is already stiff compared to the column, it is more advantageous to increase the

2.75 *Structures which depend on continuity of members or rigid joints can be classified as frames.*

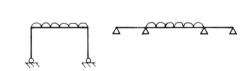

2.76 *Frame with pinned feet and three-bay continuous beam have similar bending moment patterns.*

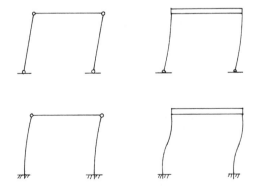

2.77 *Mechanism, top left, and post and beam structure, bottom left, transformed into full frame structures, right, by rigidly connecting to stiff beams.*

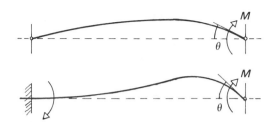

2.78. Deflected shape due to applied moment on beam that is pinned or fixed at far end.

column stiffnesses rather than to make further increases in beam stiffness, and vice-versa; see Tables 2.11 to 2.15 .

The *stiffness* in bending of an individual beam or column element is a measure of its resistance to rotation when a moment is applied at one end. For an element which has pinned connections at both ends (*2.78*), the stiffness, *s*, is given by:

$$s = \frac{M}{\theta} = \frac{3E.I}{L} \text{ unit moment/radian}$$

where   *M* is the bending moment applied at one end in N-mm (lb-ft);

   θ is the rotation at the end of the element where the bending moment is applied;

   E is the modulus of elasticity of the material in N/mm² (lb/in²);

   I is the moment of inertia of the element about the axis of bending in mm⁴ (in⁴); and

   L is the length of the element in mm (in).

For an element which is pinned at one end, where the moment is applied (*2.78*), and is fixed at the other end, the stiffness, *s*, is given by:

$$s = \frac{M}{\theta} = \frac{4E.I}{L} \text{ unit moment/radian}$$

In practice for a beam or column element in a frame, the degree of fixity provided at each end of the element is not known at the start; as the frame is usually made of the same material, the stiffness often simply refers to the ratio *I/L* .

Frame Analysis

Practical building frames are indeterminate structures but, as in the case of continuous beams, may be made into determinate structures, or mechanisms, which serve as models for

preliminary analysis, by inserting pin joints near the points of inflection which are known to occur in the real structure under load. Because the deflected shape depends on the type and direction of the load, there will be different models for the analysis depending on which loads are under consideration; the loads, and deflected shapes, to consider are those due to vertical loads on the floors (*2.53* and *2.81*) and horizontal loads on the frame (*2.83*). For preliminary analysis of regular building frames it is usually sufficient to consider the effects of uniformly distributed vertical load on one or more of the horizontal spans and the effects of a horizontal load applied at each floor level. In both cases the object is to find the worst bending moments, in the span and at junctions, and the worst axial loads in columns for preliminary sizing

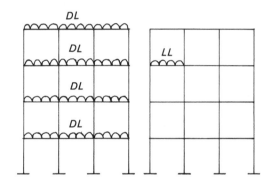

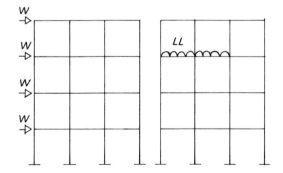

2.79 Four basic load cases, due to wind and gravity load, which may be factored and combined in various ways to find the worst axial loads and bending moments in the frame.

of the elements of the frame by any likely combination of dead load, live load and wind load (*2.79*). Practical building frames can be divided into braced and unbraced frames. *Unbraced frames* are those in which the frame is required to resist both vertical gravity loads as well as the horizontal, or lateral, loads. Unbraced frames resist the horizontal loads, such as wind or earthquake loads, by *frame action*, that is by the bending action of the column and beam elements (*2.83*). *Braced frames* are those in which the lateral stability of the building, that is its resistance to horizontal forces, is assured by vertical stiffening systems, such as shear wall or core structures, to which the frame is connected; see Table 2.15 . The frame is then only required to resist gravity loads (*2.80*).

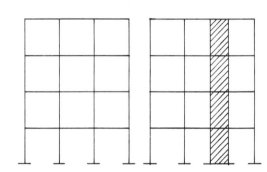

2.80 Braced and unbraced frame with vertical stiffening system in braced frame shown shaded.

Beam and Column Elements in Frames

For preliminary analysis, the floor beams in a building with a braced frame, may be designed as if they were continuous beams with knife-edge supports (*2.81*). This is equivalent to assuming that the columns have pinned connections at the top and bottom, where they connect to floor beams, and that they take axial loads but no bending moment. On the same assumption, interior columns may be designed to take axial load only. However, if the floor beam supported by the column has a grossly different span on one side of the column than the other, there is likely to be

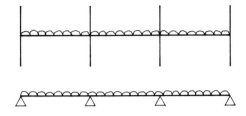

2.81 Floor beams in frames can be treated for analysis as if on knife-edge supports.

bending in the column and the assumption is no longer valid. For the same reason, the last column at each end of a continuous beam is likely to pick up bending moment as well as axial loads (*2.82*). At a preliminary stage, all the exterior columns may be designed in the same way as the end column of a single-storey multibay frame. Alternatively they may be designed as columns carrying axial load only, the axial load used being much greater than the actual axial load to take account of bending; see Table 2.6 . The floor beams in unbraced frames carry gravity loads in the same way as braced frames. However unbraced frames must also carry horizontal loads and in this case both columns and

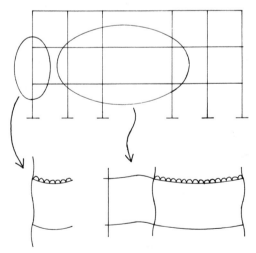

2.82 Bending in columns caused by vertical load on end spans or on unbalanced interior spans.

beams are put into bending in addition to that already present due to the vertical load. A common assumption, for preliminary analysis, is that the deflected frame has a point of inflection at midspan of the beams and at midheight of the columns; pin joints are then put in these positions in the structural model for the preliminary analysis (*2.83*). Note that, in general, all columns in unbraced frames are put both into bending and compression. In braced frames the combination of bending and compression is only likely to be

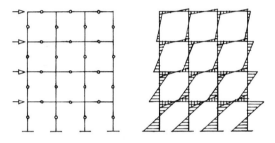

2.83 Unbraced frame transformed into a determinate structure for analysis of horizontal load, by insertion of pin joints, left; resulting bending moment under horizontal load is shown, right.

significant in end columns. The axial forces in the floor beams and slabs of braced or unbraced frames, due to horizontal forces, is not high enough to be significant in the calculation of their sizes. In both braced and unbraced frames the floor slabs can generally be designed to take vertical load only. Although floor slabs usually also function as horizontal diaphragms, in order to transfer horizontal load to the vertical stiffening systems, this action, vital as it is, does not have as significant an effect on the initial sizing of the floor slabs as bending does.

FLOOR AND ROOF SYSTEMS

Beam Grids

One particular arrangement of beams is the *beam grid* structure which may be used for floors and roofs. It consists of beam elements rigidly connected to each other in a two-way grid. To

make efficient use of material the beam grid needs to be supported on all four edges and the plan shape of the supported grid should be as close to a square as is possible. *Rectangular grids* are those which have beam elements at right angles to the lines of support. Beam grids work principally in bending but, by sketching the way in which they deform under load, it is clear that the beam elements also work in torsion (*2.84*). The torsional stiffness of all the beam elements increases the overall stiffness of the grid, as against an arrangement of beams in which the beams in each direction are in two different layers, the one either resting on the other or connected by a flexible tie (*2.85*). In the latter case only the bending stiffness of the beams affects the overall stiffness. If the plan shape of a beam grid is substantially different from a square shape then the only elements making a significant contribution to the stiffness of the beam grid are the beam elements spanning the

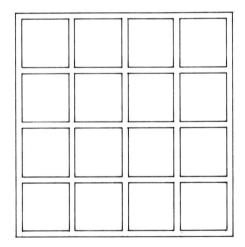

2.84 Plan and section through rectangular grid showing torsion of grid elements under load.

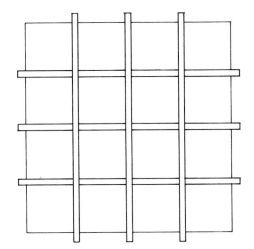

2.85 Plan on two-layer arrangement of beams.

shorter of the two span directions. For both beam grids or flat plate structures, if the longer span is more than about one and a half times the shorter span then two-way action is not significant and the beam grid or plate spans in the short direction only. *Skew grids* are those which have beam elements at an angle to the lines of support (*2.86*). Because the beam elements of skew grids 'cut the corner', like a skew space frame, they reduce the effective span and can be more efficient than rectangular grids. In addition the loss of two-way action that occurs in rectangular grids that are not

2.86 Plan on skew grid.

square on plan can be considerably reduced. Grid beam structures having a large grid spacing are sometimes used for roofs and for floors with or without a slab on top that is integral with it.

Slab Systems

As previously noted, *plates* or *slabs* may be modelled by bars, either in tension or compression, in a space frame arrangement. The bars may be imagined as having pinned connections in a preliminary design. However plates and slabs also

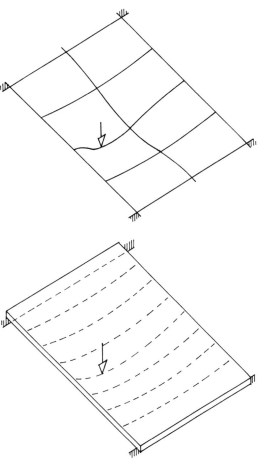

2.87 Point load on beam grid, top, and on one-way spanning slab, bottom, showing deflected shape.

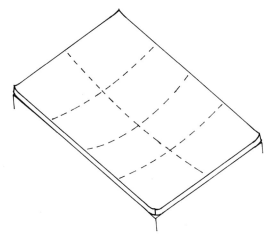

2.88 Simply-supported two-way spanning slab showing lifting of corners under load.

behave in similar ways to a beam grid and their structural action becomes clearer if they are thought of as a series of beam elements spaced very closely together. In particular the torsion which occurs in slab elements is more easily visualised this way. A *one-way slab* which is simply supported on two opposite sides and carries a uniformly distributed load may be imagined as a series of beam elements. There is no torsion. With a point load, however, the beam grid model shows torsion must be induced either side of the point load (*2.87*). A *two-way slab* which is simply supported on four sides and carries a uniformly distributed load also works in bending and torsion; in this case the torsion in the slab elements would cause the four corners of the slab to lift off from their supports (*2.88*). In practice floor slabs in multibay structures are usually continuous from one bay to the next and integral or firmly held down on their lines of supports so that lifting of the corners cannot occur (*2.89*); the fixing of the slab at the supports and the effect of the torsion considerably reduces the bending moment at the centre of the slab compared to that in the simply supported slab.

For preliminary analysis, slabs supported on walls or by a grid of deep beams may be sized by considering a slab strip running in each direction

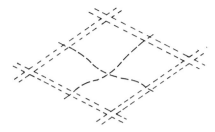

2.89 Continous two-way spanning slab showing supports and deflected shape.

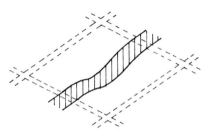

2.90 Strip of slab considered to be one-way spanning for preliminary design.

through the centre of the slab (*2.90*). Each slab strip can be analysed as a continuous beam assuming it to carry, for preliminary design, the actual uniformly distributed load or an equivalent uniformly distributed load which allows it to be treated as a continuous beam, depending on the proportions of the panel and the stiffness of the supports on all four sides of the slab; see Table 2.4 . However in many cases it is not possible to have a line support along all four edges of the slab, such as is provided by a wall or a deep beam. An extreme case is the *flat slab* or *flat plate* floor structure in which there are no beams, the columns directly supporting the slab, sometimes with a drophead or thickening of the slab at the top of the column. Flat slabs are almost always continuous over several bays and for preliminary analysis may be sized by considering slab strips running in each direction through the centre of the slab and other slab strips running in each direction over the column positions (*2.91*). Each slab strip can be analysed as a continuous beam assuming it to

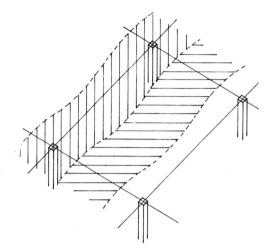

2.91 Column and middle strips, of equal width, used for design of flat plates and slabs.

carry a uniformly distributed load which is slightly less and slightly more, respectively, than the actual uniformly distributed floor load on these widths of strip; see Table 2.4 .

A case which is intermediate between the flat slab, which is only supported at the column

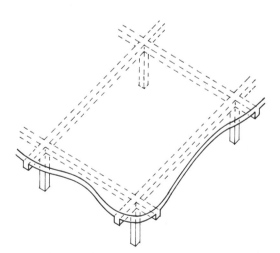

2.92 Two-way spanning slab and supporting beams.

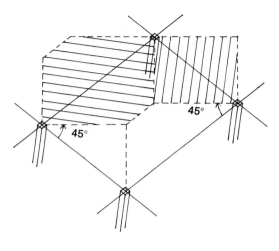

2.93 Tributary areas for beams lying on the column grid.

positions, and the two-way slab, which is continuously supported along all four panel edges, is the two-way slab and beam structure, this having beams in each direction along the column grid (*2.92*). If the beams are very deep then they may be designed as continuous beams

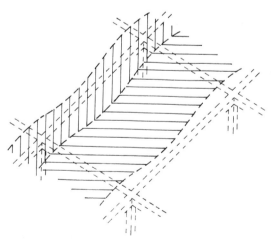

2.94 Column and middle strips, of unequal width, used for preliminary design of two-way spanning slab and beams.

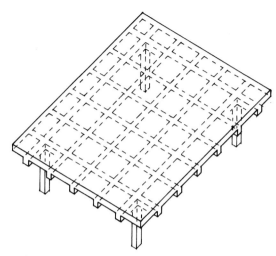

2.95 Waffle slab with closely-spaced ribs.

supporting their tributary load (2.93) or, more conservatively, as supporting a floor strip one bay wide, which carries the actual uniformly distributed load; see Table 2.4 . The beam in the direction at right angles is assumed to carry the same load. The slab can be assumed to behave as a two-way slab continuously supported on all four edges. If the beams are shallow then the system behaves more like a flat slab. The beam could then be designed as a continuous beam assuming it to support a floor strip, one-third of a bay wide, carrying twice the actual uniformly distributed load; a central strip two-thirds of a bay wide is then assumed to carry half of the actual uniformly distributed load and may also be analysed as a continuous beam (2.94); see also Table 2.4 . Note that the total load on each bay must still equal the actual total load on each bay. *Waffle slabs,* which consist of a beam grid with an integral slab, in which the beam or rib elements are closely spaced, may be treated structurally like a solid slab of the same overall depth (2.95).

Membrane Action of Slabs

A rectangular plate, or a thin slab, which initially is flat and supported along all four edges, will deform into a curved shape when a vertical load is applied. The plate initially resists these loads in bending.

However if the plate is thin it will have a low stiffness in bending so that the deflection of the plate may be significant. If the plate is restrained at its edges in any way, so that it is unable to move horizontally, then membrane action will quickly develop, coexisting with the bending action (2.96). *Membrane action* means that the structure is resisting load by direct stresses of tension or compression in the plane of the structural element. If the slab is restrained at the edges, membrane action becomes increasingly significant as the deflection increases. If the deflection of the rectangular plate exceeds about twice the thickness of the plate then almost all the load is carried by membrane action rather than by bending; for very thin plates this amount of deflection is reached even under light loading.

2.96 Slab in which deflection is nearly equal to slab thickness.

BUILDING SYSTEMS

Shear Wall and Frame Systems

For medium-rise or high-rise buildings the structural system adopted is usually a choice, in one form or another, between loadbearing wall systems, also known as shear wall systems, and frame systems (2.97). Frame and shear wall systems may be combined in the same building (2.98). A *loadbearing wall* is one used to carry gravity load but is known as a *shear wall* if it also transfers horizontal forces to ground. Whatever structural system is adopted, it must be able to carry the vertical loads associated with gravity forces, and the horizontal loads associated with wind and earthquake forces. Earthquakes may cause additional vertical forces to act on the structure but damage is most likely to occur as a result of the horizontal forces on the building due to earthquakes. The horizontal forces are of paramount importance in the design of high rise buildings. *High rise buildings* may be said to be those buildings for which the scale effect of an

2.97 Plans of buildings stabilised by shear walls, left, and by frames, right.

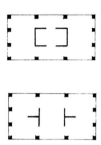

2.98 Plans of buildings with frames and shear walls.

increase in height has a significant influence on the structural design. In general this scale effect is associated with buildings above about twenty storeys in height for which the ratio of height to least horizontal dimension is greater than five. As buildings increase in height, more efficient ways of providing lateral stiffness are necessary to control horizontal movement and acceleration and these can have a significant influence on the form. *Medium rise buildings* may be said to include buildings which are lower than high-rise buildings but still more than about five storeys in height.

Various methods are used to resist the horizontal forces on a building. *Shear walls* are efficient at resisting horizontal loads which are applied in their own plane (2.97). As horizontal

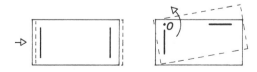

2.99 Unsatisfactory arrangements of shear walls causing lateral sway, left, or rotation about a point, right.

forces may be applied in any direction, the shear walls must be placed in at least two different directions and, in addition, must be placed such that they cannot rotate about a point (2.99). Each shear wall should carry as much gravity load as possible in order to prevent tension occurring under horizontal forces. Shear walls deflect like vertical cantilevers in which, under a uniformly distributed load, the storey-height drift, that is the horizontal deflection between one storey and the next, is greatest at the top of the cantilever (2.102). Under a uniformly distributed load, the shear force varies linearly with the height and the bending moment varies with the square of the height (2.110). Typical examples of shear wall systems are loadbearing masonry buildings, cast-in-place concrete loadbearing walls and precast concrete panel systems. Outside earthquake areas, unreinforced masonry may be satisfactory even for high buildings because of the prestressing of the masonry by gravity load. Although thick steel plates may be used to provide vertical bracing, usually steel is used in the form of a *shear truss*. The steel shear truss acts in an equivalent way to the shear wall. It consists of a truss placed vertically and triangulated in any convenient way (2.100). Like shear wall systems in masonry or concrete, the shear truss may be used as a planar element, for example, in a steel frame, or several shear trusses be combined to form core structures.

A fundamental difference between shear wall

2.101 *Deflected shape of frame due to bending of beams and columns.*

and shear truss systems, on the one hand, and frame systems, on the other hand, is in the way they deflect under horizontal load (2.100 and 2.101) : shear walls deflect like cantilever beams and, assuming their height is greater than about five times their length they take a smooth curved shape in which almost all deflection is due to bending. Shear trusses also deflect like cantilevers. Assuming the cross-bracing is properly sized, almost all horizontal deflection in the shear truss under a horizontal load is due to the column extension or shortening on the windward and leeward side of the shear truss respectively. Like all

triangulated frameworks, there is no significant bending moment in individual members, but the whole shear truss action resembles the action of a cantilever. The storey-height deflection, Δ_h, of a shear wall or shear truss is approximately given by (2.102) :

$$\Delta_h = \frac{Q.h}{6E.I}\left(H^2 - \frac{y^3}{H}\right) \text{mm (in)}$$

where Q is the total uniformly distributed load on the shear wall or truss in N (lb);

h is the storey height in mm (in);

H is the total height of the shear wall or truss in mm (in);

y is the distance from the top of the shear wall or truss to the storey concerned in mm (in);

I is the moment of inertia of the shear wall or truss, which for a truss $\approx A.L^2/2$ where A is the area of each leg and L is the depth of the shear truss, in mm^4 (in^4).

By contrast, when *rigid frames* deflect under horizontal load, they have a racking type of deflection shape, in which almost all the deflection is due to the bending of the beams and columns and only a small part, normally under 10%, is due to column extension or shortening (2.101). However as the height of the frame increases the deflection due to column extension or shortening has an increasing effect.

Building Frame Design

Two approximate methods are used for a preliminary analysis of the shear force, bending moment and axial forces in building frames under horizontal load: the portal method and the cantilever method. In the *portal method*, it is assumed that there are points of inflection at the midspan of all beams and at midheight of all columns (2.83). It is further assumed that the horizontal shear on all interior columns at any one level is equal and twice that on all the exterior columns (2.103). In the *cantilever method*, points of inflection are also assumed at midpoints of beams and columns (2.81), but with the further assumption that the axial stress in each column, due to horizontal load is proportional to its distance from the neutral axis of the building frame (2.104). The frame is a highly indeterminate structure but the assumptions in each method make the structure determinate and allow an

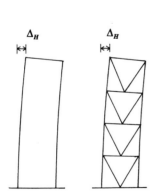

2.100 *Deflected shapes of shear wall, left, and shear truss, right.*

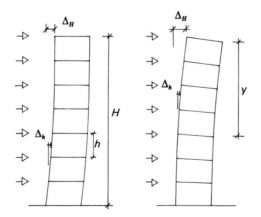

2.102 *Overall deflected shape of framed building, left, and cantilevered building, right.*

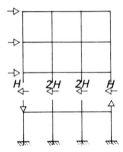

2.103 Section on building in which interior columns take twice the shear of exterior columns.

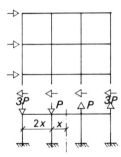

2.104 Axial loads in columns as assumed by the cantilever method.

estimate to be made of the forces in each member; see Table 2.13 . The portal method is generally assumed to give a reasonable estimate of the bending moments and axial forces if the building is less than about twenty storeys high and the ratio of height to width is less than four. The cantilever method gives a better estimate of the axial forces in the columns if this ratio is greater than about three. The portal method assumes the frame to have a racking type of deflection shape; it gives a better estimate when the frame is 'well-proportioned', that is when the horizontal spans are equal, the moments of inertia of the beams at each level are equal and the moments of inertia of the interior columns are twice those of the exterior columns (*2.103*). The cantilever method assumes the frame has the deflected shape of a cantilever. A modification, due to Spurr, for use with the cantilever method, is that the moment of inertia of each beam be adjusted so that it is proportional to the shear force on it and to the square of its span. This has the effect of ensuring that all columns, including interior columns, help in resisting horizontal load. The portal method, by contrast, ignores column extension and shortening under horizontal load and assumes that only the exterior columns carry the additional axial loads due to horizontal forces.

In steel frames the stresses in the members are generally not as critical as the horizontal deflection or drift of the frame. The total horizontal deflection at the top of the frame, Δ_H, as a proportion of the total height needs to be controlled as well as the relative deflection between storeys as a proportion

of the storey height. Assuming points of inflection at midheight, a good approximation of the storey-height deflection, Δ_h, at a typical level, not those at the top or bottom of the frame, is given by [4] (*2.102*) :

$$\Delta_h = \frac{F.h^2.\Sigma K_c}{12E} + \frac{F.h^2.\Sigma K_b}{12E} \text{ mm (in)}$$

where F is the total horizontal shear at the floor level considered in N (lb);

h is the storey height in mm (in);

E is the modulus of elasticity of the material in N/mm² (lb/in²);

ΣK_c is the sum of h/I for each column at the floor level in 1/mm³ (1/in³); and

ΣK_b is the sum of L/I for each beam in the floor immediately above the columns in 1/mm³ (in³).

For a frame with pinned feet at ground floor, the ground floor storey-height deflection, Δ_h, is given by:

$$\Delta_h = \frac{F.h^2.\Sigma K_c}{3E} + \frac{F.h^2.\Sigma K_b}{8E} \text{ mm (in)}$$

For a frame with fixed feet at ground floor level, the ground floor storey-height deflection is somewhat less than that given by the formula for storey-height deflection at a typical level. The formulae clearly show the different influence of the stiffness of the beams and columns on the storey-height deflection. For estimating the total frame deflection, Δ_H, the cantilever deflection due to column extension and shortening must also be included. For preliminary calculation the total deflection may be split into that due to the beams, with very stiff columns pinned at midheight, that

due to the columns, with very stiff beams, and that due to column extension and shortening, with two very stiff cross-braces which are not connected to each other and free to slide over each other; see Tables 2.13 and 2.14 . Because the total horizontal shear at each floor increases, going down the building, the stiffness of the beams and columns will also need to increase.

Stability of Buildings under load

As in steel beams, where it is necessary that the vertical load be lined up with the shear centre at any vertical section through the beam (*2.48*), so the horizontal load on a building should coincide, as far as possible, with the shear centre at any horizontal section taken through the building. The shear centre is the centre of stiffness of the building at any horizontal section taken through it. If the resultant horizontal load always passes through the shear centre at each level, then the building experiences no torsional moment. The resultant horizontal load on a building may be due to wind or earthquakes. Earthquakes cause accelerations of the ground so that inertial forces then act on the building structure. The resultant inertia force acts through the *centre of mass*, or centre of gravity, of the building; therefore in earthquake areas, the centre of mass should as far as possible coincide with the shear centre in order to minimise the torsional moment on the building. This may be achieved by placing the building's mass and the building's vertical stiffening systems symmetrically with one another (*2.105*). Even in those areas that are not subject to earthquakes, the dynamic effect of wind forces will cause the building to twist if the centre of pressure of the

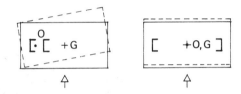

2.105 Ground movements causing lateral displacement and twist, left, or pure lateral displacement where centre of mass (G) and shear centre (O) coincide, right.

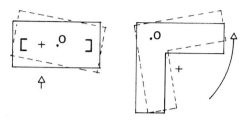

 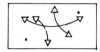

2.108 Building with separate translational and
twisting modes of vibration, left, and building in
which these modes are coupled, right.

2.106 Plans of buildings in which shear centre (O)
does not coincide with centre of pressure.

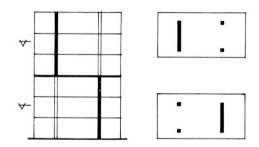

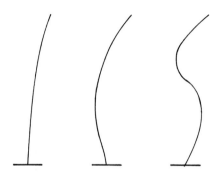

2.107 Vertical and plan sections of building in which
plan position of shear centre varies with height.

2.109 Schematic drawing of first three modes of
translational movement in a tall building.

rotational movements there are a series of modes
for each type of movement, of which the
fundamental modes are the most important
(2.108). The natural frequencies of building
elements may be measured or estimated by
calculation. The fundamental natural frequency,
ω_0, of a frame or a single mass on a cantilever is
given by:

$$\omega_0 = \frac{1}{2\pi}\sqrt{\frac{g}{\Delta}} \text{ Hz}$$

where Δ is the deflection at the top of the structure
when the dead load of the frame, which is a
distributed load, or the weight of the mass on
the cantilever, which is a point load, is
applied horizontally; for the mass, this
deflection,

$$\Delta = \frac{W.H^3}{3E.I} \text{ mm (in)};$$

g is the acceleration due to gravity in mm/s²
(ft/s²);

W is the weight of the mass in N (lb); and

H, I, E are the height, moment of inertia and
modulus of elasticity of the cantilever.

An approximate figure for the fundamental
frequency of a building, ω_0, is given by:

$$\omega_0 = \frac{20}{\sqrt{\Delta}} \text{ Hz}$$

where Δ is in mm (in)

The object in the design is to prevent *resonance* of
the building and to damp out the vibrations which
do occur as quickly as possible by arranging that
the important natural frequencies of the building
are different and therefore out-of-phase with the
forcing frequencies of the wind or earthquake
movements. Most structures have a sufficient
amount of natural damping to prevent the
continuance of vibration. However in high-rise
buildings of steel construction, for example,
measures may need to be taken to increase the
natural damping of the structure.

HIGH RISE BUILDINGS

Frames and Tubes

A large number of high-rise buildings use shear
walls to provide lateral stability (2.97). A
development of the shear wall is the *core structure*
in which a number of shear walls are placed

wind forces, that is the place where the resultant
wind force acts, and the shear centre of the
building are not close together; this is especially
true in high-rise buildings (2.106). In addition,
high-rise buildings in which the plan position of
the shear centre changes significantly within the
height of the building will cause torsional
moments to occur (2.107). If possible the shear
centre and the centre of mass should coincide
throughout the height of the building to prevent
twisting movements and oscillations occurring. As
noted previously, shear walls and frames must be
placed so as to resist horizontal forces from any
direction whether they are translational or
rotational in character (2.99).

Dynamic Forces on Buildings

The response of a building to earthquake forces or
to wind buffeting may be significantly affected by
the natural frequencies of the building structure,
because these forces are dynamic rather than static

in nature. In general a dynamic analysis of a
building structure becomes necessary if the
frequencies of the earthquake or wind buffeting
are close to, or of a similar order of magnitude to,
the natural frequencies of the building. A building,
like other building elements, for example a steel
beam, has natural frequencies associated with
translational movements about the two principal
axes of bending. In addition there are natural
frequencies associated with rotation about the
shear centre (2.108). For each of these three types
of movement there will be a series of natural
frequencies, the first or fundamental mode, second
mode, third mode and so on, of which the
fundamental mode is the most important (2.109).
If the shear centre and the centre of mass do not
coincide throughout the structure, as is usually the
case in practice, then there will still be three types
of movement but *coupling* will occur, in which the
three types will contain both translational and
rotational movements. As for pure translational or

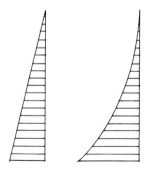

2.110 *Variation of shear force, left, and bending moment, right, with height for cantilever under uniform horizontal load.*

together, usually enclosing lifts, stairs or services to form tubes or other plan shapes (*2.98*); compared to a single wall the core or shaft structures have 'flange' as well as 'web' portions to resist horizontal forces. However the overall shear and bending moment patterns in shear wall and core structures follow that of a cantilever (*2.110*). A practical difficulty arises because of the need to provide openings in the core structure for service runs or doorways. With only small openings the core structue will be unaffected but larger openings will require strengthening round the openings, especially at sharp corners. Most core structures are of poured concrete construction in which extra reinforcement may be placed as necessary but cores may also be built in reinforced

or unreinforced masonry. Where a high-rise concrete frame of cast-in-place construction is used, it is natural, and advantageous, to connect the frame with shear walls so that they interact with each other. In *shear wall and frame interaction*, the frame is proportioned to help restrict deflection in the shear wall at the top while the shear wall helps to restrict deflection in the frame at the bottom (*2.111*). The effect is that wind shear forces are largely carried by the frame in the upper storeys and by the shear wall in the lower storeys(*2.112*). In steel buildings, the equivalent combination is that produced by *shear truss and frame interaction*. A further increase in stiffness against horizontal forces can be provided in steel buildings by using a *shear truss and frame with belt trusses*. In this system deep horizontal outrigger trusses are connected to the central shear trusses which are vertical, and to a horizontal belt truss in the perimeter of the steel frame (*2.113*). As the shear truss deflects the outrigger trusses force the perimeter windward and leeward columns into axial tension and compression respectively, thus increasing the plan area of the building which takes part in the structural action (*2.114*). In order to prevent bending moment being introduced into the perimeter columns, the connection between them and the belt trusses can be a pinned one. There are certain optimum locations for the belt trusses: if two belt trusses are used they would be best placed somewhere near the half and three-quarter points in the height of the building; if only one belt truss is used, it would be best placed somewhere between these two

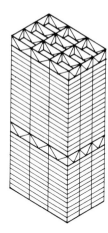

2.113 *Building with outrigger trusses connected to two perimeter belt trusses.*

positions, although in practice the highest belt truss is often placed at the top of the building.

The most effective way of resisting horizontal loads, for any given plan area, is to use a cantilever with a solid section; however hollow tubes are more efficient in that they are almost as stiff but use very much less material than a solid section cantilever (*2.115*). The direct stresses of tension and compression and the shear stresses are those associated with a pure cantilever (*2.110*). Solid

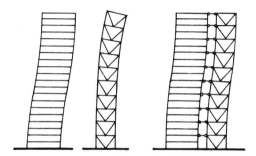

2.111 *Deflection of frame and shear truss and frame-shear wall combination.*

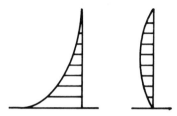

2.112 *Proportion of shear force carried by frame, left, and shear wall, right, over height of building in a frame-shear wall combination; with uniform horizontal load, addition of the two shears produces a straight line.*

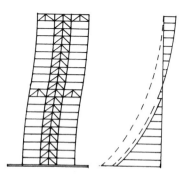

2.114 *Section through building with outrigger and two belt trusses, left, showing bending moment on vertical shear truss, right; dotted lines show bending moment with only one belt truss acting and with shear truss acting alone as cantilever.*

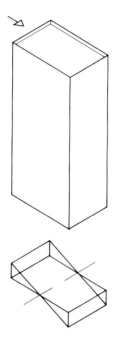

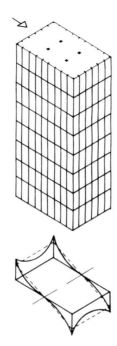

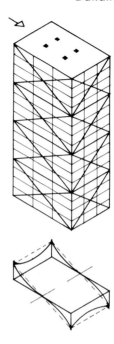

2.115 Pure tube showing distribution of vertical forces at bottom of tube under horizontal load (shown dotted in following three diagrams).

2.116 Schematic diagram of external framed tube showing distribution of vertical forces at bottom under horizontal load; in practice beams and columns have large widths to ensure rigidity of the frames on the facade.

2.117 Schematic diagram of diagonal truss tube showing distribution of vertical forces at bottom under horizontal load.

sections are not practical forms and hollow sections without openings are generally only feasible for towers, chimneys and other such uses. However high-rise buildings can still be designed to exploit the inherent efficiency of tube action by an appropriate choice of form. An objective, if tube-type systems are used, is to increase the plan area of the tube as much as possible, that is to increase the effective section area of the cantilever, and to make the structural behaviour as close as possible to that of the the hollow tube without openings in it. As window openings are necessary for the building, the perimeter structure is weaker and more flexible than that of the pure tube. However buildings do have the compensating advantage of being stiffened by the floors, which act as a series of horizontal diaphragms and prevent distortion of the cross-section of the building throughout its height. One general type

of high rise structure is the *framed tube*, which can be built in steel or concrete. In this system the perimeter columns are very closely spaced, and as wide as possible, and act in combination with deep spandrel beams (*2.116*). The whole framed tube cantilevers, causing axial forces in the perimeter columns. However the 'web' faces of the framed tube tend to deflect like frames and, as well as this, the 'flange' faces suffer from 'shear lag' so that, compared to a pure tube, there are increased axial loads in the columns near the corners and reduced axial loads elsewhere. Cast-in-place concrete construction provides the rigid frame construction necessary for framed tubes. Steel is also used but here the rigid joints required need to be made by welding and, as many such joints are required, this can be expensive. An improvement on framed tube construction is the *diagonal truss tube*. In this system, diagonal members are placed

on the perimeter making a fully triangulated framework on each face of the building. The diagonal members are arranged to intersect the columns and beams at column-beam joints (*2.117*). Columns may be spaced further apart than in a framed tube. Because of the large number of columns and beams which need to be provided anyway, each face consists of more than a simple truss system: the diagonals on the 'web' faces of the building act largely as cross-bracing to prevent shear deformation of the building under horizontal load; on the 'flange' faces, and on all faces when there is no horizontal load, the diagonals act more as inclined columns ensuring an even distribution of vertical load between the columns, in proportion to their stiffness under load. For this reason it is not strictly necessary for vertical columns to be continuous down the face of the building (*2.118*). Diagonal truss tubes have been

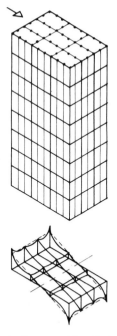

2.118 Schematic diagram of bundled tube showing distribution of vertical forces at bottom under horizontal load.

built both in steel and concrete. The efficiency of the diagonal truss tube may be improved by inclining the corner columns inwards. An ingenious method of reducing the flexibility and load concentrations associated with the framed tube is to form several smaller tubes connected together (2.119), which is then known as a *bundled tube*. This system is particularly applicable to buildings of large plan areas and allows interior columns to participate in carrying horizontal load. The effect of building several tubes into one larger tube is to reduce the shear deformation associated with bending of the beams and columns and to allow more of the horizontal forces to be taken by cantilever action, that is by axial forces in the columns (2.104). The bundled tube system may be used with any tube system including the diagonal truss tube. As with a single tube system, each tube in the bundled tube may have almost any plan shape as long as it forms a

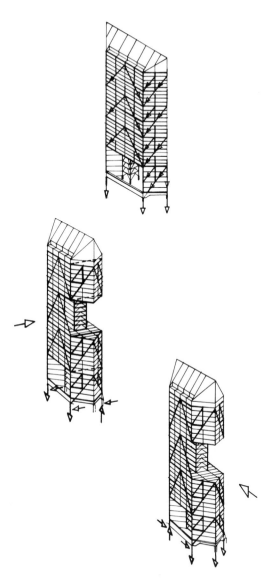

2.119 Large scale trussing used in high-rise building; structure has external diagonal trussed tube with internal core, which in combination carry gravity load, top, and wind loads, middle and bottom; main diagonal members are eight storeys high; some vertical perimeter columns are not continuous; main loadbearing members shown bold (drawn using ref.5 and material supplied by structural engineer: Le Messurier/SCI).

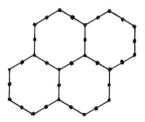

2.120 Plan on bundled tube building made up of hexagonal units.

closed plan shape (2.120). The stiffness of framed tubes may also be used by improved by connecting it to shear walls or core structures which may be present in the building anyway. This then gives *framed-tube and shear wall interaction* which is a variant on basic frame and shear wall interaction and works in a similar way (2.112). If the shear wall is in the form of a core structure then this is often known as a *tube in tube* system (2.121).

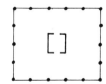

2.121 Tube in tube system using a perimeter frame and core.

PROPERTIES OF SURFACES

Curvature

An important property of a plane curve at any position along its length is its *curvature, c*, which is the change in angle of the curve, $d\theta$, in moving a very small distance, ds, between two points at the position concerned. The radius of curvature, r, is obtained by taking normals to the curve, that is lines at right angles to the curve, at the two points and finding the distance from the curve at which the two normals intersect (2.122). The one is the reciprocal of the other and defined by:

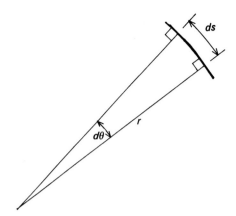

2.122   Radius of curvature of curve defined by tangents of two points close together.

$$c = \frac{d\theta}{ds} = \frac{1}{r} \; 1/mm \; (1/in)$$

A sign convention normally adopted is that curves concave downwards are positive while curves concave upwards are negative. By analogy with a plane curve, the curvature of a three-dimensional surface at any position, known as the *gaussian curvature, K,* is defined as the solid angle, $d\beta$, subtended by a small area, dA, when it is transferred onto the surface of a sphere with unit radius, with every point on the original contour which surrounds the small area, dA, having a corresponding point on the surface of the unit sphere; the corresponding point is found by drawing a radial line through the centre of the unit sphere which is parallel to the normal at the point on the contour surrounding the small area on the original surface, dA (*2.123*). The area enclosed by all these points on the unit sphere is equal to the solid angle, $d\beta$. The normal to a surface at any point is the line which is at right angles to the tangents at the point on any two plane sections taken through the point. Note that any contour on the surface of a unit sphere, whatever its shape, subtends a solid angle equal to the area contained by the contour; the whole surface of the unit sphere has an area of 4π, which is equal to the solid angle surrounding the point at the centre of the sphere, or any other point in three-dimensional space.

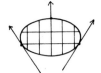

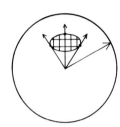

2.123   Contour surrounding small area dA on a smooth surface showing normals to the surface at the contour line, top; corresponding contour line on unit sphere with normals parallel to those on the original surface, bottom.

Gaussian Curvature

Consider a point on a smooth surface in which the normal to the surface has some known direction, represented by a line with an arrow head. If a plane section is taken in any of the directions which pass through the normal line, then the curvature, c, of the surface in the direction chosen over a small length, ds, may be found (*2.122*). The normal is assumed to pass through the middle of the small length of line ds. If, as well as in the middle, normals are also drawn at each end of the small length, ds, it will be seen that, in general, these two normals have rotated with respect to each other about the line ds (*2.124*). The angle is seen by looking along the section line. Calling this angle $d\varphi$, and by analogy with curvature, the *twist* of the surface in that direction, t, at the point concerned, is defined as:

$$t = \frac{d\varphi}{ds} \; 1/mm \; (1/in)$$

If other vertical sections which pass through the normal are taken, they will also have a certain curvature and twist. It is a property of any smooth surface, however, that there are two directions on the surface, at right angles to each other and to the normal, for which there is no twist. Further, in

these two directions, known as *principal directions*, the surface has, at this point, its maximum and minimum curvature (*2.122*). The curvatures are known as the *principal curvatures, c_x and c_y*. It can be shown that there is a relationship between the principal curvatures and the gaussian curvature at any position on a surface given by:

$$K = \frac{d\beta}{dA} = c_x.c_y \; 1/mm^2 \; (1/in^2)$$

By the use of the notion of gaussian curvature, surfaces may be divided into three distinct types: *synclastic surfaces*, such as domes, in which the principal curvatures have the same sign so that the gaussian curvature is positive; *anticlastic surfaces*, such as saddle surfaces in which the principal curvatures have opposite sign so that the gaussion curvature is negative (*2.125*); and *developable surfaces*, such as cylinders in which one of the principal curvatures is zero so that the gaussian curvature is also zero. One way of thinking about the gaussion curvature of smooth surfaces is to imagine the surface as made up of small triangular 'tiles', the connections between the vertices of the triangles lying on the actual surface concerned. If the surface is a closed surface, then the small triangles make it into a polyhedron, that is a closed surface made up of flat polygons (*2.130*). Each

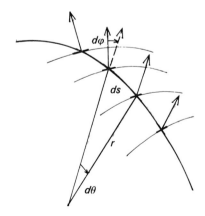

2.124   Plane section through a surface showing curvature and twist on surface at a point on this section.

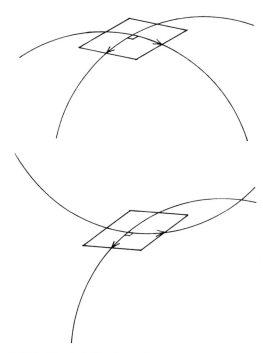

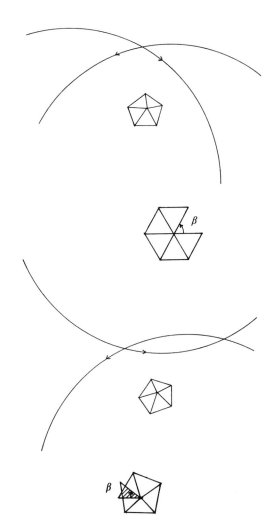

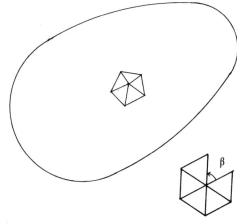

2.125 Principal directions of curvature on a synclastic surface, top, and an anticlastic surface, bottom.

2.126 'Tiles' around a point on a closed surface, formed by drawing straight lines between adjoining points on the surface; when flattened these give the 'left over' angle at the point, β.

2.127 'Tiles' shown when on a synclastic surface, top, and an anticlastic surface, bottom, and when both are flattened out.

vertex of the polyhedron subtends a certain solid angle. It can be shown that this solid angle, $β$, is equal to 2π minus the sum of all the angles each triangle makes at the vertex or, more graphically, the angle 'left over' if the triangles surrounding the point are flattened out (2.126). For triangles modelling a synclastic surface there is not enough angle in the triangles at the apex point and the

material opens up if laid flat while for an anticlastic surface there is too much angle in the triangles at the apex point and the material overlaps if laid flat (2.127). By making the triangular 'tiles' sufficiently small, a good approximation to the gaussian curvature, K, at any point on a closed surface, or any other smooth surface, is given, from the definition, by:

$$K \approx \frac{β}{A} \quad 1/mm^2 \; (1/in^2)$$

where $β$ is the solid angle or 'left-over' angle at the relevant vertex on the surface in radians; and

   A is the area of the polyhedron associated with this vertex which is equal to a third of the sum of the areas of all the triangles surrounding the vertex (2.128).

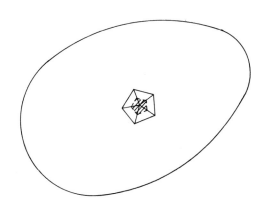

2.128 Point on surface surrounded by 'tiles' with area associated with point shown shaded.

MEMBRANE STRUCTURES

Membrane Equation

A *membrane* is any thin, flexible plate or sheet material. Membranes usually take on a three-dimensional surface shape and carry loads by any combination of tension, compression or shear but with all three types of stress acting in the plane of the surface (2.31). Examples of membrane structures are thin shells made of rigid materials, which can work in tension, compression or shear, or tents made of films or fabrics, which can only

2.131 Dome surface represented by bars in triangular arrangement.

2.132 Generation of dome surfaces by rotation about an axis.

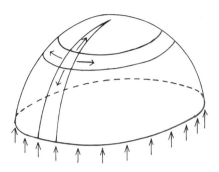

2.134 Hemispherical dome showing typical arch segment and hoop ring; the support reaction at the base is assumed to act in a vertical direction only.

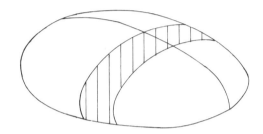

2.133 An elliptical paraboloid can be generated by translation of one parabola over another parabola of a different shape; a typical strip, for use in preliminary design, is shown shaded.

2.135 Point load on a thin dome causing bending (meridional and circumferential lines drawn on shell).

pure membrane action, can be made into a determinate structure if some assumption is made concerning the support reactions; for example the dome, if evenly loaded, may be assumed to have a uniformly distributed reactions at its base (*2.134*). The framework model assumes that a small area on the surface can be represented by a one-dimensional bar element. A more sophisticated model for the action of continuous shells with membrane action is provided by assuming the surface of the shell to consist of a large number of *finite elements*. The finite element is a 'tile' element with an area. One way of connecting triangular finite elements together is to connect them at the three apex points of each triangle; just as it is assumed that the strain at any point down the length of a bar can be calculated in terms of the movement at the two ends of the bar, so it is assumed the strains, and therefore the stresses, within each finite element can be calculated in terms of the movements of the node points of the triangular finite elements. For membrane action, the finite element can be assumed to take only membrane stresses. Other shapes of finite elements and other types of finite element which take both membrane and bending stresses are in common use for the analysis of practical shell structures.

Domes

Many shell structures which are thin but possess some bending stiffness work substantially by membrane action. A dome is a typical example. The *dome* is produced by revolving a curve about a vertical axis through its apex so as to make a three-dimensional surface (*2.132*). Alternatively one curve can be run over another, of a different shape,

to produce surfaces such as the elliptic paraboloid dome surface (*2.133*). Like a fabric membrane, the dome works with direct stresses in the plane of the dome. Unlike a fabric, however, the dome is able to develop substantial tangential shear stresses between one small element on the dome surface and the next. The stresses in the dome surface may be defined by considering a small rectangular element and the direct and shear stresses acting on the element in the meridional and circumferential directions, which are at right angles to each other. Dome, which are intact, do not behave like a series of narrow arch segments, fitted together, because the dome is able to generate hoop stresses in the circumferential direction (*2.134*); a uniformly distributed load on any arch segment, cut from the dome, which was not funicular for that arch shape would cause bending (*2.66*) but the same uniformly distributed load over the whole dome would not, because of the effect of the hoop and

shear stresses in the dome. The dome, and shell surfaces in general, have the property of behaving like funicular surfaces, that is surfaces that do not develop significant bending moment with any well distributed load. The single arch element, by contrast is funicular for only one particular load pattern. However bending moments do develop if there are sudden changes in the curvature of the shell or if point loads are applied (*2.135*). For example bending will develop near the base of the dome if lateral movement there is restrained; in theory, to prevent such bending, the supports should supply forces to the dome which only act in the plane of the dome and allow displacement and rotation in any other direction (*2.134*). In practice this is hard to achieve so that there is usually some secondary bending near the supports to the dome which necessitates an increase in shell thickness. In general any load or support reaction which is not well distributed causes bending moments to

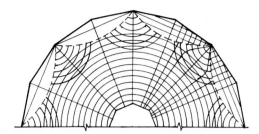

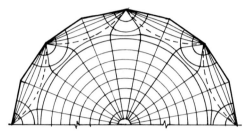

2.136 *Section through dome showing bending moment caused by incompatibility between the deformation of the shell under load and its support.*

2.138 *Half plan of shell in 2.137 showing how the disposition of reinforcing bars, left, closely follows the stress-flow lines, right.*

develop. However in a synclastic structure, such as a dome, the bending is only local and the dome can still carry almost all the load by membrane action (*2.136*); in anticlastic shell structures based for example on the hyperbolic paraboloid, bending action at the edges may propagate long distances. One common type of support for the dome is a tension ring at the base to counteract the outward thrusts from the dome; local bending arises in this system because the tension ring expands outwards and, in doing so, pulls the shell with it, thus producing additional forces on the shell; such a dome is said to have incompatibilities of displacement. An effective way of minimising the outward movement and avoiding cracking is to prestress the ring beam in compression (*2.137*). The *buckling* of domes is a major consideration in domes of long span and low rise, both because the meridional stresses are high and because the curvature of the dome surface in the two principal

directions of curvature is likely to be low. Buckling is potentially dangerous because any local deflection of the shell from its design shape makes buckling more likely to occur. This may be contrasted with cable or fabric structures in which buckling, or creasing, of the surface has no serious effects and in which the deflection generally leads to a better distribution of stresses within the curved surface. *Concrete domes* are usually in the form of thin shells, which however have low stresses in the surface and are given as much curvature as possible (*2.138*). *Masonry domes* are a special case of the membrane structure. Although masonry domes are thick, they are usually unreinforced and therefore have little bending or tensile strength. Hence they must work as membrane structures making use of their compression and in-plane shear resistance. Cracks will occur before significant tensile stresses develop (*2.139*). Closed shell surfaces, such as egg shells, are stronger and stiffer than open surfaces such as domes. In addition it is easier to ensure that the reactions on a closed surface are well distributed so that better membrane action can develop, for example that which occurs when an egg shell is pressed between the palms of the hand.

Steel domes and *wood domes* are almost always in the form of *reticulated structures*, either single-layer or double-layer. A general distinction may be made between reticulated domes set out on radial lines and these on a regular grid. An intermediate type is the network or lamellar grid, which is based on the use of approximately parallel rings of members but in which, unlike radial domes, the lengths of the members are

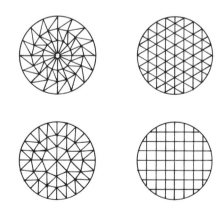

2.139 *Unreinforced masonry dome showing cracking at base originated by hoop stresses; the dome requires sufficient thickness to enable it to work partly by an arch action; in a reinforced spherical shell under self-weight, the hoop stresses change from compression to tension below the hoop ring that makes an angle of 51.8° with the vertical at the centre of the sphere, assuming a membrane state of stress.*

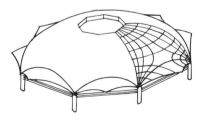

2.137 *Reinforced concrete shell by Torroja having post-tensioned cables at base with stress-flow lines shown over one sector; cylindrical canopies at the base absorb outward thrusts from the shell.*

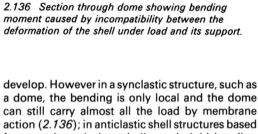

2.140 *Dome plans based on braced radial ribs, top left, network pattern, bottom left, three-way grid, top right, and two-way grid, bottom right.*

approximately equal (2.140). Radial rib domes can be shaped to be funicular, in cross-section, for the full design load, so that other loads, especially unbalanced loads, can then be taken by the hoop or circumferential members. In practice the dead load of a radial rib dome is not as significant as live load but the idea is important and could be used as a starting point in the development of a suitable form. Cross-bracing or stiff joints may be used to take shear stresses in the plane of the shell.

Grid Shells

The *grid shell* is made up of elements initially on a regular grid, whether rectangular or skew, which are made into any non-developable and three-dimensional surface shape (2.140). A distinction may be made between grid shells with two-way and three-way grids. The *two-way grid shell* is made up of continuous elements with some bending stiffness, such as timber beams and steel tubes, which, however, can rotate, and in some cases slide, relative to the members going in the other direction. The grid shell takes compressive stresses, like a membrane, in the plane of the surface, but unlike a continuous membrane, or a three-way grid, which is triangulated, it is unable to take shear stresses in the plane of the surface. Grid shells may be thought of as flat beam grids pushed into a three-dimensional shape and anchored at their base so as to work like a series of interconnected arches. The grid shell is a mechanism but, once in position, the complete structure is stabilised by its supporting system. Because of its lack of shear stiffness and, usually, its limited bending stiffness, it is made to have a funicular shape for the important load pattern on it, which may be the dead load. In practice, as with the case of radial domes, cross-bracing can be added between the intersection points of the grid shell, or the joints made to give restraint against rotation in the plane of the shell, in order to add shear stiffness. Hanging cable nets automatically take funicular shapes when the loads are applied and this may be used to establish a funicular shape for the grid dome by upturning the shape given by a hanging cable structure which has the same loads on it as the dome. Grid domes are mirror images of hanging net structures.

Cable Structures

Hanging cable roof structures have similar geometries to domes; usually they have either a radial arrangement of cable elements or an orthogonal grid (2.140). The cables act in tension and have a suspended concave shape (2.71); they are covered by sheets or panels which, when connected together can function as a shell structure so that the cables would then behave as reinforcement to the shell. Tension from the cables may be absorbed by leading them to ground or, more usually, by connecting them into a ring beam, around the edge of the cable roof structure, which is shaped to be funicular with the full uniformly distributed load on the roof (2.141). Bending moment in the ring is therefore controlled. For a hanging roof of spherical shape, whether the cables be arranged radially or on a uniform orthogonal grid, there can be equal tension in all cables under any uniformly distributed vertical load (2.142). The ring beam is funicular if it is given a circular shape. For a roof of an elliptic paraboloid shape, the ring beam is funicular for any of the ellipse shapes produced by taking a horizontal section through the elliptic paraboloid surface, assuming the vertical load is uniformly distributed. Cables running in the same direction, in the orthogonal grid of the elliptic paraboloid, are all shaped by the same parabola and have the same horizontal force in them, in spite of their different lengths. This is so because, if there is a uniformly distributed vertical load on each cable, the horizontal component of the force in the cable is proportional to the ratio of the square of the cable span to its sag which is a constant for any length of the same parabola. If the cable forces in the two directions are adjusted so that the horizontal components of the cable forces are equal within each set then the elliptical edge beam can be made to be funicular and, under full uniformly distributed load, each cable in the orthogonal grid will carry exactly half of the strip of tributary load on it (2.143); this is true whether the cables are hanging freely under their own weight or whether they are stressed against each other in the later stages of construction; in the final condition the behaviour of the edge beam may be affected by any shell action of the roof. Note that the orthogonal grid net on a spherical surface is a special case of the elliptic paraboloid. In the case

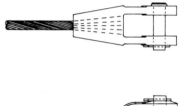
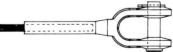

2.141 *Socket terminal, top, and swaged terminal, bottom, for attaching cables to rigid boundary.*

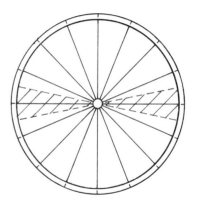

2.142 *Cable roof in a radial arrangement showing tributary load for a typical cable.*

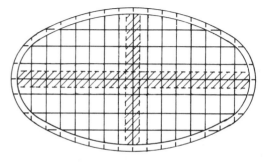

2.143 *Plan on elliptical paraboloid roof showing tributary load for the two middle cables.*

of a spherical surface with a radial arrangement of cables the tributory load is segment-shaped and, for a cable with this loading, the circular shape is funicular so that there are no significant hoop stresses in such a spherically shaped dish, assuming the sag is not excessive (2.71).

Hyperbolic Paraboloid Structures

As well as domes and hanging structures with surfaces in the form of a sphere or elliptic paraboloid, another classic shape for a three-dimensional roof surface is that of the hyperbolic paraboloid. The *hyperbolic paraboloid* is formed by running a downward curving parabola along an upward curving parabola thus producing a 'saddle' surface (2.125). The 'saddle' has negative gaussian curvature, that is, of the two principal curvatures on any element of the surface, one is curving upwards and the other has opposite sign and curves downwards. Hyperbolic paraboloids can also be formed by running a set of lines, which are parallel on plan, across two edge lines which are also parallel on plan but not coplanar (2.144). The hyperbolic paraboloid surface, so formed, contains another set of lines parallel on plan to the two edge lines. The two sets of lines are known as straight line generators. The property of being able to be formed by straight line generators is an important reason for the use of the hyperbolic paraboloid shape in construction. If the downward-curving generator parabola runs along an upward-curving directrix parabola of the same shape, then the hyperbolic paraboloid (HP) so formed is said to be 'rectangular' and the two sets of straight line generators are at right angles to each other in plan. HP shells, like other shells, are normally built with edge beams. In an HP shell cut out from the middle of the saddle zone with edges parallel to the straight line generators, uniformly distributed load is mainly carried by a series of 'arches' and 'cables', which are parallel to the two principal directions of curvature. In a rectangular hyperbolic paraboloid having a square plan with edges along the straight line generators, the horizontal forces of the 'cables' on the edge beams exactly balance those of the 'arches' on the edge beams and the remaining unbalanced forces have a resultant which acts straight down the line of the edge beams which therefore act principally as columns. Note that the edge beam, although

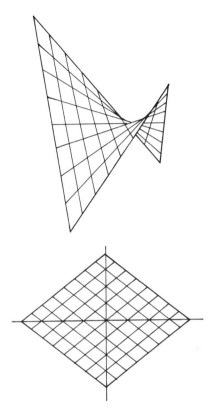

2.144 *Side view and plan on hyperbolic paraboloid with edges parallel to the straight line generators; the two principal directions of curvature run parallel in plan to the lines joining the two high points together and the two low points together.*

straight, must twist down its length in order to remain in the same plane as the HP shell. The shell requires only two points of support and light stabilising cables or rods to prevent rotation about the line of the supports. HP shells with both square and rectangular plans forms have been built in wood, in reinforced and prestressed concrete, plastic, ferrocement and steel sheet. At a much larger scale the hyperbolic paraboloid shape has been used in cable roofs. These are *prestressed cable nets,* the HP shape allowing prestressing of cables in one direction against those in another as a means of stabilising the cable network. As with

hanging cable roofs, the cables are usually laid out on an approximately equal orthogonal grid. In such a roof with uniformly distributed load on it, the horizontal component of the force in each set of cables running in the same direction can be made equal because, as for the elliptic paraboloid, the ratio of the square of each cable span to its sag determines the horizontal component of the force in the cable, and this ratio is constant for the same parabola no matter what length is considered. If a rectangular HP surface is used then the forces in the two sets of cables can be made equal so that the ring beam to which the cables are attached needs to be circular in plan to be funicular. If the horizontal components of the forces in the two sets are unequal the ring beam must be an ellipse in plan. The fact that the ring beam is not planar causes only minor additional forces in it. Other shapes are possible with prestressed cable roof structures including types with intermediate point supports, such as bell-shaped network structures (2.145). In all cases the main requirement is that every small element of the surface, wherever it is, has an anticlastic shape; for large span structures in which the radius of curvature in the two directions is large, the prestressing forces in the

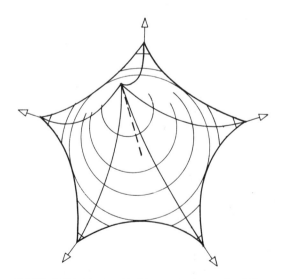

2.145 *Bell tent supported by mast edge and radial cables with hoop lines drawn on to show curvature.*

work in tension and are prestressed against a boundary; other examples are provided by air-supported structures in which the film or fabric is slightly prestressed in tension by air pressure. An unusual example of membrane action is provided by soap films, which can be a matter of only a few molecules thick and have a uniform tension in all directions on their surface as a result of the action of surface tension. A soap film may be described as a material with strength but no stiffness so that it can behave in a different manner from a normal elastic film or sheet material. Its ability to change shape in response to the action of surface tension, without creasing, allows it to form minimum surfaces between a rigid, closed boundary. In membranes made of films or coated fabrics, however, in general, the tension is not uniform in all directions. Films or fabrics will buckle, that is they crease, before compressive stresses can arise. In elastic films creasing occurs when the tensions in the two principal directions of stress are far enough apart for significant shear stresses to develop, to which they have little resistance. Fabrics, being made of fibres that are woven in two directions, are not continuous materials and the concept of principal directions of stress does not strictly apply. Nevertheless the fibres can be arranged to line up, as far as possible, with the principal directions of curvature which, in a material without significant shear resistance, should line up with principal stress directions (2.146). In coated fabrics there is a practical limit to the ratio of stresses of the fibres in the warp and weft (fill) directions of about five. Membrane action is always present and the only way of

supporting loads for materials such as films and fabrics which have no bending stiffness. However surfaces which are rigid against in-plane shear and have only limited bending stiffness, such as timber and wood shells, can also be designed to work substantially by membrane action. For membranes with loads that are normal to the surface, the direct forces at any point in the membrane can be related to the pressure or uniform load at that point by the *membrane equation*, which is as follows (2.129):

$$p_r = \frac{N_x}{r_x} + \frac{N_y}{r_y} \text{ N/mm}^2 \text{ (lb/in}^2\text{)}$$

where p_r is the normal pressure or uniform load at at the point considered in N/mm² (lb/in²);

N_x, N_y are the direct forces over a small area at the point considered in the two principal directions of curvature in N/mm (lb/in); and

r_x, r_y are the principal radii of curvature at the point in mm (in).

For spheres or cylinders, which are regular surfaces, the principal radii of curvature are equal at all points on the surface and the membrane equation becomes:

$$p_r = \frac{2N}{r} \text{ N/mm}^2 \text{ (lb/in}^2\text{) for the sphere}$$

where r is the radius of the sphere in mm (in); and

$$p_r = \frac{N}{r} \text{ N/mm}^2 \text{ (lb/in}^2\text{) for the cylinder}$$

where r is the radius of the circular cross-section through the cylinder in mm (in).

The membrane equation shows that, under loads normal to the surface, the direct forces in the membrane are proportional to the membrane curvatures.

Models of Membrane Action

A way of thinking of a smooth, continuous membrane surface is as a triangulated framework of small, straight bars with the connection points between bars lying on the membrane surface. If the membrane only works in tension, the bars can be thought of as lengths of cable. All joints between the bars are ball joints allowing rotation in any direction, so that the bars can only take direct tension or compression. As the triangles may be arranged in any way, two sides of each triangle may be chosen to be in the principal directions of stress, for example, with the third side supplying stiffness in shear (2.131). As noted previously any such framework would be

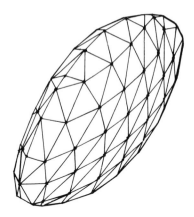

2.130 *Closed surface represented by bars in triangular arrangement.*

determinate if:
$$n = m + r - 3j = 0$$
In this model the support reactions must act in directions which are tangential to the surface at the edge of the shell, if distortion of the shell is to be prevented. A closed shell surface, if triangulated in this way, takes a polyhedral shape (2.130); for such a framework with triangular faces, it can be shown that:
$$m + 6 = 3j$$
The triangulated model is therefore a determinate structure if there are six support reactions, which is the minimum number needed to fix an object in space (2.3); one possibility is for there to be three support points each supplying restraint against movement in two directions which are tangential to the surfaces. In a real closed shell, point or line supports, even if they act within directions tangential to the shell surface, will cause some local bending of the shell to develop, because of incompatibilities of deformation ignored by the membrane theory. The membrane action of a dome may also be modelled by a triangulated framework; the framework would have an open top and reactions at the base which were tangential to the surface (2.131); actual reticulated domes with this arrangement of bars are known as Schwedler domes. The framework model for the dome, like that for the closed shell, is determinate. A real continuous shell, which has

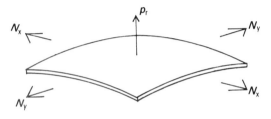

2.129 *Small curved area of membrane showing direct stresses in the two principal directions of curvature.*

cables will need to be correspondingly large in order to stabilise the roof against wind forces, as indicated by the membrane equation; the prestress required in the cables is determined by wind and other unbalanced loads rather than the maximum uniformly distributed load that is determinant for hanging cable roofs. The prestressed cables can be clad with panel or sheet materials like those in hanging roofs.

Fabric Structures

Prestressed tent structures are designed on similar structural principles to prestressed cable nets. However they are usually much smaller in scale and generally use fabric both as a structure and as a covering material. Like prestressed nets, they have almost no stiffness either in compression, shear or bending and must therefore work as membranes in tension; they are shaped so that each element of the surface has an anticlastic shape, at all points on the surface; very often the shapes are based on HP surfaces or on bell-shaped surfaces (*2.145*). Because fabric is relatively weak, it is important that the radius of curvature in the two principal directions is as small as practical so that the prestress in the fabric required to prevent flutter is as low as possible and well inside the tear strength of the fabric. The prestressed tent must be supported at its edges and by intermediate supports if necessary. A useful starting point in design is to find the soap-film surface formed between a wire frame which is geometrically similar to the actual boundary supports for the tent. The soap film so formed is anticlastic, and is a minimum surface, that is, it has the smallest surface area possible for any surface shape with those boundaries. The soap film also has the desirable property of having equal surface tension, whatever direction on the surface is considered. Therefore the principal directions of curvature at any point on the surface are opposite and equal. For practical use, however, the soap film surface may have insufficiently small radii of curvature. Models of the prestressd tent may also be made in highly stretchable fabrics which approach the performance of a soap film in being able to adapt themselves over a large range of extension so that wrinkles do not form on the surface. Prestressed tents are often supported at their boundaries by flexible edge cables: assuming the edge cables

and the adjacent areas of fabric to exist in one plane, then the shape of the cable is circular if the stresses in the fabric are equal in all directions at all points along the cable, as in the case of a soap film; in practice the stresses in the two principal directions of curvature may be significantly different so that the circular shape of the edge cable would be modified. Cables are also used in fabric structures to reduce the span of the fabric and ideally would be placed along the principal directions of stress for the shape concerned (*2.146*). Arches may be used in the same way to act as edge supports for the fabric (*2.147*). Prestressed tents, having taut, well-tensioned surfaces, have high natural frequencies which are outside the normal frequencies of wind gusts and buffeting. One practical difficulty with prestressed tent structures is to devise methods, at the construction stage, for introducing the desired level of prestress into all areas of the surface.

Air-supported structures use slightly pressurised air as the structural medium to support a light fabric covering material. As in the case of prestressed tents, the fabric works as a membrane in tension, most fabrics having negligible shear stiffness, as noted previously. The ideal shape for an air-supported structure is a spherical one, the

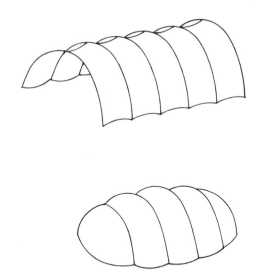

2.147 *Space covered by prestressed tent on arches, top, and by air-supported membrane supported by cables, bottom.*

radius of the sphere depending on the pressure difference required across the fabric and the strength of the fabric. Soap film surfaces can be used to model the behaviour of air-supported structures by applying a pressure difference across a soap film on a fixed rounded boundary; sharp corners on the boundary give rise to anticlastic areas which are difficult to fabricate (*2.148*) and are therefore avoided in practice (*2.149*). In a soap bubble, the tension is equal in all directions on the

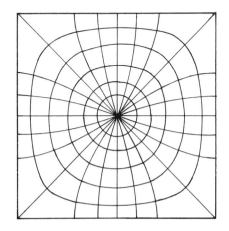

2.146 *Stress-flow pattern for an elastic film supported by a square frame and at a higher central point.*

2.148 *Shape formed by soap film on square frame with pressure difference across film.*

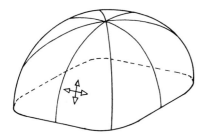

2.149 Air-supported membrane with synclastic shape showing principal directions of curvature; shape is close to that of a sphere and tensile stresses in the two directions shown are nearly equal.

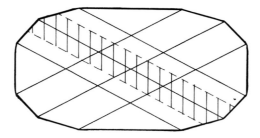

2.151 Plan on cable reinforced air-supported membrane showing tributary load for a central cable; the actual load on the cable must be less than this.

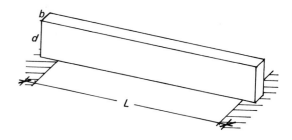

2.152 Simply supported beam with dimensions.

surface, which is ideal. However as the stresses in air-supported fabric structures are low, the stresses in one direction on the fabric may be up to about five times greater than those in the direction at right angles and still be satisfactory so that many other shapes then become possible. For example an air-supported membrane with a half-cylindrical shape and rounded ends has a tensile stress in the circumferential direction of the cylinder which is twice that in the longitudinal direction but is still satisfactory in practice (2.150). Air-supported structures may also be used in conjunction with reinforcing cables; the fabric spans between the cables and this enables it to have a small radius of curvature, thus reducing the stress in it. The air pressure acts at right angles to the surface of the fabric upwards but otherwise, the horizontal force in the cable is found in exactly the same way as for

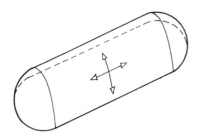

2.150 Air-supported membrane with half-cylindrical shape showing stresses in principal directions of curvature.

a cable under gravity load (2.151). As with other cable structures a horizontal ring beam may be provided which is shaped to be funicular for the load that is transferred to the ring beam when the fabric is inflated (2.151). Compared to prestressed tent structures the air-supported structure is tolerant of variations in material properties of the fabric and in the shape of the tent. Air-supported structures are susceptible to wind gusts and buffeting because of their natural frequency range. However the natural frequency can be altered, to avoid the wind excitation, by altering the inflation pressures. *Air-inflated structures* are different from air-supported structures in that they are closed surfaces and have very high inflation pressures, like car tyres. The basic idea of such pneumatic structures is that the air be used to prestress the enclosing fabric of the pneumatic structure in tension so that fabric does not go into compression over any significant area of the fabric when loads are applied to it. In this way beam or arch elements may be made out of fabric.

STRUCTURAL FORM AND SCALE

Scale Effects

The scale at which a structure is built, whether natural or man-made, has a fundamental influence on the form and material used for the structure. For example paper may be a suitable material for a model but is inadequate at the scale of a building because it has insufficient strength and stiffness; a straight rolled steel joist has a suitable, and

convenient, form for the spans commonly found in buildings but is an inadequate or grossly inefficient form at the scale of the spans found in bridges, which are designed as suspension structures. As an example of the effects of changes in scale, consider a beam, simply supported at its ends, which has a solid rectangular section and only supports its own weight (2.152). It has a bending stress, f, and a deflection, Δ, in the middle of the beam given by:

$$f = \frac{\rho.b.d.L^2}{8Z}$$

$$= \left(\frac{3\rho.L}{4d}\right)L \quad \text{N/mm}^2 \text{ (lb/in}^2) \text{ and}$$

$$\Delta = \left(\frac{5\rho.L^2}{32E.d}\right)L^2 \quad \text{mm (in)}$$

where Z is the section modulus of the beam in mm^3 (in^3);

ρ is the density of the material of which the beam is made in N/mm^3 (lb/in^3); and

b, d, L are the breadth, depth and length of the beam in mm (in).

If two such beams are built of the same material and with exactly the same proportions but with one beam having all dimensions say five times larger than the other, then the equations show that the bending stress is five times larger and the deflection is twenty-five times larger in the larger beam than the smaller beam. In this case the bending moment in the beam goes up in proportion to the fourth power of the linear dimensions while the section modulus only rises by a third power. Acceptable deflections for floor and roof beams normally depend on the deflection ratio, that is deflection to span length; this ratio, too, increases with the span length. The example illustrates that it is not possible simply to scale up a model either from the point of view of an adequate strength or an acceptable deflection and illustrates what may be called a *scale law*. For example the use of steel or precast concrete beams and columns with standard forms and sizes implies that the elements are built within a certain range of scales that are typical in building; at a larger scale these elements are not suitable. Because any material has a certain limiting ultimate strength, σ, there is always a limit to the span for the material, whatever form the structure takes. For example in the case of the self-supporting beam considered above and, in general, any cases where the live load is low, such as in roof beams, the maximum span depends on the strength to weight ratio for the material, σ/ρ. This is an important material property. To overcome the effects of the operation of the scale law, the proportions of the structure may need to be altered. In the example considered the depth of the beam would need to increase not in proportion to the span but to the square of the span in order that the bending stress does not increase. This change of proportion as scale increases is general and applies to the animal world as well. For example, birds increase their wing size by disproportionately large amounts, and their wing-beat frequency decreases, as their overall size increases. Again it is fundamentally a matter of scale that allows insects to walk on vertical surfaces.

In building structures the scale law can be overcome by changing the proportions, by changing the form of the structure or by changing the material from which it is built. For example the section of a beam could be altered from a solid one to a more efficient shape for bending such as an I-shaped or tubular section; alternatively a sandwich construction using lighter materials could be used. Overall changes in form are another way of allowing increases in scale. For example road bridges change from simply-supported concrete slabs to concrete beams, to steel beams and trusses, continuous steel plate girders and trusses, prestressed concrete box beams and then to steel or concrete arches and finally to steel suspension bridges using cables, as the scale, that is the span of the bridge, increases (*2.153*). In bridges of any

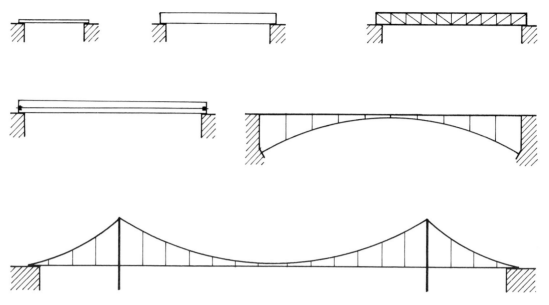

2.153 *Schematic diagrams of bridges showing changes in proportions or in structural system as a response to increases in span.*

size, self-weight is much larger than the other applied loads so that, as bridge spans increase, it is logical to transfer material from the middle of the span to the supports where the weight of the material can be directly taken by the bridge piers, thus helping to minimise bending moment (*2.154*). Thus form changes with scale. In

buildings there is a similar transformation from frame systems to shear wall systems to tubular systems as the height of the building increases and, to a lesser extent, as the height to width ratio increases. The behaviour of flexible structures also illustrates the effects of scale; flexible elements are those which have no stiffness against bending.

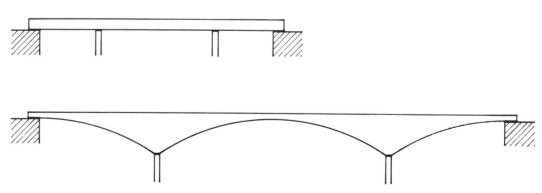

2.154 *Concrete bridges have a form with a uniform or varying depth depending on span.*

Cables spanning short distances, for example, may be in relatively flat curves, while those spanning long distances, such as suspension bridge cables, need to have a different curve shape with a larger sag in order to limit tension in the cables. A mercury drop on a glass plate can also be regarded as a flexible structure in which the surface tension provides the resistance to hold the drop in shape.

2.155 Drops of mercury on glass plate with form depending on size of drop.

The drop tends to a spherical shape when small but takes a much flatter shape as the drop increases in size (*2.155*). In this case, the surface tensions acting on the outside of the drop are constant and a new form is the only way to adjust to the new balance of forces. Note that in practical structures it is the loss of stiffness rather than the loss of strength which is of concern as the scale increases. However in some forms of construction, the requirement is not so much for stiffness or strength, as for stability. For example, some columns, which take only moderate lateral forces, are governed by the need for stability which is largely a matter of the proportions between the height and the thickness so that, in this case, a simple scaling up of proportions is likely to be satisfactory. Indeed in masonry construction, where stability is a principal consideration, proportional rules have a long history.

Theory of Models

Although it is not possible simply to scale up the proportions and loads on models to larger structures without regard for the materials or loading, it is possible to form true models which behave in identical ways to a larger structure if certain conditions of similarity are obeyed. The

formula given for the deflection of a rectangular section beam under its own weight, shows that a true model of the deflection characteristics of a full-size structure in bending will be obtained if the dimensionless quantities,

$$\frac{\Delta}{.L}, \quad \frac{\rho.L}{E}, \quad \frac{L^2}{d^2}$$

are equal in the model and the full-size structure. The first of the three terms is equal to the deflection ratio and the last term shows that the model must have the same proportions as the full-size structure. *Dimensional analysis* produces the same result, without the need to find the exact formula for deflection, by considering a complete list of the independent variables which affect deflection. A set of dimensionless ratios is formed from these variables which are then made equal in the model and the full-size structure. A so-called π rule gives the number of dimensionless ratios there should be.

Dimensional analysis to investigate the bending deflection, when a point load, F, is applied at any point to a simply-supported beam and to a frame indicates that, respectively, the following dimensionless ratios are relevant for the model:

$$\frac{\Delta}{L}, \quad \frac{F.L^2}{I} \quad \text{for the beam and}$$

$$\frac{\Delta}{L}, \quad \frac{h}{L}, \quad \frac{I_b}{I_c}, \quad \frac{F.L^2}{E.I_c} \quad \text{for the frame}$$

where F is the applied load in N (lb);
   I is the moment of inertia of the simply-supported beam in mm⁴ (in⁴);
   h, L are the height and length of the portal frame in mm (in); and
   I_b, I_c are the moments of inertia of the frame beam and column respectively in mm⁴ (in⁴).

In the above two cases the deflection is proportional to the load. For a light cable which is initially straight but not prestressed, the deflection, Δ, under a point load, F, is not proportional to load. The following dimensionless ratios are relevant for this model:

$$\frac{\Delta}{L}, \quad \frac{A}{L^2}, \quad \frac{F}{E.L^2}$$

where A is the area of the cable in mm² (in²);
   L is the span of the cable in mm (in); and
   E is the modulus of elasticity of the material, which is assumed to be linear-elastic, in N/mm² (lb/in²).

LOAD PATHS

Load Paths to Ground

A *principle of stiffness* operating in structural design is that the loads acting on a structure will always travel to ground down the paths that are stiffest. For example, a point load applied above a central column at the top of a multistorey frame building will be carried to ground almost entirely by that column, rather than the adjacent columns(*2.156*). This is because the central column is very stiff, that is, it has a very small deflection under the load, compared to all the alternative paths for this load, which transfer load to the other columns by causing bending of the beams. If the main loadbearing column were to be removed, the deflection under the point load would be some 500 times that of the column, if it alone supported the load (*2.156*); this indicates that the column takes 500 times more load than all the remaining load paths together. Another example is afforded by a straight beam bent into a portal shape with a point load applied at the apex. If the feet of this frame are pinned then there is no bending in the frame, only axial compression, as in a pure arch (*2.157*). However if one of the feet were to have a sliding support, it would be impossible to develop a horizontal reaction at the base and the frame would then work like a bent but simply supported beam and there would be significant deflections under the load. With pinned feet this bending action is suppressed. If a central column, of the same section size as the rest of the

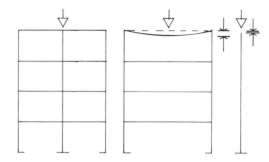

2.156 Frame with point load on central column, left, and relative deflections of component parts under a point load, right.

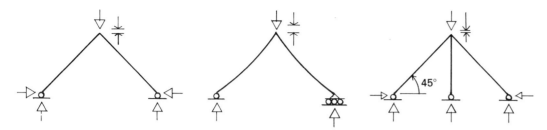

2.157 *Different types of A-frame structure having variable stiffness under a vertical load.*

frame, is added to a frame with a 45° angle slope, 75% of the load now passes down the column, reflecting the relative stiffnesses of the column and frame when they act separately. Another important example of the principle of stiffness is provided by a steel truss girder in which the individual members are rigidly connected to one another, as is normally the case (*2.158*). In spite of the method of jointing, the truss still behaves substantially like a truss with pinned joints because truss action of the girder, in which members are in tension or compression, is stiffer than the vierendeel action, in which members go into bending (*2.63*). Secondary bending in the individual members, therefore, is small. There are other examples: a thin plate initially works in bending but as the deflection increases more and more turns to membrane action (*2.96*); the continuous shell surface of a dome attempts to work as a membrane structure, the way in which it is stiffest, before bending will develop. Note that a choice of action or load path implies that the structure is indeterminate; determinate structures may only carry load in one way.

Foundations

Foundations are selected and sized by the need to ensure that the ground underneath is sufficiently strong so as not to fail in shear (*2.159*) and that the movement of the foundation over the long or short term, whether it be heave or settlement, is satisfactory. In particular the differential movement, the relative movement between one part of the building and another, must be such that it will not cause damage either to the structure or to doors, windows, partition walls or affect the usefulness of the building in any way. Usually the foundation design is governed by the need to limit differential settlement, rather than the need to prevent the ground failing in shear. Note that the type of settlement and the shearing resistance of the soil depends not only on the type of soil but also on whether ground water is present in it.

On good ground, the normal way to support a point load, as from a column, is to use a *pad foundation*, also known as a spread or column footing; *combined footings* are those that incorporate two or more point loads on the same foundation (*2.160*). To even out the bearing pressure as far as possible the combined footing is

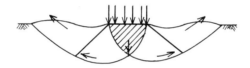

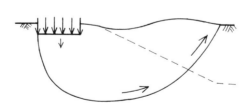

2.159 *Two models used for calculation of the pressure that would cause failure in shallow foundations: disturbed soil above a sliding surface is displaced outwards, except for the soil wedge below the foundation, shown shaded, which moves downwards, top; disturbed soil rotating along a sliding surface, bottom, this method being applicable to clay soils, particularly with sloping ground (shown by dashed line).*

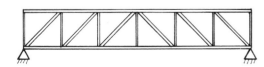

2.158 *Truss beam with welded connections between members.*

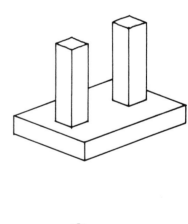

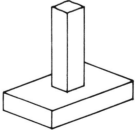

2.160 *Individual pad and combined footing.*

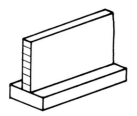

2.161 Strip footing.

designed so that the resultant of all the point loads coincides with the centroid, or 'centre of gravity', of the pad foundation. Walls or a series of point loads may be supported on a *strip footing*, also known as a line footing (*2.161*). Where the building must be founded on poor ground, a *raft foundation*, also known as a mat foundation, may be used to support the entire building. The object in the design of the raft foundation is to spread all the loads of the building from the raft and into the ground so that the bearing pressure on the ground is as even as possible, thus making maximum use of the available area. Another aim is to reduce differential settlement. The raft is particularly suitable where good ground is at a considerable distance below the surface. Rafts are often combined with the bottom slab of a basement structure. The design of a raft is similar to that of a continuous floor slab, except that now the load is applied by the ground from below and that unlike gravity loads on floors, the distribution of pressure from the ground is not generally known with any degree of accuracy. As with floor structures, flat slabs or one-way and two-way spanning slabs on beams may be used. If good ground is available at a reasonable depth or raft foundations are inadequate or unsuitable, *pile foundations* may be used. Except for piles of large diameter, piles are usually used in conjunction with pile caps. To ensure stability, isolated pile caps usually have at least three piles (*2.162*). The piles should be symmetrically placed under the loads and, in general, the spacing between piles should be three times the pile diameter. Piles can be split into end-bearing piles and friction piles (*2.160*). *End-bearing piles* transmit the load on them to the ground at the bottom of the pile while *friction piles* transfer the load in them to the ground, gradually,

down the length of the pile by friction between the pile and the ground. In practice piles may work in both ways. *Caissons* are very large diameter cylinders that are cut or drilled into the ground (*2.163*). Caissons for building are usually filled with concrete, subsequent to the installation of the hollow caisson. Their function is similar to that of an end-bearing pile. Note that the resultant axial load supported by pad foundations, combined footings, individual piles or pile groups, may not pass through the centroid of the foundation or pile group because of bending moment in the columns or because, in the case of combined footings or pile groups, the load is not symmetrically placed with respect to the centroid; in these cases, the load on the ground is not uniform or, in the case of pile groups, some piles carry more load than others. All foundations must be designed to carry horizontal forces from wind or earthquake forces as well as vertical loads due to gravity.

Basement floors may be required in buildings both to provide extra space and to compensate for the extra weight of the building on the ground by the removal of soil; one storey of excavated soil weighs at least as much as five storeys of a concrete frame building. Retaining walls are required around the perimeter of the basement and, in the final condition, may be supported over their height by the basement floors. Temporary

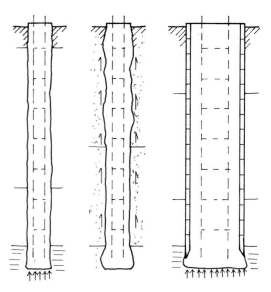

2.163 Piles work mainly in end-bearing, left, or in friction, centre; caisson piles work mainly by end-bearing, right.

steel sheeting may be necessary in order to retain the earth while construction of the basement takes place. One way of avoiding this is to use a *slurry-trench*, also known as a diaphragm wall. This consists of excavating a trench about 600mm (2ft) wide under a bentonite slurry which prevents the sides of the trench collapsing. When a section of the wall has been excavated to its full depth, reinforcement is placed in the trench and then concrete is added at the bottom of the trench, down a tremie pipe gradually displacing bentonite at the top of the trench which is reused. The concrete is then left to harden. Slurry trench walls may be used in conjunction with 'top-down' construction in which the first basement floor is cast before excavation for the basement floors below. The basement floors are able to stabilise the slurry trench wall during construction. Excavated soil is taken through holes in the basement floor slabs. For basement subject to uplift from the hydrostatic pressure of ground water, tension piles or high strength ties may be necessary to prevent uplift of the basement.

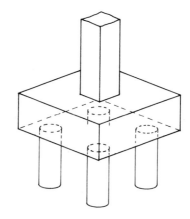

2.162 Column and pile cap supported by piles.

Table 2.1   Bending Moments and Deflections in Single Span Beams or Slabs

Description	Position	Beam with Applied Load and Bending Moment Diagram	Bending Moments in Span or at Support	Deflection in Span or at End of Span	End Slope
Simply Supported beams - ud load	span and support		$M_C = \dfrac{W.L}{8}$	$\Delta_C = \dfrac{5W.L^3}{384E.I}$	$\theta_A = \dfrac{W.L^2}{24E.I}$
- central point load	span and support		$M_C = \dfrac{W.L}{4}$	$\Delta_C = \dfrac{W.L^3}{48E.I}$	$\theta_A = \dfrac{W.L^2}{16E.I}$
- bending applied at each end	span and support		$M_A = M_B = M$	$\Delta_C = \dfrac{M.L^2}{8E.I}$	$\theta_A = \dfrac{M.L}{2E.I}$
Cantilevers - ud load	support and free end		$M_A = \dfrac{W.L}{2}$	$\Delta_B = \dfrac{W.L^3}{8E.I}$	$\theta_B = \dfrac{W.L^2}{6E.I}$
- point load	support and free end		$M_A = W.L$	$\Delta_B = \dfrac{W.L^3}{3E.I}$	$\theta_B = \dfrac{W.L^2}{2E.I}$
Fixed End Beams - ud load	span and support		$M_A = M_B = \dfrac{W.L}{12}$ $M_C = \dfrac{W.L}{24}$	$\Delta_C = \dfrac{W.L^3}{384E.I}$	$\theta_A = 0$
- central point load	span and support		$M_A = M_C = \dfrac{W.L}{8}$	$\Delta_C = \dfrac{W.L^3}{192E.I}$	$\theta_A = 0$
- point load	span and support		$M_A = \dfrac{W.b^2.a}{L^2}$ $M_B = \dfrac{W.a^2.b}{L^2}$	$\Delta_{max} = \dfrac{2W.a^2.b^3}{3E.I(3L-2a)^2}$	$\theta_A = 0$
Beams with Fixed or Pinned Ends - forced displacement	supports		$M_A = M_B = \dfrac{6E.I.\Delta}{L^2}$	$\Delta_A = \Delta$	$\theta_A = 0$
- bending applied at one end	span and supports		$M_A = 0.5M$ $M_B = M$	$\Delta_{max} = \dfrac{M.L^2}{27E.I}$	$\theta_B = \dfrac{M.L}{4E.I}$
- bending applied at one end	span and supports		$M_A = 0$ $M_B = M$	$\Delta_{max} = \dfrac{M.L^2}{15.62E.I}$	$\theta_A = \dfrac{M.L}{6E.I};$ $\theta_B = \dfrac{M.L}{3E.I}$

Table 2.2 Bending Moments in Continuous Beams or One-Way Slabs - Equal Spans

Description	Position	Beam with Loads and Bending Moment Diagram	Bending Moments

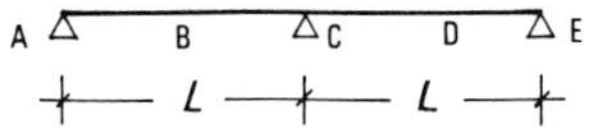

Two spans
- Dead Load — End and interior spans

$$M_B = M_D = \frac{W_d.L}{12}$$

$$M_C = \frac{W_d.L}{9}$$

- Live load — End spans

Interior support

$$M_B = \frac{W_l.L}{10}$$

$$M_C = \frac{W_l.L}{9} \text{ (diagram as for DL)}$$

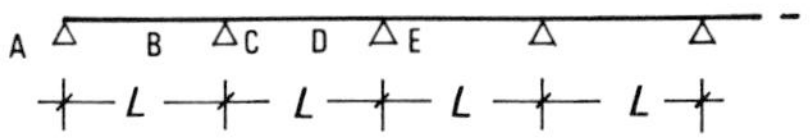

Three or more spans
- Dead load — End and interior spans

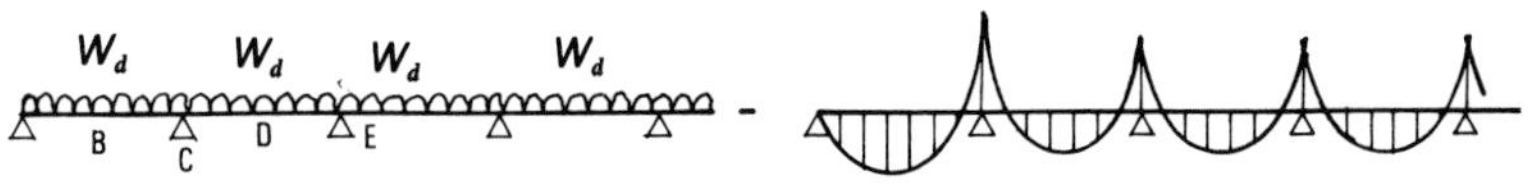

$$M_B = \frac{W_d.L}{12}; \quad M_C = \frac{W_d.L}{10}$$

$$M_D = \frac{W_d.L}{24}; \quad M_E = \frac{W_d.L}{12}$$

- Live load — End spans

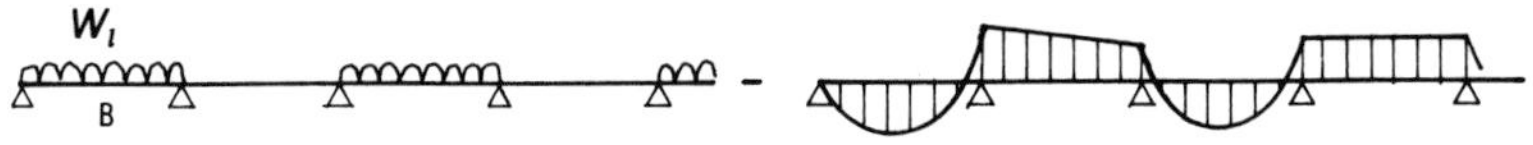

$$M_B = \frac{W_l.L}{10}$$

End Supports

$$M_C = \frac{W_l.L}{9}$$

Interior spans

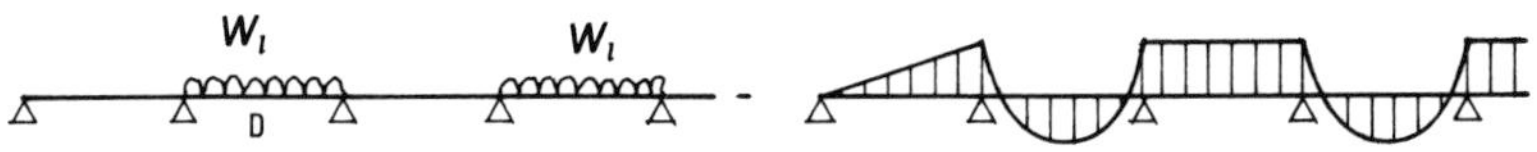

$$M_D = \frac{W_l.L}{12}$$

Interior supports

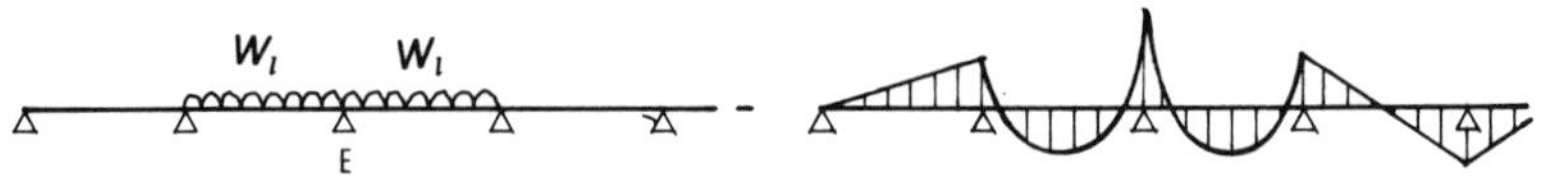

$$M_E = \frac{W_l.L}{9}$$

Continuous beams
- Dead load(DL)
and live load(LL)

for total bending moment
add dead and live load moments
i.e. *M = M(DL) + M(LL)*

Formulae usually sufficiently good for
spans that do not differ by more than
15% of smaller span

Table 2.3   **Bending Moments in Continuous Beams or One-Way Slabs - Unequal Spans**

Description	Position	Beam and bending moment diagram	Bending moments
Two spans - Dead load	End and interior spans		$M_B = \dfrac{W_{d1}.L_1}{8} - \dfrac{M_C}{3}$ $M_C = \dfrac{W_{d1}.L_1^2 + W_{d2}.L_2^2}{8(L_1 + L_2)}$
- Live load	End spans		$M_B = \dfrac{W_{l1}.L_1}{8}\left(1 - \dfrac{L_1}{3(L_1 + L_2)}\right)$
	Interior support		$M_C = \dfrac{W_{l1}.L_1^2 + W_{l2}.L_2^2}{8(L_1 + L_2)}$
Three or more spans - Dead load	End and interior spans	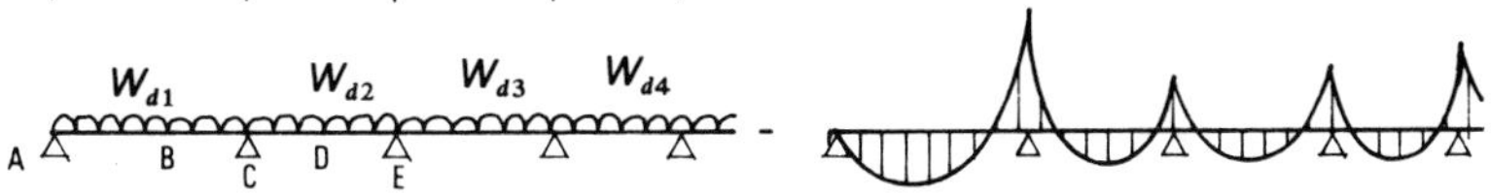	$M_B = \dfrac{W_{d1}.L_1}{8} - \dfrac{M_C}{3}$ $M_C = \left(\dfrac{W_{d1}.L_1^2}{8} + \dfrac{W_{d2}.L_2^2}{12}\right)\dfrac{1}{L_1 + L_2}$ $M_D = \dfrac{W_{d2}.L_2}{8} - \dfrac{M_C + M_E}{3}$ $M_E = \left(\dfrac{W_{d2}.L_2^2}{12} + \dfrac{W_{d3}.L_3^2}{12}\right)\dfrac{1}{L_2 + L_3}$
- Live load	End spans	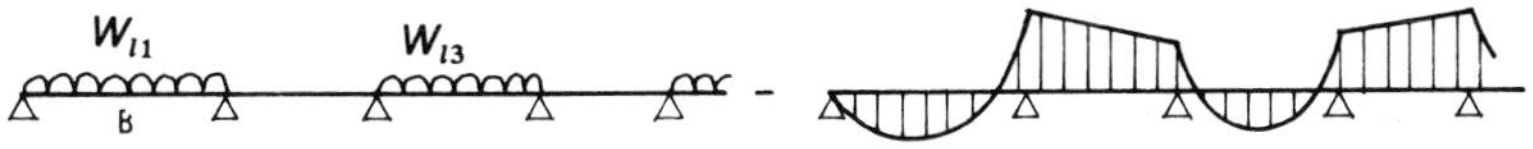	$M_B = \dfrac{W_{l1}.L_1}{8}\left(1 - \dfrac{L_1}{L_1 + 0.86L_2}\right)$
	End supports		$M_C = \left(\dfrac{W_{l1}.L_1^2}{8} + \dfrac{W_{l2}.L_2^2}{9}\right)\dfrac{1}{L_1 + L_2}$
	Interior spans	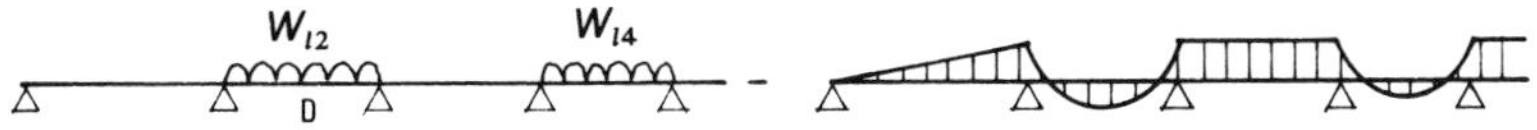	$M_D = $ $\dfrac{W_{l2}.L_2}{8}\left(1 - \dfrac{L_2}{3}\left[\dfrac{1}{L_1 + L_2} + \dfrac{1}{L_2 + L_3}\right]\right)$
	Interior supports	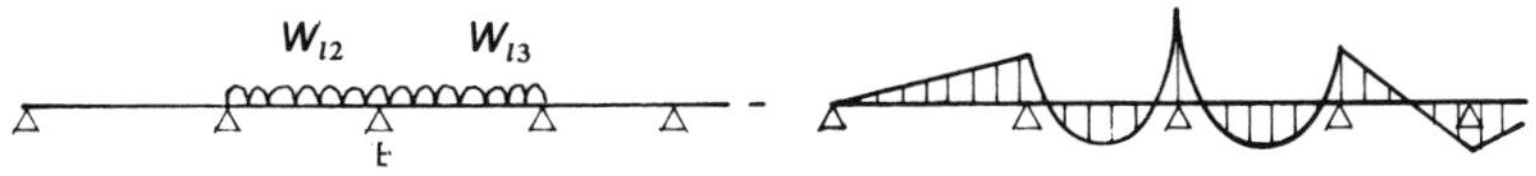	$M_E = \left(\dfrac{W_{l2}.L_2^2}{9} + \dfrac{W_{l3}.L_3^2}{9}\right)\dfrac{1}{L_2 + L_3}$
Continuous beams - Dead load(DL) and live load(LL)		for total bending moment add dead and live load moments i.e. *M = M(DL) + M(LL)*	Exact moments given at two-span support; other moments approximate

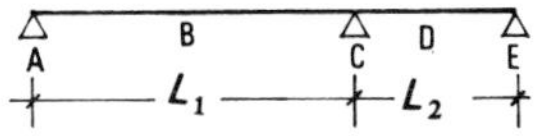

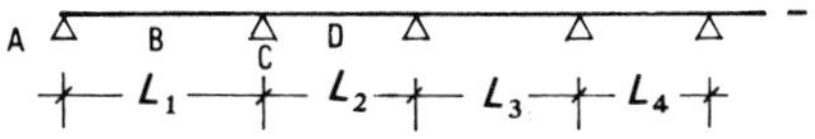

Table 2.4 **Load for Calculating Bending Moments in Concrete Beam and Slab Systems**

Vertical Load(W) or Equivalent Vertical Load(W_{eq}) for calculation of beams and slab strips as one-way spanning elements

Description and Section of System	Plan of System	Description and Section of System	Plan of System
One-way beams and slab 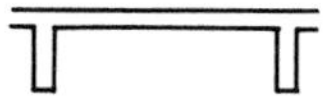	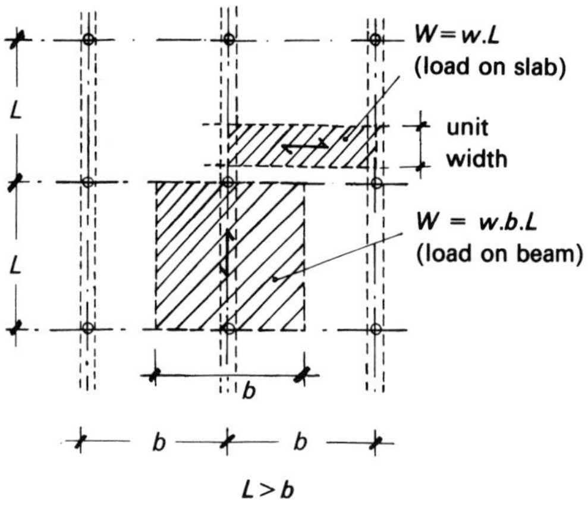 W = w.L (load on slab) unit width W = w.b.L (load on beam) L L b b b L > b	Flat slab or Waffle slab 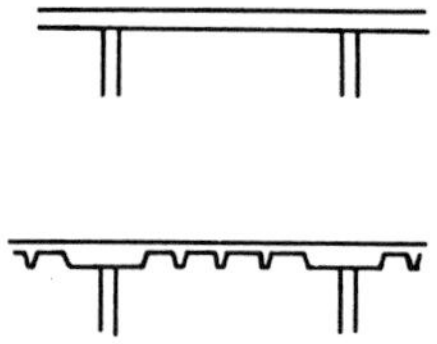	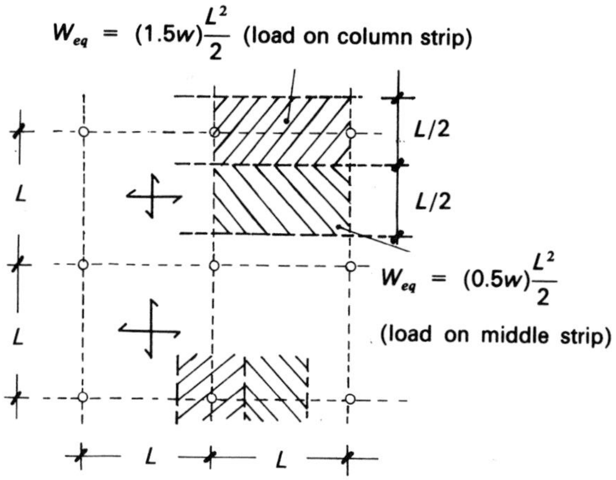 W_eq = (1.5w) L²/2 (load on column strip) L/2 L/2 W_eq = (0.5w) L²/2 (load on middle strip) L L L L
Beams and ribbed slab or Main beams, secondary beams and slab 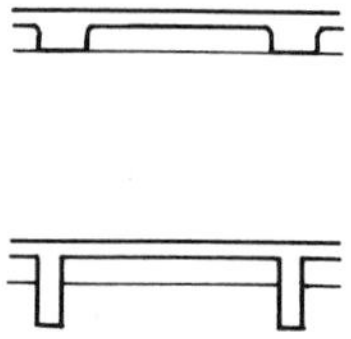	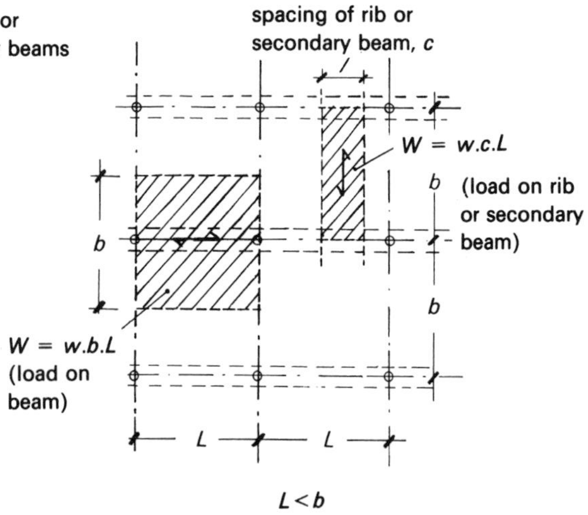 spacing of rib or secondary beam, c W = w.c.L (load on rib or secondary beam) b b b W = w.b.L (load on beam) L L L < b	Two-way beams and slab 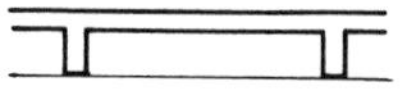	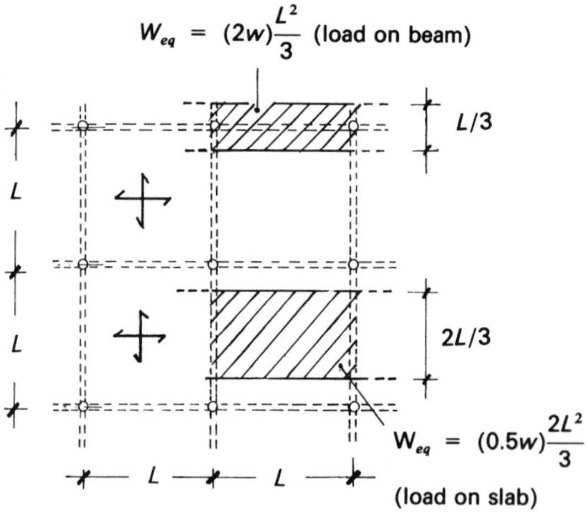 W_eq = (2w) L²/3 (load on beam) L/3 2L/3 W_eq = (0.5w) 2L²/3 (load on slab) L L L L

Tables 2.1 to 2.3 give bending moments for one-way spanning elements

Table 2.5   Sizes of Elements carrying gravity load - Masonry

Plan on Element	Vertical Section	Sizing Formulae	Remarks
Single wall		 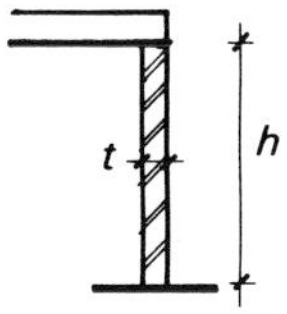 $\dfrac{h}{t} < 20$	Formula valid when lateral movement is prevented at top and bottom of wall, at right angles to wall; such restraint usually provided by floor and roof construction Wall has greater bending strength in the horizontal direction so that vertical supports would be preferred to horizontal supports Walls fail by crushing if $h/t < 10$ or by buckling and crushing if $h/t > 10$
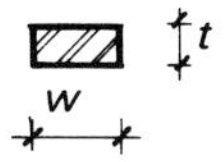 Column $t < w < 4t$	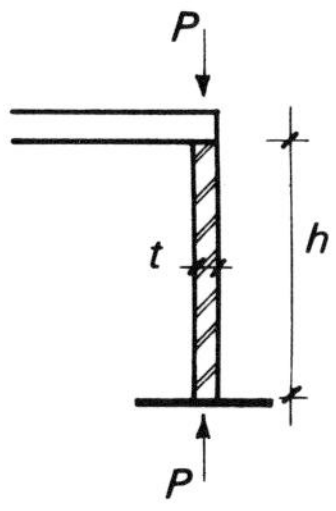	$\dfrac{h}{t}$ and $\dfrac{2h}{w} < 20$ $P < \dfrac{t.w.u}{5}$ where u is ultimate compressive strength of small masonry sample	Column illustrated given lateral restraint at top in one direction only and effective height of column in that direction taken as actual height; effective height in direction at right angles taken as twice actual height Columns fail by crushing if slenderness ratio, $h_{ef}/t < 10$ where h_{ef} is effective height and t is thickness of column P is working value of load applied near centre of column
Cavity wall		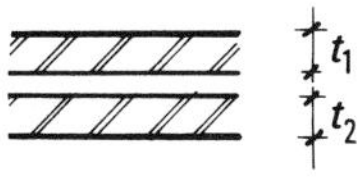 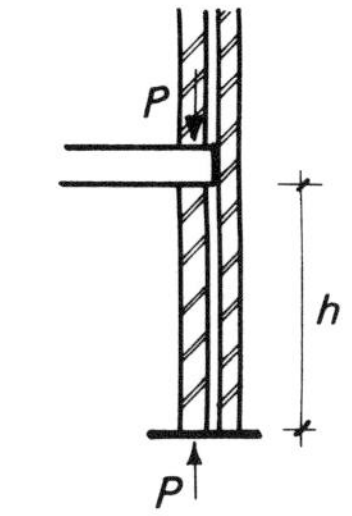 $\dfrac{h}{t_{ef}} < 20$ where t_{ef} is greater of t_1, t_2 or $2/3(t_1 + t_2)$	t_1 and t_2 are thicknesses of leaves of cavity wall which are tied together Wall illustrated has vertical load from floor taken by inner leaf only
Single wall with piers or intersecting walls		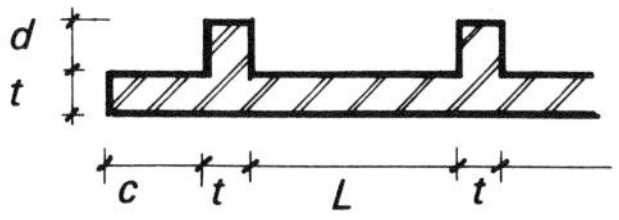 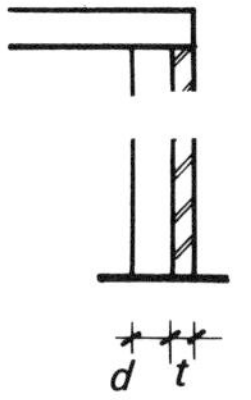 $\dfrac{L}{t} < 20$ $\dfrac{2.5c}{t} < 20$	Vertical piers or intersecting walls used to restrain walls as alternative to horizontal supports at top and bottom of wall Dimension c is distance of outhang from last vertical support d is depth of pier or intersecting wall which should be greater than 500mm (20in)

Table 2.6 — Sizes of Elements carrying gravity load - Concrete

Horizontal Section on Element	Elevation on Element	Sizing Formulae	Remarks
Prestressed tie		$P < \dfrac{A.u}{3}$ where A is area of tie P is working value of tie force u is ultimate compressive strength of concrete by standard cylinder test ($= 0.8$ x ultimate strength by standard cube test)	Minimum working force in prestressing cables is at least equal to P
Reinforced column 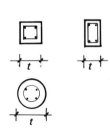	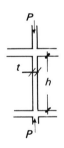	$P < \dfrac{A.u}{3}(1 + 0.14n)$ where A is area of column P is working value of axial load n is percentage of mild steel longitudinal reinforcement $\dfrac{h}{t} < 15$ where t is least width of column and h is height between lateral supports	Concrete columns in buildings are usually 'short' i.e. $h_{ef}/t < 15$; formulae given for 'short' columns, axially loaded with longitudinal reinforcement and link bars With more reinforcement reduction in area possible e.g. with 4% reinforcement there is a possible 20% reduction in area compared to 2% reinforcement; typical percentages vary from 2% to 6% For building laterally braced, for example by stair or elevator shafts, the effective height of columns, h_{ef}, is not greater than the actual height; for slender columns, those with $h_{ef}/t > 15$, there is a decrease in load compared to that for 'short' columns e.g. for column with $h_{ef}/t = 30$ area required is double that for same load on 'short' column To take account of bending, if present, as well as the compression in columns, multiply vertical load on column by $\dfrac{s + x}{s + 1}$ and treat factored amount as axial vertical load where s is the number of storeys above the column considered and $x = 1.25$ for interior columns, $x = 2.00$ for corner columns and $x = 1.50$ for all other exterior columns For 1 hr fire rating, minimum length of side of column $= 200mm$ ($= 8"$) and for 2 hr rating length $= 300mm$ ($= 12"$)

Table 2.6 continued — Sizes of Elements carrying gravity load - Concrete

Vertical Section on Element	Elevation on Element	Sizing Formulae	Remarks
Simply supported reinforced beam showing effective section at midspan 	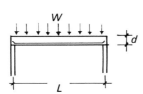	$\dfrac{L}{d} = 18$ (rectangular beams) or $\dfrac{L}{d} = 15$ (T and L beams) giving $\Delta \approx L/240$ where d is overall depth of beam and L is span	Span to depth ratios given for beams with about 1% tension reinforcement at a stress of 240 N/mm^2 (= 34 ksi); higher values of L/d up to about 1.5 those given are possible for wide beams or those with heavier reinforcement; for long spans L/d should be reduced

Span to depth ratios given are for rectangular and T and L beams having similar flange widths; T and L beams give considerable savings in concrete section and weight, compared to rectangular beams designed for same task, and can be assumed to have same L/d ratio as a narrow rectangular beam

For T beams at midspan $b = L/5$ and for L beams $b = L/10$

Typical total percentages of reinforcement in beam are between 2.5% and 4.5%

More efficient use of material is had with high values of L/d; however to prevent lateral instability restraints required, usually by floor or roof construction e.g. for a beam with $d/b = 4$ maximum span between lateral restraints = 60b

Economic value of d given when

$$\frac{M}{u.b.d^2} = 0.03 \text{ to } 0.05$$

with maximum value ≈ 0.09 where M is working value of bending moment b is width of top of beam

Bending moment in middle of beam, $M = W.L/8$ where W is total u.d. load on beam and shear at supports = $W/2$

Required area of steel in tension $= \dfrac{M}{P \times 0.8d_1}$

where p is allowable working stress in steel d_1 is the effective depth of the beam equal to the distance from the centre of the reinforcement to the top of the beam

For 1 hr fire rating minimum width of beam = 120mm (= 5″) and for 2 hr fire rating width = 200mm (= 8″)

$$\frac{V}{u.b_1.d} < 0.06$$

with maximum value ≈ 0.15 where V is working value of shear force at supports b_1 is width of web of beam

Table 2.6 continued   Sizes of Elements carrying gravity load - Concrete

Vertical Section on Element	Elevation on Element	Sizing Formulae	Remarks

Continuous reinforced beam showing effective section at midspan, left, and at support, right

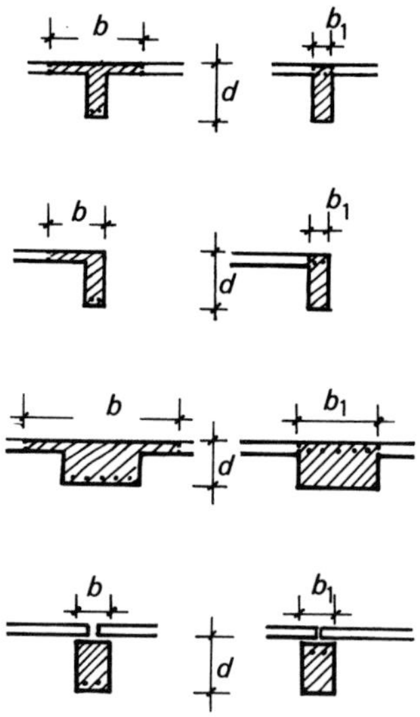

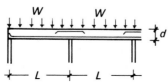

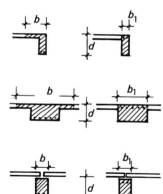

$\dfrac{L}{d} = 22$

(rectangular beams)

or

$\dfrac{L}{d} = 18$

(T and L beams)
giving $\Delta \approx L/240$
where d is overall depth of beam and L is span

Economic value of d

given when $\dfrac{M}{u.b.d^2}$ or

$\dfrac{M}{u.b_1.d^2} = 0.03$ to 0.05
with maximum value
≈ 0.09 where
M is working value of bending moment
b is width of top of beam at midspan and
b_1 is width of beam web at support
u is ultimate strength of concrete by standard cylinder test ($=0.8$ x ultimate strength by standard cube test)

$\dfrac{V}{u.b_1.d} < 0.06$
with maximum value
$= 0.15$
where V is working value of shear force at supports

At support points T and L beams have an effective section which is rectangular
For T-beams at midspan $b = L/7$ and for L-beams $b = L/14$
Bending moment at middle of end span = $W.L/11$ and at first interior support = $W.L/9$ where W is total working u.d. load on span, all spans are equal and dead load is greater than live load
Shear at supports = $0.6W$
Required area of steel in tension = $\dfrac{M}{p \times 0.8d_1}$ where p is allowable working stress in steel and d_1 is the effective depth of the beam
Notes on span to depth ratios as for simply supported beams
For 1 hr fire rating minimum width of beam = 120mm ($=5''$) and for 2 hr fire rating width = 150mm ($=6''$)

Table 2.6 continued   Sizes of Elements carrying gravity load - Concrete

Vertical Section on Element	Elevation on Element	Sizing Formulae	Remarks
Cantilevered reinforced beam showing effective section at support 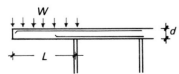	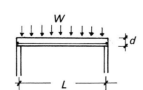	$\dfrac{L}{d} = 8$ where d is overall depth of cantilever L is length of cantilever Economic value of d given when $\dfrac{M}{u.b_1.d^2} = 0.03$ to 0.05 with maximum value ≈ 0.09 where M is working value of bending moment b_1 is width of web of beam $\dfrac{V}{u.b_1.d} < 0.06$ with maximum value $= 0.15$ where V is working value of shear force at supports	For cantilever beam with $d/b = 4$, maximum distance between end and last lateral restraint $= 25b$ Bending moment at support $= W.L/2$ where W is total u.d. load on cantilever and shear is W Notes on fire resistance and on span to depth ratio as for simply supported beams
Simply supported prestressed beam 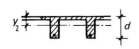 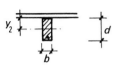 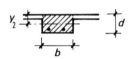		$\dfrac{L}{d} = 34$ (rectangular beams) or $\dfrac{L}{d} = 28$ (T and L beams) $Z = \dfrac{I}{y_2} = \dfrac{1.40M}{u}$ (rectangular section) or $Z_2 = \dfrac{I}{y_2} = \dfrac{1.45M}{u}$ (double T-section)	y_2 is the distance from the centroid to the top of the concrete section I is the moment of inertia of the section about the centroid Z is the section modulus, which, for rectangular sections, is equal to $b.d^2/6$ M is the working value of the bending moment Depths of prestressed beams are about 65% of those required in reinforced concrete Minimum working values of the prestressing force in cables are $M/0.5d$ for rectangular sections or $M/0.6d$ for double T sections, where M, as above, is the maximum working value of the bending moment in the beam

Table 2.6 continued   Sizes of Elements carrying gravity load - Concrete

Plan on Element	Vertical Section	Sizing Formulae	Remarks
Simply supported one-way solid slab 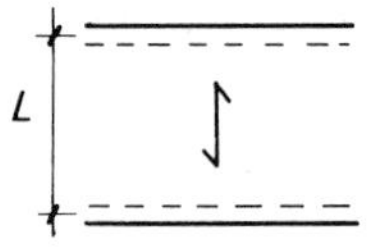	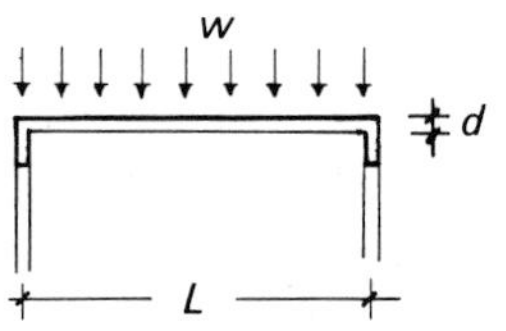	$\dfrac{L}{d} = 20$ giving $\Delta \approx L/240$ where d is overall depth of slab and L is span	Span to depth ratio given for slabs with about 0.5% tension steel reinforcement working at a stress of 240 N/mm^2 (=34ksi) with effective depth of slab = 0.85d; higher values of L/d up to about 30 possible with more reinforcement Typical percentages of reinforcement in one-way slabs $\approx$ 1% Bending moment at middle of slab = $w.L^2/8$ per unit width where w is load per unit area For cantilever slabs span to depth ratio $L/d = 9$ with bending moment = $w.L/2$ Required area of steel in tension $= \dfrac{M}{p \times 0.8d_1}$ where M is working value of bending moment, p is allowable working stress in steel, d_1 is the effective depth of the slab For 1 hr fire rating minimum, depth of slab d = 95mm (=4″) and for 2 hr fire rating d = 125mm (=5″)
Continuous one-way solid slab 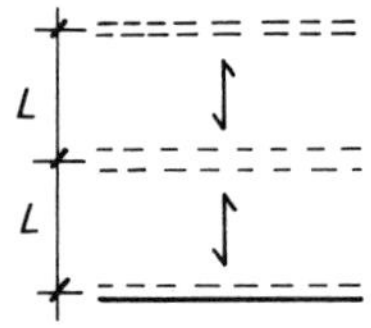	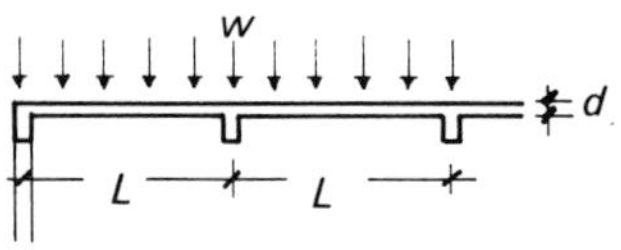	$\dfrac{L}{d} = 25$ giving $\Delta \approx L/240$	Span to depth ratio given for slabs with about 0.5% tension steel reinforcement working at a stress of 240 N/mm^2 (=34ksi) with effective depth of slab = 0.85d; higher values of L/d up to about 35 possible with more reinforcement For 1 hr fire rating minimum depth of slab d = 95mm (=4″) and for 2 hr rating d = 125mm (=5″) Bending moment in middle of slab = $w.L^2/12$ per unit width and bending moment at interior supports = $w.L^2/9$ where w is total load per unit area and dead load is greater than live load
Continuous two-way solid slab 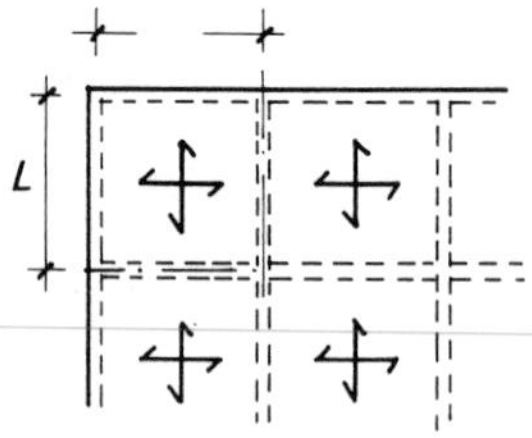	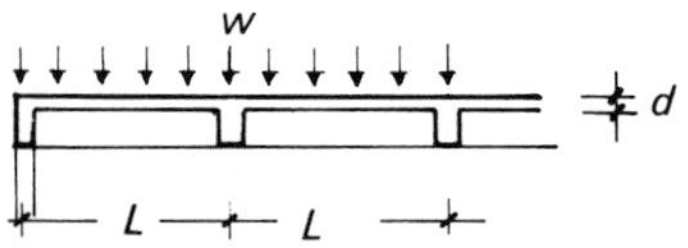	$\dfrac{L}{d} = 32$ giving $\Delta \approx L/240$	Span to depth ratio given for square slabs supported along the edges with 0.25% tension steel reinforcement, in two directions, working at stress of 240 N/mm^2 (=34ksi) with effective depth of slab = 0.8d; higher values of L/d up to about 40 possible with more reinforcement Typical percentages of reinforcement in two-way slabs $\approx$ 0.8% Bending moment at middle of slab = $w.L^2/24$ per unit width and bending moment at interior supports = $w.L^2/18$ where w is total load per unit area and dead load is greater than live load (see Table 2.4) Notes on fire resistance as for one-way slabs

Table 2.6 continued   Sizes of Elements carrying gravity load - Concrete

Element	Vertical Section	Sizing Formulae	Remarks
Continuous one-way ribbed slab	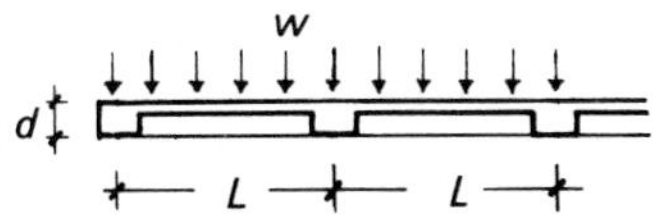	$\dfrac{L}{d} = 16$ giving $\Delta \approx L/240$ where d is overall depth of slab and L is span $\dfrac{V}{u.b_1.d} < 0.014$ where where V is working value of shear force on each rib b_1 is width of rib and d is overall depth of slab	Span to depth ratio given for slab with about 0.5% tension reinforcement, based on gross cross-sectional area including voids, working at a stress of 240 N/mm^2 ($=$34ksi) with effective depth of slab $= 0.85d$; higher values of L/d up to about 30 possible with more reinforcement Bending moment on each rib at centre of slab $= c.w.L^2/12$ and bending moment on each rib at support $= c.w.L^2/30$ with wide support beam or $= c.w.L^2/9$ with narrow support beam where c is spacing of ribs and w is load per unit area (see Table 2.4) For 1 hr fire rating minimum width of ribs and depth of slab between ribs $= 90$mm ($=3\frac{1}{2}$″) and for 2 hr rating these dimensions $= 115$mm ($=4\frac{1}{2}$″)
Continuous two-way waffle slab	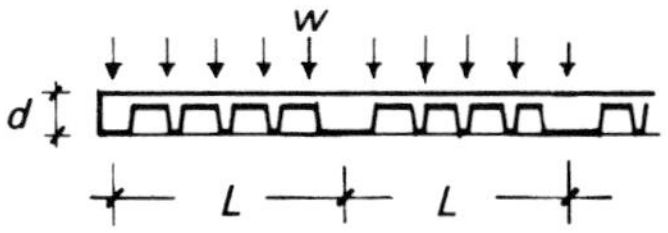	$\dfrac{L}{d} = 26$ giving $\Delta \approx L/240$ $\dfrac{V}{u.b_1.d} < 0.014$ where V is working value of shear force on each rib of waffle slab	Span to depth ratio given for slab with 0.25% tension reinforcement in two directions, based on gross cross-sectional area including voids, working at a stress of 240N/mm^2 ($=$34ksi) with effective depth of slab $= 0.80d$; higher values of L/d up to about 35 possible with more reinforcement Bending moment on beams with the same depth as the slab are as for T-beams in two-way beam and slab systems (see Table 2.4) M at midspan $= \dfrac{2w.L^2}{3}.\dfrac{L}{12}$ and at support $= \dfrac{2w.L^2}{3}.\dfrac{L}{9}$ where w is total load per unit area with dead load greater than live load Bending moment on each rib at centre of slab $= c.w.L^2/24$ and at support $= c.w.L^2/18$ where c is spacing of ribs of waffle slab

Table 2.6 continued   Sizes of Elements carrying gravity load - Concrete

Element	Vertical Section	Sizing Formulae	Remarks
Flat slabs without drop panels	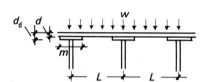	$\dfrac{L}{d} = 29$ $\dfrac{w.L^2}{u.d(4t + 12d)} < 0.014$ where t is diameter of round column or length of side of square column	Span to depth ratio given for square panels having 3 equal bays in each direction with 0.25% tension reinforcement in two directions working at stress of 240 N/mm² (=34ksi); higher values of L/d up to 32 possible with more reinforcement Bending moments on column strip at midspan = $w.L^2/8$ per unit width and over columns, without redistribution, = $w.L^2/6$ per unit width where w is full load per unit area and dead load is greater than live load; bending moments on middle strip as for two-way solid slabs (see Table 2.4)
Flat slab with drop panels		$\dfrac{L}{d} = 32$ $\dfrac{w.L^2}{u.d_d(4t + 12d_d)} < 0.014$ where d_d is depth of slab plus depth of drop panel	Span to depth ratio given for square panels having 3 equal bays in each direction with 0.25% reinforcement in two directions working at stress of 240 N/mm² (=34ksi); higher values of L/d up to 36 possible with more reinforcement Bending moments as for flat slabs without drop panels Typical value of length of side of drop panel, m, is between $0.3L$ and $0.5L$

Table 2.7 — Sizes of Elements carrying gravity load - Steel

Element	Section and Elevation on Element	Sizing Formulae	Remarks
Tie		$\dfrac{P}{A_1} < p_t$ where P is working-value of tie force A_1 is net area of tie p_t is allowable working stress of steel in tension $= 110$ N/mm^2 $(=16$ksi$)$ $\dfrac{L}{r_{min}} < 240$ where r_{min} is minimum radius of gyration of tie section L is length of tie between supports Extension $e = \dfrac{P.L}{A.E}$ should be checked where A is gross area of tie E is elastic modulus of steel $= 2.1$ x 10^5 N/mm^2 $(=30,000$ksi$)$	At bolted connections, area of tie is reduced by holes and this is the net area, A_1 Area of tie usually decided by connection detail and need to limit extension If connection points markedly eccentric to centroid of tie, area of tie may need to be increased Increasing the width of the joint, whether bolted or welded, increases strength more than increasing overlap of joint Joints subject to alternating tension and compression need special consideration to prevent fatigue
Column		$\dfrac{P}{A} < p_c$ where P is axial load in column A is area of column p_c is allowable working stress of steel in compression which depends on slenderness ratio h_{ef}/r_{min}, see below, where h_{ef} is effective height of column; slenderness ratio must not exceed 200 and should normally be less than 180 $\dfrac{h_{ef}}{r_{min}} = \quad p_c =$ 10 150 N/mm^2 $(=21$ksi$)$ 50 120 N/mm^2 $(=17$ksi$)$ 80 100 N/mm^2 $(=14$ksi$)$ 150 40 N/mm^2 $(=6$ksi$)$ 200 20 N/mm^2 $(=3$ksi$)$	Dimension b is width of column along x axis, d is depth of column along y axis and c is width of column at right angles to v axis (axis of minimum moment of inertia and radius of gyration) For buildings which are laterally braced for example by cross-bracing or cores, effective height of columns, h_{ef} is not greater than actual height between floors h Given formula valid for columns carrying axial load; for columns carrying bending moment as well as axial load see Table 2.9 Steel columns are usually slender and more efficient use of column material is had by collecting loads into one rather than several columns; an efficient section shape for each individual column is one with a low value of A/r_{min}^2 e.g. A/r_{min}^2 for square or circular sections varies from 0.8 to 2.5 and for I-sections varies from 2 to 7

$r_y/b = \quad r_x/d =$

0.22   0.38

0.25   0.42

0.38   0.38

$r_y/b = \quad r_x/d =$

0.41   0.35

0.35   0.35

0.60   0.35

Table 2.7 continued   Sizes of Elements carrying gravity load - Steel

Element	Section and Elevation on Element	Sizing Formulae	Remarks
Simply supported rolled steel beam	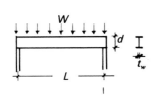	$\dfrac{M}{Z} = f_{bc} < p_{bc}$ where M is working value of bending moment on beam Z is the section modulus of the beam p_{bc} is allowable working stress of steel in bending $= 165$ N/mm^2 ($=24$ksi) $$\Delta = \frac{5W.L^3}{384E.I} = \frac{5f_{bc}.L^2}{24E.d} \text{ where}$$ W is u.d. load on beam L is span Δ is midspan deflection I is moment of inertia of beam E is elastic modulus of steel $= 2.1 \times 10^5$ N/mm^2 ($=30{,}000$ksi) f_{bc} is actual bending stress in beam at midspan Typical maximum span to depth ratios, L/d, are 28 for roof purlins 25 for roof beams in flat roofs 22 for floor beams giving total dead and live load deflections $\Delta = L/220$, $L/250$ and $L/280$ respectively if beam fully stressed, from above formula If live load deflection limited to $L/360$ then $E.I > 3.98W_l.L^2$ where W_L is u.d. live load on beam $\dfrac{V}{d.t_w} < p_v$ where V is working value of shear force on beam t_w is the thickness of web of beam p_v is allowable working stress of steel in shear $= 105$ N/mm^2 ($=14$ksi)	Given allowable stress in bending p_{bc} assumes top flange restrained against buckling, and horizontal forces if any, with maximum distance between lateral restraints $= 85r_{min}$; if distance between restraints $= 150r_{min}$ then $p_{bc} = 100$ N/mm^2 ($=14$ksi) where r_{min} is minimum radius of gyration of top flange spanning between any lateral restraints Steel sections symmetrical about the y axis have shear centre (O) in vertical line with centroid of section (S); for sections not symmetrical about y axis, loading along vertical line through centroid requires lateral restraint to prevent twist and/or lateral deflection of the section; e.g. channel sections twist, Z-sections deflect laterally and angle sections twist and deflect laterally without such restraints; normally restraints provided by floor or roof construction Bending moment in middle of beam, M, $= W.L/8$ and shear force at supports $= W/2$

Table 2.7 continued — Sizes of Elements carrying gravity load - Steel

Element	Elevation on Element	Sizing Formulae	Remarks
Continuous rolled steel beam	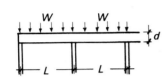	$\dfrac{M}{Z} = f_{bc} < p_{bc}$ where M is working value of bending moment on beam Z is the section modulus of the beam p_{bc} is allowable working stress of steel in bending $= 165$ N/mm² ($= 24$ksi) $\Delta = \dfrac{5f_{bc}.L^2}{24E.d}$ or less where L is span of beam Δ is midspan deflection E is elastic modulus of steel $= 2.1 \times 10^5$ N/mm² ($= 30{,}000$ksi) f_{bc} is actual bending stress in beam at midspan $\approx \dfrac{1}{Z}\left(M_S - \dfrac{M_A + M_B}{2}\right)$ where M_S is $W.L/8$, M_A and M_B are moments at supports, all at working values, W is u.d. load on beam, Z is section modulus of beam $\dfrac{V}{d.t_w} < p_v$ where V is working - value of shear force on beam t_w is the thickness of web of beam p_v is the allowable working stress of steel in shear $= 105$ N/mm² ($= 14$ksi)	Assuming W is total u.d. load on each span, all spans are equal and dead load is greater than live load, bending moment in span of beam, M, $= W.L/12$ and bending moment at interior supports $= W.L/9$ except first interior support for which bending moment $= W.L/8$ Shear at supports $V = 0.6W$ Notes on allowable stress and unsymmetrical sections as for simply supported beams

Table 2.7 continued Sizes of Elements carrying gravity load - Steel

Element	Section and Elevation on Element	Sizing Formulae	Remarks
Simply supported composite steel and concrete beam	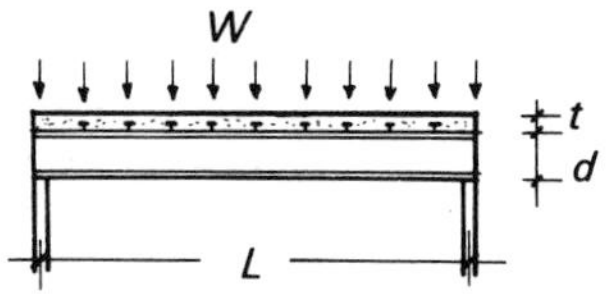 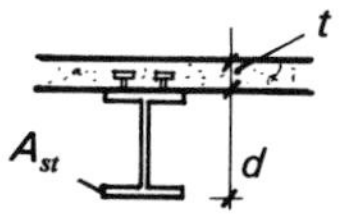	$\dfrac{M}{A_{st}(0.5d + 0.8t)} < p_t$ and $\dfrac{M_d}{Z_{st}}$ $< p_{bc}$ where M is working value of total bending moment on beam $\dfrac{M}{Z_{comp}} < p_{bc}$ where $\dfrac{Z_{comp}}{Z_{st}}$ $< 1.35 + 0.35M_l/M_d$ [(1)] and M_l is working value of bending moment due to live load $\Delta_d = \dfrac{5W_d.L^3}{384E.I_{st}}$ and $\Delta_l \approx \dfrac{5r.W_l.L^3}{384E.I_{st}}$ where r has a value between 0.3 and 0.5	Typical values of $\dfrac{L}{t+d}$ are 24 or 20 for those with vibration Given formulae assume that steel beam is not propped during construction and carries dead load alone but that live load is carried by composite action M_d is working value of bending moment due to dead load A_{st}, Z_{st} and d are area, section modulus and depth of steel beam and t is depth of concrete slab p_t and p_{bc} are allowable working stresses for steel in tension = 125 N/mm² (=18ksi) and for steel in bending = 165 N/mm² (=24ksi) Z_{comp} is section modulus of composite section Δ_d and Δ_l are deflections due to dead and live loads W_d and W_l are working values of dead and live u.d. load on span I_{st} is the moment of inertia of the steel section
Simply supported truss	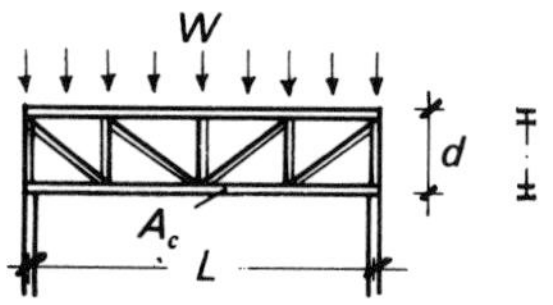	$\dfrac{M}{d.A_c} < p_c$ where M is working value of bending moment on truss at midspan A_c is area of top or bottom chord of truss at midspan d is depth of truss between chord centre lines p_c is allowable working stress of steel in compression $\approx$ 150 N/mm² (=21ksi) $\Delta \approx \dfrac{10W.L^3}{384E.I}$ where I is moment of inertia of top and bottom chords about centreline of truss = $A_c.d^2/2$ If live load deflection limited to $L/360$ then $E.I > 7.96W_l.L^2$ Economic value of L/d = 10 to 14	Given formulae apply to trusses with top chord restrained against buckling Forces in truss members largely axial and are checked under tension or compression Deflection in truss is greater than that of beam with same moment of inertia because of shear deflection in truss due to change in length of diagonal and vertical members

Table 2.7 continued   Sizes of Elements carrying gravity load - Steel

Element	Elevation and Plan on Element	Sizing Formulae	Remarks
Simply supported vierendeel girder	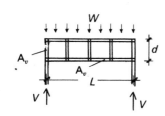	$\dfrac{M}{d.A_v} < p_c$ where M is working value of bending moment on girder at midspan A_v is area of top or bottom chord of girder at midspan d is height of girder between chord centre lines equal to horizontal panel dimension $\dfrac{V}{2A_v} + \dfrac{M}{Z} < p_c$ where A_v is area of vertical member above support and of adjacent top and bottom chord members M_v is working value of bending moment on end chords and verticals $= V.d/4$ where V is equal to vertical reaction at each support Economic value of $L/d = 6$ to 10	Given formulae apply to girder with top chord restrained against buckling Members in vierendeel girder subject to shear forces, axial forces and bending moments; although vierendeel girder inefficient form becomes relatively more efficient with increase in size Estimate of deflection of truss established by frame analysis of girder taking account of flexibility of members in bending and shear
Double layer space frame	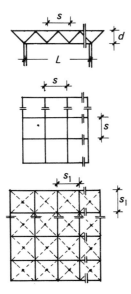	Economic value of $\dfrac{L}{d} < 15$ for space frame supported at corners or $\dfrac{L}{d} < 20$ for space frame supported around perimeter where L is span and d is depth of frame $s \approx \sqrt{2d}$ to $2d$ and $s \approx L/10$ for L up to 50m ($=160'$) or $s \approx L/10$ to $L/15$ for L above 50m where s is module size of bottom layer of frame $s_1 \approx s$ to $\dfrac{s}{\sqrt{2}}$ where s_1 is module size of top layer of frame	Wide variations in span to depth ratios from those given are possible The number of joints and members in a space frame is proportional to the inverse of the square of the module size; therefore economy of space frame increased by larger number of supports, moderate span to depth ratio as well as by larger module size

Table 2.8   Sizes of Elements carrying gravity load - Timber Softwood

Element and Horizontal Section	Elevation on Element	Sizing Formulae	Remarks
Solid timber tie	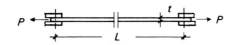	$\dfrac{P}{0.8A} < p_t$ where P is working value of tie force A is gross area of tie p_t is allowable working stress of timber softwood in tension $= 3.5$ N/mm² $(=0.5\text{ksi})$ $\dfrac{L}{t} < 70$ where t is least dimension of tie cross-section L is length of tie between supports	Area of tie at connection assumed to be 80% of gross area Given span to width ratio assumes tie may take small amount of compression Actual area of tie usually decided by type of connection detail; because of difficulty of tension connections steel rods often used in place of timber ties Given allowable stress is for long-term (2 month) load on construction grade softwood
Solid timber column	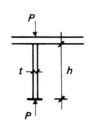	$\dfrac{P}{A} < p_c$ where P is working value of compression in column p_c is allowable working stress of timber in compression which depends on slenderness ratio h_{ef}/t see below, where h_{ef} is effective height of column; slenderness ratio should not normally exceed 50 $\dfrac{h_{ef}}{t} =$ $\quad p_c =$ 10 9.0 N/mm² $(=1.28\text{ksi})$ 20 6.0 N/mm² $(=0.86\text{ksi})$ 30 2.8 N/mm² $(=0.40\text{ksi})$ 40 1.5 N/mm² $(=0.21\text{ksi})$ 50 1.0 N/mm² $(=0.14\text{ksi})$	For buildings which are laterally braced for example by cross-bracing, effective height of columns h_{ef} is not greater than actual height h between floors Given formula valid for columns carrying axial load Given allowable stress is for long-term (2 month) load on construction grade softwood

Table 2.8 continued   Sizes of Elements carrying gravity load - Timber Softwood

Element and Horizontal Section	Elevation and Section on Element	Sizing Formulae	Remarks
Simply supported solid timber beam		$\dfrac{M}{Z} < p_{bc}$ where M is working value of bending moment on beam Z is the section modulus of the beam p_{bc} is allowable working stress of softwood in bending $= 7 \text{ N/mm}^2$ $(= 1\text{ksi})$	Formulae assume top of beam is laterally restrained or has ends held in position; in general $d/b < 7$ and if $d/b > 6$ beam requires bridging as well as lateral restraint where b is width of beam Given allowable stress is for long-term (2 month) load on construction grade softwood Typical spacing of beams in floors, c, is 450-600mm (18-24in)
		$\Delta = \dfrac{5W.L^3}{384E.I} = \dfrac{5f_{bc}.L^2}{24E.d}$ where W is total u.d. load on beam L is span and d is depth of beam Δ is midspan deflection I is moment of inertia of beam E is elastic modulus of timber including effects of creep which depends on duration of load f_{bc} is actual bending stress in beam at midspan To prevent ponding on flat roofs $E.I > c.\rho_w.L^4/50$ [(2)] where I is moment of inertia of roof beams at spacing c E is short-term elastic modulus of softwood $= 11 \text{ kN/mm}^2$ $(= 1560\text{ksi})$ ρ_w is density of water $= 10 \text{ kN/m}^3$ $(= 62 \text{ lb/ft}^3)$ L is span of roof beams given camber $> 2.5\Delta_d$ where Δ_d is dead load deflection of beams at midspan	If total deflection limited to $L/330$ then $E.I > 4.34W.L^2$
Simply supported glued-laminated timber beam 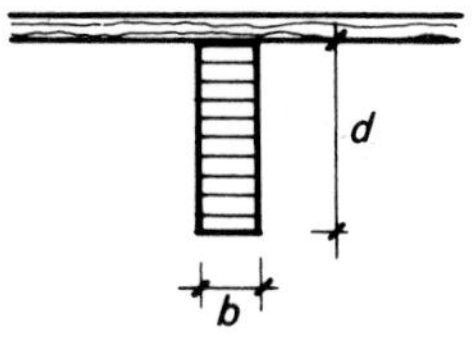	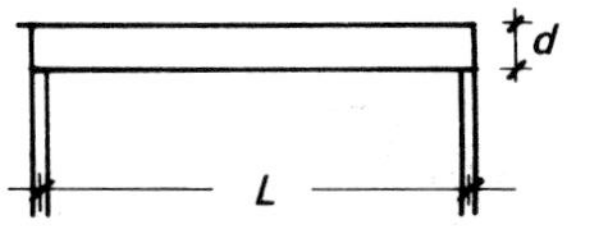 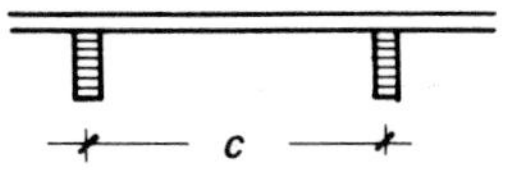	$\dfrac{M}{Z} < p_{bc}$ where p_{bc} is allowable working stress in bending $= 12.5 \text{ N/mm}^2$ $(= 1.8\text{ksi})$ To prevent ponding on flat roofs $E.I > c.\rho_w.L^4/50$ where E is short-term elastic modulus of laminated softwood $= 12 \text{ kN/mm}^2$ $(= 1750\text{ksi})$	Notes and formula for deflection as for solid timber beams

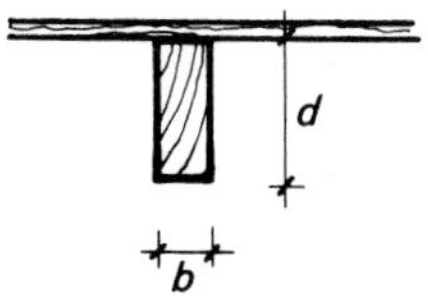

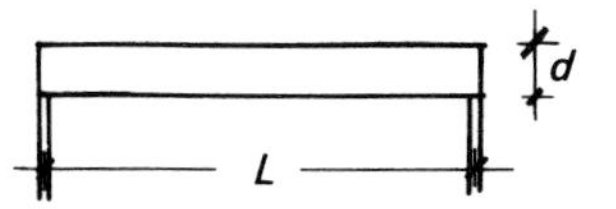

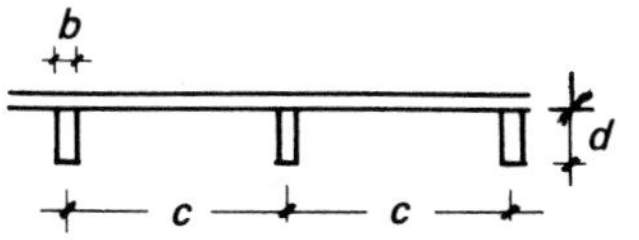

Table 2.9   Sizes of Columns under bending and axial load - Concrete and Steel

Element and Horizontal Section	Elevation and Graph for Element	Sizing Formulae	Remarks

Reinforced concrete column (braced)

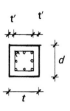

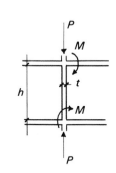

$\dfrac{h}{t} < 15$ where h is height of column and t is least dimension of rectangular cross-section with dimensions of t and d

Eccentricity of load on column is $e = \dfrac{M}{P}$ where

P is working value of axial load
M is working value of bending moment on column
If $e \leqslant t/3$ then there is a maximum allowable axial load, P_{max}, for any particular eccentricity, and an associated bending moment $e.P_{max}$, where

$$P_{max} = \frac{u.d}{2.25} . \frac{3(0.5t-e)}{2}$$

u is ultimate compressive strength of column by standard cylinder test ($= 0.8$ x strength by standard cube test)
If $e > t/3$ then there is a maximum allowable bending moment in column for any particular eccentricity found by interpolating between M_1 and M_0, associated with an eccentricity of $t/3$ and with zero axial load, respectively (see graph);

$$M_1 = \frac{u}{2.25} . \frac{d.t^2}{12} \quad \text{and} \quad M_0 = 0.8 p_{st} . A_{st}(t - t')$$

t' is distance from centre of steel in tension to nearest concrete face
A_{st} is area of steel in tension t' from face of concrete
p_{st} is the allowable working stress of steel in tension $= 140$ or 210 N/mm² ($= 20$ or 30 ksi)
M_1 is the maximum allowable working value of the bending moment in column when eccentricity is $t/3$
M_0 is the maximum allowable working value of the bending moment in column when there is zero vertical load
Given formulae valid for columns, bending about one axis, symmetrically reinforced about the axis of bending with 2% longitudinal reinforcement; formulae consider bending about minor axis of a rectangular column but also valid for major axis bending with d and t interchanged.

Steel column (braced)

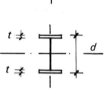

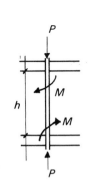

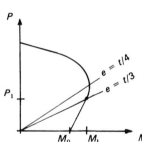

$\dfrac{h_{ef}}{r_{min}} < 100$ where h_{ef} is the effective height of the column and r_{min} is the minimum radius of gyration of the column section

$\dfrac{f_c}{p_c} + \dfrac{f_{bc}}{p_{bc}} < 1$ where $f_c = P/A$ and $f_{bc} = M/Z$ are working stresses, about one axis, in compression and bending respectively
P and M are working values of vertical load and bending moment
A and Z are the area and section modulus of the steel column section about the axis of bending
p_c and p_{bc} are the allowable working stresses in compression and bending respectively; p_c depends on slenderness ratio h_{ef}/r_{min} and is obtained from entry for steel column in Table 2.7; p_{bc} is taken = 150 N/mm² ($= 22$ksi)

Dimension b is width of column along x axis, d is depth of column along y axis and t is thickness of flange of column
Given formula valid when slenderness ratio, h_{ef}/r_{min}, < 100 and $d/t < 50$
For buildings which are laterally braced for example by cross-bracing, effective height of column, h_{ef} is not greater than the actual height between floors h; for unbraced frames h_{ef} may be taken $= 2h$
For load combinations involving dead, live and wind or seismic loads allowable stresses may be increased by 25%

Table 2.10   Bending Moments and Deflections - Single Bay, Single Storey Frames

Description	Frame and Applied Loads	Bending Moment Diagram and Reactions	Deflected Shape	Stiffness of Beam compared to Column (k)	Bending Moments and Reactions	Horizontal Deflection Factor (β)	Remarks
Single bay frame with pinned feet - Vertical load				0 (stiff column)	$M_A = 0.09W.L$ $M_B = 0.05W.L$		$k = \dfrac{h.I_b}{L.I_c}$
				0.5	$M_A = 0.07W.L$ $M_B = 0.07W.L$		
				1	$M_A = 0.05W.L$ $M_B = 0.08W.L$		With pinned feet,
				5	$M_A = 0.02W.L$ $M_B = 0.11\ W.L$		$M_A = \left(\dfrac{3}{3+2k}\right)\dfrac{W.L}{12}$
				∞ (stiff beam)	$M_A = 0$ $M_B = 0.13W.L$		$M_B = \left(\dfrac{1+2k}{3+2k}\right)\dfrac{W.L}{8}$
- Horizontal load				0.5	$M_A = 0.50F.h$	4.0	$R_A = 0.50F$ and $V_A = F.h/L$ and
				∞	$M_A = 0.50F.h$	2.0	$\Delta = \beta\dfrac{F.h^3}{12E.I_c}$ with $\beta = 2 + 1/k$ for pinned feet frame
Single bay frame with fixed feet - Vertical load				0 (stiff column)	$M_A = 0.09W.L$ $M_B = 0.05W.L$		
				0.5	$M_A = 0.07W.L$ $M_B = 0.06W.L$		$M_C = 0.5M_A$ for all values of k, where M_C is bending moment at fixed feet
				1	$M_A = 0.06W.L$ $M_B = 0.07W.L$		
				5	$M_A = 0.03W.L$ $M_B = 0.11W.L$		
				∞ (stiff beam)	$M_A = 0$ $M_B = 0.13W.L$		
- Horizontal load				0 (stiff column)	$M_A = 0$ $M_C = 0.50F.h$	2.0	$\Delta = \beta\dfrac{F.h^3}{12E.I_c}$
				0.5	$M_A = 0.19F.h$ $M_C = 0.32F.h$	0.87	with $\beta = \dfrac{2+3k}{1+6k}$ for frame with fixed feet
				1	$M_A = 0.22F.h$ $M_C = 0.29F.h$	0.71	
				5	$M_A = 0.25F.h$ $M_C = 0.26F.h$	0.55	Columns in each frame are identical
				∞ (stiff beam)	$M_A = 0.25F.h$ $M_C = 0.25F.h$	0.50	I_b and I_c are moments of inertia of beam and column

Table 2.10 continued   Bending Moments and Deflections - Single Bay, Single Storey Frames

Description	Frame and Applied Loads	Bending Moment Diagram and Reactions	Deflected Shape	Stiffness of Beam compared to Column (k)	Bending Moments and Reactions	Horizontal Deflection Factor (β)	Remarks
Single bay frame with semi-rigid footings - Horizontal load	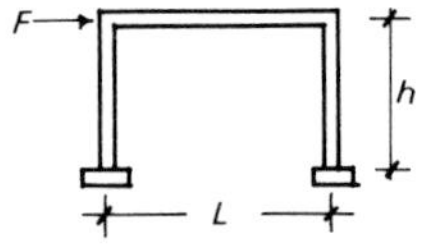	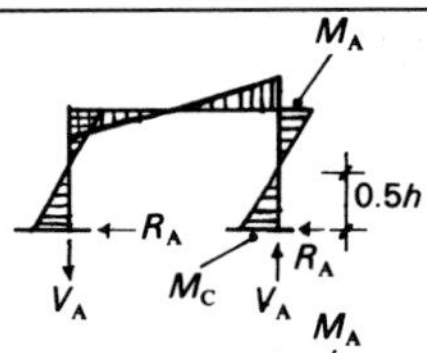		0.5	$M_A \approx 0.25F.h$ $M_C \approx 0.25F.h$ $R_A = 0.5F$		Bending for vertical load intermediate between that for fixed and pinned feet
	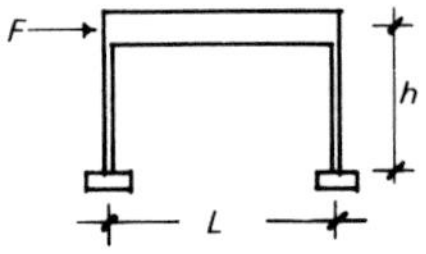	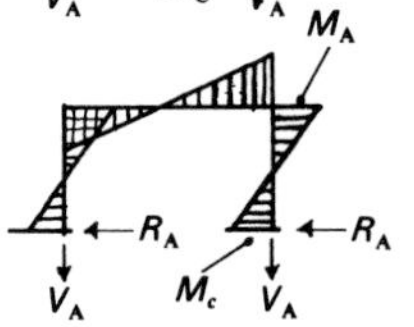		∞	$M_A \approx 0.35F.h$ $M_C \approx 0.15F.h$		$V_A = F.h/L$ All columns identical

Table 2.11   Bending Moments and Deflections - Multibay, Single Storey Frames

Description	Frame and Applied Loads	Bending Moment Diagram and Reactions	Deflected Shape	Stiffness of Beam compared to Column (k)	Bending Moments and Reactions	Horizontal Deflection Factor (β)	Remarks
Two bay frame with pinned feet - Horizontal load	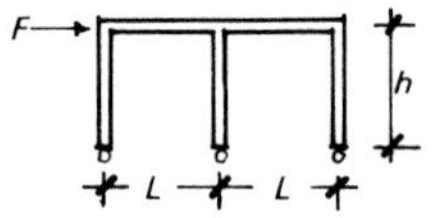	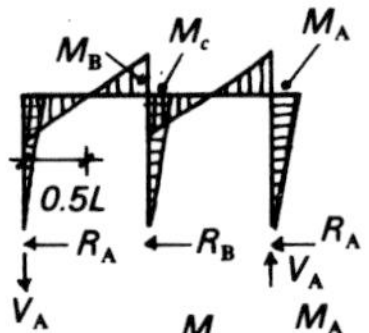		0.1 (stiff column)	$M_A = 0.25\,F.h$ $M_B = 0.25F.h$ $M_C = 0.50F.h$ $R_A = 0.25F$ $V_A = 0.50F.h/L$	$1.5 +$ $0.5/k$	$k = \dfrac{h.I_b}{L.I_c}$
	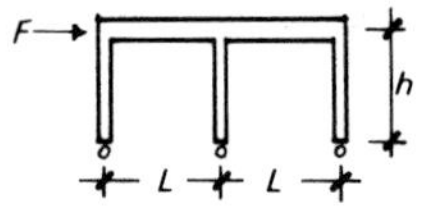	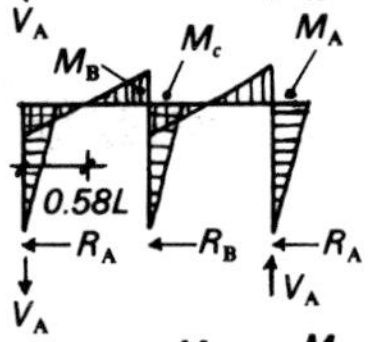	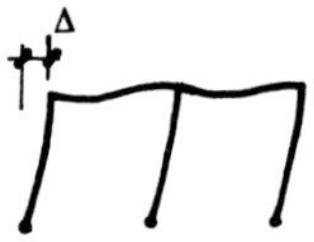	1	$M_A = 0.29F.h$ $M_B = 0.21F.h$ $M_C = 0.42F.h$ $R_A = 0.29F$ $V_A = 0.50F.h/L$	1.92	$R_B = F - 2R_A$ for all 2 bay frames
	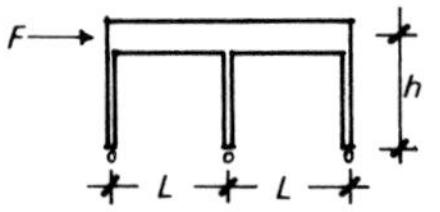	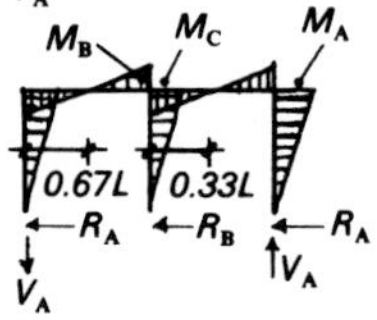	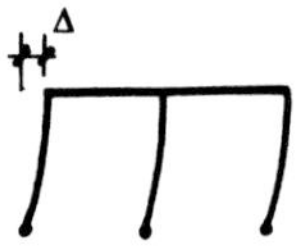	∞	$M_A = 0.33F.h$ $M_B = 0.17F.h$ $M_C = 0.33F.h$ $R_A = 0.33F$	1.33	$\Delta = \beta\dfrac{F.h^3}{12E.I_c}$
Three bay frame with pinned feet - Horizontal load	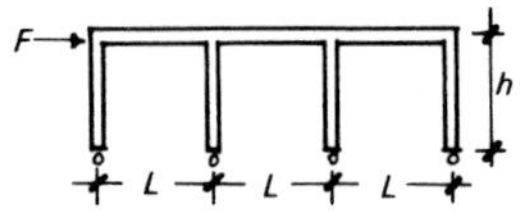	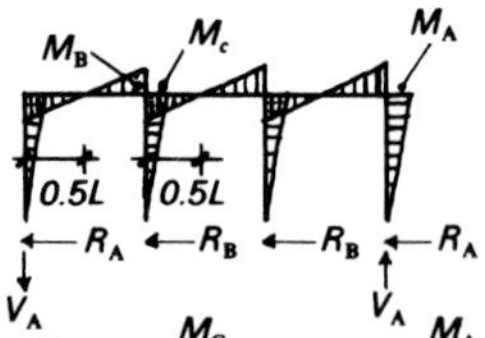		0.1 (stiff column)	$M_A = 0.17F.h$ $M_B = 0.17F.h$ $M_C = 0.33F.h$ $R_A = 0.17F$ $V_A = 0.33F.h/L$	$1.11 +$ $0.33/k$	$R_B = 0.5F - R_A$ for all 3 bay frames
	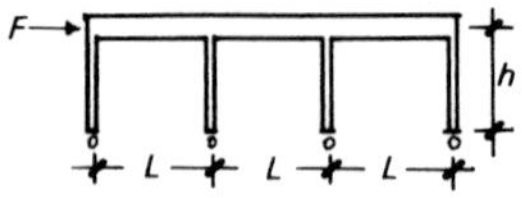	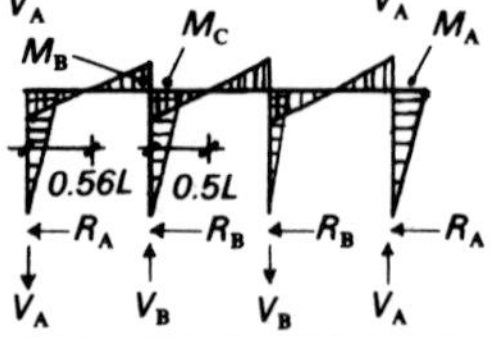		1	$M_A = 0.21F.h$ $M_B = 0.17F.h$ $M_C = 0.29F.h$ $R_A = 0.21F$ $V_A = 0.38F.h/L$ $V_B = 0.14F.h/L$	1.38	Columns in each frame are identical I_b and I_c are moments of inertias of beam and column

Table 2.11 continued   Bending Moments and Deflections - Multibay, Single Storey Frames

Description	Frame and Applied Loads	Bending Moment Diagram and Reactions	Deflected Shape showing Point of Inflection	Stiffness of Beam compared to Column (k)	Bending Moments and Reactions	Horizontal Deflection Factor (β)	Remarks
Three bay frame with pinned feet - Horizontal load	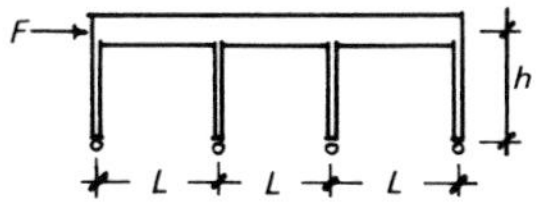	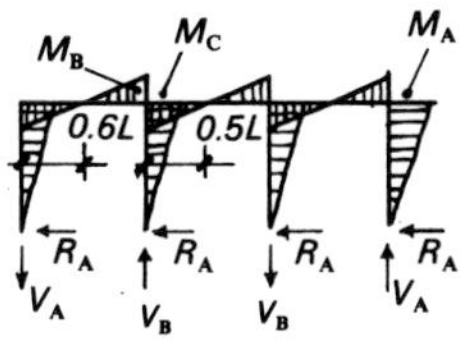		∞ (stiff beam)	$M_A = 0.25F.h$ $M_B = 0.17F.h$ $M_C = 0.25F.h$ $R_A = 0.25F$ $V_A = 0.42F.h/L$ $V_B = 0.25F.h/L$	1	
Two bay frame with fixed feet - Horizontal load	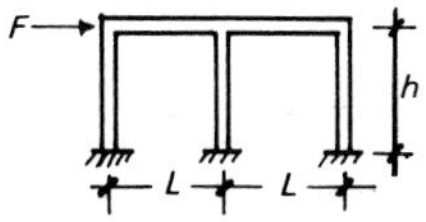	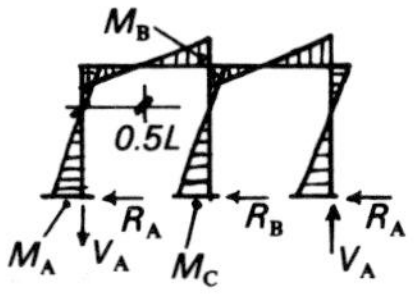	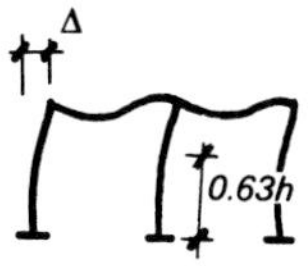	0.1 (stiff column)	$M_A = 0.26F.h$ $M_B = 0.07F.h$ $M_C = 0.22F.h$ $R_A = 0.31F$ $V_A = 0.13F.h/L$	0.58 + 0.034/k	$k = \dfrac{h.l_b}{L.l_c}$
	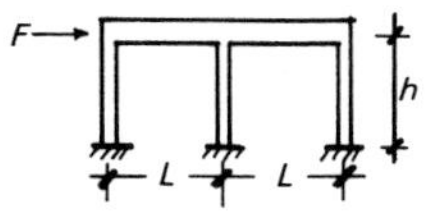	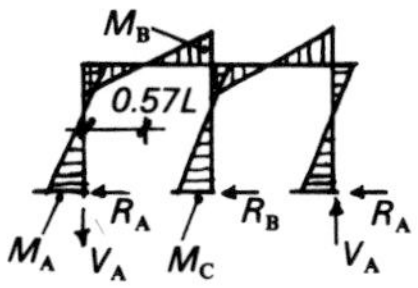	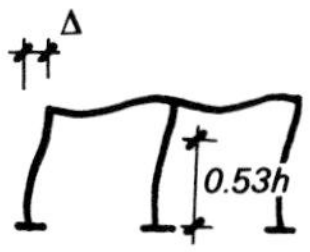	1	$M_A = 0.18F.h$ $M_B = 0.11F.h$ $M_C = 0.21F.h$ $R_A = 0.30F$ $V_A = 0.22F.h/L$	0.46	$R_B = F - 2R_A$ for all 2 bay frames
	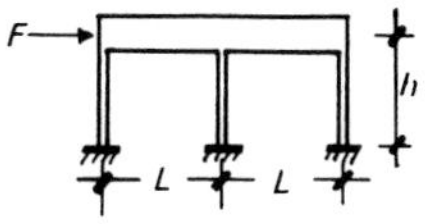	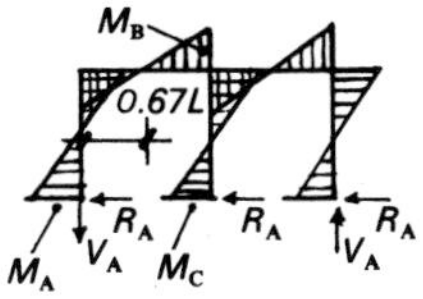	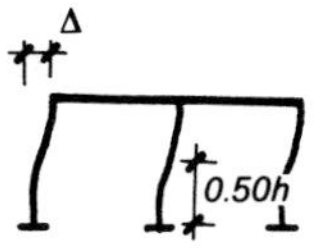	∞ (stiff beam)	$M_A = 0.17F.h$ $M_B = 0.09F.h$ $M_C = 0.17F.h$ $R_A = 0.33F$ $V_A = 0.25F.h/L$	0.33	$\Delta = \beta \dfrac{F.h^3}{12E.l_c}$
Three bay frame with fixed feet - Horizontal load	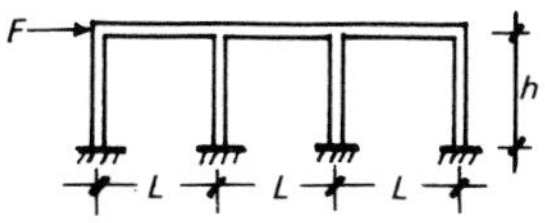	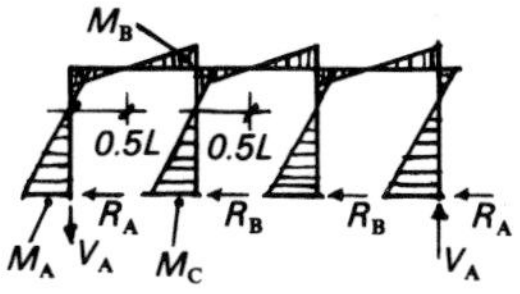	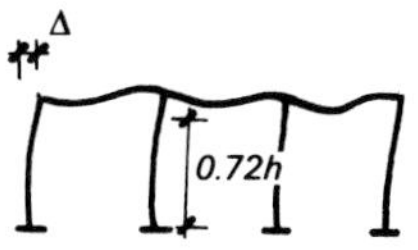	0.1 (stiff column)	$M_A = 0.18F.h$ $M_B = 0.04F.h$ $M_C = 0.20F.h$ $R_A = 0.22F$ $V_A = 0.08F.h/L$	0.48 + 0.018/k	$R_B = 0.5F - R_A$ for all 3 bay frames
	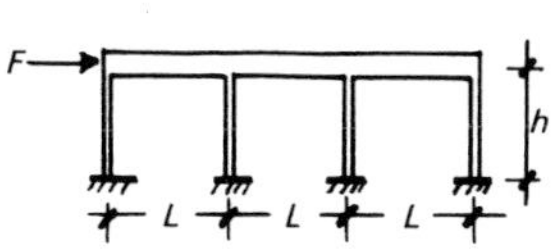	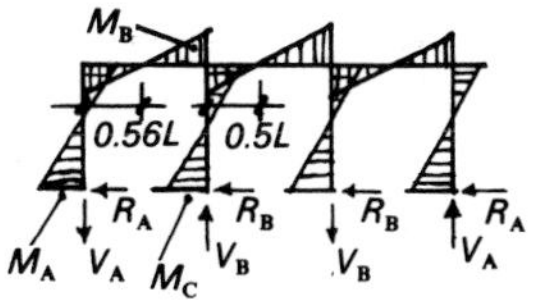	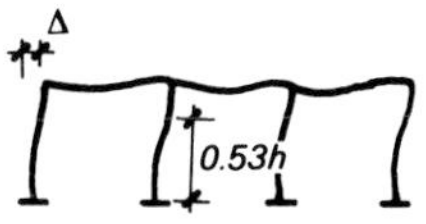	1	$M_A = 0.13F.h$ $M_B = 0.07F.h$ $M_C = 0.15F.h$ $R_A = 0.22F$ $V_A = 0.16F.h/L$ $V_B = 0.05F.h/L$	0.33	Columns in each frame are identical
	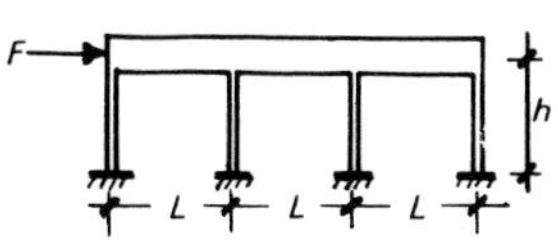	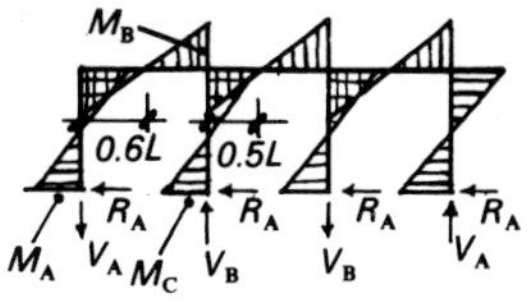	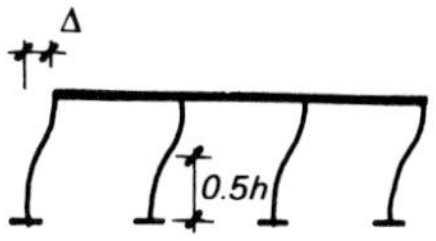	∞ (stiff beam)	$M_A = 0.12F.h$ $M_B = 0.08F.h$ $M_C = 0.12F.h$ $R_A = 0.25F$ $V_A = 0.21F.h/L$ $V_B = 0.12F.h/L$	0.25	l_b and l_h are moments of inertia of beam and column

Table 2.12   Bending Moments, Axial Forces and Deflections - Multistorey Frames

Description	Frame and Applied Loads	Bending Moment Diagram and Reactions/ Deflected Shape	Bending Moments, Reactions and Horizontal Deflections	Remarks
Single bay frame - Vertical load	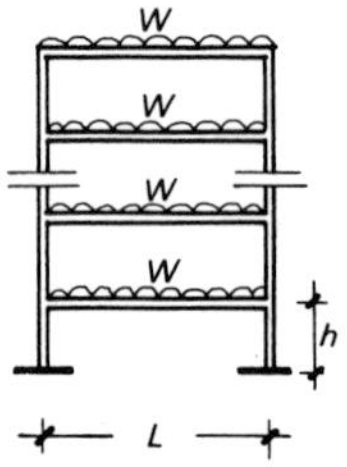	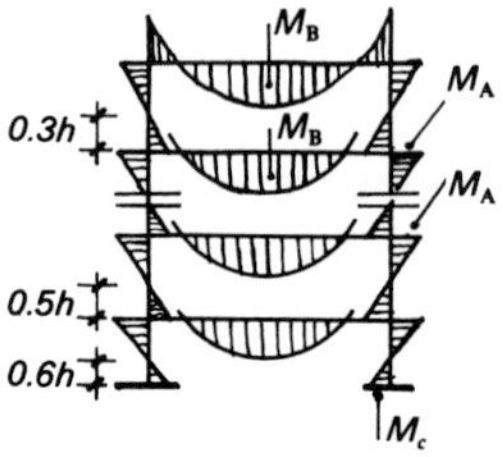	$M_A = 0.024W.L$ $M_B = 0.080W.L$	$k = \dfrac{h.I_b}{L.I_c} = 1$
- Horizontal load	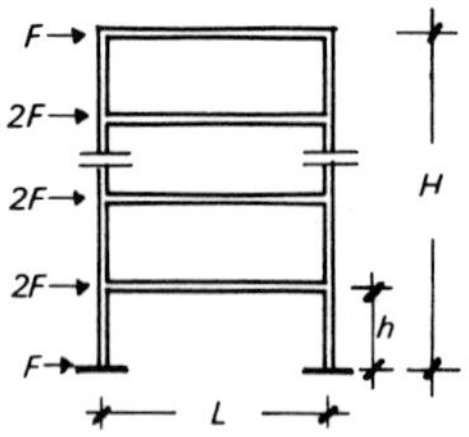	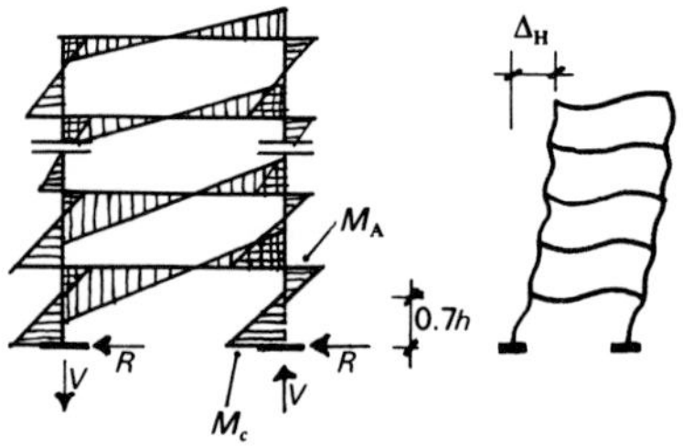	$M_A = 0.25(2n-1)F.h$ $M_C = 0.37(2n-1)F.h$ $R = (n-0.5)F$ $V = \dfrac{n.F.H}{L}$ with n equal to the number of storeys	$\Delta_H = \dfrac{F.h^3}{24E.I_c}\left(3n^2 + 8n - 5\right)$ for pinned feet $\Delta_H = \dfrac{F.h^3}{24E.I_c}\left(3n^2 - 2.5n + 0.25\right)$ for fixed feet $\Delta_H \approx \dfrac{F.h^3}{24E.I_c}\left(3n^2 - 1\right)$ for semirigid footings $2F$ is the horizontal force at each intermediate floor level
Multibay frame - Horizontal load Bending moments and axial loads at base of frame (portal method)	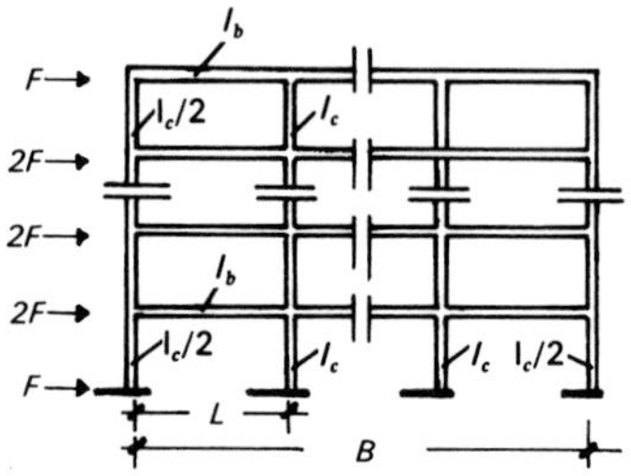	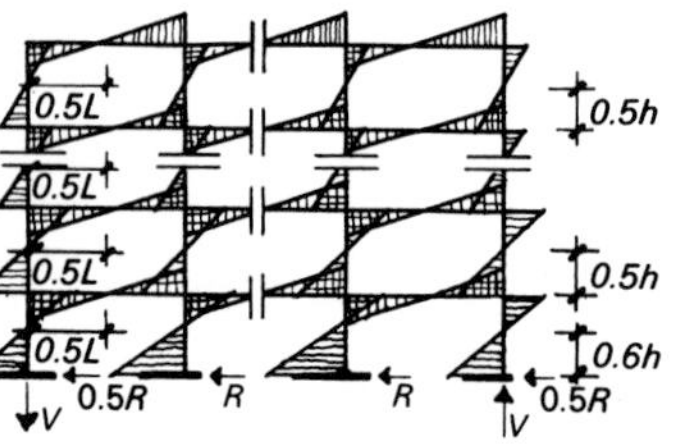	$M_A = 0.5R.h$ $M_B = 0.7R.h$ $M_C = 0.5M_B$ with $R = \dfrac{(2n-1)F}{m}$ $V = \dfrac{n.F.H}{B}$	Moments and forces given for portal method assume internal columns have twice stiffness of external columns Number of storeys in frame $= n$; number of bays in frame $= m$ so $H = n.h$ and $B = m.L$ The portal method gives a reasonable estimate of moment and axial forces when $H/B < 4$ and $n < 25$
Axial loads at base of frame if $H/B > 3$ (cantilever method)		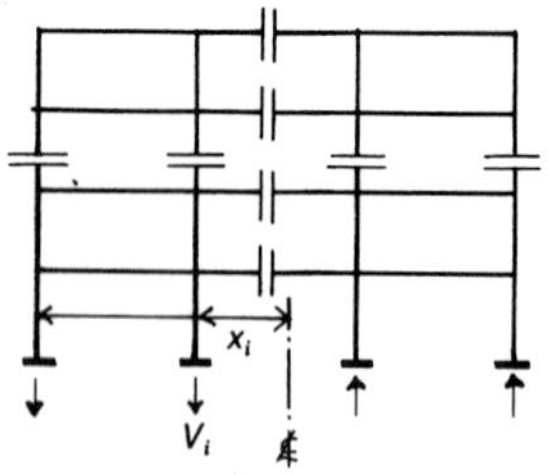	M on base $= n.F.H$ $I = \sum A_i.x_i^2$ $V_i = \dfrac{A_i.x_i.M}{I}$ $\left(= \dfrac{x_i.M}{\sum x_i^2}\right.$ if equal-sized columns $\Big)$	M is moment over whole of base due to axial loads in columns I is moment of inertia of all columns together about their centroid x_i is distance of each column from centroid V is axial load in column at base

Table 2.13 Sidesway in multistorey Frames - Equal Bays with Uniform Beam and Column Sizes throughout height

Description	Frame and Applied Loads or Deflected Shape	Sidesway due to flexibility of beams or columns or to change in length of columns	Total sidesway due to flexibility of beams and columns and to change in length of columns in three particular cases	Remarks

Multibay frame
- Horizontal load

Total sidesway at top = Δ_H
where $\Delta_H = \Delta_B + \Delta_C + \Delta_L$

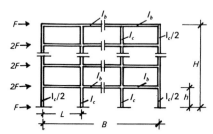

	case 1	case 2	case 3	$k = \dfrac{h.l_b}{L.l_c}$
	2 storeys $(n=2)$	5 storeys $(n=5)$	10 storeys $(n=10)$	
	4 bays $(m=4)$	4 bays $(m=4)$	4 bays $(m=4)$	
	$k=5$	$k=2$	$k=1$	
	$h/L=0.4$	$h/L=0.4$	$h/L=0.4$	
	$H/B=0.2$	$H/B=0.5$	$H/B=1$	

Sidesway due to flexibility of beams, Δ_B
(stiff columns)

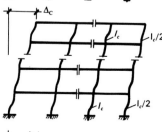

$$\Delta_B = \frac{F.h^3}{E.l_c} \cdot \frac{n^2}{12m.k}$$

	case 1	case 2	case 3
$\Delta_B \times \dfrac{E.l_c}{F.h^3} =$	0.017	0.26	2.07
$\dfrac{\Delta_B}{\Delta_H} =$	17%	33%	48%

Number of storeys in frame = n; number of bays in frame = m
All columns assumed to have same area, A_c, but internal columns assumed to have stiffness, l_c, twice that of external columns

Sidesway due to flexibility of columns, Δ_C
(stiff beams)

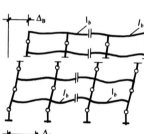

$$\Delta_C = \frac{F.h^3}{E.l_c} \cdot \frac{n^2}{12m}$$

	case 1	case 2	case 3
$\Delta_C \times \dfrac{E.l_c}{F.h^3} =$	0.083	0.52	2.08
$\dfrac{\Delta_C}{\Delta_H} =$	83%	66%	49%

Sidesway due to change in length of columns, Δ_L
(stiff crossbraces free to slide on each other)

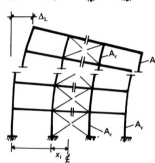

$$\Delta_L = \frac{F.h^3}{E.A_c} \cdot \frac{n^4}{4\sum x_i^2}$$
$$= \frac{F.h^3}{E.l_c} \cdot \frac{n^4}{m^2} \cdot \frac{t^2}{L^2} \cdot \frac{1}{48\sum c_i^2}$$
$$= \frac{F.h^3}{E.l_c} \cdot \frac{n^4}{m^2} \cdot \frac{1}{6912\sum c_i^2}$$
with $L/t = 12$

	case 1	case 2	case 3
$\Delta_L \times \dfrac{E.l_c}{F.h^3} =$	0	0.009	0.145
$\dfrac{\Delta_L}{\Delta_H} =$	0%	1%	3%

t is depth of internal column
x_i is distance of each column from centroid of all the columns
$x_i = c_i.B = c_i.m.L$

	case 1	case 2	case 3
$\Delta_H \times \dfrac{E.l_c}{F.h^3} =$	0.10	0.79	4.29

Table 2.14   Sidesway in multistorey Frames - Equal Bays with Beam and Column Sizes varying linearly with height

Description	Frame and Applied Loads or Deflected Shape	Sidesway due to flexibility of beams or columns or to change in length of columns	Total sidesway due to flexibility of beams and columns and to change in length of columns in two particular cases	Remarks

Multibay frame
- Horizontal load

Total sidesway at top $= \Delta_H$
where $\Delta_H = \Delta_B + \Delta_C + \Delta_L$

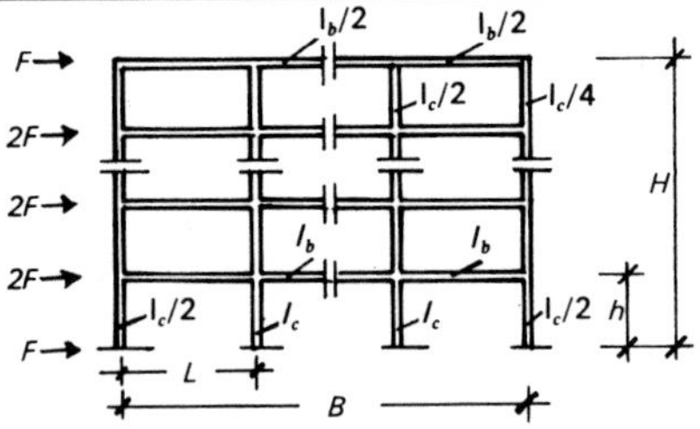

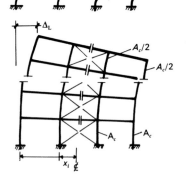

Sidesway due to flexibility of
beams, Δ_B
(stiff columns)

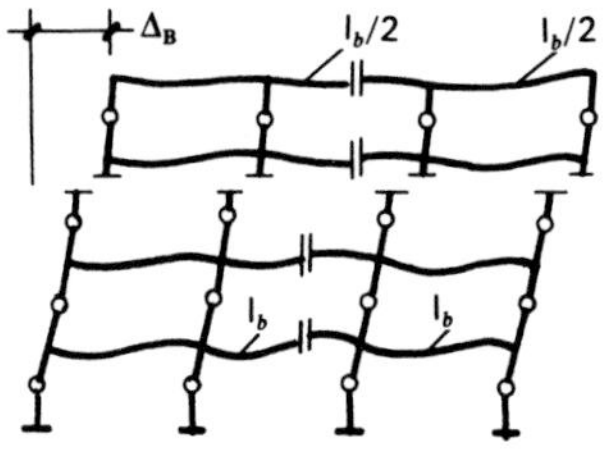

$$\Delta_B = \frac{F.h^3}{E.I_c} \cdot \frac{r.n^2}{12m.k}$$

with $r \approx 1.1$ for buildings
less than 10 storeys and
≈ 1.2 for buildings
10 storeys or above

Sidesway due to flexibility of
columns, Δ_C
(stiff beams)

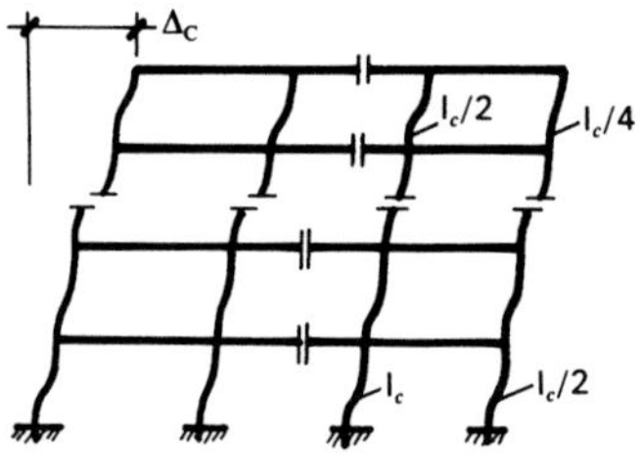

$$\Delta_C = \frac{F.h^3}{E.I_c} \cdot \frac{r.n^2}{12m}$$

with r as above

Sidesway due to change in
length of columns, Δ_L
(stiff crossbraces free to slide
on each other)

$$\Delta_L = \frac{F.h^3}{E.A_c} \cdot \frac{r.n^4}{4\sum x_i^2}$$

$$= \frac{F.h^3}{E.I_c} \cdot \frac{r.n^4}{m^2} \cdot \frac{t^2}{L^2} \cdot \frac{1}{48\sum c_i^2}$$

$$= \frac{F.h^3}{E.I_c} \cdot \frac{r.n^4}{m^2} \cdot \frac{1}{6912\sum c_i^2}$$

with $L/t = 12$ and r as above

	case 1	case 2
	20 storeys	40 storeys
	(n = 20)	(n = 40)
	4 bays	4 bays
	(m = 4)	(m = 4)
	k = 0.6	k = 0.5
	h/L = 0.4	h/L = 0.4
	H/B = 2	H/B = 4
$\Delta_B \times \frac{E.I_c}{F.h^3} =$	16.66	80.00
$\frac{\Delta_B}{\Delta_H} =$	57%	49%
$\Delta_C \times \frac{E.I_c}{F.h^3} =$	10.00	40.00
$\frac{\Delta_C}{\Delta_H} =$	34%	25%
$\Delta_L \times \frac{E.I_c}{F.h^3} =$	2.66	42.59
$\frac{\Delta_L}{\Delta_H} =$	9%	26%
$\Delta_H \times \frac{E.I_c}{F.h^3} =$	29.32	162.59

Remarks:

$k = \frac{h.I_b}{L.I_c}$; number of storeys in
each frame $= n$; number of
bays in each frame $= m$
Columns at each level assumed
to have same area but internal
columns assumed to have
twice stiffness of external
columns

Stiffness of beams and
columns, and areas of columns,
assumed to vary linearly with
height, being I_b, I_c and A_c
typically at bottom and half this
at top

Beams assumed to have same
stiffness at any one level

Deflection between one storey
and next, due to flexibility of
beams and columns, is

$$\Delta_h = \frac{R.h^3(1 + 1/k)}{12E.I_c.m}$$ where

R is total shear force at storey
level considered

t is depth of internal column

x_i is distance of each column
from centroid of all the columns
and

$x_i = c_i.B = c_i.m.L$

Table 2.15 Horizontal Deflection of Vertical Stiffening Systems in Buildings

System	Building Section	Building Plan	Deflected Shape	Plan on System	Horizontal Deflection at Top (Δ_H)	Remarks
Shear wall	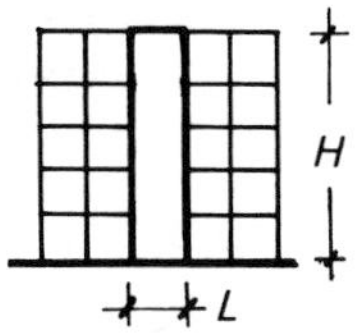	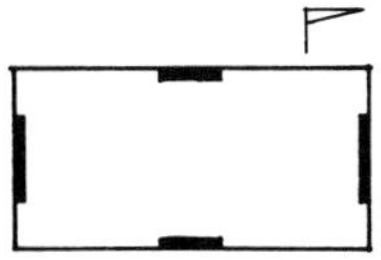	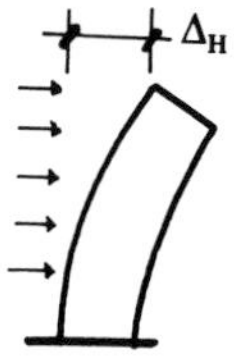	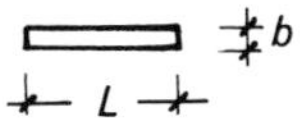	$\Delta_H = \dfrac{Q.H^3}{8E.I}$ with $I = \dfrac{b.L^3}{12}$	H is total height, Q is total distributed horizontal load over height H, E is modulus of elasticity. Base assumed to provide fixity
Core	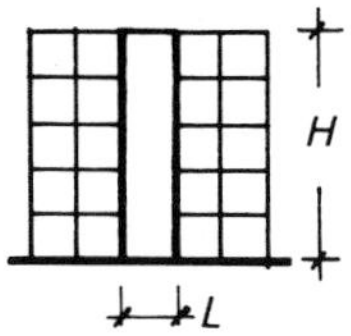	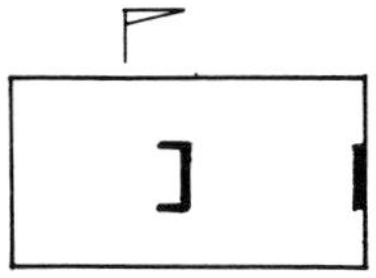	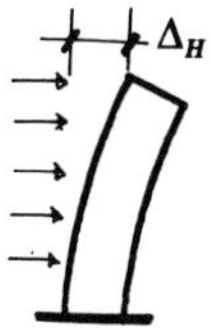	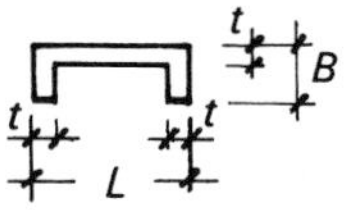	$\Delta_H = \dfrac{Q.H^3}{8E.I}$ with $I = \dfrac{b.L^3}{12}$ $-\dfrac{(b-t)(L-2t)^3}{12}$	Base assumed to provide fixity
Frame with shallow connecting beams	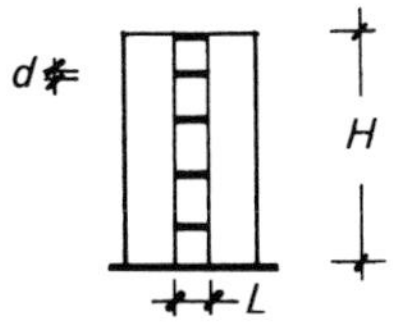	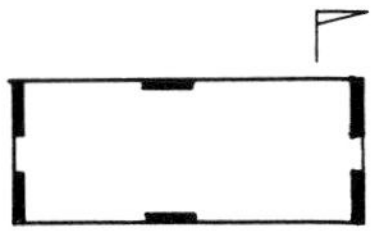	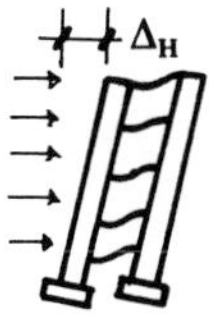	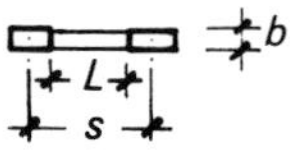	$\Delta_H = \dfrac{v.L^2.H}{12E.I} = \dfrac{Q.L^2.H^2}{24E.I.n.s}$ with $v = \dfrac{V}{n} = \dfrac{Q.H}{2n.s}$ n = number of connecting beams I = moment of inertia of each beam $= \dfrac{b.d^3}{12}$ s = spacing between column centres L = length of beam V = vertical reaction at each base due to force, Q	Each base assumed to allow rotation but not settlement

Table 2.15 continued Horizontal Deflection of Vertical Stiffening Systems in Buildings

System	Building Section	Building Plan	Deflected Shape	Plan on System	Horizontal Deflection at Top (Δ_H)	Remarks
Frame	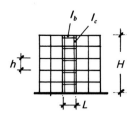	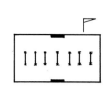	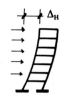		$\Delta_H =$ $$\frac{Q.H^3(n^2 + 1/k[2n^2 - 1])}{48E.I_c.n^4}$$ with $k = \dfrac{h.I_b}{L.I_c}$ n = number of beams I_b and I_c are moments of inertia of beams and columns	Each base assumed to provide partial fixity with no settlement
Shear truss	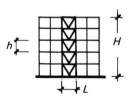	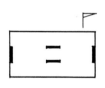			$$\Delta_H = \frac{Q.H^3}{2A.E.L^2}$$ with A = area of each column L = spacing between column centres	Each base assumed to allow rotation but not settlement
Connected shear walls	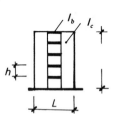	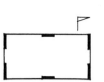			$$\Delta_H = \frac{\beta.Q.H^3}{8E.I}$$ with $I = \dfrac{b.L^3}{12}$ and $\beta \approx 1$ if $\alpha.H > 8$ or β between 2 and 5 if $\alpha.H < 4$ assuming that $a/L < 0.3$ in both cases, where $\alpha.H$ $$= n\sqrt{\frac{2h.I_b}{a.I_c}\left(1 + \frac{L}{a} + \frac{L^2}{a^2}\right)}$$ and $n =$ number of connecting beams	Connected shear walls tend to behave like single wall if $\alpha.H > 8$ and like frame if $\alpha.H < 4$ (3) Each base assumed to provide fixity with no settlement

Chapter Three

Building Physics

Building physics is the term coined for the study of those aspects of physics which are relevant to the practical design of buildings. It includes lighting, ventilation, air flow, acoustics and those subjects concerning the control and use of energy, especially energy in the form of heat; it also includes the study of the microclimate, that is the study of conditions in the immediate environment of the building. Study of these subjects should help to produce better comfort, safety and economy in building design. Normally the stiffness, strength and durability of the building structure and cladding elements and any other topics connected with the structural mechanics of the building are the concern of the structural engineer. Those topics included in building physics are the concern of the building services engineer. The two disciplines come together in *systems engineering*, which is the study of methods for the general optimisation of the form, organisation, structure, equipment and servicing of the building. Usually the object of the optimisation is good value for money, however defined, rather than the absolute optimisation of one criterion, such as lowest cost, fastest construction time, minimum number of site operations and so on. Most often optimisation consists only of evaluating several schemes in the initial stages but where meaningful numerical values can be assigned to the items which must be optimised, methods such as linear programming may be suitable, the exact solutions to the numerical problem being obtained by computer. With any design some trial and error is inevitable, because of the many criteria that have to satisfied in the chosen design solution.

INTERNAL ENVIRONMENT

Comfort Conditions

The human body generates heat by metabolic action but maintains itself at a constant temperature of approximately 37°C (98.6°F). Therefore heat must be lost from the body, but at a controlled rate, so that the subject does not feel chilly or, at the other extreme, does not become so hot that the body needs to perspire in order to dissipate the excess body heat. The object of thermal design is to provide conditions which will allow an appropriate heat loss from the body. Hence although it is possible to insulate oneself with clothing against excessive cold, it is not possible to insulate oneself against excessive heat, except temporarily. As the body generates more heat when active than when still, for example walking generates about twice that heat produced by sitting still, the thermal conditions required in each room or area will depend more on the clothing worn and activities likely to be undertaken there than on any other factors. Heat is lost from the body by convection, radiation or evaporation of body moisture. At moderate air temperatures most heat is lost by convection and radiation but at higher air temperatures most heat is lost by evaporation and all heat is lost by evaporation when the air temperature is greater than or equal to the body temperature of 37°C (98.6°F). Although the body must lose heat, the rate of loss may be slowed down if the body absorbs radiation from a hotter surface or is in warm air. The factors normally controlling comfort are the air temperature, the relative humidity of the air, the air movement and the amount of radiation between the body and the surrounding surfaces. The designer may influence these four factors to a degree that depends on the sophistication of the design. For example in many air-conditioning systems all four factors may be altered more or less independently. The conditions which provide comfort are to some extent subjective and vary from country to country. Broadly speaking, by varying the amount of clothing worn a subject sitting still may be comfortable within a temperature range two or three degrees C either side of 22°C (four or five degrees F either side of 72°F) and with the relative humidity between about 20% and 60% (3.25). However these are only partial guides to the comfort of a room as experienced by the user. For example, a room at high temperature and humidity may still be comfortable if there is enough through ventilation and, conversely, rooms with a low air temperature may be comfortable if the mean radiant temperature of the room surfaces is high. If people become accustomed to certain conditions, they are sensitive to changes in it. For example in offices, temperature changes need to be kept to within about 2°C (4°F) of some mean temperature. For reasons of economy and comfort, design room temperatures are usually set higher in summer than in winter.

The most important measurement, with reference to comfort, is the air temperature, as measured by a *dry-bulb thermometer*. An instrument which also takes account of radiation from the surrounding surfaces and some account of air movement is the *globe thermometer*, consisting of a dry-bulb thermometer placed at the centre of a copper globe painted black. The thermometer records a higher temperature than the air temperature if the surrounding surfaces are at a higher temperature than the air. Humidity can be measured by a *wet-bulb thermometer*. The wet-bulb thermometer has its bulb wrapped in a damp cloth and the temperature recorded is the temperature of the saturated water vapour around the bulb, which is very nearly equal to the dew point of water vapour at that particular partial pressure, see section on condensation. The wet-bulb temperature is lower than the dry-bulb temperature, assuming the water vapour in the air is unsaturated, because of cooling due to evaporation of water. The difference between the wet and dry bulb temperatures gives an indication of the relative humidity of the air.

As well as the air temperature, an index of temperature often used in calculations is the *environmental temperature, T_{ei}*, which takes account of radiant heat as well as air temperature, and is defined by:

$$T_{ei} = \tfrac{2}{3}T_r + \tfrac{1}{3}T_a \text{ °C (°F)}$$

where T_r is the mean radiant temperature of the surrounding surfaces in °C (°F); and

T_a is the air temperature in °C (°F).

It is found that the black globe thermometer gives a good estimate of the environmental temperature. A useful indicator for the purposes of comparison is the *effective temperature* which takes into account several factors but chiefly air temperature and humidity. It may be defined as the temperature of still air with a relative humidity of 50% which in the absence of radiation is assumed to give the same degree of comfort as the air in the room under consideration.

HEAT TRANSFER

Methods of Heat Transfer

Heat may be transferred by conduction, convection or radiation. *Conduction* is transfer of heat between one part of a body and another, or between two bodies in contact, by molecular collision. The rate of heat transfer, Q, through a unit area is given by:

$$Q = \frac{\lambda . \Delta T}{d} \text{ W/m}^2 \text{ (btu/ hr ft}^2)$$

where λ is the thermal conductivity of the material in W/ m °C (btu in/ ft² hr °F);

ΔT is the temperature difference between the two points under consideration in °C (°F); and

d is the distance between the two points in m (in).

For a material of a homogeneous composition, the thermal conductivity is closely related to density, the conductivity increasing as the density decreases (Table 3.1).

Convection is an important method of heat transfer and occurs when a liquid or gas moves past a surface and a heat transfer occurs between the surface and the liquid or gas, for example that occurring when air flows over heating pipes. There is mixing when the hotter liquid or gas expands, becomes less dense and therefore rises setting up circulation. The amount of heat transferred, Q, is given by:

$$Q = \alpha . \Delta T \text{ W/m}^2 \text{ (btu/hr ft}^2)$$

where α is the surface conductance of the boundary layer at the surface in W/ m² °C (btu/ hr ft² °F); and

ΔT is the temperature difference in °C (°F).

Thermal radiation is energy in the form of electromagnetic waves. All bodies emit electromagnetic waves but, in general, a hot body emits more heat than a cool one so that there is a net transfer of radiant heat between them. The amount of heat, Q, radiated by a body is given by:

$$Q = \sigma . \varepsilon . T^4 \text{ W/m}^2 \text{ (btu/ hr ft}^2)$$

where σ is a radiation constant equal to 5.77×10^{-8} W/ m² °K⁴ (1.73×10^{-9} btu/ hr ft² °R⁴);

ε is the absorptivity of the surface being about 1.0 for a black body going down to about 0.2 for a shiny metal surface (Table 3.2); and

T is the temperature in °K (°R), based on absolute zero which is equal to -273°C (-460°F).

For buildings, the most important radiation is that received from the sun; it has wavelengths ranging from 0.25 to 3.00 μm (1 μm = 1 x 10^{-6} m). However, energy re-radiated from building surfaces, after exposure to the sun, has longer wavelengths between 2.5 and 100 μm. Solar

Table 3.1   Thermal Properties of Building Materials

Material	Specific Gravity $\dfrac{\rho}{\rho_w}$ dimensionless	Thermal Conductivity λ $\dfrac{W}{m°C}$	Thermal Conductivity $\dfrac{btu\ in}{ft^2\ hr\ °F}$	Thermal Diffusivity $\dfrac{\lambda}{\rho.c}$ $\dfrac{mm^2}{s}$	Thermal Diffusivity $\times 10^{-3}\ \dfrac{ft^2}{hr}$	Thermal Absorption $\lambda.\rho.c$ $\times 10^6\ \dfrac{W^2\ s}{m^4\ °C^2}$	Thermal Absorption $\dfrac{btu^2}{hr\ ft^4\ °F^2}$
Limestone	2.2	1.3	9	0.78	30	2.2	19
Brickwork	2.2	0.9	6.2	0.4	15	2.0	17
Concrete	2.4	1.2	8	0.7	27	2.1	18
Iron and steel	7.8	45	312	11	426	184	1586
Timber	0.4	0.14	1	0.12	4.6	0.16	1.4
Plywood	0.6	0.11	0.76	0.13	5.0	0.09	0.78
Chipboard	0.7	0.14	1	0.15	5.8	0.13	1.1
Gypsum plaster	1.3	0.40	2.8	0.40	15.5	0.40	3.5
Fibre insulation board	0.3	0.06	0.42	0.11	4.2	0.03	0.26
Glass wool	0.06	0.04	0.28	0.8	31	0.002	0.0017
Cork and carpeting	0.11	0.05	0.35	0.23	8.9	0.011	0.10
Solid plastic	1.2	0.20	1.39	0.12	4.6	0.33	2.8
Expanded polystyrene	0.02	0.034	0.25	1.15	44	0.001	0.009
Polyurethane foam board	0.03	0.028	0.2	0.73	28	0.001	0.009
Air	0.0013	0.024	0.17	18.5	720	0.00003	0.00027
Water	1	0.6	4.16	0.14	5.4	2.6	22

radiation which is incident on the surface of a material may be partly absorbed, partly reflected and partly transmitted. The ability of a surface to absorb radiation is measured by its *absorptivity* which is defined as the ratio of radiation absorbed on the surface to the total incident radiation. At any given temperature and wavelength, the absorptivity is equal to the *emissivity*, the emissivity being a measure of the surface's ability to emit radiation. Note that surfaces may have low absorptivity at short wavelengths but emit at longer wavelengths for which the emissivity, and absorptivity, is different (Table 3.2). Black or darkly coloured surfaces have greater absorptivity than white or light coloured surfaces, especially for the wavelengths present in solar radiation.

The glass used in buildings may be classified by the proportion transmitted, absorbed and reflected of the solar radiation in the visible range from 0.4 to 0.8 μm and in the infrared range from 0.8 to 3.0 μm. Clear glass does not transmit any significant

Table 3.2 Average Values of Absorptivity and Reflectivity of Surfaces

Surface	Absorptivity (or emissivity) to Low-temperature Radiation (long wave radiation)	Absorptivity (or emissivity) to Solar Radiation (short wave radiation)	Reflectivity to Solar Radiation (short wave radiation)
Red brickwork	0.9	0.7	0.3
Yellow brickwork	0.9	0.4	0.6
Grey concrete	0.9	0.7	0.3
Black concrete tiles	0.9	0.9	0.1
Asphalt	0.95	0.9	0.1
Aluminium paint	0.5	0.4	0.6
White paint	0.9	0.25	0.75
Polished aluminium	0.04	0.2	0.8

amount of radiation outside these two ranges but has between 80% and 90% transmission in the visible range and between 75% and 85% transmission in the infrared range (3.1). When sunlight penetrates glass windows in a room it heats up the air and material in that room. The greater the heat absorbed by the material in the room, the smaller the immediate rise in the air temperature. The amount of heat absorbed by the enclosing elements and other material in the room depends on the surface area of the materials exposed to the heat and the thermal absorption, v, of each material, see section on intermittent heating and cooling. The emitted radiation from the material has wavelengths longer than $3\mu m$ so that radiation is trapped by the glass and more heat is introduced into the room than can escape. This is known as the *greenhouse effect*. The amount of heat transmitted through windows may be altered by external blinds or by blinds fitted within double-glazing or by solar control glasses. Solar control glasses are those whose transmittance of solar infrared radiation is deliberately curtailed. They are customarily split into *heat-absorbing glasses* which directly transmit between 20% and 60% of the solar infrared radiation, most of the rest being absorbed and *heat-reflecting glasses*, which directly transmit between 10% and 25%, reflect between 25% and 50%, the rest being absorbed. All heat absorbed in glass is released, afterwards, both to the inside and outside (3.1). The *shading coefficient* is the proportion of the total solar infrared radiation transmitted by a glass, including that part which is absorbed but released afterwards to the inside, divided by 0.87, which is the proportion of the total infrared radiation transmitted by a thin clear glass, used as a standard for comparison (3.1). The directly transmitted infrared radiation has short wavelengths that heats up solid material in the room, but not the air, so that there is a delay before the air is heated by long wave radiation from the material, the delay depending on the total thermal capacity of the material. By contrast, the released infrared radiation from the glass is longwave and, as the glass only has small thermal capacity, it is able to heat the air almost immediately. High glass temperatures, particularly on the inner glass of double-glazed units, can have a significant effect on the mean radiant temperature and on comfort

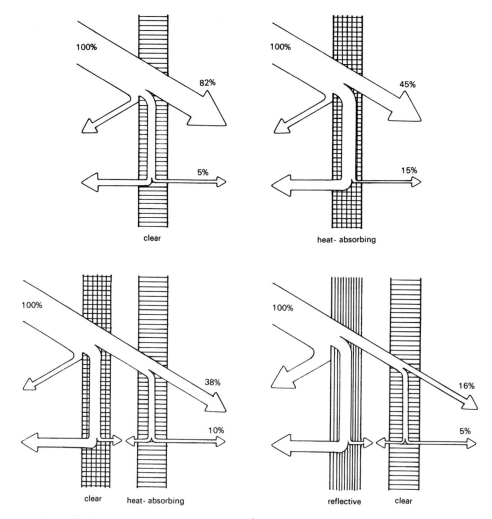

3.1 Single and double glazing system showing proportions of solar radiation reflected, transmitted and absorbed; radiation absorbed is subsequently re-radiated.

or discomfort in the perimeter zones. For double glazed heat-absorbing glasses the shading coefficient can go down to about 0.35 and that for double-glazed heat-reflecting glass down to about 0.15. In the latter case a metallic coating is usually placed on the inner surface of the outer pane of glass to reflect the infrared radiation. The visible light transmittance for such double glazing is usually somewhat less than 50%. However as

the eye is able to adapt to changes in lighting level this need not be a problem. Note that the transmission properties of glass will change depending on the angle of incidence of the infrared radiation. As the shading coefficient is based on a comparison with clear glass, it is a more or less constant figure whatever the angle of incidence.

Insulation

Insulation, more accurately *resistive insulation*, refers to materials which prevent the passage of heat by conduction and thus have low thermal conductance. Resistive insulation, if it is needed, is more effective on the outside of any building construction because it can then keep the interior construction near the design indoor temperature, thus helping to smooth out temperature peaks and, in cold climates, to reduce the risk of condensation (*3.2*). However the response time for heating is slower with insulation on the outside. *Reflective insulation* helps to prevent the absorbance of radiant heat by use of a material to reflect the radiant energy (Table 3.2).

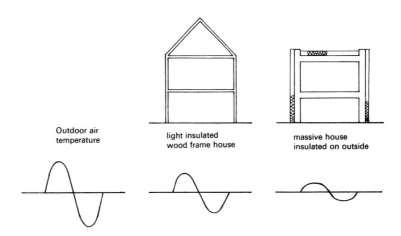

3.2 Diagram showing periodic variations in interior temperature for light and heavy forms of construction for same insulation and outdoor temperature variation.

Heat transfer through elements

Heat is lost through the walls and roof of a building by conduction, convection and radiation. A calculation of the heat transfer through the walls and' roof may be done in terms of the thermal conductance of a surface, representing the transfer of heat by radiation and convection at the surface, and the thermal conductance of a solid layer of material, representing the transfer of heat through it by conduction. For heat conducted through a wall with several parallel layers the quantity of heat passing through unit area, Q, is given by:

$$Q = U.\Delta T = \frac{\Delta T}{R} \text{ W/m}^2 \text{ (btu/hr ft}^2)$$

where U is the thermal transmittance (U-value) in W/ m² °C (btu/ hr ft² °F);

  R is the thermal resistance in m² °C/ W (hr ft² °F/btu); with

$$R = \frac{1}{U} = \frac{1}{\alpha_o} + \frac{d_1}{\lambda_1} + \frac{d_2}{\lambda_2} + \ . \ . +\frac{1}{\alpha_i} \text{W/m}^2 \text{°C (btu/ hr ft}^2 \text{°F);}$$

  α_o and α_i are the surface conductances of the outside and inside surfaces in W/ m² °C (btu/ hr ft² °F);

  λ is the thermal conductivity of each layer in W/ m °C (btu in/ hr ft² °F);

  d is the thickness of each layer in m (in); and

  ΔT is the temperature difference across the complete wall construction in °C (°F).

The formula assumes that the temperatures on

both surfaces of the construction are near those air temperatures on the inside and outside that are used to calculate the temperature difference. For purposes of calculation, the temperature difference could be based on the inside environmental temperature and the outside dry-bulb air temperature. If the outside surface is in direct sunshine, the outside temperature used in the calculation should take account of solar radiation as well as the air temperature. The *sol-air temperature*, T_s, takes account of both these factors. Ignoring heat re-radiated from the surface, it is given by :

$$T_s = T + \frac{a.I}{a_o} \text{ °C (°F)}$$

where T is the outside dry-bulb air temperature in the shade °C (°F);

  a is the absorptivity of solar radiation on the surface of the building;

  a_o is the surface conductance in W/m² °C (btu/ hr ft² °F); and

  I is the intensity of solar radiation, which depends on the season and the orientation of the surface, in W/m² (btu/ hr ft²).

Table 3.3 gives approximate values for the thermal transmittance (U-value) of some typical wall and roof constructions in moderate conditions of exposure.

INTERMITTENT HEATING AND COOLING

Thermal Capacity

The heat transfer calculation given above assumes a steady state, meaning that the temperature difference between the two sides of the construction remains constant. If the temperature varies it is necessary to consider not only the thermal conductivity of each layer of the construction but also the *thermal capacity, s,* and the *thermal diffusivity, h,* of the materials of construction. These factors are given by:

  $s = \rho.c$ J/ m³ °C (btu/ ft³ °F)

where ρ is the density of the material in kg/m³ (lb/ft³)

  c is the specific heat capacity of the material in J/kg °C (btu/lb °F); and

$$h = \frac{\lambda}{s} = \frac{\lambda}{\rho.c} \text{ m}^2\text{/s (ft}^2\text{/hr)}$$

If there is not a steady state, the heat flow through the construction will vary. There is always a reduction in the heat flow through a wall or roof when thermal capacity is taken into account. A building with large thermal capacity, that is high thermal inertia, such as one with thick masonry walls, requires more heat to increase its temperature than one with walls made of gypsum board and wood planking, for example, which has small thermal capacity, that is low thermal inertia.

Table 3.3   Thermal Transmittance (U-Value) of Building Elements

Element	U-Value (= 1/R Value)	
	$\dfrac{W}{m^2\,^\circ C}$	$\dfrac{btu}{hr\,ft^2\,^\circ F}$
Solid wall		
with 225mm (=9") brickwork wall and 12mm (=½") gypsum plaster	2.25	0.40
Cavity wall		
with 105mm (=4") outer skin of brickwork, 25mm (=1") cavity, 25mm (=1") board insulation, 100mm (=4") inner skin of lightweight concrete block and 12mm (=½") lightweight plaster	0.56	0.10
with 105mm (=4") outer skin of brickwork, 50mm (=2") cavity, 20mm (=¾") plywood on timber frame, 100mm (=4") mineral wool and 12mm (=½") gypsum plasterboard	0.30	0.052
Window		
with single glazing in metal frame	5.6	1.00
with double glazing in metal frame	3.2	0.56
with double glazing in wood frame	2.5	0.44
Flat roof		
with built-up roofing, 50mm (=2") insulation board, 150mm (=6") concrete slab and 12mm (+½") lightweight plaster	0.50	0.088
with 12mm (=½") screed, 50mm (=2") woodwool slabs on timber joists, ventilated cavity, 50mm (=2") insulation board 12mm (=½") foil-backed gypsum plasterboard	0.43	0.076

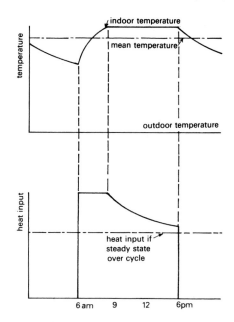

3.3 Heat input and temperature response over 24-hour cycle in winter months for building in daytime use (from ref. 1).

By the same token, however, the building with large heat capacity cools more slowly and this can help to prevent the occurrence of peak temperatures or troughs of low temperature inside the building (3.2); as noted previously, such evening out of the temperature in the building could help to prevent surface condensation, see section on condensation.

In design work it is a question of matching the thermal properties of the building fabric to the climate, to the speed of response of the heating or air conditioning system, to any ambient or internal heating or cooling which may be available for part of the day and to the pattern of use and zoning of activities in the building (3.3). With so many factors involved, the calculation of inside temperatures may be complex. However for a building in almost constant use it is, in general, desirable for the building fabric to have low thermal diffusivity, both to smooth out temperature variations and to reduce heat losses and gains. If the thermal diffusivity, which is a material property, is low and combined with thick walls or roof constructions then the walls or roofs are said to exhibit *thermal lag*. Buildings with thermal lag are desirable in climates with high daytime and low nighttime temperatures. However quick rises or falls in temperature may be desirable properties in buildings which are only used intermittently and need rapid heating up or cooling down and in these buildings, high diffusivity could be an advantage, even though this also gives rise to higher heating and cooling losses through the building fabric. A better composite indicator for buildings only heated or cooled intermittently is the *thermal absorption, v*, of the materials of the building fabric, given by:

$$v = \lambda.\rho.c \ W^2\,s/\,m^4\,^\circ C^2 \ (btu^2/\,hr\,ft^4\,^\circ F^2)$$

For a room heated intermittently from the inside, it is the thermal absorption of the inner layers that has most effect on changes in the air temperature; in the initial stages of heating, only the surfaces have any influence on the rate at which the room temperature rises. For a wall made of a single material heated from one side, with heat flow to the other side, the rate at which the surface temperature, T_w, rises can be estimated from the expression [1]:

$$T_w = \frac{q}{2}\sqrt{\frac{5t}{v}} \ °C \ (°F)$$

where t is the time in s;

v is the thermal absorption of the surface material in W^2 s/ m^4 $°C^2$ (btu^2/ hr ft^4 $°F^2$); and

q is the rate of heat input in W/m^2 (btu/ hr ft^2).

The surface temperature stops rising when the heat input is just sufficient to maintain a steady state. Surfaces with low thermal absorption, such as light insulating materials, give rapid changes in surface temperature and would therefore be preferred for buildings heated or cooled only intermittently, while surfaces with high thermal absorption, such as metals and, to a lesser extent, concrete, will give slow changes in surface temperature. The thicknesses of wall and roof constructions for buildings heated or cooled intermittently should be increased as much as possible. Note however that, as with acoustic insulation, there are diminishing returns as these thicknesses increase. Some buildings have large internal heat gains and may need to lose heat even in the winter months. Clearly for such buildings the thermal insulation and thickness of the wall or roof construction would need to be reduced as much as possible.

Ventilation

Rooms require a minimum turnover of the air in the room in order to remove carbon dioxide, cooking smells and so on and to introduce fresh air with oxygen. The turnover is usually expressed in air charges per hour depending on the type of room. The minimum turnover is about 0.1 to 2.0 air charges per hour. In many cases *natural ventilation* provides a sufficient number of air changes. Natural ventilation may also be used to lower the air temperatures and is especially effective at night when the outside air is cooler. In other cases exhaust fans may be used and, in more extreme cases, full mechanical ventilation will be necessary.

CLIMATE

Effects of Climate

To a much greater extent than the structural design, the strategy adopted to achieve comfort in buildings depends on the climate of the area and the microclimate of the particular site. Most of the habitable regions of the world could be divided into four climatic zones: cold, temperate, hot-humid and hot-arid. An approximate indication of the different amounts of winter heating necessary in any area over a year is given by the *degree days*. It is estimated by subtracting the mean daily outdoor temperature from a reference temperature, usually of 18°C (65°F), and then adding together the differences for each day of the year, when they are positive numbers (Table 3.4). At a temperature of 18°C (65°F) it is assumed that no heating is required. It is also possible to use a degree day method as an indication of the amounts of cooling required, using the same base temperature as for heating.

In *cold climates*, summers are cool and winter is cold or very cold. Heating equipment is essential for use during a large part of the year. The amount of heating required is about 3000 degree C days (5400 degree F days) or above. The cooling load could go down to about 260 degree C days (500 degree F days) or less. The design needs to concentrate on reducing heat losses by a substantial amount of insulation. Active or passive solar heating should be considered. Condensation can be a problem but good insulation, by keeping inside surface temperature high, would prevent condensation on the inner surface of the walls. Vapour barriers should be provided on the warm side of the insulation to prevent interstitial condensation within the wall or roof construction. Ventilation and infiltration should be minimised to save heat. If two vapour barriers are used, for example in roof constructions, then the space between the vapour barriers must be ventilated to prevent condensation. In *temperate climates*, summer is slightly too hot and winter much too cold. Heating equipment is essential for the winter months unless efficient capture of solar or other ambient energy is possible. Good insulation is economic in almost all cases. Shading of windows

Table 3.4 — Required Annual Heating in Degree Days

City Area	Type of Climate	Degree Days base=18°C (=65°F)	City Area	Type of Climate	Degree Days base=18°C (=65°F)
United States:			**Europe:**		
Honolulu	hot-humid	0	Bath	temperate	2625
Miami	hot-humid	100	Oxford	temperate	2800
Houston	hot-humid	750	Aberdeen	cold temperate	3900
Phoenix	hot-arid	980	Paris	temperate	2440
San Francisco	temperate	1660	Marseille	temperate	1300
Washington	hot and cold	2340	Rome	temperate	1310
New York	cold temperate	2900	Hamburg	cold temperate	3450
Chicago	cold	3680	Stockholm	cold	4530
Anchorage	cold	6020			
			Australasia:		
Canada:			Darwin	hot-humid	0
Winnipeg	cold	5930	Sydney	temperate	970
Resolution Island	very cold	8900	Wellington	temperate	1900

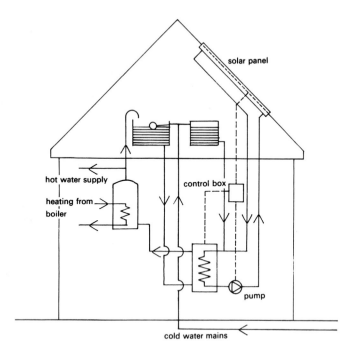

3.4 Solar panel used in domestic hot water system.

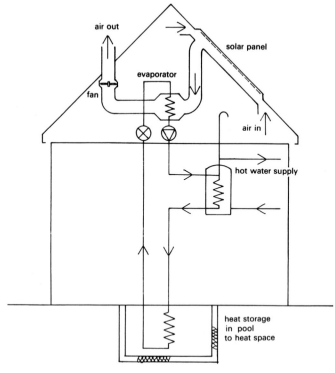

3.5 Heat pump used with solar panel to increase its efficiency; the condenser coils release heat in the hot-water tank and the heat storage pool.

to exclude summer sun but admit winter sun is advantageous. Ventilation and infiltration should be minimised. In humid areas, ventilation or air conditioning may be needed in the summer. In *hot-humid climates*, the weather in winter is cool rather than cold whereas in summer the relative humidity may go up to 90% and the temperature up to 37°C (98.6 °F), the temperature of the body. The cooling load in a year may amount to 2200 degree C days (4000 degree F days) or more. The design should concentrate on making comfortable conditions in the summer months by shading of windows and good ventilation or air conditioning. The difference between daytime and night time temperatures is smaller than in other climates so that in order to prevent excessive heat being stored during the day which would be released during the night, low thermal inertia is desirable. Almost no heating is required as measured in degree days. Air conditioning, when used, can make the interior more comfortable by reducing the humidity and

temperature but air movement is the cheapest way of providing reasonable comfort; a velocity no greater than and usually less than 0.5 m/s would be required. In *hot-arid climates*, the weather in winter may be slightly cool or cold and in summer it is dry and much too hot. The temperature often exceeds 37°C (98.6 °F), the temperature of the body. Shading of windows, roofs or walls from the sun is helpful and good insulation is necessary. Because nights in summer can be cool, the thermal inertia of the building should be high to allow it to soak up heat during the day which can be released at night. Ventilation is unhelpful but cooling by evaporation of water helps to reduce temperatures and increase the humidity to more comfortable levels. Passive solar designs may supplement the effects of high thermal inertia of the building fabric by exploiting the alternation of hot and cold

periods both in winter and summer. For example cool night air may be drawn through the building or over thermal stores, allowing this thermal mass to lose heat at night by convection and radiation and so help to keep down the interior daytime temperatures.

Solar Energy

Ambient energy is the energy available from the surroundings, that is from the tides, wind, plants and the sun and is currently exploited in buildings for daylighting, natural ventilation, space and water heating and power. Ambient energy is, in principle, a renewable source of energy. For buildings, the sun is the most important source of energy. Some way of extracting the energy must be found. An *active solar system* is one which uses a device to collect the sun's radiation in order to

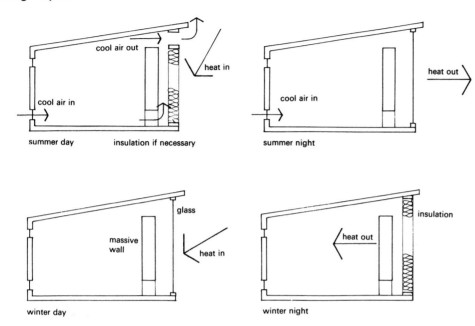

3.6 Diagram showing strategies for control of solar gain in summer and winter months using ventilation, insulation and trombe wall of large thermal capacity.

heat a fluid, often water. The heated fluid is most often used for hot water heating or in heating and air conditioning equipment (*3.4*). Energy from the sun, and other sources of heat energy, may be supplied to these systems at reasonably high temperatures by a heat pump; *heat pumps* collect heat from ambient air or water, waste heat from lighting or mechanical plant or available heat from any other source to provide a heat input to the evaporator of the heat pump (*3.10*). Heat rejected at the compressor of the heat pump is then available for space or water heating or any other purpose (*3.5*).

A *passive solar system* is usually one in which the building itself receives the solar radiation and in which there is no major input of energy from other sources such as the electricity supply. The basic idea of passive solar design for heating purposes is that, while heat from the sun is available during the day, it should be stored in materials of high thermal capacity, such as concrete or masonry walls and floors, so that the

heat may be released later in the day, or at night, when the solar heat is no longer available. More flexibility in use, and greater endurance time, before heating is needed, is obtained by increasing the size of the thermal store (*3.5*). However this can be costly and inconvenient. More heat can be collected by using a greenhouse, or glass enclosure on the side of the building facing the The effectiveness of such a design may be improved by insulating the heat storage materials at night so that less heat is lost (*3.6*). Passive cooling systems consist of heat storage materials which soak up heat during the day and release it during the night thus evening out the inside temperature. This system may also be improved by insulating the heat storage during the day, to minimise heat gain, and removing the insulation at night to maximise heat loss by radiating heat to the outside (*3.6*). These strategies need to be integrated into the building services design (*3.7*). In winter, in the northern hemisphere, windows on the south face of buildings will have the greatest

exposure to solar radiation, so that, as a general guide, it is best to elongate a building in the east-west direction with most windows facing south. For buildings in the southern hemisphere, the windows would face north. In summer, the heat gain on the south face (north face for buildings in the southern hemisphere) is greatly reduced by the high altitude of the sun, although the sun's rays would be able to penetrate to the back of rooms on the east and west faces at each end of the day when the sun is at a low altitude (*3.8* and *3.9*).

HEATING AND COOLING LOADS

Heating Loads

By assuming that the outside temperature and the inside temperatures of all the rooms in a building are known and remain constant, it is possible to calculate the heat loss from a room or from a whole building. The inside environmental temperature and the outside air temperature can be used for such calculations. In practice the outside design temperature is often based on standard figures for each particular location but must be carefully chosen to suit the premises on which any calculation is based. First the thermal resistance of the wall or roof construction must be estimated. Where there are air spaces in the construction, known values of thermal resistance can be used, to represent the loss of heat by radiation and convection. A cavity wall consisting of two leaves separated by an air gap has an overall thermal resistance, R, given by:

$$R = \frac{1}{\alpha_o} + \frac{t_1}{\lambda_1} + R_a + \frac{t_2}{\lambda_2} + \frac{1}{\alpha_i} \text{ m}^2 \text{ °C/W}$$
(hr ft² °F/btu)

where α_o and α_i are the surface conductances of the outside and inside surfaces in W/m² °C (btu/hr ft² °F);

λ_1 and λ_2 are the thermal conductivities of each leaf in W/m °C (btu in/ft² hr °F);

d_1 and d_2 are the thicknesses of each leaf in m (in); and

R_a is the thermal resistance of the air gap in m² °C/W (hr ft² °F/btu)

The total heat loss from a building, Q, is due to heat lost through the total surface area of the fabric and due to ventilation and infiltration of air from the outside:

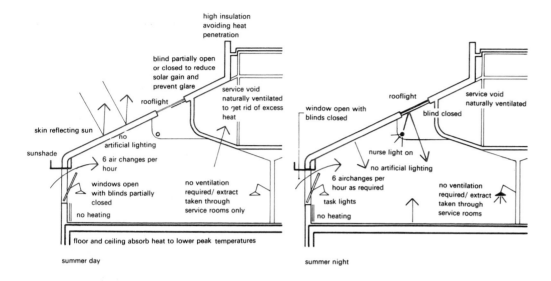

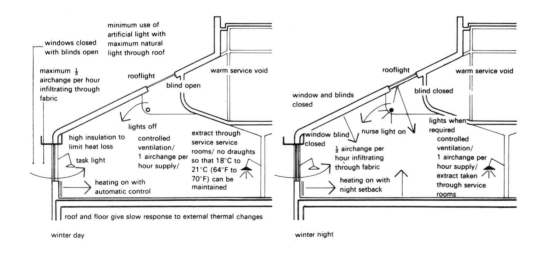

3.7 *Diagram showing strategies for energy conservation in an hospital (courtesy of Ahrends, Burton and Koralek, architects, Building Design Partnership, services engineers, and Gifford and Partners, structural engineers).*

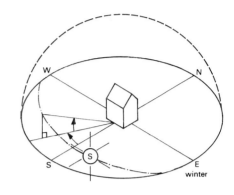

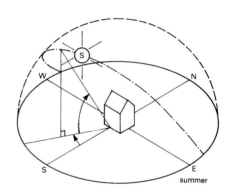

3.8 *Path of sun in northern hemisphere showing altitude and azimuth angles at winter and summer solstice (21st December and 21st June); at equinoxes (21st March and 21st September) the sun rises at 06.00 in the east and sets at 18.00 in the west everywhere on the earth's surface (see 3.9).*

$$Q = \left(\frac{\Delta T_1 . A_1}{R_1} + \frac{\Delta T_2 . A_2}{R_2} + .. \right)$$
$$+ c.\rho \left(\Delta T_1 . V_1 + \Delta T_2 . V_2 + .. \right)$$
$$= \left(\sum A.U.\Delta T + c.\rho \sum V.\Delta T \right) W \text{ (btu/hr)}$$

where ΔT is the design temperature difference between each room and the outside in °C (°F);
A is the exterior surface area of each room in m² (ft²);

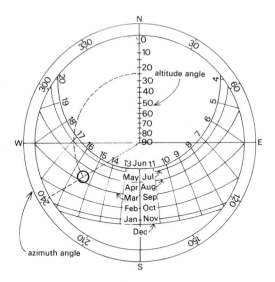

3.9 Sunpath diagram for a location of some given latitude in the northern hemisphere giving altitude and azimuth angles on twenty-first day of each month for any hour of daylight on the 24-hour clock; dotted line and arc gives 240° azimuth and 25° altitude at 15.30 true local time on 1st April at the given latitude.

R is the thermal resistance of the exterior construction of each room in $m^2°C/W$ (hr ft^2 °F/btu), see Table 3.3 ;

V is the volume of air in each room lost by ventilation and infiltration to the outside in m^3(ft^3); and

$c.\rho$ is the specific heat multiplied by the density of air $\approx$ 1,200 KJ/m^3 °C ($\approx$ 18 btu/ft^3 °F).

This kind of calculation can be sufficient for sizing heaters in rooms or estimating the total energy required for heating a building, taking due account of the fact that the heating plant will not necessarily be required to heat all the spaces to their full design loads simultaneously. In assessing the energy input some allowance must be made for the energy consumed by pumps or any form of energy not connected with losses through the building fabric or from ventilation.

Cooling Loads

The temperature in a building, and the heat absorbed by the building, can rise very rapidly if there is a sudden increase in radiation from the sun. The air temperture in the building and temperature of the building fabric will both undergo changes as this heat is absorbed. Temperatures in the building would normally take several hours to reach a steady temperature, even if the new heat load was to remain constant. However, in general, the heat load varies too. Steady state conditions do not obtain, therefore, and account must be taken, among other things, of the thermal inertia of the building fabric and the previous heat loads on the building. For design purposes it is often only necessary to consider the conditions in the perimeter zones, which are adjacent to the windows and liable to solar gain and any other rooms which are liable to become uncomfortable. Typical daily weather patterns are assumed for the purposes of a steady state calculation. The cooling load at any time depends on the normal transmission of heat through the whole building envelope due to the higher outside temperture as well as solar gain through the windows and heat introduced by people, ventilation, mechanical equipment and lighting, in the room or zone of the building which is under consideration. It is necessary to know what sunshading is provided and the thermal properties of the building fabric, especially its thermal admittance, thermal diffusivity and the reflectivity and emissibility of the surfaces. Calculations are often complex and best done by computer but some quick hand methods are available.

One method of estimating the swings in room temperature as a result of intermittent heating or cooling is based on the use of thermal admittance. The *thermal admittance* of a room is the change in heat output that is required in order to change the room temperature by one degree, the thermal admittance of the room being made up of the thermal admittances of all the individual elements of construction in the room. The thermal admittance, Y, is a property of internal surfaces, like the surface thermal absorption, v, to which it is closely related (Table 3.5). Thermal admittance takes account of the heat transmitted through the surface, as calculated by its U-value, and the amount of heat required to raise the temperature of the surface, so that for light constructions it is nearly equal to the U-value while for heavy construction the thermal admittance is consider-

ably greater than the U-value. If a steady state does not exist so that there is intermittent heating in a room, as is generally the case, a mean environmental temperature in the room, T_{ei}, may be estimated using the formula:

$$Q = (\textstyle\sum A.U + c.\rho.V)(T_{ei} - T_o) \text{ W (btu/hr)}$$

where Q is the mean heat input to the room over that period being considered in W (btu/hr);

A and U are the areas in m^2 (ft^2) and the transmittances in W/ m^2°C (btu/ hr ft^2 °F) of the individual external surfaces of the room, heat transfer across internal floors and walls being assumed to be small;

$c.\rho$ is the product of the specific heat and the density of the air in J/ m^3 °C (btu/ ft^3 °F);

V is the volume of air in the room changed in unit time by ventilation and infiltration to the outside in m^3/s (ft^3/hr);

T_{ei} is the mean environmental temperature in °C (°F); and

T_o is the design mean outside temperature in °C (°F).

The swing in the environmental temperature about the mean environmental temperature may then be calculated from the swings in the heat input to the room, ΔQ, about the mean heat input to the room, Q. The calculation substitutes values of admittance in place of the transmittance used in steady state or mean value calculations:

$$\Delta Q = (\textstyle\sum A.Y + c.\rho.V)\Delta T_{ei} \text{ W (btu/hr)}$$

where ΔQ is the swing in heat input from the mean at the time being considered in W (btu/hr);

A and Y are the areas in m^2 (ft^2) and the admittances in W/ m^2 °C (btu/ hr ft^2 °F) of all the surfaces of the room; and

ΔT_{ei} is the swing in the environmental temperature from the mean temperature at the time being considered.

The two expressions enable an estimate to be made of environmental temperatures either as a result of intermittent operation of a heating or cooling plant, in cold or hot weather respectively, or as a result of intermittent heating of rooms by casual heat gains, solar radiation and high outside temperatures in hot weather. In most cases the mean temperature would be calculated over a 24 hour period, which is assumed to have a repeating pattern of temperature changes and of heating or cooling output from plant (*3.3*). In hot weather, it is normally the peak environmental temperature

Table 3.5   Thermal Admittance of Building Elements

Element	Admittance (Y-value)	
	$\dfrac{W}{m^2\,°C}$	$\dfrac{btu}{hr\,ft^2\,°F}$
Solid wall		
with 105mm (=4″) brick and 16mm (=$\frac{5}{8}$″) gypsum plaster each side	4.1	0.72
with 225mm (=9″) brick and 16mm (=$\frac{5}{8}$″) gypsum plaster each side	4.4	0.77
with 75mm (=$\frac{1}{2}$″) lightweight concrete block with 16mm (=$\frac{5}{8}$″) gypsum plaster on each side	2.6	0.46
Cavity wall		
with 105mm (=4″) brickwork inner and outer skins with 50mm (=2″) cavity and 16mm (=$\frac{5}{8}$″) gypsum plaster on inside (heat applied from inside)	4.3	0.76
with two fibreboard sheets and cavity (internal partition)	0.3	0.05
Floors		
with concrete	6.0	1.06
with concrete and carpeting	3.0	1.03
with wood	2.0	0.35
with wood and carpeting	2.0	0.35
Ceilings		
with plastered concrete	6.0	1.06
with timber laths and plaster on wood	2.0	0.35
with 16mm (=$\frac{5}{8}$″) gypsum plasterboard on 10mm (=$\frac{3}{8}$″) wood with air space between	0.3	0.05

adapted from refs. 2 and 3

that needs to be assessed and this is calculated for that time of day at which the peak solar gain has most effect on the internal room temperature. If the peak environmental temperature is high then cooling may be required. Obtaining good estimates of the environmental temperature depends, in practice, on obtaining suitably accurate data for the casual heat gain, solar radiation and mean outside temperature. It is clear that, for example, for a room with large windows exposed to the sun, increasing the thermal insulation of the room construction against radiant and conducted heat but maintaining the admittance value of the internal surfaces, reduces the temperature swing; decreasing the admittance of the surfaces, for example by carpeting of concrete floors, but maintaining the thermal insulation value, increases the temperature swing.

THERMODYNAMICS

First Law of Thermodynamics

Energy may be transferred from one body to another and may be transformed from one form of energy, such as mechanical work, to another, such as heat. Thermodynamics is concerned with the study of energy and the processes and effects of the transfers and transformations of energy. Of particular interest is the relationship between heat and work and with the properties of systems. A system is defined as any collection of matter with known boundaries. It follows that the principles of thermodynamics are relevant to the operation of plant and the changes in state of matter connected with regulating the internal environment of buildings. The state of matter is to do with its form, whether solid, liquid or gas, and with other properties such as its temperature and pressure. All such properties are associated with different energy contents of the matter. The *first law of thermodynamics* states that, although energy can be transferred between matter and can be converted into different forms, it cannot be created or destroyed. As applied to a closed system, such as gas in a piston, the first law states that the increase in internal energy of the system, ΔU, if it changes state, is equal to the heat transfer to the system, ΔQ, minus the work done by the system, ΔW, that is:

$$\Delta Q = \Delta U + \Delta W \text{ joules (btu)}$$

A closed system is defined as a system which cannot exchange matter across its boundaries but can exchange energy which, generally, is in the form of heat and work. If no transfer of work occurs, changes in the internal energy of the system are exactly equal to the transfer of heat. As well as internal energy, another important property of a system is its *enthalpy, H*, defined as:

$$H = U + p.V \text{ joules (btu)}$$

where p is the pressure in N/m² (btu/ft³);

  V is the volume in m³ (ft³);

  U is the internal energy of the system in joules (btu).

If a closed system changes state at constant pressure then the change in enthalpy, ΔH, is given by:

$$\Delta H = \Delta U + p.\Delta V$$
$$= \Delta U + \Delta W$$
$$= \Delta Q \quad \text{joules (btu).}$$

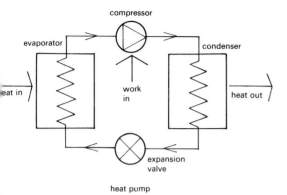

3.10 Diagram of action of a heat pump working on the compressive-refrigeration cycle like that shown in 3.29.

Hence in a closed system at constant pressure, for example a unit weight of air and water vapour going round an air-conditioning system, changes in enthalpy are equal to the changes in the heat transfer. Therefore enthalpy may be thought of as a measure of the heat content of the system, for example the heat energy contained in a unit weight of air and water. Note that the work done by a system at constant pressure is equal to that pressure times the increase in volume, ΔV. For a closed cyclic system, for example the whole apparatus of a heat pump, the initial and final states of the system are identical whatever the time interval, so that by the first law, the work done on the system, for example by the compressor of a heat pump, must equal the net transfer of heat from the system in the same time (*3.29*). A heat pump, of which one example is a refrigerator, exchanges heat with two reservoirs, one at the condenser and one at the evaporator (*3.10*). Changes to a system that occur without any energy crossing the boundaries of the system are said to be *adiabatic* changes. For example, the water in a contained mixture of air and water may evaporate causing a drop of temperature in the container but without any heat being transferred to or from the container. This change is adiabatic.

Second Law of Thermodynamics

The opposite of a heat pump is a heat engine which exchanges heat with two reservoirs and produces work as a result of this exchange (*3.11*). One statement of the *second law of thermodynamics* is that it is impossible to construct a heat engine, working in a cycle, such that it produces work but exchange heat with only one reservoir. For example, in a steam engine, the boiler, which is the first reservoir, applies heat to the water to make steam but some of this heat will be lost to the surroundings at the condenser, the second reservoir, in bringing the water vapour back to a liquid and is not available for producing useful work. If installed in a ship, the engine would not be able to power itself merely by exchanging heat with the sea, which constitutes a single reservoir. However, the reverse operation is possible. For example, the work done on a block pushing it over a surface can all be converted, by friction, to heat which is exchanged with one reservoir, the surface. This last process is therefore an irreversible one according to the second law. The concept of reversible and irreversible processes is basic to the second law. Reversible processes are ideal processes in which there are no sudden flows, movements or shocks, no friction effects and in which heat transfers take place

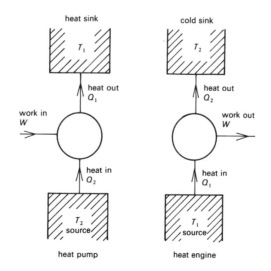

3.11 Diagrams showing transfers of work and heat for a heat pump and a heat engine.

across infinitely small temperature differences and work done by a piston, for example, is only done by infinitely small differences in pressure across the face of the piston. Actual processes can, at best, only approach the behaviour of reversible ones and must therefore be classified as irreversible. Good examples of irreversible processes are those involving friction, heat transfer, mixing of gases or the unrestrained expansion of a gas to a lower pressure. The notion of an *irreversible* process is closely tied up with a property of matter known as its *entropy*. Irreversible processes always increase the entropy of a system, while in a reversible process the entropy would remain constant. As all actual processes are irreversible there is always an overall increase in entropy during a process. If all the operations in a heat engine or a heat pump were reversible then the heat engine and heat pump would have their maximum possible efficiency; the theoretical efficiency of plant having reversible processes may be used as a base for comparison with the actual efficiencies of plant and other equipment.

In an isolated system, which is defined as one in which no matter and no energy cross its boundaries, the entropy also has a tendency to increase. This is because increases in entropy are associated with changes to a state where things are more random and unstructured than they were previously, associated with changes to a state of equilibrium and of higher probability. If a closed system is not in the most probable state, it is not in equilibrium and thus tends to move to a state such that it then becomes in equilibrium. For example an isolated system, such as a container with gas in it, may have more gas particles at one end than the other, but the system tends to move to the most probable state in which the gas particles are more evenly distributed and the gas pressure is uniform throughout. Similarly if the gas is hotter at one end, so that the gas particles move faster at that end, the effect of collisions between slow and fast particles is to cause an averaging out of velocities around a mean value so that the gas has a more uniform temperature at an equilibrium state. Both these changes are associated with increases in entropy.

One aspect of the second law, already noted, is that there is always a limit on the amount of heat that can be converted to work in any given conditions. Any system at a temperature above absolute zero (-273 °C) possesses energy but there is a certain maximum amount of work that can be done by the energy in any system known as the *available energy*. The remainder of the energy in the system is known as the unavailable energy. A corollary of the second law is that a system cannot do work as a result of its temperature, unless this temperature is above the temperature of the surroundings. Therefore, of the heat energy that is transferred to a heat engine, for example, the available energy of the heat transferred is that part of it connected with the higher temperature the fluid of the heat engine has over the surrounding temperature. The total available energy of a closed system, for example that consisting of a unit weight of hot gas, can be defined as the maximum possible work that the system can deliver as it changes from its initial state to a state that is similar to that of its surroundings; for example, in its final state, the gas would be at the same temperature and pressure as the surroundings. To make use of all the available energy, for example the heat energy of a gas, all processes involved in producing work would have to be reversible ones. The importance of the concept of available energy lies in the standard it provides for the efficient use of energy for any given temperature of the surroundings. The classification of heat sources as 'high grade' or 'low grade', can be given meaning in terms of the larger proportions of available energy in the former than in the latter. For example water just above the outside air temperature can be said to be a low grade heat source because it has only a small proportion of available energy in these conditions, whatever its actual size or energy content.

All actual thermodynamic processes are irreversible so that heat transfer, or any other irreversible process, always involves a loss of available energy; however, by the first law, there can be no overall loss of energy, the loss of available energy being balanced by an increase in unavailable energy. An increase of unavailable energy in any system means there is an increased proportion of the energy in that system that is not able to produce work. An increase in unavailable energy at any particular temperature, as it is brought about by irreversible processes, always

causes a proportional increase in entropy. All real processes, being irreversible, cause increases in unavailable energy, as well as increases in entropy. Worldwide, therefore, there is a general overall increase in entropy and a continual transformation of available energy, energy in a form that is concentrated so that it can produce work, to unavailable energy that cannot.

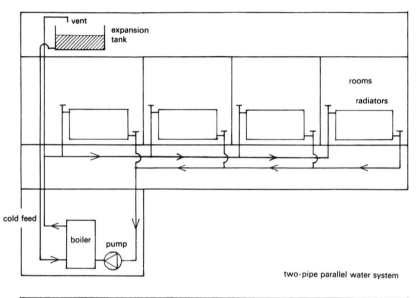

two-pipe parallel water system

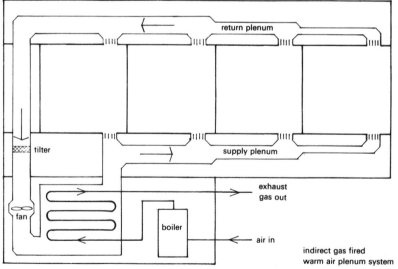

indirect gas fired
warm air plenum system

3.12 Schematic drawing of hot-water and warm-air heating systems for buildings.

AIR CONDITIONING

Heating and Cooling

By definition, air conditioning equipment is used to provide both heating and cooling in buildings. However in many cases only simple heating of the room spaces is required and cooling equipment is unecessary. There are two ways of *heating* rooms: either heating units can be installed in each room, as required, or heat may be supplied from one large central boiler plant. If central heating is used, then the heat from the boiler must be transferred to the rooms concerned, either by warming and then pumping air through ducts to each room or by heating water which is then pumped through pipes to radiator units in each room (*3.12*). The water pipes may be relatively small in diameter, compared to the dimensions of air ducts; water has a higher specific heat than air and therefore can transfer the same heat energy with less volume. A disadvantage of water systems is that they require radiator units in order to release the heat effectively. Other methods of heating room spaces consist of warming the room surfaces, for example by heating the floors with electric cables, or or providing high radiant heat sources, for example gas fires.

Air conditioning is necessary when cooling cannot be effected by natural ventilation or by passive means. The principle of air conditioning is as follows: conditioned air is sent from a plant room, where the air handling unit is situated, via a supply duct and in most cases is returned to it by a return duct (*3.13*). In an all-air system, all heating and cooling is provided by the air; in an air-water system, hot or chilled water is supplied to room units as well as conditioned air in the supply ducts (*3.14*). Air conditioning implies the ability to control not only air temperture but also air humidity, air movement and, to some extent, the cleanliness of the air too. Some types of air conditioning allow these items to be controlled by the users in each room or zone of the building.

In some climates no mechanical plant for heating or cooling may be needed, while in other climates it may only be necessary to provide heating plant for use during the winter. Natural ventilation, or mechanical ventilation of the air with electric fans, may be helpful in either of these cases. In large buildings, buildings with no

windows or no openable windows, buildings where large amounts of heat or foul air are generated or buildings where special conditions of humidity or cleanliness are required, air conditioning will generally be necessary whatever the climate. Large buildings tend to favour the use of air conditioning because of the difficulty of altering environmental conditions in rooms or zones, which have no outside walls, by natural means. There is also a scale effect. As buildings become larger their surface area reduces in proportion to their volume so that it becomes more difficult to dissipate internal heat gains through the building fabric during summer, as well as easier to heat, during winter. In harsh climates, that is where there are extremes of heat or

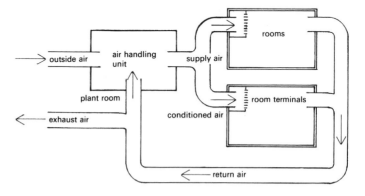

3.13   Schematic drawing of the action of an all-air air-conditioning system.

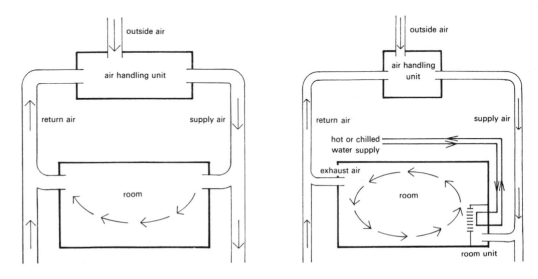

3.14 Air conditioning using all-air system, left, and air-water system with secondary air circulated by a room unit, right.

humidity, air conditioning may need to be provided for most types and sizes of building.

The most important of the controls provided by air conditioning is that of temperature, the humidity being allowed to vary over a much larger range. In an all-air system the room temperature and humidity is controlled by the amount and temperature of the conditioned air supplied to each room and this replaces the air extracted from the room. In a typical air-conditioning system with central station plant, the extracted air is returned to the plantroom via the return air duct system. At the air handling unit, the return air is mixed with air from the outside in a mixing chamber and passed through filters, the amount of air coming from outside being controlled by dampers. In winter the air is heated by heating coils, sometimes supplemented by preheat coils, which are linked to a boiler; when on heating cycle, the cooling coils are switched off and the air temperature is controlled by the proportions of outside and return air. In summer the air passes straight from the filters to a cooling coil, which cools and dehumidifies the air. From the heating or cooling coil the conditioned air is pumped by a fan through the supply air duct system (3.15). Room terminals, which may contain air dampers to control the flow of air, or reheat and cooling coils, to alter the air temperatures, give a degree of individual control of the conditions in each room.

In winter, it is sometimes necessary to preheat the outside air, or the mixture of outside and return air, to prevent condensing and freezing on air filters and freezing in chilled water cooling coils. Air cooling is not required in winter so that the cooling coils can be used for heat recovery: in this, warm water is passed through the coils, which cools the water but heats the air passing over it. If the air is too dry, a steam injection humidifier can be used to increase humidity. In summer, the coil surface temperature operates at a set dew point temperature, which is designed to be sufficiently low to allow moisture to be condensed out of the air (3.26). If, as a result, the air temperature is too low a reheat coil must be used either in the air handling unit itself or in the room terminals (3.28). A method using less energy which however does not give such good control of humidity, is to pass part of the air over a very cold coil, the rest bypassing the coil, the resulting mixture having a

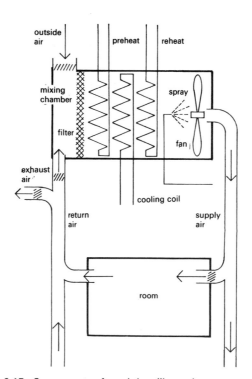

3.15 Components of an air handling unit.

sufficiently high temperature without the use of reheat. Proper control of the dampers in the mixing chamber is important. In winter, the reuse of a very large part of the return air can save energy. In summer, an 'economizer cycle' will allow as much as 100% of outside air to be used for cooling if it is found to be cooler or drier than the return air. In this case the air damper system rejects all return air to the outside. Note that foul air from kitchens or similar work areas is usually exhausted direct to the outside without using the return air duct system.

In a building that requires air conditioning there will be different heating and cooling loads in different rooms and, sometimes, different loads between one part of a room and another. A building is therefore split into *zones* where the requirements for heating and cooling are similar. In a simple building or a large room, there may only

be an interior zone and one or more perimeter zones (3.16). The perimeter zones may be subject to rapid heating by solar radiation, in summer, but may be uncomfortable in winter because of cold downdraughts and low radiant temperatures on the glass windows; the perimeter zone is usually considered to extend inwards from the windows a distance of 4 to 5 metres (12 to 15 feet). By contrast, the temperature in the interior zone will fluctuate much less. In large buildings there will be many different zones, each space in the building being allocated to a particular zone depending on the times when it is occupied, the purpose of the space, the equipment installed in it, its orientation to the sun and so on.

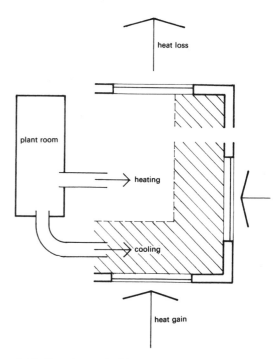

3.16 Part plan on building having an interior and perimeter zones with heating and cooling required simultaneously, in mid-season, as shown; in other zoned buildings, in winter, cooling may be required in the interior zones and heating in the perimeter zones; recovery and transfer of heat from hot to cold zones may be economic.

All-air Systems

In an all-air system, the treated air from the main plant is supplied at a higher temperature in winter and a cooler temperature in summer, than the design temperature of the zone. To alter the air temperature in a zone either more air from the plant should be supplied or its temperature should be increased. In a *constant air volume system* (CAV), the temperature of the air supplied must be altered. In a *variable air volume system* (VAV), it is the volume of air that is increased or decreased. *Singlezone CAV conditioners* supply conditioned air at the required temperature and humidity to one zone, which may consist of several rooms but which in total requires the complete output of the air conditioning plant (*3.17*). For smaller zones, *multizone CAV conditioners* can serve several

zones; hot and cold air is supplied separately by a hot deck and a cold deck in the air handling unit (*3.18*). The supply duct for each zone is connected to the hot and cold decks and takes a mixture of hot and cold air, the proportion being controlled by dampers depending on the requirements of each zone. The multizone air conditioner can supply up to about twelve different zones. The control of humidity is imperfect. For economy the hot air supplied should be no hotter than the conditioned air required by any one of the zones and the cold air no cooler than the conditioned air required by any zone. In both the singlezone and multizone CAV systems, further control of conditions within each zone may be provided by room terminals containing reheat or cooling coils (*3.18*). It is

inefficient for a multizone conditioner to have the required air temperatures in the hot and cold deck determined by two very small areas one of which requires very hot conditions and one of which requires very cool conditions; it is in such circumstances that reheat or cooling coils in room terminals are particularly worthwhile. An alternative to the multizone air conditioner, where the areas in each zone are large, is to use several different air handling units, one for each zone, supplied by the same central plant (*3.19*). A *dual duct CAV system* is similar to the multizone air conditioner; two ducts containing hot and cold conditioned air, supply the whole building and are only mixed in mixing boxes in the room terminals (*3.20*). The hot and cold air is usually supplied at medium or high velocity in order to keep the size of

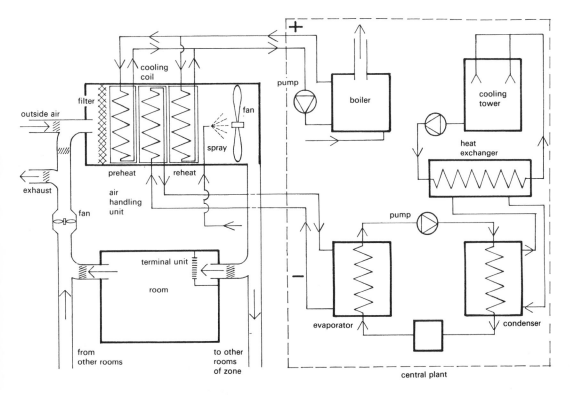

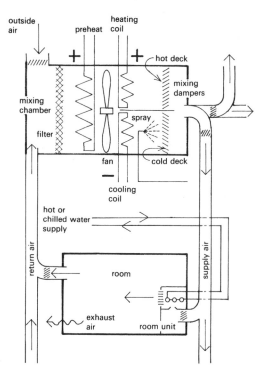

3.17 *Single zone constant air volume (CAV) air-conditioning system.*

3.18 *Air conditioning using multizone air handling unit and room terminal units.*

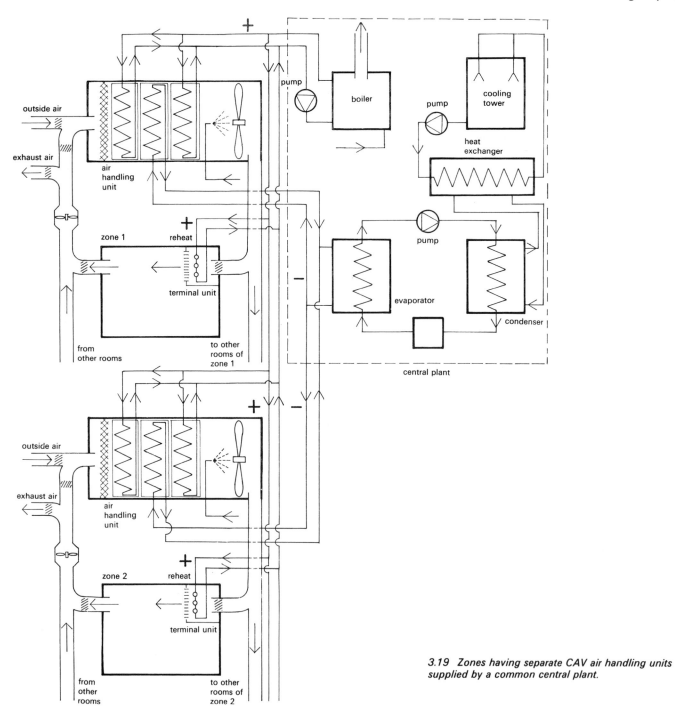

3.19 Zones having separate CAV air handling units supplied by a common central plant.

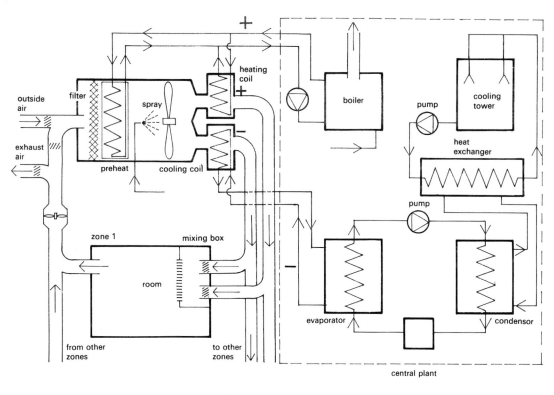

3.20 Dual duct CAV system.

ducts to a minimum. A dual duct system, although it requires a large number of ducts, would be able to heat one room in a building and to cool another in a different part of the building. The system is usually designed so that the volume of air passing through each mixing box is constant whatever the proportions of hot and cold air, so that the air supply outlets in each room, the registers, can be matched for known air speeds. It is clear, however, that in all cases where hot and cold air is mixed, there is an overall increase in entropy, a loss of available energy and a consequent waste of the

energy that has been used to provide the separate hot and cold air supply. The *variable air volume system* (VAV), does not waste energy in this way and has much simpler ductwork (*3.21*). There is only one supply duct; this can be made sufficiently large so that the air velocity is low and only moderate inputs of energy are required to drive the fans. It is, in principle, a cruder and more inflexible system than the dual-duct system, both because the 'throw' distance of the air from the registers is altered by the volume of air supplied and because of the effect this change of air volume has on the

supply of conditioned air at other registers. However methods are available to alleviate this problem including the use of fan-powered mixing boxes, in which conditioned air from the supply duct is mixed with room air in each room terminal unit, and the use of by-pass room terminal units, in which the proportion of the supply air passing through the register is varied by by-passing some of it. Generally the VAV system does not need to supply as much air as a CAV system because of the way it can more easily exploit the casual and solar heat gains. Even smaller quantities of air are

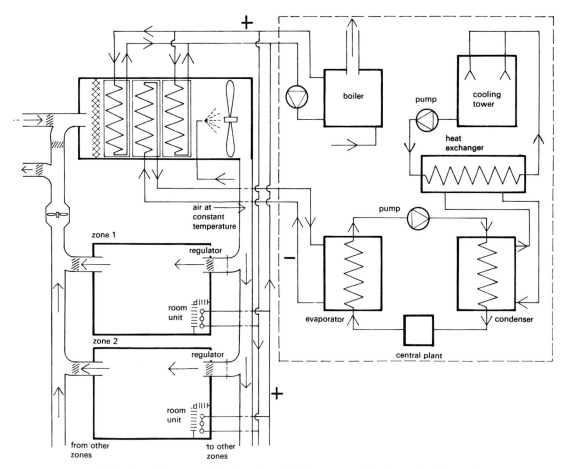

3.21 Zones having variable air volume (VAV) system with perimeter heating units.

supplied at part load, providing further savings relative to a CAV system. A basic VAV system cannot provide heating and cooling simultaneously but, as with CAV systems, reheat and cooling coils can be provided in the room terminal units and heating or cooling units placed around the perimeter, as necessary (*3.21*).

Air-water Systems

Air-water systems supply hot or chilled water to each zone from the main plant as well as air. In general the air-handling unit supplies as much conditioned fresh air, the *primary air*, as is necessary for proper ventilation or other purposes. The hot or chilled water is supplied to induction units, or fan-coil units, which then heat or cool the adjacent air and force circulation of this air (*3.14*). The recirculated air is known as the *secondary air*. Air-water systems are often used in the perimeter zones of buildings, the induction or fan-coil units being placed below or beside the windows, with an all-air system being used in the central zones (*3.16*). The main advantage of the air-water system is that it only needs to supply about a quarter of the conditioned air that would be needed in the all-air system, so that air ducts can be smaller; the hot and chilled water supply pipes only occupy small amounts of space. Induction or fan-coil units fitted with dampers are more economic than those without and give better individual control (*3.22*).

Many variations are possible on the basic all-air and air-water systems previously described. Air-water systems may work with two pipes, one supply and one return, connected to each fan-coil or induction unit, or four pipes with two supply

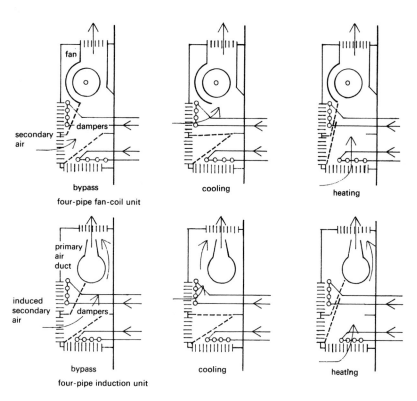

3.22 Four-pipe fan-coil and induction terminal units with dampers in bypass, cooling or heating operation.

and two return pipes. The *two pipe system* can only supply either hot or chilled water to each unit an any one time (*3.18*), while the *four pipe system* can supply hot and chilled water to heating and cooling coils in each unit simultaneously (*3.23*). Sometimes the two pipe system uses chilled water at the units to provide all the cooling with primary air to provide heating. It is possible to effect a changeover whereby the two-pipe system carries hot water in winter. Four pipe systems are inherently more flexible in use, allowing control of the flow rate of hot and chilled water to the heating and cooling coils and further control of the temperature of the air drawn through the units by use of the dampers to direct air over the heating or cooling coil or to by-pass both (*3.22*). The primary air is designed to supply sufficient ventilation to the rooms. Four pipe fan coil units have the

advantage over four pipe induction systems in that they can be turned off when necessary; also the primary air does not need to be pressurised to the same extent as that in the induction system. Apart from systems using air handling units positioned in plantrooms or on the roofs of buildings, it is also possible to use *unit air conditioning* in which the air handling unit is incorporated into terminal units in each room. A popular system with many energy-conserving features is the *reverse cycle unitary system* which uses water at a constant temperature of about 26°C (80°F) supplied from a central plant to each unit. In winter the unit acts as a heat pump rejecting heat into the room while in summer the heat pump cycle is reversed, heat being rejected to the constant temperature water supply and cooled air being drawn into the room (*3.24*).

Ducts

The depth and cross-sectional area of the supply and return air ducts are important for general planning and for sizing of the fan motors. The required cross-sectional area of a duct, *A*, is given by:

$$A = \frac{Q}{V} \text{ m}^2 \text{ (ft}^2\text{)}$$

where Q is the rate of air flow in m³/s (ft³/s); and

V is the velocity in m/s (ft/s).

In general the main air ducts are the most difficult to incorporate into the building structure. Concrete flat slab floors are often used to limit the depth of the floor structures and provide more headroom for services. If beams are necessary then holes may be made through the beams for the main ducts. Structurally the holes are best if circular and

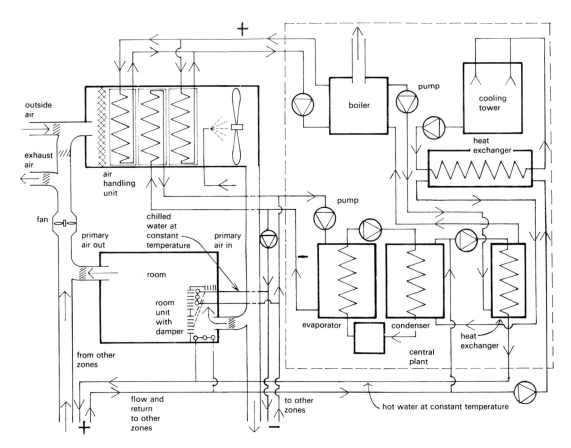

outside
air

exhaust
air

fan

air
handling
unit

primary
air out

chilled
water at
constant
temperature

primary
air in

room

room
unit
with
damper

from other
zones

flow and
return
to other
zones

to other
zones

boiler

pump

cooling
tower

heat
exchanger

pump

evaporator

condenser

central
plant

heat
exchanger

hot water at constant temperature

3.23   Four-pipe air-water system with fan-coil or induction room terminal units; the central plant uses a heat recovery system.

placed at quarter span points where the bending moment is less significant. Castellated steel beams or trusses usually have large enough openings for ducts to pass through them.

PLANT OPERATION

Room Sensible Heat Ratio

For spaces which require air conditioning, in general, there should be a check on the air movement and the mean radiant temperature of the room surfaces but, as noted previously, the

main control provided by the air-conditioning system is on the temperature and relative humidity of the air. The air conditioning plant influences the air temperature and humidity of the supply air by adding or removing heat and moisture. The *enthalpy* of a mixture of air and water vapour at a more or less constant pressure is a measure of the total heat contained in it, both in the form of *sensible heat,* which is the energy required to raise the temperature of the mixture from freezing point, and the *latent heat,* which is the energy required to change the water vapour in it from a liquid state to a vapour state. In summer when room air needs to

be cooled, the sensible cooling load on the equipment is said to be that which lowers the temperature and the latent cooling load that which dehumidifies the air. The cooling loads come from internal heat gains due to people, lights and equipment, infiltration of outside air and external gains through the building skin due to solar radiation and transmission through the building fabric. The sensible heat gain from lights and electric equipment can be taken equal to the electrical power input. Electrical equipment normally gives no latent heat gain; however gas-fired equipment will cause a latent heat gain. Each

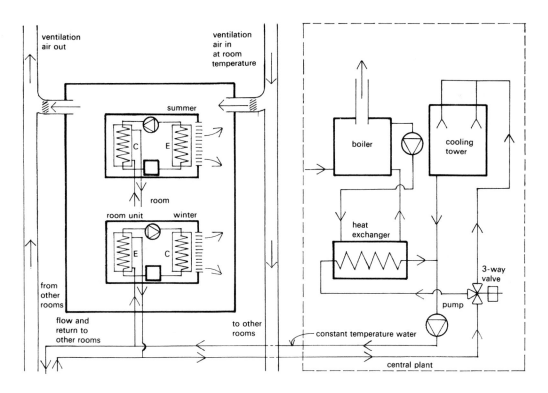

3.24 Reverse cycle system showing summer and winter operation.

person causes a sensible heat gain of about 130 watts (450 btu/hr) and latent heat gain of about the same amount due to perspiration. Infiltration of outside air also causes sensible and latent heat gains. In summer, the air-handling units must supply sensible and latent cooling for the total calculated ambient gains. In winter the building is more likely to require sensible and latent heating, that is the air would be heated and humidified (*3.26*). The ratio of the sensible heat gain to the total sensible and latent heat gain in each room or zone is known as the *room sensible heat ratio* (RSHR).

Psychrometric Chart

The various stages of the air conditioning process can be shown on a *psychrometric chart*. The assumed temperature and humidity ranges, to ensure conditions of comfort, can be plotted on this psychrometric chart (*3.25*). The chart plots the vapour pressure or the *humidity ratio* of the air, which is the amount of water vapour by weight per unit weight of dry air, against the dry bulb temperature. If these two quantities are known then the relative humidity and enthalpy of the air in question can be found. The psychrometric chart is

drawn for air and water vapour which are at standard atmospheric pressure. At other pressures the relative humidity and enthalpy of the air would be different for the same water vapour content and dry bulb temperature. The psychrometric chart is in effect a plot of latent heat against sensible heat so that air which changes state, such that it moves along any straight line drawn on the chart, will have changes in enthalpy with the same proportion of latent to sensible heat. The psychrometric chart has lines plotted on it, showing the wet bulb temperatures, so that the condition of air can be established directly by wet

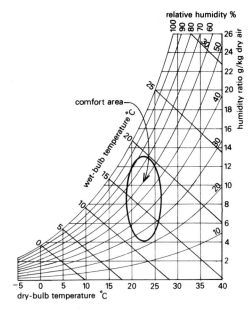

3.25 *Psychrometric chart showing approximate comfort conditions for sedentary office workers.*

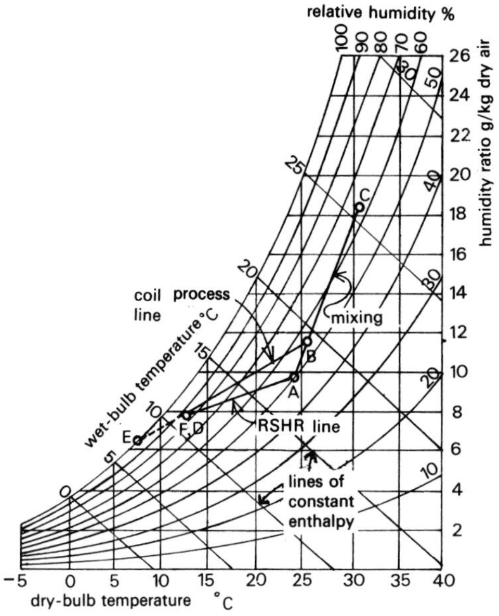

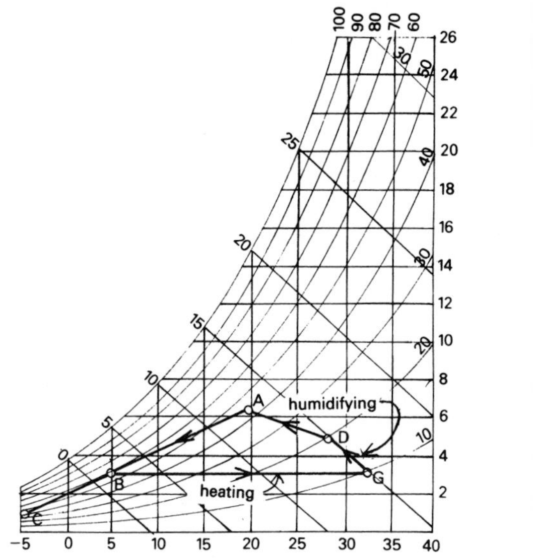

cooling cycle

heating and humidifying cycle

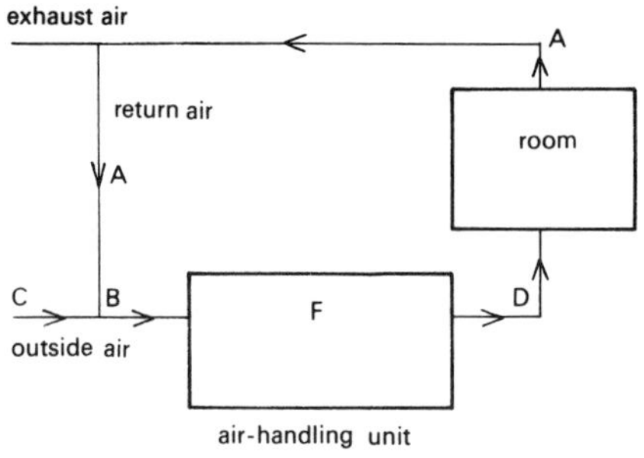

air-handling unit

3.27 *Cooling and heating and humidifying processes for typical installation as shown on psychrometric chart.*

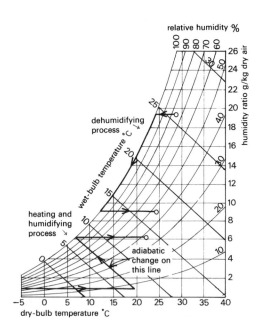

3.26 *Humidifying and dehumidifying processes with sensible heating or cooling to bring air to room temperatures.*

and dry bulb temperature readings. The wet bulb temperature lines are also lines of constant enthalpy and air moving along any of these lines undergoes only an adiabatic change of state (*3.26*), see section on condensation. However the values of enthalpy given are for saturated air and need to be corrected for the condition of the air as it actually is. The correction is very small and given by curved lines on some charts.

The cooling provided in summer by the air conditioning process is represented on the psychrometric chart as follows (*3.27*). The required indoor air temperature and relative humidity at the extract register are known (A). The RSHR is also known so that a straight line can be drawn on the chart representing the change in the condition of the air in the room as it leaves the fan of the air-handling unit (D) to the point at which it is extracted from the room. This is known as the *RSHR line*. The closer point D is to point A, the smaller the difference in temperature between the air supplied and the air extracted from the room, and the more conditioned air that needs to be supplied to maintain the desired conditions. The air extracted from the room is mixed with a known proportion of outside air, at the assumed outside conditions (C), so that the condition of the air as it leaves the mixing box (B) can be established. A line must now be drawn from point B representing the change effected by the cooling coil. This is known as the *coil process line*. The coil process line, if extended, should be able to intersect the saturation curve (E), indicating that part of the air, at least, can be cooled to its dew point and that proper dehumidification of the air is possible. All the full lines drawn represent the average condition of the air. The average condition of the air as it leaves the cooling coil is represented by point F. The air passing very close to the coils can be considered to be as cold as the cooling coil itself and it is air in this condition that is represented by point E on the chart. This point is known as the *apparatus dew point*. The actual drop in temperature of the air from point B to point F divided by the maximum possible drop in temperature if the cooling coil were 100% efficient (B to E) is known as the *coil factor* and gives a measure of the efficiency of the cooling coil. In some cases the air leaving the cooling coil is too cold and reheating by a coil is necessary (*3.28*); in the other cases points D and F coincide (*3.27*). The use of reheat is wasteful of energy but is sometimes necessary. It represents the extra refrigeration needed in order to dehumidify air with a high moisture content.

The proportion of sensible to latent cooling provided by the plant air conditioner is determined by the surface temperature of the cooling coil. The cooler the coil, the greater the proportion of latent cooling, or condensation, which is provided. A cooler coil also means that less air needs to be

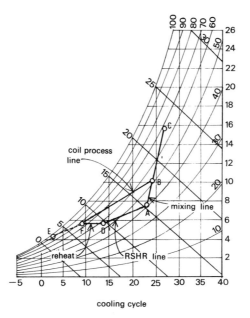

coil process line

mixing line

reheat

RSHR line

cooling cycle

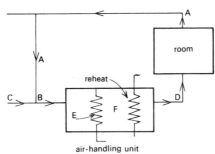

room

reheat

air-handling unit

3.28 Air-conditioning cycle with reheat shown on a psychrometric chart.

circulated for the same cooling effect. In practice the amount of cooling supplied by the air conditioner plant does not exactly match the sensible and latent cooling loads on it so that there is a 'drift' from the specified room conditions until a balance is reached between the actual room conditions and the capacity of the air conditioner plant to provide sensible and latent cooling. For example if the relative humidity of the air in the room can be allowed to rise above that specified

then the plant does not need to provide so much latent cooling. At the same time the latent cooling capacity of the plant rises the more humid the air is. When the latent cooling capacity matches the latent cooling load a balance is established at some new value of the relative humidity in the room, albeit that this is higher than that originally specified. Similarly if the latent cooling capacity of the plant is reduced, because chilled water is supplied at a higher temperature than previously, a new balance point will be established, also giving higher relative humidity in the room.

Heating Plant

Central plant for heating air or for providing hot water and steam is usually powered by oil, gas or coal or, sometimes, by electricity. Local heaters , for each zone, are mostly powered by electricity or gas. Central plant for cooling air or for providing chilled water to a local air handling unit is based on using either the *mechanical refrigeration cycle* (*3.29*) or, sometimes, the *absorption-refrigeration cycle* (*3.30*). The former is usually powered by

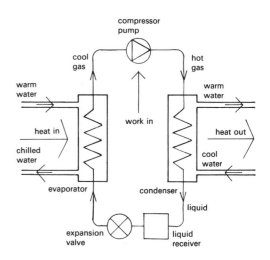

compressor pump

cool gas

hot gas

warm water

warm water

work in

heat in

heat out

chilled water

cool water

evaporator

condenser

liquid

expansion valve

liquid receiver

Compressive-refrigeration cycle

3.29 Compressive-refrigeration cycle; cooling at the evaporator is effected by a pressure drop of the refrigerant at the expansion valve causing it to take on latent heat from the surroundings.

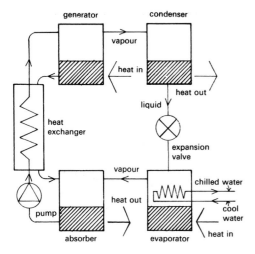

3.30 Absorption-refrigeration cycle; cooling takes place at the evaporator, after passing through the expansion valve, the cold refrigerant vapour being absorbed by a solution in the absorber; the refrigerant vapour is recondensed in the condenser; the cycle is driven by the heat supplied at the generator which separates the absorbed refrigerant as a vapour from the absorber solution which returns via a heat exchanger to the absorber.

electricity, to drive the compressor, while the later usually uses steam from a boiler unit as a way of increasing the strength of the salt solution. Local air conditioners for cooling air generally use the mechanical refrigeration cycle with electric power. *Heat pumps* are similar in principle to local air coolers and use the same mechanical refrigeration cycle. In this case it is the rejected heat from the condenser that is used to heat the air in a room. In suitable climates, heat pumps may be used to heat and then cool the building by reversing the direction of flow of the refrigerator (*3.24*).

The main advantage of a heat pump is that the output of energy, in the form of heat, is greater than the input of energy, usually in the form of electricity, which is needed to drive it. The ratio of output to input is known as the *coefficient of performance*, (COP), for heating:

$$COP = \frac{\text{actual heat output}}{\text{work input}} = \frac{Q_1}{W}$$

where Q_1 and Q_2 are the heat rejected at the compressor and the heat absorbed at the evaporator respectively in joules (btu); and W is the work input at the compressor which, by the first law of thermodynamics, is equal to $Q_1 - Q_2$ joules (btu)

For a heat pump in which all processes are reversible (*3.11*) the coefficient of performance, COP_r, is given by:

$$COP_r = \frac{Q_1}{W} = \frac{Q_1}{Q_1 - Q_2} = \frac{T_1}{T_1 - T_2}$$

where T_1 and T_2 are the temperatures at the condenser and evaporator respectively in °K (= °C + 273) or °R (= °F + 460).

The formula shows that heat pumps are increasingly inefficient at providing heat as the temperature at the evaporator drops and as the difference between the output temperature, T_1, at the condenser, and the input temperature, T_2, at the evaporator, increases. The efficiency may be able to be increased by exploiting solar radiation (*3.5*). Typical values of COP vary from two to three. The heat pump makes good use of the heat supplied to it but the decision to install a heat pump will depend on the operating conditions and offsetting capital and maintenance costs. In cold weather, because the heat pump works so inefficiently, supplementary heating provided by electricity or fossil funds is usually necessary. Solar energy may be used for pre-heating water but, at present, it is unable to provide water at sufficiently high temperatures for direct use in hot water heating systems or in place of the steam in air conditioning equipment using the absorption-refrigeration cycle.

WALLS AND ROOFS

Function of the Enclosure

The enclosure of a building is taken to include the walls and the roof of the building. The enclosure has several functions: it must moderate the effects of the outside temperatures so as to maintain a reasonably even inside temperature throughout the year (*3.2*); it must be made so as to reduce as far as possible the energy required to heat or cool the building, largely by providing high thermal

insulation but also by exploiting or excluding solar radiation, as necessary. It must admit sufficient daylight; it must prevent rain or dampness penetrating to the ceiling or the inner surface of the wall or to any insulation that could degrade in damp conditions. In cold climates, it must be made as airtight as possible to prevent draughts or loss of heat by air infiltration, although some 'leakage' can be allowed. Ventilation either natural or mechanical, must be allowed so as to exhaust polluted air and to provide the air movement necessary for comfortable conditions. In addition, it must prevent interstitial condensation in the roof or wall or condensation on any interior surfaces (*3.55*), see below. The enclosure must also reduce the penetration of noise, to a degree depending on circumstances. It should have as high a thermal capacity as possible in order to reduce temperature movements of the enclosure and thus the need for joints to accommodate it, assuming this to be compatible with minimising the energy requirements of the building. Other functional requirements of the building enclosure include good access, security and appropriate cost, stiffness and strength, dimensional stability, durability, ease of erection and ease of maintenance. In general the conditions of exposure are more severe for the roof than for the walls of a building so that, in general, different methods of enclosure are needed for these two elements of construction.

Damp Penetration

Damp may be excluded from the inside of buildings by three principal methods: the use of a thin layer of impermeable material, such as glass, plastic or metal sheeting; the use of a layer of material of low permeability to water, such as brick or concrete, of sufficient thickness to provide resistance to rain penetration; the use of cavity wall construction, either with permeable or impermeable materials, in which water or dampness, which penetrates through the outer leaf of the wall at joints or because of the porous and permeable nature of the material, is drained or otherwise dispersed from the cavity and thus cannot reach the inner leaf of the wall. If possible, the wall materials on the outside surface should provide good resistance to rain penetration while still allowing water vapour from within the wall construction to be dispersed to the outside (*3.55*). Cavity wall construction can be seen as a reliable way, in temperate climates, to prevent penetration of rain and dampness while allowing water vapour to escape.

Some permeable materials like masonry or concrete may benefit from water-repellent coatings, such as paints or renders, on their external faces. Porous materials, including masonry and concrete, are made up granules with continuous voids between them, providing a path for water to be drawn through the voids. If they are small enough, water is drawn through by capillary suction, that is by surface tension. Assuming the material is permeable then water will eventually transfer from one face of the wall which is kept wet to the opposite one which, initially, is dry. In practice as the external face of a wall is not continuously wet, water can evaporate through one or both faces as a vapour and thus prevent water as a liquid reaching the inner face of the wall. The wall should have a thickness, depending on the climate, such that it has sufficient capacity to hold the water absorbed, before warm, dry external air allows evaporation of this water. Note that materials with a large number of voids, which could therefore be described as porous, may nevertheless have low permeability if the voids are not continuously linked. And materials which have voids of a very large size, even if continuously linked, may have low permeability because capillary suction is largely absent. No-fines concrete, that is concrete made from cement and large, regular aggregate only, is one example of such a material, the voids in this case being sufficiently large to function as cavities rather than as pores. By contrast masonry walls are prone to develop cracks between the masonry units and these can provide an easy path for water to the inner face, because of the effect of capillary action. One way to prevent such capillary action is the use of an internal groove or break. The passage of damp must also be prevented through the basement and ground floor of the building, as well as through the walls. If the ground is likely to remain damp for long periods, this can be done by providing waterproof layers to surround the basement construction or, if there is no basement, by damp-proof membranes at ground floor level with damp-proof layers to prevent the passage of

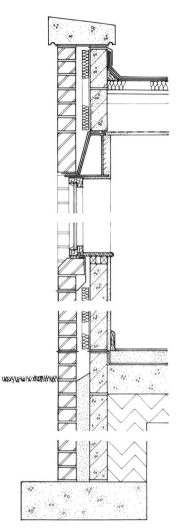

3.31 *Masonry cavity wall construction with steel lintel and having 'cold roof'.*

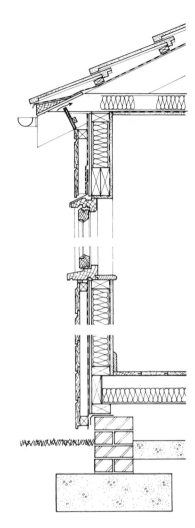

3.32 *Timber frame wall with pitched roof; the wall incorporates a vapour barrier on the inside and a breather paper on the outside of the insulation; the suspended floor is also insulated.*

damp up the walls (*3.31* to *3.33*). Because the damp-proof layers at ground floor and basement levels are protected from puncturing and are not exposed to the weather, unlike roof membranes, they are not usually a source of problems if properly installed.

Wall Cladding

For many buildings, the external walls act both as enclosing and as structural elements. Common examples are houses, and some other building types, which use loadbearing masonry (*3.31*).

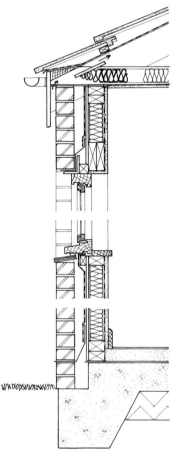

3.33 Wall construction with sloping roof having timber frame inner leaf and masonry outer leaf tied to it.

loadbearing element. The wall cladding may consist of masonry, supported by the frame, curtain walling, patent glazing or any of a very large number of panel systems made of various materials. The most common types of external wall panel, excluding metal panels, are: precast concrete panels, made of reinforced or prestressed concrete; glass fibre reinforced cement (GRC) panels, made of glass fibre reinforcement in a matrix of hardened cement paste; and glass reinforced polyester (GRP) panels made of glass fibre in continuous or chopped lengths set in a polyester resin matrix. Metal panels may be divided up into three main types: profiled metal sheeting which may be flat or curved and used either as single sheets or as composite insulated panels; sheet metal panels, which may also be supplied flat or curved but have greater metal thicknesses than profiled metal sheeting; and composite sheet metal panels, which are of a thin sandwich construction.

Concrete and GRC panels can usually be attached directly to the building, because of their rigidity and strength. Concrete and GRC panels are commonly used either as full-height panels without glazing, or with glazing incorporated into the panel (*3.34*) or are used as spandrel panels, in which there is a separate band of glazing between the spandrels (*3.35*). The fixings for these panels need to allow for dimensional errors arising in manufacture and during construction. The panel should be easy to put into position and there must be a method of adjustment that allows the panels to be accurately lined up with one another (*3.36*). Once in position, the fixings should allow for dimensional variations caused by shrinkage or temperature changes, for example. In a typical case there might be four fixing points at each corner of a flat panel (*3.37*). Normally, the two fixings at the bottom would carry the weight of the panel, so that the top fixings could then be simple restraints which would prevent movement at right angles to the panel but still allow movement in the plane of the panel. The bottom fixings should also allow horizontal movement in the plane of the panel, either at one or both sides (*3.37*). Corner panels, with a sharp or right angle bend in them, should preferably be suported near the corner, rather than at the ends, in order to allow free movement at these points. Spandrel panels may be

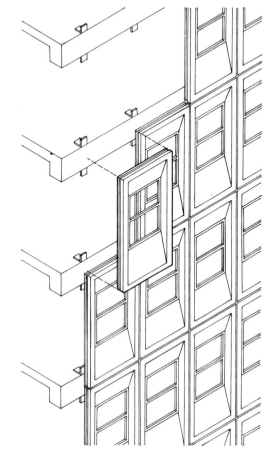

3.34 Storey-height precast concrete panel incorporating window.

attached directly to columns (*3.35*) or to the spandrel beams. The attachments to the spandrel beams serve either as the main connection points or, if used in conjunction with column fixings, as points of restraint to help prevent movement of the panel relative to the glazing (*3.38*).

Profiled metal sheets are almost always supported off a secondary framework; they usually consist of an outer steel or aluminium sheet with insulation behind and a liner panel on the inside. However composite panels incorporating insul-

Wood framed panels or concrete panels can also be connected together to make stable, three-dimensional *loadbearing* assemblies. Wood panels may be used in combination with an outer layer of shingles, boarding or tiles or an outer leaf of masonry (*3.32* and *3.33*). In buildings larger than houses, the frame is more common. In this method of building, the frame provides the structural strength and the wall cladding only needs to carry the wind loads on the panel and its own weight and is therefore termed a *non-*

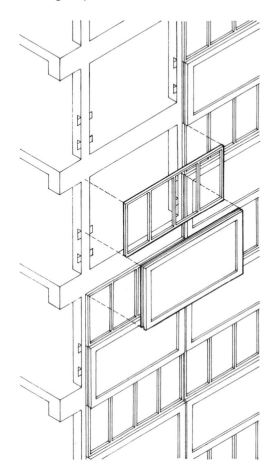

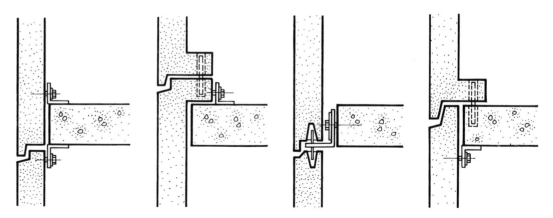

3.36 Various methods of fixing storey-height precast concrete panels to floors using slotted metal angles and dowel bars; packing shims and weatherproofing not shown.

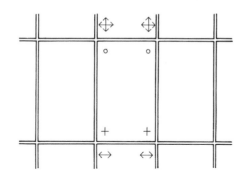

3.35 Spandrel precast concrete panel with separate framing for window strip.

3.37 Panel supported at four points so as to allow movement in plane of panel; one bottom fixing can be held in position if necessary.

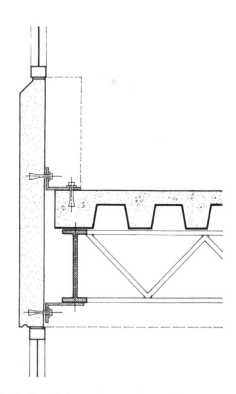

ation between two sheets of metal are also available (3.39). External wall *metal panels* are made in greater thicknesses than profiled metal sheets. There are two principal types: framed panels consisting of steel or aluminium sheets at least 2mm thick, which have stiffening ribs on the back that bolt to secondary framing; and sandwich panels which consist of two thinner metal sheets sandwiching insulation, the composite panel so formed having good stiffness and strength (3.40); both these types usually have a separate insulation

layer and a liner board behind. *GRP panels* are used sometimes and are either attached to the main structure or to a secondary frame (3.41). They are usually used as a single skin panel, slightly shaped for stiffness, but can also be made as a double skin panel incorporating insulation (3.42).

Patent glazing consists of glass panes supported by thin secondary framing members usually of a T-section shape (3.43). A more sophisticated cladding system, with very much

3.38 Spandrel precast concrete panel showing attachments to spandrel beam and floor.

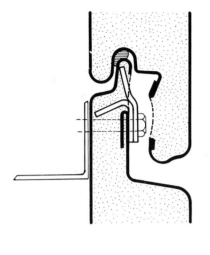

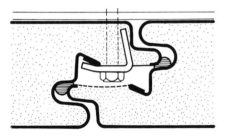

3.39 Vertical section, top, and horizontal section, bottom, on joints between composite metal panel with secret fixing to horizontal rail; the two-stage vertical joint uses sealant tape outside and a compressible sealant strip inside (redrawn from information supplied by H.H. Robertson).

higher performance and therefore a larger range of uses, is curtain walling. *Curtain walling* is normally taken to include all those cladding systems using a rectangular grid of horizontal and vertical secondary framing members which support glass and other infill panels, whether transparent, translucent or opaque. The secondary framing members are metal sections, usually of aluminium,

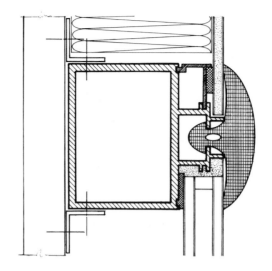

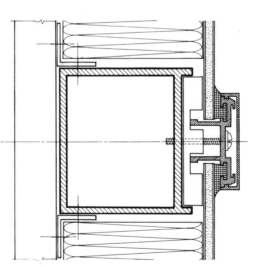

3.40 Horizontal or vertical section through laminated metal panel system showing attachment of mullion/transom to cladding rail; weather sealing done with push-fit gasket, top, or 'top hat' section and gaskets, bottom.

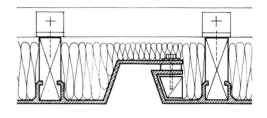

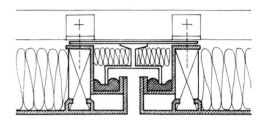

3.41 Single skin GRP panels with timber stiffeners attached to horizontal rail; joints are made by an overlap sealant joint, top, and with channel strip and compressible sealants, bottom.

and are attached to the main structure. The principal division among the systems available is between those supported on a vertical mullion system, the so-called stick system (*3.44*) and those incorporating secondary structural members on the perimeter of each panel unit, the so-called unit system (*3.45*). The *stick system* uses mullions one or two storeys high which are attached to the main frame. The connection between the mullions has a type of sliding joint which allows vertical movements to take place and also provides a tolerance for erection. In order that this movement can take place freely, a horizontal joint must also be provided between the panels at or near this level (*3.46*). Horizontal movement of the transoms can usually be absorbed by the transom to mullion joint (*3.47*). In the *unit system*, each unit is independent of the others and temperature movements can take place freely at the boundaries of each panel unit. Curtain walling systems can be

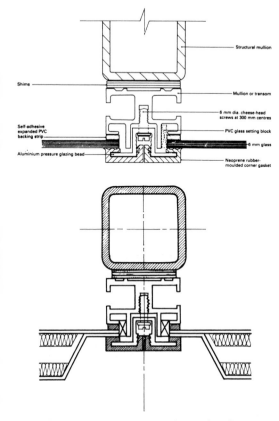

Structural mullion

Shims

Self-adhesive
expanded PVC
backing strip

Aluminium pressure glazing bead

Mullion or transom

6 mm dia. cheese-head
screws at 300 mm centres

PVC glass setting block

6 mm glass

Neoprene rubber-
moulded corner gasket

3.42 *Joint using a 'top hat' section and gaskets to support glazing, top, or a double skin GRP panel with insulation, bottom (top diagram by architects Farrell Grimshaw).*

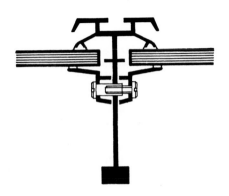

3.44 *'Stick' system for attaching curtain wall cladding with vertical movement joints at 'stick' connections.*

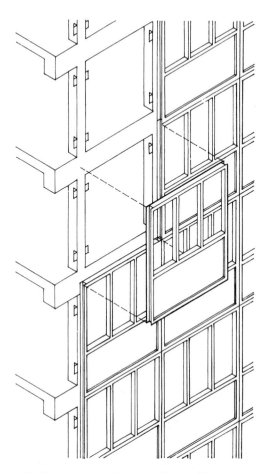

3.45 *Unit curtain wall system allowing horizontal and vertical movement at perimeter of panels.*

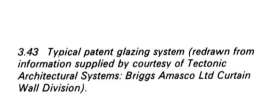

3.43 *Typical patent glazing system (redrawn from information supplied by courtesy of Tectonic Architectural Systems: Briggs Amasco Ltd Curtain Wall Division).*

used to span between spandrel beams (3.48 and 3.49), if the required specification were not such as to allow the use of patent glazing.

Joints in Walls

Wall cladding is exposed to the weather, undergoes significant changes in dimension as a result of its exposure, and therefore must incorporate movement joints. In general, these movement joints will be positioned at the same places as the supports to the cladding. Most materials used for walls need specific provisions to

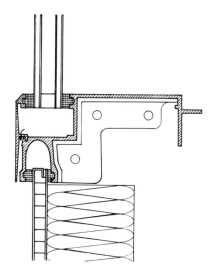

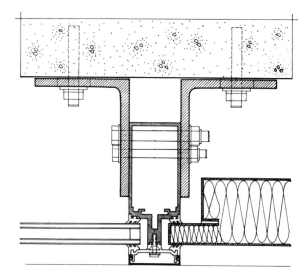

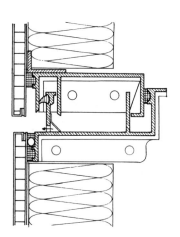

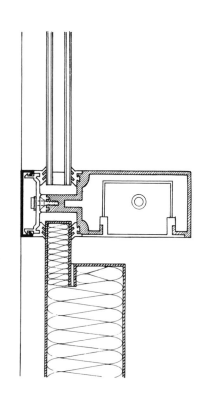

allow for the movement. An exception is wood, in which such movement as does occur can be accommodated at the connections between the timber elements. Weathering of movement joints used in cladding systems is usually achieved by sealants or gaskets. Joints can be classified as one-stage joints, in which there is only one barrier to rain penetration or, as two-stage joints with two barriers to rain penetration. For example, sealants are often used as one-stage joints, while the open-drained joint and the pressure-equalised joint are important examples of the two-stage joint. The *sealant joint* provides a watertight barrier by adhesion of the sealant to the cladding material each side of the joint (*3.50*). The width of the joint must be large enough to accommodate the expected movement, and, as important, large enough so that the percentage extension or contraction of the joint is within the limits of the sealant material. Loss of adhesion of the sealant to the cladding is a danger. Eventually, a sealant will lose its elastic properties and require renewing. Sealants are used both with butt and overlap joints, the overlap joint giving greater protection against the weather (*3.41*). Sealant joints are in common use for masonry cladding and for precast concrete panels. They can also be used for joints in GRC and GRP panel systems and in profiled metal sheeting. Profiled metal sheets generally have overlap joints which in many cases do not require the use of a sealant. The *gasket joint* relies on a gasket being put into compression between the two faces of the joint or gap it is required to seal, thus keeping it in position. Gasket joints are commonly used in GRC, GRP and metal panel

3.46 Curtain walling system using glazing and laminated metal panels showing fixed horizontal joint, top, and moving horizontal joint, bottom; the moving joint would be suitable for a stick or unit system; both joints use pressure equalized zones with drain holes (redrawn from information supplied by courtesy of Cupples Products).

3.47 Stick curtain walling system using glazing and thick insulated metal panels showing horizontal section through mullion at its fixing point, top, and vertical section through transom, bottom; the joint uses gaskets secured by a pressure screw with a thermal break; the enclosed voids make pressure-equalized chambers which are drained; angle brackets at the fixing points, top, incorporate slotted holes which allow adjustment in three directions (redrawn from information supplied by courtesy of Tectonic Architectural Systems: Briggs Amasco Ltd Curtain Wall Division).

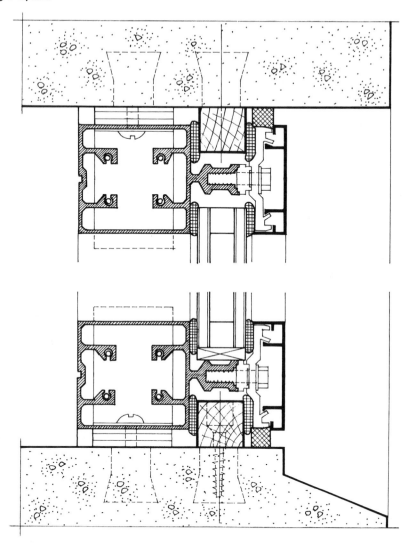

3.48 Vertical section through ribbon curtain wall system showing shims and fixing brackets to secure mullions to head and sill units and to transoms; hardwood battens are secured above and below the double glazing (redrawn from information supplied by courtesy of Mellowes ppg).

systems (*3.40, 3.41* and *3.50*). Gaskets can also be used for fabric joints made on site (*3.51*).

The *open-drained joint* is a two-stage joint, having two zones separated by a loosely-fitted baffle. Driven rain collects in the outer zone from where it is drained at the foot of the panel. The inner zone forms a ventilated cavity with an airtight barrier at the back, often achieved by the use of a sealant in compression. Any water reaching the inner zone may also be drained away. The barrier at the back of the inner zone must remain airtight so as to maintain an air pressure in the inner zone which is nearly equal to that in the outer zone and, by this means, prevent rain penetration to the inside (*3.50* and *3.52*). The open-drained joint is most commonly used with precast concrete panels but can also be specified for use with GRC and GRP panels too. The *pressure-equalized joint* describes the type of joint used in metal cladding systems but the term is general and could, in theory, be applied to any joint working on the principle of equalizing air pressures on either side of a weather barrier. It is similar to the open-drained joint in its operation. The pressure-equalised joint is a two-stage joint that consists of an outer barrier layer which is sealed against the cladding to prevent the entry of driven rain as far as possible, but is designed to allow air in or out at other points, for example at drain holes; these points are not directly exposed to the weather (*3.48*). There is also an inner barrier layer which should make an airtight seal with the frame to prevent loss of pressure, relative to that outside. Normally the zone between the two barriers is subdivided into a series of small chambers, to help ensure that each part of the zone is at the same pressure as the outside air nearby and that there is thus no tendancy for air to be sucked into the joint. Pressure-equalized joints are commonly used in curtain walls and in other cladding systems (*3.47*). The joint must also prevent the ingress of water through gravity or capillary action.

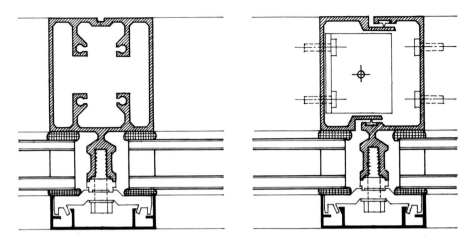

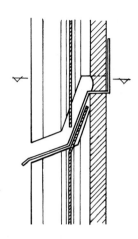

3.49 Horizontal sections through standard and split mullions used in 3.48 ; standard mullion drawn at mid-height and split mullion at base to show fixing brackets (redrawn from information supplied by courtesy of Mellows ppg).

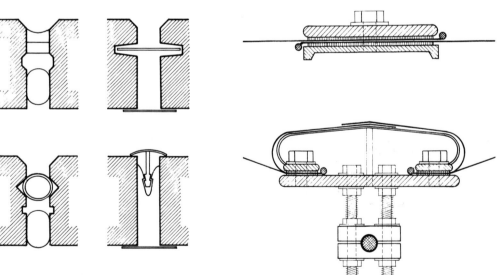

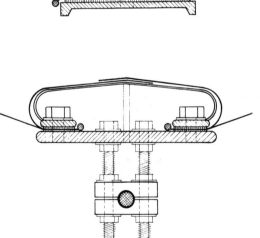

3.50 Joints for precast concrete panels: two-stage sealant joint, top left; open-drained joint with perforated tube and sealant strip behind, bottom left; open-drained joint with baffle and backstrip, top right, gasket joint with backstrip, bottom right.

3.51 Pressure joints with gasket strips used for fabric materials; joint with overlapping material, top, and with steel cable, bottom.

3.52 Vertical section, top, and horizontal section, bottom, at junction of vertical and horizontal joints in precast panel system; the horizontal joint has a one-stage sealant joint and the vertical joint an open-drained joint with a baffle and sealant strip; a flashing piece is used at the cross-over point; sealant strips shown shaded.

Temperature Movements in Panels

Panels will pick up stresses if their free movement due to shrinkage or temperature changes are prevented or restrained. For example, a panel which was completely fixed at both ends and underwent a uniform temperature fall, ΔT, below that at which it was installed, would experience a tensile stress in the panel, σ, given by:

$$\sigma = \alpha.\Delta T.E \ N/mm^2 \ (lb/in^2)$$

where α is the coefficient of thermal expansion per °C (°F);

ΔT is the temperature fall in °C (°F); and

E is the elastic modulus of the material in N/mm^2 (lb/in^2).

If the same panel has pinned joints at both ends and undergoes a temperature rise then the panel is most likely to bow and lock in bending stresses. Even if the panel is simply supported, so that it is free to move in its own plane, a temperature gradient across the panel which was linear, with the temperature difference between one face and the other being ΔT, would cause a bow, Δ, in the middle of the panel given by:

$$\Delta = \frac{\alpha.\Delta T.L^2}{8d} \ mm \ (in)$$

where h and d are the length and depth of the panel respectively in mm (in).

Stresses and movements induced in panels by temperature effects will be reduced in panels with large thermal capacity which are able to slow down temperature rises in the panel. Even panel fixings giving only moderate restraint to free movement may nevertheless induce tensile stresses which are sufficient to cause cracking in some panel materials. The bowing produced by temperature gradients across the panel may also give rise to cracking or delamination of insulation cores from the faces of laminated panels. This is particularly likely to be the case for curved corner panels where the fixings are likely to provide restraint against the free movement necessary to remove temperature stresses.

Roofs

Roofs pitched at not less than 18° to the horizontal may be covered with tiles, slates, shingles or impermeable sheeting with appropriate details, depending on the material used and on the exposure of the roof (3.32 and 3.33). There is usually a waterproof sheet immediately below

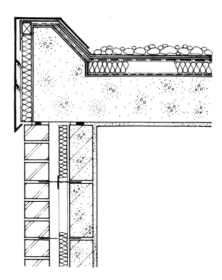
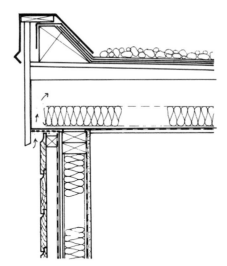
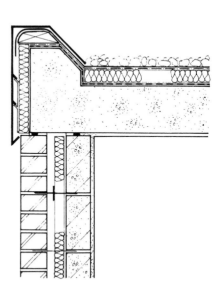
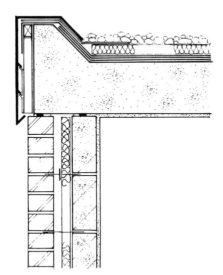

3.53 Cold roof of timber construction relying on ventilation from below the fascia board and through the roof cavity to disperse water vapour; the vapour barrier put below the insulation is only partially effective, top left; inverted roof (protected membrane roof), with built-up roofing, dispensing with need for separate vapour barrier, bottom left; warm roof using built-up roofing with breather layer below (shown dotted); water vapour in the breather layer is dispersed along the upstand edge, top right; warm roof using single membrane with breather layer immediately below, bottom right; in warm roof construction the vapour barrier can be made fully effective.

tiles, and other unit coverings, to drain snow or rain driven between them to eaves level. Compared to walls, where at least three methods of water exclusion are available, only the use of a thin layer of impermeable material is practical in most cases for flat roofs. The problem of excluding rain and damp is much more onerous for flat roofs than for pitched roofs, both because rainwater may accumulate on the roof, and is only slowly dispersed, and because the roof, more than the other surfaces of the enclosure, is subject to solar radiation and thus to large variations in temperature which, in turn, give rise to large differential movements between the waterproofing layer and the roof deck. These effects can cause cracking in the waterproof layer where it bridges gaps or joints in the decking or insulation immediately below it. The cracks may then let water in. Cracking is less likely if the waterproof layer is made of a material that has good tensile strength and does not soften excessively in summer or become brittle in winter.

There are three common types of flat roof construction, the so-called cold roof, the warm roof and the inverted roof. The most efficient but the most expensive to construct is the *inverted roof*, also known as the protected membrane roof. A type that is cheaper to construct but prone to interstitial condensation, if not well ventilated, is the *cold roof*. The most common type is the *warm roof*, which can have good long-term performance, if it is properly specified, but is still reasonably economic to lay (*3.53*). A major advantage of the warm roof is that it is possible to form a reliable and almost completely effective vapour barrier with average care during construction (*3.54*). In warm roofs, the insulation used between the roof deck and the waterproof layer may allow differential movement to take place between the structural deck and the waterproof covering, but if the covering is bonded, or partially bonded, to the insulation, the movement is restrained by the stiffness of the insulation boards. As noted previously, a breather layer within the warm roof construction would be able to relieve pressure from water vapour that has entered, from inside or outside, but would be unable to cope with leaks in the waterproof layer. The breather layer would generally be installed above the insulation layer in a warm roof and may

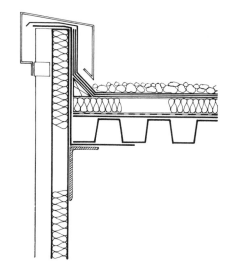

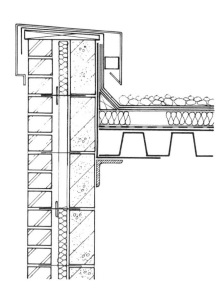

3.54 Edge details of metal deck roofs with profiled sheet metal cladding, top, or masonry cladding, bottom; both roofs use warm construction with rigid board on top of deck.

serve as a separating layer, if differential movement between the insulating layer in the warm roof and the waterproof layer is thought to be desirable.

If a vapour barrier is specified for a warm roof, it would be placed immediately below the insulation (*3.53*). As an alternative, an underlay may be used, in the same position as the vapour barrier, to prevent dampness penetrating the insulation from below, for example during drying of a cast-in-place concrete roof slab. The underlay might not be required as a vapour barrier in the long term and, in that case, it would normally be reasonably permeable to water vapour. Usually the insulation in a warm roof, whether there is a vapour barrier or not, would be fully bonded to the structural deck; however partial bonding might be used if movement was likely over joints in the structural deck.

Two coats of mastic asphalt or three or more layers of fibre-reinforced, bitumen-impregnated felts laid in hot bitumen are the two principal in-situ methods of surfacing a flat roof. Bitumen felts may be separated, partially bonded or fully bonded to the structural deck or the roof insulation depending on circumstances. Mastic asphalt is normally isolated from the deck by sheathing felt. An alternative is the use of a partially bonded, loosely fitted polymer sheet with as few joints as possible made in-situ. Other methods include the use of metal sheets, such as lead, copper, zinc and aluminium, or profiled metal sheets, such as those made from aluminium alloy or protected steel. Movement has to be allowed for. The joints are usually made with standing seams or by overlapping the sheets.

CONDENSATION

Dewpoint

Condensation may cause problems in buildings in two ways: firstly, surface condensation in which water vapour in warm humid air, from the inside of a building, condenses as water on the inner surface of the wall or roof construction which is at a temperature below the dew point; secondly, interstitial condensation in which warm humid air from inside the building condenses within the thickness of the wall or roof construction at the place within the construction where the temperature drops below the dew point (*3.55*).

Air in the atmosphere has as one of its constituents a certain quantity of water vapour per unit volume, that is water which is in a gaseous state. The water vapour exerts a gas pressure, the water vapour pressure, and this pressure together with the pressures due to other gases in the air makes up the total atmospheric pressure. The more water vapour contained, the higher is the water vapour pressure. However, it is found that, at any particular temperature and pressure, there is a known maximum quantity of water vapour which may be present per unit volume of air. Air in this state is said to be *saturated* and has a known *saturated water vapour pressure, P_s*. The saturated water vapour pressure is lower at lower temperatures. Lowering the temperature of air which is alredy saturated causes condensation to occur, such as the surface condensation that occurs on the inside of single glazed windows during the winter months. Looked at another way, for air with a given quantity of water vapour per unit volume, there is a known temperature at which condensation starts to occur, if the air is cooled at some known constant pressure (*3.25*). This temperature is known as the *dew point*. An indication of how near the water vapour in the air is to condensing is given by the *relative humidity, RH*, of the air at the given ambient temperature where:

$$RH = \frac{P}{P_s}$$

where P and P_s are the water vapour pressure and the saturated water vapour pressure of the air under consideration.

The relative humidity can also be defined, with good accuracy, as the ratio of the quantity of water vapour present in the air to that which would be contained in air that was saturated at that temperature. Air with 100% relative humidity is *saturated* air, anything less is *unsaturated* air. The relative humidity is conveniently measured by a wet-and-dry-bulb thermometer, the wet-bulb thermometer recording a lower temperture, for the same dry-bulb temperature, as the relative humidity decreases. The wet and dry bulb temperatures are identical in saturated air.

Interstitial Condensation

Typically the inside air has a relative humidity of about 50%, much lower than that of the outside air in winter, which may be about 80%. Nevertheless the hotter inside air has a higher water vapour pressure and contains more water vapour than the outside air. The inside air, however, being at a higher temperature, is further from its dew point. In these conditions, if the wall construction is permeable to water vapour, then there is a transfer of water vapour from the inside, which has a high water vapour pressure, to the outside, which has a low water vapour pressure. The greater the pressure difference the greater the rate of transfer of moisture. If an estimate can be made of the water vapour pressure at each intermediate position between the inner and outer surfaces of the wall construction then the dew point, that is the temperature at which condensation starts, can be found for each of these positions. With a single

3.55 Variation of temperature compared to dewpoint temperature and of vapour pressure compared to saturated vapour pressure across a single-leaf construction; with insulation on the inside, left, there is condensation but none if the insulation is on the outside, right.

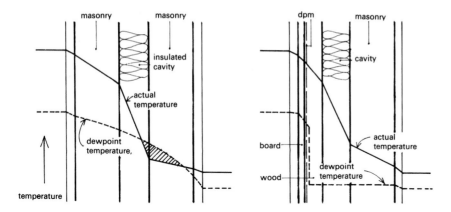

3.56 Variation of temperature compared to dewpoint temperature across cavity wall constructions; condensation occurs in outer leaf of cavity wall, left, but when vapour pressure is kept low by membrane condensation is prevented, right.

layer wall, the water vapour pressure is found by interpolating between given vapour pressures on its inside and outside surfaces (*3.55*). The object of the design is to arrange the thermal insulation and vapour checks in such a way that the temperature within the construction does not drop below the dew point at any particular position within the wall (*3.56*). If it does, *interstitial condensation* will occur. Interstitial condensation may always be avoided if the layers of the wall or roof construction are arranged so that the thermal resistance of each layer, d/λ, increases, going from the inside to the outside, while the vapour resistance of each layer, R or d/δ, decreases going from inside to outside. There are standard values for the vapour resistance of thin sheet materials; the vapour resistance is equal to the reciprocal of the permeance (Table 3.6). For thick materials, the vapour resistance is given by:

$$R = \frac{\mu.d}{\delta} x 10^9 \text{ N s/gm (1/perm)}$$

where d is the thickness of each layer in mm (in);
δ is the vapour permeability of the material in gm mm/ N s (perm-inch).

In practice this ideal state, in which there is increasing thermal resistance and decreasing vapour resistance going from inside to outside,

may be difficult to arrange. In a flat roof, for example, the outer layer is vapourproof and waterproof. In addition, a vapour barrier on the inside of the construction may be ineffective, for example, because it is not properly sealed, and in these circumstances it may be better if it were omitted altogether. In practice, many vapour barriers are not completely vapourproof and could be more accurately referred to as vapour retarders. However it is possible to provide effective vapour barriers on the inside surfaces which at the very least would be able to slow down the transfer of water vapour and may possibly prevent it altogether. It is also possible to provide thermal insulation on the outside surfaces of both walls and roofs. Also the outer layers of many types of wall construction are permeable to water vapour: a masonry wall is permeable to water vapour and can dry out through its external and internal faces; a sloping and tiled roof is waterproof but completely pervious to water vapour and this is a major advantage of this form of construction.

If interstitial condensation does occur it may cause material degradation and loss of thermal insulation in the insulating layers. In other cases interstitial condensation may not be harmful. For example in cavity wall construction, with

insulation provided in the cavity, there is usually no requirement to provide a vapour barrier on the inside surface of the inner leaf because condensation on the inside surface of the outer leaf, assuming it does not freeze, may be drained at the bottom. Alternatively it may be dispersed by air circulation and diffused as vapour to the outside, at the top of the wall or through the outer leaf (*3.56*). Interstitial condensation is usually allowable over the winter months if the condensate can be re-evaporated over the summer months. In a roof or wall, condensation occurs because of diffusion of vapour from the inside to the outside; if the amount of water vapour condensed over the winter period is G, then assuming a steady state, G is given by (*3.55*) :

$$G = \left(\frac{P_1 - P_2}{R_1} - \frac{P_s - P_2}{R_2} \right) t \text{ gm/m}^2 \text{ (lb/ft}^2) \text{ of wall}$$

where P_s is the average of the saturation vapour pressures, each side of the band where condensation takes place, in N/m^2 (lb/ft^2);
P_1 and P_2 are the vapour pressures on the inside and outside of the roof or wall construction in N/m^2 (lb/ft^2);
R_1 and R_2 are the vapour resistances of the construction on the inner and outer side of the condensation band in N s/gm (x 0.495 x 10^6 1/perm) and
t is the period expressed in seconds (hours) of the winter season, often taken as lasting sixty days.

In summer when re-evaporation takes place, the same formula is used with t representing the period of the summer season and G, having a negative value, representing the amount evaporated. The minimum vapour saturation pressure within the construction thickness is higher, during summer, than the vapour pressures on the inside and outside so that drying out may be able to occur through diffusion inwards as well as outwards, as for example in a permeable wall. In a flat roof with a vapourproof membrane on the outside, the diffusion outwards may lead to blistering of the roof material, see below. The formula gives the maximum amount of water that could be re-evaporated which must exceed that which can condense. For roofs which have a waterproof layer on the outside which is vapourproof, or has a high vapour resistance, the second term in the formula is negligible and can be ignored. Note that interior

Table 3.6 — Vapour Permeability of Materials

Material	Vapour Permeability	
	$\times 10^{-6}\ \dfrac{\text{gm mm}}{\text{N s}}$	perm in
Brickwork	10-40	7-27
Dense concrete	10-20	7-14
Lightweight concrete	20-35	14-24
Wood	12-22	8-15
Plywood	0.16-0.6	0.11-0.41
Expanded polystyrene	1.6-10	1.1-6.9
Foamed polyurethane	1-32	0.7-22
Gypsum plasterboard	16-22	11-15
Air	182	125

	Vapour Permeance	
	$\times 10^{-9}\ \dfrac{\text{gm}}{\text{N s}}$	perm
Aluminium foil (0.025mm)	0	0
Polythene sheet (0.1mm)	5	0.08
Asphalt (100kg/m^2)	5.7	0.1
Built-up roofing (hot)	0	0
Bitumenised paper	90	1.6
Gloss paint	58	1.0

vapour barriers will prevent drying out of the construction to the interior and may need to be be omitted for this reason, particularly in flat roof construction. Flat roofs are most likely to suffer damage from material degradation and from vapour blistering due to interstitial condensation. *Vapour blistering* occurs in roofs in hot weather: as the condensate revapourises in the heat, the vapour pressure rises and blisters form under the impermeable layer. Vapour which does not diffuse downwards may be dispersed by vents which penetrate the roof membrane or by a pressure-relieving layer which disperses the vapour at the roof edges (*3.53*).

Surface Condensation

The prevention of surface condensation can be achieved by more insulation and good circulation of air near the affected area. Problems are most likely to occur at the corners of external walls where, in winter, there is a greater external area for dispersal of heat than in the middle of a straight wall, for each unit area of inside surface. Hence the temperature on the inside surface is lower. As air circulation is also lower near the corners this is the likely position for surface condensation. Note that insulation to prevent surface condensation may be placed in the inner or outer layers of a wall construction but not so as to then result in

interstitial condensation. Other potential sources of condensation are *cold bridges*. A cold bridge will occur over any area of the building enclosure which has poor thermal insulation and may be a result of oversights in design or construction. If concrete balcony slabs or structural steel members, which both have relatively high thermal conductivity, have to penetrate a layer of thermal insulation, they form cold bridges, unless the slab or the steel member is specially insulated over the cold surfaces near the penetration point. A cold bridge not only causes a decrease in the average value of the insulation for the enclosure but, because of its low surface temperature, collects surface condensation. Note that any condensation may cause yet further losses in the insulation at the cold bridge, owing to the high thermal conductivity of the water that condenses on or within the cold bridge.

LIGHTING

Electromagnetic Spectrum

A part of the electromagnetic spectrum contains visible light. Visible light occurs between wavelengths of 0.38×10^{-6}m and 0.78×10^{-6}m, (0.38μm and 0.78μm), a particular colour being associated with light of a particular wavelength.

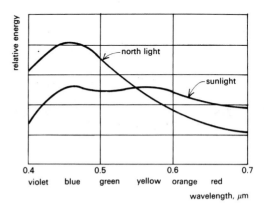

3.57 Energy distribution curves for daylight from north or direct sunlight from south, in northern hemisphere (after ref. 2).

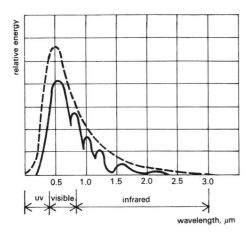

3.58 Energy distribution curves for solar radiation above the earth's atmosphere (dotted line) and as received after passing through the earth's atmosphere (full line).

Luminance and Illuminance

The human eye alters the amount of light reaching the retina by adjusting the size of the pupil in the eye. In addition the eye can adjust the sensitivity of the receptors on the retina so that it is better able to cope with dull or very bright light. Because of this,

Some of the principal colours in the visible spectrum, listed in increasing order of wavelength, are violet, blue, green, yellow, orange and red (3.57). Light which contains energy over almost all the wavelengths in the visible spectrum, in approximately equal amounts, is known as white light. The sun produces white light. However the sun emits radiation over a larger range of wavelengths than those contained in white light. In total the sun emits radiation with wavelengths between 0.25 and 2.50 μm, (0.25 x 10^{-6}, and 2.50 x 10^{-6}m), that band with shorter wavelengths than the visible spectrum being known as ultraviolet radiation and that with longer wavelengths being known as infrared radiation (3.58). The solar radiation incident on a building is made up of direct radiation and of diffuse radiation, the latter being the radiation that is reflected off the ground and other buildings.

the amount of lighting required for any purpose may be allowed to vary over a large range and still be acceptable. The thermal conditions required for reasonable comfort are much more restricted, by contrast. A general guide to the overall power of a light source, as perceived by the eye, is given by the *luminous flux, F,* of the light source as measured in lumens. It is a measure of luminous power output, not the power input which is always greater. A measure of the luminous power of a point light source, at any particular angle from that light source, is given by the *luminous intensity, I,* and is measured in candelas. For light uniformly emitted in all directions, the luminous intensity would equal the luminous flux passing through a unit solid angle subtended at the light source (3.59). Alternatively, considering any spherical area surrounding the light source, the luminous intensity, *I,* is given by :

$$I = \frac{F}{4\pi} \text{ candelas}$$

where   *F* is the luminous power of the point light source in lumens.

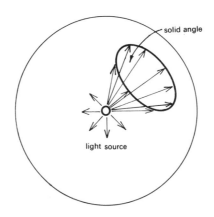

3.59 Imaginary unit sphere placed around a point source of light showing the area on the sphere subtended by a solid angle at the light source; for a unit area, of any shape, on a sphere of unit radius, the solid angle is equal to one steradian; if the light is uniformly emitted over the unit area, the luminous intensity in candelas is equal to the luminous flux in lumens passing through that area.

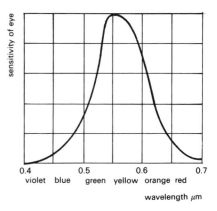

3.60 Curve showing sensitivity of eye to light of different wavelengths (after ref. 2).

. Solid angles are measured in steradians, there being 4π steradians subtended by a sphere at its centre. For light which is not uniformly emitted, the general case, the luminous intensity equals the luminous flux in a small solid angle divided by the size of the solid angle in steradians. As an observer moves away from a point light source, the luminous intensity is unaltered, being a property of the light source and the angle of the source to the observer, but the illuminance provided on a surface by the light source decreases. The *illuminance, E,* on a surface is the luminous flux falling on it per unit area and is measured in lux. A lux is equal to one lumen per square metre. Photometers, containing light-sensitive cells, are calibrated to measure illuminance. However because the eye is more sensitive to some colours than others most photometers are 'colour corrected', that is, they do not have a linear response to light but give relatively larger readings for light to which the eye is known to be sensitive, thus attempting to mimic the eye's response to light (3.60).

The illuminance on a surface gives a guide as to whether there is sufficient lighting reaching anything to be seen on that surface, for example print on the page of a book. The *inverse square law* for illuminance gives the illuminance on any surface, which is at right angles to the light rays, in terms of the luminous intensity of that light source,

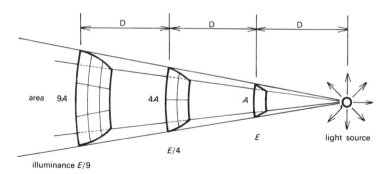

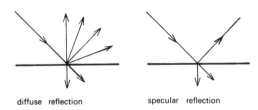

diffuse reflection   specular reflection

3.61 The illuminance provided by a point source of light varies in inverse proportion to the square of the distance from the light.

3.63 The incident light arriving on an opaque surface is absorbed and reflected; perfectly diffuse reflected light is scattered and has the same luminance wherever it is viewed from, left; specular reflected light, in general, has varying luminance depending on the angle of incidence of the light seen, right.

at the particular angle it is viewed from. The illuminance, E, is given by (*3.61*) :

$$E = \frac{I}{r^2} \text{ lux}$$

where I is the intensity of the source in candelas and
 r is the distance from the light source in m.

If the surface is not normal to the light rays the illuminance, E_1 is given by (*3.62*):

$$E_1 = E.\cos\theta$$

where θ is the angle of incidence of light on the surface and
 E is the illuminance on a surface at right angles to the rays of light.

The objects seen alter in appearance depending on

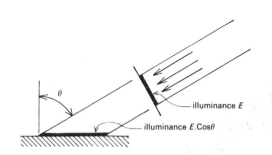

3.62 Diagram showing how illumination is progressively reduced on a surface as it departs from making a 90° angle with the light rays; the illuminance is inversely proportional to the area projected on the surface by a unit area which is at 90° to the light rays.

the amount of light they emit or reflect towards the eye. The *luminance* or brightness of a surface is a measure of the amount of light emitted and reflected by that surface. It is measured in lumens of light emitted per square metre, apostilbs, (the same type of units used for illuminance) for a diffusing surface and in candelas per square metre for polished surfaces or surfaces that emit light. A matt, perfectly diffusing surface scatters the reflected light such that the surface has the same brightness whatever angle it is viewed from. By contrast, a polished surface or a light source may have a different brightness depending on the particular angle of view, so that the appropriate unit is then the intensity of the light per unit area.

Polished surfaces or mirrors give *specular reflection*, in which the angle of incidence of light equals the angle of reflection, while matt surfaces give *diffuse reflection* in which the reflected light is scattered in all directions. Most actual surfaces exhibit a combination of these properties (*3.63*).

The inverse square law shows the illuminance at any position due to a point source of light to vary in inverse proportion to the square of the distance from the source. However a point source of light applies to only a minority of actual light sources. A more practical case is a plane surface that emits light, such as a window or the diffusing panel of a luminaire belonging to a light. The plane surface may be thought of as a series of small elements, which may have different intensities. Assuming, however, that the small elements have a uniform intensity, then the illuminance at any position due

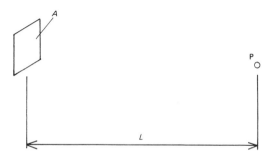

3.64 Illumination at a point due to a small planar area of light; the average illumination from all directions arriving at the point depends on the luminance of the planar area and the solid angle it subtends at the point concerned; the solid angle decreases as the projected area of the planar source, A, seen from the point, decreases and as the distance, L, increases.

to the planar source is proportional to the area of the planar element and inversely proportional to the square of the distance from the element, by the inverse square law, that is (*3.64*):

$$E = \frac{k.I.A}{d^2} = \frac{k.I}{\omega} \text{ lux}$$

where E is the average illuminance of the light arriving at the position concerned from all directions in lux;
 I is the intensity of light in the direction concerned in candelas;
 d is the distance, large compared to the dimensions of A, in m;

A is the area of the planar source in m²;

ω is the solid angle subtended at the position concerned by the light source in steradians; and

k is a constant.

The average illumination at a point, therefore, depends not on the distance from the planar source but on the solid angle subtended at the point by the source. Another area source of light is the hemisphere, which is used as a model for estimating the illumination at ground level due to the luminance of the sky (*3.65*). For a point on a plane surface surrounded by a uniformly luminous diffusing hemisphere, representing the sky, the horizontal illumination on the surface can be shown to be equal to the luminance of the sky. Note that, as for a planar source, the illuminance is independent of the distance of the luminous hemisphere from the central point. As the hemisphere can be drawn in any position, the illuminance is the same at any position on the planar surface.

GLARE

Types of Glare

The luminance or brightness of an object, is an important guide as to whether the eye will be comfortable or able to distinguish the features of the object in sufficient detail. However the uniformity of lighting is also important. An object with sufficient luminance against a dark background will have a lower *apparent brightness* if the background is made lighter; in some cases, the object may need to have its luminance increased in order to be seen properly. However if this contrast between the brightness of the object and the background brightness is excessive, glare is experienced. *Glare* is caused by any excessive contrast in brightness in the field of view which normally takes in objects over an angle of about 45 degrees, seen in section. In general to avoid glare the luminance ratio or *brightness ratio*, that is the ratio of the luminance of the object to be seen to that of its background, should not exceed three, if the background is near to the object, or ten, if the background is some way behind the object. Glare is caused both by a bright light or object against a dark background, as with car headlights seen at night, and by dark objects against a light background, as with pictures, placed next to windows, that are obscured by high sky luminance. If, as in the latter case, there is an object to be seen, the glare is best cured by restricting brightness in the normal field of view. *Disability glare* is glare that prevents detail being seen clearly and could stop some tasks being done at all. *Discomfort glare* only causes visual discomfort and may often be cured by shielding the light sources or by moving position. Another type of glare is *veiling reflection*, caused by the reflection of a bright light on the working surface. Veiling reflections may be reduced by reducing the reflectance of the working surface or by changing position relative to the light source. Preferably light to illuminate a horizontal working surface should not come from that zone above and just ahead of the observer, because the light may reflect into the observer's eyes. It is a common practice for those working at desks to face parallel to or away from the windows and to be placed midway between continuous rows of artificial lighting and facing parallel to the rows (*3.66*). A 'batwing' distribution of light from the strip light luminaire would be suitable (*3.79*). It is found that, generally, the observer's line of sight to the task makes an angle with the vertical of between about 20° and 40°. Therefore a luminaire that gives

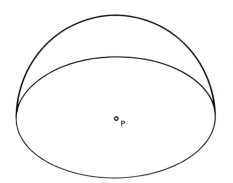

3.65 Sky represented as a luminous hemisphere surrounding any point on the ground's surface; if the hemisphere has a uniformly diffusing luminance then the horizontal illuminance at the point, that is the illumination on the horizontal plane, is equal to the luminance of the sky, if expressed in the same type of unit.

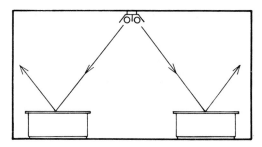

3.66 Placing of desks with respect to strip lights and windows either side of desks in order to reduce veiling reflections; the direction of view should be parallel to the strip light and window lines.

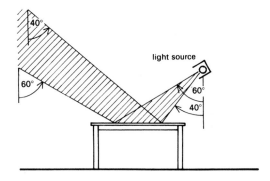

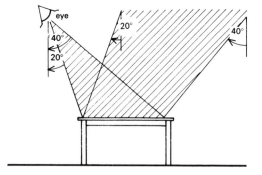

3.67 In order to reduce veiling reflection, the reflected angles of any light source on the task viewed, top, should be different from the normal lines of sight, bottom.

out light mostly between 40° and 60° to the vertical, in the plane defined by the light, the observer and the task, greatly reduces the veiling reflections on a horizontal working surface (3.67). If relatively low ambient lighting is provided but topped up by local task lighting then the observer should be able to move the task light so that veiling reflection can be minimised. At the other extreme veiling reflections, as well as glare, can be reduced by uniform or diffuse lighting of low intensity, for example that produced by a completely luminous ceiling. However this kind of light makes objects look 'flat' and without much shadow. Often it is not possible to substantially eliminate direct glare and veiling reflection when the lighting also gives high illumination levels and good contrast.

Veiling reflections are substantially dependent on the reflectance of the surface looked at. The *reflectance* of a surface is defined as the percentage of incident light on the surface that is reflected; the rest of the light is absorbed or transmitted by the material (3.68). The reflectance of most mirrors is more than 90% but it is nearly zero for a matt black surface, which is almost 100% absorbent. Reflectance depends to some extent on the angle of incidence of the light. The *transmittance* is the percentage of incident light on a material that is transmitted, being about 90% for clear glass. The transmittance of the material, in general, will vary with the wavelength of the light and quoted figures are given for light of a particular wavelength or are averages over a particular range of wavelengths.

COLOUR

Trichromatic Theory

The trichromatic colour theory is the one most widely used in discussing colour. It assumes that the cones in the eyes are of three types, each type being sensitive to light of different wavelengths; the response of the three types is mixed and interpreted by the brain as a particular colour. The theory assumes that colour is received and interpreted by the eye and brain in similar fashion to the way it is received in a colour television camera; the camera works by separation of any colour into three primary colours (3.69), which can then be remixed by the additive process when the picture is received (3.70). In practice colour vision is more complex than this because of the part the brain takes in interpretation. For example, the colour of an object is not perceived as different even when it is viewed under a range of very different lighting conditions. This phenomenon is known as *colour constancy*. But there are limits to the change in lighting that are possible without the objects also appearing to change in colour. Basic to the an understanding of how colours change are the processes of colour addition and colour subtraction.

Light of one particular wavelength is known as monochromatic light and is associated by the eye with a particular colour. If two monochromatic lights are shone onto the same white screen, the eye mixes them and sees a new colour, which is always lighter than either of the two original colours. For example red and green produce a yellow light and red, green and blue produce white light (3.70). This process is known as *colour addition*. The properties of surfaces are important. As noted previously, surfaces of materials either transmit, reflect or absorb the light impinging on them (3.68). A white surface reflects almost all the light on it with very little absorption whereas a black surface absorbs almost all the light on it, reflecting almost nothing back. A blue surface appears blue because it reflects only the blue

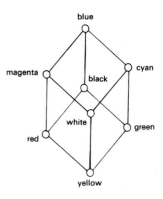

3.69 Red-green-blue model for colours with their complementary colours shown on opposite corners of the cube; addition either of the three primary additive colours (red, green, blue) or the three secondary colours (yellow, cyan, magenta) or any two complementary colours can produce white; subtraction of any of the two primary colours from each other produces black.

component of the light and absorbs the other colours in the incident light, which are green and red in the case of white light (3.71). Similarly a blue filter transmits only blue light, absorbing all other colours (3.72). For a surface to appear blue the incident light must contain blue in it. Thus,

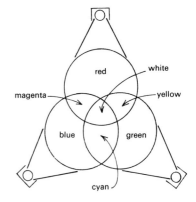

3.70 Colour addition with red, green and blue lamps to produce white light and the secondary colours, magenta, yellow and cyan.

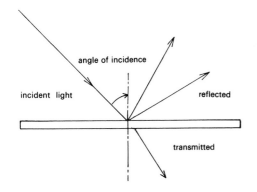

3.68 Incident light falling on a material is reflected and transmitted in amounts depending on the type of material; that not reflected or transmitted is absorbed on the surface.

because a sodium lamp emits mostly yellow light, with very little blue and because a blue surface absorbs all other colours, blue appears black under a sodium light. This process is known as *colour subtraction,* the surface or filter emitting light always being darker than the original incident light on it. Colour subtraction takes place on the surfaces of two paints of different colours when they are mixed together, so that the resultant colour is always darker than any of the two original colours. Subtraction of any of the three primary colours (red, green and blue) from each other always gives black; subtraction of any two of the secondary colours (yellow, cyan and magenta) from each other gives a primary colour; for example, yellow and cyan, if colour subtracted, give green, which is the common component of the two colours (*3.69*).

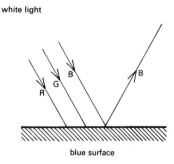

3.71 Substraction of colour on a surface; subtraction also occurs when coloured paints are mixed, the resulting surface of the paint appearing darker than either of the original colours.

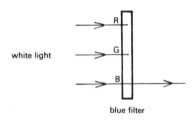

3.72 Subtraction of colour with a filter.

DAYLIGHT

Daylight Factor

The amount of daylight in the sky, is greater near the equator than in the temperate regions of the earth which have higher degrees of latitude. Generally buildings which rely on natural lighting will have large window sizes, especially in the temperate regions. However the thermal design of the building will also affect the window sizes, and, in general, has an overriding influence. Acoustics must be considered too. For example large windows increase outside noise as well as the thermal losses in winter, although both these effects may be reduced by double or triple glazing. Solar gain is an important consideration too. Solar gain through large windows facing the sun on southern or eastern elevations in the northern hemisphere (northern or western in the southern hemisphere) can usually be controlled by sun shading or, possibly, the use of reflective glass while still allowing enough daylight to enter the room from sunlight reflected off the sky, the ground or nearby buildings.

The amount of outside light available varies not only between different regions of the earth but also due to changes in weather from day to day and from hour to hour in each local area. Hence the amount of daylight entering a room can only be imperfectly controlled. By contrast artificial light is completely controllable. A design which uses natural lightning must try to take these variations into account. Any method used must estimate the brightness or luminance of the sky at any particular angle from the building. For preliminary design purposes, however, it is often the practice to assume that the sky is a uniformly luminous hemisphere. As noted previously, this would provide an illuminance, on an open area of the ground surface, of the same value as the luminance of the hemisphere; the luminance of the sky could be taken as having a fixed value of about 5000 lux, irrespective of the actual cloud cover or weather conditions.

Even with a constant value for the exterior daylight illuminance, the illuminance on any plane within a room still depends on a large number of factors. It is common practice to consider the illuminance on a horizontal working plane at a reference point near to the back wall, furthest

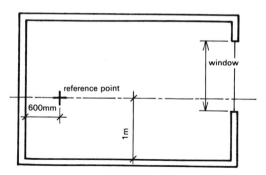

3.73 Typical position of reference point in the back of a room for calculation of the minimum daylight factor.

away from the window. There are two principal methods of calculating the amount of daylight in a room: the *daylight factor method* considers the ratio of the illuminance on a horizontal working plane at the reference point in the room to the illuminance on a horizontal plane outside which is not obstructed from the light by neighbouring buildings, trees and so on (*3.73*). The daylight factor, *DF*, depends on the solid angles the reference point makes with the windows which surround it, with the other internal surfaces and with buildings nearby which obstruct the light, as well as on the reflectances of the ground surface and nearby buildings and on the reflectances of the walls, floors and ceilings in the room. The daylight factor, thus, depends on direct light received from the sky, the sky component, *SC*, as well as the externally reflected components, *ERC*, and the internally reflected components, *IRC* (*3.74*). The daylight factor for the room is defined as that occurring under an overcast sky. However, as the daylight factor is a ratio of values, it is largely a property of the room and does not depend, to any significant extent, on the weather or the level of exterior illumination, and this is a major advantage of this method of calculation. Note that the daylight factor does depend on the amount of transmittance of light through the windows, which may be reduced by dirt on the window, the formulation of the glass or the size of the window frames, for example. Typically the daylight factor would be about 2% for a reference point near to the

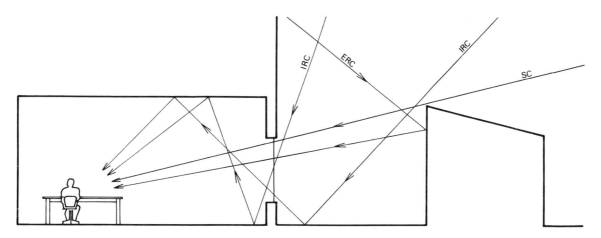

3.74 Sky component, externally reflected component and internally reflected components of light received at a desk.

back of a room and about 10% for a reference point near to a window in the room (Table 3.7). Places near the back of the room are unlikely to be well lit by daylight if the sky component is less than 1%. Where there are external obstructions to daylight, it is useful to draw the 'no-sky' line on a room plan; the 'no-sky' line is the line connecting the points on the working plane at which the sky just ceases to be visible.

For the purposes of the preliminary design of windows, it may be useful to calculate an *average daylight factor*. If the average exceeds 5%, then supplementary artificial lighting will only be required occasionally in rooms of normal shape in most climates; if below 2%, then artificial lighting will be needed almost continuously in most of the room. The average daylight factor for a shallow room lit by vertical side windows, or a room lit by rooflights, is given by [4]:

$$\text{Average DF} = \frac{0.85W.\theta}{A(1-R^2)} \%$$

where W is the net area of glazing in m²;

θ is the angle in the vertical plane subtended by the sky from the centre of a window or a roof light (*3.75*);

A is the total area of indoor surfaces, including the window and rooflight areas and

R is the average reflectance of the indoor surfaces, including windows and rooflights.

The *lumen method* of estimating light levels treats each window as a luminous panel, with the illumination on the working plane at the reference point being split into that due to direct light from the sky and that due to reflected light from the external surfaces. In other respects it is similar to the daylight factor method. In practice the various factors used in both methods are awkward to calculate and best obtained from standard computer programs or charts. Another useful method for daylight design of rooms is to construct a model of the proposed building. The model may be used indoors, with artificial lighting, or outdoors by transporting it to the site of the proposed building or anywhere else with a similar climate. As the illuminance at any point in the room depends only on the intensity of the light and

Table 3.7	Required Daylight Levels	
Type of Space	Average Daylight Factor %	Minimum Daylight Factor %
Kitchen	5	2
Living room	5	1
Bedroom	2	0.5
Offices	5	1
Drawing office	5	3

values given for working plane: artificial lighting would generally be required anywhere daylight levels fall below the given minima

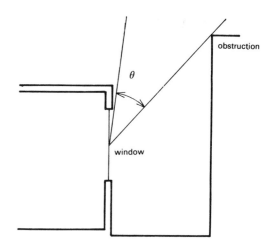

3.75 Vertical angle subtended at the centre of a window for calculation of the average daylight factor in a room.

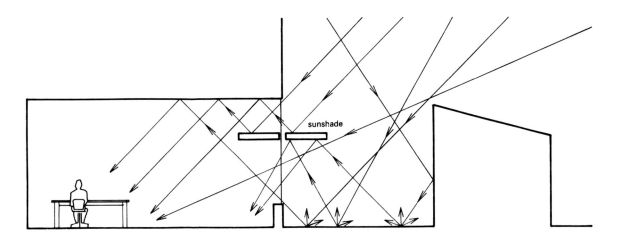

3.76 Paths of light into a room using natural lighting.

the solid angles subtended at the point by the windows and walls, as noted previously, the model is exact and may be used to measure illuminance at any point in the room, in various weather conditions, whatever the scale at which the model is built. However the model must have the same surface reflectances as those in the actual room.

Skylights provide a good source of daylight not only because they face upwards, the direction in which the daylight illuminance tends to be high, but also because, if not obstructed, they receive daylight at all times of the day, and give more illumination on the horizontal work plane than light arriving from lower levels. Glare and overheating can cause problems, which may be resolved by the use of north lights or shading devices. In deep buildings, if it is impossible to provide skylights, it is necessary to have high ceilings and high windows to enable daylight to reach the far ends of the room (*3.76*). Sunshades can be made to act as light shelves to reflect daylight into the interior of the room (*3.77*). As a rule, natural light may be used for most of the time in a zone which extends in plan from the windows a distance of about twice the window height. Beyond this artificial light may be used to supplement or replace the natural light (*3.78*).

Artificial light must also be used at times when daylight illumination is insufficient, which, generally, is when the level of illumination on the workplane is less than about 400 lux.

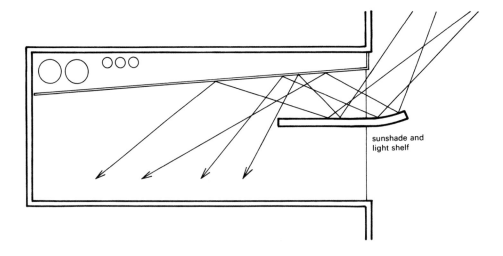

3.77 Room with tilted sunshade and sloping ceiling to maximise the natural light received in the interior.

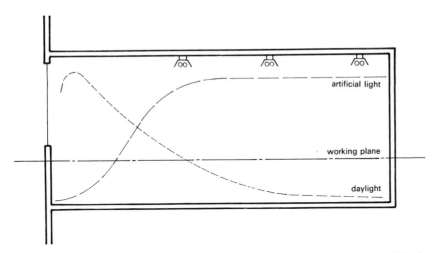

3.78 Integrated lighting system using daylight, supplemented by artificial light when the daylight factor at the back of the room is less than a fifth of that near the windows.

ARTIFICIAL LIGHT

Lamps

Artificial light is generally produced by incandescent lamps or by discharge tubes such as the tubular fluorescent lamp. The amount of light given out in any direction from the lamp depends not only on the lamp but also on the shape of the luminaire used with the lamp. Luminaires may be classified by polar curves which show the luminous intensity at any angle from the light and have a similar pattern whatever the power of the lamp in the luminaire (*3.79*). The lamp itself may be classified by the power it gives out at each particular wavelength. For each type of lamp a graph of power or relative energy against wavelength has a characteristic pattern which is referred to as its colour distribution pattern (*3.80*). The temperature at which the lamp operates gives a good indication of its colour; more precisely a lamp is classified by its *colour temperature*, which is the temperature of a black body that most nearly has the colour distribution of the lamp in question. Lamps may be classified by how well they render various colours compared to a reference source of light. This property of a lamp is known as its *colour rendition*. The colour rendering index gives a guide as to the average performance of a lamp tested on a range of colours. Another useful indicator of the lamp's performance is its *luminous efficacy* which is the ratio of luminous flux emitted by a lamp in lumens to the electrical input in watts. Table 3.8 lists characteristics of some common types of lamp.

A lamp which produces a large proportion of light of a wavelength to which the eye is very sensitive, such as yellow-green light, will have a higher luminous efficacy than a lamp which produces a large proportion of say, infrared radiation which has wavelengths outside the visible spectrum altogether (*3.60*). Lamps with low luminous efficacy produce large amounts of heat which may need to be extracted by an air conditioning system. If the building requires cooling, lights will add to the cooling load and increase running costs. Some ducting systems

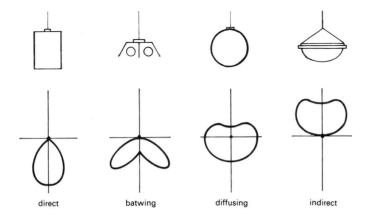

3.79 Types of luminaire used to modify the distribution of light from the source; the polar diagram below each luminaire gives the luminous intensity of the luminaire at any particular angle in the plane being considered.

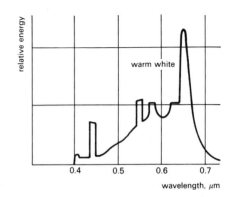

3.80 Energy distribution curve for 'warm' white fluorescent light.

Table 3.8   Types of Electric Filament and Discharge Lamps

Type of Lamp	Efficacy	Life	Colour Temperature	Uses
	lumens/watt	hours	°C	
Tungsten filament	9-18	1000-2000	<3000	general lighting
Tungsten halogen filament	20-30	2000-4000	<3000	shops and area lighting
High pressure mercury tungsten discharge (mercury blended)	10-30	5000-8000	3000-4000	long-life general lighting
High pressure mercury discharge (mercury fluorescent)	35-55	5000-10000	3000-4000	factories and area lighting
Low pressure mercury discharge (tubular fluorescent)	20-70	5000-10000	3000-6000	offices and shops
High pressure mercury discharge (metal halide)	70-90	5000-10000	3000-6000	factories, shops and area lighting
High pressure sodium discharge	50-120	6000-12000	<2000	factories and area lighting
Low pressure sodium discharge	70-150	6000-12000	(Yellow light)	where distortion of colours by yellow light is acceptable

adapted from ref. 5

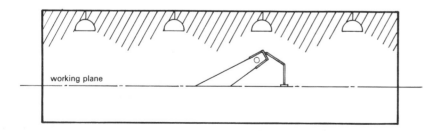

3.81 Ceiling lights being used to provide nearly uniform illuminance at the working plane; extra illuminance can be provided, on the horizontal plane, by task lights and by daylight or wall lights on vertical surfaces.

remove heat from the lamps by extracting exhaust air from the room past the lamps.

In simple cases it is possible to estimate the number of luminaires required for a given illumination level. If a sufficient number of luminaires are fitted then the average horizontal illuminance may be calculated using the lumen method. The average illuminance on a horizontal working plane due to artificial lighting, E, is given by (3.81):

$$E = \frac{n.F.CU.LLF}{A} \text{ lux}$$

where n is the number of luminaires;

F is the output of each luminaire in lumens;

A is the total horizontal area of the workplane in m²;

CU is the coefficient of utilisation and represents the proportion of the lamp lumens that reach the workplane; it depends on the type of lamp and luminaire, the proportions of the room and the reflectance of the walls, ceiling and floor surfaces and

LLF is the light loss factor, or maintenance factor, which allows for loss of output of the lamp due to dirt or deterioration of the lamp.

Scalar Illuminance

In most cases, as above, the lighting level is specified in terms of the illumination on a horizontal plane. However if the light only flows in one direction, in the above case vertically downwards, objects in the room may seem 'flat' and the room may appear drab, even if there is sufficient light reaching the horizontal plane. It is generally desirable to introduce light flowing in a nearly horizontal direction, if light is already flowing in the vertical direction, so as to light up the vertical and inclined surfaces. The concept of scalar illumination is useful, in this respect, as a means of specifying the amount and direction of light available. The *scalar illumination* is the average of the illuminance arriving from all directions at the point being considered. It can be defined as the average illuminance reaching the surface of a very small sphere placed at the point. It is instructive to compare the light received by a disc of unit radius, facing a unidirectional source of light, to that received on a sphere of the same radius at the same point: the same amount of light falls on both surfaces; however the surface area of the sphere is four times that of the disk so that the scalar illumination at the point, with this lighting, is a quarter of the illuminance on the side of the disk that faces towards the source. Inside a sphere of uniform luminance, the two kinds of illuminance are equal: in the sphere, the scalar illuminance is equal to the luminance of the sphere; and, as previously noted, the illuminance on a flat disc at the centre of the base of a uniformly luminous hemisphere (3.65), or the illuminance on a disc at the centre of a uniformly luminous sphere, is also equal to the luminance of the sphere. The concept of light arriving from all directions and falling on a small sphere also provides a method of defining the resultant direction of 'flow' of the light at any point. The direction of flow is defined by the line, passing through the centre of the sphere, which joins up the points of maximum and minimum illuminance on the surface. In general, the direction of flow of light will vary from point to point, in which case the lines of flow are not straight lines. Preferably, the direction of flow of the light should make an angle of between fifteen and forty-five degrees with the horizontal in order to give pleasant lighting effects.

SOUND

Sound Pressure Level

Sound is caused by vibration in an elastic material and its velocity, c, in the material is given by

$$c = \sqrt{\frac{E}{\rho}}$$

where E is the elastic modulus and
ρ is the density of the material.

Airborne sound is caused by changes in air pressure which are detected by the human ear and cause vibrations take place in it. The rate at which these vibrations take place is known as the frequency of the sound. The ear is very sensitive to changes in air pressure and can detect some frequencies of sound at air pressures down to about 2×10^{-5} N/m². Each frequency of sound is associated with a particular wavelength, the wavelength multiplied by the frequency of the sound being equal to the velocity of the sound through the air at the place concerned. Audible sound occurs between frequencies of about 20 Hz to 20 kHz (20

Table 3.9 — Octave Band Analysis of Sound Levels(dB)

Sound	Octave Band Centre Frequency(Hz)							
	62	125	250	500	1000	2000	4000	8000
Ringing telephone	20	40	50	60	60	70	60	50
Centrifugal fan	40	38	35	30	25	25	20	15

to 20 000 cycles per second), corresponding to wavelengths of about 17m to 17mm (3.82). In general a sound can be identified as containing particular frequencies; the ear is able to distinguish the different audible frequencies which are transmitted simultaneously. The eye, by contrast, sees only one mixed colour when different frequencies of light are emitted from the same source. The most common method of specifying sound is based on using a scale divided into octave bands centred on 62, 125, 250, 500, 1000, 2000, 4000 and 8000 Hz; an interval of an octave

between two sounds indicates that one sound has twice the frequency of the other.

A particular sound source can be analysed by dividing up all the frequencies present in the sound into bandwidths having nearly similar frequencies. The narrower the frequency bandwidths used, the more accurate the analysis. Typical bandwidths are an octave or a third of an octave wide (Table 3.9). The sound pressure levels due to each bandwidth in several sound sources can be combined to give a resultant sound pressure level for each bandwith. Compared with light, audible sound has large wavelengths and a consequence of this is that sound can diffract round obstacles, as well as reflect off them (3.83). Some sound energy is also absorbed (3.84). Diffraction is the bending of sound into the 'acoustic shadow' behind an obstacle when its wavelength is greater or nearly equal to the height or width of the obstacle on which it impinges. Hence a free-standing wall provides only limited protection from noise because of the diffraction of sound at the top (3.83). The sound power, W, of a sound source is measured in watts and the sound intensity, I, in watts per square metre. The sound intensity at any distance from a point source of sound radiating into free space may be found by the inverse square law for sound:

$$I = \frac{Q.\,W}{4\pi r^2} \; W/m^2$$

where r is the distance from the source in m and
Q is a directivity factor which for sound uniformly radiating into a free space is one; if the source is put on a plane reflecting surface, radiating into a hemisphere, Q is two and so on.

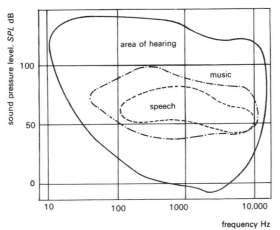

3.82 Areas in terms of pressure level and sound frequency for audible sound, music and speech; the upper limit for audible sound represents the threshold of pain.

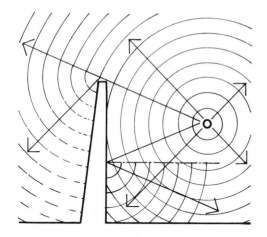

3.83 Sound striking a solid wall is reflected and absorbed at the surface; sound at the top of the wall diffracts into the 'shadow', the low frequency sounds diffracting more than high frequency sounds; the arrows represent the direction of movement of the sound pressure waves.

The sound pressure is usually measured on a logarithmic scale in decibels, dB, and is then known as the *sound pressure level, SPL* :

$$SPL = 20 \, Log_{10}\frac{P_1}{P_0} \, dB$$

where P_1 is the sound pressure in N/m^2 at the point considered and
   P_0 is a reference level usually taken as 2×10^{-5} N/m^2, the threshold of hearing.

As a guide, background noise in a quiet area gives an *SPL* of about 40 dB and loud music about 100 dB. Because the subjective response to an increase in sound level does not go up in proportion to the sound pressure but is more nearly proportional to the percentage change on the existing sound pressure, a measurement using a logarithmic scale gives a better indication of the human response to sound level changes. The relationship of sound intensity to pressure is given by :

$$I = \frac{P^2}{\rho.c} \, W/m^2$$

where P is the sound pressure in N/m^2 and
   $\rho.c$ is the impedance of the air in rayls.

Because of this relationship the *SPL* is also given by:

$$SPL = 10 \, Log_{10}\frac{I_1}{I_0} \, dB$$

where I_1 is the sound intensity at the point considered and
   I_0 is the reference sound intensity for a pressure of 2×10^{-5} N/m^2; the impedance, $\rho.c$, is generally taken as 410 rayls in which case I_0 is nearly equal to 10^{-12} W/m^2.

The sound power, *W*, may also be measured on a logarithmic scale and is then known as the *sound power level, PWL*.

$$PWL = 10 \, Log_{10}\frac{W}{W_0}$$
$$= 10 \, Log_{10}W + 120 \, dB$$

where W_0 is the reference sound power, taken as 10^{-12} W.

From the foregoing definitions, the *PWL* of a point sound source placed on a reflecting surface radiating into free space can be related to the *SPL* at any point:

$$SPL = PWL - 20 \, Log_{10}r - 8 \, dB$$

where r is the distance of the point from the sound source.

Sound levels are measured by meters. The meters can measure the average (root mean square) pressure of the sound which is converted to a meter reading. Most meters as well as having a direct linear response to the sound levels also have weighted A and B scales in which the response of the meter to a constant pressure level varies depending on the frequency of the sound. The weighted scales aim to mimic the response of the human ear which finds sounds at some frequencies to be louder than others which have the same pressure level (*3.82*). However, many other scales for the measurement of sound or noise have been developed for specific purposes. In all cases the scales are designed to indicate, as far as possible, the subjective effects of sound or noise on those listening.

To find the effect on the ear of several sources emitting sound simultaneously it is necessary to convert sound pressures to sound intensities which may then be added together; sound pressure levels cannot be added arithmetically. The total sound insensity, *I*, due to several sources is given by:

$$I = I_1 + I_2 + I_3 + \ldots$$
and the sound pressure level in decibels,

$$SPL = 10 \, Log_{10}\frac{I}{I_0} \, dB$$

As an example, it is found that two sound sources of equal power do not seem twice as loud as a single source. The increase in the *SPL*, by the above formulae, is only 3dB for this case and corresponds, approximately, with the increase in sound as perceived by the ear.

Sound may be transmitted through a solid or liquid elastic medium or in the air. Airborne sound is said to occur in a *free sound field* if it is able to propagate unimpeded over a large sector. In this case the sound intensity decreases with distance in accordance with the inverse square law. By contrast in a closed room with reflecting surfaces sound is propagated from the source in all directions, both as *direct sound* and as *reflected sound*, which is the sound reflected off all the surfaces in the room. Shortly after a sound source is turned on, a more or less uniform sound pressure level is established in most of the room, known as the *reverberant sound pressure level*. The room is then said to have a *diffuse sound field*. Reverberation may be defined as that continuation of audible sound after the sound source is cut off and is a property of the room concerned.

SOUND ABSORPTION

Methods of Absorption

Materials on which sound impinges may be classified in accordance with the way they absorb sound power. As with light, some of the sound reaching the surface is reflected, some is transmitted through the material and some is absorbed and converted to heat (*3.84*). Materials specified for use because of their abilities to absorb sound are known as *sound absorbers*. The *absorption coefficient, α*, of a material is the apparent absorption of the material in a room to a listener in that room. The sound said to be absorbed also includes that which is transmitted:

$$\alpha = \frac{I_A}{I_1}$$

where I_A is the non-reflected sound energy and
   I_1 is the incident sound energy impinging on the material.

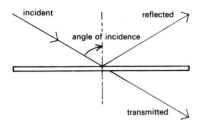

3.84 Sound striking a thin panel is reflected, absorbed and transmitted; the arrows represent the direction of movement of the sound pressure waves.

If $\alpha = 1$, all the incident sound energy is said to be absorbed, even if, as is the case with open space, all the sound is transmitted through the material. In practice most fibrous acoustic absorbents allow large amounts of transmittance, as well as providing absorbance.

Sound absorbers are of two main types, porous absorbers and resonant absorbers. *Porous absorbers* admit the sound waves down a large number of pores where the flow resistance of the pores reduces the sound energy (3.85). The porous absorber is most efficient when the sound wave passes through it at the position where the wave has maximum amplitude; for this to be so, the thickness of the absorbent should be at least equal to a quarter the wavelength of the sound

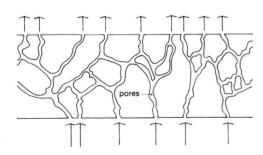

3.85 Section on porous absorber which works by converting sound energy to heat; the thickness must be at least equal to a quarter of the sound wavelengths to be absorbed and such as to give sufficient flow resistance; the pores impede flow but must also allow the sound to penetrate the surface.

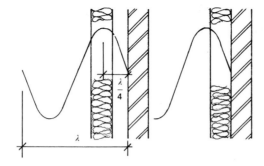

3.86 A porous absorber in front of a solid wall can be placed to intercept a particular sound frequency at the optimum position, a quarter of the sound wavelength from the wall, left; if placed against the wall it is most efficient in absorbing higher frequency sounds, right.

absorbed (3.86). As the range of audible sound frequencies normally designed for have wavelengths ranging from about 50mm to 3.5m, porous absorbents, in practical thicknesses, are not effective with low frequency sound. *Resonant absorbers* can usually be classified either as vibrating panels or Helmholtz resonators; both these types of resonant absorber can be designed to absorb sound in the low to medium frequency ranges but only over narrow bandwidths. They

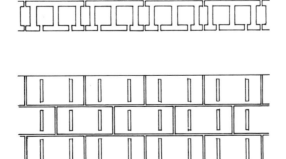

3.87 Section and elevation of absorbent hollow blockwork working on the Helmholtz principle; the resonant frequency depends mostly on the width and depth of the slots in the blockwork.

both work on a mass-spring principle: the vibrating panel consists of a thin, dense panel, representing the mass, with air behind representing the spring; the Helmholtz resonator consists of a plug of air in the neck of the resonator, the mass, with a large volume of air behind it, the spring (3.87). The perforated vibrating panel works on the same principle as the Helmholtz resonator (3.88). Practical wall constructions can be designed to provide absorbance by a combination of these means (3.89). Sound insulation and sound absorption may be provided simultaneously by absorbent attached to a solid wall, the thickness and distance of the absorbent from the wall depending on the frequencies of the sound that need to be 'soaked up' (3.86).

The absorption of a surface is given by $S.\alpha$ in square metres; a measure of the total sound absorbency of a room is given by the room constant, A, where :

$$A = \frac{S.\bar{\alpha}}{1-\bar{\alpha}} \text{ m}^2$$

where S is the surface area of the room in m^2 and
$\bar{\alpha}$ is the average absorption coefficient from all surfaces in the room and equal to
$$\frac{S_1.\alpha_1 + S_2.\alpha_2 + ..}{S_1 + S_2 + ..}$$
with α_1 etc and S_1 etc being the absorption coefficients and areas of the different surfaces in the room.

Sound absorption is measured in a reverberation chamber with sound arriving at various angles of incidence. The absorption of any particular material will vary depending on the frequency of the sound impinging on it (Table 3.10).

SOUND INSULATION

Airborne Sound

Sound transmission between adjacent rooms or spaces is usually split up into two components: the *airborne sound* is that transmitted through the air from the sound source, which, in turn, causes vibrations in the surrounding walls, floor and ceiling (3.90); the *structure-borne sound* is that originating in the structure, for example that caused by a direct hammering action on a wall; the vibrations of the structure then cause sound to be transmitted through the air to the listener in the

Table 3.10   Absorption Coefficients (α) at various frequencies

Element	Frequency(Hz)			
	125	500	2000	4000
Brickwork	0.05	0.02	0.05	0.05
Fibreboard on solid wall	0.05	0.15	0.3	0.3
Glass wool 25mm thick on solid wall	0.15	0.7	0.9	0.9
Glass wool 50mm thick over 25mm air space on solid wall	0.35	0.9	0.95	0.9
Pile carpet on thick felt on concrete floor	0.07	0.5	0.6	0.65
Plywood panel over air space against solid wall	0.3	0.15	0.1	. .
Hardboard panel backed with bitumen felt and mounted over air space on solid wall	0.9	0.25	0.1	0.1
Curtain in folds over 25mm air space against solid wall	0.05	0.35	0.5	. .

adapted from ref. 2

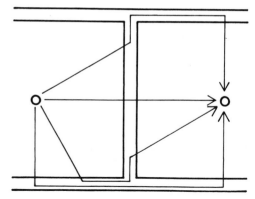

3.90 Four routes for the propagation of airborne sound to an adjacent room; the three routes not passing directly through the separating wall are the 'flanking' transmissions, which may be reduced by discontinuous construction.

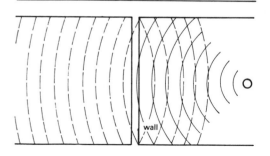

3.91 Direct sound transmission through a separating wall with some stiffness; the sound causes vibration of the wall which itself acts as a secondary sound source leading to transmission and reflection of the original sound.

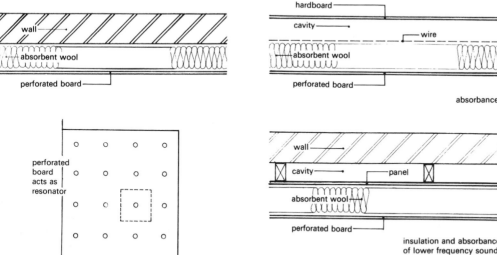

3.88 Section and elevation on sound absorbent construction using perforated board on a solid wall; each perforation and the space behind, shown dotted, acts like a Helmholtz resonator; the wall also provides sound insulation.

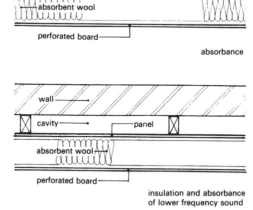

3.89 Porous absorber used on timber frame construction, top, and on solid wall, bottom; absorbance at the solid wall is achieved by use of an absorbent wool on a resonant panel thus giving sound absorption over a wide band.

receiving room (3.91). Airborne sound passing through anywhere except the main partition wall separating the two room spaces is known as the flanking transmission (3.90).

To reduce the transmission of airborne sound it is necessary to provide a barrier or sound insulant. The sound transmission loss, TL, or the sound reduction index, R, of a wall is given by:

$$R = 10\text{Log}_{10}\frac{1}{T}$$

where T, the transmission coefficient of the wall, is equal to the ratio of the transmitted to the incident sound energy on the wall.

For a wall with door or window openings the average transmission coefficient T_{AV}, should be used and is given by:

$$T_{AV} = \frac{T_1.S_1 + T_2.S_2 + T_3.S_3 + ...}{S_1 + S_2 + S_3 + ...}$$

where T_1 etc and S_1 etc are the coefficients and areas of each part of the wall.

The sound transmission paths work 'in parallel' and the formulae show that even a small area with a high transmission value has a significant effect on the average value, leading to significant losses in sound reduction. The loss is proportionally greater in heavier walls (3.92). The values of the sound reduction coefficient, R, are measured under laboratory condition and give values of R over a range of frequencies (Table 3.11). For convenience, a single figure is often used to characterise the insulation of a wall or other partition. An *average sound reduction* and a

Table 3.11   Sound Reduction of Elements at Various Frequencies (dB)

Element	Frequency (Hz)					
	125	250	500	1000	2000	Average 100 to 2150
Wall 110mm thick plastered	34	36	41	51	58	45
Wall 220mm thick plastered	41	45	48	56	58	50
Wood floor with tongue and groove boarding and plasterboard ceiling	18	25	37	39	45	34
Wood floor with t and g boarding floating on glass wool and 50mm sand on 3-coat ceiling on metal lath	36	42	47	52	60	49
Concrete floor 126mm thick	35	36	41	49	58	45
Single glazing with 4mm glass	17	21	25	26	23	22
Double glazing with 4mm glass tightly sealed and 200mm air space with absorbent in reveals	30	35	43	46	47	39

adapted from ref. 2

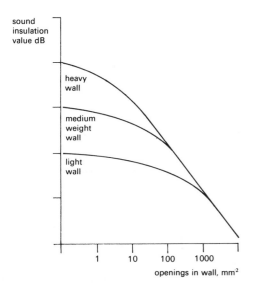

3.92 Curves showing loss of sound insulation in light, medium and heavy walls caused by openings in the walls.

weighted sound reduction index are among those used, the latter being obtained by fitting a standard shaped line, weighted to take account of the ear's perception of sound, to the graph of the experimental figures over the range of frequencies used in the test. In practice, the laboratory test does not usually take into account the flanking transmission, the methods of fixing, the size of the partition or the sound absorption of the receiver room for the particular case being considered. The last two factors are taken into account, however, by the *level difference, D*, or *noise reduction, NR :*

$$NR = R - 10\text{Log}_{10}\frac{S}{A}$$

where S is the area of the wall in m^2 and
        A is the total sound absorbency of the receiver room in m^2.

As noted previously, low sound insulation values of the doors or windows will greatly reduce the overall insulation of the wall or partition. However poor seals or small holes in the wall can also have a noticeable effect; the loss in sound insulation is significant for sound frequencies whose wavelengths are comparable to or less than the dimensions of the opening through which the leakage occurs (3.93).

An approximate guide to the sound reduction of a wall or partition is given by the mass law, which, in its simplest form, states that there is an increase in sound reduction, R, of 6dB for each doubling of the mass of the wall (3.95). The mass of the wall is the best, single guide to its insulation value, although the law only properly applies to materials without stiffness. Because actual building materials have stiffness, they provide less insulation than that assumed by the mass law, only amounting to about 4 or 5 dB each time the mass of the wall is doubled (3.94). The stiffness that materials possess causes them to resonate, particularly at high frequencies, and it is this that is responsible for the decrease in the sound reduction from that predicted by the mass law. Resonance effects also occur in cavity walls, especially ones with narrow cavities, and in panels

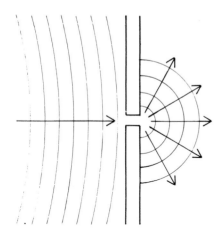

3.93 Diffraction of sound through small hole in a separating wall.

Table 3.12   Approximate Critical Frequencies

Material	Thickness mm	Surface Mass kg/mm²	Critical Frequency Hz
Brick	215	400	100
Brick	102	200	200
Lead	18	200	15000
Plasterboard	10	9	2900-4500
Plasterboard	20	18	1400-2300
Glassfibre reinforced gypsum board	10	18	2000
Plywood	10	7.5	1300
Steel	3	25	4000

after ref. 6

attached to single walls, for example dry plasterboard linings attached directly to walls or separated from them by a layer of thermal insulation.

In single-leaf walls the frequency at which resonance occurs is known as the *critical frequency* and occurs due to a *coincidence* effect. As coincidence is only noticeable above the critical frequency of the wall, it is important to make the critical frequency as high as possible by increasing the density and decreasing the thickness and elastic modulus of the material (*3.95*). Walls can be said to be *pliable* if the critical

frequency is above about 2000 Hz and *rigid* if it is below about 200 Hz . Table 3.12 gives typical critical frequencies for various forms of construction. There are dimishing returns in continually increasing the mass of a single-leaf wall as a way of improving its sound insulation. Beyond a certain point it is better to use a second wall which, in general, gives greater improvements in the sound reduction for the same additional thickness. Unfortunately the two walls cannot be placed close together without the air between the two walls acting as a resonator and coupling the motion of the two walls causing a loss in the sound reduction (*3.95*). The frequency at which this coupling occurs in double-leaf walls is the

resonant frequency, f_R, (*3.95*). The resonant frequency is given by:

$$f_R = \sqrt{\frac{k.E_D}{d}\left(\frac{1}{m_1} + \frac{1}{m_2}\right)} \text{ Hz}$$

where k is a constant;
   E_D is the dynamic modulus and d is the thickness of the intermediate layer and
   m_1 and m_2 are the masses of the two leaves per unit area.

As the advantage of double-leaf construction is only apparent above the resonant frequency, it is important to try and lower this frequency by increasing the mass of both walls and the distance between them. The intermediate layer, between the two leaves, is usually air. At high frequencies, coincidence effects on both leaves individually reduce the sound reduction that would otherwise be possible; the effect is particularly marked if coincidence occurs simultaneously for both leaves, although this can be minimised by leaves having different characteristics, for example different thicknesses. Between the resonant frequency and the frequencies at which coincidence effects occur, the mass law shows that, in theory, it would be possible to have a 12dB increase in sound reduction for every doubling of the mass of the wall, assuming that the two walls are spaced sufficiently far apart so as to act independently. Double-leaf walls are also subject to losses in sound reduction due to standing

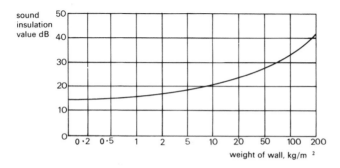

3.94 Approximate actual sound insulation value of single-leaf wall.

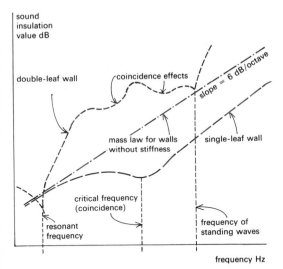

3.95 *Approximate shape of theoretical variation of sound insulation with frequency for single-leaf and double-leaf walls by reference to the insulation of a flexible single-leaf wall according to the mass law.*

elsewhere, the maximum sound pressure amplitude occurring at positions a half-wavelength from each node point (*3.96*). By contrast in a normal travelling wave, the sound pressure amplitude varies by the same amount at each point over a wavelength. A standing wave is formed by the superposition of two sound waves travelling in opposite directions and is caused in this case by continuous reflection off the two parallel surfaces.

The best insulation is provided by heavy walls but the insulation of lightweight can be significantly improved by double-leaf construction, the percentage increase in sound reduction being greater in lightweight walls. (*3.97*). As noted previously, to prevent the coincidence of each leaf occurring simultaneously, it is best if each leaf has different characteristics. However this may have to be balanced against the need to keep the resonant frequency low, which is a minimum when the two leaves have equal mass per unit area. For lightweight construction it is particularly important that the two leaves are spaced as far apart as possible. In practice high sound reduction depends on good detailing and workmanship, especially in ensuring that elements are acoustically isolated from each other. Preferably, sound-absorbing material should be hung in the intermediate layer. As noted previously, sound insulation can be combined with sound absorption on the outer surfaces (*3.89*).

waves (*3.95*). *Standing waves* will occur when the frequency of sound is such that the distance between the two parallel leaves is an exact multiple of the wavelength; a standing wave gives no sound at some positions, the nodes of the sound pressure wave, but amplified sound

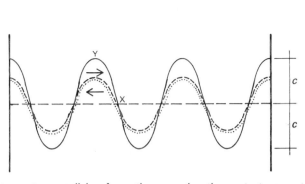

3.96 *Standing wave between two parallel surfaces, three wavelengths apart, at moment when amplitude is greatest; the standing wave is made up by superposition of sound waves travelling left and right (shown dotted); at the node points X the sound pressure is always at atmospheric pressure; at Y the sound pressure varies between atmospheric plus c and atmospheric minus c.*

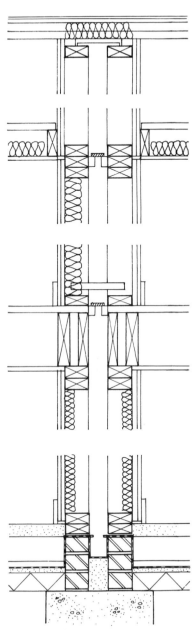

3.97 *Vertical section through lightweight, double-leaf separating wall as used in timber framed houses with pitched roofs; except at the ground floor and roof, only the firestops, shown shaded, and light flexible ties at level 2 bridge the cavity; cavity width between the inside faces of the double layers of gypsum board is about 250mm (after ref. 7).*

Structure-borne sound

Structure-borne sound is that which arises by impact on the walls but, more usually, the floors of a room. The impact sound insulation of a floor is measured by the airborne sound level in the room below, when the floor receives impacts from a standard tapping machine. The impact sound insulation of a single homogenous floor element is poor and protection against impact noise is best provided by covering the floor with a resilient layer, by suspended ceilings or by floating screeds on top of insulants resting on the main floor structure. Floating screeds work on similar principles to a double-leaf wall; the resonant frequency of the system should be as low as possible and this is done by increasing the mass of the floor screed and by decreasing the stiffness of the intermediate layer under dynamic load as much as possible (3.98). The thicker the intermediate layer, the smaller the stiffness. As the mass of the supporting structure is usually much greater than the screed, an increase in the mass of the floor structure produces only a small improvement in the overall insulation value. Practical floor and wall constructions must incorporate ways of minimising both airborne and structure-borne sound (3.99 and 3.100). Suspended ceilings below a floor are most effective in giving impact sound insulation if they are heavy, reasonably

flexible, well sealed at the edges and placed as far as possible from the floor soffit (3.101). Preferably sound absorbent material should be placed above the suspended ceiling.

Vibrating machinery may be treated by placing on resilient supports or by placing on a heavy base on resilient supports using the mass-spring principle of the floating screed (3.102). A layer of viscoelastic material may be used to provide damping as well as elasticity. The construction and thickness of the insulant layer may be altered to reduce the transmission of dominant or important frequencies which may be present.

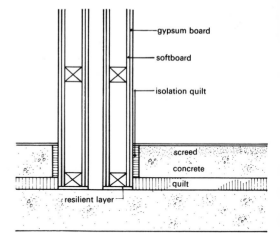

3.100 Vertical section through base of discontinuous, double-leaf timber separating wall; softboard and gypsum board is used on the inside and outside of each leaf; the clear width of the cavity is about 50mm.

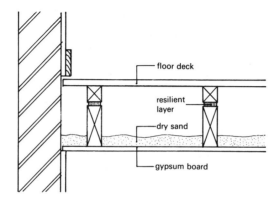

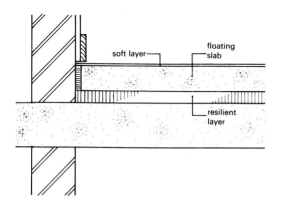

3.98 Mass-spring principle used to provide impact sound reduction in floors; the floating screed should be as heavy as possible.

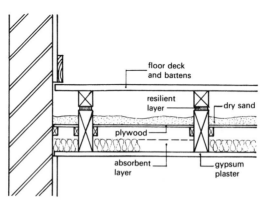

3.99 Typical constructions used in timber floors to limit airborne and structure-borne sound transmission.

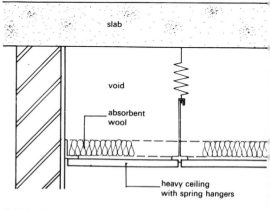

3.101 Typical construction of suspended ceiling to reduce airborne sound caused by impact on floor slab above.

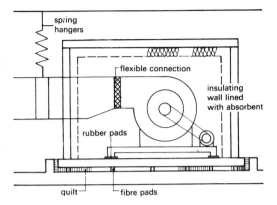

3.102 Typical construction used to reduce airborne and structure-borne sound emissions from air-handling plant.

Noise Control

Sounds that cause disturbance are termed as noise. Noise may be controlled by reducing the power of the noise source, by natural attenuation, by reducing the transmission of sound and by acoustic treatment of surfaces in the receiving room. Principal sources of noise within buildings are those due to the components of air conditioning systems such as the fans, water pumps, compressors or ducts, in the choice of which the designer has an opportunity of reducing the noise emitted (*3.103*). Natural attenuation

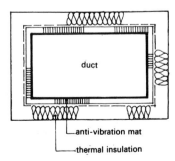

3.103 Lagging of air ducts with heavy mats to increase sound insulation.

consists simply of separating noisy areas from quiet areas as far as possible. This leads to the idea of zoning quiet and noisy areas in a building. In an open field natural attenuation by the inverse square law gives a 6dB reduction in the sound pressure level every time the distance from the noise source is doubled. In practice the attenuation is likely to be less than this, outside, because of the ground surface, temperature changes and other effects of the weather. Some sound sources are highly directional, emitting higher sound pressures than the average in particular directions. There are several methods of reducing sound transmission most of which consist of good sound insulation. In particular, low sound transmission through walls depends on mass, the control of resonance effects, the sealing of air paths and the elimination of flanking transmissions by the use of discontinuous construction (*3.97*).

An effective method for reducing the sound level in a room is by covering the room surfaces with sound-absorbing material. In an enclosed space, assuming the sound pressure level due to reverberation is uniformly distributed throughout the room, the reverberant sound pressure level due to a point sound source at any position not in the near field of the source is aproximately given by:

$$SPL = PWL + 10\text{Log}_{10}\left(\frac{Q}{4\pi r^2} + \frac{4}{A}\right) \text{dB}$$

where Q is the directivity factor;
   r is the distance from the source in m and
   A is the room factor in m^2

In such a diffuse sound field, the output of sound energy at the source is equal to that lost by absorption. The second term within the brackets is the *SPL* due to the reverberant sound. To calculate the *SPL* in a free field, where there is only direct sound radiated over non-absorbent ground, the same formula is used with $Q = 2$ and with the second term within the brackets, due to reverberant sound, being omitted.

ROOM ACOUSTICS

Reverberation Time

Room acoustics are concerned with providing a good quality sound at sufficient volume in all parts of a room and reducing unwanted noise either from a source within the room or outside. Noise

from outside is best reduced by arranging the walls, roofs and floor of the room to give high sound insulation. Listeners could be protected from loud noise within the room by a low wall acting as a barrier placed near to the noise source. However the noise will reflect off the barrier and surrounding walls and is also able to diffract or bend round the edges of the barrier, especially low frequency sound. If possible the noise source should be completely shielded by an enclosure which has high sound insulation and which is lined with a sound absorbent to reduce the reverberant sound within the enclosure (*3.104*). With unwanted noise at an acceptable level, the design can concentrate on giving an even distribution of the required sound in all parts of the room. The sound may be reinforced by reflecting surfaces in some parts of the room and muted by absorbents in other parts. The shape of the reflectors will alter the way the sound is propagated (*3.105*). The reflecting surfaces should avoid focusing the sound at particular points (*3.106*). Flutter is also to be avoided. *Flutter* is caused by sound repeatedly reflected off parallel surfaces, which give rise to standing waves that occur at all frequencies for which the distance between the two parallel leaves is an exact multiple of its wavelength (*3.96*). This causes variations in sound level and distortions. To cure it, the surfaces should be covered with absorbent or made non-parallel.

Sound reflected off the walls or other surfaces

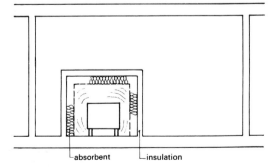

3.104 Heavy enclosure lined with an absorbent to limit intensity of of noise from source.

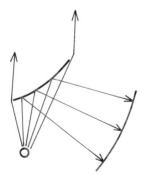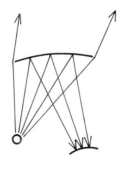

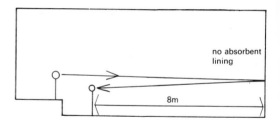

no absorbent lining

8m

3.108 Sound reflected off back wall causing echo.

3.105 Reflectors made to disperse or concentrate sound power; because of diffraction at the edges, the reflector must be large compared to the wavelength of the sound in order for it to be effective.

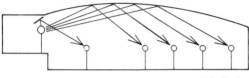

sound distribution

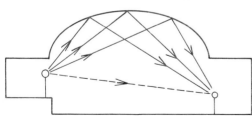

sound focusing

3.106 Ceiling shape giving good distribution of sound, top, and one causing excessive focusing, bottom.

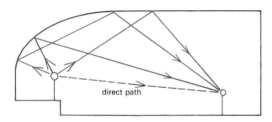

direct path

3.107 Sound received at point by direct and reflected sound.

will reach the listener slightly later than the sound on the direct path from the sound source (*3.107*). However reverberant sound will blend with the direct sound assuming the time gap is less than about 50ms (50×10^{-3} s). Reflected sound with a larger time gap than this will be perceived as an echo. This time gap corresponds to a travel distance of about 16 metres (*3.108*). Thus a sound source directly in front of a listener reflecting off a wall 8 metres directly behind the listener gives rise to an echo; in practice the maximum travel distance should not be more than about 10m, if possible. Concert halls and other similar types of space should have absorbents at the back of the space, to prevent echoes, and reflectors at the front, to help distribute the sound. In practice the behaviour of sound in a room is extremely complex and depends on the frequency of the sound, the type and amount of absorption and the three-dimensional geometry of the room surfaces.

An important acoustic property of a room, which may be measured, is the reverberation time. Sound lingers in a room after it is emitted because of the reverberant sound. The *reverberation time, t,* is the time taken for a sound to decay by 60 dB, that is, to a millionth of its original sound intensity. Rooms with low reverberation times, less than about 0.8 seconds, feel 'dead' while those with long reverberation times, greater than about 1.5 seconds, cause interference with the direct sound and loss of intelligibility. Sabine's formula states that :

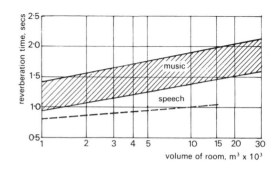

3.109 Typical recommended reverberation times for speech and music.

$$t = \frac{0.16V}{A} \text{ seconds}$$

where V is the volume of the room in m³ and
       A is the room constant, or absorbency, at any particular frequency

Typical reverberation times which have been found to be satisfactory are about one second for a lecture hall and about two seconds for a concert hall, where the longer reverberance, in the latter case, can increase the sound quality (*3.109*). For a room with a reasonable level of reverberant sound, the reverberation time is more or less constant in all parts of the room. Normally the designer should aim to have similar values for reverberation time at all the different audio frequencies. However, concert halls may have slightly longer times for the lower notes. As with assessments of daylight illuminance, it is often difficult to predict the acoustic performance of a room by calculation and, in some cases, models may be useful. The effect of the shape of the room on the propagation of sound waves within the room may be investigated, in two dimensions, by a ripple tank. This consists of a shallow tray of water in which a shape representing any particular cross-section through the room is placed. A vibrator, representing the sound source, causes surface ripples which then give a ripple pattern representing the way the sound waves would propagate. Several of the cross-sections may be tried. For final design a three dimensional model may be built to a scale. The time is changed in the same scale-ratio so that the model would be tested at ten times the normal audio frequencies, if the model is built at a tenth scale. The internal surfaces of the model should have the same absorption properties at these frequencies as the actual surfaces have at normal audio frequencies. A scale model can also be used with an analogue light source, instead of the sound source, and light reflectant surfaces, instead of the acoustically reflectant surfaces of the actual room. The illuminance levels in the model than represent the sound pressure levels. Computer models of the acoustic performance of the room can also be valuable in design work.

Chapter Four

Fire Safety

The possibility of a fire has a major influence on building design, both at the initial and final stages of the design. Fire precautions in buildings are concerned with the prevention of fire, for example by removal of combustible material, safe handling procedures, choice of lining materials and so on, and, should this fail, with the protection from fire of people and property. Under the term of *fire protection* are measures designed to allow means of escape for the occupants of the building as well as measures to prevent the spread of fire both within a building and from one building to another. In most countries the statutory fire regulations vary according to the type and use of the building and, in general, attempt to cover both life safety and protection of the building and its contents. Although there are arguments, on the grounds of a more effective use of resources, that statutory regulations only cover life safety requirements, the preventive measures taken may be beneficial on both counts. For example protection against collapse of the building saves lives as well as the building structure and its contents.

Fire is associated with *combustion,* which is a reaction between some chemical substance and oxygen that gives out heat and produces a flame.

Some substances can react with oxygen at room temperatures but do not give out sufficient heat for combustion to take place and do not produce a flame. Only certain substances are readily combustible, many building materials being classified as non-combustible. In general, even if a combustible substance is in contact with oxygen, combustion will not start without heat being applied. In a combustible substance, oxygen and the heat given out by the combustion are both necessary in order for the combustion to be able to maintain itself. If it does, development of the fire can be very rapid.

COMPARTMENT FIRE

Ignition and Growth

The behaviour of materials under fire is complex and depends on many factors, of which the most important is the type of fuel for the fire. For example, many new finishing materials contained within the building enclosure are highly flammable and, when alight, the flames can spread across them at speeds greater than walking speeds. Other materials may only smoulder when set alight. Another important factor is the ventilation, which is the amount of air reaching the fire. To limit the number of variables in the disussion of the behaviour of fires in buildings, a useful concept is that of the compartment fire. A *compartment fire* is one in which the fire starts and reaches a fully developed stage in a single enclosure or compartment which may be a room, a hall or a whole building. The compartment fire can be considered as having three phases, ignition and growth, full development and decay. *Ignition* is said to have occurred only when the heat given out by combustion is just sufficient to maintain combustion after the applied heat, which started the fire is removed. For ignition to occur the temperature of the combustible substance, the fuel, must be raised to some minimum temperature. This temperature can be measured, although the exact conditions of measurement need to be defined, as far as possible and, even then, the variations may still be very significant. For *liquids*, ignition depends on there being a suitable proportion of vapour and air present at the surface. The *flash-point* of a liquid is the lowest temperature at which the vapour above the liquid will ignite when a small flame is brought near to it. Volatile liquids such as acetone or petroleum spirit (gasolene) have low flash-point temperatures, igniting immediately at room temperatures; others such as paraffin (kerosene) have to be heated above room temperatures before they will ignite in this way. For *solid materials* an indicator of the likelihood of ignition is the flash ignition temperature. The *flash ignition temperature* of a material is said to be the lowest temperature at which ignition can occur. The ignition temperature of wood is approximately 200°C (400°F). Although it is possible to have self-ignition, in which the temperature is raised by internal reactions, normally, as noted previously, an applied heat is necessary for ignition to occur and comes from an external source, such as a flame. The source must not only be hot itself but has to transfer enough heat to the fuel to be able to raise it to its ignition temperature. For example sparks, although hot, generally contain insufficient energy to do this.

The *ignitability* of the fuel is the ease with which it may ignited. The three material factors which have most influence on ignition are the ignition temperature, the surface area ratio, the ratio of

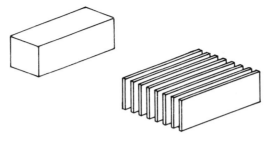

4.1 A wood block sawn into thin strips has a higher surfaces area ratio and is easier to ignite.

surface area to mass of the material, and the surface thermal absorption. An illustration of the signifance of the surface area ratio is provided by comparing the ease of ignition of thin strips of wood or wood shavings, with a large surface area, to a block of wood of the same mass (*4.1*). Similarly a foamed plastic ignites more easily than a solid piece of plastic. A material in the form of thin strips or a foam requires less heat to raise it to any given temperature than if it is in the form of a solid block. Hence it is easier to ignite. When alight, a material with a high surface area ratio, such as foamed plastic, burns faster and releases

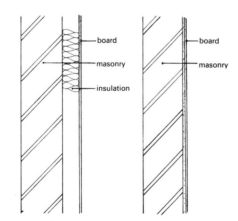

4.2 Thin board backed by insulation has low thermal absorption, left, and is easier to ignite than one without insulation, right.

heat and toxic gases more quickly than solid material. Combustion of a solid, being nearly always a reaction between vapours from the solid and external oxygen, occurs at the surface of the solid, so that an increased surface area increases the rate at which heat is produced. The third factor, the *thermal absorption, v,* is also significant, particularly for wall and ceiling lining materials which, if ignited, may allow rapid spread of the fire. The thermal absorption is defined by:

$$v = \lambda.\rho.c \; \text{W}^2 \, \text{s}/ \, \text{m}^4 \; ^\circ\text{C}^2 \; (\text{btu}^2/ \, \text{hr ft}^4 \; ^\circ\text{F}^2)$$

where λ is the thermal conductivity of the material in W/ m °C (btu in/ ft² hr °F);

ρ is the density of the material in kg/m³ (lb/ft³); and

c is the specific heat of the material in J/ kg °C (btu/ lb °F).

In a material having low surface thermal absorption, *v*, any heat applied at the surface concentrates particularly at that point, so that there is a rapid rise of temperature at the point and ignition is achieved with relative ease. Note, for this same reason, a thin sheet material backed by an insulant is more likely to ignite than one backed by a material with good conductivity (*4.2*). The rise in temperature at a distance in from the heated face is very slow compared to that on the surface itself, so that, above a certain minimum, the thickness of the material has no significant influence on the rate of heating, the rate of heating on the surface, over these short periods, being similar to that of an infinitely thick material. Note that ignition does not always cause immediate flaming. Some materials may smoulder for long periods and then catch fire because of a change in conditions, for example a sudden increase in ventilation.

Full Development and Decay

In a compartment fire, after the ignition stage, the fire starts to grow and in doing so generates an increasing amount of heat, as the fuels decompose; the fire is then able to spread and does so at an ever-increasing rate. The initial rate of spread depends on how much of the heat generated goes to heating up fuel, as well as on the surface area ratio and the surface thermal absorption of the materials. If there are no easily ignitable materials nearby, the fire could go out. However if the fire develops, ever more heat is produced so that the compartment and its contents increase in temperature, at a corresponding rate. The flames grow in size and soon reach ceiling level in a room. At this stage the type of wall and ceiling lining still has a decisive influence on the rate of spread of the fire. As the fire develops further, the radiation from hot surfaces, particularly from the ceiling, becomes a more decisive influence than convection or the general rise in air temperature. Burning materials may start to fall from the ceiling. As each combustible part of the compartment rises in temperature it gives off volatile gases. More and more parts give off more and more vapour. *Flashover* occurs when these gases all ignite, often in sudden fashion, such that the whole compartment is filled with fire. When this happens the fire is said to be *fully developed*. A fire which reaches flashover point in less than about three minutes may give insufficient time for evacuation and may lead to loss of life.

A fully-developed fire is associated with a rapid rise in temperature, even if the rate of increase declines, and is almost always *ventilation controlled*, that is the severity of the fire is only limited by the amount of air available; unburnt gases find their way out of the compartment taking fire as they encounter more oxygen. Clearly escape from the compartment must take place before flashover, as at this point the whole atmosphere inside the compartment is poisonous. For compartments with large window areas or small amounts of fuel it is possible for the fire to be a *free-burning fire,* or fuel-controlled fire, in which the severity of the fire depends largely on the type and arrangement of the fuel; more air would not increase the rate of burning. As the fire continues, eventually a point is reached where the temperature inside the compartment peaks, the fire starts to run out of fuel and *decay* is said to have started. The fire ceases when all available fuel has been burnt.

TEMPERATURE AND DURATION OF FIRE

Rate of Burning

An important idea is that fire can be contained by an enclosure in such a way as to prevent spread of the fire. For this to be possible the elements of the enclosure must have fire resistance. The *fire resistance* is applied to elements of construction such as walls, floors and beams and is an indication of the extent to which these elements will resist a fully-developed fire. The term 'fire resistance' has to be defined more precisely for specific purposes, such as fire regulations. Normally standard fire tests are used to establish nominal values, in hours, for the 'fire resistance' of building elements; the fire tests do not necessarily reproduce actual fire conditions but are useful as a basis for comparison of different forms of construction. The term 'fire rating' is often used in place of 'fire resistance' to reflect the fact that this is a relative rather than an actual measure of fire resistance. The actual required fire resistance of an element, in order that it behaves satisfactorily, will depend on the *fire severity*, the most important aspects of which, for these purposes, are the duration of the fire and the maximum temperature reached during the fire. The total heat released during a fire, in which there is a complete burnout, depends on the amount of fuel present, that is the *fire load* (Table 4.1). In a ventilation-controlled fire, the rate of burning can be increased by increasing the ventilation through the openings to the compartment, which, in a building, are almost always window openings; ordinary glass usually shatters soon after the fire is fully developed. The rate of burning, R, in such a fire in a room with an opening is approximately given by [1]:

Table 4.1   Values for Fire Load Density

Building Type	Fire Load Density (wood equivalent)	
	lb/ft^2	kg/m^2
Residential	5	25
Institutional	5	25
Office	5-10	25-50
Shop	<50	<250
Factory	<30	<150
Assembly halls	5-10	25-50
Storage	<100	<500

values given are indicative only
from ref.2

$$R = \frac{0.18}{E}(1-e^{-0.036\eta}) \quad kg/s$$
$$= \frac{1.22}{E}(1-e^{-0.065\eta}) \quad lb/s$$

where $E = \frac{1}{A}\sqrt{\frac{D}{W.h}}$ kg/ s m$^{5/2}$ (lb/ min ft$^{5/2}$);

$\eta = \frac{A_t}{A\sqrt{h}}$ m$^{-1/2}$ (ft$^{-1/2}$);

A is the area of the opening to the room in m^2 (ft^2);

A_t is the area of the room floor, ceiling and walls, excluding the area of the opening, in m^2 (ft^2);

h is the height of the opening in m (ft);

D is the depth of the room in m (ft);

W is the width of the room in m (ft); and

e is the base for natural logarithms.

The factors, E and η, are only connected with the geometry of the room and its opening. The rate of burning increases both as the area of the opening and the width of the room increase as a proportion of the room depth. If the total fire load is known then an estimate can be made of the fire duration; the fire load is usually expressed as the mass of wood which would have a similar effect as the actual fire load. The *fire duration, τ* is given by:

$$\tau = \frac{L}{R} \quad s \ (min)$$

where L is the fire load in kg (lb).

If the fire is free burning then the fire duration depends on the form and type of the fuel. Table 4.1 gives typical values of fire load density.

Temperature of Fire

The average temperature reached during a fire, the other component of fire severity, depends on the fire load, but to a lesser extent than the fire duration, and on the room geometry factor, η; with large openings, that is low values of η, the rate of heat release is high but this is balanced by high heat losses; with small openings, the heat released is small but losses are also small. The result of this is that there is not a particularly wide variation in the average fire temperature. Experiments give the *average fire temperature* as not exceeding about 1200 °C (2200 °F) with η equal to 15 m$^{-1/2}$ (25 ft$^{-1/2}$), dropping quickly as η decreases and more slowly as it increases; the temperature is about 800° C (1500 °C) with η at four times this value.

SPREAD OF FIRE AND SMOKE

Fire Spread

In a building fire spreads from the room where ignition took place by passing through gaps in the room enclosure. The fire consists of flames, as well as hot gases which take flame as they encounter oxygen. Fire may also spread from the room where ignition took place by conduction through the room enclosure, allowing the material on the other side of the wall to become hot enough to ignite spontaneously. The flames and hot gases can escape from the room through windows, doors, along suspended ceilings, raised floors and, more insidiously, through service ducts, cable trays or through the gap around pipes that penetrate the room enclosure. As the flames and gases escape from the room enclosure, they are then free to spread along corridors, stair and lift cores, service shafts and cavities within the construction between the rooms. The spread can be extremely rapid. As already noted, one way of preventing fire spread in a building is *compartmentation,* which is the division of a building into compartments which are enclosed by fire-resistant construction. For the compartmentation to be effective, any gaps or openings in the compartment enclosures, such as those due to ducts or pipes, must be properly plugged by fire stops or, in the case of duct openings, closed by fire shutters which can operate as soon as a fire is detected (*4.9*). Note that the barriers to the fire provided by the compartment may prevent easy access to cables and ducts for the purpose of maintenance or for changes to the mechanical systems. Providing smokeproof construction is even more onerous in this respect.

Another important path for the spread of flames is via windows. In most buildings the windows will shatter in the heat soon after the fire is fully developed so that flames and hot gases could spread to the floors above and may be able to ignite combustible materials there and allow spread of the fire upwards. The height of the flame tip above the bottom of the window increases as the rate of burning, *R*, increases but decreases as the width of the window increases. Equally important for fire spread is the horizontal gap between the flame tip and the face of the building above the fire. For a window of constant height,

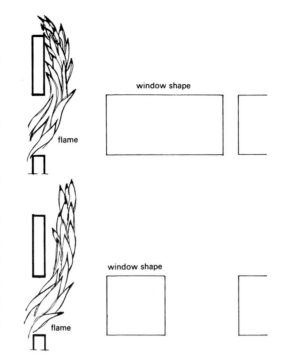

4.3 Section and elevation on open window, at typical floor of multistorey building, showing variation in flame shape, due to internal fire, for window with a square or a rectangular shape; in the latter case the flame turns back into the building and could set fire to the floor above.

with the same rate of burning, this gap decreases as the window width increases (*4.3*). With wide windows or continuous strips of glazing the flame tips will curl back and touch the face of the building. At this point the temperature of the flame would be about 540°C (1000°F). With continuous glazing strips the exposed spandrels may be protected against flames by a wide flame shield at the bottom of the spandrel but the flames may still be able to enter the floor above and set light to combustible material (*4.4*).

Fire may also spread from one building to another, adjacent to it, by flames, flying brands or radiation from the building already on fire. Of these methods of spread, the most important is the

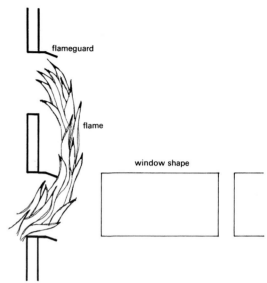

4.4 Section through windows showing use of flameguards to protect spandrel beams from internal fire in lower storey.

radiation which, commonly, can have intensities sufficient to cause ignition at a considerable distance from the fire. The radiation from the fire varies with distance in the same way as the illuminance does from a light source. The radiation intensity, *I*, at a point away from the fire depends on its distance from the fire, on how much of the area on fire is facing towards the point (the projected area) and on the radiation intensity at the fire, I_0, which, in turn, is very dependent on the fire temperature. The intensities are related by:

$$I = \varphi.I_0 \text{ kW/m}^2 \text{ (btu/ ft}^2 \text{ min)}$$

where φ is a factor depending only on the geometrical relationship of the point concerned to the building, known as the configuration factor.

The configuration factors in respect of several different fire areas may be added together to calculate the total radiation intensity at any point. In general the radiation at any point on a building adjacent to a building on fire should not exceed about 12.5 kW/m² (65 btu/ ft² min), which corresponds to the radiation which would cause wood to ignite if a flame were present. In this case

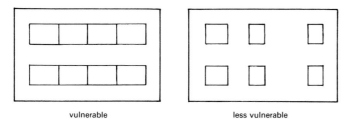

4.5 A building, which is next to a building on fire, may be vulnerable to ignition, if the adjacent building has a large area of window facing towards it; it is less vulnerable if the window area is small.

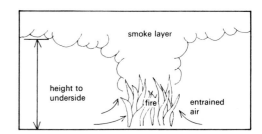

4.6 Diagram showing build-up of smoke cloud at ceiling in an enclosed space.

a flame might be brought by a flying brand. The radiation can be reduced by reducing the configuration factor, for example reducing the number of openings in the walls facing the adjacent building or increasing the separation between them (4.5). In addition the outsides of buildings, particularly roofs, should be designed to minimise the risk of ignition if they are subjected to flames and radiation from an adjacent building. Standard tests can be used to grade particular forms of roof construction in terms of their ability to prevent ignition and spread of fire.

Smoke

The single most important threat to the occupants of a building, as distinct from that to the building itself, is the smoke produced by a fire. Smoke may spread and still be at lethal concentrations in a building even at great distances from the fire. Another and important hazard of smoke is that it reduces visibility to the extent that it may slow down or even prevent escape from the building. Smoke consists of the gases given off by the combustible material, of sooty particles from the fire and of the air entrained by the plumes of hot gases as they rise from the fire. The hot gases near ceiling level will be at a higher pressure than the atmospheric pressure at that level and those gases near floor level at some lower pressure than this; if vents were provided, the smoke would be expelled at the top, thus pulling in fresh air at the lower level. If no vents are provided then the layer of smoke will spread sideways and downwards and occupy more and more of the volume of the room. Almost all of the volume of smoke produced

consists of the entrained air; the rate at which air is entrained and therefore, approximately, the rate of production of smoke depends on the perimeter length, P, and on the heat output of the fire and, for a fire within a room, on the vertical distance between the seat of the fire and the bottom of the cloud of smoke which forms under the room ceiling, y (4.6). Once the fire is established, the rate of production of smoke is rapid and in an enclosed space, without vents, the cloud of smoke can quickly extend horizontally across the ceiling and then downwards to reach head height. An estimate of the time in seconds, t, taken for smoke to get down to any particular height is given by [3]:

$$t = \frac{20A}{P\sqrt{g}}\left(\frac{1}{\sqrt{y}} - \frac{1}{\sqrt{h}}\right) s$$

where A is the plan area of the room in m² (ft²);
P is the perimeter length in m (ft);
g is the acceleration due to gravity = 9.81 m/s² (32 ft/s²);
y is the bottom of smoke to floor distance in m (ft); and
h is the height of the room in m (ft).

Using this formula, a calculation of the time taken for smoke to reach head height in a room of the size of a classroom with the fire of a size that would engulf a table, is about 30 seconds. As all smoke from fires contains toxic products, the emphasis when considering life safety is on rapid means of escape. The toxicity of the smoke produced during combustion depends on the type of fuel but the smoke from fires always contains carbon monoxide, a product of incomplete combustion, and in quantities that, commonly in buildings, are fatal even for short periods of exposure. Table 4.2

lists some of the toxic gases and vapours produced by combustion of materials that are commonly found in buildings. Table 4.3 indicates the large quantities of toxic gases that can be produced by combustion. As well as their noxious effect, due to toxicity, the hot gases of combustion may cause irritation, burning and vitiation of the available oxygen, which, even by itself, could cause loss of consciousness. It is important to recognize that the rate of burning will generally have as much influence on the danger of the fire as the toxity of the gases produced; rapidly burning materials, such as foams, can generate large volumes of smoke very quickly and limit the time available for escape.

PASSIVE FIRE PROTECTION

Aims

Fire protection is necessary when fire prevention, which should help to prevent fires starting, has failed. Fire protection falls into two categories: *active* measures are concerned with direct intervention in the fire, manually or automatically providing, for example, early detection of the fire, suitably loud alarms, suppression of the fire, smoke control and any necessary access or communication; *passive* measures are concerned with the layout and construction of the building and access to it. The two paramount aims of passive fire protection are the provision of means of escape, to save life, and the containment of any fire to a compartment where the outbreak started, to limit fire damage and give time for evacuation.

Table 4.2   Toxic Compounds Produced by Combustion

Material	Toxic gas or vapour with maximum allowable concentrations for prolonged exposure (parts per million) given in brackets
Combustible materials containing carbon	carbon dioxide (5000) carbon monoxide (100)
Celluloid, polyurethanes	nitrogen dioxide (5) and other nitrogen oxides
Wool, silk, leather, plastics containing nitrogen; cellulosic plastics, rayon	hydrogen cyanide (10)
Wood, paper	acrolein (0.5)
Rubber, thiokols	sulphur dioxide (5)
Polyvinyl chloride, fire-retardant plastics, fluorinated plastics	halogen acids including hydrochloric acid hydrobromic acid hydrofluoric acid (3) phosgene (1)
Melamine, nylon, urea formaldehyde, resins	ammonia (100)
Phenol formaldehydes, wood, nylon, polyester resins	aldehydes
Polystyrene	benzene (25)
Foamed plastics	azo-bis-succino-nitrile
Fire-retardant plastics (some types)	antimony compounds
Polyurethane foams	isocyanates

dangerous concentrations of gas for short periods of exposure are approximately twenty times those given above
after refs. 2, 4 and 5

Table 4.3   Amounts of Carbon Monoxide and Hydrogen Cyanide produced by Combustion of 1 kg (2.2lb) of various substances

Substance	Carbon Monoxide				Hydrogen Cyanide			
	kg	lb	m^3 at 20°C	ft^3 at 68°F	kg	lb	m^3 at 20°C	ft^3 at 68°F
Cellulose (cotton)	0.50	1.10	0.4	14	..	..	..	..
Wood	0.23	0.51	0.18	6.4	0.12	0.26	0.1	3.5
Nylon	0.44	0.97	0.35	12	0.11	0.24	0.09	3.2
Acrylic fibres	0.3	0.66	0.24	8.5	0.26	0.57	0.21	7.4
Polyurethane foam	0.55	1.21	0.44	16	0.035	0.08	0.028	1.0

the volumes of gas at 300°C (= 570°F) would be double those at 20°C (= 68°F)
after ref. 4

Every effort should be made to prevent smoke moving from the compartment where the fire started to the other compartments in the building. As noted previously, concentrations of smoke can cause fatalities long distances from the fire itself. In practice, making compartments smokeproof requires great care in construction, especially at openings, and, therefore, is expensive.

Escape Routes

Escape from buildings is by designated routes that are protected, as far as possible, against the entry of fire and smoke. It is convenient to divide up the escape route into four stages: stage one leads from any point in a room to the room exit; stage two leads from the room exit to the exit from the storey level, or to a protected place, usually a protected stairway at that level; stage three leads downwards, or upwards, to the escape level; stage four leads from the protected place to the final exit at the same level, or to another place of safe refuge (*4.7*). The escape routes must always lead to places of safe refuge. In this context *safe refuges*

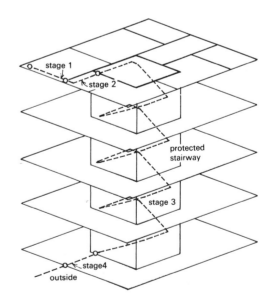

4.7 Schematic diagram of the various stages of escape from a room to a place of safety outside.

would include an exit point leading away from the building, a protected stairway, a compartment which is separated from the fire by a fire wall and leads to an exit, or a protected corridor or lobby leading directly to an exit or a protected stairway. The protection required for refuges against fire and smoke is much more stringent that that required for the route there. Two important notions connected with means of escape are the travel distance and the alternative route of escape. The *travel distance* is the shortest distance travelled from any point in the building to some specific point, for example to a protected place. It is usual to specify maximum travel distances, to safe refuges or to protected places, in fire regulations. The maximum allowable travel distance will depend on the likely speed of the occupants towards the refuges and the likely time available before the fire would prevent movement in safety to those refuges. If the occupants of a building are not close to a safe refuge then *alternative routes* of escape should be available to reduce the chance that occupants will be trapped by fire (*4.13*). The principle is that, whenever possible, there is an alternative route for occupants of the building, wherever the fire starts.

Ventilation of Smoke

Allied with the need to allow escape, is the need for smoke venting to the outside (*4.8*). The aim of *smoke venting* is to prevent dangerous accumulations of smoke without unduly feeding the fire by allowing in more air. The movement of the smoke is controlled by normal air movement as well as the general movement upwards of the hot, lower density smoke and gases. Hot smoke will rise to ceiling level and thus allow a short period of time for escape but cool smoke, for example, that which may be fed through the air-conditioning system, may hang at head height and would be a hazard. Vents to exhaust smoke can be placed at roof level or above windows in the rooms. Vents may be opened manually, or automatically by smoke detectors, and may use fans or natural convection. The venting is much more effective if the smoke at roof level can be prevented from spreading horizontally away from the vents either by positioning the vents in pockets in the roof or by hanging screens (*4.8*). In single storey buildings where the flames from a fire are within reach of the

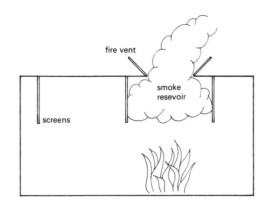

4.8 Smoke vents and ceiling screens used to exhaust . smoke and prevent its spread.

roof, it may be possible to provide ventilation by roofing in a plastic material, such as acrylic or polycarbonate, which can be designed to collapse in the area above the fire, before it ignites, and thus provide venting. Note that effective venting also relies on supplies of fresh air coming in at lower levels.

Compartmentation

As noted previously, the *compartmentation* of a building consists of subdividing it into compartments, with fire-resisting walls, floors or roofs. The subdivision is made in order to limit the spread of fire and restrict damage to the building and its contents. Maximum compartment sizes are usually set by the need to restrict losses and ease fire fighting. A fire compartment may consist of one wing of a building or a complete floor level or part of a floor level. As a general guide, large floor areas would have compartment walls at maximum intervals of about 45m (150ft) in each direction. Specific hazards such as boilers, fuel or general stores would generally be in separate compartments however small they might be. Automatic sprinklers can be installed to help dowse any fire that does break out and to help prevent fire spread. At the very least, they would delay fire spread and thus give extra time for the firefighters. As sprinklers help to reduce the chance of fire and contain its spread, it is logical to increase the size of fire compartments, if they are installed. If vertical

shafts penetrate floors that are fire compartments then these vertical shafts must be protected to prevent the passage of fire between floors via the shaft (*4.7*). The shaft is generally of non-combustible material which has a fire resistance rating at least equal to that of the compartments, although it is often less for the access doors into the protected shaft. In addition, attention also has to be paid to penetration of the compartment walls or floors, and penetration of the protected shafts, by service installations. These services would include cabling, plumbing and air ducts. The openings around pipes or ducts, where they penetrate compartments or shafts, must be fire stopped by intumescent fire sleeves, mineral wool pillows, bonding vermiculite mixes or, for small gaps, by gypsum plaster.

In the case of air ducts, fire dampers must be installed within the ducts where they penetrate the compartment walls, or else the duct itself must be of a fire-resistant construction as it passes through each compartment and have no openings into the compartment. Alternatively, ducts can be placed in separate fire compartments (*4.9*). If dampers are used then they may be operated automatically by fusible links or by honeycomb dampers based on the use of intumescent coatings that swell in the heat and block the duct; they may also be operated manually from a central control room. By similar reasoning, all cavities within the building construction need, as far as possible, to be divided up into smaller areas by lines of fire stops. Preferably the surfaces of the cavity should be non-combustible or have a low surface spread of flame. As a general rule, a cavity within any element such as a wall panel, should not communicate with a cavity in an adjacent floor or wall panel. If a fire-resistant wall or floor abuts a cavity construction, then, in general, a fire stop should be provided in the cavities in the same plane as the wall or floor (*4.10*). In practice these recommendations are often difficult to carry out, both because of difficulties in construction and because of the need, in some cases, to allow ventilation. An obvious place where there is a potential passage for fire is in suspended ceiling voids. In this case, a suspended ceiling either of gypsum board with a mineral fibre seal or of metal lathing sprayed with an intumescent spray would provide a barrier to fire spread, and possibly to the

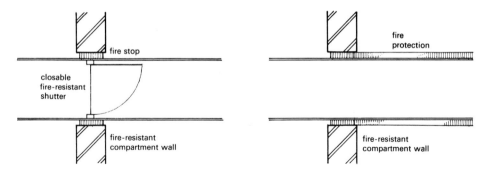

4.9 Air-conditioning ducts penetrating fire compartments should have fire-shutters, left, or be fire protected, right, to prevent spread of fire and smoke.

spread of smoke. Alternatively, lines of fire resistance can be provided by carrying up corridor and partition walls through the ceiling void to the floor slab soffit (4.11). The passage of smoke through the ducts may also present a hazard and this could call for the installation of smoke detectors.

Fire Tests

The building structure must have sufficient fire resistance in order to carry the loads put upon it, so that there is no structural collapse either within the compartment where the fire is or elsewhere. The general principle is that the compartment

enclosure be able to withstand a complete burn-out of all combustible matter within it and that the building structure be able to withstand a complete burn-out of all combustible matter in the whole building without loss of function in either case. The function of the building structure is resistance to collapse and, in particular, sufficient stiffness and strength; the compartment enclosure needs stiffness and strength but also resistance to flame penetration and sufficient insulation to prevent high temperatures on those faces not exposed to the fire. For example, ordinary wired glass is only partially suitable as an enclosing material; although it will remain in place and prevent the passage of flames for short periods, it transmits radiant heat to the extent of preventing passage of the occupants of the building past the glass and it may also allow fire spread. The fire resistance required for building elements, whether they form part of the building structure or the compartment enclosure, will depend on the fire severity, and to a lesser extent on how much of the heat produced is transmitted to the element. As it is based on a probability concept, the required period of fire resistance of an element will also depend on how serious are the consequences of failure. For example a long period of fire resistance is required for high-rise building structures or basement structures where, in general, in both cases, the elements support large floor areas.

As noted previously, elements can be graded

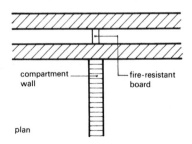

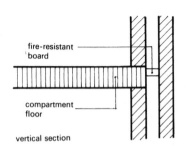

4.10 Fire stops used in cavities to prevent fire spread around compartment wall, top, or compartment floor, bottom.

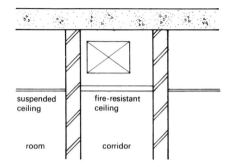

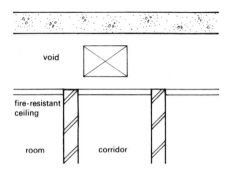

4.11 Separation of air-conditioning ducts from adjacent rooms can be achieved by taking walls up to ceiling soffit, left, or by building a complete fire-resistant ceiling, right.

relative to one another in terms of the time they resist a standard fire which follows a defined time-temperature curve. It is then possible to talk of elements having a certain *fire resistance* grading or *fire rating*. Various tests have been devised in order to be able to compare other aspects of the fire performance of building materials or building elements. Among tests in common use are those connected with measuring combustibility, ignitability, the surface spread of flame and the propagation index, that is the rate at which the material contributes heat to a fire and thus helps to propagate it. In general the results of these standard tests will depend both on the material and the form it is in, so that, as with the fire resistance test, results have to be given separately for all the different types of elements of construction. As most measurements cannot be said to be measurements of known fundamental properties, because these results cannot usually be explained theoretically and do not describe known states, the exact conditions of the test need to be defined in order to establish their relevance in any strategy for design against fire. All of these four standards tests are designed to be relevant to the selection of *lining materials* for rooms, corridors or stairways where the requirement is to reduce, in some degree, the chances of ignition and then, if ignition does occur, to limit the rate of spread of fire across the lining during the growth of the fire. Although fire spread over linings occurs on the surface, in many cases the 'surface' should be understood to include backing materials when they influence results. As already noted, one established property which influences fire ignition and growth is the surface thermal absorption. Many materials can be treated to reduce their ignitability and surface spread of flame, although most treatments against ignition do not significantly affect the rate of burning once the materials have been ignited.

ACTIVE FIRE PROTECTION

Equipment

Active fire protection measures consist principally of detection, alarm, fire suppression, control of smoke and air conditioning systems, use of lifts and evacuation procedures. *Alarm systems* are

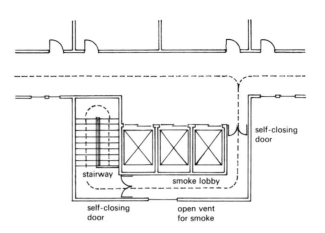

4.12   Smoke lobby with doors and vents to prevent smoke spread into protected stairway.

necessary in most buildings and must be sufficiently loud so as to wake up the building occupants if they are asleep. The alarms could be triggered manually, by wall switches or automatically, by fire detectors or by the opening of escape doors. The alarms would have an independent power supply. *Fire detectors* are important in that they give valuable extra time in which to allow the building to be evacuated and the fire to be extinguished. Various types of detector are available: those which respond at a fixed temperature or to rapid changes in temperature; those which respond, with varying sensitivity, to smoke; those which respond to the infra-red or ultra-violet light in a flame. There are particularly good grounds for installing detectors in places where fire or smoke is likely to remain undetected or in any place where a fire is more likely to cause loss of life or material because, for example, the fire develops rapidly or because evacuation may be slow. Typical positions for smoke detectors would be in cable duct cupboards, air-conditioning return ducts, vertical shafts for cables, conveyors or other services, store rooms and rooms adjacent to service shafts and stairways. *Control of smoke* in rooms with air conditioning requires control of fans and dampers, either by automatic devices or manually from a fire control centre. Air-conditioning systems which recirculate return air via the central plant rooms

can distribute smoke to all parts of the building served by that plant and poison the atmosphere far away from the seat of the fire itself. A minimum requirement, in a fire, is that the air circulation be shut down, for example after an alarm is sounded. More sophisticated systems would allow all the return air to be exhausted directly and the supply air to be all outside air, which does not contain smoke. It is very desirable to prevent the spread of smoke to places outside the immediate area of the fire. This can be done by pressurizing the spaces surrounding the fire; in general return ducts in the building would be closed and supply ducts open but, to extract smoke in the fire area itself, return ducts here would be open and supply ducts closed. Similarly in places of safe refuge or in protected stairways the atmosphere could be kept clear of smoke by pressurization with outside air; the pressurization should not be so high as to prevent opening of the doors. Alternatively a smoke lobby would allow ventilation to the outside (*4.12*). These provisions are particularly relevant to high-rise buildings.

Of those installations directly concerned with suppressing or extinguishing a fire, as distinct from those helping escape, the most useful is the sprinkler system. *Sprinklers* operate either as dry pipe or wet pipe systems. A wet pipe system is one completely filled with water. In freezing conditions, anti-freeze can be added to the water.

Otherwise a dry pipe system, which discharges a pressurized gas before the water reaches the sprinkler head, can be used. The sprinkler heads are normally triggered when they reach a fixed temperature or there is a rapid change in temperature. Adequate discharge rates, over the floor area concerned, for a moderate fire hazard, would be about 4mm (0.16in) depth of water per minute over the area covered; this could be provided by sprinklers on a 4.5 x 4.5 m (15 x 15 ft) grid. Typical sprinkler grids go down to about 3 x 3 m (10 x 10 ft). Sprinkler heads usually work independently of one another but may be designed to operate in blocks if there is a high fire hazard. They could also be activated by smoke detectors. Many systems have sprinkler heads which are closable and thus help to limit damage by water after the fire has been extinguished. Sprinklers are useful for suppressing the growth and size of fires and, being an automatic system, are one of the best means of protection against spontaneous combustion. Because of their potential to limit the size of a fire, sprinklers may be used either to reduce the fire grading required for the building structure and fire compartment walls or else allow increases in the floor areas of fire compartments. This may help open the way to the use of open plan floor arrangements.

Although sprinklers may hold a fire in check they may not be sufficient to extinguish it. The most effective general method of extinguishing fire is with large diameter high pressure water hoses manned by the fire services. In low-rise buildings hoses can be coupled together from street level up the protected stairway, assuming this does not interfere excessively with exit from the building. Above about seven storeys, however, the time taken to connect hoses together is excessive. At these heights, it is also difficult to fight the fire with hoses or other equipment from the outside. Therefore the fire must be fought from inside the building using *rising mains*. Hoses are connected, at any level, to these rising mains which run the full height of the building, normally within a stairway enclosure. The hoses are normally connected to outlets at, or one floor below, the fire level. As well as water a large number of gas, liquid, foam and powder systems are available for specific fire hazards. In high-rise buildings, besides good access for firefighting

equipment at street level, the fire services will require access up protected stairways and control of all lifts. People inside lifts could be trapped if power supplies fail and would be asphyxiated if the lift shafts become smoke pathways. Firemen's lifts would be provided to allow the fire services rapid access to higher levels; these lifts would have secure power supplies and be protected from fire and smoke by lobbys at each floor level. They would be linked to protected stairways to provide a means of escape, if necessary.

FIRE PRECAUTIONS IN BUILDINGS

Escape Routes

In multi-storey *hotels,* where a central corridor provides access to the rooms the places of safe refuge are usually the enclosed stairways and the escape route is down the corridors, through the enclosed stairway to the outside. Typical fire protection measures on each floor are indicated in what follows. Doors opening onto the corridors from the rooms, preferably, should be self-closing and provide resistance to the fire and smoke for a short period. At intervals of about 18m (60ft), the corridors should have fire doors, generally providing fire resistance and smoke control, but where there is little danger of fire, only smoke control may be required. Walls and ceilings should have some resistance to surface spread of flames. Any services running in the corridor should be of low fire risk or provided with a fire-resisting ceiling below them (*4.11*). Fire regulations will generally specify a maximum compartment size and a fire rating both for the building structure, to prevent collapse, and for the walls separating the fire compartments. As noted previously, the fire rating should reflect the likely severity of any fire; this depends on the fire loads and thus, in turn, on the compartment size and the type and contents of the building (Table 4.1). All material in the staircase enclosure would have resistance to surface spread of flame and, apart from finishes, would be non-combustible. For the purposes of escape, the enclosure to the stairways would have a half-hour period of fire resistance.

To prevent smoke contamination of the stairs, no rooms apart from wash rooms would open directly into the stair enclosure or, as an

alternative, access to the stair enclosure would be via a smoke lobby with self-closing doors (*4.12*). The stair enclosure must be arranged in such a way that if a fire was to break out in any of the stairways, smoke could not reach the corridors and prevent use of an alternative route of escape. The maximum stage one travel distance from any point in a room to the room exit would be 9m (30ft). If the room was large then two separate room exits would be provided and the travel distance to the nearest exit could increase to 18m (60ft). The maximum stage two travel distance from the room exit to the stair enclosure, from a dead end, where only one escape route was available, would be 7.6m (25ft) but, where alternative routes were available, could increase to 18m (60ft) to the nearest stair enclosure (*4.13*). If fire were to break out in one of the rooms then the self-closing doors would help to limit the speed with which the fire and smoke could spread. If the fire did spread to the corridor then the fire or smoke doors would help to limit its effects to a local area. Assuming alternative routes of escape are available then it will be possible for occupants not in the immediate area of the fire to bypass it. Where rooms give onto a 'dead end' corridor, the corridor leading to the stairway should be made of walls with a half-hour fire resistance; this helps to reduce the chance that a fire in the corridor would prevent escape. The general fire grading of elements would be for one hour and the building structure and fire compartments, in particular, would require at least this period of fire reistance. A fire compartment in the hotel building may comprise one complete floor, in which case the floor slabs become compartment floors. The enclosure to the stairways as noted, would have a half-hour period of fire resistance where required as escape routes. However if the stairways are compartments themselves, or penetrate between one floor compartment and another, the enclosing walls must have a fire resistance at least equal to that of the compartment floor to prevent spread of fire and provide the same overall resistance to fire as that of the floor. Doors leading to stairways that penetrate fire compartments, but are not fire compartments themselves, the general case, could have half this specified fire resistance, because the fire would need to penetrate two doors to pass between one fire compartment and another; the stairways

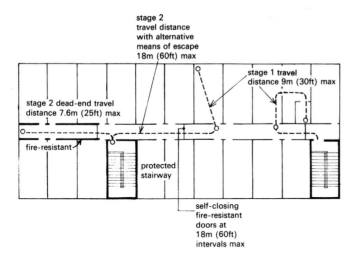

stage 2
travel distance
with alternative
means of escape
18m (60ft) max

stage 1 travel
distance 9m (30ft) max

stage 2 dead-end travel
distance 7.6m (25ft) max

fire-resistant

protected
stairway

self-closing
fire-resistant
doors at
18m (60ft)
intervals max

4.13 Typical specified travel distances to protected stairways in an hotel building.

should not contain combustible matter.

In multi-storey *office buildings,* fire protection measures are similar, in principle, to those in hotels but planning tends to be more open and there are less likely to be concentrations of people. The maximum stage one travel distance from any point in a room to a corridor giving alternative routes of escape would be 12m (40ft), with the total travel distance from this point to the nearest place of safety, the stage one and two distances, being 45m (150ft) (*4.14*). The total stage one and two distances from a dead end would be about 18m (60ft). Corridors would be subdivided into 45m (150ft) lengths by fire doors. In open plan offices, with no corridors the maximum travel distance from any point in a room to a place of safety would be about 12m to 18m (40ft to 60ft), if there is only one escape route available. If an altenative route exists, the maximum travel distance to a place of safety would be about 30m to 45m (100ft to 150ft) (*4.15*). Within fire compartments smoke vents may be provided at high level, above windows for example. Each fire compartment in the office may encompass several floors, or even the whole office, so that stairs between floors need not be enclosed. This is a common requirement. If this is the case, however, separate enclosed stairways are still necessary to provide an escape

route. Note that as these staircases are not fire compartments they do not require the fire resistance of a compartment but only protection against smoke and that fire resistance required for an escape route. In general this would be for half an hour. Although it is preferable to provide

alternative routes for escape, this is not always practicable or justified by circumstances.

In *low-rise buildings,* with corridors, where the escape routes along the corridors were short, only one enclosed stairway may be necessary. However access to the stairway would be through a smoke lobby and the final route away from the stairway would be short and contain no fire hazard. Even in buildings up to ten storeys, one enclosed stairway may be adequate. In such cases more emphasis is put on having small fire compartments and on the use of sprinklers. Doors onto the corridor would be self-closing and the corridors would be non-combustible as well as able to prevent the spread of flame. The stairway may be pressurised with fresh air to prevent smoke contamination or else a smoke balcony provided, allowing any smoke brought through the smoke lobby to vent to the outside before it reached the stairway itself (*4.12*). The stairway would be fire-proof, that is able to ride out a fire of whatever length, and constructed of non-combustible materials.

In *high-rise buildings,* there are special problems to be overcome in extinguishing fires, as noted previously. Unlike other building types, it is not possible to arrange for quick evacuation of the building in a fire and because most of the building is beyond the range of the fire fighting equipment

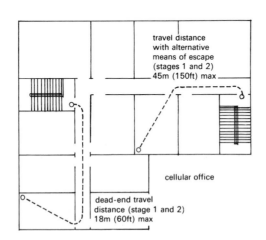

travel distance
with alternative
means of escape
(stages 1 and 2)
45m (150ft) max

cellular office

dead-end travel
distance (stage 1 and 2)
18m (60ft) max

4.14 Typical specified travel distances to protected stairways in an office building.

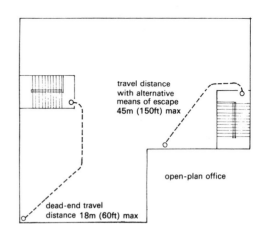

travel distance
with alternative
means of escape
45m (150ft) max

open-plan office

dead-end travel
distance 18m (60ft) max

4.15 Typical specified travel distances to protected stairways in an open-plan office.

available, the fire has to be fought from inside. High-rise buildings are subject to *stack effect*, in which, with lower outside temperatures, air tends to enter the building at low levels and exhaust at high level causing draughts, especially in vertical shafts. These draughts can speed the spread of fire and smoke. More than most, high-rise buildings benefit from active fire protection measures including not only those of fire detection and suppression but also those connected with pressurising stairways, the use of lifts, lighting, communication and alarm systems and management of the fire from a central control room which would include the manipulation of the air-conditioning system to exhaust the smoke and prevent its spread. The basic tactic is to move the occupants of the building to places of safety at each floor or to places of safety within a few floors of any affected floor level. Occupants would be evacuated from these places of safety on a controlled basis. In many cases evacuation would not be complete before the fire had run its course. Clearly places of refuge must be built to stringent standards.

In large *single spaces* such as factory floors, shopping centres, halls and atriums, where there are no corridor escape routes, the approach is to minimise or separate fire loads and to provide sprinkler coverage. This helps to limit the size of any fire. Smoke would be extracted by automatic vents. Typical sprinkler coverage might be on a 3 x 3 m (10 x 10 ft) grid, which it could be assumed would limit the fire perimeter to 12m (40ft) and the heat output of the fire to 5MW (5 x 10⁶ W). For spaces which contain no floors above the bottom level, or at most two floors above the bottom level, as in shopping centres, the automatic vents could be designed to extract the smoke for a 5 MW fire, or whatever maximum size of fire the sprinklers are assumed to allow. In spaces containing or being overlooked by many floors, the size of the fire might be greater as the possibility exists for fire spread between floors, to some extent fanned by the stack effect. In such cases the automatic vents should be designed for greater volumes of smoke.

PROPERTIES OF MATERIALS IN FIRE

Relevant Properties

The actual fire resistance of structural elements depends on the form of the element and on the material. The materials used for structural elements vary widely in their behaviour in a fire. Desirable material properties are stiffness and strength at high temperatures, low thermal expansion and low thermal diffusivity. A low coefficient of thermal expansion reduces movement and the potential disintegration of parts of the building in a fire. Low thermal diffusivity limits the area of an element affected by high temperatures and therefore the loss in strength of the element. The thermal diffusivity, h, is given by:

$$h = \frac{\lambda}{\rho.c} \text{ m}^2/\text{s (ft in/hr)}$$

where ρ is the density of the material in kg/m³ (lb/ft³);
   c is the specific heat capacity of the material in kJ/ kg °C (btu/ lb °F); and
   λ is the thermal conductivity in W/ m °C (btu in/ ft² hr °F).

Other factors which affect the temperature rise within the building element are the heat transfer coefficients. The heat absorbed by an element, I, at any time is given by:

$$I = (\alpha_c + \alpha_r)\Delta T \text{ in W/m}^2 \text{ (btu/ ft}^2 \text{ hr);}$$

where α_c and α_r are the heat transfer coefficients for convection and radiation in W/ m² °C (btu/ hr ft² °F);and
   ΔT is the temperature difference between the gas surrounding the element and the surface of the element in °C (°F).

Concrete

A difficulty in discussing the behaviour of concrete in a fire is the extreme variability in composition of the concretes in use. It is convenient to divide the aggregrates used in concrete into four groups: siliceous and carbonate aggregrates, as used in normalweight concrete, and lightweight and sand-lightweight aggregrates, as used in lightweight concrete. In general, normalweight concretes only start to lose strength above 320°C (600°F), having half their room temperature strength at about 550 °C (1000°F). Lightweight and carbonate aggregrate concretes have better fire resistance than this because the aggregates in these concretes do not cause the spalling common

with the siliceous aggregate concretes in general use. Lightweight and carbonate aggregate concretes have half their room temperature strength at about 700°C (1300°F). Greater high-temperature strength is usually attained by mixtures rich in cement. If concrete does not spall, the reinforcement in it will not attain a high temperature, and thus be able to maintain most of its strength; concrete has low thermal diffusivity. The temperature reached during a hot one-hour fire, 25mm (1in) from the surface of the concrete, only reaches that corresponding to about a 50% loss in strength compared to the strength at room temperature. In most concrete elements, therefore, large parts only suffer a modest drop in strength, and steel reinforcement bars, even a small depth from the heated face, are to a large extent protected. The temperature reached by concrete during a fire is indicated by its colour. Concrete changes to a pink or red-brown colour as it starts to lose strength turning to grey before turning buff, at which point it has lost about 50% of its room temperature strength.

Masonry

The fire resistance of masonry is found to be good, depending on the details of construction. Concrete masonry has similar thermal properties to the normalweight or lightweight concrete of which it is made. However the form of the masonry may be important, too, in that joints between the masonry units can give relief to thermal stresses which would otherwise develop in a continuous wall. Loadbearing walls are generally required to carry vertical load and provide fire separation. They will deflect towards the fire, as the side nearer the fire expands. Eventually the bulge may be sufficient to cause a loadbearing wall to fail.

Steel

The fire behaviour of steel is of particular interest, because of its effects on the costs of fire protection and therefore on the economics of steelwork construction. The loss in strength of steel, as the temperature rises, varies depending on the type of steel used. Mild steel and high strength alloy steels maintain or increase their strength up to about 350°C (650°F) after which point they start to decline in strength and have lost 50% of their room temperature strength at about 500°C (950°F).

Cold drawn and heat treated prestressing strands revert to their untreated strengths at about this temperature and therefore do not retain any significant amount of the extra strength they have over mild steel at room temperatures. They lose 50% of their room temperature strength at about 400°C (750°F). The elastic modulus of steel also drops sharply with temperature. Because steel has very high thermal diffusivity, steel sections require protection against high temperature, unless they are very thick or could only be exposed to a fire for short periods because, for example, the fire load is low. Generally a thermal insulant would be used, if protection were necessary. Any of the following might be suitable: an encasement of the members with masonry, cast-in-place concrete or fire-resistant boards; sprayed material using vermiculite or mineral fibres with a binder which could be cement powder; intumescent paint. In a standard fire resistance test, the time taken for a steel member with thermal insulation to reach any critical temperature, often that associated with a 50% loss of strength, is dependent on a section factor, S, which is given by:

$$S = \frac{\lambda.H}{d.A} \quad \text{W/ °C m}^3 \text{ (btu/ °F hr ft}^3)$$

where H is the length of the perimeter of the section that is exposed to the fire in m (ft);

d is the thickness of the insulating material in m (ft); and

A is the cross-sectional area of the member in m² (ft²).

If the steel member is not protected by an insulant then the section factor would be equal to H/A. As a guide, a steel column in a fire with a fire load of about 15 kg per sq m (3 lb per sq ft) of floor area, with a section factor of 165 1/m (50 1/ft) would not attain a temperature of more than about 500°C (950°F).

Steel sections may be unprotected if the fire load is low or if the steel members are placed outside the building such that they cannot reach a critical temperature. In the latter case the building enclosure could protect the steel members from flames or radiated heat. Some steel and concrete composite structures may attain a grading of half an hour in a standard fire resistance test without further protection because of their thermal capacity. Typical examples of such composite structures are floor slabs consisting of profiled metal deck and concrete, complete floor structures consisting of steel beams with shear studs with a concrete slab on top, and columns of hollow steel tubes infilled with concrete. The extra fire resistance of composite over pure steel structures is associated with the concrete and its steel reinforcement. Another method of fire protection, which relies on increasing the thermal capacity rather than the thermal insulation, is to fill hollow steel members with water; usually the water will be designed to circulate in the event of a fire, to provide continuous cooling. A difficulty with exposed steework is its large thermal expansion in a fire which may cause structural damage to other elements.

Wood

Wood is a combustible material which nevertheless can be used for elements requiring fire resistance. The fire resistance of wood elements depends on the ability of wood to char and the protection afforded by the charred outer portion to the inner portion of the wood section. For timber exposed to a fire on one face the average charring rate is between about 30 and 50 mm/hr (1¼ and 2 in/hr); it has not been found to be particularly affected by the temperature of the fire. The charred portion is very stable and has low thermal diffusivity so that the uncharred portion retains almost all its original strength. A common practice is to oversize structural elements such as beams and columns to allow for charring and to provide as long a period of fire resistance as is necessary. Wood panels, however, are less satisfactory in providing fire compartmentation than masonry; fire tends to attack the wood panels at the joints and other weak points. Note that, in general, retardants to slow down the surface spread of flame have little effect on the charring rate. Among the timber species, the dense hardwoods have the lowest rate of charring. Intumescent coatings can reduce the initial charring rate for periods up to ½ hr, but beyond this, the charring rate is as for untreated timber.

Plastics

Plastic is often used in buildings as a material for claddings, linings, insulation and, in the case of transparent plastics, as window lights. All plastics are combustible. The fire resistance of most plastic materials as utilized in buildings is negligible. The ignitability and surface spread of flame characteristics however are important, particularly if plastic material is used as a lining to walls or ceilings or as an insulant within the construction. Although plastics will always burn in an already established fire, many plastics are available with fillers and retardants to make the plastic less easy to ignite. Note however that such treatments are often at the expense of other properties such as durability. Thermoplastic materials soften and then melt in a fire and, of these, some will fall away from their fixings before they ignite and therefore do not usually add to the fire spread, although the hot drops of plastic may be a hazard. Those plastics which stay in place, however, whether thermoplastics or thermosetting plastics, can significantly contribute to fire spread. Plastics are commonly used as foam insulants in wall or roof panels and in this form burn fiercely, particularly the thermoplastic foams; polyurethane, polyisocyonurate and polystyrene are typical thermoplastics in such use. Many other plastics are used inside buildings; for example polyurethane, neoprene and polyamide foams may be found in furniture upholstery. When burnt, all these plastics give off gases or vapour of varying quantities and toxicity (Table 4.2): polystyrene gives off benzene; polyurethane gives off a mixture of isocyanates, including hydrogen cyanide. Acrylic fibre, which may be present in covering materials, also gives off hydrogen cyanide when burnt. Rigid polyvinyl chlorides, used in panels, windows, pipes and roof coverings gives off halogen acid vapour when burnt. Like all combustible matter, plastics also produce carbon monoxide. In small rooms toxic concentrates of gas are quickly exceeded even with moderate fire loads (Table 4.3). Some plastics give off dense smoke when they burn and this can be as much a hazard as the toxicity because it affects the ability of occupants to escape and that of the firefighters to control the fire. The range of properties of plastics is very wide. Some plastics only support combustion at high temperatures and may have good resistance to ignition. Others may only produce moderate amounts of heat and smoke when they burn. Fire retardants may be used to improve the fire behaviour of plastics but note that some fire retardants may themselves give off toxic products, such as halogen acid vapours, if they burn. Measures taken to limit fire hazards must balance advantage against disadvantage. The measures may include changes in chemical composition, special fixing details and protecting shields or barrier coats of non-combustible inorganic compounds. As noted previously, the ability of plastics to fall away or burn through may be exploited in roofs as a method of venting smoke and toxic gases. Many plastic materials form the basis of *fabrics*. Glass-fibre woven fabrics coated with ptfe only support combustion at high temperatures, combustion ceasing if the source of heat is withdrawn. Glass-fibre woven fabrics coated with silicon have similar fire performance. Polyester-fibre woven fabrics coated with polyvinyl chloride will melt when heated but do not contribute significantly to the propagation of fire.

Glass

Glass is a non-combustible material but cracks and falls away from its frame when exposed to fire. Toughened or laminated glass is no better than ordinary annealed glass in this respect. However wired glass provides a measure of fire resistance if it is not allowed to sag excessively in a fire. Note that almost no protection is given against infrared radiation by ordinary soda-lime glasses. Some formulations of calcium-silica glass have moderate periods of fire resistance and offer reasonable protection from infrared radiation. Borosilicate glasses are available with high melting points and maintain their integrity for long periods. Other methods of fire protection include the use of laminated glasses that incorporate an intumescent resin-gel which provides fire resistance, including reasonably good protection against infrared radiation.

Chapter Five

Houses and Community Buildings

The buildings in this chapter are bracketed together as houses and community buildings, having a similar type of use and being built to a similar scale. A scale is measured relative to an exact standard size or to some known, if approximate, size, for example in architecture the human size. In the way it is generally used, the 'scale' of a building refers both to the actual size of the building and its elements and to its apparent size. In fact, usually a series of scales is revealed in approaching and moving through any building. The buildings considered in this chapter are all small, which gives them a pleasingly small scale appearance and also allows a freedom to the design not always possible in larger buildings. With buildings this size, it is possible to give full play to local circumstance, and even individual whim, in what can be seen, in many cases, as a reaction to the uniformity of official and commercial architecture. In particular, the designer has maximum opportunity to develop a scale and system of dimensions which is related to the way people use and experience the building. A correct scale, whether related to the human scale or not, should be one which makes for a sense of harmony, to be contrasted with the dispiriting, and even disquieting, effect of a badly judged system of dimensions. As a practical matter, good design is probably most easily achieved at this small scale and it is from the successes of these small buildings, in overall design terms, that large buildings need to take their cue. A technical aspect of building small, is that, having smaller ratios of volume to surface area, these buildings react more quickly than large buildings to heating or cooling from the outside, so that the construction materials chosen for the walls and the roof and the use made of ambient energy are of an especial importance. In addition, the forces put on the elements in these buildings, and the connections between the elements, are small and the movements of the building under any kind of changes in load or temperature are small. These two factors, in large measure, guarantee that the buildings have good stiffness and strength against any likely forces that may be put on them and, therefore, increase the available choice of form and material.

Woolstone Houses,
Milton Keynes, England

Introduction

Brick is one of the oldest and the first man-made building material and, in time, overtook stone as the principal material for masonry construction. The idea of making small standard-sized units for assembly into complete buildings is almost as basic as the idea of division and number. That brick is still so popular is largely due to this geometrical idea and the consequent flexibility it allows both in the plan shape and massing of buildings. A brick is a size of masonry unit, smaller than a block, and might be made of any of a large number of ceramic materials. The size is important because this introduces a suitable scale and allows the bricks to be laid with one hand. The large number of indigeneous materials, such as clay, concrete or silica, which may be used to make masonry units, give a good range of properties and allow choices in colour, texture, durability, compressive strength, thermal mass and even thermal insulation, although this last property tends to work against a desirable acoustic mass and compressive strength. This group of houses, part of a larger development of similar construction, is a classic example of the application of brickwork in a temperate climate in which an external cavity wall construction is used to protect the inner leaf (wythe) from the weather, particularly rain. Each house provides, at budget prices, well-insulated spaces for people, including a double-height living room facing the south-east.

Description

The six-person house contains three main walls in the long direction; these support the two monopitch roofs and the floor above ground level on the north-west side. On the south-east side is a double-height living room with stairs neatly placed in the corner, leading up to an open balcony overlooking the room and giving access to the rooms upstairs. The house is unusual in that the main central wall is both an internal and an external wall and is therefore of cavity construction throughout. This arrangement dispenses with the need for timber trusses while taking advantage of all space up to the undersides of the rafters and is of particular importance in

View of a house from E.

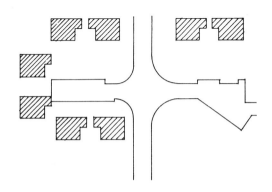

Overall plan on group of six-person houses.

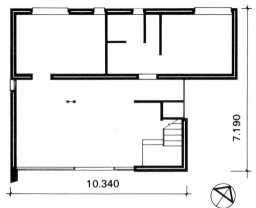

Ground floor plan.

7.190

10.340

WOOLSTONE HOUSES (1982)

Description:
Two-storey houses of brick cavity construction with timber
roofs
Architects:
Aldington, Craig and Collinge

Axonometric
of six-person
house from S:

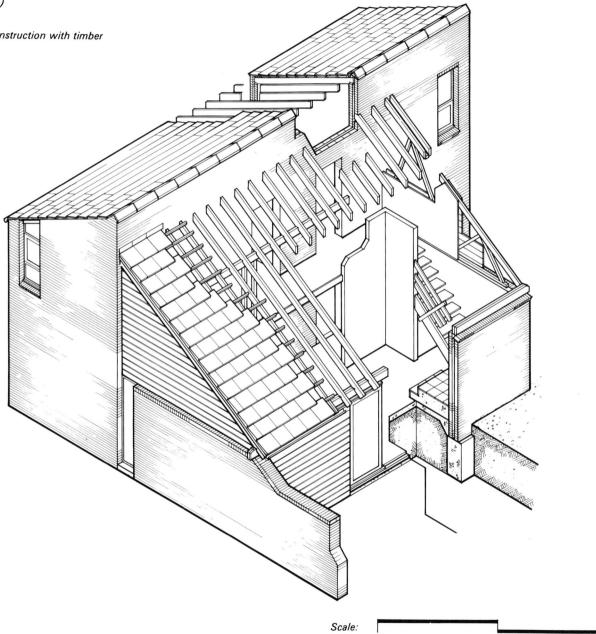

Scale:

6 m

20 ft

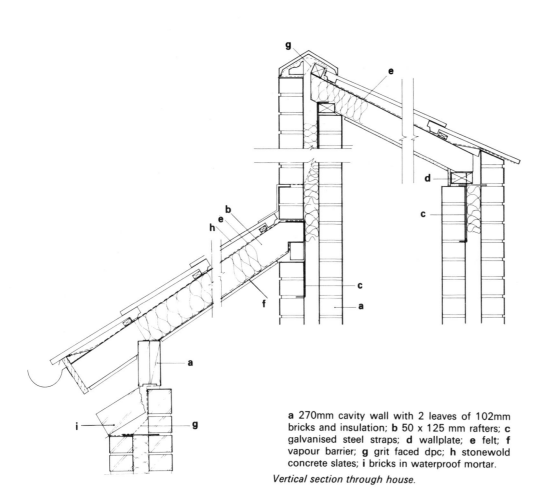

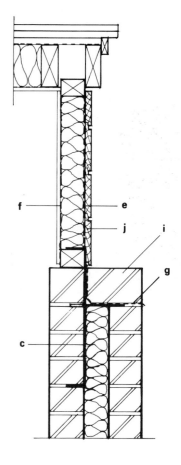

a 270mm cavity wall with 2 leaves of 102mm bricks and insulation; b 50 x 125 mm rafters; c galvanised steel straps; d wallplate; e felt; f vapour barrier; g grit faced dpc; h stonewold concrete slates; i bricks in waterproof mortar.

Vertical section through house.

j timber rebated boarding.

Vertical section through timber gable.

tightly planned houses such as these. The central wall has enough thermal mass to significantly dampen the swings in internal temperature. The house is well insulated especially in the roof. Window sizes are moderate except for the large window on the south-east side where the solar

gain into the living room more than outweighs the loss of heat from reduced insulation. Horizontal timber boarding is used on the south-east face as well as in the roof gable ends of the living room and provides a good contrast with the brickwork.

Structural Action

The object of the structural design is to keep the masonry everywhere in compression, under which it is strong, and reduce tension, under which it is weak. This is best achieved by applying gravity

View of a house from S.

View on living room.

loads down the centre of walls, as here on the south-east wall for example, and providing frequent lateral supports to the walls so that bending and tensile stresses, due to lateral wind forces on walls, are low. The usual disadvantage of masonry, its instability, a direct result of its poor tensile strength, is not an important factor in buildings at the scale of this house; roofs, floors and walls at right angles are all available to provide lateral support to the walls. With the seating details adopted here, gravity loads do not cause the sloping rafters to exert horizontal forces at the top of the support walls but do provide the necessary lateral support.

Construction

This group of eight houses is part of a larger group of twenty-six houses of the same construction and space that were built over a period of nine months. All openings in the walls occur at brick module heights.

Conclusion

The design makes good use of modest resources and this is particularly true of the living room: on elevation, there is varied treatment of the external surfaces; inside a special space has been made in the main living room area by means of a balcony, a sloping roof and the relatively large perceived volume, which neatly incorporates almost all the circulation space, including the stairs. Whenever possible construction detail is exposed, as that on the stairs, on the balcony and on top of the south-east wall. The detailing is chunky and rustic and adds a flattering simplicity to suburban living.

Keldy Castle Forest Cabins, Cropton, Yorkshire, England

Introduction

In this development, accommodation for visitors to a large forest area is provided in 58 separate wood cabins of three distinct types, although only three units were built of one of these types. The two common types each have a plan area of 30 sq m and fit in a living space and beds for five people and one of these two types provides a space in the loft. All cabins are made from wood elements and panels which were prefabricated, for manhandling and rapid erection on-site. With foundations in place, the building fabric of each cabin was completed in a single day by four men. This scheme is an excellent demonstration of the potential of wood as a material for industrialised building. Most components are mass produced but those components used only in small numbers can still be made at a moderate unit cost.

Description

The cabins are supported by 100 x 300 mm timber beams which rest on concrete ground beams or braced timber posts going to ground. This arrangement allows cabins to be positioned on steep slopes. All cabins are made up from the same prefabricated panels and parts, only the lengths of floor and roof beams being different between types. Floor panels, made of joists and floor boards, were fabricated in height or width modules of one, two or three metres, with a special dished panel for the shower room; external wall panels, made of 50 x 50 mm studding with ply and sawn boards, were fabricated in modules of one or two metres.

Special panels for each type were made for the gable ends above the 2m module height line because of the different roof slopes. Roofs consist of rafters supported at the eaves and near the ridge by 75 x 250 mm timber beams. These rafters support either ply deck with built-up roofing and stones or, for types with pitched roofs, 50 x 50 mm battens with a board-on-board covering. The boards are 150 x 25 mm in section, placed at 225mm centres in two layers, which overlap, and are nailed to the battens. Because of the way they are placed, the boards cup inwards and there is little leakage at the overlaps but slater's felt is

Exterior view of cabin (photo by architect).

KELDY CASTLE FOREST CABINS (1979)

Description:
Prefabricated cabins of wood panel construction
Architects:
Hird and Brooks
Structural engineers:
Chapman and Smart

Axonometric
of cabin
with loft:

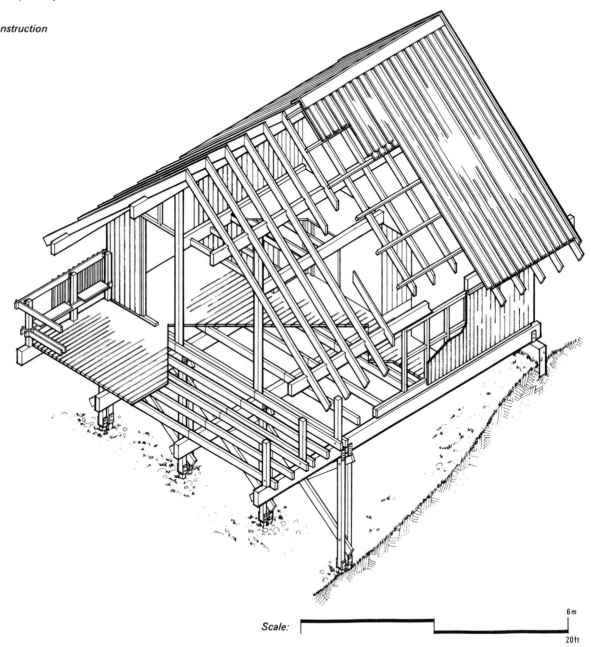

Scale:

6 m

20 ft

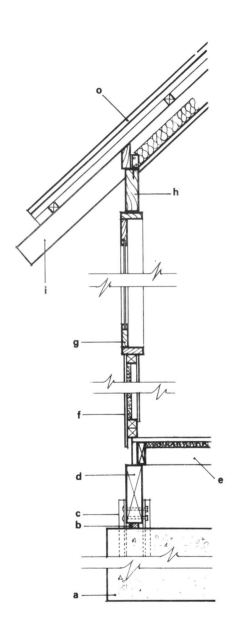

Interior view of cabin (photo by architect).

a concrete ground beam; **b** oak pad on dpc; **c** steel angle with 2/ 22mm bolts; **d** 100 x 300 mm floor beam; **e** floor panel with 25mm t and g boards and 50 x 125 mm joists and 38mm insulation; **f** solid wall panel having 19 x 100 mm softwood boards on 6mm ply on 50 x 50 mm uprights and crossmembers with 38mm insulation; **g** window panel; **h** 75 x 250 mm roof beam; **i** 25 x 150 mm boards on 50 x 50 mm battens on felt on 50 x 125 mm rafters at 600mm centres with 60mm insulation.

Vertical Section through wall.

draped over the rafters to catch what leakage does occur. The cabin type with loft space has floor panels in the loft which are similar to those at the main level; they are supported by 75 x 250 mm beams. The walls consist either of solid panels, panels with small windows, panels glazed top to bottom or panels with sliding or swing doors, some of them glazed. All softwood used in manufacture of the panels was european redwood.

Connections between the panels and timber beams are generally made by galvanised steel screws, 3.2mm in diameter, with mastic in the

Construction

The shell of each cabin was transported, erected and then glazed all in one day. Installation of the internal partitions and finishing required a further five days. Good accuracy was required to enable the glazing, which was precut, to fit into positions. There were 18 assembly drawings for each cabin, referenced to a set of 80 standard details, as well as about 100 fabrication drawings of the panels and all parts used in these three cabin types. All panels were manhandled into position. The 58 cabins were built in a period of 18 months with work in the factory starting two months ahead of that on site.

Conclusion

The very large roof overhangs used here not only protect the cabin against sun and rain but also provide an appropriate motif connected with the idea of shelter. An attribute of this architecture is the way that the structure and method of building are left in evidence. For the cabin type with loft space, fabrication amounted to 65% of the final cost, excluding foundations, with erection and transport coming to 16%; figures for the other types were similar. Because of the construction method, the lengths of cabins may be increased at will, using the same parts and panels, as long as the length increases are in modular amounts. Developed versions were made of some of the cabin types used here.

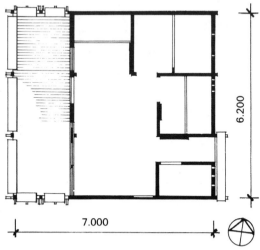

Ground floor plan.

6.200

7.000

joints. For the holding down details near the four corners, a 12mm galvanised steel bolt is used to connect the wall panel to the roof beam above and long screws connect it to the floor panel below; the floor panel is connected to the floor beam by galvanised steel straps. Other important connections also have steel straps or clips and brackets with bolts or screws. Most of these connections are exposed to view and reinforce the simplicity, which is part of the quality of this design. Services are connected through the floor of each cabin, heating and hot water being done electrically.

Structural Action

All joints between elements act like pin joints. All elements and panels are attached to each other and to the foundations so that the cabin behaves as one unit with wind forces taken by the roof and the wall panels acting in shear. Wind forces at right angles to the ground posts are taken by the concrete ground beam. Enough connections must be made to overcome local wind pressure and suction, especially near the eaves.

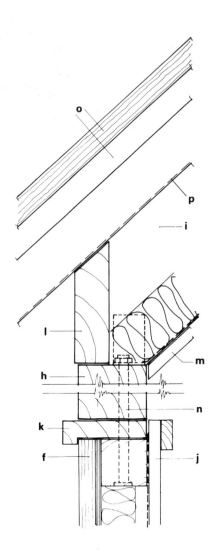

j 12mm softwood boards on vapour barrier; k wallplate; l infill piece; m roughsawn board; n 12mm steel bolt; o 150 x 25 mm roofboards; p reinforced slater's felt over rafters.

Eaves section through solid panel near corner.

IBM Exhibition Pavilion, Europe

Introduction

Two examples were made of this pavilion building, each being made in a kit form to house exhibitions for the general public. The pavilion is specifically designed to be easy to demount, transport and re-erect. It is entirely clad in a transparent plastic, which also doubles up as part of the structure; in a temporary building, the long term fall-off in properties of the plastic is unimportant. The plastic is moulded into units which are stackable, light and pyramid-shaped for strength. The detail and shaping of the connection pieces is exceptionally elegant. The whole building, including its air conditioning equipment, can be transported in 22 container trucks and erected in four weeks.

Description

The design of the superstructure is essentially concerned with the design of a single arch element which, on each side of the arch, consists of six transparent polycarbonate plastic pyramids with a single outer laminated timber chord, joining the tops of the pyramids together, and with two inner laminated timber chords, attached to the base corners of the pyramid. These inner chords are 1.20m apart and are joined to each other near the pyramid corners by timber cross-members, at right angles to them, thus forming a 'ladder'. The two halves of the arch unit are joined to each other at the apex by pin connections between the two timber 'ladders'; there is no structural connection between the polycarbonate pyramids at the apex. Thirty-four such arches placed side by side at 1.40m centres, with a joint between each one, make up the superstructure. Apart from some minor variations in those at the ends, the arch units are identical.

The arch units spring off a raised steel floor structure. It consists of 450mm deep light steel lattice trusses, which are at 1.40m centres, on the joint lines, and span between short steel legs at each side and in the centre of the arch span; each leg is made of a threaded bar and tube which allows adjustment for height. These trusses connect on each side, in the centre and at two other intermediate points, to other trusses of the same depth at right angles to them. The floor

Side view of pavilion (photo by engineer).

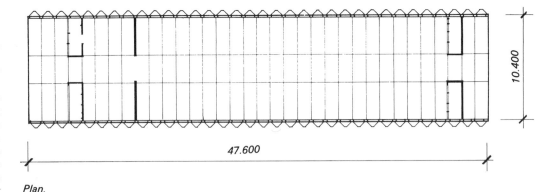

Plan.

47.600

10.400

IBM EXHIBITION PAVILION (1984)

Description:
Single-storey pavilion with trussed arches of polycarbonate
plastic and laminated timber
Architects:
Renzo Piano/ Building Workshop
Structural engineers:
Ove Arup and Partners

Axonometric
view on end:

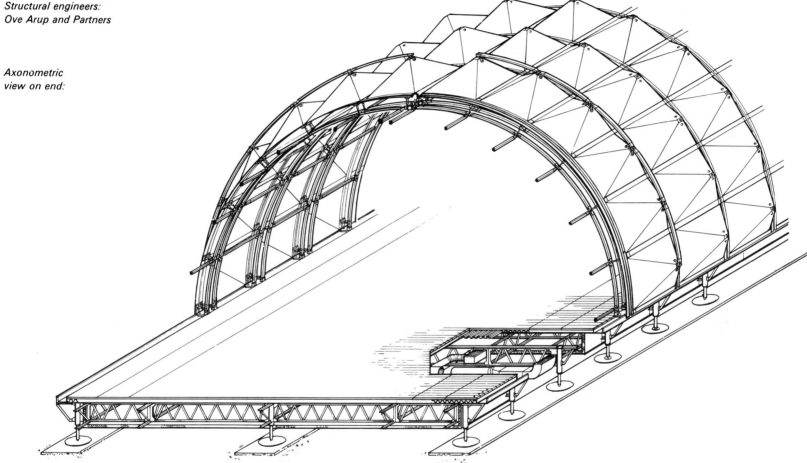

Scale:

6 m

20 ft

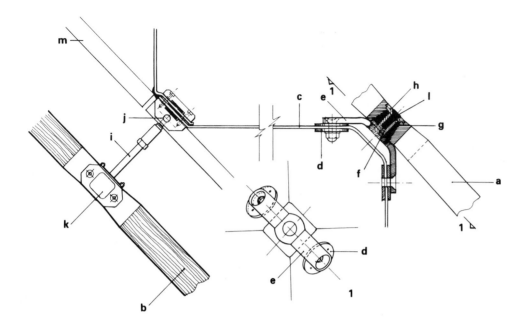

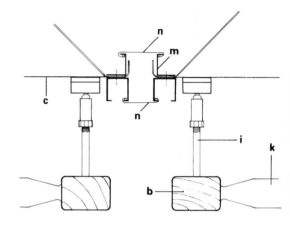

a outer chord; b inner chord; c 5mm plastic; d stainless steel discs glued to plastic; e 12mm stainless steel plate; f 25mm rod with internal thread; g rubber block; h cover plate; i stainless steel rod with rubber block; j rotating cross-pin in stainless steel block; k cross-member; l locking screw; m aluminium stiffener sections bolted through polycarbonate pyramids.

Vertical section through wall at or near centre of chords.

n clear flexible plastic strip for weatherproofing.

Horizontal section at junction between arch units.

panels are 1.40m wide and span between the trusses. They consist of a 55mm deep corrugated steel deck which supports 20mm larch floor board through bent metal strips. Phenolic foam fills the voids and provides insulation and 'deadening' for the board.

The polycarbonate pyramids are vacuum formed from 6mm thick, flat sheets, three pyramids being made from each sheet. The chords are made from laminated beech. Short lengths are connected together at the cast aluminium nodes, to which the pyramids are attached, using glued finger joints. At the top of the pyramids, stainless steel discs are shop-glued in two places to either side of the polycarbonate and to these is bolted a

bent stainless steel plate, from which a rod with a rubber block cast on it projects radially. The rubber block has a push fit with the outer aluminium nodes; it is secured by an outer cover plate with a screw fitting to the rod.

At the base of the pyramid, a stainless steel block, with a rotating cross-pin, is glued to the polycarbonate. A stainless steel rod about 200mm long, but adjustable in length, is threaded and screws to the cross-pin, at one end, and, at the other end, has a rubber block with a push fit to the inner aluminium nodes; it is secured by a plate with two bolts. This detail was necessary to allow the pyramids to move circumferentially and radially relative to the chords, the polycarbonate having a

coefficient of thermal expansion about twenty times that of the wood. Most movement takes place near the apex joint. Although free to rotate radially, the cross-pin is fixed in the building's long direction so that wind forces in this direction are transferred to the 'ladders', which act as frames; the 'ladders' are connected to each other at the apex and mid-point on each side of the building. The cross-members of the 'ladder' are attached to the radial members with bolts. To prevent buckling, the inner radial edges of the pyramids, adjacent to joints, are stiffened by extruded aluminium channels each side of the polycarbonate; the channels are bolted together through the polycarbonate, using slotted holes to allow differential thermal movement, and do not carry any axial load. The joint between the arch units is weatherproofed by an internal and external strip of transparent pvc, the edges of both strips being wrapped round wires and placed within the stiffening channels.

A consequence of the use of a single skin of polycarbonate is that air conditioning was necessary to cater for the climatic conditions. A two-dimensional study of airflow patterns, by computer, indicated that the number of air changes necessary in hot conditions could be reduced by increasing the height of the pavilion so that pockets of hot air were at least 2m above the floor. Opaque double-skinned insulated panels, fitting inside the pyramids, were placed as necessary to reduce light levels and increase the thermal insulation. Six free-standing air-handling units were placed down the length of the building; these supply ducts within the depth of the floor trusses that discharge via floor grilles at the perimeter and elsewhere. There are additional air handling units within the voids of the flat enclosing walls at each end of the pavilion; these supply fresh air, heated or not, to the internal volume and also to a central high-level duct from which smaller ducts, placed in the space between the arch units, discharge on to the inner surface of the pyramids at high level to prevent condensation.

Structural Action

The structural design is dominated by the need to allow for thermal movement of the polycarbonate. As the inner edges of the pyramids increase in length their radius of curvature also increases. This movement is largely unrestrained because of the pinned joints used, only small secondary moments arising in the elements. Both the outer chord to pyramid joints and the inner chord joints allow rotation. The superstructure works as a series of three-pinned arches. Each arch unit has two parts, the pyramids and outer chords working in unison but largely independent of the inner chord; the pyramids and outer chord have greater bending stiffness but, being discontinuous at the apex, must transfer forces into the inner chord near this point. The connections between the 'ladders' of the arch unit allow horizontal forces to be distributed through the whole building structure.

Detail at junction of arch units (photo by engineer).

Detail at base of arch units (photo by engineer).

Construction

The need to transport and erect the pavilion was a major influence on the design. For transport, the superstructure is split into its component chords, cross members and pyramids. Most of the building's weight is in the raised floor structure and the flat enclosing walls at each end supported off it. All components can be manhandled, the only plant used being a forklift truck and a purpose-made jack for lifting each half of the arch unit. The use of push-fit joints allowed the building to be erected without difficulty even when the joints were slightly misaligned. Erection of the building took less than four weeks.

Conclusion

From transparent plastic, mostly, the designers have created a well lit arcade with a bold pattern given by the reflecting planes. Compared to most thermoplastics, the polycarbonate has good flammability characteristics and good impact resistance; however it needs care when drilling to prevent cracks. Its 'milking' or slight loss of transparency over time are no disadvantage here. The costs of forming the pyramids and the costs of purpose-made stainless steel and cast aluminium joints are high. When in service, the air-conditioning load per unit volume is considerable because of the transparency of the plastic. The joints are brilliantly conceived and detailed and are a major element in the proper working and appearance of this sophisticated building kit.

South Poplar Health Centre, London, England

Introduction

Especially in the central areas of towns and cities, sites can become temporarily vacant, because of delays and uncertainties in the planning process. This local health centre building is designed to capitalize on this. It has high quality finishes and full facilities for health care but is, nevertheless, relocatable, breaking up into lorry-mounted units that can be reassembled on other sites. The whole process, up to recommissioning of the building, need only take two weeks on a prepared site where ground works have been done.

Description

The building is single storey, square on plan and divided up by a modular grid with dimensions of 3.30 x 6.60 m, the area occupied by each of the container-shaped removable modular units. Sixteen of these units, together with a clear 6.6m square central space, make up the complete building. Hollow section members spanning between opposite modular units support the floor and roof of this central space. The removable modular units, surrounding the central space, are also hollow section members; at the top four corners, a screw fitting allows them to be lifted by crane. After positioning, these fittings are also used to attach adjacent units to each other via a steel plate screwed to each fitting; at the bottom a similar plate is bolted to angles on each unit. In both cases neoprene washers are sandwiched between the steel surfaces to reduce transmission of structure-borne sound. The modular units simply rest on a steel bearing plate set on top of brick piers on concrete pad foundations. By raising the building off the ground, the design eliminates the need for damp-proofing and allows space to accommodate the distribution of main services to the various modules. The roof floor, external walls and internal partitions, that provide enclosure use standard timber framing which is bolted to the steel frame of the unit. Double partitions and staggered studs in single partitions are used to increase sound insulation. Rainwater pipes run within these partitions. The cladding is made from red-coated steel panels that are slightly raised in the centre for extra stiffness and supported by

View of Health Centre from N (photo by Fabienne de Backer).

neoprene gaskets, set into aluminium sections. Each unit has piped services that are linked up to those in the adjacent units by flexible connections. Only the panels between the modules at floor, wall and roof level and some service connections need to be removed to allow the fully equipped modular unit to be lifted away and resited.

Structural Action

As is very often the case with prefabricated components, for example large precast concrete units, the greatest forces on the modules are dynamic and occur during transport and erection. An effect of the small scale of each unit, however, is that they have great stiffness and strength. In position, gravity and wind loads are taken by frame action. Connections are made by welding and bolting.

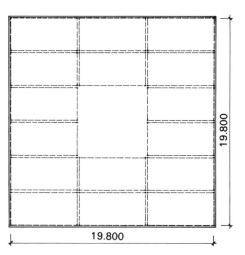

Plan on roof.

SOUTH POPLAR HEALTH CENTRE (1980)

Description:
Relocatable single-storey health centre of modular steel unit
construction with removable steel panels
Architects:
Derek Stow and Partners
Structural engineers:
Ove Arup and Partners

Axonometric
view from NE:

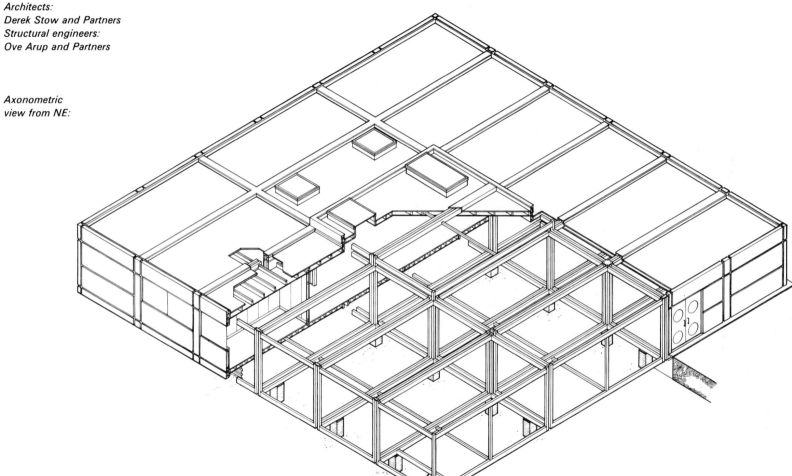

Scale: 6 m
20 ft

View of W side of health centre (photo by Fabienne de Backer).

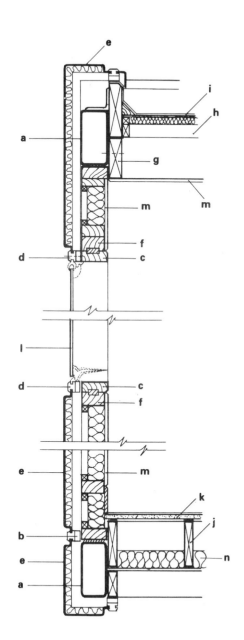

View of NE side of health centre (photo by Fabienne de Backer).

Construction

The units are designed to be made and fully fitted with engineering services in the factory. In these conditions installation or relocation can be done in a matter of weeks.

a 200 x 100 mm steel hollow section; b aluminium section; c hardwood; d neoprene gasket system; e steel panel with polyester powder coating, insulated with 25mm polyurethane foam (inside face sealed with fire-resistant board); f softwood; g 150 x 50 mm roof joist; h 6.5mm plywood and 25mm urethane foam with foil lining; i built-up roofing; j 175 x 38 mm floor joist; k carpet on 22mm chipboard on felt cushion strips; l frameless toughened (tempered) glass; m fire-resistant board; n 100mm foamglass.

Vertical section through wall.

Conclusion

For removable buildings, metal frames have an almost unassailable advantage in their resistance to shock, ease of transport and speed of erection, the direct result of their high strength, strength to weight and ductility. Steelwork is usually the economic choice. The need to make the building transportable has increased the cost of the structure, for example the four columns at internal supports. However these units may be stacked and put in many other plan configurations and the cladding, being held only by neoprene gaskets, is removable and reusable for any new arrangement. The pattern made by these gaskets on elevation is most successful and gives scale and unity to an already bold piece of design.

Sixth Form College, Alton, Hampshire, England

Introduction

This single-storey school building has a deliberately informal appearance and a variety, both in plan form and roof shape, but uses a traditional central quadrangle to pull the design together and create a protected space. The individual planning of spaces has been accommodated without compromising the design and without the additional expense that would be incurred in large buildings. Moreover, the method of construction adopted here is extremely economic, when the internal volumes are subdivided, so that roof spans are small, and an appropriate use is made of the principal materials, which are wood and masonry. The building is representative of a large class of buildings such as schools, health centres and community halls that use this form of construction, which, in effect, is a stretched or scaled-up versions of ordinary house construction.

Description

The school contains classrooms, offices, a dining room, a library and a hall. The hall has an octagonal plan and a pyramid shaped roof. The other areas are covered by trussed rafters, in which all the members are in the same plane and connected together by metal plates, or by one of eight types of truss, in which members are in different planes and connected together by split ring or toothed plate connectors. The external walls are of double-leaf construction using 100mm thick calcium silicate bricks with a 50mm cavity between. The internal walls are also 100mm thick and are freely arranged to suit the planning requirements. The trusses rest on a timber wallplate, on top of the walls, or on piers which are formed in the walls, as necessary, to provide a suitably large bearing area. On three sides of the building, the two kinds of roof truss are used in a a split level arrangement that allows natural light into the middle of the building and also gives convenient positions for air extracts: the trussed rafters spanning 5.55m are spaced at 600mm centres while the trusses, spanning 7.35m, are at the larger spacing of 2.70m between centres. The hall has a 13m distance between opposite faces of its octagonal plan which is

View of main entrance from SW.

spanned by a $17\frac{1}{2}$ degree pitch pyramid roof using four principal 35 x 495 mm laminated timber beams. These beams rest on neoprene pads on concrete padstones set in the inner leaf of the cavity wall; the feet of the beams are tied into horizontal steel bars of 24mm diameter to prevent sidethrust on the walls. The outer leaf of the cavity wall is stiffened by a pier at these positions. The high walls, which form the hall space, are stabilised by the roof and the wall panels on either side. The floor slab in the building is 125mm thick concrete laid directly on hardcore but thickened and having strip footings where there are significant line loads from the internal masonry walls.

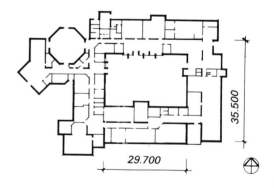

35.500

29.700

Ground floor plan.

ALTON SIXTH FORM COLLEGE (1978)

Description:
Single-storey school of brickwork construction with timber
roofs
Architects:
Hampshire County Council
Structural engineers:
Gifford and Partners

Axonometric
view from SW:

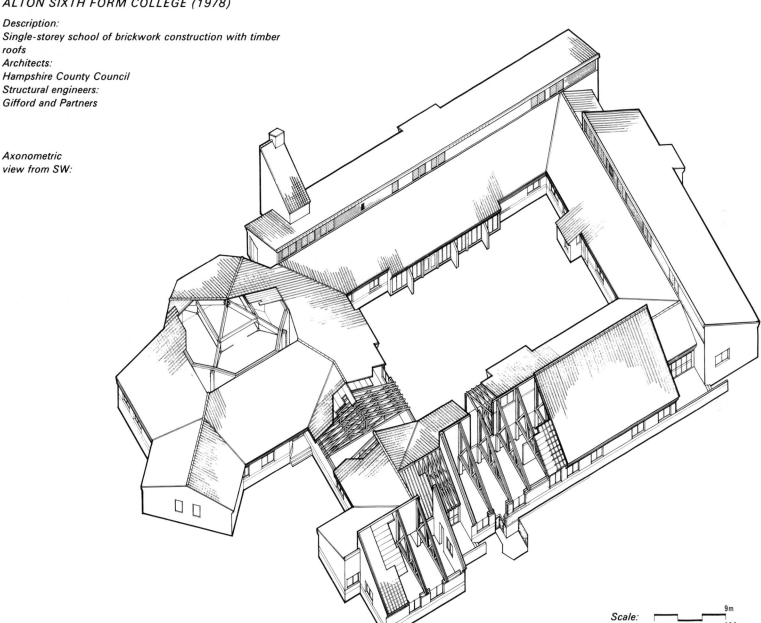

Scale:

9m
30 ft

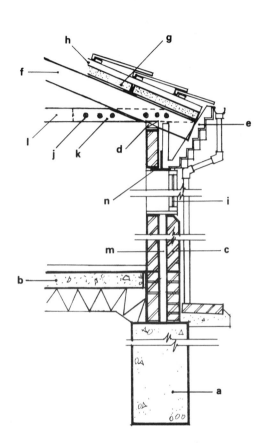

View of split-level roof and entrance from SW.

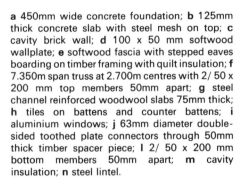

a 450mm wide concrete foundation; b 125mm thick concrete slab with steel mesh on top; c cavity brick wall; d 100 x 50 mm softwood wallplate; e softwood fascia with stepped eaves boarding on timber framing with quilt insulation; f 7.350m span truss at 2.700m centres with 2/ 50 x 200 mm top members 50mm apart; g steel channel reinforced woodwool slabs 75mm thick; h tiles on battens and counter battens; i aluminium windows; j 63mm diameter double-sided toothed plate connectors through 50mm thick timber spacer piece; l 2/ 50 x 200 mm bottom members 50mm apart; m cavity insulation; n steel lintel.

Typical vertical section at window.

Structural Action

Vertical movement joints are provided in the external walls at intervals of about 9m and, generally, are positioned where weakening occurs because of door or window openings. As a result the building behaves like a series of individual units. The principal problems are in ensuring the stability of individual walls and the overall resistance of the building to horizontal forces. In this case the individual walls are stabilised by the other walls to which they are attached and by their connections to the ground floor slab and roof. The overall resistance of the building is assured by shear walls which are mostly in one of two directions at right angles to each other, these walls all being attached at the top to the roof structure, which acts as a diaphragm. There is diagonal bracing in the plane of the roof and in one of the planes formed by the web members of the roof trusses. The principal truss spanning 7.35m has members in three separate vertical planes so that the members overlap; split ring and toothed plate connections are used to join them together, with spacer pieces as necessary. At each joint the centre lines of the members meet as near as possible in one point to minimise secondary bending moments.

View of hall from W.

View of NE corner of courtyard.

Typical wall and window construction in courtyard.

Construction

The total period for construction was 21 months.

Conclusion

In this irregular plan, loosely based on the idea of a quad, the key architectural element is the tiled roof and it is this which, in the end, helps to organize the layout. The construction, here, is typical of many other buildings of this general type. The brickwork walls are multipurpose, giving an appropriate texture and scale to the building, as well as providing the enclosure, taking gravity loads and acting as shear walls against horizontal forces. The tensile stresses that develop in shear walls, due to wind or other horizontal forces, must be suppressed by the gravity loads, as in all loadbearing masonry structures. However, in single-storey buildings, such as this, the tensile stresses due to wind are extremely small. Timber with a high strength to weight ratio and good workability is an obvious choice of material for the roof construction. It is difficult to achieve rigid or even semi-rigid connections between timber members but, as the truss only relies on pinned connections at node points, this is a suitable form for it to take. Connections between the wall and roof elements are vital to ensure that each building unit is a stable structural entity.

Schulitz House,
Beverly Hills, California, USA

Introduction

Sited on a very steep slope with spectacular views south is this steel frame, clad with aluminium panels, and all but unrecognizable as a house. The building has none of the weight or sense of enclosure commonly associated with housing, but instead is open, flooded with light and excels in its fixing details, regularly spaced columns and surfaces of glass and metal. This is perhaps the best example in more than twenty years of the use of off-the-shelf mass-produced components put together in a completely individual way. The design does not compromise its use as a house and the simple frame makes a setting for the different textures provided by wood slats, shades, venetian blinds, carpets, bookshelves and all the paraphernalia associated with living rooms in use. This small house represents, in a very accomplished form, an important idea about building methods which has great potential but which, as yet, is unrealised to any great extent.

Description

There are three levels to the house, the top level being at street level. The house is a steel frame with 6 x 6 in (150 x 150 mm) square tubular columns that, in general, support two main channel beams on either side; these support steel open-web joists of standard length, in their turn supporting a metal deck and lightweight concrete floor slab. The four lines of columns are supported by three rows of circular concrete stub columns, cast on top of piles, and by the retaining wall at street level. The stub columns are stabilised by a grid of reinforced concrete tie beams cast on the surface of the sloping ground. The cladding is of aluminium panels on a light gauge secondary framing system with insulation. Trim elements and window frames are also in aluminium. It is these secondary items and the standard lengths in which they are supplied by the manufacturers that has determined the dimensioning system and, through that, the dimensions of the main frame. The dimensions are modular, that is multiples of a unit, which here is 4in (100mm) in both horizontal directions and 6in (150mm) vertically. The various building elements must fit within this modular grid with sufficient

View of house from S (photo by architect).

tolerance to allow easy erection, and any dimensional variations or errors whether in construction or in manufacture of the components.

Structural Action

The house is in an earthquake area so that the forces on it are due not only to wind or gravity loads but, more significantly, to ground accelerations, which produce horizontal and vertical forces on the structure. However the house is light so that these inertial forces are low. Except at the top, where the cantilever action of the column is sufficient, cross bracing is used to take the horizontal forces and, therefore, the steelwork joints are simple and cheap and can allow generous erection tolerances.

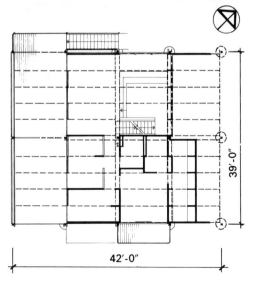

Middle level floor plan.

SCHULITZ HOUSE (1976)

Description:
Three-storey house with steel frame and standard aluminium
wall panels
Architect:
H. C. Schulitz
Structural engineer:
Kurily and Szymanski

Axonometric
view from S:

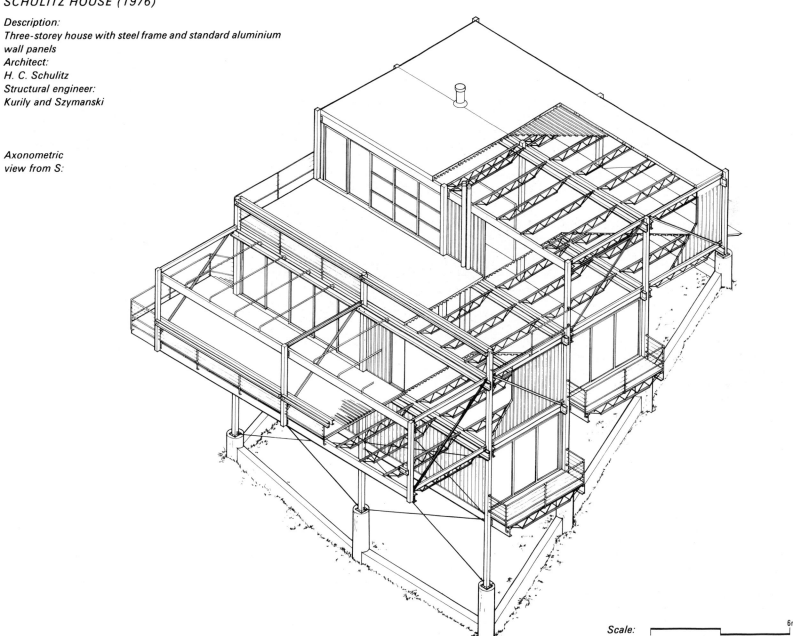

Scale:

6m

20ft

View of house from SE (photo by architect).

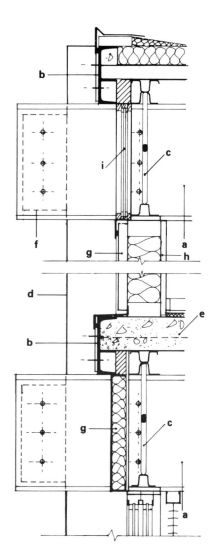

Construction

The total period of construction was nine months due to the fact that the architect did much of the infill-construction work himself. However the steelwork erection, as usual, was very fast, taking only two days to complete.

Conclusion

The method of building adopted here has been called an 'open system', meaning that it has been assembled with a maximum number of off-the-shelf parts. Every house of an open system could have a different appearance. This method of building has been developed in reaction to closed systems, such as proprietary concrete panels and wall frame systems, which have suffered from their

generally monotonous appearance; it also contrasts with metal building systems, which, although they are more flexible, are still purpose-made and can be used only as a defined system. The costs of such closed systems are greatly increased by components which are only required in small numbers and are therefore uneconomic to produce. But 'open' systems are yet to win, not only public approval, but also the approval of architects and builders, since open systems require a rigorous principle of selection, coordination and joining of parts. However the quality of the design in this building should increase the acceptance of this kind of collage of elements. The light sections and quick connections possible with steelwork have been used here to excellent advantage.

a 12″ x 20.7 lb/ft steel channel; **b** 6″ x 8.2 lb/ft steel channel; **c** open web joist at 4′ centres; **d** 6″ x 6″ x ¼″ thick steel tube; **e** 4″ lightweight concrete floor slab on metal deck; **f** connection plates welded to tube; **g** aluminium panel with metal studs, fibreglass insulation; **h** gypsum board; **i** window in aluminium frame (or fascia board).

Vertical section through wall on NW and SE sides.

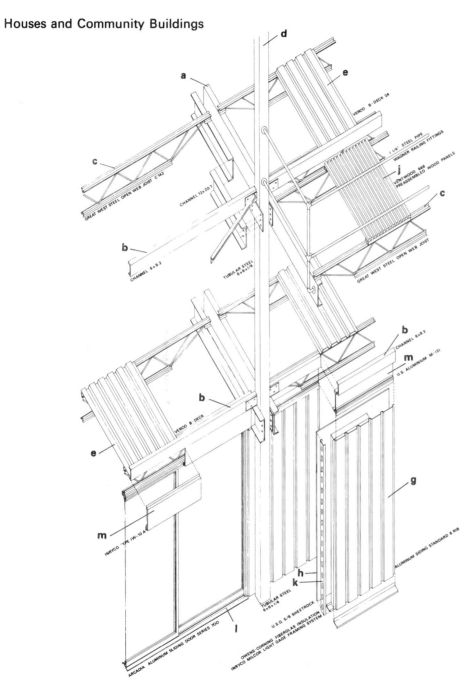

Steel framework under construction (photo by architect).

Detail of junction on SE side (photo by architect).

j wood panels; k metal stud; l aluminium sliding door; m aluminium fascia board.

Exploded view of construction on NW and SE sides (drawn by architect).

Marin Tennis Club,
San Raphael, California, USA

Introduction

As a natural composite material, wood has
mechanical properties which, as yet, are quite
unmatched by artificial composites. For the
designer, timber also provides an almost endless
and unforced variety of natural colour and grain
patterns with surface textures varying from the
rough sawn to the smooth and varnished. One
disadvantage of the use of wood is the difficulty of
making rigid connections which, compared to
steel and concrete, has restricted its use as a
material for building frames. For small buildings
the disadvantage is insignificant and in this tennis
club building it simply provides an opportunity for
the use of some distinctive steel cross-bracing and
robust steel brackets. The main building of the
tennis club is a two-storey timber frame which
both provides an indoor space, protected from the
weather, and continues beyond the cladding line
to provide an outdoor shelter around the perimeter
with views onto the courts. The building makes
marvellous use of wood both on interior and
exterior surfaces, the almost wholesome nature of
the wood, reinforced by the simplicity of the frame
which is set out on a standard grid.

View of clubhouse from E (photo by Joshua Freiwald).

Description

The building frame is on a 10ft (3.00m) square
grid, with 6 x 6 in (150 x 150 mm) Douglas Fir
columns two storeys high that carry the mezzanine
floor and roof beams. Floor and roof beams,
typically, are 6 x 10 in (150 x 250 mm) to span 10ft
(3.00m), but are increased in depth where spans
or loadings increase. The ground floor of the main
building is given over to a lounge with a kitchen
and bar in the east corner and a shop and office in
the middle. Double-height glass walls in a timber
surround are set back from the perimeter of the
wood frame and allow views out in almost all
directions. The space is double-height but for a
mezzanine floor which extends into the central
area of the lounge and provides a high-level
viewing gallery. Also at the mezzanine level is the
plant room providing hot water to the kitchen and
to the showers which are housed in a separate
building on the north-east side of the main
building. The exterior cladding to the kitchen and

plant room areas is in Western Red Cedar
boarding. The roof and the mezzanine floor deck
use Hemlock planks. The foundations are concrete
pads.

Structural Action

Stability against horizontal forces, such as those
due to wind or earthquakes is provided, on three
elevations, by cross-bracing using steel rods. On
each elevation two bays, one at each end, is
braced. On the fourth elevation, the north-east
side, the exterior cladding provides the necessary
rigidity. The roof deck acts as a horizontal
diaphragm to tie all the columns into one structural
unit. This type of construction, when all elements
are properly tied to each other, has particularly
favourable characteristics in earthquake areas,
wood being light, having good impact resistance

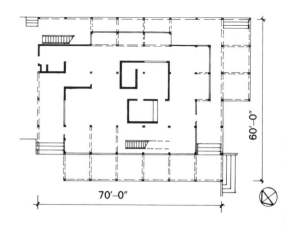

Ground floor plan.

MARIN TENNIS CLUB (1974)

Description:
Two-storey clubhouse of wood frame construction
Architects:
Backen, Arrigoni and Ross
Structural engineer:
J.S. Papp and Associates

Axonometric
view from W:

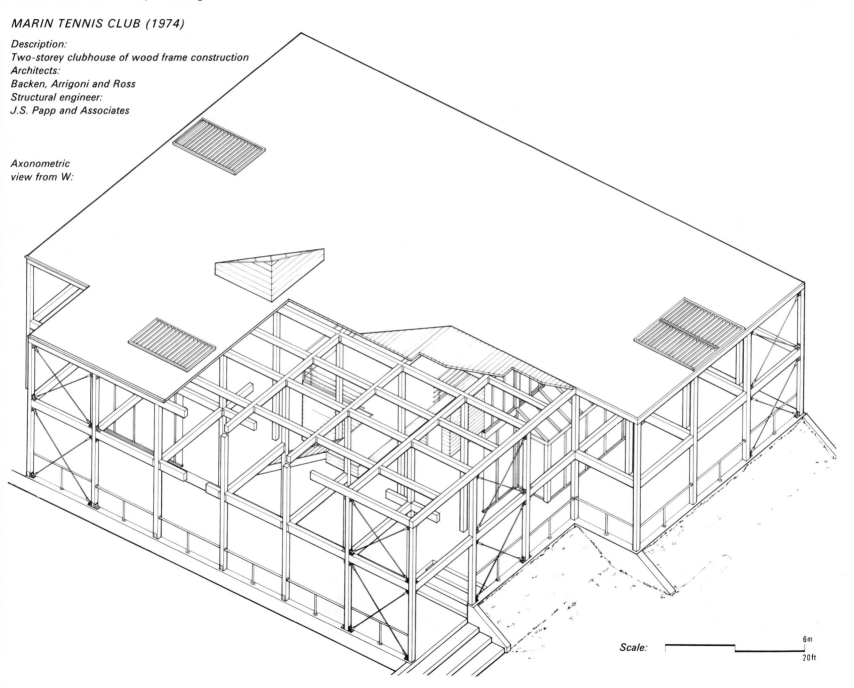

Scale:

6m

20ft

View of terrace on SW side looking SE (photo by Joshua Freiwald).

View along SW side (photo by Joshua Freiwald).

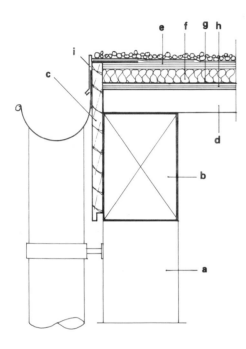

a timber column; **b** 6″x 8″ timber edge beam; **c** 1″ cedar fascia board; **d** 2″ tongue and groove timber decking; **e** built-up asphalt roof; **f** 1″ rigid insulation; **g** waterproof membrane; **h** plywood sheet; **i** sheet metal flashing and gravel stop.

Vertical section through edge of roof.

Inside view looking E (photo by Joshua Freiwald).

and having connections able to absorb substantial deformation while remaining intact.

Construction

The period of construction for both clubhouse buildings was 12 months.

Conclusion

The three-dimensional structural grid, along which the frame is set, is always visible and the design makes extremely good use of it as a reference interval and ordering principle for the building. The frame also allows a gradual transition from indoor to terrace to outdoor spaces. There is plenty of visual detail associated with the frame and, inside, a further nice contrast between the roughness of the frame and the carefully worked details and finishes.

Dune Houses,
Atlantic Beach, Florida, USA

Introduction

From the beach, what distinguishes this building is its earth mound with two openings, that seem to caricature a bird gazing wide-eyed but abstractedly out to sea. In fact, each oculus is a window into a small apartment recessed into the face of a sand dune. There are two such apartments, each a mirror image of the other and separated by a concrete wall. The walls and roof are made of sprayed concrete and are good examples of the use of such concrete to form awkward, doubly-curved surfaces. The building has two levels but manages to disappear into the sand dune to take advantage of a stable thermal regime below ground level, while maintaining the view out to sea.

Description

The lower level floor is a 4in (100mm) thick cast-in-place concrete slab, which is turned up slightly at the edges and, in the middle, is recessed over a small square area. Two egg-shaped shell structures of sprayed concrete are built on top of this slab. The upper level floor, inside the shell, is wooden and supported by wood posts on one side and the dividing wall on the other. The entrance to each apartment, reached down some garden steps, is on the west side at the upper level, as is the bathroom and bedroom; from here wooden stairs lead to the dining and living room areas on the lower level. Contrary to the general case with underground buildings, there is no insulation on the outside of the shells because the ground here is at a steady year-round temperature of about 70°F (21°C), maintaining the inside at near the same temperature; at least 20in (500mm) of soil covers the shell and this is enough to even out temperature fluctuations. Heat gain through the oculus in the mornings is controlled by reflective blinds. Electrically powered heating and air conditioning is available, if required. The air conditioning is provided by a water-cooled, reverse-cycle heat pump and humidifier in each apartment. A waterproof membrane, on the outside of the construction, and fans from the kitchen and bathroom exhausting through the top are sufficient to control humidity in most

View of building from NE (photo by architect).

circumstances, without the need for special equipment. Sound reverberation is controlled by carpeting and wood slat surfaces. The interior of the shell is sprayed concrete, trowelled smooth, but could also have been finished with an acoustic plaster.

Structural Action

The shell is a doubly-curved synclastic surface that is prestressed in compression by the soil backfill. The shape was determined so as to practically eliminate bending stresses due to the weight of the shell and the sand cover; therefore stresses, are very low and no reinforcement is necessary in the shell, for structural purposes, except that around the oculus, which does undergo some bending. A structural model having

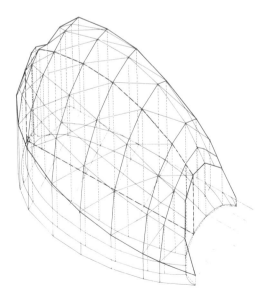

Model of shell for structural analysis.

View from SE with plywood templates and bars in position (photo by architect).

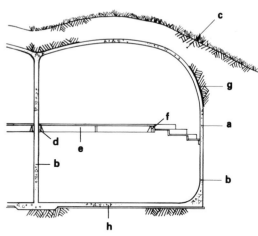

a 4" sprayed concrete with $\frac{3}{8}$" bars at 12" centres each way; **b** 5" sprayed concrete; **c** 20" earth; **d** 2" x 8" wood section fixed to wall with $\frac{3}{8}$" bolts; **e** 2" x 8" wood joists at 1'–4" centres; **f** 2/ 2" x 8" joists on wood posts; **g** bituminous waterproof membrane; **h** 4" cast-in-place concrete slab.

N-S section through apartment.

triangular finite elements was used to check the shape of the shell and the levels of stress.

Construction

After pouring of the lower level slab and wall upstands, $\frac{3}{8}$in (9mm) steel bars at 12in (300mm) centres each way were placed one at a time and bent to the required shape, using plywood templates at the outer edges and a line of support down the centre of each shell; these bars lap with other bars of the same size which project from the walls. Most steel bars were only needed as a temporary support for a metal lath, rather than as reinforcement. The metal lath was laid on top of the bars, fixed and then sprayed with concrete on the outside to a thickness of less than 1in (25mm) which was nevertheless sufficient to make a rigid form. After removal of the templates inside, the curved shell was brought up to a total thickness of 4in (100mm) by spraying concrete from inside.

Walls were sprayed to a thickness of 5in (125mm). The construction of the concrete shells took six weeks.

Conclusion

Although only one window opening is provided in each apartment, it has a considerable area. The idea of such an opening can be extended to buildings in which the whole of one side is glazed, other sides being covered with an earth berm, and in which heat or coolness from the outside is absorbed or rejected at the glass line, as necessary. Even without elaborate thermal controls, the use of the earth backfill around this building provides insulation and thermal capacity which is estimated to almost half the electricity that would be required by a conventional, well insulated timber building above ground. In extreme climates this method of construction offers even greater benefits.

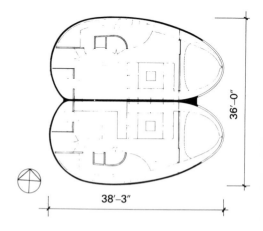

Lower floor plan.

ATLANTIC BEACH DUNE HOUSES (1975)

Description:
Underground houses of sprayed concrete shell construction
Architects:
William Morgan Architects
Structural engineer:
Geiger Berger Associates

Axonometric
view from SE:

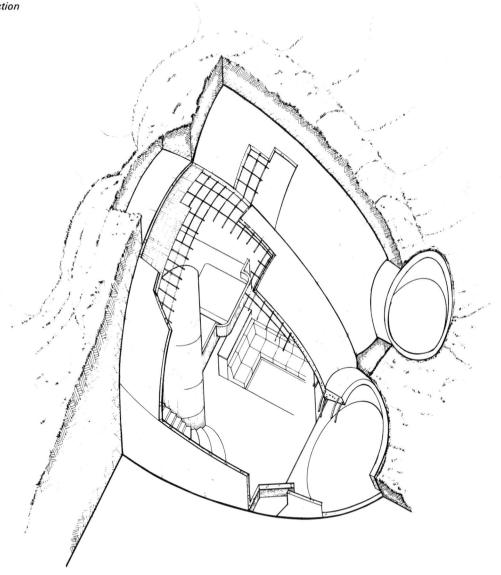

Scale:

6m

20 ft

West Beach Bathhouse, Chesterton, Indiana, USA

Introduction

This single-storey precast concrete building is a typical symptom of the importance attached to preserving the natural environment. It is designed to blend into its sand dune setting and to minimise the disturbance to the dune during construction. The key element in the scheme is a precast concrete unit, in the shape of a column capital, that connects the beam and column elements together. This capital unit is positioned at floor and roof levels and provides a generous amount of space to allow connections to be made easily. In a more general sense, it acts as a device for turning corners which is distinctive and has been repeated throughout to allow the division of the building into smaller units. This gives flexibility to the planning and helps to reduce the visual impact of the building.

Description

The building provides changing facilities for a lakeshore beach. The columns, which are cast in place in circular forms, are set out on a 27ft 5in (8.37m) square grid and are supported by pad footings. At floor levels, octagonal-shaped precast concrete capitals are placed on top of the concreted column, eight reinforcement bars from the column passing through $2\frac{1}{2}$in (63mm) diameter holes in the capital, which were formed by casting in corrugated pipe. At both floor and roof levels, the capital sits on a mortar bed which allows adjustment for line and level. Precast prestressed beams, on a two-way grid, are placed between the capitals and in turn support precast prestressed hollow core planks, either 10in (200mm) deep at floor levels or 8in (150mm) deep at roof levels. Hardboard pads, $\frac{1}{8}$in (3mm) thick, are used to spread the load at the bearing of the planks on the floor beam. A 2in (50mm) concrete topping covers the planks at floor level.

At roof level the planks are covered with rigid insulation and built-up roofing. Eight large clerestory windows allow light into the interior. The clerestories are built from 8in (200mm) precast wall panels bolted to the support beams and attached to 6in (150mm) precast roof planks via weld plates cast into both unit types. The

View during construction with some clerestory elements in position (photo by architect).

clerestory glazing has aluminium frames with spacer blocks between the frames and the precast concrete units. At floor level the cladding is mostly in brick. An important aspect of the design is that the cladding is not made to abut the columns but passes to one side on lines at 45 degrees to the grid.

Structural Action

The building has a two-way grid of beams between the columns, unlike most commercial precast concrete frame systems in which, apart from perimeter beams, all the beams run in a single direction and are tied together by the slab. In this building all tie forces are taken by the beams; the slabs are simply placed on top of them. The connection of the beam to the capital unit is worthy of note: two vertical $\frac{5}{8}$in (16mm) anchor

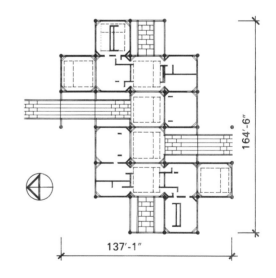

Floor plan.

164'-6"

137'-1"

WEST BEACH BATHHOUSE (1977)

Description:
Single-storey bathhouse of precast concrete construction
Architects and structural engineers:
Howard, Needles, Tammen
and Bergendoff

Axonometric
view from NW:

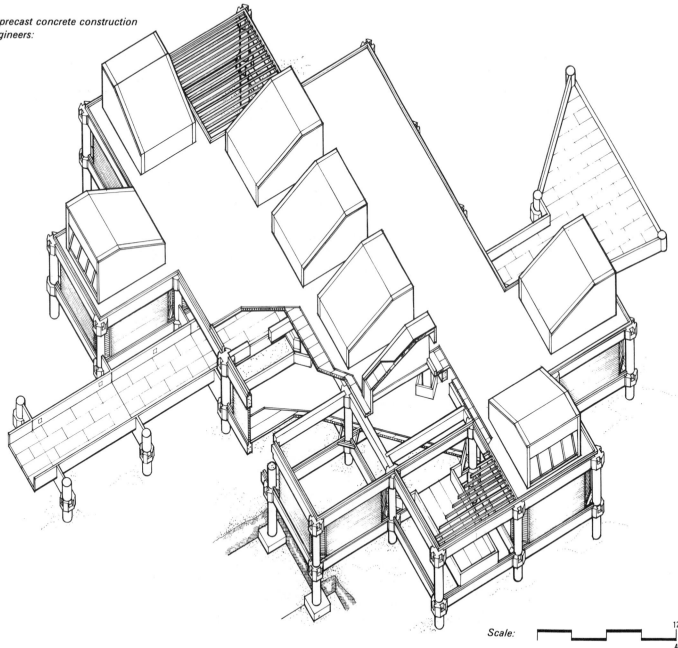

Scale:

12 m

40 ft

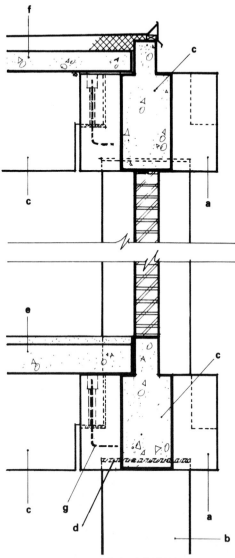

a precast concrete capital unit 2'-8" high with grid of W12 x 22lb/ft steel beams in lower half; **b** 2'-8" diameter cast-in-place column; **c** 3'-8" x 1'-6" prestressed concrete beam; **d** 1¼" mortar bed; **e** 10" concrete planks with 2" concrete topping; **f** 8" concrete planks with rigid insulation and roofing; **g** 2/ ⅝" anchor bolts embedded in capital unit.

Vertical section through wall.

Close-up view of finished building (photo by architect).

View of bathhouse during construction with floor complete (photo by architect).

bolts from the capital fit into 1½in (63mm) sleeves at each end of the beam unit. The bottom of the sleeve is filled with a compressible filler but, at the top, a nut on the anchor is bolted tight against the beam; the pocket for the nut is then grouted up. This detail allows sufficient movement to prevent the build up of large forces due to shrinkage and temperature movements, while still developing a sufficient tie force. There is no bending moment at this joint. The building resists wind and other horizontal forces by cantilever action of the columns; higher buildings than this would need to incorporate cross-bracing or shear walls. There is a nominal gap of ½in (12mm) between the ends of the beams and the concrete capital to allow for dimensional changes and the inevitable variations in the sizes and in the positioning of the units. Large tolerances, although convenient for construction purposes, can sometimes give unacceptable variations in joint width and affect the strength of the joint. The capital connection detail adopted here is particularly satisfactory on these counts.

Construction

Precast units more than about five tons in weight can sometimes increase the cost of a precast concrete building. Only one crane was needed on this site and, in general, lifting weights were moderate. Beam and floor units were placed after all the capitals were in position at each level. The total period on site was nine months with manufacture of the units starting six months before the start on site.

Conclusion

Even on a relatively small project such as this, there are still five types of beam, eleven types of wall panel and several different widths for the floor units. The variations with small production runs can make such precast concrete construction expensive. However the variations here are mostly achieved by different box-outs of the same mould forms. Precast concrete is put to good use, the building units being almost maintenance free, having excellent straightness of line and a sandblasted finish which in colour and texture matches that of the dunes.

Chapter Six

Office Buildings

In its present form, the office building is typified by a block with flat faces and nearly identical floors stacked one upon another. The unity necessary to the design is achieved, typically, not by detailed design with variations on some underlying theme but by the more facile device of extreme geometrical simplicity and the repetition of modular elements. The simplicity reduces the design time. However, a really appropriate and compelling form may be difficult to find, within the given constraints, and the blocks produced by such abbreviated design procedures are not unusual. Typically the floors in an office are required to have a minimum distance between columns varying from six to nine metres, that is from thirty to forty feet, and must be flexible in use. With these spans, no one type of structure is especially suited, so that the structure, which can be one of the most powerful influences on form, provides no obvious starting directions for the design; neither do the service requirements which are usually modest and can be accommodated in ceiling and floor voids. Flexibility in use of the offices is also required because of the rapid changes in the size and composition and in the equipment and methods of work of the organizations using the office space. The requirement for flexibility has had a major but not always beneficial effect on the design. One result has been a tendency to produce neutral, layered space between the surfaces of the floor and the suspended ceiling, in order to allow easy rearrangement of the space, including the repositioning of bulky office equipment and machinery and to pass what remains of the original requirements to be resolved by the interior design. However, given the modest cost of the offices, compared to their great economic importance or to the salaries of the buildings' users over the life of the offices, it can be expected that, increasingly, designers will be expected to enlarge the scope of the design, to take a view on what an office should be and to provide more specifically for the well-being of the office worker. This chapter, and the subsequent chapter on high-rise buildings, includes examples of buildings where this has happened, as well as those where concerns about cost and flexibility have had the predominating influence. The buildings included in this chapter have been selected so as to demonstrate the use of various forms and types of materials.

if needed

required

TRADA Offices,
High Wycombe, England

Introduction

There is office accommodation of up to three storeys in this building. The top two storeys are of timber construction and have stressed skin panel external walls, made of ply on softwood studs but, inside, have a timber framework using hardwood columns and joists. There is a basement storey below this which is of brick construction. The timber construction used provides all the necessary structural stiffness and strength as well as an enclosure which can conveniently incorporate very high thermal insulation. The building comes as light pre-assembled parts, in effect a prefabricated system that does not pay the factory overheads or site craneage associated with precast concrete. The long span of the floors is a reminder of the range of properties of structural timber, this hardwood having about three times the bending strength and twice the stiffness of softwood. The finishing details are worthy of further application and make the best of the advantages and, especially, the disadvantages of using timber.

Description

As the site slopes towards the north-east, the basement storey occupies only that part of the plan area on the north-east side. The timber ground floor above this occupies the full plan area and is supported by 200 x 100 mm exposed hardwood beams on the long south-west and north-east sides and by a reinforced concrete retaining wall which provides a line support in the middle. The hardwood beams, at the back, on the south-west side, rest on concrete filled pipe sections and at the front, on the north-east side, on the basement brick walls. The hardwood joists of the first floor and roof are supported by 600 or 750 mm deep plyweb panel beams at window head level on the long sides of the building and by a line of hardwood posts and beams in the middle. The panel beams are simply nailed on to the wall panels below and covered on the outside by a horizontal band of wood boards. All panels use ply, only 9.5mm thick, nailed and glued to 50 x 75 mm softwood studs. The joints between the wall panels are covered on the outside by softwood

View of part of NE elevation.

vertical strips. Ventilation ducts and other services run in a false ceiling in the corridor blowing hot or cold air into the room at high level. As is usual in timber framed construction, the building is well insulated but with low thermal capacity. Some heat is recovered from the light fittings by the return air. Because of the difficulty of providing a flat ceiling soffit with long span beams, softwood battens are nailed to the underneath and provide a fixing for the ceiling boards as well as space for wiring alongside. The building is detailed to allow for movement of the timber structure due to

changes in moisture content. A polythene vapour barrier is provided on the inside of the wall to prevent condensation within the wall which would reduce the insulation value and could lead to high moisture content in the timber.

Structural Action

The post and beam construction on the middle line takes gravity loads but no wind loads so that only simple beam to column connections are required. The wall panels take the remaining gravity load and all wind loads. This arrangement provides

TRADA OFFICES HIGH WYCOMBE (1976)

Description:
Three-storey office block of timber framework with plywood panel walls
Architects and structural engineers:
TRADA

Axonometric
view from E:

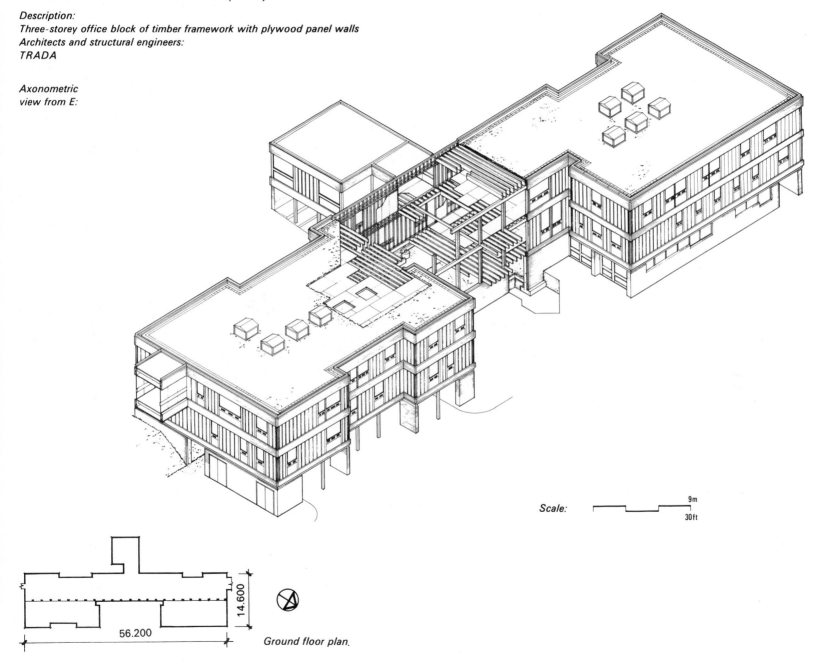

Scale: 9m / 30ft

14.600

56.200

Ground floor plan.

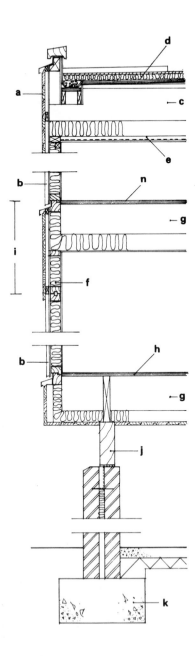

Typical wall and window construction.

View of part of SW elevation.

a 19mm shiplap boarding; **b** 9.5mm stained plywood fixed to 50 x 75 mm softwood studs; **c** 63 x 300 mm hardwood roof joists at 400mm crs; **d** insulation on built-up roofing; **e** clear space for wiring; **f** 75mm mineral wall insulation with 65μm polythene vapour barrier and 6mm medium density fibreboard; **g** 75 x 300 mm hardwood floor joists at 400mm crs; **h** 16mm plywood; **i** 600mm deep plyweb panel beam; **j** 100 x 280 mm hardwood beam; **k** 600 x 300 mm concrete foundation.

Section through external wall on S face.

clear space inside as well as being a good strategy against fire; the post and beam frame are of thick section and protected by charring of their surface while the more vulnerable but less heavily loaded panel walls still have their ply sheets and studs protected by mineral wool insulation and the internal lining board. The fire resistance required here was half an hour, although a one-hour fire rating could easily have been provided by thicker sections for posts and beams and extra fire resistant lining boards for walls and floors. In the design of timber floors it is often the stiffness required that determines the size of joists and so it is the increase in elastic modulus of the hardwood compared to softwood that is significant rather than the increase in bending strength. In such cases a typical 60% increase in elastic modulus gives a 25% increase in span. The hardwood joists used here can be cheaper than plyweb beams, laminated timber or steelwork beams, although compared to steelwork they have about twice the depth for the same span.

Construction

This method of building allows rapid erection of building units. Each unit is nailed to the adjacent units, with bolting being used at the corners. Units were designed for handling by two men although the hardwood frame members required a crane to lift them into position.

Conclusion

In practice timber buildings are often found at up to three and sometimes to four storeys height, but comparatively rarely higher than this. This is partly due to reservations about fire performance, but also to the general appearance and supposed durability of timber buildings. The fire performance is moderately good: timber structures are not easily ignited and provide reliable resistance to fire; by contrast steel and concrete structures, which are subject to large temperature movements, can destroy the structural integrity of a building and may break up any fire protection provided. Nevertheless wood is a combustible material, like plastic, and may not be used where there are statutory requirements for non-combustible materials, for example in stairways.

1111 Nineteenth Street NW, Washington DC, USA

Introduction

The long horizontal bands of window and cladding, and the sleek, industrial styling of this building seem to emphasise the movement of the traffic along the street. In fact, the elevations were designed, in a straightforward way, to reflect on the exterior the long floor spans inside. The building is indented at ground level where there are shops and the chance for a change of scale for those on foot. Most of the energy of this design has gone into an almost copybook example of maximising office rental space in a building which had a strict limit imposed on its height. The building contains more than 230 000 sq ft (21 360 sq m) of usable office space as well as parking for more than 250 cars in three basement levels. These requirements are well met by floors of prestressed, post-tensioned cast-in-place concrete construction which have kept down the floor depth while still allowing large clear spans inside.

Description

The building is of cast-in-place concrete construction with three floor bays spanned by prestressed beams in the north-south direction. At a typical office floor, the maximum spans are approximately 54, 36 and 54 ft (16.46, 10.97 and 16.46 m), these large spans being required both to allow flexibility in the layout of the offices and to give the clear spaces in the basement necessary for efficient circulation in a large car park. The floor area in the basements is slightly larger than that at a typical office level, the floor slab spiralling downwards and spanning to the retaining walls instead of the perimeter columns, but the structural arrangement is otherwise similar. Floors from levels 4 to 11 are identical. Prestressed beams at 20ft 4in (6.20m) centres are 2ft x 1ft 8in (600 x 500 mm) deep, the slab is 5½in (139mm) deep and interior columns are 2ft (600mm) square with external columns 2ft x 1ft 6in (600 x 450 mm) in section. The beams are not continuous across the three bays but stopped at third points in the middle bay, which provides both space for horizontal ducts and a convenient position for the anchorages of some of the prestressing strands in the beam. Other prestressing cables in the beam

View of building from W (photo by Harlan Hambright and Assoc.).

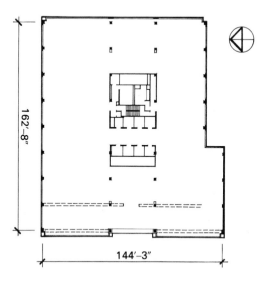

Typical floor plan.

are continuous across the complete width of the building and run in the slab depth over the middle third of the centre bay. The total prestressing force in the two outer bays is typically about 260 tons (235 tonnes) and that in the centre bay about 160 tons (145 tonnes). The stressing of the cables takes place from anchorage points around the perimeter of the floor structure. The floor slab, which spans 20ft 4in (6.20m), is also prestressed, at a level of 7.5 tons per ft run (22.35 tonnes per m).

The building has precast concrete spandrel panels alternating with bands of window and column cladding. The spandrel panels are about 20ft (6.10m) long and supported off the floor slab by three pairs of fixings. Above level 11, the building is stepped back on the north and south faces, to preserve rights of light in adjacent buildings, and the columns here are sloped.

Most mechanical equipment, including the elevator motors and the cooling tower, is housed in a plant room on the roof, also of prestressed

concrete construction. The floor slab of the plantroom is 8in (200mm) thick but has a 2in (50mm) resilient layer and a 6in (150mm) slab on top of this where there is vibrating machinery. Services run vertically down openings on either side of the core. A VAV air conditioning system is used with electrical reheat available in the perimeter terminal units. At a typical floor, the maximum sizes of ducts leading from each vertical opening are 3ft 6in x 1ft (1050 x 300 mm) deep and 4ft 2in x 10in (1250 x 250 mm) deep. Conditioned air passes through a VAV control box at the head of each interior supply line or to the perimeter terminal units, which are at about 10ft (3.00m) centres, and contain their own 1 kilowatt heater as well as a control box and 4ft (1.22m) linear diffuser. On the east and west sides 1ft x 6in (300 x 150 mm) deep holes have had to be provided at intervals in the prestressed beams to allow air supply to the perimeter units. Wet risers for firefighting run against interior columns near the east and west ends and are boxed in.

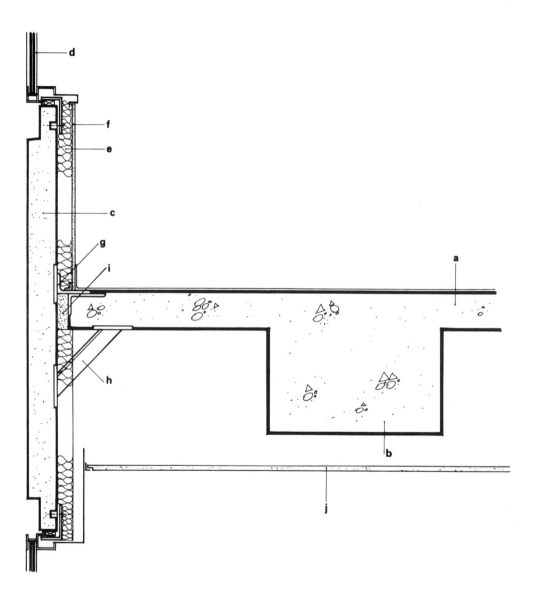

Structural Action

The span to depth ratio of the beam is 30 and that of the slab 45, indicating typical benefits obtained by prestressing. The strands in the beams have been prestressed to virtually eliminate downward deflection or upward camber under dead load and also to cancel out the bending stresses produced by dead load. To do this the prestressing strands need to follow the stress flow lines, which are parabolic. The same principle also applies to the slabs. Because of their slenderness, prestressed floor structures can be subject to vibration, although this is not a concern in offices or car parks.

Construction

The sequence of operations for each floor consisted of erection of formwork, taking about three days, laying of tendons, taking one day and placing of concrete, taking the following day. Only a modest quantity of ordinary reinforcement was necessary. The concrete used developed a strength of 3000 psi (21 newtons per sq mm) after three days, at which time it could be prestressed. An 8ft 6in (2.59m) square hole was left in the slab for a tower crane. The total period of construction was approximately 12 months, all concrete work being completed in approximately 5 months.

Conclusion

This building uses a simple beam and slab system which allows flexibility in the plan arrangements. However prestressing has been extensively used in two-way flat slabs, both with and without drop panels, for buildings with regular column arrangements in both directions on plan. Drop panels or beams give useful extra depth, saving on prestressing strand, as well as providing space for the anchorages. This building has a clean, spare appearance, makes excellent use of space and, at a price, gives generous and unobtrusive car parking space.

a $5\frac{1}{2}$" prestressed slab; b 2'–0" x 1'–8" prestressed beam; c 4'–10" x $4\frac{1}{2}$" precast concrete spandrel panel; d 5'–7" window with 1" double glazing; e $2\frac{1}{2}$" semi-rigid insulation; f $\frac{1}{2}$" wallboard; g 3" x 5" x $\frac{1}{2}$" x 4" long steel angle welded to recessed plates; h $2\frac{1}{2}$" x $2\frac{1}{2}$" x $2\frac{1}{2}$" x $\frac{1}{4}$" steel angle welded to recessed plates; i fire stop; j suspended acoustic tile ceiling.

Vertical section through wall on E and W sides.

1111 NINETEENTH STREET WASHINGTON (1979)

Description:
Twelve-storey office block of prestressed concrete
construction
Architects:
Weihe, Black, Jeffries and Strassman
Structural engineers:
Keith Thornton and Associates

Axonometric
view from NW:

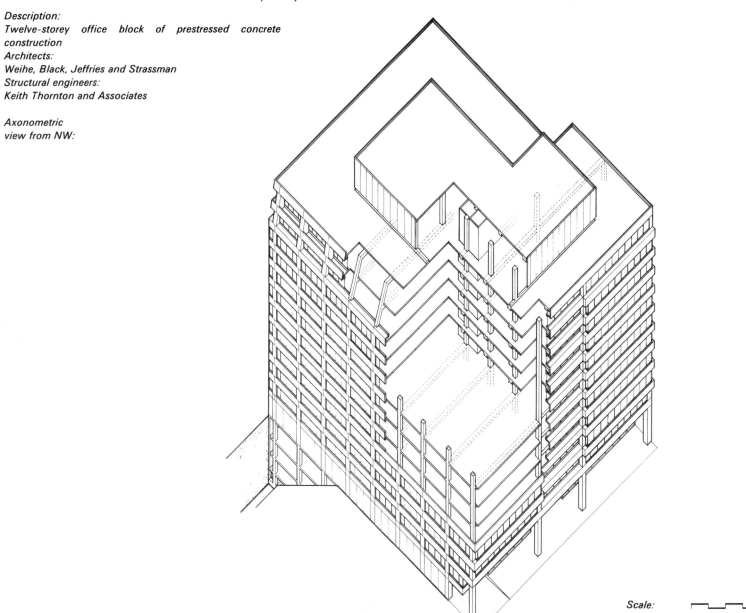

Scale:

12 m

40 ft

Chloride Technical Offices and Workshop, Swinton, Manchester, England

Introduction

Building materials come laden with status and values such that they are often impossible to use even if, technically, wholly suitable. Rather at the opposite end of commercial civilisation from the polished marble or shining glass of office blocks comes corrugated metal sheet associated with the down-at-heel and humble manufacturing origins of the products before these are shot into the bright world of advertising. Typically enough, corrugated sheet, like almost all new types of material, was first used by artless engineers before being discovered and understood by all the design professions. However the new materials still have to win general acceptance. This building is one of few that make an accomplished and complete use of corrugated sheet. The fact that the offices are in an industrial area and incorporate a workshop is indicative of the distance this material still is from respectability. However, the steel frame with corrugated sheet is a classic method of construction for industrial sheds and has long been available in the form of standard prefabricated systems. This building indicates the real quality achievable with this type of construction.

Description

The offices occupy two storeys on the south side of the building and the workshop, connecting with an existing workshop, the single storey on the north side; they are separated by a 450mm brick wall. The building has the same height and roof span throughout. The offices consist of six steel portal frames at 6.09m centres having UB columns and sloping beams, with a haunched connection at the eaves. There are 203 x 133 mm tie beams connecting the tops of the columns in the long direction. The top floor of the offices is a 250mm concrete flat slab supported by the portal columns and 254 x 254 mm UC internal columns on a 6.10 x 7.32 m grid; the slab is increased to 300mm thick at column positions. The workshop has the same kind of construction as the offices but the sloping beams, although having the same serial size, are heavier, increasing in weight from 51 to 92 kg per m and, to give clear space, two columns on the

View of building from SE (photo by architect).

west side are omitted, the roof beam loads being taken by a UB 602 x 228 x 101 kg/m eaves beam which transfers them to the one remaining, and slightly heavier, portal column on that side of the workshop. The building is clad, both on the walls and roof with a composite metal cladding system, coloured dark brown on the weathering face. However the curved metal sheets at the eaves are single skin sheets with separate fibreglass insulation and a gypsum board lining, curved composite sheets not being available at the time. An aluminium subframe carrying 6mm bronze glazing is set between the panels as required. The horizontal distance between the glazing and corners is such that, generally, cutting of sheets along their length is unnecessary. Nevertheless some cutting of the sheets to widths smaller than the 715mm standard widths was necessary, for example on the roof and, for walls, on the frame lines of the workshop. The position of cut-offs is clear from the incorrugated flash piece strips which cover them and which in fact, create a nice rhythm on elevation; similar pieces cover junctions at corners and between windows and metal sheets. The panels at the top of the gables and at the tops of the housing for the air-conditioning units were cut in length on site. These air-

conditioning units are placed outside the main office spaces and are supported by an extension of the top floor slab and, below, by a steel bracket off the ground floor slab; they are clad with the same composite sheet and include air inlet and exhaust grilles. The roof sheeting is supported by 200mm deep cold-formed steel purlins at about 2m centres and the wall sheeting by four horizontal

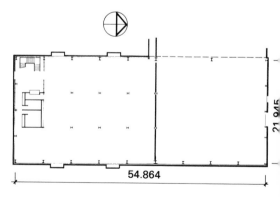

Ground floor plan.

CHLORIDE TECHNICAL OFFICES (1978)

Description:
Offices and workshop of steel portal frame construction with
composite metal roof and wall cladding
Architects and structural engineers:
Building Design Partnership

Axonometric
view from SE:

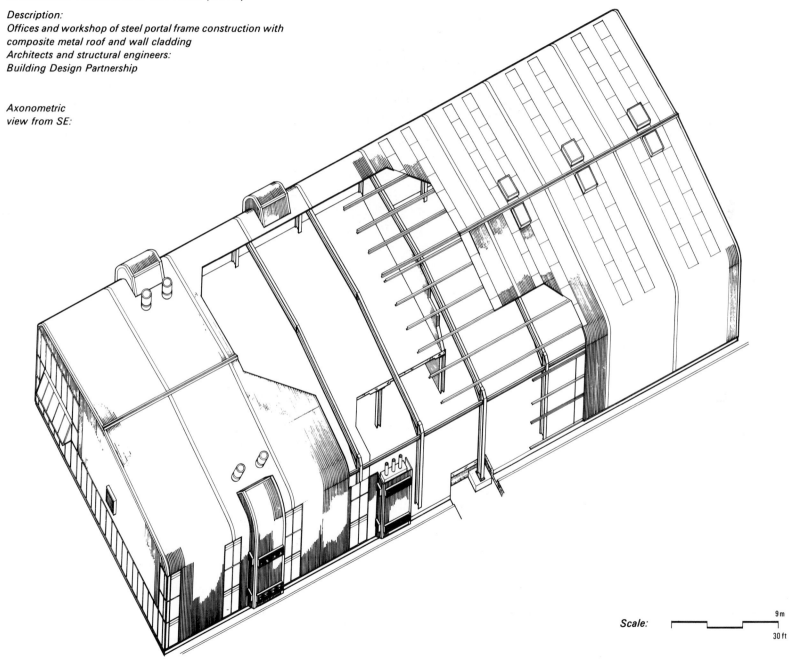

Scale:

9 m

30 ft

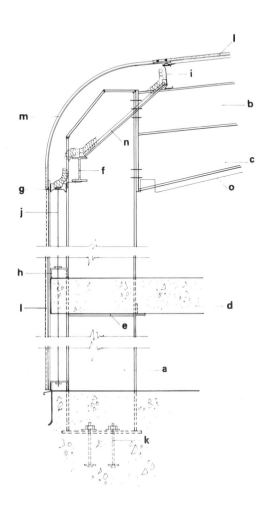

View on housing for air-conditioning equipment (photo by architect).

at the apex of the roof and strips of translucent sheet provide natural lighting.

Structural Action

Wind forces across the building are taken by the portals acting as rigid frames with pinned feet; the portal column baseplates are bolted to the foundation by four 19mm bolts set out on the corner of a 200mm-sided square. Wind forces in the long direction are taken by frame action of the concrete slab and columns; internal columns have bolts on a 400mm-sided square with a 30mm baseplate and make a semi-rigid connection. A typical office portal column carries a vertical load of 34 tonnes and exerts a horizontal sidethrust of nearly 5 tonnes.

Construction

The building was completed over a period of eighteen months. Temporary cross-bracing was provided on the north, west and east faces of the building. Columns with semi-rigid bases were self-supporting at erection.

Conclusion

The building has an unassuming air of utility. Each office floor has a usable area of 670 sq m which makes a useful working size for an office. The juxtaposition of glass and steel sheet is a happy one and the discipline of working with the module of the sheet was fully accepted. Such metal composite claddings as these are expected to last more than 20 years, assuming the problems of differential temperature movements between inner and outer faces are properly designed out, for example by providing good separation between the faces and by allowing the outer face to expand and contract freely, somewhat like a bellows. Allowance has been made here for damaged panels to be removed, from the outside, but they must be replaced by separate inner and outer metal sheets, with loose insulation between. The vocabulary of sheet metal construction, which includes the infill panels and the corrugations and joints, is well used. What is provided here is a building in what has become an industrial vernacular style, looking, perhaps suitably, not quite permanent.

a 602 x 228 mm UB column; **b** 356 x 171 mm UB beam; **c** haunch at eaves; **d** 300mm shearhead at column; **e** 100 x 20 mm steel plate support welded to column; **f** 203 x 133 mm UB tie beam; **g** cold-formed steel rail; **h** 152 x 76 mm channel; **i** 200 x 75 mm cold-formed steel purlin; **j** 12mm steel sag rod; **k** 4/ 19mm bolts 305mm long with 20mm baseplate; **l** composite steel cladding panel; **m** single skin steel sheet; **n** gypsum board and insulation; **o** suspended ceiling.

Vertical section through wall near office column.

steel rails, either channel or purlin sections which are attached to the main columns and to each other with sag rods at midspan. There are no gutters in this building; wide flashing pieces are used at tops of windows and most rain runs down the walls to be collected in a precast channel at the bottom. End laps of sheeting occur on the roof and are sealed by double runs of butyl mastic to prevent leaks. There are four air-conditioning units for each office floor, two feeding an inlet duct which runs down each side of the offices feeding, in turn, branches to the diffusers; this is hidden by a suspended ceiling. Fans in the roof allow input of fresh air or extraction of stale air, if the air conditioning is switched off. Lighting strips in the ceiling at about 2m centres supply 550 lux at the working plane. Carpet and fissured mineral fibre tiles on the ceiling provide good sound absorbence. In the workshop there are extract fans

Havas Conseil Offices, Neuilly, France

Introduction

From the street, this building stands out because of its strong lines and its coherence as a design. It is of steel construction and is unusual for the large amount of steel which it exposes to view, amounting to 45% of the total tonnage, and for the serious attempt to use steel in a simple but decorative fashion. The building is upheld largely by six powerful two-storey high steel box portal frames in order to free space at street level, these frames being supported by a separate concrete substructure with six basement floors below street level. Prestressed composite steel beams are used for the main building spans.

Description

The glazed cylinder, placed asymmetrically, about one third down the length of the building, forms a counterpoint for the rest of the building and contains reception areas, lifts, stairs and ducts for vertical distribution of services. It is constructed of one central steel tubular column 457mm in diameter with twelve 300mm diameter steel tubular columns around the periphery supporting ring and radial steel beams; these support the floor slab which consists of a 15m diameter concrete disc pierced where necessary for openings. The columns are infilled with concrete and painted with intumescent paint to achieve 30 minutes' fire resistance. The rest of the building is supported, at street level, by just six external portal frames which consequently are heavily loaded: each portal column carries a load approaching 1200 tonnes. The portal frames consist of heavy box-section steel columns, 700 x 1200 mm in section, resting on 740 x 1000 x 48 mm neoprene bearing pads at street level, and a box-section transverse member of the same size overhanging the top of each column by 3.50m. The two middle portal frames, in the larger of the two rectangular parts of the building, have heavy longitudinal beams rigidly connecting the tops of the columns together. The frames are thereby stabilised against horizontal forces from any direction. In the storeys above this, there are rigid internal frames in the same plane as the main, street-level portals, to which they are welded; these frames are attached to each other by

View of building from S (photo by Christophe Demonfaucon).

internal longitudinal beams. The longitudinal beams are prestressed composite steel beams with an overall depth of 650mm. Parallel to them are the facade beams which are purpose-made and have a 1200mm deep I-section shape.

A 160mm concrete slab spans the 5.40m between these longitudinal beams, resting on top of the internal beams and on shelf angles on the facade beams, the angles being welded to the inner face of the facade beams at mid-depth. Because of the small number of portal frames, the longitudinal beams have to span large distances, up to a maximum of 23.40m for the facade beams and 15.30m for the internal beams. The facade beams are completely exposed and are infilled by a window band set behind them; the beams are supported by 300mm deep I-section stud columns bolted to the beam across reinforced neoprene

pads, so giving a pinned joint which allows thermal movement of the beams along the facade. A cold-formed channel section is attached to the outside face at mid-depth and radically changes, for the better, the perceived scale and visual interest of the facade. Internal longitudinal beams, unlike those on the facade, could not be deep without hindering the circulation; their 650mm depth is made up of the concrete slab, composite with a 450mm deep rolled steel beam to which a heavy 400 x 40 mm steel flange plate has been welded on the underside to give additional strength. To limit deflection, the beams were prestressed. To this end the steel beams were cambered 74mm in the middle by means of two inclined hangers, which were attached to the beam at its quarter points. The hangers were tensioned to a force of 73 tonnes against the rest of

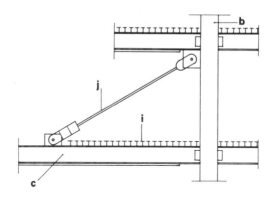

i 90mm high 22mm diameter shear studs; j steel
hanger and hydraulic jack.

*Diagram showing prestressing of internal longitudinal
beam before pouring of slab.*

*View of box-section portal frame on N face of building
(photo by André Martin).*

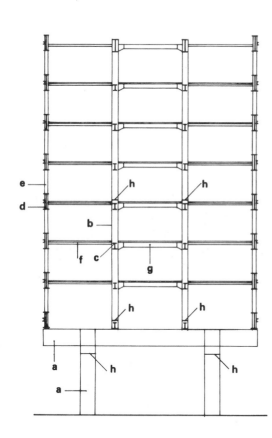

a 700 x 1200 mm deep fabricated steel box
section; b steel box section column; c HE 450B I-
section longitudinal beam with 400 x 40 mm
bottom flange plate and 160mm composite
concrete slab; d 1200mm deep I-section beam; e
HE 300B I-section column; f HE 160B I-section
tie beam; g HE 360B I-section transverse beam; h
joint welded on site.

Vertical section through building.

the structure by a hydraulic jack at one end of each
hanger. The concrete slab was then poured and,
after it had cured, the jacks were released thus
leaving a net compression in the top of the
concrete slab and in the bottom of the steel beam.
Allowing for the effect of dead load, shrinkage of
the concrete and relaxation of the prestressing, the
beams still have a net upward camber in the middle
of some 7mm, before live load is applied.

Structural Action

Vertical and horizontal forces acting on the
structure are largely taken in bending, that is to say
by elements acting as beams or as part of a frame
action. Lateral stability of the cylindrical part
depends on its connection at each floor level to the
rest of the building. Because of temperature
movement, a large number of pinned-type points
have been incorporated in the exposed structure,
particularly those at the feet of the main portal
frames.

Construction

The ground floor portals were shop fabricated in
three parts and welded together on site at joints
near the top of each column. The internal box-

section columns were brought to site in sections
either three or four storeys high and then site
welded to beams, cross-bracing being used before
the welds were complete. Each facade beam on
the long side, which is continuous, was fabricated
in four sections and welded at three points where
there was very low bending moment. All purpose-
made elements were fabricated in the shop by
automatic welding of steel plate. Manual welding
on site was checked by x-ray examination or
ultrasonic testing if welds were not accessible.

Conclusion

The building was relatively expensive to construct
because of the welding and prestressing on site
and the heavy framing required. A total of 950
tonnes of steel was used. However this is a
thoroughly professional piece of work, well
proportioned, strong enough to stand out over the
roaring street below and makes simple, decorative
use of metal. This is a direction in which present-
day designers still have ground to catch up on the
elegant fashioning of cast iron by their
predecessors.

HAVAS CONSEIL OFFICES (1973)

Description:
Nine-storey office of steel frame construction with six basement levels
Architects:
M. Andrault, P. Parat, J-P. Sarrazin
Structural engineers:
Haiat and Dziewolski

Axonometric view from SE:

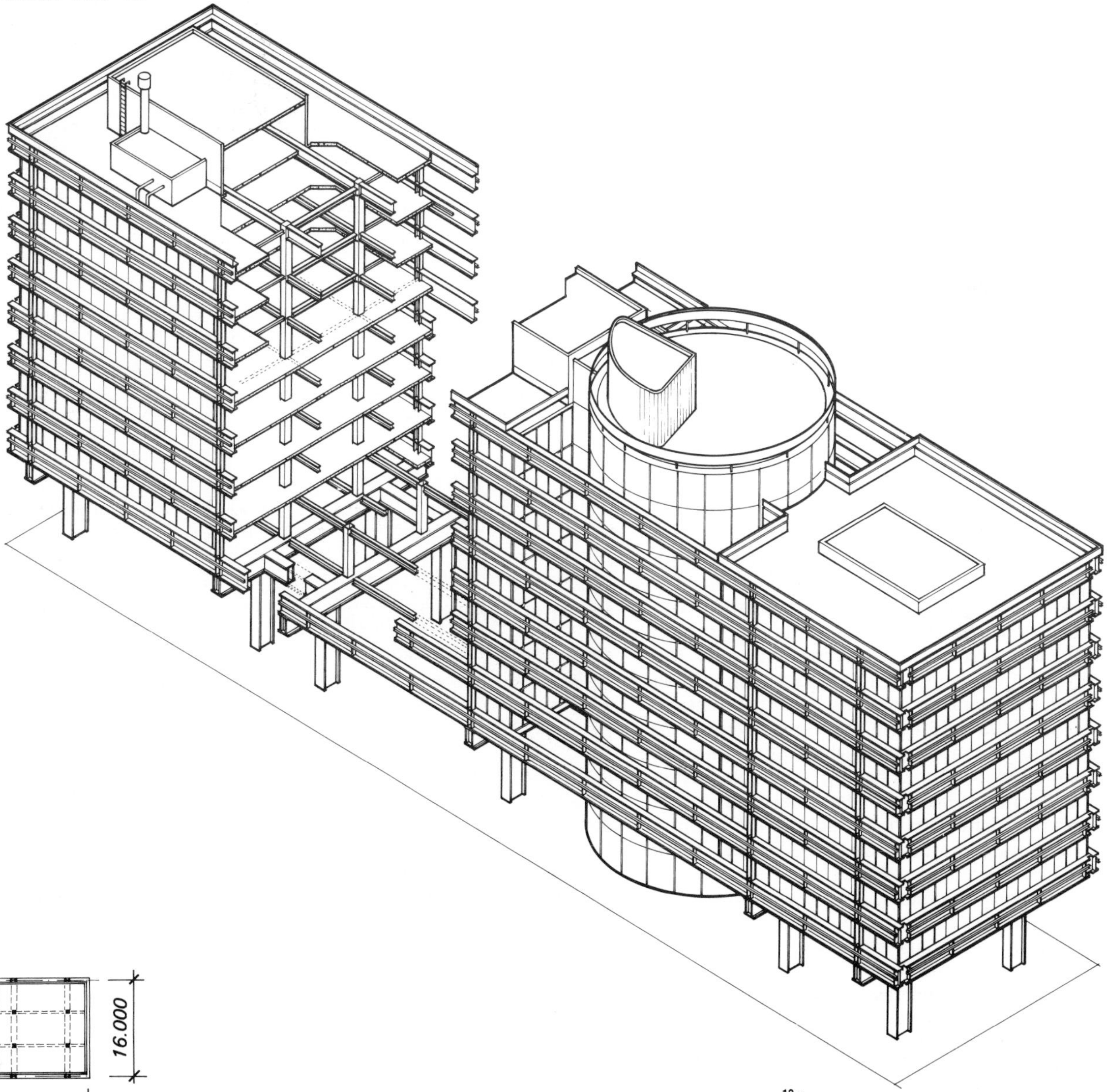

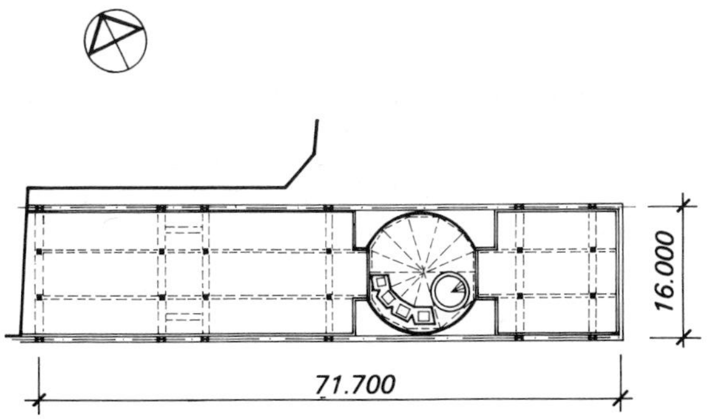

Typical floor plan.

16.000

71.700

Scale:

12 m

40 ft

Banque Belge Offices,
London, England

Introduction

Occupying an important corner site and well set
back from the road this seven-storey office
building manages to look appropriately opulent
but discreet, movements inside being only barely
discernible through the darkened glass. The
building is characterised by a smooth outside
surface, consisting of generously sized and well
proportioned windows set in a grid of thick bands
of bronze aluminium curtain walling. Behind this,
a light framework of steel supports the floors and
the cladding and is itself attached to a cast-in-
place concrete core structure.

Description

A steel framework was selected here because the
perimeter columns needed to have a plan size,
including fireproofing, of less than 275 x 225 mm
in order to look sufficiently slender, and because
there are no internal columns; the floor beams have
to span 12m from the perimeter to the concrete
core and this was achieved with an overall
structural floor depth of 742mm. The floor consists
of a UB 610 x 229 x 101 kg/m steel beam at 3m
centres with a 140mm thick lightweight concrete
slab on metal deck on top acting compositely with
the beam; pairs of 20mm shear studs 100mm high
at 305mm centres make the action composite. The
relatively low weight of this floor helps to limit
load on the perimeter columns; these columns are
UC 203 x 203 x 86 kg/m at ground level except
either side of the entrance where purpose-made
square tubular columns having 50mm plate were
used. Slots in the bottom of the metal deck provide
support for 'fishtail' fixings which, in turn, support
the false ceiling and services. To avoid the use of
formwork, the outside edge of each floor slab is in
precast concrete which is cast in with the rest of
the floor and is supported by a perimeter lattice
girder with two shear studs welded to its top
flange fitting into pockets in the precast units. At
midspan the main beams are connected to each
other by light transverse lattice girders to dampen
out any vibration which could occur. At ground
floor level, the perimeter columns on the long
facade are supported by a concrete beam to allow
clear space in the basement. There are two

View of office from SW.

BANQUE BELGE OFFICES (1977)

Description:
Seven-storey offices of steel frame construction with concrete floor and aluminium curtain walling
Architects:
GMW Partnership
Structural engineers:
Scott, Wilson, Kirkpatrick and Partners

Axonometric view from SW:

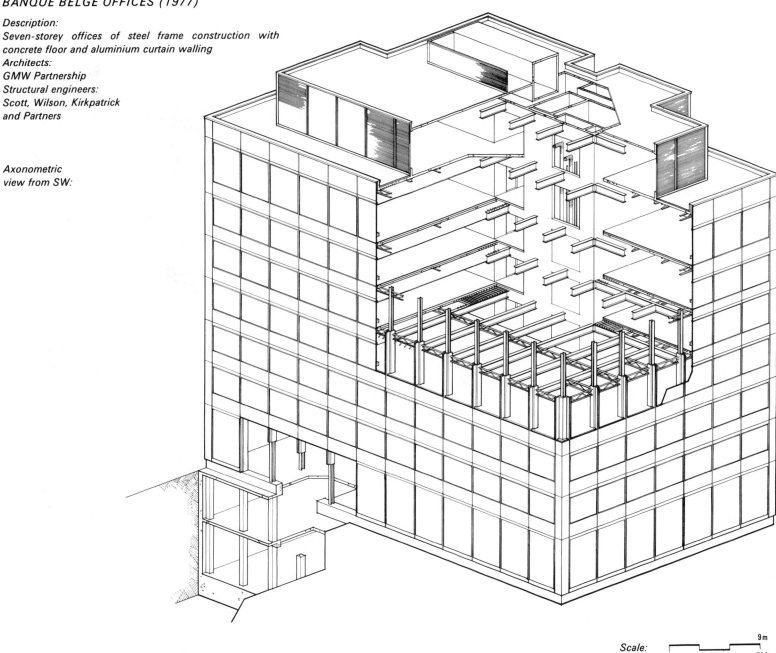

Scale:

9 m

30 ft

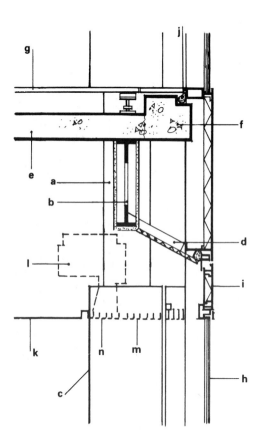

Interior view showing air-conditioning ducts (photo by E.J. Studios).

a UC203 steel column; b 455mm deep lattice girder cased with vermiculite board; c faced vermiculite board; d firestop; e 140mm concrete slab on metal deck; f precast concrete edge beam; g raised floor; h 6mm heat-absorbing pane with 12mm clear pane and 12mm air gap; i smoke vent; j fire resistant filler; k false ceiling; l induction unit; m air intake; n air supply.

Vertical section at typical floor.

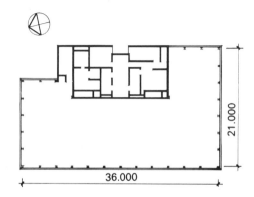

Typical floor plan.

basement levels. The whole building is supported on a 2m thick raft bearing directly on clay.

The building is air conditioned and uses induction units above the false ceiling around the perimeter. The plant room is on the top of the building and vertical distribution of services is via the core. Heating ducts and pipes run at the same height, parallel to the main floor beams, but cross through circular holes in the web of the beam where necessary. Double glazing is used with a darkened heat-absorbing glass on the outer and a clear glass on the inner pane. From the inside there appears to be good natural light even at the back of the room thanks to the area and height of the glazing. The curtain wall frames are a storey high by 3m wide and connect to adjustable brackets

View of underside of floor before installation of suspended ceiling system (photo by E.J. Studios).

NW elevation at installation of curtain wall (photo by E.J. Studios).

fixed to the columns. A modular raised floor is used for distribution of wiring and, at the ground floor, for heating ducts. Two hour fire protection is given to main structural members, using a mineral spray for beams and aluminium faced vermiculite board for columns. The perimeter lattice girders are also cased and form part of a 900mm break against fire spread from floor to floor, with a smoke vent below.

Structural Action

Half the gravity load and all horizontal forces are taken by the concrete core structure containing lifts, stairs and services. The perimeter columns are slender enough not to pick up any substantial bending moment either from gravity or horizontal forces. The floor slab works as a stiff diaphragm to transfer horizontal load to the core.

Construction

The total period of construction was 28 months. The soil under an existing foundation on one side of the site was retained by placing steel columns at 3m centres and infilling with concrete as excavation proceeded. The raft and basement were poured first and, following that, the core using timber formwork. Steel erection was next, taking 15 weeks including 4 weeks for placing the metal deck. Temporary plan bracing was used before the metal deck was in place. Vertical alignment of the columns was kept within 25mm over the full height of the building; column to column connections were end bearing, requiring accuracy in fabrication and trial lining up at the works. The curtain wall and glazing were fixed, without scaffolding, from the inside. The lightweight concrete was pumped to all floors, because of restrictions on space and the speed of construction necessary.

Conclusion

This is a typical example of a well executed commercial office building with 70 per cent of net usable space per floor. The facades of the building have an apparently impenetrable gloss so that these offices look new, almost permanently.

Slough Estates House, Slough, England

Introduction

The pre-eminent formal arrangement of this office building suggests a derivation from the classical orders, flattened-out and streamlined for the modern age but, seen closer-to, the weight of the classical pile is missing. In fact the elevations are made from glass and precast concrete panels, and the vertical joints indicate that this is a panel construction. Indeed behind the 100mm panel thickness of the horizontal bands are voids with air-conditioning ducts, pipes and their services and, beyond this, column-free space, suspended ceilings and all the equipment necessary for a modern office. The sober virtues of the building lie, above all, in sound construction, good finishes to cladding, low external maintenance and, by a suitable choice of form, efficient use of energy and space. The offices are typical in their requirement for perimeter offices with a view, as well as divisible, open-plan floor areas behind. The overhanging floors are unusual and give the building protection from the sun and aircraft noise overhead as well as making the building distinctive.

Description

The shape of the offices is close to the optimum shape for reduction of heat loss in a rectangular building, which is one with equal losses through all faces, or a cube if the surfaces have similar insulation values. The same reasoning applies to heat gain which, here, is further reduced by the overhangs. Because of the scale effect, these losses and gains diminish, relative to the total heating or cooling required, as the building increases in size; at the scale of this building, in this climate, losses and gains are modest. The square plan shape also reduces the area of cladding required for the same floor area, although this is at the expense of access to daylight; Where perimeter offices do block off light, at least one side, or its equivalent length, is left clear and provides views out for those working in the central open-plan areas.

The largest vertical elements are two cast-in-place concrete core structures, one housing the two lifts and the other the staircase and a vertical

View of building from NE (photo by Henk Snoek).

services duct. The floors and roof consist of cast-in-place waffle slabs, 400mm deep, or in the case of the ground floor slab, solid slabs 400mm deep with 4.80m square, 400mm deep dropheads at column positions. They are supported by the two cores, which have a minimum wall thickness of 150mm, two internal columns, which are 600mm square increasing to 700mm square below the ground floor slab, and sixteen 375 x 900 mm perimeter columns. There is a large basement for car parking and mechanical plant. Except at ground floor level, the slabs are supported by 3.60m wide internal beams; at level 2, the internal beams are contained within the slab depth, but at all other levels these beams are slightly deeper than the slabs.

All the internal beams are on a 10.80m square grid but the perimeter beams, which are 9.60m from the internal beams at levels 2 and 3, move out to 11.85m from them at level 4, which is the roof level. The 300 x 900 mm perimeter columns supporting the roof are in their turn supported by cantilevering out the beams at level 3 from the main perimeter columns; at the columns these cantilevers are a massive 1m deep, and still 3.60m wide, but taper to 600mm deep, 2.40m inside from the main column centreline. The perimeter beams and columns are clad in precast concrete panels, nominally 1.20m wide, with a cream aggregate finish. The precast concrete cladding panels are cleverly chamfered at the bottom, so reducing their apparent height and pointing up the inverted pyramid shape of the building. Windows are double-glazed with a pvc frame and have a

SLOUGH ESTATES HOUSE (1975)

Description:
Three-storey offices and basement of concrete construction
with precast panels
Architects:
Salmon Speed Associates
Structural engineers:
Campbell, Reith and Partners

Anonometric
view from E:

Scale:

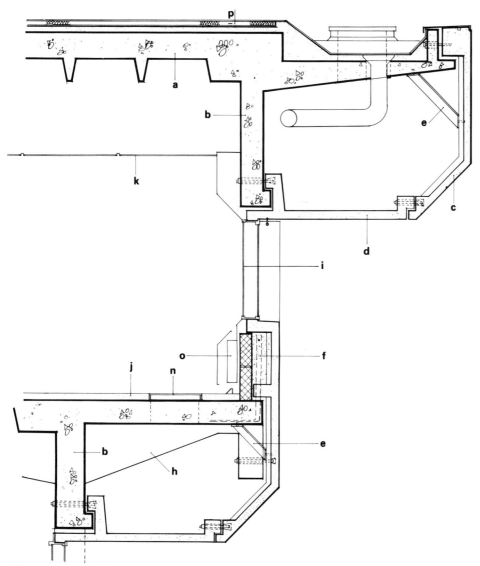

a 400mm concrete waffle slab; b downstand beam supporting cantilever with openings for services and access to void; c vertical precast panel with Derbyshire Spa aggregate; d horizontal precast panel; e steel bracket fixing; f cast-in-place concrete connection between panel and slab; g 375 x 900 mm cast-in-place column behind; h 3600 x 1000 mm cantilever behind to support column above; i double glazing in pvc frame with 12mm anti-sun outer glass and 6mm clear inner glass; j 75mm screed; k suspended ceiling with air extract zone above; l 400mm solid slab; m 375mm retaining wall with waterproofing; n access to duct below; o induction unit fed from duct; p 2 coat mastic asphalt on felt on 50mm cork on vapour barrier on screed.

Vertical section through top of wall.

200mm space between the outer and inner glasses for sound reduction at levels 2 and 3. The windows, the internal partitioning and the ceiling panels are all set out on the same 1.20m module grid as the cladding; this grid is offset from the structure grid so that there is no obstruction of one by the other. In principle partitions could be erected anywhere on this grid and linked into the window mullions. However, the office floors are divided into two air-conditioning zones and only the outer zone, within a 6m perimeter band, can be supplied by the perimeter induction units, so that only here is the arrangement truly flexible. In the centre zone, air is supplied and extracted through the ceiling and partition layouts must not interfere with the design air flows. Fluorescent lighting is set in shaped ceiling panels which reduce glare and break up and localise reflected sound; return air is extracted round the lights. These panels are set on a chequer-board pattern; the remaining ceiling panels there are flat and sound-absorbent. At joints between panels there are air supply diffusers. Where partitions are installed, for example for offices at the perimeter, a sound baffle is built in the ceiling above the partitions to prevent sound transmission.

All plant for air conditioning, lift room equipment, batteries, meters, switch room, transformers and compressors is located in the basement. Separate plant is used to supply the perimeter zone and the centre zone. The perimeter zone uses a four-pipe induction system with a control damper passing the secondary air over heating or cooling coils, each hot or chilled water coil being supplied from the basement boiler or refrigeration plant. The centre zone is a high velocity all-air system with terminal reheat. Heat exchanges in the basement recover some of the heat from the return air. The air-conditioning plant is automatic in operation, controls being operated by compressed air. Cabling is contained within the thickness of the screed at each floor level.

Structural Action

Wind forces are taken by the two cores and by frame action. A 300mm deep cast-in-place post-tensioned concrete floor was developed as an alternative to the waffle slab but rejected on grounds of cost and because of limits placed on openings. The sizes of columns were determined

View of SE elevation.

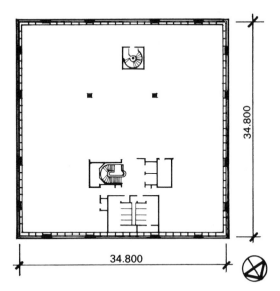

Plan at level 3.

34.800

34.800

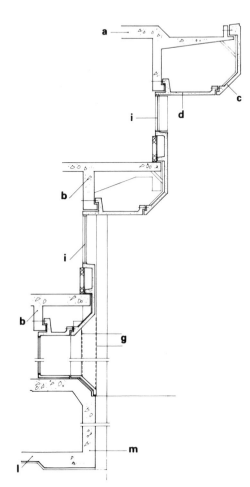

Vertical section through wall and basement.

by the need to avoid dropheads at the two central columns at office levels. Pad foundations were used for all columns.

Construction

The building, including the basement and all ancillary site work, was completed in a period of 20 months. The external faces of the precast panels were sandblasted and treated with acid. The panels were erected by crane from the top down, and after the roof mastic asphalt had been laid, so that finishing work was able to start inside immediately. Scaffolding was needed temporarily to support the horizontal panels before the vertical one was in place. The manufacturing tolerance for panels was 6mm on dimensions more than 3m and 3mm on dimensions less than this, with a tolerance on twist of 3mm for each panel as measured from a plane defined by three points on the external surface. The nominal joint between panels was 18mm which was sufficient to cope with errors in position and manufacture. Particular care was needed in positioning corner units as well as column units and those units next to them.

The columns are clad by front and back units, the front units being fixed by bolts passing through holes in the cast-in-place column.

Conclusion

This is a well planned and efficient building which completely satisfies the stated requirements. The gross floor area just exceeds 5000 sq m. The technical solutions adopted give both durability and low maintenance. The staining pattern on the cladding, for example, would be acceptable even in a very polluted atmosphere. Inside, the spaces are, in practical terms, as flexible as they could be, although the appearance of the existing partitioning system with its small scale divisions, while better than most such systems, does not match the standards achieved in the permanent architecture. Outside there is only a limited amount of detail for the eye to linger on, but the building has a really positive presence in its somewhat barren surroundings. The entrance is very unobtrusive for a building of this type and size.

Scottish Mutual House,
Leeds, England

Introduction

In its resolution, a design should pull all the disparate elements together and should impose a visual unity such that a building has recognizable characteristics and qualities. This city-centre office has such a unity not just on elevation but throughout its volume and is based on a construction idea, rather than any particular characteristic of the space or geometry. The building is made from precast concrete, which is not easy to use on an infill site, but has still provided a most efficient means of solution to all the logistical problems of building. The precast units on the main elevations are distinguished by their fine proportions.

Description

The building is almost exclusively of precast concrete. The office areas of the building which are on the east and west sides are spanned by prestressed, precast double-T units just under 35ft (10.66m) long, these floor units being 1ft (300mm) deep and acting with a 3in (75mm) deep cast-in-place topping; The core area between the two office spaces has 5in (125mm) deep precast concrete slabs with a 2in (50mm) deep cast-in-place topping; the stairs and lift shaft in the core are also made up from precast items. Support for the floors is provided, in the vertical plane, by precast concrete frames, but in some places, individual precast beams are also used. Apart from the lift shaft and one stair wall, all vertical divisions in the core are made by infilling the frames with masonry. At the suspended ground floor over the basement, arrangements are more complex, due to difficult ground, and here extensive use is made of cast-in-place construction. Of all elements, the most important are the precast rectangular-shaped box frames, which stack on top of each other and are all exposed to view on the facades. On the east and west faces of the building, which look on to streets below, these precast rectangular-shaped box units are designed as a pure work of architectonics without need of embellishment. Double column precast units are used at ground floor level on the west side with a precast L-beam on top. On the

View of building from SW (photo by William Hamer).

north and south sides, the elevations overlooking the inner wells have frames with a double beam and columns each end; those sides against the existing buildings use precast beams infilled with masonry. Each box unit used on the east and west faces has four 8in (200mm) square stub columns with steel shoes at the end, which subsequently are site welded and connect it to the units above and below; each adjacent pair of shoes is covered on the outside by a small precast panel. The connection between adjacent precast units is by a 1½in (38mm) steel bar welded to angles cast into the four corners of all the units.

The choice of precast concrete construction on a site, in a city centre, between two existing

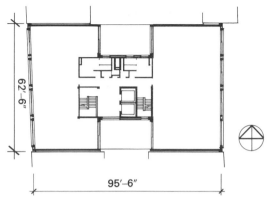

Typical floor plan.

buildings is unusual especially where, as is often the case, the site is irregular in plan but must still be fully utilised. The technique for overcoming these difficulties was simply to abut the frames at the four corners of the waisted, middle section of the building, the columns at each corner being joined by cast-in-place concrete; this joint can be adjusted to allow any angle on plan. Cast-in-place concrete is also used to join the precast beams, running against the existing building to the rest of the floor structure and provides a dimensional tolerance. All exposed precast units are made of high strength white concrete with a ground finish. The precast box units contain a gutter which drains down to rainpipes placed between the two precast columns at the four corners of the building. The building has no air conditioning, but heating is provided by hot water radiators under the window sills; the boiler is placed in the basement and feeds each floor via a vertical duct, next to the boiler flues in the core. Windows placed within the box precast units are horizontal sliding ones in an aluminium frame and allow natural ventilation. Cables run in tracks in the 2in (50mm) floor screed; There are no suspended ceilings in the offices, the soffit of white double-T units being exposed to view. The lift motor room and storage tanks are housed in the top storey of the core.

SCOTTISH MUTUAL HOUSE (1969)

Description: Seven-storey offices using white precast concrete frames and floor units
Architects:
E.G.V. Hives and Sons
Structural engineers:
Jan Bobrowski and Partners

Axonometric
view from SW:

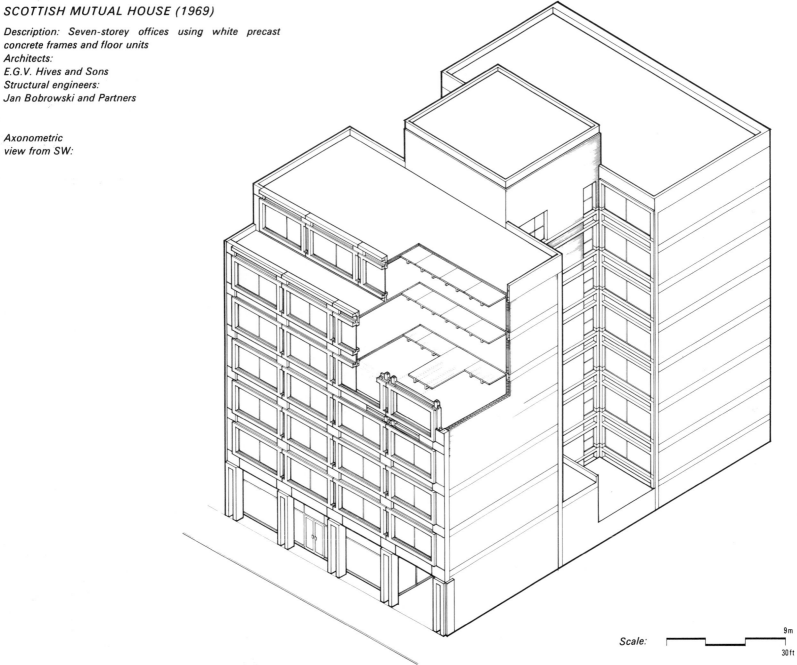

Scale: 9m

30 ft

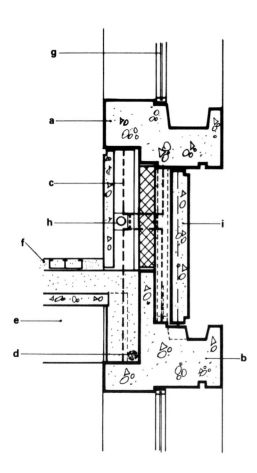

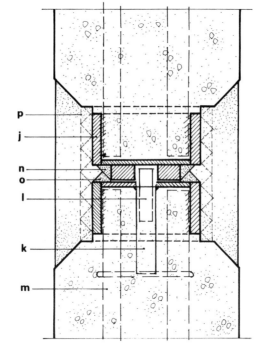

Installation of prestressed floor unit (photo by Sydney W. Newbery).

a precast box unit 15'–0" x 10'–0" overall; **b** top of box unit; **c** 8" square stub column and welded steel shoe connection behind; **d** 1½" bar welded to adjacent units; **e** 1'–0" deep, 7'–6" wide double-T precast concrete unit with 3" concrete topping; **f** 2" screed with cable track; **g** sliding aluminium window; **h** hot-water heater; **i** precast panel covering shoes.

Vertical section near end of box unit.

j ½" steel plate welded to each end of channel section, to make shoe, and to column reinforcing bars; **k** 4½ ton lifting socket; **l** 1¼" steel locating pin; **m** column reinforcing bars; **n** shop weld; **o** site weld around shoe; **p** metal lath welded to shoe.

Typical column connection detail.

Structural Action

Precast units are joined together by site welding and reinforced cast-in-place concrete. With all joints completed the forces on the building are taken by shear walls in the core and to a lesser extent by frame action between precast frames and double-T floor units.

Construction

The building was put up as quickly as steelwork, the total period of construction, including groundwork, being 20 months. One tower crane positioned next to the core was used to erect the units. The principles of construction are that connections between columns, between beams and between beams and floor units are separate so that they can be made easily. Stability at each level was assured after the cast-in-place concrete joints

Close-up on rectangular-shaped box unit (photo by Dorchester Photographers).

View of well on N side (photo by Dorchester Photographers).

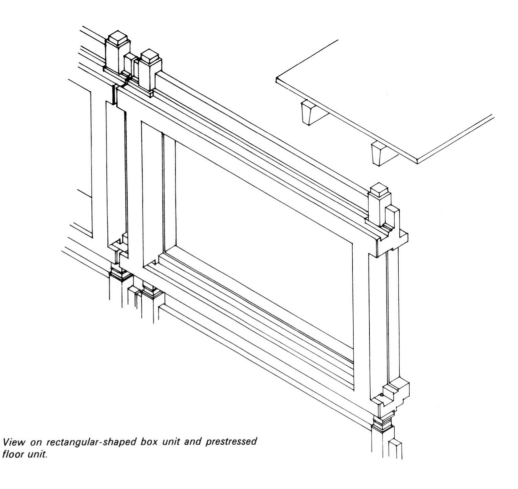

View on rectangular-shaped box unit and prestressed floor unit.

had gained sufficient strength, but this could also have been achieved by site welding. Floor units were propped at midspan during erection until the concrete topping was cured; the units have an upward camber in the centre of about $1\frac{1}{2}$in (38mm) which is levelled out by a cast-in-place topping of varying thickness.

Conclusion

This is a building without undue artifice that fulfills all requirements simply. The decision to use precast concrete was a brave one and the difficult details and non-standard elements which inevitably result have not prevented this scheme being economic. The main facades are highly successful inventions and could have been further refined by the expression of each individual shoe connection of the box units on the elevations. Thorough and detailed knowledge of a technique has resulted in good value for money.

Mercantile Bank Tower,
Kansas City, Missouri, USA

Introduction

Office buildings positioned on small sites in central areas often require building heights of about 20 storeys to provide sufficient total usable space and would require areas on each floor of about 20 000 sq ft (1860 sq m) with clear spans of between 30 and 40 ft (9.14 and 12.19 m) to allow for rearrangement. In the sense that it has a similar size, this building is a representative one but it also provides a very satisfactory solution to the awkward problem of providing clear space at street level. A steel frame has been chosen, partly because of this last requirement. The building has deep exposed spandrel beams, which are both structure and cladding, and is built with impeccable regard for structural logic.

Description

From level 5 to the top, there are 24 columns spaced on a regular 28ft (8.53m) grid. Between levels 4 and 5, an 18ft (5.48m) high space truss collects the load from twenty of these columns into five larger columns, the four columns around the elevator core continuing straight to the ground. The exterior framework, above level 5, occupies half of the elevational area. It is made up of 5ft 6in (1.67m) deep spandrel beams welded to the columns, thus forming rigid frameworks on all four sides of the building; these carry the wind forces and part of the floor loads. Windows are fitted between the spandrel beams. There is no cladding apart from that needed to protect the fireproofing on the columns and on the perimeter members of the space truss. All interior beams and columns are fireproofed as is the space truss and the interior of the spandrel beam. The outer surface of the spandrel is unprotected being shielded from flames by a downturn on the bottom flange.

The five large columns at street level are made up from four standard columns welded together, to form a hollow section. This is filled with water and connected to an expansion tank and gives fire protection. The space truss consists of 45 degree inverted pyramids above each of the large columns, with secondary framing and a composite concrete floor slab at the top and bottom levels to create a complete unit. Because the eight internal

View of building from NW (photo by Hedrich-Blessing).

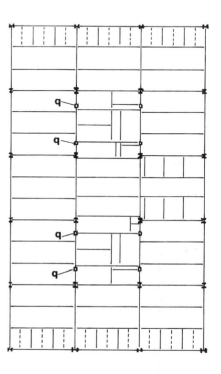

Typical floor steel framing plan.

columns, at typical floor levels, are more heavily loaded than the external columns there are, predominantly, compression forces in the top slab and tension forces in the bottom slab, these tension forces being taken, to a large extent, by post-tensioned high strength steel strands running diagonally to the core. A large space is left within the truss for mechanical plant.

Structural Action

Floor loads either travel down the four columns of the core or are transferred into the five large cruciform columns by the space truss. These cruciform columns are pinned at each end, and

thus always have pure axial loads in them, shear and bending moment, which make the columns more prone to buckling, being eliminated. The effect is to reduce the column sizes. Because buckling is the governing factor, that is all columns whatever load they carry require a minimum width, it can be shown that less material is used if there are a small number of large columns rather than a large number of smaller columns. The advantage is balanced, in this case, by the need for a space truss. All the wind forces above level 5 are taken by the exterior framing, all overturning moments at level 5 being resisted by axial forces in the large columns below and all horizontal shear at this level

MERCANTILE BANK TOWER, KANSAS CITY (1974)

Description:
Twenty-storey steel frame office tower with lattice core and space truss
Architects:
H. Weese and Associates
Structural engineers:
J.D. Gillum and Associates

Axonometric view from NW:

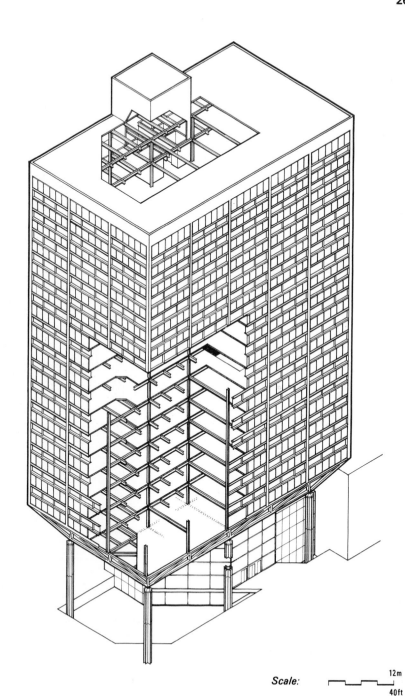

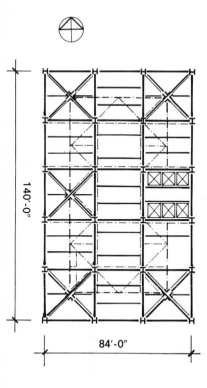

Plan on space truss with bold lines for top layer, dotted lines for bottom layer and full lines for diagonals.

140'-0"

84'-0"

Scale:

12m
40ft

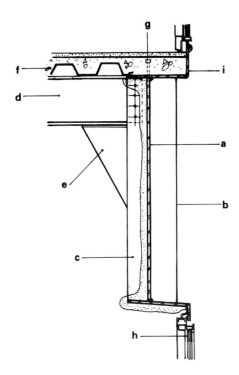

a spandrel beam made of $\frac{3}{8}''$ steel plate in web and flanges; b $\frac{3}{8}''$ stiffener plate at 9'-4'' centres; c $\frac{3}{8}''$ stiffener plate at 4'-8'' centres; d W14 x 26 lb/ft steel beam; e $\frac{3}{8}''$ bracing plate; f $6\frac{1}{4}''$ concrete slab on metal deck; g shear studs at 2'-4'' centres; h 1'' gold reflective double glazing; i $\frac{3}{8}''$ bent steel plate.

Vertical section through E wall.

View of office block at construction (photo by Fotodesigns Inc.).

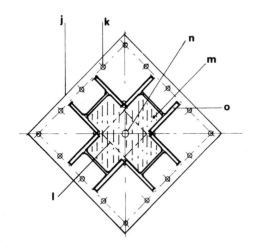

j 4'-6" x 4'-6" x 6½" baseplate; k 1⅝" holes for bolts at 12" centres; l diaphragm plates; m anti-freeze liquid; n hole for circulation of liquid; o W14 x 202 lb/ft section, 4 in all.

Horizontal section near base of large built-up column.

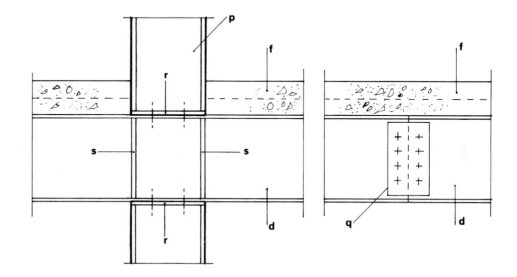

p W14 column; q ¼" shear plate each side at splice; r ⅝" plate; s stiffener plate.

Typical interior column to beam connection and beam to beam splice.

being transferred to the core by the space truss. Hence a frame action takes the wind forces at the top and a shear truss action those at the bottom. Reference to a typical building that uses a frame-shear truss interaction over its full height shows the frame action to be most effective towards the top and shear truss action to be most effective towards the bottom, so that the separation of these two actions here is done without loss. Because the core is offset to one side of the building, it has to take torsion as well as shear forces. The shear centre, that is the point through which the resultant of all the shear forces must pass to prevent twist of the building, is nearly on the same line as the outside face of the tower. Because the resultant of the wind shear forces is in the middle of the building, large torsional movements are

produced. Rotational movements are more easily perceived than pure lateral movements and, sometimes, the torsional stiffness and strength can be difficult to provide. In this building with a 90 mph (40.20m/s) wind on the shorter face maximum corner movement was 6.6in (168mm) and dynamic analysis showed that the peak accelerations were just perceptible. With the same wind on the longer face the lateral displacement was 10.3in (262mm), the rotations being small. A 70mph (31.26m/s) wind, however, likely to occur once every fifty years, gave low accelerations.

Construction

A temporary trestle was needed to erect the fabricated sections of the space truss. However above this level erection procedure was

conventional, one tower crane being used for lifting. The time on site including construction of caisson foundations and the low level precast concrete building was only nine months.

Conclusion

Total quantity of steelworks used averaged 16½ lb per sq ft (80.55 kg per sq m), a slightly higher figure than normal for a building of this height and largely attributable to the use of deep spandrels. However the overall cost is lower than that for a building with standard 2ft (600mm) high spandrels, there being almost no separate cladding and, conveniently, no core bracing above level 5, wind drift being controlled by the frame. This is an ingenious and thoroughbred design.

Baring Brothers Offices,
London, England

Introduction

Considering the preference of the constructors of buildings for simplicity, it is natural that an elevational style based on a repetition of fine line elements and well-proportioned rectangular panels should have become popular. At the same time, the feeling that such builidngs have been done to death is due not just to numbers built or to these buildings' vulnerability to clumsy detailing but also to a more general feeling that building design anyway has become too abstract and impersonal. This mood now obscures the original purpose and technical achievement of the curtainwall building with its regular structure and open floors designed not as entities in themselves but as clear spaces gridded for an appropriate subdivision. This 23-storey office block derives from the same construction rationale, to achieve reasonable first costs, but also to have durable finishes, make good use of a valuable site and thus maintain its market value.

Description

Perhaps contrary to expectation the building structure of the office block is in concrete, with columns set out on a 7.45m square grid. The curtain wall, which makes a smooth skin rather than a delineated grid, is set forward from the edge of the concrete slab; the mullions of the curtain wall are at 1.50m centres and at these positions the edge of the slab is indented by an area 300 x 155 mm to allow the mullion to pass up with a clearance all round; The mullions are attached to the slab by steel angles. Typical floors consist of a 300mm deep waffle slab on two-way wide, shallow beams of the same depth with a downstand beam around the perimeter. The columns and the core, which is eccentrically placed, are supported by a 2m deep concrete raft resting on 900mm diameter concrete piles. Interior columns vary in size from 800mm square at the top to 1000mm square at the bottom, each being supported by four piles; perimeter columns are slightly smaller, each resting on three piles. On three faces of the building a void is left between the perimeter columns and the cladding to allow vertical distribution of pipes for the perimeter

View of building from NW (photo by Crispin Boyle).

BARING BROTHERS OFFICES (1981)

Description:
Twenty-three storey office block of concrete construction
with aluminium curtain walling
Architects:
GMW Partnership
Structural engineers:
Scott Wilson Kirkpatrick and Partners

Axonometric
view from SW:

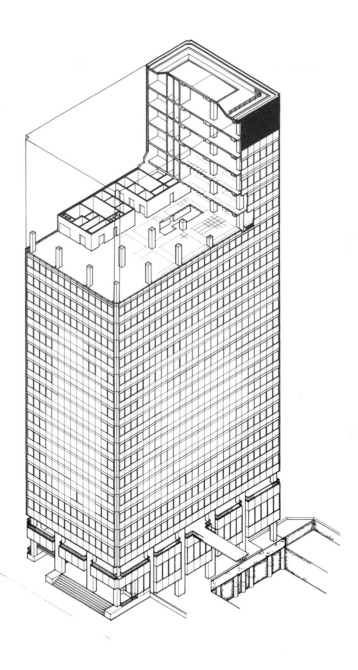

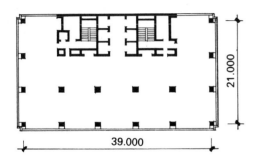

21.000

39.000

Typical floor plan.

Scale: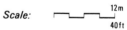

12 m

40 ft

window; this may also be used for ventilation. Over two bays, between levels 12 and 18, a 150mm thick solid slab spans across a 3m square opening in the centre of each bay and may be removed, if necessary, to accommodate stairs.

Structural Action

Wind forces on the building are resisted by cantilever action of the core together with the frame action given by the columns and beams over the rest of the building. For purposes of analysis, the core is simplified into a system of interconnected shear walls which have a pin joint connection with each line of frames. Transference of wind forces to the core is facilitated by a solid slab adjacent to the core. Wind on the narrow face of the building produces tension on the core, which, however, it is well able to resist.

Construction

The building was constructed in 36 months. The substructure was built as a separate contract from the superstructure. At topping out of the concrete structure, the finishing trades were one third of the way up the tower.

Conclusion

This office block is typical of many in big cities in its spare and straightforward design and in its reliance on interior design to create a suitable place for work. Outside all design values are surface values. The block was easy to build; for example, the cladding has relatively few variations and was erected from the inside without scaffolding. Although a steel frame would have shortened time on site and given some saving in the areas of column on plan, concrete was chosen in preference on account of the moderate overall depth of floor structure it allowed and the stability provided by the concrete structure; such a slender tower in steelwork would have required substantial amounts of bracing. The savings in the depth have had a significant effect on the overall height of the building. The core of the building occupies 20% of the gross area, giving 80% of net usable area, slightly above the norm with this plan area. The cost of the cladding is high, amounting to some 28% of the total contract price compared to 35% for the building structure and foundations.

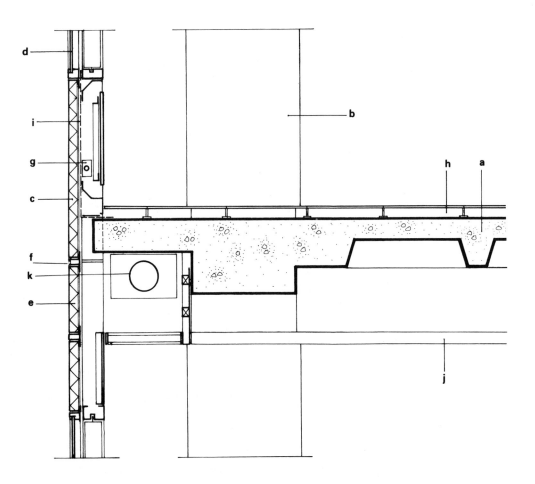

a 300mm deep waffle floor with ribs at 800mm centres; b 650 x 800 mm column; c cladding panel with 6mm bronze-anodised aluminium sheet with integral insulation and fire resistant backing; d double glazing unit with bronze-tinted outer glass; e openable smoke vent flap; f expansion joint at mullions; g finned radiator unit; h 125mm raised floor zone; i 915mm high fire break between service ducts; j suspended ceiling; k 200mm diameter air-conditioning duct.

Vertical section through wall.

heating. Heavy plant is located in the basement with other plant and air handling units on the top two floors. An escape staircase, wet riser and fireman's lift are placed at the north-east corner of the building and give directly on to the street. Smoke extracts from the basement are also placed here. At typical floor levels, smoke is extracted through a small openable panel above each

View of W face of building at street level.

Federal Reserve Bank, Minneapolis, Minnesota, USA

Introduction

Although there are several office blocks with floors hung from the top of the building, this office block must be unique in being hung across a 270 ft (82.29m) gap. This magnanimous if extravagant gesture was justified both by the feeling that the plaza, in which the building stands, ought to be clear of obstructions and the knowledge that columns would interfere with the operations of that part of the building which is below the plaza. In effect the building has been broken into two separate entities, a vast three-level underground structure, with a plan area at each level of some 140 000 sq ft (13 000 sq m) and, contrasting with that, a long ten-storey office block hung above the plaza, each level having a plan area of some 16 800 sq ft (1560 sq m). The building is notable for its daring and boldly expressed structure, and for the clarity of the design solution, the building being handled like a giant, abstract composition. The offices make a landmark, which is to say that they largely refer to the urban scale.

Description

Below the plaza, the upper two levels house all the secure areas of the bank, as well as the parking and reception areas for trucks with cargoes of money. The upper level of the areas below the plaza houses also the entrance level for the office block above. The pedestrian entrance, and access for trucks, is on the south-east side of the building. The bottom floor of the substructure consists of parking for 280 cars, access being from two entrances on the north-west side of the plaza. The substructure is of concrete construction, founded on limestone, has no windows and is completely air conditioned. The offices above the plaza can only be reached from the main lobby by elevators in the central core, which is structurally independent of the offices and of the two end cores. These end cores contain stairs, toilets, service elevators and mechanical ducts. All vertical and all transverse horizontal loads are taken by the end cores, which are H-shaped, 200ft (60.96m) high, and have a 61ft (18.59m) long, 2ft 6in (0.76m) thick 'web' and 18ft (5.49m) long, 4ft (1.21m) thick 'flanges' at each end. Concrete

View of building from W showing access to parking (photo by Balthazar Korab).

walls built either side of the 'web' contain a 48 x 21 ft (14.63 x 6.40 m) area. Longitudinal horizontal loads are carried by the interacting elements of the concrete end cores and the stiffened catenary. Each catenary is of welded steel plate an average of 3ft (0.91m) deep and contains 4in (100mm) diameter post-tensioning cables. There are eight cables at the top of each catenary, reducing to six, then to four, then to two cables at the bottom. The horizontal thrust at the top of the post-tensioning cables is taken by a box-truss, 28ft (8.53m) deep and 60ft (18.29m) wide, the lines of action of the truss, the catenary and the core meeting on a single line. The vital connection between the three

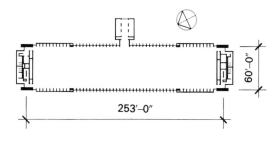

Typical floor plan.

FEDERAL RESERVE BANK OF MINNEAPOLIS (1973)

Description:
Ten-storey office block using braced catenary supports
Architects:
G. Birkerts and Associates
Structural engineers:
Skilling, Helle, Christiansen, Robertson

Axonometric
view from N:

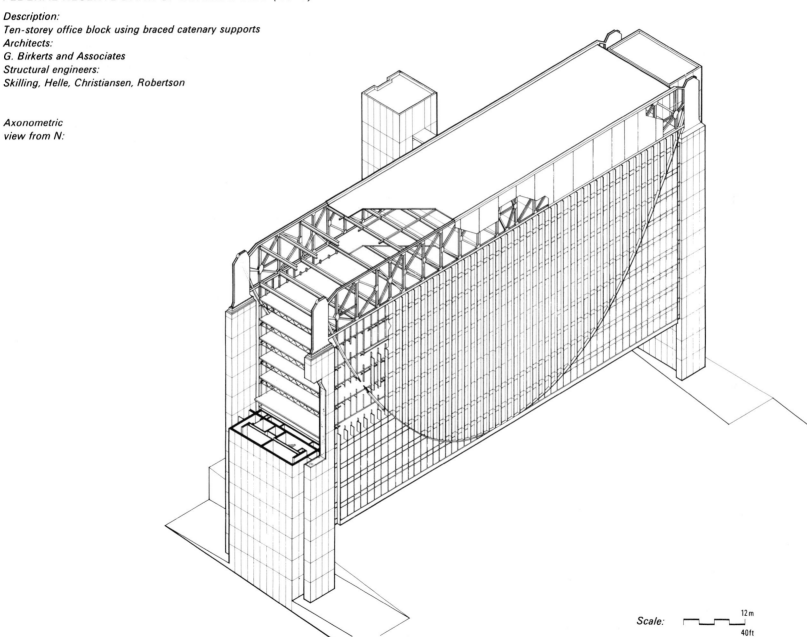

Scale:

12 m

40 ft

elements is made by a 92 ton (85 tonne) anchor piece of welded high strength steel. Each of the four anchor pieces is attached to the concrete core by forty 8ft (2.44m) long anchor bolts embedded in the concrete; each anchor piece carries a vertical load of 6500 tons (6000 tonnes).

The floors are of concrete on steel deck carried by light steel trusses, 10ft (3.04m) on centre, across the 60ft (18.29m) width of the offices. The trusses above the catenary are supported by columns and those below are carried up to the catenary by steel flats. The office spaces are completely free of columns or other obstructions. Clear, reflective double glazing set on the line of the columns above the catenary but about 4ft (1.21m) out from this, on the outer end of the vertical steel fins, below the catenary, define the line of the facade. In the morning, at ten in midsummer, the sun can shine in almost unobstructed, but the fins progressively restrict the amount of solar gain and later, between about noon and two in the afternoon in midsummer, the fins completely block direct solar radiation from reaching the inside. Thereafter solar gain is limited. The air conditioning system makes use of radiant panels with either hot or chilled water and conditioned air that is supplied through light fixtures. The plant room is housed within the top-floor box-truss.

Structural Action

The building is supported by the post-tensioned catenary system. The vertical component of the load at the end of each catenary is taken by the end cores and the horizontal component by one of the two 28ft (8.53m) deep elements that form the sides of the box-truss. At office floors, the spandrels on the two long sides of the building serve as horizontal stiffeners tying the columns and hangers at each floor level together so that each facade then acts like a frame in resisting lateral loads. All vertical loads on the floors are taken by the catenaries and all horizontal load by the diaphragm action of the floor slab which carries the load to the end cores. The end cores are designed as I-beam cantilevers, but with wind against the short side, these cantilevers are stiffened by the catenary system. The top-floor box-trusses also act as horizontal stiffeners where the catenaries are not uniformly loaded. Assuming

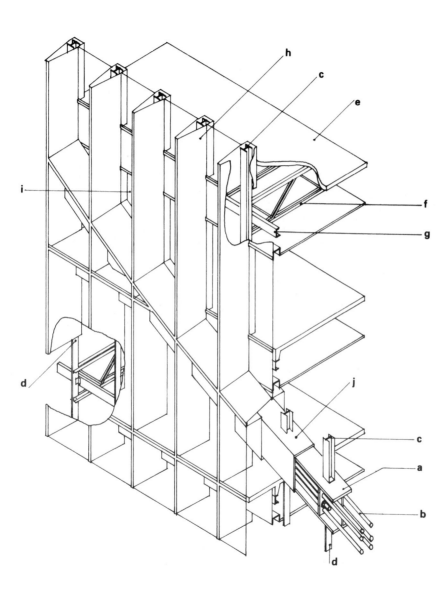

a steel catenary member; **b** 4″ strand cables; **c** 8″ wide column; **d** 1″ x 8″ hanger; **e** concrete slab; **f** 3′–0″ deep steel joist; **g** 10″ deep channel cross-member; **h** steel fin; **i** 1″ double glazing; **j** fireproofing.

Detail of office wall.

Interior view by catenary (photo by Balthazar Korab).

View from NW with catenary and box-truss in position (photo by Balthazar Korab).

the catenary is placed over the full height and all floors have equal loads, the horizontal component of the load at each end of the catenary is the same, whatever the height of the building. The same would be true of an arch system. This led to the idea of supporting any future extension on top of the existing building by use of an arch whose outward thrust could exactly balance the inward thrust imposed by the existing catenary. The planned extension has a height of five storeys.

Construction

Construction of the steelwork was done from the top downwards. First the concrete end cores were cast using a three-level climbing rig; the top level was used for placement of reinforcing bars and concrete, the middle level for positioning of rigid insulation and granite cladding, which serve as permanent formwork, and the bottom level for checking of alignment. Temporary steel erection towers were placed between the end cores, providing support for the top-floor box-truss until it was completed. The catenaries were built in parallel, being hung from the box-truss by the columns. With 80% of the steelwork in place the erection towers were removed. Stressing of the cables in the catenary was done in three stages as the loads on the catenaries increased with the

addition of more and more construction load. After the final stressing, all columns were in compression and the top-level box-truss had an upward camber of $1\frac{1}{2}$in (38mm). The stressing was done from a cable end cap at the top of the anchor piece.

Conclusion

This building is an extraordinary example of the use of a catenary system for the spanning of large distances and might have potential for further application. It is equally extraordinary in the size and purity of its shape.

Gateway House,
Basingstoke, England

Introduction

The architects' aspirations to encapsulate randomness but also a certain fixed order within their buildings reflects what, in a different context, Baudelaire called the 'mysterious and contradictory love of the spirit for surprise and symmetry'. The idea informs the design of this office block, a building with 19 000 sq m of floor space, in which the working hours of nearly 1000 people are spent and in which, except for its views, is on an unpromising site between two roads. The problem is typical and in need of good solutions. Here a random element may be seen in the clutter of office work and the views out, particularly those on to the luxuriantly planted terraces outside, and order in a 7.50m square grid to which the building structure and cladding system have to conform. The grid is sufficiently large for a building of this size to prevent it becoming mechanically repetitive but remain suitable for all the many technical requirements. A notable feature of the building is the thorough integration of the architectural ideas and the construction method, which gives the design an immediate authority.

View of building from SE (photo by Trevor Waller).

Description

The building is in the form of an L-shape that in all major respects is symmetrical about a diagonal line running south-east from the main entrance on the north-west corner. The building cascades down in a series of terraces on the inside edges of the L-shape but all the other facades are vertical. The terraces are heavily planted and there is an enclosed courtyard at level 2. This has the effect of creating a focus outside the building. Those people facing the terraces, and others more fleetingly, can be made aware of their position in relation to the rest of the building. The main entrance, which is at level 3, leads to a reception area which also has a view across the terrace. To the north and west of the reception area are double-height spaces for the plant room and restaurant respectively. The site slopes steeply to the south and parking has been provided lower down over the whole of level 1, the lowest level, and over about half of level 2.

The structure is a concrete frame which makes extensive use of precast items. Columns are cast-in-place with overall dimensions of 450 x 450 mm but are scaled down by their cruciform shape; they are set out on a strict 7.50m square grid which is suitable for the office spaces and allows adequate arrangements for car parking below. Two types of floor are used: a ribbed floor slab with an overall depth of 500mm for parking and other utility areas and a precast concrete pyramid floor with an overall depth of 1.85m that contains a void with a maximum height of 1.12m for services. The pyramid units are used in all office areas; they are made up of four identical precast quadrants each weighing 3.5 tonnes which are jointed along the diagonal lines of the pyramid. Precast concrete lattice beams run on the grid lines along the sides of each pyramid and help to support the floor slab above. The floor, which is a 150mm thick concrete slab cast on metal decking, is supported not only by the lattice beams but also by the collar at the apex of the pyramid and by the columns. The joint between the pyramid quadrants, the lattice beams

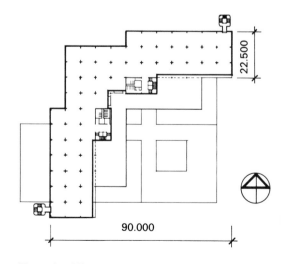

Plan at level 5.

GATEWAY HOUSE (1976)

Description:
Six-storey office building of concrete frame construction
with aluminium cladding panels
Architects and structural engineers:
Arup Associates

Axonometric
view from SW:

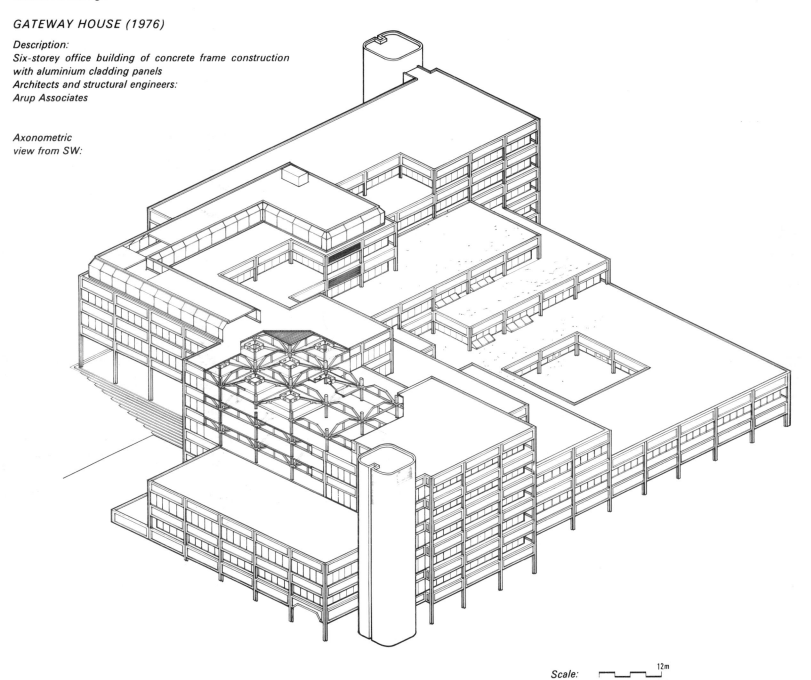

Scale: 12m
40 ft

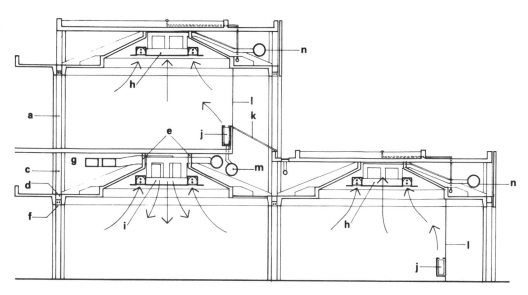

a 450 x 450 mm cruciform cast-in-place column; **b** 150mm concrete slab on metal decking; **c** 450 x 450 mm octagonal connecting column; **d** 1.60m deep lattice truss; **e** quadrant of ceiling pyramid; **f** position of light fitting; **g** services void; **h** light fitting and return air unit; **i** light fitting and air unit; **j** induction unit; **k** roof light; **l** glass line; **m** supply air; **n** return air.

Section through office area.

View across terrace from conference room (photo by Brecht-Einzig Ltd.).

and the column is cast-in-place; within the depth of the void the column has an octagonal section which allows extra room for supports and reinforcing bars.

The interest and good broad scale provided by the heavy pyramid is reinforced by the lighting arrangements. Illumination is given principally by strip lights running on grid lines, and recessed between the edges of the pyramids, to form an outer square; an inner square of light is provided in the apex and helps to set the pyramid into relief. To provide reasonably uniform conditions, both fittings required reflectors giving a 'batswing' distribution of light; two tubes were required, one above the other, to increase precision on the control of the quantity and direction of light. The maximum light output is angled between lines at 25 and 35 degrees to the vertical. In the inner square, the fitting also incorporates a cross-blade

louvre and air handling slot, all return air being extracted through this fitting. The ceiling of each pyramid unit is level over a 1.50m wide strip around the perimeter of each unit and this conveniently allows an overhang beyond the glass line on the external bays facing east or south. This eliminates all the nearly vertical natural light and allows better perception overall by reducing contrast; therefore, and perhaps contrary to expectation, lower levels of artificial light can be specified. The overhangs combined with the use of blinds limit solar gain and this taken with a moderate lighting level helps to lower the cooling load for the building. Other energy saving measures include bronze-tinted glass, good insulation in external walls as well as the high thermal capacity provided by the concrete structure. The walls consist of aluminium cladding panels and double glazing sealed with neoprene.

Full air conditioning is provided. There are four air-conditioning zones for the offices which are defined by a vertical plane that makes a diagonal line on plan and a horizontal plane that passes through level 5. An induction system is used, about four volumes of secondary air being induced by each volume of primary air. The induction units are placed below the perimeter glazing at 1.5m centres and serve a depth of 7m. One air-handling unit is allocated to each zone, two units being placed on the roof, in glass enclosures, and two at level 2. Each unit comprises a mixing chamber for the fresh and return air, a roll filter, humidifier, cooling coils, a centrifugal fan and a silencer through which air passes to a plenum chamber and then to the supply ducts. In cold weather, local temperature control is provided by heater batteries within each supply duct. The system is designed to maintain a dry-bulb temperature indoors within

Interior view of offices (photo by Martin Charles).

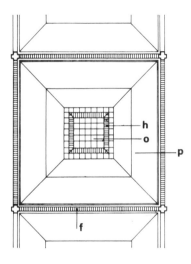

o acoustic tile; **p** textured paint.
Reflected plan of 7.50m pyramid ceiling.

2°C of 22°C with a relative humidity near to 50%; outdoor design conditions in summer are taken as 28°C dry bulb and 18°C wet bulb. A general feature of all such induction and fan-coil systems is the reduction in the sizes of ducts and the air-handling equipment because of the small volume of the primary air, which is about a third of that handled by an equivalent all-air system. Equipment in the main plant room consists of two centrifugal chiller units with a total capacity of 2490 kilowatts and three gas-fired heating boilers, the two used in winter having a total capacity of

2340 kilowatts; the plant room also contains two calorifiers, a cold water booster set, hose reel water boosters and duplicate pumps for hot and chilled water circuits and the condenser water. For a ten-hour office day the actual annual consumption of gas has been about 180 000 therms or less and that of electricity just over 3 million kilowatt-hours; of the electricity used just under a third is used for lighting and just under a half for operation of the air conditioning plant.

Dehumidification is largely provided by treatment of the primary air in each zone and

sensible cooling by the induction units. A control valve operates between one and three units giving a measure of local control of the air temperatures but not of the humidity. In those parts of the offices beyond the reach of the induction units, conditioned air is supplied through grilles in the side of the pyramid ceiling fed from constant volume room terminal units with heater batteries. Also, two air-conditioning units are located in a void adjacent to the service cores at each floor level, in order to provide for the concentrations of people that may occur in any area that is

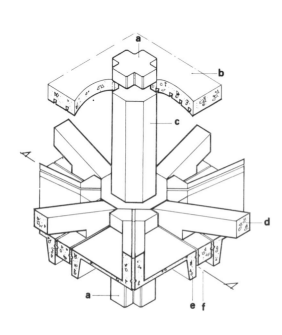

View on column in services void.

View of building from SW.

requisitioned as a conference room; the conditioned air is supplied down a spine duct in the service void and can be taken to any module in the office areas. Special provisions are made for air conditioning of the kitchens and computer suites.

The office areas which have a net area of over 14 500 sq m are designed to accomodate both open office space and small individual offices. A conflict occurs because of the narrow plan, with windows on both sides, that would be required by the latter and the large square spaces, with minimum obstruction of daylight, required by the former. The problem is solved to some extent by the provision of different kinds of plan at each floor level. However the office spaces always have the same unifying elements at all levels, the major ones being the modular grid and the structure on it.

Structural Action

Because of support provided by the apex of the pyramid and along the grid lines, the office floor slab acts like a continuous slab spanning 3.50m in two directions between point supports. Load on the apex of the pyramid is taken down the diagonal lines to the column joint. Excluding the column itself, there are no less than twelve separate elements to be joined at each internal column joint; because of lack of space, the side thrust along the diagonal lines has to be counteracted by the bottom chord of the lattice truss rather than within the pyramid unit itself. Horizontal forces on the building are taken by frame action and by the core elements.

View of terrace (photo by Trevor Waller).

Vertical section through services void.

Construction

The total period of construction amounted to 29 months. All precast units required propping until jointing was complete; the cast-in-place office slabs had to be propped off the pyramid unit below until cured.

Conclusion

This is an invigorating design. One of the most successful aspects, and important in large buildings, is the clear, visible relation of each part to the whole; moving round the building there are shifts of scale within and between floors and a continuous unfolding of different views of familiar places. In most places the potential monotony of grids and smooth surfaces is held off by relief, changes of direction, planting and other incidents and the permanent architectural elements always succeed in imposing themselves. This is a highly accomplished piece of work in the sense that, although not cheap, it might be said that the added value easily exceeds the extra cost. In terms of practical achievements in the design of large buildings, this one stands near a pinnacle. The building structure represents about 17% of the final costs compared to nearly 40% for services and 13% for windows and cladding.

Centraal Beheer Offices,
Apeldoorn, Holland

Introduction

Industrialisation is the most fundamental change yet to patterns of life in those countries affected by it, with enormous repercussions on established habits and ways of thought, disguised only by the slow, continuous nature of the change. The benefits and economies of scale usually associated with industrialisation can be exploited not only for operations in manufacturing but also for those in retailing, administration, passenger handling and even housing and health care. The advantages can be generally associated with high economic growth but there are costs. One consequence, largely initiated by the potential for economies of scale, has been the specialisation of tasks and the concentration of facilities with the accompanying effect on building designers that they have had to solve sometimes complex organizational problems, at a larger physical scale, and all in one go, rather than slowly and piecemeal. While design must aim to be systematic, often, only the most basic and obvious general features of its problems are abstracted and looked at, let alone solved. With pressure on time and resources the large-scale operation, most often, has brought into being buildings which are large and impersonal too.

Naturally there has been opposition to this tendency. However, in the field of office building the alternatives to the anonymous, undifferentiated office space have been difficult to formulate and have been discouraged by the primary requirement to simplify construction of the building to achieve low first cost. This office building for an insurance company is exceptional because it has avoided tight financial constraints and because of its designers' hope and belief that there is no necessary opposition between the large and systematically designed building and each user's most individual needs. The design is famous but unique. It provides space for 1000 office workers but attempts to attach each of them to a group space in a beehive arrangement inside the building. The inside is open, like a framework, and allows reference outside the group areas, where each individual is positioned, so that a necessary corporate identity is maintained. This highly

View of building from NW (photo by Aerophoto Schiphol).

organized form is continued on to the outside.

Description

The building may be split into four quadrants, each perforated by full height internal corridors crossing each other at right angles. The focal point is a central space to which all the corridors lead, containing lifts and escalators. Each corridor and the central space extend upwards to perspex rooflights which allow sunlight to penetrate inside. All quadrants of the building contain office space except the east quadrant which has social facilities, such as the restaurant and the recreation areas. The building is constructed as a series of nine-metre square towers of varying height with a three-metre space between. Typically the towers are separate and linked only by bridges, so that

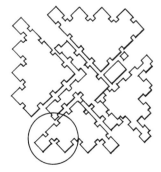

General plan of building.

CENTRAAL BEHEER OFFICES (1972)

Description:
Five-storey office block of concrete frame construction with
extensive use of precast elements
Architects:
Herman Hertzberger/
Lucas and Niemeijer
Structural engineers:
Dicke and Boogaard

Axonometric
view from NW:

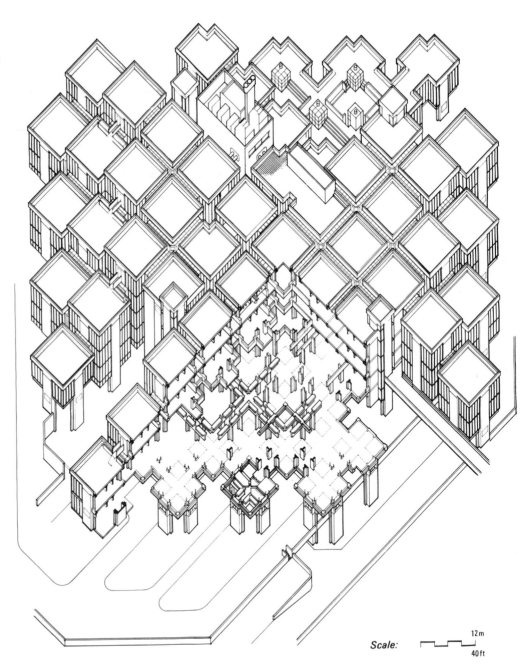

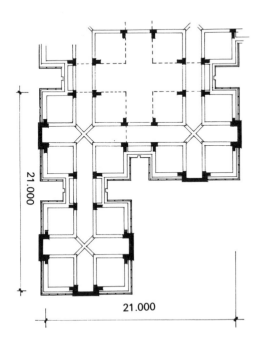

21.000

21.000

Part plan of building.

Scale:

12 m

40 ft

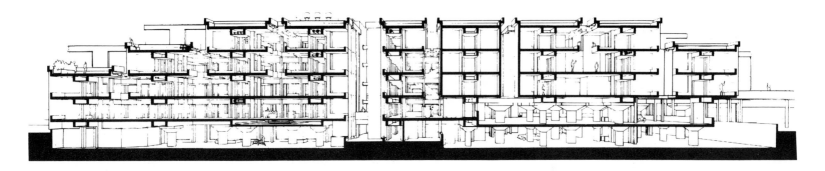

E-W section through offices (drawn by architect).

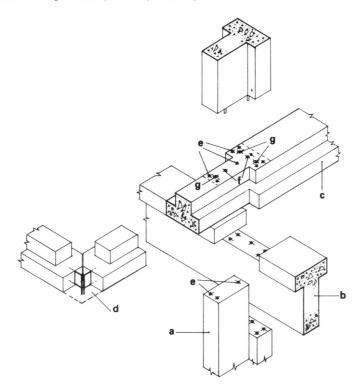

a 900mm deep T-shaped precast column; **b** precast main beam with 830mm effective depth below flange; **c** 450mm deep precast edge beam; **d** cast-in-place joint with immediate connection by means of bolt and 2 steel plates with 45° slots in opposite direction; **e** 8 dowel bars; **f** 2 dowels from column above; **g** 3 adjusting bolts for column above.

Details of corner and column connections.

floors in other towers are visible through the open space; this arrangement provides a view from each position. In other areas the floor slab is continuous across several towers, providing larger floor areas where these are required. As well as the desire to provide congenial spaces, another determining feature of the interior architecture was the need to provide a grid of services to run in two directions under the floors of each tower; these carry services from the central plantroom, which is placed adjacent to the central space to minimise service runs. The structural system of a typical internal tower works on a balanced cantilever system, the cantilevers projecting into each tower from the eight perimeter columns. The main cantilever beams are connected to each other in the centre of the tower by diagonal cross-beams 450mm deep, still leaving a depth of 830mm below this, to the bottom of the main beams, for a service channel to run in both directions between the beams. At the perimeter of the building, and at many places in the interior, the tower units cannot be linked to other units on all sides; these tower units therefore work, not as balanced cantilevers, but as spatial frames, leaning into the central cross-beams on the same principle as a three-hinged arch.

The main beams of the tower are precast concrete, as are the edge beams resting on top of these main beams. Precast concrete slabs are used in the four corner quadrants. The remainder of the slab and the central cross-beams are cast in place. The important joint, connecting together the main beam, the edge beam and the columns above and below, uses eight dowel bars to connect the two beams to the column below, with two dowels projecting from the column above that fit into pockets in the top of the edge beam. Adjustment of the position of the column above is by means of three adjusting bolts set into the edge beam. The joint between the main beam and the column below is moment resistant, and ensures that the frame is stable. This basic framework is infilled largely with glass panes and concrete and glass blocks to provide solid or void, openness or enclosure as required. The masonry blocks are carefully laid and the surface finish to precast items is excellent. The elevations also use concrete block but consist mostly of large areas of glass curtain walling, nicely divided by purple aluminium mullions, providing views out over every one of the many external corners of the building. The curtain walling is supported off L-shaped steel brackets which are bolted back to the concrete edge beam.

Part of the lowest two floor levels, of the five levels in the building, are given over to parking. As the columns of the towers do not fit the parking pattern, four tower columns were supported by just one cast-in-place column, with a very large mushroom head, on an 8.50 x 8.50 m grid in these parking areas at the lower levels. The cast-in-place columns carry a load of 500 tonnes and the mushroom head works something like an upside-down pilecap, with top reinforcement across the diagonals of the head. Columns are supported on pad foundations about one metre thick with deep ground beams between these pads to help even out settlement on a ground of variable quality.

Environmental conditions have been given the same degree of attention as the building fabric. In the office areas, the design aims to control the air temperature and radiant heat, the relative humidity, the lighting level and background noise level. A general lighting level of 400 lux is provided by light panels in the ceiling and this can be brought up to 800 lux by desk lamps and extensions from the ceiling. Background noise was specified not to exceed a noise rating index of 30 and this was achieved by placing mufflers behind suction ventilators and in front of the extraction ventilators in the roof, by acoustic isolation of air ducts and by mounting of vibrating machinery on isolating pads. The control of the thermal environment is more difficult. The building is heavy but has large areas of glass so that in

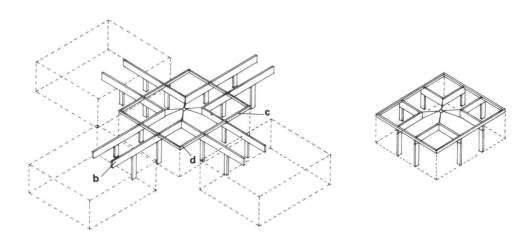

Structural arrangement of tower using balanced cantilever frames or hinged spatial frame.

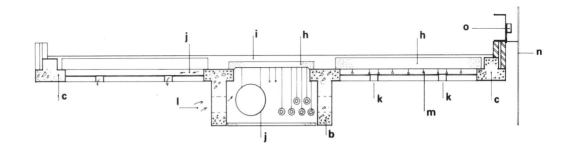

h precast floor panels; i concrete topping; j primary air; k fluorescent light panels; l secondary air; m hot or cold water pipes; n single glazing in aluminium frame; o radiator.

Cross-section through tower.

winter a lot of heat is needed to warm it up, while in summer a lot of heat must be removed, even though the building only heats up slowly. Air conditioning is therefore necessary. The amount of heating or cooling required is greatly influenced by the solar gain which depends on the type and area of the glass and the sunshading provided and on the internal heat gain which is largely dependent on the lighting levels. To keep the costs of air conditioning down it was decided that 80% of the direct solar gain had to be eliminated. Clear single glazing is used in conjunction with electrically operated exterior sunshades. Primary conditioned air is distributed from ducts in the service channels to perforated plates in the ceiling system. There is an induction unit in the service channel which recirculates room air. The open internal architecture allows return air to be extracted from the voids below the rooflights. The amount of radiant heating or cooling is influenced by aluminium plates below the ceiling which are clamped to pipes and become hot or cold as water in the pipe is hot or cold. To counteract downdraughts by the windows and below rooflights, radiators are placed at the bottom of windows and in the spaces below rooflights. Holes provided in the main beams allow services to cross through. The central plantroom, serving the whole building, has six levels including the roof level, each with a plan area of 140 square metres. In the basement are three gas engines turning three electricity generators each rated at 560 kilowatts; these generators and three transformers supply part of the electrical energy. The basement also contains heat recovery vessels which take exhaust gas from the engines to produce steam for the absorption cooling plant. The large air intakes have mufflers fitted. At level one are telecommunications, at level two the air distribution system, at level three the air treatment system and boilers, at level four cooling machines and storage vessels and at roof level the cooling towers and gas reduction station.

Structural Action

The building achieves lateral stability through frame action. The rigid connection ensuring this is that made between the main beams and columns by dowel bars grouted in position. All gaps between the slabs and beams had to be filled with

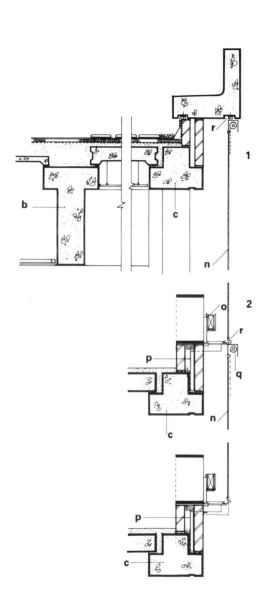

p steel bracket fixed to beam; q sunshade; r movement joint.

Vertical section through outside wall.

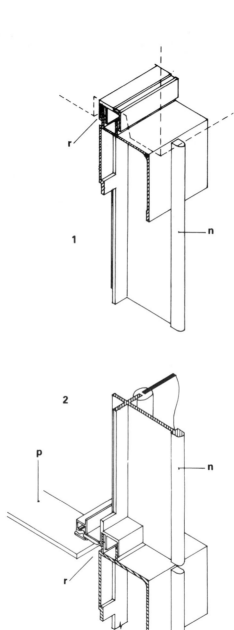

Details of wall.

mortar and the screed and infill positions poured before the structure was able to function as an integral unit.

Construction

Although the concrete framework of the building is relatively complex, there is a large amount of repetition. To minimise time on site, elements of the frame needed in large numbers were precast, the prefabricated elements being produced before the start on site. The remaining parts and a large number of the joints were in cast-in-place concrete. The elements were sized by the demands of construction, rather than the load carried, main beams and columns being oversize and edge beams undersize. An important part of the cost of a precast scheme is the craneage and storage of units. A huge travelling bridge crane ran in an east-west direction across the site, running on one rail to the south of the building, near the storage area, and another rail going through the middle of the building plan, the rail resting on the roofs of the building after this part had been completed. Two tower cranes were placed to the north of the site. Total construction time on site amounted to 42 months.

Conclusion

The physical form of this building is organized by the three-dimensional grid, one for circulation, one for services and one for structure, each offset one from the other. Within this strong form, different purposes may be accommodated by suitable secondary elements and furnishings, so that the building is flexible in use to some, limited, degree. The building is about an idea, for a social organization which is friendly and not overtly hierarchical; the arrangements inside, outside and at the entrances are deliberately informal. Because the overall organization is taken care of and the relationship of part to whole is everywhere so evident, users are encouraged to exercise choice over the detailed arrangements. Most areas are well served with daylight. Inevitably the large areas on elevation and the 'puzzle' frames make the building relatively expensive. Groundworks and concrete work account for slightly more than a third of the total cost, services slightly under a third and finishing, cladding and permanent fitting the remainder.

Interior view of tower units linked to each other (photo by Willem Diepraam).

View between tower units showing rooflights (photo by Willem Diepraam).

One Finsbury Avenue, London, England

Introduction

The not unusual requirements for this office block were that it be a 'quality' building with large floor areas built at maximum speed and minimum cost. The finished building is a paradigm of resourceful architecture and unusual in the measure to which the requirements were met. The design consists of pulling together a wide range of detailed knowledge about the building process and the manufacture of individual parts and of selecting the key elements in the overall design concept. Broadly speaking, the method here takes the form of maximum repetition of several general design themes but with ingenious variations to provide changes in massing and elevation and in the views to the outside and across the atrium. A deft touch is the use of screens, internally and externally, to control the scale in a way that is both effective and cheap.

Description

The building uses the whole of the available site but helps to create its own sense of place with its large full-height atrium space and a varying plan area between the ground floor and roof. The building solves as many problems as possible at the fundamental levels of the plan and massing arrangements: both the shape and the scale effect of the huge volume enclosed, amounting to a maximum of eight storeys in height and nearly 57 x 84 m in plan, combine to reduce the exposed area to volume ratio and thus the energy losses too; the plan provides a large amount of usable space around the perimeter and against the atrium where, even at lower levels, there is a high level of natural light. The large areas of floor space provided at each level are of a convenient size, the step-back of the building on elevation at high level being compensated for by a smaller area of atrium; the smaller rooflight area, which is then possible, helps to regulate the transmission of heat and light. The particular positioning of the lifts and services allows subdivision of the floor into separate offices, if required.

The building is of steel frame construction using columns on a 6 x 6 m grid, increased to 6 x 7.5 m on two central strips to allow a corridor space or larger

View of building from NW.

ONE FINSBURY AVENUE (1984)

Description:
Eight-storey office block of steel frame construction
Architects and structural engineers:
Arup Associates

Axonometric
view from NE:

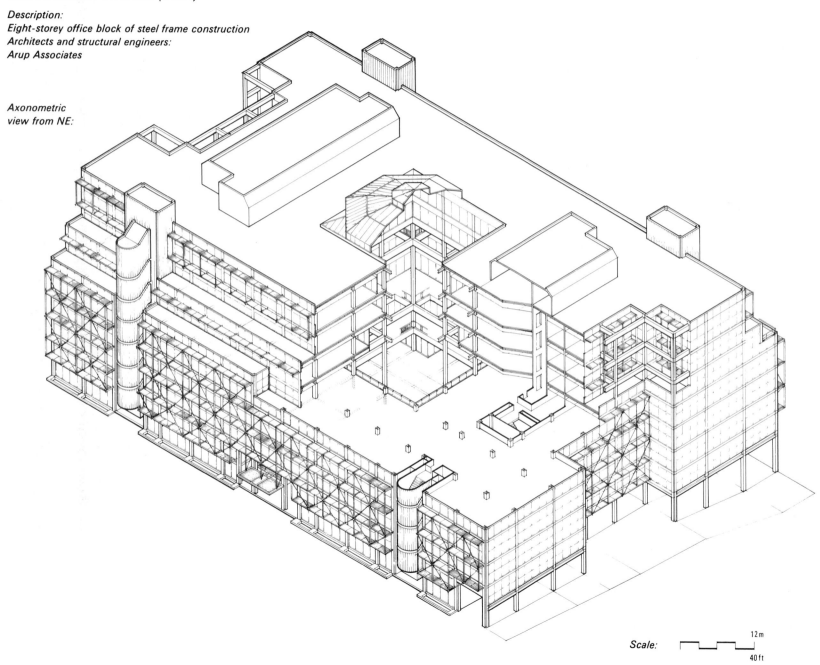

Scale:

12 m

40 ft

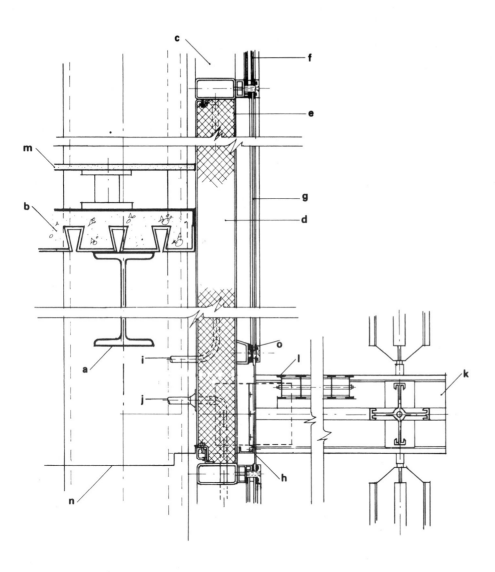

a UB 406 x 39 kg/m steel beam; b 130mm concrete slab on metal deck; c 120 x 60 x 5 mm rectangular steel tube subframe heated; d 120mm insulation; e 3mm aluminium sheet and vapour barrier; f bronze tinted double glazing; g single toughened spandrel glazing in front of ventilated cavity; h 3mm bronze-anodised aluminium cladding; i hot water supply; j hot water return; k cross-shaped aluminium extrusion fixed via stainless steel brackets to curtain wall subframe; l aluminium grille; m raised floor; n suspended ceiling; o neoprene glazing section with anodised aluminium pressure plate bolted to fitting on subframe.

Vertical section through wall (drawn from material supplied by J. Gartner and Co.).

column-free areas. Simple bolted connections were used, with 20mm diameter bolts specified as standard and used wherever possible. A 130mm deep lightweight concrete floor slab, of a specified strength of 30 newtons per sq mm, acting compositely with a 50mm deep profiled metal deck spans 3m between steel secondary beams which in turn span between the lines of the main beams. Generally the beams are of the same serial size being about 400mm deep and composite with the slab. There is a clear space of 395mm between the bottom of the beams and a suspended ceiling; this carries cables, VAV ducts supplying ceiling air diffusers and piping to supply sprinkler heads, as well as serving as a path for the return air. The ceiling consists of perforated metal ceiling tiles, with backing providing acoustic absorbency and some acoustic insulation, and fluorescent light fittings to give an average of 500 lux in the office areas. A raised floor is provided above the slab for cabling and consists of metal-faced chipboard supported on adjustable pedestals at 600mm centres both ways. Smoke barriers are provided at about 18m intervals in this void. The external cladding, in general, is made in 3.30m high by 5.60m wide panels, slightly less than the standard storey height and bay width. It consists of lightly tinted double glazing, in the top half, and single glazing in front of rigid insulation, in the bottom half, both in bronze-anodised aluminium external surrounds; they are set in a grid of 120 x 60 x 4 mm rectangular steel tubes which is a subframe and attaches directly to the concrete floor. There are five vertical and two horizontal tubes in each panel, of which the upper half is connected to hot water pipes. The hot water circulates inside the tubes and provides heating at the perimeter. The infill column and horizontal cladding strips are 400 and 350 mm wide of 3mm thick aluminium with insulation behind. The projecting screens, used on all except the north and south elevations, are made of aluminium I-sections and supported by cross-shaped aluminium extrusions, which, at one end, are fixed via stainless steel brackets to the curtain wall subframe and, at the other end, are connected to 30mm diameter stainless steel cross-bracing rods. Cladding to the external stairs and other exposed elements is also in aluminium. For greater durability, at the ground floor only, granite cladding is used for door and window surrounds.

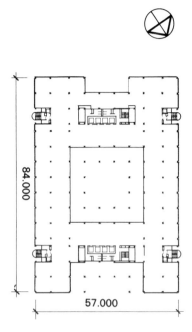

84.000

57.000

Third floor plan.

View of part of SE elevation.

Rooflight over atrium (photo by architect).

Screens are also provided at the higher levels of the atrium acting both as sunscreens and as visual foils.

A concrete basement contains sports facilities, plant rooms and a car park. Other plant is placed on the roof either side of the atrium rooflight, vertical service ducts being placed either side of the lifts. Except for the basement areas and part of the ground floor, only one hour fire protection was required, the external steelwork, at the perimeter, being cased in concrete for fire and corrosion protection, steelwork in the ceiling void being sprayed and other internal steelwork being clad in steel-faced fire resistant board but not protected against corrosion. The steel-faced board was also required to take out rolling and constructional tolerances in the steelwork, this being particularly important in the long atrium columns. The glazing separating the offices from the atrium is not fire resistant but prevents the passage of smoke.

Access is available through a lobby to four external staircases, as well as two adjacent to the lifts. Sprinklers are expected to limit the size of any fire such that the smoke produced is in quantities that can be extracted by openings in the vertical sides of the atrium rooflight. Reinforcement was provided in slabs for fire resistance.

Structural Action

Vertical loads are taken by frame action and horizontal forces by diagonally braced frames surrounding the two lift areas and transferred to the ground floor slab. The steel columns were placed directly over large diameter underreamed piles, about 15m long, with a capacity of 3600 kilonewtons.

Construction

The total period of construction was 18 months, of which the steel amounting to some 1600 tonnes

took only 15 weeks to erect. Two tower cranes were used, one in each lift shaft. Concrete was pumped. Columns were erected in three-storey heights. Standard beam sizes, bolts and details were adopted. No treatment was given to the internal steelwork except an initial cleaning. Stairs were shop-made in steel, stair treads being filled on-site in concrete. As much work as possible was done off-site, including encasement of beams at ground floor level and welding of some shear studs. Cladding panels were erected complete, including glazing, and only needed connections to the floor slab and to the hot water supply and return pipes. The infill panels and cover strips between panels were put in place subsequently. Generally the steel beams and profiled metal sheet required no propping. The very fast erection of the steelwork can be attributed to the regularity of the grid, the repetitive nature of the floor system, although as noted the floors vary in area, and to the fact that no concreting was necessary during the erection of the steel, the frame being stable in its own right.

Conclusion

This office block, although slickly put together, avoids being either flat or glossy and, in spite of its actual volume, the building even manages to achieve a confectionery lightness, on its long sides. The atrium space is used most effectively and gives rise to all kinds of views and angles without opposite sides being obtrusively close. The potential of the design was compromised to some extent by the usual requirement for a flat ceiling, which makes the space 'endless', although it does allow flexibility in the arrangement of partitions. The repetitive use of elements, which is either disguised or used to reinforce the design, and the judicious allocation of resources demonstrate bedrock professionalism. Nearly 30% of the cost of the buildings is in the services, with 50% in the fabric and the remaining 20% in the finishes including the granite at ground floor. Of the fabric cost, more than 40% is attributable to the cladding and only 10% to the building frame. The steel used in the frame above ground averages 45 kg per sq m.

View across atrium (photo by architect).

Chapter Seven

Public Buildings

One issue that particularly confronts the designer of public buildings is what attitude to adopt to monumental architecture. In the past, the deliberate aggrandisement, which is part and parcel of monumental architecture, has been used to express differences of status or to symbolise what have been thought to be important ideas, such as the omnipotence of the law or other kinds of authority, divine or secular. But it has also been, consciously or not, a vehicle which expresses a ruling ethos, in the way that bourgeois liberalism is represented by the Corn Exchanges in England or by the decorous residences which were contemporary in other parts of Europe. In recent times, however, the formal satisfactions provided by these kinds of buildings is less evident and, in general, the stylistic expressions are less confident. The church building, which more than any other, is the prototype for monumental architecture, has had its scale and impact reduced. Shops and department stores, described by Zola as 'the poetry of modern society', are no longer thought of as grandiose halls for display but as facilities to allow individual choice. Museums, art galleries, libraries and schools are no longer monuments of civic pride. What still distinguishes public architecture, where conditions allow, is its enhanced scale, most often seen in civic, government or corporate architecture. The buildings in this chapter cover a range of scales and a variety of approches to the design of public buildings but are representative of a generally more ambivalent attitude to monuments, whatever influence this kind of architecture still exerts. The buildings are selected to show off a variety of materials and building techniques.

St. Anne's Church, Fawley Court, Henley-on-Thames, England

Introduction

A church is a place that embodies ideas of community and of sanctity. Without the idea of the sacred, some basic concepts lose weight, values become relative and are therefore depleted. A sacred building can be seen as one which, beyond its inert physical materials, contains elements of drama, like other buildings, but also has a direct personal appeal, in the way it can be understood, to reinforce the sense of human freedom of action and purpose. This church reflects some of these ideas, using steeply angled planes of roof surface meeting along ascending ridge lines and high natural light to illuminate the inside. But the plan area is modest and there is a simple choice of wood or brick surfaces.

Description

The design abandons any symmetrical plan arrangement in favour of a more intense piece of abstract design. The crypt and narthex on the west side are triangular shaped rooms with vertical brick on glass walls but the main body of the church is formed by two lines of laminated timber A-frames which meet, at an angle to each other, on a line at the centre of the nave. On this common line both ridge lines are at their respective highest points; the end frame from the east set fits over that from the west set and, on the north side, the higher of the two frames springs off the lower by means of a flitch joint but has its own connection with the concrete floor on the south side. the span of the lower frame is 62ft (18.89m); The area between these two A-frames is glazed, except where this gap becomes very narrow. The two sets of A-frames are independent structural entities with cross-bracing in the end bays of each set. The frames have pinned joints at the base and the apex and members are tapered near these points to give them a more slender appearance. All frames in the west set are different; the members have a width of $4\frac{3}{4}$in (120mm) and depths in the middle of their span varying from $12\frac{3}{4}$in (324mm) to $36\frac{1}{8}$in (918mm). The members in the east set have a size of $4\frac{3}{4}$ x $36\frac{1}{8}$in (120 x 918 mm) except the end member on the joint line which is 6 x $27\frac{7}{8}$ in (150 x 620 mm) because of the flitch joint. The A-frames

View of church from W (photo by S. Baynton).

are covered with fair-faced $2\frac{1}{2}$in (64mm) thick tongued and grooved wood planks which are covered in copper roofing with a standing seam joint. There are no longitudinal members, apart from those along ridges and a single line of members to support the roof over the north-west corner of the building. This roof has cranked laminated timber beams spanning between the main A-frames and the brick external wall. Freestanding brickwork is used both for internal and external walls.

Structural Action

The main A-frames behave like a three pinned arch in carrying gravity loads. Straight members are structurally less efficient than curved members, although only slightly so with steep frames, but are very much cheaper. Under horizontal loads the two principal planes of the roof could behave like folded plates if the wood planks were connected

along their joints but, here, it was more convenient to fix crossbracing at the end bays of each structural unit.

Construction

The building was constructed in a period of 18 months. An end bay of each structural unit, with its crossbracing, was erected first and frames erected subsequently were stabilised against it by temporary longitudinal members.

Conclusion

The building is fitting and makes excellent use of its laminated timber. Better definition and considerable economies were effected by use of straight members as compared to curved or bent members. A significant part of the total cost is associated with the roof planking and fair-faced finish to this and other timber elements.

ST ANNE'S CHURCH (1972)

Description:
Church of laminated timber frame construction
Architects:
W.Crabtree and Jarosz
Structural engineers:
Taylor Whalley and Spyra/
Rainham Timber Engineering

Axonometric
view from W:

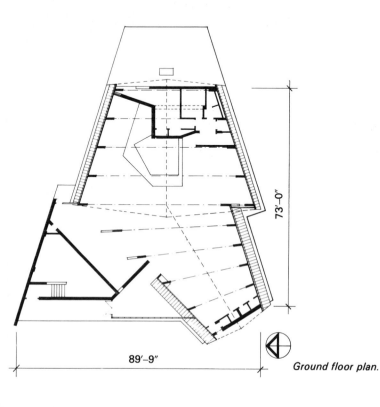

73'-0"

89'-9"

Ground floor plan.

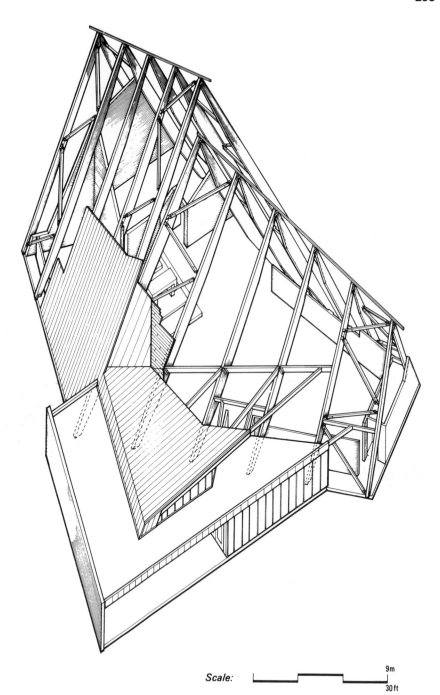

Scale:

9m

30ft

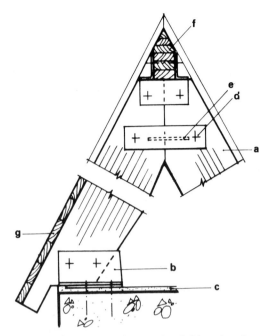

a laminated timber rafter member; **b** 2/ steel angle anchor plates using $\frac{3}{4}''$ bolts through timber and to concrete slab; **c** 1" mortar; **d** 2/ steel plates using $\frac{3}{4}''$ bolts; **e** $\frac{3}{4}''$ diameter steel rod; **f** ridge member; **g** $2\frac{1}{2}''$ wood planks.

Typical vertical section through apex.

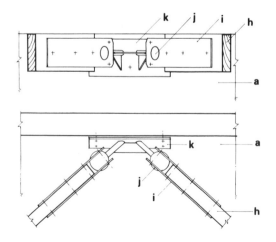

Inside view looking E (photo by S. Baynton).

h $2\frac{3}{4}''$ x $8\frac{3}{4}''$ timber bracing; **i** $\frac{1}{4}''$ steel plates with 3/$\frac{3}{4}''$ bolts; **j** steel ball joint with 2/ $\frac{1}{2}''$ bolts; **k** steel plate bolted to rafter.

Elevation, top, and plan, bottom, of rafter connection to wind bracing.

Kron Apotheke,
Stuttgart, West Germany

Introduction

The siting of this multi-use building is typical of innumerable buildings in town centres that are hemmed in on awkwardly shaped areas by existing buildings and road and pavement lines. As the building is also in an area of medieval origin, the urban plan makes a particularly tight constraint. The design overcomes all these difficulties and, in the process, gives a virtuoso demonstration of suitable fashioning for a building in cast-in-place concrete. The elevations in concrete and glass make use of relief but are pleasantly spare in their use of material. The regularly spaced structural mullions, and some additional non-structural mullions, and the lines of the floors stepping out at the higher levels achieve a small scale and help to create a modern idiom for building in this area.

Description

There are six levels in the building including a basement for storage, a chemist's shop at street level and surgeries in the space above, with two flats occupying the attic storey and a part of the storey below the attic. Halfway down the west side of the building are the stairs, lifts, vertical service ducts and the flue pipes. The last three extract through a concrete shaft at roof level. Most of the washrooms are grouped round this service core. The wall adjacent to the existing building is of solid concrete, generally 270mm thick with 40mm of rigid insulation and 10mm gypsum board inside. Opposite it, on the west elevation, is an exposed concrete frame consisting of a pattern of non-structural mullions and of columns at approximately 4m centres. Seven concrete frames, spaced at up to about 4.5m centres down the length of the building, join these two long sides together, the two end frames, with some additional concrete mullions, being made into gable elevations that are similar in appearance to the west wall. Except in one position, where only one column could be allowed, each frame has two interior columns 240mm square with a beam of 350mm depth and 240mm width supporting a 160mm slab. In the basement the slab is 250mm thick and the walls have a minimum thickness of 300mm in order to give a reliable quality of

Lowest three storeys on N elevation (photo by Friedhelm Thomas).

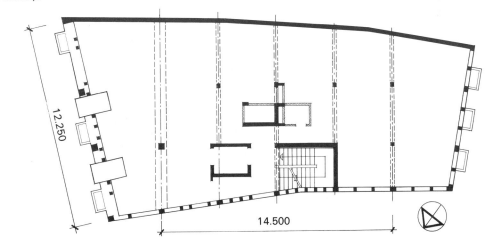

Ground floor plan.

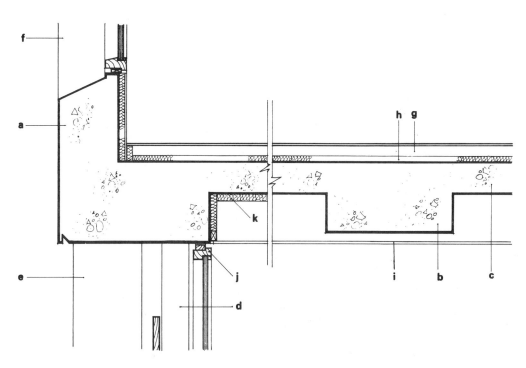

a 310 x 710 mm upstand beam; b 650 x 350 mm interior beam; c 160mm slab; d 140 x 175 mm mullion; e 350 x 350 mm column behind mullion; f 240 x 175 mm mullion; g screed with finish; h foam and mineral fibre isolation; i ceiling; j window frame; k 30mm rigid insulation.

Vertical section through floor at level 2.

View of building from NE (photo by Friedhelm Thomas).

concrete against water seepage. Windows are set in wooden frames, the vertical members of which are set behind the concrete columns and mullions and not seen on elevation. The roof rafters are of timber, excepting the gable rafters which are made of concrete.

Structural Action

As usual in a building with complex planning, only a one-way spanning slab gives the necessary flexibility in arranging columns and other vertical supports. For its purpose the beam and slab floor system is economic and adaptable, the spans of the slab being nearly optimum. In the shop, beam widths rather than depths were increased, to save overall height. The perimeter beams are a mixture of upstand and downstand beams, which emphasise the floor lines on the elevations. Wind loads on the building are insignificant and, such as they are, taken by frame action. Indeed the building could suffer considerable structural damage without this affecting its overall stability.

Construction

About half the cost of cast-in-place concrete is attributable to formwork and, in most buildings, economy dictates constant reuse of formwork and a high rate of turnover. In this kind of building, however, which is on a small and irregularly shaped site, these standards cannot applied and unit costs are always high. The exposed concrete on elevation has a boardmarked finish to give grain to the surface and, for this reason, was preferred to precast concrete which was felt to look too 'flat'.

The concrete is expected to weather without the darkening, due to accumulations of dirt, that occurs in more polluted atmospheres. All concrete was pumped. The total period of construction was 18 months.

Conclusion

A concrete framework has been designed that, on elevation, integrates the structure and enclosure as well as giving window arrangements suited to the interior spaces at a scale suitable for the area. The frame is a rugged, fireproof structure which is relatively easy to build even on an awkward site but which also gives scope for different internal plan arrangements.

KRON APOTHEKE (1977)

Description:
Five-storey building of concrete frame construction
Architect:
Werner Luz
Structural engineer:
A. Stumpf

Axonometric
view from N:

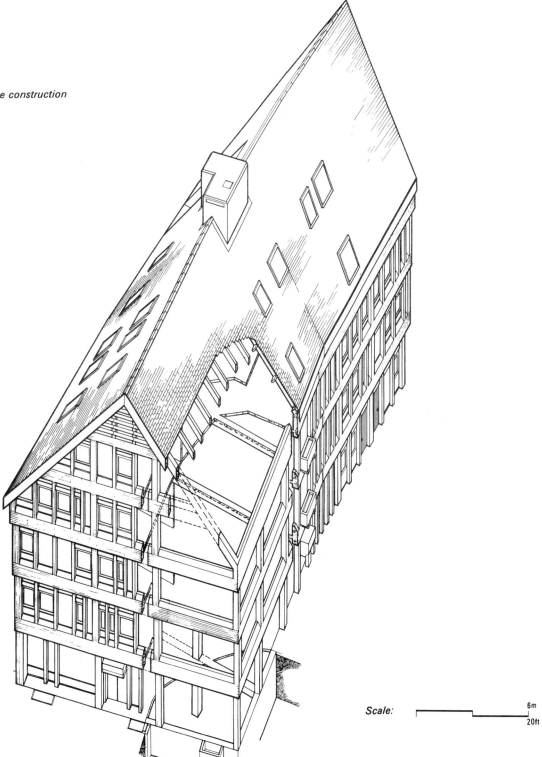

Scale:

6m

20ft

South Holland Centre, Spalding, England

Introduction

Not many buildings have deeply modelled elevations with such a medley of different elements in them as this. The treatment is a response to the almost toytown character and scale of the market square which this building overlooks and can be seen as a conscious attempt to echo the variegated appearance of the townscape. But these elevations are not merely free compositions. For those familiar with it, this particular piece of iconography has meaning in terms of the room functions and the technical requirements of the building structure. The Centre is a large, multipurpose public facility containing halls, meeting rooms, exhibition and storage spaces and also includes a lounge bar and a kitchen. The structure of the building is interesting on account of its use of fully engineered loadbearing brick, a somewhat neglected form of construction with medium or long floor spans; because this structure rests on compressible soil it has had to be designed to cope with differential movement. The construction is notable, too, for the range of standard techniques adopted in all its various parts.

Description

The building can be thought of as four separate entities with front, middle and back units and a small plant room block at ground floor level on the south corner of the building. These divisions correspond with planning divisions but, more particularly, with the structural arrangement, each unit being a separate structural entity with a 25mm movement joint separating them. The two movement joints separating the three principal blocks run straight across the building, being reflected by parapet lines in the roof, and extend right down through the foundations. The front unit, on its north-west elevation, overlooks the market square and contains four single-storey height floors above ground level, as well as a basement below; in this unit are contained the entrance and foyer at ground level, toilet facilities above this, a lounge and bar above this level and overlooking the square, with utility rooms and a balcony on the top floor. The middle unit, with the

View of centre from NW.

SOUTH HOLLAND CENTRE (1974)

*Description: Four-storey building of loadbearing masonry
with precast and cast-in-place concrete
Architects:
Ruddle Wilkison and Partners
Structural engineers:
Stirling Maynard and Partners*

*Axonometric
view from N:*

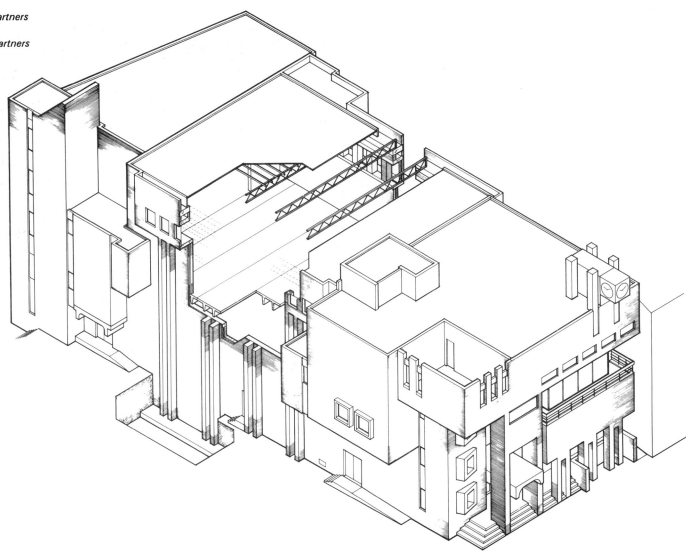

Scale: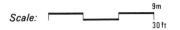

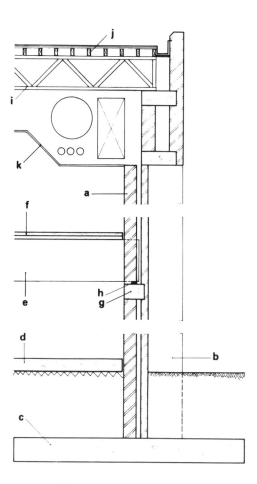

a 381mm brick cavity wall with 225mm inner leaf and 108mm outer leaf; b 2/ 340 x 573 mm piers at 4.21m centres; c 3600 x 350 mm concrete strip foundation; d 200mm floating ground floor slab; e 16 125 x 2388 x 711 mm prestressed double-T units with 10 cables in each rib; f 50mm topping; g 345 x 200 mm concrete bearing strip; h 120 x 100 x 10 mm neoprene bearing pad under each rib; i 127 x 711 mm deep cold-formed steel trusses at 3m centres; j 50 x 150 mm softwood joists at 600mm centres on firring strips; k suspended ceiling with acoustic plaster and ventilation ductwork above.

Vertical section through wall on NE side.

View of piers on NE side.

same overall height, contains two double-storey height floors, a small hall, meeting room and kitchen at ground floor level and a main hall at the level above this. The back unit has two single-storey height floors below the main hall floor level, which contains changing rooms, a workshop and a store, and above this level there is a double-storey height space for a stage and fly tower. The principal stair access is a square-shaped spiral staircase, in the front unit, against the south-west side, leading from the basement to the main hall level; from ground floor level up, it is supported only off the ends of the three slabs it connects together. There is also an enclosed stairway next to

the lift in the front unit, the lift motor room being positioned above them at roof level; another escape stairway is provided at the east corner and another lift near the south corner of the building.

Generally the building has cast-in-place concrete floors supported by brickwork walls and columns, although, outside on the north-west elevation, the six small columns and the two large columns either side of the entrance are concrete with a brick surround and in the middle unit of the building, the floor of the main hall is precast concrete. The structure of the middle unit consists of two 381mm thick brick cavity walls with the main hall floor and roof spanning them. These side walls are buttressed by 340 x 573 mm deep piers at 4.21m centres giving an overall depth at pier positions of 954mm; the main hall floor consists of prestressed precast concrete double-T floor units, 2388 x 711 mm deep with a 50mm cast-in-place topping; adjacent units are welded together by means of steel inserts at 2.40m centres along the edges, the floor thus forming a rigid diaphragm. The strip foundations to the side walls are taken below a soft clay layer to sand which, however, contains peat and is liable to settlement; the width of the foundation is a minimum of 3.60m because of this. The stability of the whole middle unit of the building is assured by four 225mm thick return walls, all about three metres long, on one side or other of the wall on the south-west elevation, all being founded on the same wall strip; the two inner return walls terminate at the main hall level. All other ground floor walls at right angles to the side walls are separated from the main loadbearing walls by vertical movement joints and have separate strip foundations but only 500mm wide.

The back unit of the building is similar in principle to the middle unit but the two loadbearing walls now run across the building in a north-westerly direction with cast-in-place floor slabs spanning them; at the hall level, the slab cantilevers over the wall on the south-east elevation. The foundations for these loadbearing walls run in a continuous strip under the four walls of the unit with a minimum width of 2.35m. For both middle and back units the ground floor is mesh reinforced concrete slab floating on fill. The front unit of the building is founded on a 450mm concrete raft at basement level which is stiffened by concrete basement walls that in general are

300mm thick. This was necessary because the unit contains a multiplicity of structural forms which all work together and cannot tolerate differential movement. The concrete columns on the north-west elevation appear to be separate but, although they rest on strip foundations outside the raft foundation, they are in fact tied back to the basement by concrete shear walls below ground level and this prevents differential movement; the shear walls are 2.75m deep with a thickness equal to the overall thickness of the columns, and have to project forward from the front wall of the basement by 2.65m. Because of the presence of existing foundations on the south-west side at a higher level than the basement, the basement raft was stopped about a metre short of the boundary line and the slab cantilevered out at ground floor level to carry the weight of the new boundary wall.

Structural Action

Horizontal forces on each structural unit are taken by unreinforced brick shear walls; these are walls designed to take horizontal forces that are in the same plane as the wall. Masonry walls are very resistant to forces in their own plane, especially if the walls carry significant vertical load. The floor slabs act as rigid diaphragms to distribute any applied horizontal force between all the walls in a unit in proportion to the stiffness of each wall in its own plane. In the case of the middle unit, the roof and main hall floor planes only make a hinge connection with the side walls but the wall on the south-west elevation has a sufficient number of return walls to stabilise both. The transverse walls at ground floor level have their own narrow strip foundations separate from the main foundation strips in order to allow differential settlement to take place. Although this system would not be suitable in earthquake areas, it is adequate here. Above the main hall level the piers of both sidewalls have sufficient strength as cantilevers to resist all horizontal forces.

Construction

The building was constructed over a period of 26 months. The floor slabs were built at each level before the brickwork was taken higher. Wooden props to the existing building on the south-west side were built round until support was available from the new building.

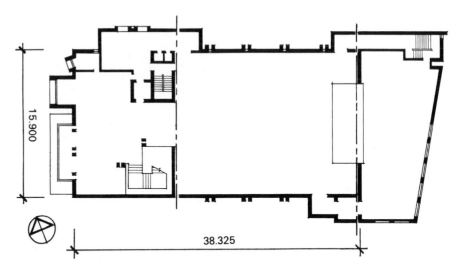

Main hall floor plan.

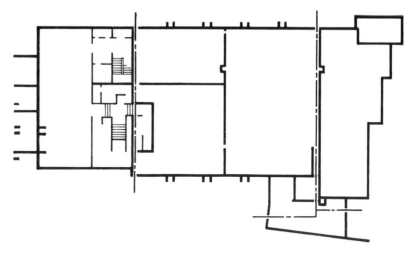

Basement plan and substructure.

Conclusion

The interior spaces are the results of patient planning and, except for the foyer and lounge, are left plain. The elevations that wrap round this assemblage of spaces are a unifying element and are as heavily featured as rubber masks to give really substantial relief and character to each face of the building. The building is original in its choice of masonry over the steel frameworks normally used to cope with differential settlement and a demonstration of the versatility of loadbearing masonry and cast-in-place concrete in handling complex forms.

St Antony's College, Oxford, England

Introduction

These dining and common room facilities were designed for a postgraduate college short of large funds but prepared to pay for a building up to the standard of the University's past, and are one of the best examples anywhere of the quality achievable in precast concrete. Flat and shaped precast concrete cladding panels are set into but kept separate from a precast concrete frame structure in which neither structure nor cladding is allowed to dominate, both forming part of an ordered composition.

Description

A basement built of 1ft (300mm) thick concrete walls occupies part of the plan area and contains a boiler, services and storage areas. The ground floor is set in from the floors above and is largely glazed on elevation. It contains dining and meeting areas and a bar on the west side. At first floor, above the bar, is a double-height dining hall with the kitchens on the east side. At second floor, above the kitchens, are common rooms. The roofs of the dining hall and common rooms have precast concrete diagrid roofs. Cast-in-place concrete is used for the floors and basement but otherwise all structural elements are in precast concrete which are exposed and help to define the interior spaces. Elements are laid to one of the two rectangular plan grids, one parallel and one skewed at 45 degrees to the sides of the building. The precast columns, being octagonal in plan, incorporate both grids, and have 6in wide faces with corbels of the same width projecting from any face, as necessary, to support 6in (150mm) wide precast beams. Vertical dowel bars project from the corbels into oversize holes at the beam ends. The beam widths are inconveniently small for detailing but were dictated by the column size and geometry. At the tops of the columns at ground floor level, a four-fin column head takes the floor slab at level 2 lining up with the skew grid. The columns were precast with a continuous 2in (50mm) central hole to take long dowel bars which make the connection between the storey-height units at each floor level. They are grouted up after erection. Double-storey columns are

View of entrance to building from W.

ST ANTONY'S COLLEGE (1971)

Description:
Three-storey college building with precast concrete frame
and precast concrete cladding panels
Architects:
Howell, Killick, Partridge and Amis
Structural engineers:
Harris and Sutherland

Axonometric
view from SE:

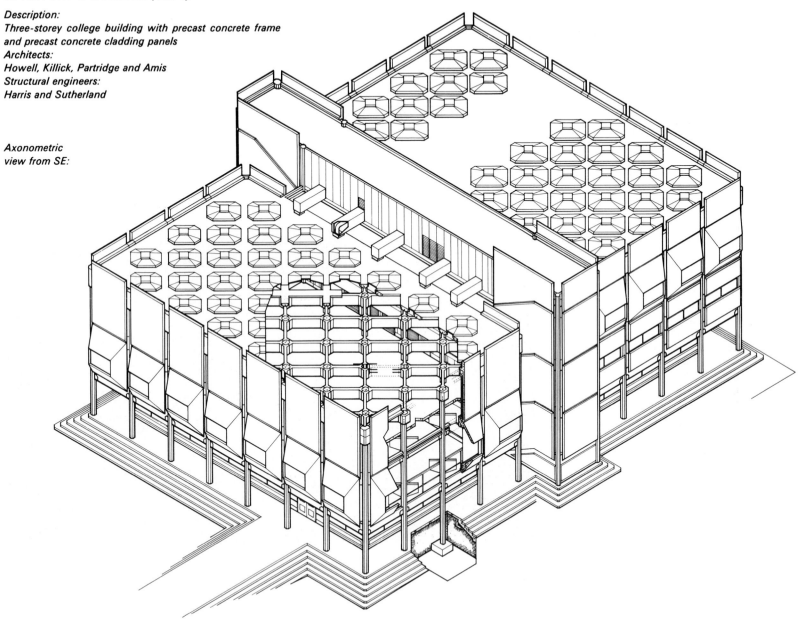

Scale: 9m / 30 ft

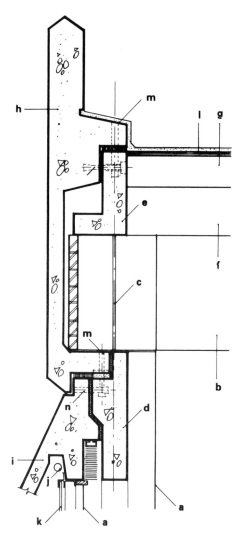

a edge of precast column; b precast diagrid unit; c joint of diagrid and column cap units; d precast beam; e cast-in-place beam; f cast-in-place flange of diagrid; g timber framing; h precast parapet unit; i shaped precast concrete unit; j lighting; k glass line; l asphalt on felt and plywood; m dowel bar; n phosphor bronze bolt and socket.

Vertical section through parapet.

View on SW corner showing four-fin column head.

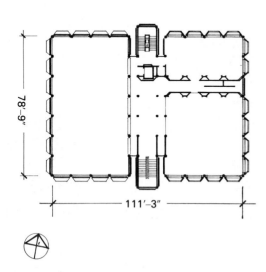

Second floor plan.

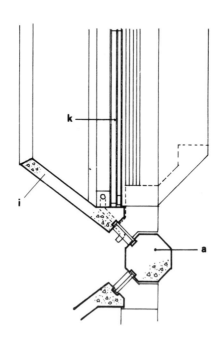

Horizontal section through column.

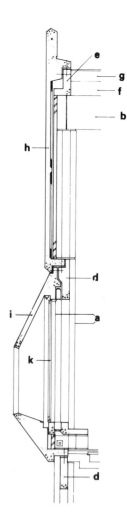

Vertical section through wall of main hall.

made by post-tensioning two units together which gives them adequate bending strength.

The floor slab at level 2 has a span to depth ratio of forty, a high figure made possible because of the fixity provided by a double row of columns around the perimeter. The diagrid roof is of considerable interest both visually, in the way it breaks a single grid pattern, and as a method of constructing slabs with two-way action even over rectangular areas. The exposed bottom part of the diagrid is made up of deep precast sections; the top part, hidden behind wooden louvres, is cast-in-place with a variable width to suit the bending moments. Because of their narrow width and the need to form neat joints the diagrid units are post-tensioned together by steel rods. Both artificial and natural lighting is provided in each square of the diagrid. The cladding of the building is made from plain or precast panels with a white aggregate granite finish. The shaped cladding units are most effective from the inside controlling glare and providing a sense of enclosure and a framed view of the outside; they incorporate space at the top for a timber slatted blind and a lighting tube to illuminate the inside surface of the panel at night. The panels are separated from the columns by a slit of glass and the main glass line is set back from the front of the unit. A plant room is placed on the roof between the two diagrid roofs. Heating elements are placed below the window sills and hidden by precast seating units.

Structural Action

The primary structure consists of precast columns and beams tied into the cast-in-place floor slabs and the diagrid roof. In the upper part of the hall, as the precast beams could not be tied into a floor slab, extra bars project horizontally from the

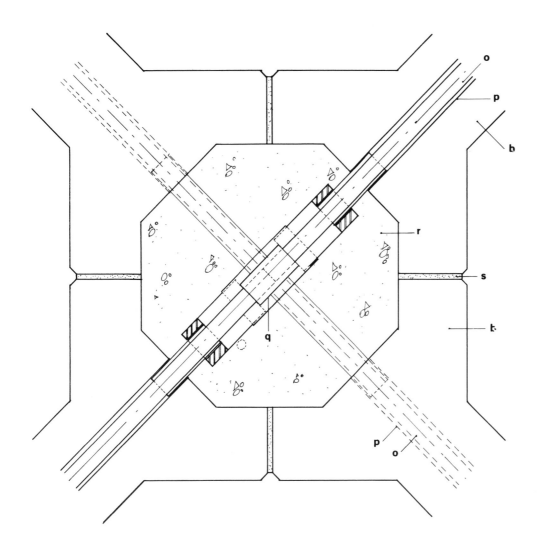

o 1″ diameter prestressing bar; p plastic tube filled with grout; q coupler; r cast-in-place concrete; s dry packed mortar.

Horizontal section on diagrid roof connection.

View on SE corner (photo by Bruno de Hamel).

column and are cast into the precast beams either side to give continuity. Wind forces are taken by frame action and the stair and lift cores. Of fundamental concern is the definition of likely construction errors and variations in dimension of the precast units in order to be able to specify figures for joint widths and tolerance. A related problem is the variation in position that the joint design allows while still maintaining the joint strength and preventing variations in joint width becoming unsightly. Here there is a nominal joint width of $\frac{3}{4}$in (20mm) between the precast columns and beams, a $\frac{3}{4}$in (20mm) vertical dowel bar projecting from the corbel being grouted into a $1\frac{1}{2}$in (38mm) hole in the beam ends.

Construction

The total period of construction was 24 months, production of precast units starting 6 months ahead of the start on site. Propping of the precast columns was avoided by using $1\frac{1}{4}$in (32mm) diameter steel bars in the 2in (50mm) diameter hole down the centre of the joint. The heaviest precast unit was the shaped cladding panel weighing about 6 tonnes.

Conclusion

The building is a good example of the successful use of modern methods to construct a building with a feel of permanence. The castellations, the bare window openings and the discipline of the geometry help to suggest the tradition in which this building takes its place. The splitting of the building into two main blocks and the almost insectile thinness of the cladding panels retain the formality of the arrangement but dispense with any grandeur that might attach to the building. The interchanging of the plain and shaped panels appears somewhat quirky but is dictated by function. The finish and precision manufacture of the precast units justifies their choice; the diagrid roofs are particularly successful. The problems raised by the geometry and joints have been satisfactorily solved. As in all precast work there is a paramount need to reduce both the number of types of unit and the number of moulds to produce them. Here there were 216 types of unit, requiring 67 drawings which was somewhat greater than half the total number of drawings.

Inside of hall.

Guilford County Courthouse, Greensboro, North Carolina, USA

Introduction

This courthouse building is one of three important civic buildings facing onto a central public plaza. The east elevation of the building, facing the plaza, has distinct classical overtones and is orchestrated to make the maximum use of relief between the different surfaces and volumes. The building makes remarkable use of precast concrete both in obtaining a very high quality surface finish, which would justify its description as 'cast stone', and in the ingenious shaping of the precast floor elements to simplify the construction process and therefore lower costs. However, cast-in place concrete is used to make the major structural connections, thereby avoiding the cumbersome details associated with joining precast elements to each other. The design is unusual for its thorough and disciplined approach, particularly in its consideration of concrete as a building material and as a method of building. The result of this is a building that gives high quality at a reasonable cost.

Description

The columns of the building are cast in place and on an alternating grid of 10ft and 42ft (3.00m and 12.80m) in the north-south direction and 24ft (7.30m) in the east-west direction. Precast double-T floor units span north-south and connect into and are supported by cast-in-place beams, in the east-west direction, which have soffits flush with the units. The precast units contain a slab, ribs and, in most cases, diaphragms connecting across the ribs. The end diaphragms are used as formwork for the cast-in-place beams. All units are 1ft 10in (0.55m) deep, 4ft (1.21m) wide and covered with a 2in (50mm) topping of mesh reinforced concrete. The columns are supported by pad foundations which are pyramid-shaped in order to save material. On the north and south faces, the units are cantilevered. In some of these cases a connection is made at the first cast-in-place beam line by welding reinforcing bars from the cantilever unit to similar bars projecting from the adjacent interior unit. In other cases a longer unit is used and is supported by the first two lines of cast-in-place beams, so that the welded

View of SE corner of Courthouse (photo by Gordon H. Schenck).

GUILFORD COUNTY COURTHOUSE (1971)

Description:
Four-storey building, with two parking levels below, with precast and cast-in-place concrete frame and precast cladding
Architects:
Eduardo Catalano
Structural engineer:
Deborah Forsman

Axonometric view from SE:

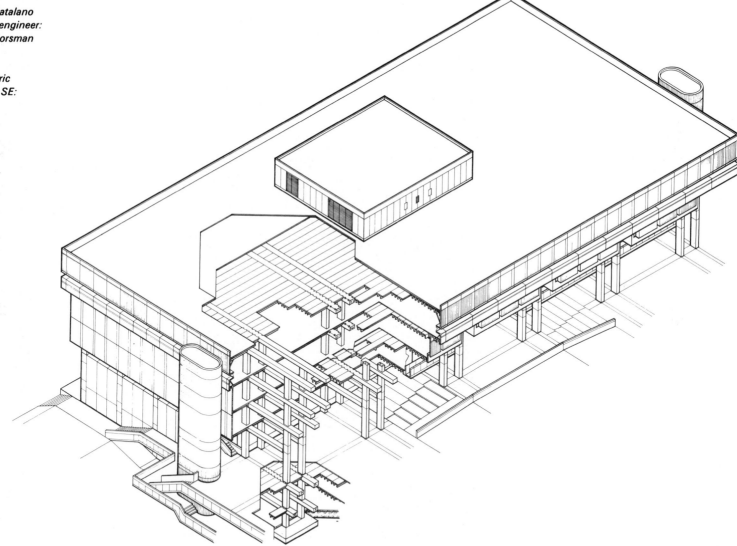

Scale:

12 m

40 ft

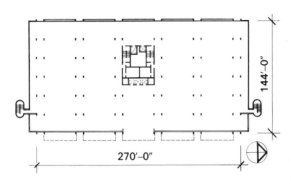

144'-0"

270'-0"

Second floor plan.

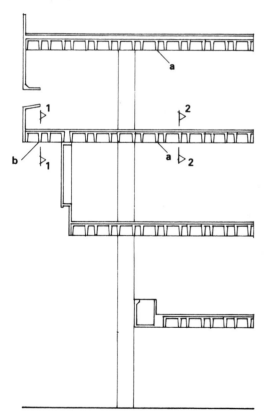

a prestressed double-T unit; **b** reinforced double-T unit.

Vertical section through E elevation.

View of S side of Courthouse (photo by Gordon H. Schenck).

connection is unnecessary. In the latter case, where this unit crosses the first beam line, its slab is eliminated and the rib reduced in depth so as not to interfere with the integrity of the cast-in-place beams, or the columns, where they occur. The units with diaphragms were used in all places where the soffit of the unit was exposed and give a pattern to it. Where a suspended ceiling was used the unit had no diaphragms and was prestressed, the anchors for the prestressing strand at each end of the unit not being visible, therefore. Precast concrete panels were used on all elevations together with some cast-in-place elements. The precast panels were welded or bolted to steel angles which in turn were welded to steel plates set into the floor structure. A buff coloured cement was used for all exposed concrete. Precast panels were sandblasted to expose coarse aggregate after the concrete had obtained a strength of at least 4000 psi (28 newtons per sq mm). Some cast-in-place surfaces using the same coarse aggregate were also sandblasted and achieved a remarkably similar appearance. The building is heated by electric coils in the air-handling units and by electric radiation. Cooling is by chilled water coils in the air-handling units. The water is chilled to 45°F (7°C) by two 350 ton (of refrigeration) centrifugal chillers on the bottom floor and piped to the air-handling units in the plant rooms on the roof.

Structural Action

The reinforced and prestressed units work differently. The cast-in-place beams are, in general, monolithic with the reinforced units and poured at the same time as the slab topping. The cast-in-place beams supporting the prestressed units, on the other hand, are cast separately, cure and are then allowed to receive the load from the prestressed units through a bearing pad. The topping is cast and, after it has attained the required strength, the props to the unit are removed and it supports its own weight by acting as a simply supported beam. By grouting up the gap between the bottom of the unit and the beam, continuous beam action is achieved for all other loads. Lateral forces on the building are taken by frame action.

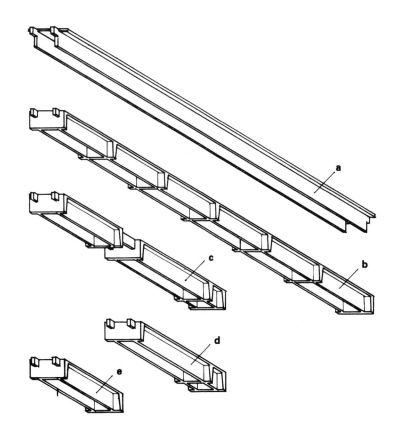

c long double-T cantilever unit; d short double-T cantilever unit used with e; e interior double-T unit.
Principal T-beam unit types.

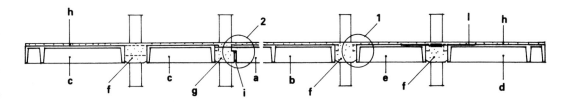

f cast-in-place beam poured with topping; g cast-in-place beam poured in two stages; h 2″ structural topping; i non-shrink grout to fill gap.
Typical vertical section through floor in N-S direction.

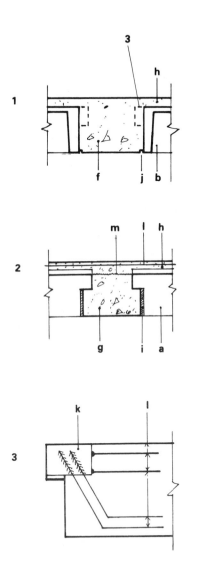

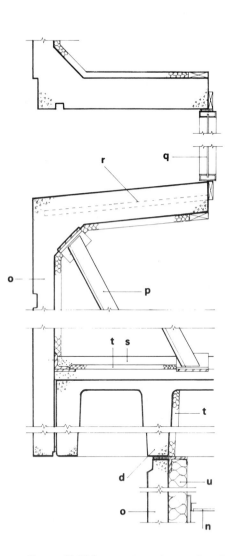

Construction

This building of over 180 000 sq ft (16 720 sq m) was completed in a period of twenty months. A very important factor in attaining good quality was the establishment of norms and control for the concrete work. Most joints in cast-in-place concrete were made with a recessed strip on the face of the concrete. In buildings with a large number of precast units a proliferation of different types of unit is inevitable. On this project many different types of floor unit were designed to be made by blocking out different parts of a single steel mould. This had a major effect on the costs of production. Most other concrete, precast or not, was cast against plastic coated plywood. Specified concrete strengths were 5000 psi (35 newtons per sq mm) for columns and precast work and 4000 psi (28 newtons per sq mm) for other work.

Conclusion

The building method adopted here seems to have squeezed all possible advantages out of the application of precast elements. The use of these components as formwork helps to simplify construction and to reduce time and cost. In some cases the frame may need to be built before the floor units are placed in order to speed up construction. Notable in this building is the high quality finish of the units in recognition of the clean atmosphere in this city. The fine, low relief would not be suitable in wet and polluted atmospheres where heavy staining may be expected. The architecture achieves its purpose giving variety in unity, appropriate scale and a strong but not too simple form. Yet the structure and construction process are relatively simple. This quality is all too rare in buildings that are highly industrialised. On this score the building must be reckoned as one of the high points in the art and science of building with concrete.

j rebate in beam; k steel plates; l reinforcing bars; m construction joint.

Detail sections in N-S direction showing cast-in-place beams (top and middle) and reinforcement at end of prestressed beam (bottom).

n ceiling; o 4" thick precast panel; p steel angle welded to plates cast into cladding and floor units; q window; r rebate (reglet) for sealant; s screed; t rigid insulation; u blanket insulation.

Vertical section through top of wall on N and S sides.

Design Research Building,
Cambridge, Massachusetts, USA

Introduction

This building uses a simple juxtaposition of large
areas of unframed glass and a mostly matt, grey
concrete. It makes excellent use of the glass.
Sandblasted concrete perimeter beams forming
horizontal bands on the elevation are held in check
by the vertical column elements, usually seen
through glass. The glass is a toughened
(tempered) one that spans between the perimeter
beams and is broken up both by these beams and
by the joints between the glass; the butted panes,
held only by small stainless steel tabs and a
silicone seal, are transparent, thus allowing the
shop goods on the lower floors to be seen from the
street while also superimposing reflections from
the sky and the surrounding areas. The balance of
transmission and reflection of light varies with the
angle, weather and time of day, giving the building
different aspects. With enough reflection on it
glass can become opaque. The faceting, or
stepping in and out of the building's frontage, and
the panes of glass at the corners, on diagonal lines,
further enhance the relief and play of light.

Description

The suspended floors and roof are all 8in (200mm)
thick concrete slabs, without beams. The columns
are placed on a two-way grid which is not
completely regular but arranged to suit the
planning. The slabs span two ways, with a
maximum span of 20ft (6.10m), in the interior, and
cantilever a maximum of 8ft (2.43m) at the
perimeter. The perimeter beam at the edge of the
slab is formed by a 4in (100mm) upstand and a
10in (250mm) downstand from the 8in (200mm)
slab, giving a suitable dimension on the elevation
as well as hiding the air conditioning duct which
runs round the perimeter. The circular columns
have 16in (400mm) diameters and are given a
spiral coil pattern by the formwork. Each column is
supported on a pad foundation about 7 x 7 ft (2.13
x 2.13 m) in plan. Below ground there is a 1ft
(30mm) thick retaining wall on a narrow strip
footing enclosing the basement. The basement
floor is a 6in (150mm) thick concrete slab floating
on compacted gravel. The toughened glass front is

View of building from SE (photo by Ezra Stoller © ESTO).

made in standard panes of 5 x 7 ft (15.20 x 2.10 m)
high, 1⅜in (35mm) thick spanning a height of 7ft
6in (2.28m) at the upper levels with two notches
on each vertical edge to accommodate stainless
steel disc fittings connecting it to the adjacent
panes. At the main entrance level, on the north
corner, the glass wall has a height of almost 13ft
(3.96m) and is split into two panes of glass over its
height with a steel T-section dropping from the
floor above to provide a support at the joint. Each
pane of glass is set into a rebate in the perimeter
beams 1½ x 1½ in (38 x 38 mm) at the sill, 1½ x 2½ in
(38 x 63 mm) deep at the head to allow
installation, and then caulked. There is a nominal
³⁄₈in (5mm) vertical gap between the panes which
is weathersealed by a translucent silicone sealant.
The inner and outer parts of the disc fittings are

held to each other by a screen thread which
tightens against a neoprene washer sealer. Other
stainless steel fittings are glued to the glass on one
side with an epoxy glue. At the bottom of some
panes there is a small area of glass, without a
frame, which hinges at its base to allow air in.
Registers coming through the floor are supplying
conditioned air from the duct below it, and are
generally provided at 5ft (1.50m) centres round
the perimeter with two smaller feeder lines down
the middle of some rooms. A masonry cavity wall
building on the roof houses the air-conditioning
plant as well as a gas boiler unit. There is a separate
condenser unit outside. Conditioned air is
supplied down a vertical shaft next to the elevator
and connects to the ducts at each floor level. There
are two staircases next to each other so that the

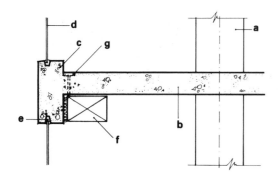

a 16″ diameter concrete column; b 8″ concrete slab; c 1′–10″ deep concrete edge beam; d ⅜″ thick toughened (tempered) glass; e 1½″ × 2½″ rebate (reglet); f duct with 1″ insulation; g floor register.

Vertical section through facade.

View of building from N (photo by Ezra Stoller © ESTO).

offices on the top two floors can have separate means of access. On the shop floors below this the slab soffit is finished by bolting 3 x 4 in (75 x 100 mm) wood plates to the slab which, in turn, receive 2 x 6 in (50 x 150 mm) fir pieces at 13in (330mm) centres. Ducts and lighting are fixed within this 10in (250mm) depth.

Structural Action

The floor slab is a flat slab without drop panels over the columns. In principle it is a two-way system with reinforced strips running in two directions over the columns. The system keeps the floor depth to a minimum and allows large holes in the slab if these are kept outside the column strips which are approximately half-a-span width across. Lateral forces are taken by frame action of

the flat slab and the stairs, elevator and service shafts which are reinforced concrete frames infilled with blockwork. The toughened glass windows have considerable extra strength and flexibility compared to ordinary annealed glass. The glass is quenched in water from a high temperature during manufacture, thus locking in a compressive stress on its surface so that considerable bending is needed before tension develops on the surface. Without internal flaws the glass can easily sustain the resulting locked-in tensile stress in the centre of the glass. All cutting and shaping must take place before the glass is toughened.

Construction

The building took 18 months to complete. Good

dimensional control was needed in positioning the rebates for the glass.

Conclusion

The surface textures and detailing of this are both carefully done and unfussy. With a similar area of glass, the use of double or triple glazing or heat-reflecting glass may be necessary in some climates in the interests of energy savings. In other types of building safety rails may be required inside the glass. Such changes to this building could subtly affect the design. In spite of technical development in joining and fixing of glass, this building remains an outstanding example of the use of glass and concrete and, in its shape and openness, a relief from both the crude and sophisticated versions of the glass box.

DESIGN RESEARCH BUILDING (1970)

Description:
Five-storey building of concrete flat slab construction with
toughened glass walls
Architects:
B. Thompson and Associates
Structural engineers:
Le Messurier Associates

Axonometric
view from SE:

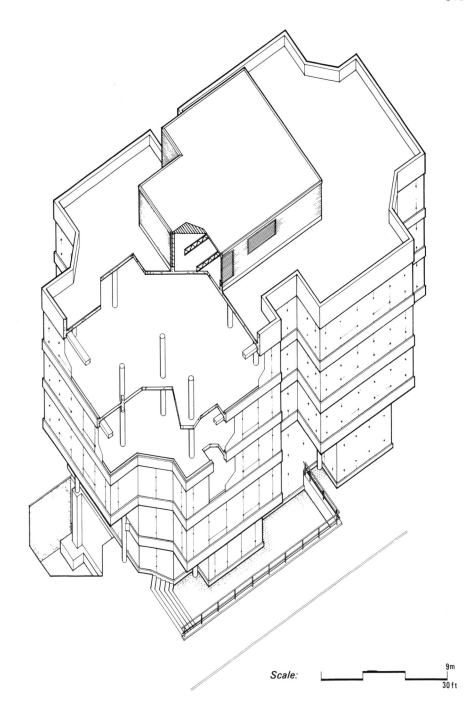

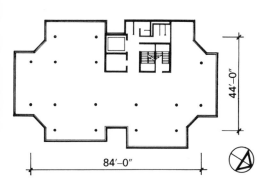

44'–0"

84'–0"

Typical floor plan.

Scale:

9m

30 ft

Centre Georges Pompidou, Paris, France

Introduction

This building became famous even before it was complete, because of its role as a national centre for the arts, and because of its uncompromising machine aesthetic. It was likened, in these two respects, to a cultural supermarket and to a process plant, the latter caricature being sharpened by the setting of the building in an historic area. Fundamental questions about the premises of the design were raised. In an attempt to get away from such questions of values, the building was declared by its designers to be a 'non-building', a neutral framework in which multifarious activities could take place to create a form of architecture based on the events themselves and the slow movement of people within the building. Even at the time, the idea of making such a refined-looking machine for the age of mass production, was not new and prefigured by ideas current in Modern Art more than fifty years before. But as a building it has no precedent in history and such direct precedents as do exist are from science fiction, a subject, appropriately for such a monument to Man's invention, with beginnings in the upheaval created by the Enlightenment. Certainly the giant size of the building and the hard sheen of the surfaces recall the imaginings of science fiction rather than anything in Modern Art. But the building is also original in its particular type of construction and detail. The space is mapped out by a structural frame more than 168 metres long and, in principle, extensible at its ends. Vertical service risers are placed outside, on the east face, and made into decorative elements. It is the structural frame which provides the organisation, controls the relief, scale and visual detail and, in the end, powers the whole design. It remains an extreme novelty: it has a vast scale bringing in new problems to do with the sizes of the spans, loadings and temperature movements, yet contains no movement joints; it makes considerable use of pinned connections, largely a consequence of its scale, to the extent that the internal primary frames become mechanisms; it contains a whole vocabulary of different types of elements and connections, including the use of cast steel connections, and it is this detail design,

View of Centre from SW (photo by Martin Charles courtesy of the Architectural Review).

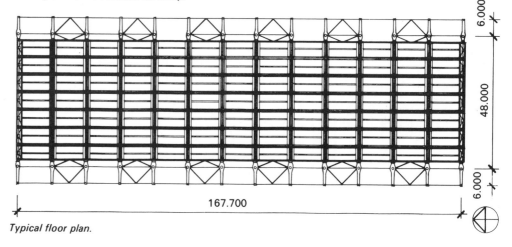

6.000

48.000

6.000

167.700

Typical floor plan.

CENTRE GEORGES POMPIDOU (1977)

Description:
Multi-purpose arts centre with six-storey articulated steel
superstructure and concrete basement levels
Architects:
Piano and Rogers
Structural engineers:
Ove Arup and Partners

Axonometric
view from NW:

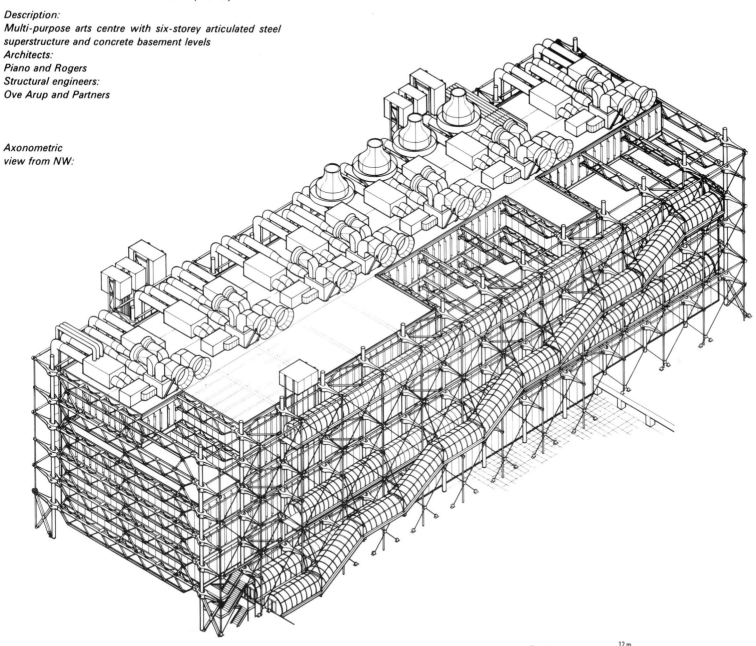

Scale: ⌐_⌐_⌐ 12 m
        40 ft

always vital in exposed steelwork buildings, that gives refinement to the structure and thus to the whole building. As a result of all the lines of structure and the way the elevational detail is set behind the structure, services and circulation routes, the cladding materials have only a secondary influence on the building's final appearance. Nevertheless the glazing used on three sides is important to the design concept of making the building appear 'transparent'.

Description

The building contains a collection of Modern Art, galleries for exhibitions, a library and other spaces including offices, terraces and a cafeteria; all these spaces are contained in the steel superstructure at piazza level and above. Below piazza level is a concrete substructure occupying an area on plan of 160 x 100 m, one part of which, below the steel structure, contains a large hall, a cinema, activity areas, storage space as well as heavy plant, the other part of which, underneath the piazza, contains parking space for 700 cars. Above piazza level, the design required six clear uninterrupted floors each 166 x 44.8 m in plan with movable suspended partitions on each floor to allow changes in use. Also a 7.60m zone each side of the 44.8m dimension was required, for movement of people on the west side, facing the piazza, and for distribution of services on the east side, facing the street. This zone mediates between the inside and the outside.

As built, the superstructure has fourteen plane frames, six storeys high, with a typical floor height of 7m, the frames being connected to each other by the floor slabs and by diagonal bracing on the long east and west facades. Each frame consists of two 850mm diameter round tubular columns, 48m apart, each column supporting six cast steel brackets which have a pinned connection with the column; each bracket takes a downward load, at its inner end, from the deep lattice truss supporting the floor, and this is balanced by the tension force in the tie attached at its outer end. The main lattice truss spanning 44.8m in the east-west direction has a midspan depth of 2.82m between the top of the twin 419mm diameter tubular top chords and the bottom of the twin 225mm diameter solid rod bottom chords. Single alternating tubular and solid diagonal members, taking compression and

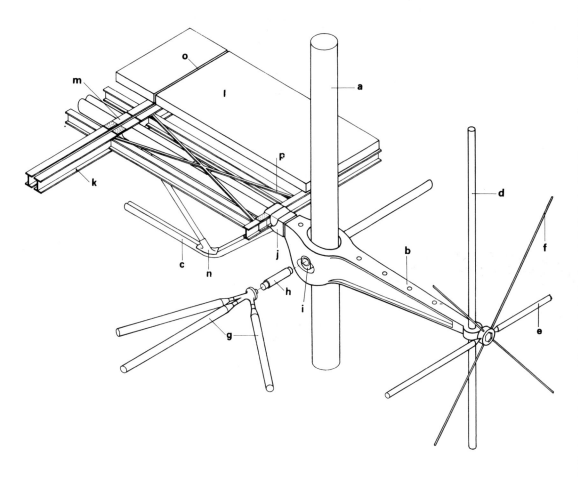

a 850mm diameter thick-walled, tubular column, water-filled for fire protection; b cast steel bracket weighing 10t with min and max wall thicknesses of 34 and 220 mm; c main lattice truss, 2.5m deep between chord centres, weighing 79t; d 200mm diameter high-strength solid rod vertical tie; e 355mm diameter tubular bracing with cast steel ends and hidden bolt; f 62mm diameter high-strength solid rod diagonal bracing; g horizontal tubular bracing with cast steel ends and hidden bolts for attachment to cast steel connecting piece; h axle piece; i doughnut-shaped unit with spherical bearing; j spherical bearing for truss; k 500mm deep rolled steel I-beam with fixed or pinned connection to truss; l 6.4m wide cast-in-place panel composite with steel beams; m position of precast concrete panel with crossbracing below; n cast steel nodes fillet welded to chord members; o joints in slab; p steel flat crossbracing connected to truss and floor beams.

Detail view of column and adjacent elements.

tension respectively, are attached to the top and bottom chords by welding to the cast steel connections that are at node points on the chords. The cast steel nodes on the top chord also receive ordinary rolled steel I-beams, generally 500mm deep, spanning in the north-south direction between the trusses. The I-beams and a 110mm deep concrete floor slab above it act compositely. Under vertical loading each internal frame functions independently of the others and joints are provided in the slab and in the steel beams to allow each truss to deflect independently of its neighbours. Resistance against horizontal forces is provided, on the east and west facades, by 62mm diameter high strength, pretensioned diagonal bars; the crossbracing is in panels two storeys high and connected to the columns and floor deck by horizontal tubular bracing in alternate bays at every other floor level. Horizontal forces transferred to the gable ends are resisted by the main lattice trusses which are connected together by diagonal tubes, 190 to 360 mm in diameter, so that each gable works like a vierendeel frame. Unfortunately the diagonal tubes could not be taken to street level between the columns, for planning reasons, and therefore heavy crossbracing has had to be provided outside the columns at this level. In general, solid round bars take tension and tubular sections take compression so that the actions of the structural members can be read and understood.

Other important elements in the composition of the facades are the secondary beams and columns for walkways, service runs, lifts and stairs: the secondary beams consist of two back-to-back steel channels usually strengthened by steel flats in tension and tubes in compression that turn it into a truss; the secondary columns consist of four steel angles symmetrically placed and connected to each other through spacers. The secondary beams span to the cast steel brackets and may easily be changed in position.

The engineering services required for the building are considerable, and complicated by the very different conditions within the building and by the fact that all services are exposed and integral to the architecture of the building. The external conditions for the design of air conditioning are 32°C dry bulb and 21°C wet bulb temperatures, in summer, and -8°C dry bulb

temperature with 80% relative humidity, in winter. Three electric boilers with a total rating of 6800 kilowatts are provided in the basement together with four storage vessels each of 115 cubic metres, which are charged overnight; three refrigeration plants with a total rating of 10 megawatts (3500 tons) are housed in the basements, two of which have double bundle condensers to recover heat from the return air system. Also in the basement are water storage and treatment facilities, electrical installations and other heat recovery equipment. Energy is distributed from the basement to users and plant rooms nearby and also, via green and yellow painted vertical risers on the east side, to the spaces above piazza level and to air-conditioning units on the roof of the building. The roof carries 26 independent air-conditioning units feeding back down large vertical ducts painted blue to each of the 13 bays of the building. To break up the bulk at roof level, each air-conditioning unit is split into its component filters, air washers, heating and cooling coils and axial flow fans; four cooling towers are also prominent on the roof. The air conditioning is a high velocity, dual duct, variable volume (VAV) system which can cater with large variations in the lighting level in any zone as well as complete shutdown of the zone. Apart from fire risers, all vertical distribution of services takes place in the zone outside the columns on the east side; there is some horizontal distribution in this zone as well as, inside the building, parallel to the main floor trusses. A 140mm high raised floor system is used at typical levels for wiring and small diameter pipes.

The curtain walls in the building are glazed except on the east side where they are opaque. The curtain wall is in line with the bearings for the main truss, 1.60m back from the column centre lines. The design has a clear, fully expressed system of pedestrian circulation. On the west side horizontal movement is through glass tubes within the outer zone and outside that, slung from the main structure like ships' gangways, diagonal glass tubes containing escalators take people up. Vertical movement is also possible by means of lifts and stairs on the inside of the glass tubes. There are four stairways on both the east and west facades for use as fire escapes. The fire precautions are extensive and all manner of techniques, active and passive, are used to protect the building

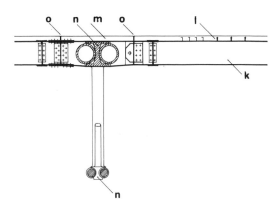

Vertical section through truss.

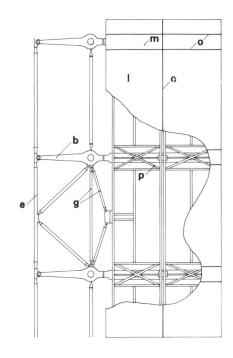

Part plan on floor.

Column at gable (photo by Harry Sowden).

against the effects of a fire. The principal structural members were required to have two hours' fire resistance, defined as steel temperatures of less than 450°C after two hours' exposure to a standard fire. The main trusses, including those on the gable ends, are clad with about 20mm of rockwool enclosed in stainless steel sheaths and the cast steel nodes are coated with a vermiculite based spray; floor beams are sprayed with rock wool. The bracing systems in the outer plane on the long facades are sufficiently far from the curtain wall, 7.60m, not to be affected by heat even from an intense fire. The cast steel brackets are shielded by fire-resistant panels in the curtain wall nearby. The columns are also protected by these panels as well as by water inside the columns, which can circulate and cool the steel such that the maximum temperature is kept below 170°C. Active fire protection is also provided in the form of sprinklers onto the brackets and onto the curtain wall. The horizontal bracing used near the curtain wall is redundant, and a large proportion of this may be lost without adverse effects. To prevent fire spread from floor to floor, the top 2.70m of the glazed curtain wall at each level has been given a fire resistance of two hours.

Additional protection behind the curtain wall is provided near stairs and lifts. Each floor is a compartment floor and each floor level is divided into two fire compartments by a fire wall. All openings in the floor or fire wall are blocked or can be blocked in the event of fire. For example a closable shutter is used in the air-conditioning ducts and where suspended ceilings are used, the voids above them are divided up by fire partitions on the lines of the trusses. Smoke extractors able to replace the air 10 to 12 times per hour are provided in the ceiling on each floor. Evacuation is by any of the eight stairways on the facades. Numerous sensors are provided as well as fire hose hydrants, sprinklers and automatic extinguishers using gas. The measures taken against fire deliberately err on the side of safety. Of all the measures taken, those principally concerned with life-saving are the sensors for rapid detection of a fire, the protected stair escapes and the smoke extract systems; the other measures are principally concerned with limiting damage. Both the compartmentation and the use of sprinklers limit the size and heat output of any fire. The safety of

the building structure in a fire was checked taking into account the abnormal temperature expansions of the structure and the ductility of the steelwork, including its increased ductility when hot.

Structural Action

The most striking and unusual features of the structural design are those brought about by the exposure and scale of the structure. Of particular note are the large number of pinned connections, such that, looked at in its own plane, each six-storey high internal frame is a mechanism, in the way that a piece of rotating machinery is; looked at in three dimensions, however, it is clear that any rotation is prevented by the floor slabs. The truss and bracket arrangement at each level is based on a Gerber system, originally devised to allow relative settlement of the piers of a bridge without affecting the distribution of forces within the bridge structure. With a distance of 48m between column centre lines and a live load of 5 kilonewtons per sq m, these floor trusses had to be heavy and comparable in size to those of a bridge. Double members were used for the top and bottom chords of the truss to minimise the truss depth and to provide it with some stability when in position. In spite of its size, large vertical movements of the truss, and therefore differential movements between trusses, had to be accepted. A result of this is that, in alternate bays of the building, floor beams have to have pinned connections with the truss at each end to allow this movement to occur; in the remaining bays the floor beams have fixed connections with trusses in order to stabilise the trusses against torsion. At this scale another movement which assumes great importance is the shortening of the top boom of any of the trusses under load; this causes considerable bending in the columns, which they must be designed to resist. On account of all these movements, the concrete floor slab is split into separate panels by 5mm joints running in the east-west and north-south directions, thus preventing stresses being induced in the slab.

Concrete panels over the truss are precast but the rest of the floor slab is cast in place. In spite of the movement joints, the slab is still able to act as a continuous horizontal diaphragm spanning between the gable walls, because the cast-in-place panels are attached to each other by small steel connectors at intervals; over the truss, steel flat crossbracing connects to a plate on the top boom of the truss and to the slabs on either side of the truss and thus maintains the diaphragm action over it. The concrete slab acts compositely with the steel floor beams, to limit overall deflection, but shear studs are only put over the central 10.40m of the 11.44m span distance in order to give some flexibility to the beams at its ends. The floor beams at the edges of the floor slab, on the long and short facades, pick up large forces from overall bending of the floor and from any temperature differences between the external crossbracing and the rest of the structure.

Other temperature differences also lock forces into the structure. The most serious of these are those caused by differential movement between the floors and between the foundations and the steel superstructure. The temperature differences are taken to be 25°C or 35°C for some bracing systems. These temperature differences cause forces in the horizontal and vertical bracing systems, which account for up to about 80% of the maximum forces in these members, as well as bending in the columns, which, however, is considerably relieved by the spherical joint at the base of the column. This joint allows a 'breathing' movement to occur. The size of members has to be optimised as any increase in size, while increasing strength, will also increase the temperature forces in the members too.

The cast steel columns, made by spinning molten steel, and the cast steel brackets, looking like rocker arms, are visible in their entirety from the outside. A pinned connection is used between each column and its brackets to avoid putting bending into the column, to which it is very sensitive, either as a result of normal floor loads or as a result of bending and rotation in the bracket due to any other cause, for example temperature movements. The bracket is supported on the column by an axle passing through the column, the bracket transferring load to the axle through a doughnut-shaped bearing unit which fits over each end of the axle; the unit can slide on the axle and the bearing inside is spherical to eliminate any problems with alignment. As the brackets are able to move, the horizontal bracing is framed directly into the axle passing through the column. The

View of Centre during construction (photo by Richard Ringoletti).

Interior view (photo by Harry Sowden).

The foundations for the column and vertical tie on each side of the frame are combined into a single wall 1m wide, up to 11m long and up to 20m deep. That part of the wall below excavation level was constructed like a diaphragm wall under bentonite mud and that above by standard cast-in-place work. The downward force of 5000 tonnes from the column and the upward force of 1000 tonnes from the tie tends to rotate the wall, and this is resisted by a basement slab at the top and by surface shear from the ground at the base and on the sides of the wall. Bursting forces immediately below the column are controlled by four pairs of prestressing cables in a thicker, flared out section immediately below the column base.

Construction

Very tight tolerances were used in the manufacture of the steel elements and connection pieces in order that they could be made to fit together on site. The tolerances are similar to those achieved in mechanical engineering. An important difference, however, is that in mechanical engineering the parts are relatively small, so that, unlike those in a building structure, the temperature at which assembly takes place is not a consideration and, anyway, can be easily controlled. In this building, once the problems concerning erection tolerances were overcome, many of the precision-made elements were self-erecting in the sense that these elements find their correct position in space because of their fit. In the case of the internal frames, because they are mechanisms during the construction phase, their final position in space is found only after the columns have been plumbed.

Each bay of this building was erected in about ten days, and the whole structure including pouring of the slabs took only eight months to complete. The main truss, which weighs 79 tonnes, was brought in as a single piece and erected by a mobile crane capable of handling this weight at a 34m radius. Two tower cranes on rails, one on the east side and one on the west side of the building, were also used for erection. The columns were brought to site in two halves that were welded together in the air; the tower cranes were used for handling the two halves. Steel erection started from the south end with the bottom halves of the first two frames: the bottom half of each column was temporarily bolted in

connection device used at the ends of the bracing is a cast steel node, which can be screwed into the axle and an internal concealed bolt at the ends of the bracing members then screws into the node. Connections to the floor deck and to other horizontal bracing members are similar.

The connections are well shaped, and help give the elements definition. At the outer end of the bracket, the ties above and below it both have a screw connection to a large nut fitting inside a seating made by machining of the bracket. At those brackets which connect to the vertical bracing panels, a large steel node is welded to the end of the bracket; the node is hollowed out to

take nuts for the diagonal and horizontal members framing into it. In all cases the use of screwed connections allows a construction tolerance by the variation possible in the depth of engagement. At the gable ends the connections between the trusses and the pairs of diagonal tubes connecting them together use a heavy pin. A spigot projects from the cast steel node of the truss and fits into a fork on the connecting member; it is held by a 150mm diameter steel pin which itself is held between steel plates at each end. A threaded connection between the fork and the rest of the member gives up to 20mm of adjustment from the central position.

position; then the first storey-height length of the vertical tie was attached to the foundations; the cast steel bracket was threaded over the top of the column and its axle driven through the column when the bracket was in position; the vertical tie was then connected to the bracket and the construction was temporarily braced. The mobile crane was then used to place the main lattice girders, and the same crane with an outrigger was also used to position the preassembled floor units, 10.54 x 6.40 m wide, consisting of steel floor beams and permanent shuttering; these bolted directly to the main lattice girders. The procedure was repeated after half the height, in each bay, was complete and after the upper half of the column had been welded on. This whole procedure was then repeated for subsequent bays of the building. Concreting of the floors followed one bay behind the steelwork erection. There was practically no welding on site, apart from that on the columns, almost all site connections being screwed or bolted. The total period of construction from the start of the substructure construction to completion of all work was 48 months.

In this contract, 65% of the 13 000 tonnes of steel used in the building was in the form of cast, rolled or forged items with thicknesses exceeding 160mm. For such thicknesses and with the defects that are present within the steel, the possibility of failure by brittle fracture has to be investigated. Fracture mechanics tests on full-size specimens with known properties gave the applied force which would initiate a brittle fracture with a known size of defect in a critical part of the steel specimen. Hence the local stress at the defect which caused fracture could be found and the necessary fracture toughness, which is a property of the metal, derived by considering that critical size of defect within metal which would cause brittle fracture under the actual stress and temperature conditions; this could then be compared with the likely size of defects in the metal as manufactured. If defects in the metal are less than the critical size, failure will not occur by brittle fracture. The minimum necessary fracture toughness for most items was calculated to be about 1500 newtons per $mm^{3/2}$. Ultrasonic testing was used to check for defects; the methods used had to be able to find defects of less than half the calculated critical size. Steel castings had two heat

treatments after demoulding: a normalizing treatment to make them more 'transparent' for ultrasonic testing and treatment to obtain a tougher microstructure. An extensive programme of tests was undertaken for the major parts.

Conclusion

The tracery of lines which make up the elevations are a magnificent invention and the better for precisely marrying appearance with utility. Inside, there is a lack of the daylight and the order that exists at the perimeter and this can be seen as a penalty of the need for adaptable space. The flexibility required meant that the interiors could not be designed as architectural entities and the more circumscribed and theatrical effects of interior design have to cope with the requirements. The gallery spaces, for example, suffer by comparison with art galleries designed from an interpretation of specific data and constraints. A question about the exact purpose of the Centre remains. The powerful framework, the circulation routes, the number of collections and exhibits and the sheer miscellany of activities are basic to the concept of the building but tend to undermine the idea of an arts centre by generating excitement, like a fairground does, at the expense of quieter space for the displays.

The popular success of the building and the redoubtable qualities of the building establish it as a reference point in recent architecture. It can be seen both as symbol for the impersonal, abstract world of technology and as a design that comes clean on the bundles of pipes and the lumps of equipment that are actually required to make large buildings work. Unlike a process plant, where the fittings are similarly exposed, the equipment and fittings here are made for display and maintenance of them is costly; the amount of detailed visual design of mechanical parts makes the building a phenomenon in itself. The building structure is notable on account of its technical innovations and its inside-out form; and, not surprisingly, its cost was high, amounting to 45% of the total cost of the building. In creating a working enterprise, the building is a major success. With its martian scale and engineering, it hints at facts about mass society and the forcing effects of technology that may not, even now, have been properly faced up to.

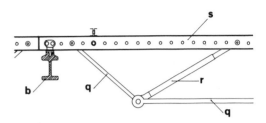

q steel flats; r steel tube; s 2 channel sections back to back.

Elevation on secondary beams.

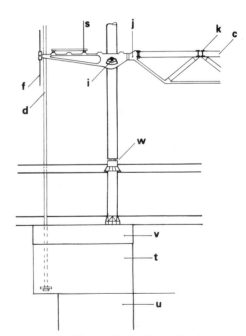

t upper part of foundation wall cast-in-place; u lower part of foundation wall cast as diaphragm (slurry) wall; v flared-out section with horizontal prestressing cables; w spherical column bearing at piazza level.

Vertical section through piazza and basement on W side.

Boston City Hall,
Boston, Massachusetts, USA

Introduction

Even when his comfort has been lavishly provided for, the hard pressed city dweller may sometimes feel some part of his dignity has been lost in the maelstroms of people and the shapelessness and confusion of modern cities. Indeed the historic role of the city as the setting for civilised life and discourse has been reduced, in many places, merely to that of providing basic facilities for commerce and government, while the major resources move to the suburbs. This building is one that helps to reverse this trend by restoring solidity, order and particular places to the city. For something as important as a city hall, it is appropriate that this is such a serious and complete piece of architecture and no mere skilful exercise in function, proportion or elevational effect. Though its style has only recent, and perhaps unfamiliar antecedents, the fundamental purpose of the building as a monument and symbol of a city is clear and, in this, the building establishes a necessary continuity with the past and appears to respond to the individual's sense of a public order and his attachment to rational values. It is a large building, there are nine floors, and the scale of the elements is vast, but this is a reassuring building to pass by and to walk through and only rarely, walking through, does a change of position fail to reveal a new aspect of the building, what has come to be a severe test of much recent architecture.

Description

The City Hall has the luck to be set in a large plaza paved with brick which allows the building to be seen from some distance as well as giving pedestrians access to the main entrances on the west and north sides. As the site slopes down from the south-west corner of the building, the north entrance is one level below the south entrance at level 3. At levels 2 and 3 are grouped those departments most frequently visited by the public; at level 1, the lowest level, are garages, storage areas and a very large plant room. The two entrances give on to generous lobby areas which are connected by a route of stairs and escalators. An open space at level 4, reached from the plaza by

View of building from W (photo by Ezra Stoller © ESTO).

outside steps on the west side, makes the building even more permeable to pedestrian traffic; this space is, in principle, dedicated to the public but it also serves to separate off the upper from the lower part of the building. The planning of the building is complex: level 5 accommodates the council chamber, offices, mayor's department, exhibition and library spaces, with each room being expressed by heavy modelling on elevation; the four remaining floor levels above are offices, the upper three of which have regularly spaced precast concrete fins, looking somewhat like a frieze.

A large well in the middle of these office floors allows a view out, and light in, from both sides. The two highest floors are stepped back from the inner perimeter line below, thus allowing more light into the well and making space for a terrace. As well as the external light well, there are two internal light wells created by shafts going straight from the roof to the lobby at level 3 near the south entrance. Above level 3 the room volumes increase and the scale stretches.

The cores at the north and south ends as well as columns, beams, walls, soffits and other exposed surfaces are mostly as struck cast-in-place concrete which is given texture by the formwork and scale by indented construction joints. These huge grey surfaces and seemingly massive elements are further pointed up and contrasted by natural or artificial lighting.

A unifying element in the design, is a special

BOSTON CITY HALL (1969)

Description:
Nine storey building of cast-in-place and precast concrete
construction
Architects:
Kallmann, McKinnell and Knowles
Structural engineers:
Le Messurier Associates

Axonometric
view from SW:

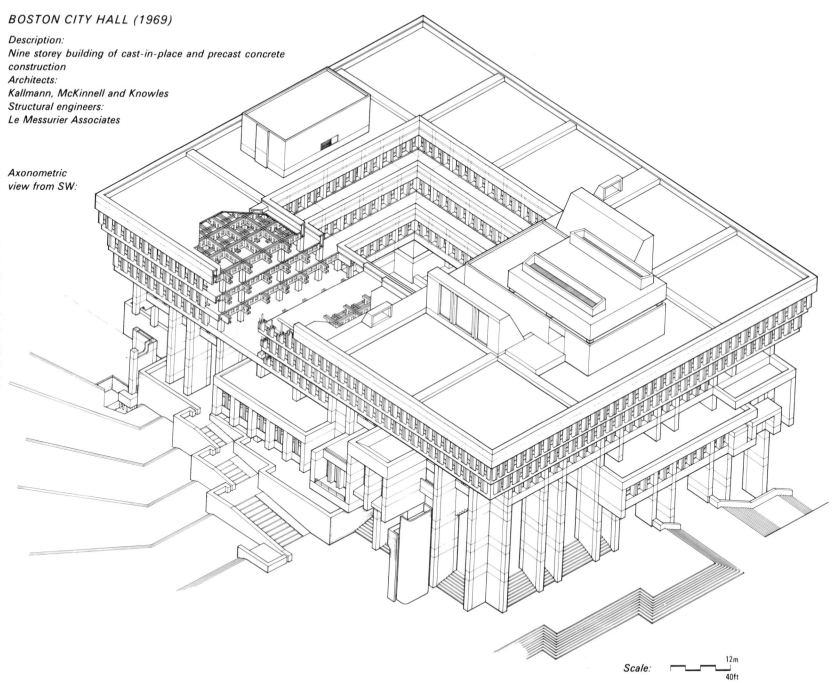

Scale: 12m 40ft

structural floor system, which is based on large concrete columns, 2ft 8in (810mm) square; these are spaced in two directions, either at 14ft 4in (4.37m) centres or double this distance. Pairs of precast concrete vierendeel trusses, 5ft (1.53m) deep and 11ft 8in (3.55m) long, run in both directions at 14ft 4in (4.37m) centres, lining up with the column faces and are joined to each other over the column which is cast-in-place or, where there is no column, by a cast-in-place joint of the same plan area. The 11ft 8in (3.55m) open squares so formed are subdivided into smaller 4ft 6in (1.37m) squares by cross-shaped precast concrete elements at ceiling level. The floor slab is cast-in-place concrete 5in (125mm) thick with a 3in (75mm) screed on top and an acoustic absorbent on the underside.

The air conditioning ducts, plumbing and electrical conduits run within the truss depth and are partly obscured by the strip lighting which is placed at the bottom between the pairs of trusses and the parallel bars of the cross unit. Below the trusses there is a clear height of 8ft 6in (2.59m) or 14ft (4.27m) at the ceremonial level, where the council chamber is housed. All columns are supported on piles. The parapet, spandrels and hollow vertical fins which form the elevation to the offices on the outer perimeter are all precast concrete units and contrast with cast-in-place concrete on lower floors. Some of the most important of these cast-in-place elements are the long fin walls, in fact made up by two standard columns with in-filling walls between them. At roof level there are two plant rooms, one incorporating a cooling tower. Above level 3 there are separate perimeter and interior air conditioning systems. The perimeter one, based on a three-pipe high velocity induction system, is fed from the roof, via pipes hidden in the hollow exterior precast fins, to induction units in the crash bar across each window; the interior system, a single duct high velocity variable volume system, is fed from the plant room at level 1 via vertical ducts in the cores to a main feeder running round the interior perimeter corridor at each floor level and, from there, to branch ducts every 14ft 4in (4.37m). The return duct for both perimeter and interior systems runs parallel with the supply duct for the interior system. Below level 3 there is also an interior system backed up by hot water radiators.

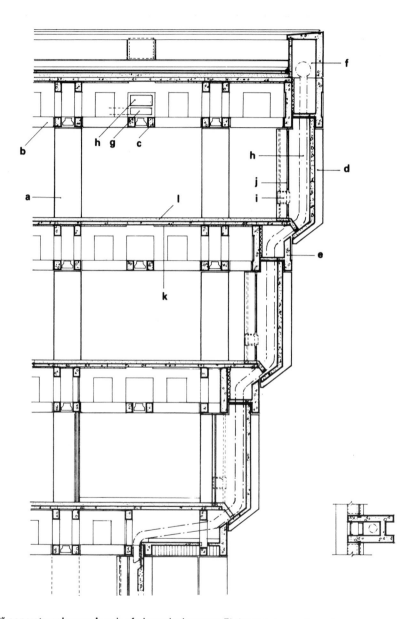

a 2′–8″ concrete columns; **b** pair of vierendeel trusses 5′ deep; **c** cross-shaped precast concrete elements; **d** precast concrete fin; **e** precast concrete spandrel; **f** ducts and piping; **g** supply duct; **h** return duct; **i** induction unit; **j** aluminium window frame; **k** acoustic absorbent; **l** 5″ concrete slab with 3″ screed.

Vertical section through facade.

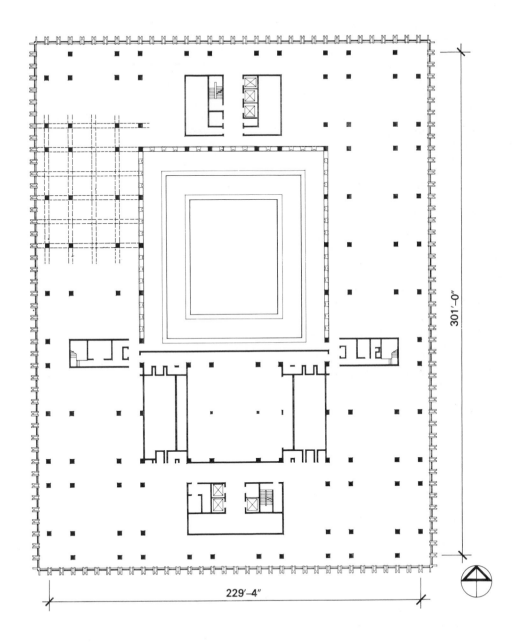

Ninth floor plan:

View of building from E (photo by Ezra Stoller © ESTO).

Interior view (photo by Ezra Stoller © ESTO).

Structural Action

Gravity loads are taken by the grid of beams which can span in two directions. Although the connections between vierendeel trusses at midspan are not to be recommended, the logic of the construction process is a more important consideration, here, than structural efficiency and the large depth of the truss helps to reduce the forces in the chords of the trusses.

Construction

The building has a total floor area of 513 000 sq ft (47 720 sq m) and complex spatial planning. In a number of areas high quality finishes to cast-in-place work were specified. In such cases, it is not possible to construct the building by means of a few simple and repeatable site operations. Therefore the organization of the building process is a major undertaking and construction costs are high. The total period for construction of the building was four years six months.

Conclusion

This project required not just expertise but resources and determination too. The organization of space in the building is excellent. The composition of the four outside elevations of the building is of a recognizable style, but done in masterly fashion, and, in its attempt to marry form and content, a fitting illustration for Pater's belief that 'all art continually aspires to the condition of music'. The elements have simplicity, weight and an appropriate interval given by the construction joint spacing and the column grid, while the frieze of precast elements at the top of the building establishes a contrasting, regular rhythm. In this more literal sense, there are parallels with music too. The elevations seem to capture some of the best qualities of concrete as an in-situ and precast material and the effect would be yet more dramatic in a sunnier climate. The decision to make a monumental form in concrete has had overwhelmingly good but occasionally bad consequences, one of these latter being the ponderousness to which concrete elements are prone. This building seems likely to remain one of the outstanding examples of the architecture of its time, however the times may change and whatever the future of the city may be.

Chapter Eight

Residential Buildings

The types of residential buildings that are included in this chapter are similar to apartment blocks and large housing schemes, except in the respect that they do not generally need to cater for permanent accommodation of family units and, therefore, are simpler to organize and plan. Looked at as structural entities, however, all these types of residential building are similar, because the subdivision of the floors, anyway at typical levels, allows use of the wall space for loadbearing elements. With the exception of those using a frame or staggered truss system, the buildings in this chapter all use the room dividing walls, themselves, as the loadbearing elements. If the walls are used as loadbearing elements, they must be lined up in plan at each floor level, in order to preserve the economy of this method of construction. The use of a loadbearing wall is an important method of building and applicable to a wide range of structures. It has more recently made a return in high rise building. In those cases where clear space is needed at lower levels, a standard frame may be used to carry the loads from loadbearing walls, or from staggered trusses, above, as some of the buildings in this chapter show.

Boulton House,
Cambridge, England

Introduction

This is a residential building in a garden setting, containing small study bedrooms for students. The elevations have a pleasing effect, attributable, in part, to good proportions and the extreme delicateness of the elements and the composition they make, including a 'layering' of the outside wall. This can be seen as a high-class exercise in the use of precast concrete elements and also as an imaginative interpretation of the needs of students in accommodation, particularly the relationship of the student rooms with other spaces.

Description

On the top three floors the building consists, essentially, of rooms, back to back, facing east and west; on the ground floor are college rooms requiring open space, so that a frame rather than loadbearing masonry was chosen as the structural system. There are 32 study bedrooms and 2 flats, as well as storage and toilet facilities behind blank panels over two bays on the west side. Each study bedroom squeezes in space for a bed, a desk, chairs as well as a basin and a built-in cupboard. A pivotal feature of this small space is a large window which opens up each room to the light. There is a window seat which projects forward from the H-frames, on elevation, and holds the aluminium window frame. This unit both frames the outside view and, closer to, provides a sheltered vantage point on it, thus making an interesting transition between the inside and outside or between private study and the vaguer but important attachments of community.

The building structure consists of eighteen stacked precast concrete H-frames around the perimeter and nine interior cast-in-place concrete columns, all supporting a heavy 9in (225mm) deep concrete slab at each floor level. The building foundations are piled, all precast columns being positioned in 2ft (600mm) deep pockets in 3ft (900mm) deep ground beams sitting on the piles. There are precast concrete infill panels between but set behind the H-frames, and these panels overlap on the columns each side. Infill panels are also used at right angles to the H-frames, having the same height as the spandrel of the H-frames.

View of building from NW (photo by architect).

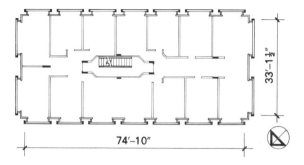

Typical floor plan.

BOULTON HOUSE(1968)

Description:
Four-storey residential block using precast concrete frames
with cast-in-place concrete slabs
Architects and structural engineers:
Arup Associates

Axonometric
view from NW:

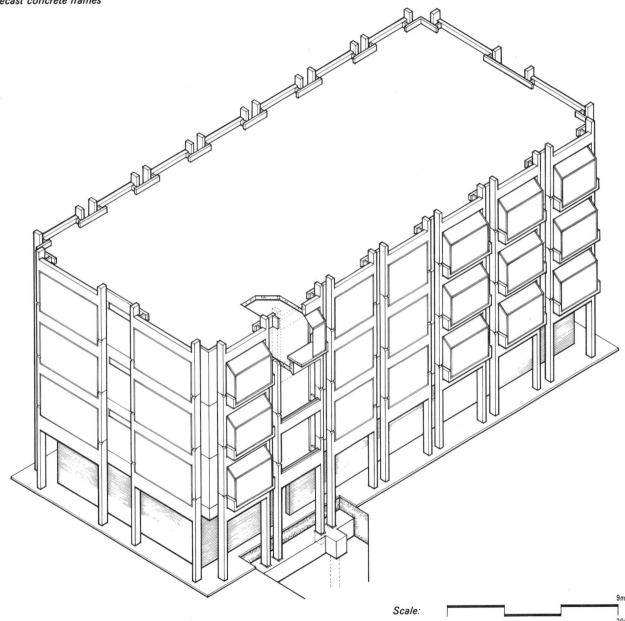

Scale:

9m

30ft

View of building from NW.

Both sets of panels and the H-frames themselves are tied into the cast-in-place floor slabs. The seating unit rests on the H-frame and is bolted back to the infill panels. The aluminium window frame fits over a recess on the seating unit, and against the vertical face of the infill panels and also into grooves underneath the spandrel-height infill panel and the spandrel of the H-frame above. There is an inward opening light on each side of the window frame to allow ventilation. The window incorporates a blind which passes round a roller at the junction of the sloping and vertical faces. A rail across the window serves as a backrest but also incorporates a heater to prevent downdraughts. All infill panels on the east and west sides as well as corner panels and the large plain wall panels on the north and south sides are 5in (125mm) thick and incorporate ¾in (19mm) of insulation.

The ground floor is set back from the perimeter and enclosed by a cavity brick wall with a clerestory light and by glass with fixed and sliding windows. Inside, the ground floor has a suspended ceiling 10in (250mm) below the slab soffit, the void containing services which then pass upwards through small holes in the floor slabs. Outside the ground floor enclosure, 10in (250mm) deep hollow clay pots are attached by light reinforcement, in 2in (50mm) concrete strips between the pots, to the slab above and are then plastered to make a flush surface; these pots serve as insulation and the spandrels of the H-frames at this level are made 10in (250mm) deeper to cover them. As well as a large common room on the south side, the ground floor also contains a kitchen, laundry, store rooms and a boiler room. There is no air conditioning; heating is provided by hot water fan convectors at the back of each study bedroom. There is only a single stairway for access or escape but this is surrounded by brickwork and fire-resistant doors at each level and at the ground floor leads through a lobby directly to the outside.

Structural Action

Internal columns are mostly at about 11ft (3.35m) centres; they are omitted at one place in the common room and here the slab has to span about 22ft (6.71m). Each floor slab carries the loads at that level, including the partition walls between study bedrooms which are 6in (150mm) heavy

View on S corner of building.

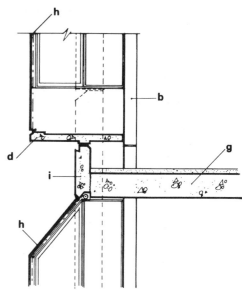

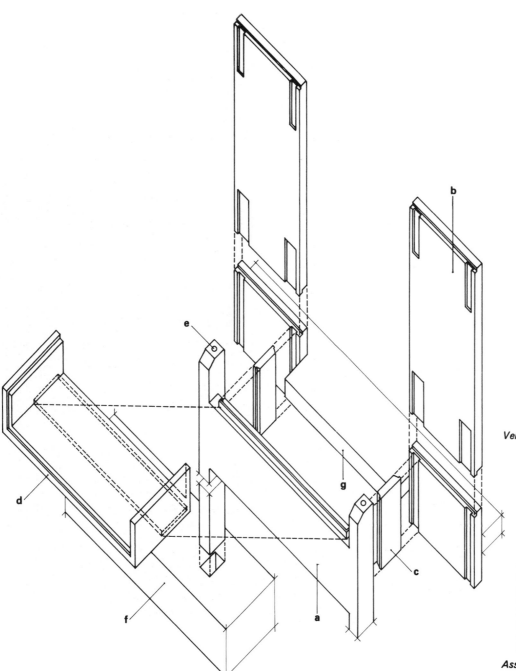

h aluminium window frame with opening light; **i** precast concrete H-frame with 1'–8" deep spandrel beam and $6\frac{1}{4}$" x $11\frac{1}{4}$" columns.

Vertical section through typical upper floor

a precast concrete H-frame with 2'–6" deep spandrel beam and $6\frac{1}{4}$" x $11\frac{1}{4}$" columns; **b** 5" infill panel; **c** 5" spandrel height infill panel; **d** precast concrete window seat; **e** $2\frac{3}{8}$" steel tube to receive lifting bolt for erection and 1" dowel bars from frame above with metal shims and mortar in final condition; **f** 3'–0" square section concrete ground beam with slots; **g** 9" cast-in-place floor slab.

Assembly of elements at floor above ground level

block plastered on both sides. Horizontal forces are taken by frame action. The precast elements have clean lines and, in general, connections between the elements are hidden. However the main joint between the H-frame columns is expressed by a 'bird's mouth' cut, a demonstration of the point made by the architect, Louis Kahn, that if designers were to draw 'stopping our pencil to make a mark at the joints of pouring or erecting, ornament would grow out of our love for the expression of method'. The joint consists of a metal shim and a dowel fitting into a tube which is then dry packed with mortar. With the joint made slightly below midstorey height, as here, the bending movements in the frame under vertical and horizontal loads are very little different from those in a four-storey frame without joints, so that in these positions the joints do not cause a loss of structural efficiency.

Construction

The total period of construction amounted to 14 months. The H-frames are erected one floor at a time and the floor slab poured before the sequence was repeated. The frames were lifted by the same threaded tubes at the column tops as are used for the dowel joint. Precast elements were made in wooden forms using white aggregates and white cement. Subsequently the window unit was acid etched and other elements given a rougher texture by bush hammering. The spandrel of the H-frame has its top sloped back towards the building so that rainwater can be led back behind the columns instead of running down the face. The bush hammering helps to disperse the rivulets of water on the surface.

Conclusion

This design is remarkable for its discrimination of the issues and its refinement, apparent in details, composition and the simple building method.

View on N corner of building.

Hyatt Regency Hotel, Lexington, Kentucky, USA

Introduction

This hotel building demonstrates both the economic use of conventional steel framing and a very apposite application of the steel staggered truss system. The upper floors are a completely 'dry' construction and a lesson in methods for building fast.

Description

Conventional steel framing is used on the lowest four floors, where open areas are required, but a staggered truss system is used in the upper part of the building, where the full-height trusses make the subdivisions of the space into hotel rooms. The lower levels have a column grid of 28 x 20 ft (8.53 x 6.10 m) and a framing scheme, which, for maximum economy, have the main beams spanning the shorter and the secondary beams the longer dimension of this grid. The floor slab is of 4½in (114mm) lightweight concrete, as usual, acting compositely both with the 3in (76mm) metal deck and the steel beams. Above the fifth level, staggered trusses are used and are spaced at 56ft (17.07m) centres at each floor level, taking the weight of two floors, one each at the top and bottom, and spanning to columns across the complete 60ft (18.29m) width of the building. Pratt type framing of the trusses, with diagonals in tension, is used. However, at the centre of the trusses, and, elsewhere sometimes, the diagonals are omitted to allow door openings. The floor here is of prestressed hollow core concrete planks, 8ft (2.44m) wide and 8in (203mm) thick, used without a topping. The vital shear connection between the floor planks and the top and bottom chords members of the truss is accomplished with shear studs welded to the chords and attached to reinforcing bars projecting from the planks. The voids are then grouted up. A steel space frame leans against one side of the building and roofs over a pleasant seven-storey air-conditioned atrium space. The external walls consist of various types of precast concrete cladding units. The internal partitions use gypsum board on metal studs. Where a truss forms the division, it is clad with two layers of gypsum board on each face. This achieves a two hour fire rating and

View of hotel from W (photo by Shin Koyama).

additionally provides for a high quality sound transmission barrier between guest rooms.

Structural Action

Wind forces on the short face of the building are taken by the frames on the long facade; moment connections between beams and columns are provided in this plane. With wind on the long face the horizontal forces are transferred from the floor

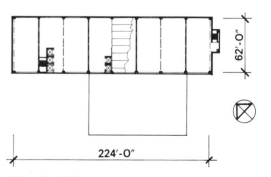

Upper level plan.

LEXINGTON HYATT REGENCY HOTEL (1977)

Description:
Thirteen-storey tower of staggered steel truss construction,
having precast cladding panels and glass atrium, with four-
storey steel frame below
Architects and structural engineers:
Ellerbe Associates

Axonometric
view of tower
from W:

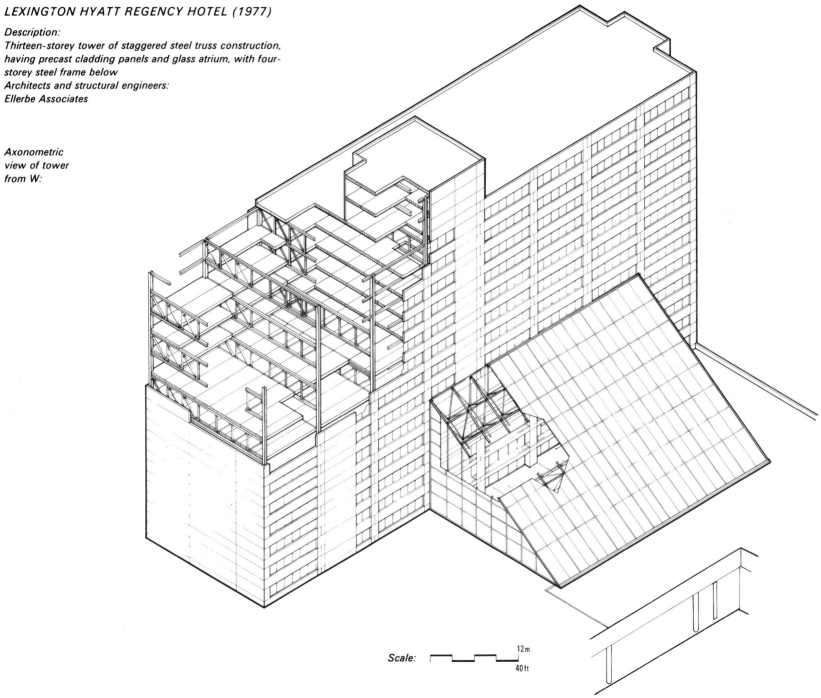

Scale: 12 m
40 ft

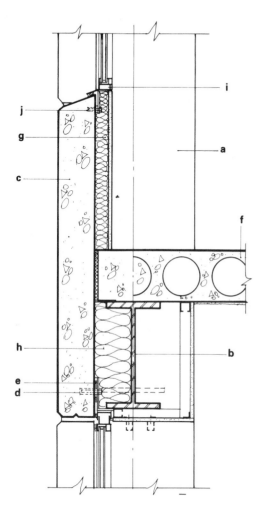

to the top of the trusses and downwards from floor to floor by the trusses and the floor slabs, which act as rigid diaphragms. Because the trusses take all the horizontal forces, in shear, there is no bending induced in the column from wind in this direction. The forces in the trusses and the floors are larger at the lower levels. At the fifth floor these wind forces are taken out of the trusses by horizontal cross-bracing in the floor and thence to ground by vertical cross-bracing, four storeys high, placed at the middle and ends of the building. It should be noted that openings in the floor for stairs and lifts greatly increase the horizontal stresses there. Double storey height trusses may be used to take extra loads, one being used here to provide a long span below level 5 and, in places, on the top two storeys.

Construction

The trusses were made up with a precamber of more than an inch (25mm) in the middle to prevent the columns being bent excessively out of line, as the truss deflects under floor load. As soon as they were erected, the floor planks were used to stabilise the trusses by welding of a plate embedded in the planks to the chords of the trusses. Total time for construction was fifteen months, all steelwork being erected within four months. A typical floor took less than four days to complete.

Conclusion

The staggered truss system is best suited to narrow shaped buildings which can accept cross walls and is thus of limited application. It is essentially a high rise system, going up to 30 stories and more, where, as in other high rise methods, as much vertical load is transferred to the outside columns to resist wind forces as is consistent with an economic floor structure. Structural steel used is about 7 lb per sq ft (34 kg per sq m) of floor area. This impressively low weight comes from the use of the truss to carry both horizontal and vertical loads and, more fundamentally, from the greater efficiency of a truss over solid I-section beams. Hence the system would not normally be used for a span of less than about 40ft (12.19m), the point at which purpose-made trusses start to become economic. This is a highly professional piece of work, built fast to a good standard.

a steel I-section column; **b** W14 steel sprandrel beam; **c** 24' long x 4' deep and 6" thick precast panel supported by steel brackets off columns at each end; **d** restraining angle welded to spandrel and bolted to panel with $\frac{3}{4}$" bolt (4 per panel); **e** neoprene washer; **f** 8" precast, prestressed concrete floor plank; **g** 2" foamed plastic insulation with gypsum board; **h** glass fibre insulation; **i** window; **j** fixing for window frame.

Vertical section through NE wall.

The Harewood Hotel,
Marylebone, London, England.

Introduction

This hotel is a first class, and very typical, example of the use of loadbearing masonry on a 'table top' of reinforced concrete construction at the lower levels. It is built on a tricky city centre site and taken right up to the height of the two existing buildings on either side.

Description

An underground railway runs across the site, so that no major loads could be founded over the area this occupies in plan. A thick reinforced concrete raft foundation is used to distribute the column loads from the cast-in-place concrete framework that goes up to the first accommodation floor, 16ft (4.88m) above street level. The beams in the floor at this level support loadbearing brick crosswalls, generally at 10ft 3in (3.13m) centres; these walls form the divisions for the bedrooms on the six floors above. Reinforced concrete almost uniquely provides the rugged construction and adaptability to all the planning requirements at the lower levels, providing clear space for a restaurant, a reception area and offices at upper ground floor level, for a lounge bar at lower ground floor level and for a boiler, electrical equipment and storage at the basement level. Two large vent shafts for the railway, as well as lifts, stairs and service ducts run right through the middle of the building. Tank and lift motor rooms as well as housings for the vent shafts, are placed at roof level.

Structural Action

The concrete frame takes all vertical and horizontal loads including modest wind forces. At the accommodation levels the brick crosswalls transmit vertical loads and wind forces in their own plane. Because the walls are placed in two quite different directions, here they are at right angles, any possible lateral movements are resisted. Rotational movements are resisted too. Wind forces in buildings less than about ten storeys high are small and the necessary overall lateral resistance is easily provided. However the stability of the individual wall elements need checking; this is almost exclusively dependent on the slenderness ratio, the effective height to the

View of hotel from SE.

Close-up on SE wall.

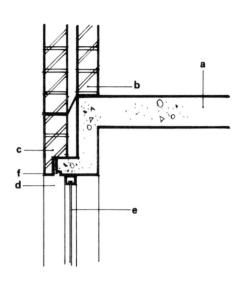

a 6″ cast-in-place concrete slab; **b** non-loadbearing brick cavity wall; **c** soldier course of brickwork supported on concrete nib; **d** horizontal movement joints for non-loadbearing masonry provided every storey at this height; **e** window; **f** drip.

Vertical section through non-loadbearing wall at front.

effective width of the wall. It is this, the sound insulation, accuracy of construction and workmanship that determine the thickness of the wall rather than the compressive strength of the masonry. The building incorporates slender reinforced concrete columns at some corners within the thickness of the brick walls to limit the area of damage and prevent progressive collapse should a substantial part of a loadbearing wall be damaged. For this purpose, return and intersecting walls can be valuable.

Construction

Construction of a loadbearing masonry building such as this requires the careful interleaving of those who lay the bricks for the walls and those who pour the concrete for the floor slabs. It is possible to arrange the work so that the trades follow each other, both following a spiralling sequence upwards. A principle is that only the minimum number of walls be constructed that are necessary to support the floor; these are the loadbearing walls; the other walls, the non-loadbearing walls, then become part of the finishing work. This building took a total period of 20 months to complete.

Conclusion

Red facing bricks have been used on the outside, giving the flexibility in plan, the scale and strong modelling not easily conceivable in other materials. The strong vertical emphasis shows the positions of the crosswalls at the accommodation levels. The discipline of the planning at the higher levels has made loadbearing crosswall construction possible although the 'table top' to support it, in reinforced concrete, is necessarily costly on this kind of site.

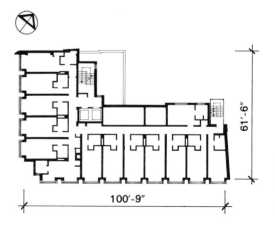

Typical floor plan.

THE HAREWOOD HOTEL (1973)

Description: Eight-storey hotel of loadbearing masonry with concrete substructure and frame at lower levels
Architects:
Lee Reading Harbison
Structural engineers:
Bylander Waddell and Partners

Axonometric view from S:

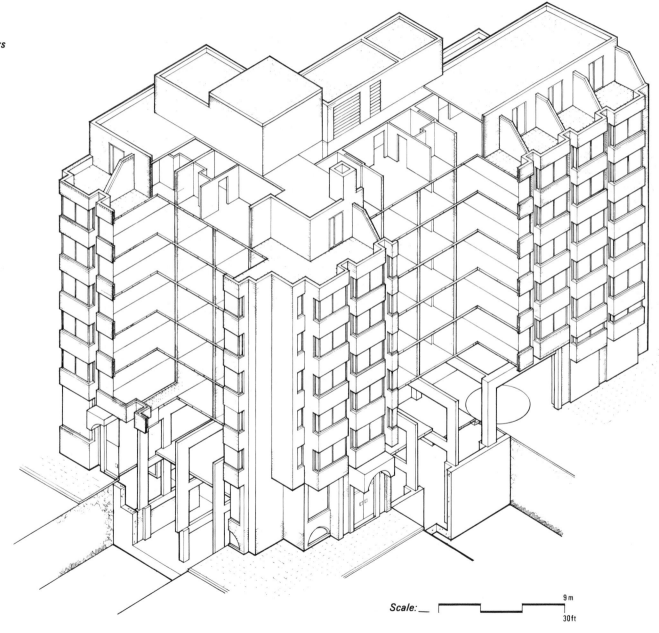

Scale:

9 m

30 ft

Elizabeth House,
Leicester, England

Introduction

Poured concrete is scaleless, constrasting as a method of building with masonry where a reference size is automatically provided by the finished brick or block units. Therefore the designer must invent a system of dimensions for each occasion, bearing in mind the human dimension, and other given dimensions, such as floor to floor heights and the overall height and width of the building. The problem is set in a typical form by this residential building, which contains flats for single people. It is 16 storeys high consisting, on elevation, of cast-in-place concrete end walls and of storey-height precast concrete panels on the long side walls. Apart from the cladding, the building is largely cast-in-place, with walls and slabs in a classic 'eggbox' arrangement.

Description

The ground floor contains a caretaker's flat, common rooms and utility rooms; the 15 floors above this are for the flats, which repeat at each level. The building consists of the external walls and a series of 175mm internal walls, all going in the east-west direction and all of cast-in-place concrete construction; each of the cellular spaces between the structural walls is made into one flat; the external walls have an overall thickness of 240mm but contain 40mm deep grooves, the ribs between the grooves being given a bush-hammered finish. There is a 125 x 500 mm precast concrete edge beam on the east and west sides connecting the walls together at their ends and helping to support the floor slab. In general the floors are 150mm thick, comprising a 75mm precast concrete plate with a smooth soffit and 75mm cast-in-place concrete topping which connects the floor to the walls and edge beams. The corridor slab is cast-in-place and 100mm thick, 150mm thick opposite the lifts, and is supported by beams on each side of the corridor. At ground floor level, the cladding consists of vertical precast concrete strips alternating with windows, but at all levels above this the precast concrete panels are shaped and contain a window opening in the centre. All loadbearing walls are

View of building from SW.

founded on heavy ground beams, typically 1200 x 900 mm in section, which in turn are supported by 750mm large diameter bored piles; the ground floor slab is supported by these and other ground beams resting on the piles.

At each typical floor level, there are a total of 15 different types of shaped cladding panels out of a total of 18 panels at each level. The differences reside mainly in slight variations in overall width which, in some cases, are taken up by the gap

between the forward vertical edges of adjacent panels; this gap varies between 70 and 175 mm. The vertical joint itself is set back near the edge of the floor slab and has a constant nominal width of 20mm. In those cases where the main part of each panel is identical, the panels can be made using the same mould. At roof level, the depth of the panel splay is reduced compared to that at typical floor levels. All panels have a blockwork inner skin behind them, while the external cast-in-place

ELIZABETH HOUSE(1979)

Description:
Sixteen-storey residential building of cast-in-place concrete
construction with precast concrete cladding panels
Architects:
J.Middleton
Structural engineers:
J.E.C. Farebrother and Partners

Axonometric
view from SW:

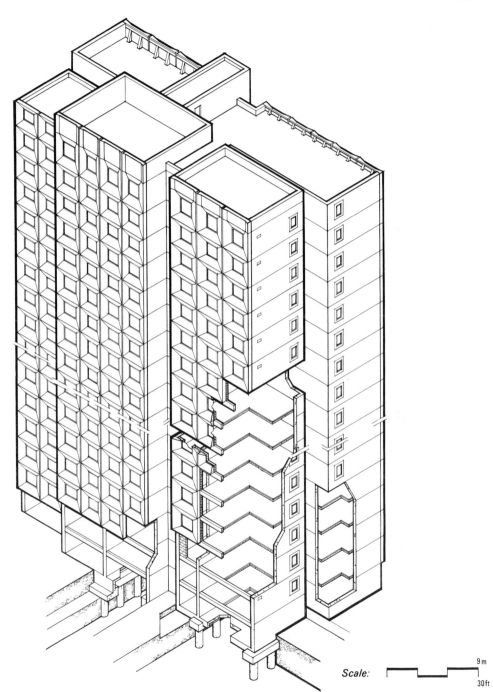

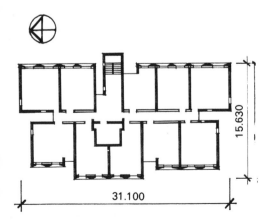

Typical floor plan.

15.630

31.100

Scale:

9 m

30 ft

View on various types of cladding panel.

walls have a 50mm dry lining with insulation and a vapour barrier. Entrance doors to the flats which open onto the corridor, or are between the corridor and the stairway, have a half-hour fire rating; lift doors have a one-hour fire rating.

Structural Action

Horizontal forces are taken by the crosswalls in the east-west direction and by the end return walls, the staircase wall and lift shaft walls going in the north-south direction; all these walls sit on the ground beams and piles.

Construction

The total period of construction amounted to 24 months. At each level, the loadbearing walls were cast 227mm above the structural floor and pockets were left for the insertion of the precast beams and plate floors; the beams and floor plates were temporarily supported by steel angles cast into the wall and packed up to their correct height; these angles were removed after the topping had been poured and cured. This process was then repeated at each level. Although each precast concrete floor plate covers the complete area of a flat, the weight of the heaviest plate is less than six tonnes. Only one tower crane, placed in the lift shaft, was needed to hoist the floor plates and other materials. The method of construction adopted meant that very few floor slabs required propping.

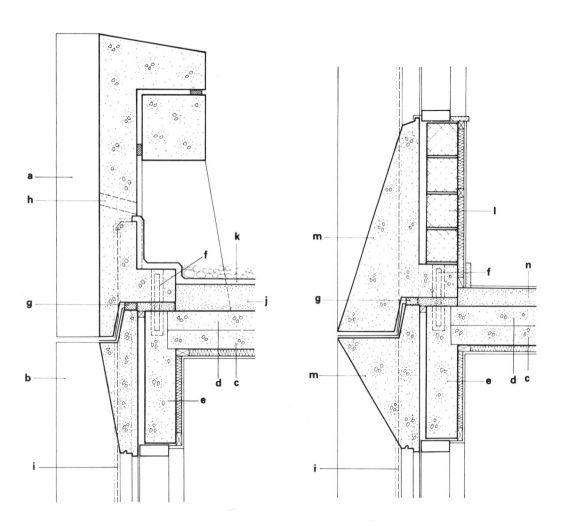

a parapet cladding panel; **b** top floor cladding panel; **c** 75mm precast concrete plate; **d** 75mm cast-in-place concrete; **e** 125 x 500 mm precast concrete edge beam; **f** dowel bar connection to beam with 30mm mortar bedding; **g** compressed sealing strip; **h** line of compressed sealing strip at vertical joint behind; **i** line of baffle at vertical joint behind; **j** lightweight screed on fibre felt separating layer; **k** 25mm asphalt; **l** 100mm blockwork; **m** typical cladding panel; **n** screed.

Vertical section through precast panels at top of building, left, and typical level, right.

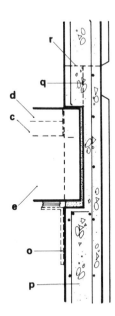

o temporary steel bracket; p 240mm external cast-in-place wall; q lines of construction joints; r line of kicker 227mm above slab.

Vertical section through edge beam at external wall.

Conclusion

The construction of this building, which consists basically of parallel crosswalls with precast panels covering the open sides, is obvious from outside; on the north and south elevations, the joint between the end panels and the end crosswalls is exposed, a valid expression of method. The deep indentations to the precast panels give a pleasing sense of thickness and good shadow although the array of panels does not succeed in generating really satisfactory proportions and rhythms. As noted previously, panels are not built to any one standard modular width. Arguably, the transition of the building to the ground could have been improved and simpler, less busy patterning used on the end walls. This is a most interesting illustration of some of the problems of building economically at a large scale and an archetypal use of cellular construction.

View on SE corner.

William Stone Building, Cambridge, England

Introduction

This is a slab block but elegantly fluted and presenting different faces on its various aspects with texture and scale provided by the brickwork used. It is eight storeys high containing study bedrooms with good views out across parkland on all floors. There is an immediate impression of mass and simplicity but the quality of this building resides in its integrity as a design and the clearing away of anything meretricious in concept or detail. The building has loadbearing brick walls and cast-in-place concrete but the building goes beyond the accepted conventions of this type of construction and its crosswall construction cannot be guessed at from the outside.

Description

The floor plans repeat at each level. The east side of the building contains most of the toilet facilities, a kitchen, a refuse chute, the main stairway and a lift; the west side is pulled out to contain the six main habitable spaces, all with good views and, excepting the room at the north end which is a bedroom, all have a southerly aspect. The elevations faithfully respect these usages: there are narrow window strips for the utility rooms on the east side, broad continous window bands on the west side and a high tower projecting above the lift and stairway which, from the east, appears to interlock with the other two parts of the building; the tower projects two storeys above the roof, containing a water tank at the top level above the lift motor room. Good, sharp vertical corner lines are used here. On the west side, the vertical lines are always offset by the horizontal lines, to a degree depending on the angle of view. The brickwork has a soft yellow-brown colour which is appropriate for the amount of surface exposed. A basement is provided for storage and service installations. All loadbearing vertical elements are brick, including the lift shaft and stairway. Generally gravity load is taken by crosswalls in the east-west direction; the horizontal forces are taken by these walls, as well as the walls going in the north-south direction. Internal walls are 9in (225mm) thick, or $4\frac{1}{2}$in (112mm) thick in the case of secondary walls; external walls are cavity walls

View of building from NW.

WILLIAM STONE BUILDING (1964)

Description:
Eight-storey residential block of loadbearing brick construction
Architects:
L. Martin and C. St. John Wilson
Structural engineers:
F.J. Samuely and Partners

Axonometric
view from SW:

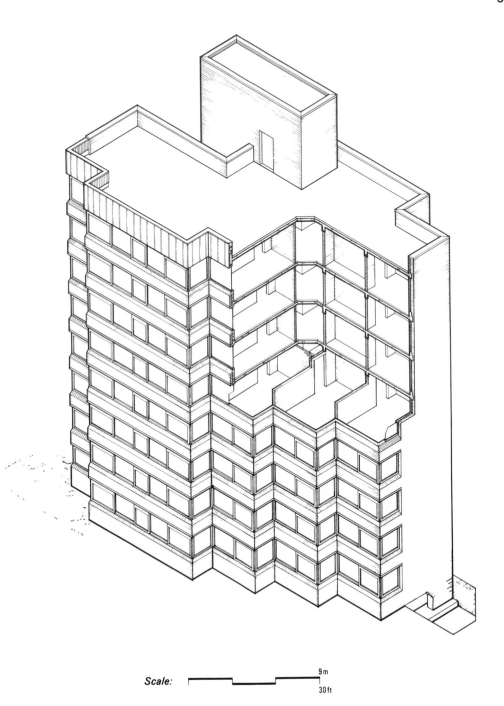

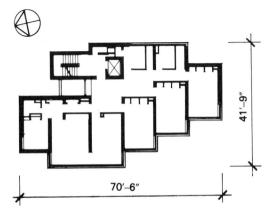

41'-9"

70'-6"

Typical floor plan.

Scale: 9 m
                                            30 ft

View of building from E.

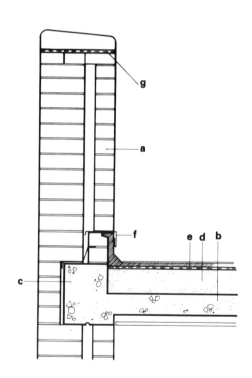

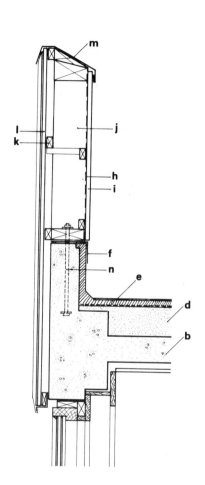

a 1'–3½" cavity brick wall; **b** 4½" concrete slab; **c** edge beam; **d** lightweight screed on felt; **e** asbestos tiles on 1" asphalt; **f** copper flashing; **g** epoxy resin dpc.

Vertical section through parapet on N side.

h felt; **i** ¾" Western Red Cedar strip boarding; **j** 6" x 2" wood frame; **k** 1" x 1½" horizontal battens; **l** lead coated copper sheet with standing seams on ¾" boarding; **m** lead coated copper capping; **n** ½" holding down bolts at 2'–0" centres.

Vertical section through cantilevered part of parapet on N side.

1ft 3½in (394mm) thick, except those round the staircase which are solid 13½in (343mm) thick walls. The external cavity walls have a 9in (225mm) outer skin with the floor structure resting on the 4½in (112mm) inner skin and the inner half of the external skin; this arrangement with a thick skin outside is unusual but has the advantage of loading both skins, and dispensing with the need for brick slips. The floor slabs are cast-in-place concrete 4½in (114mm) thick.

Along each internal crosswall there is a downstand beam, which spans across the lobby area and provides support to the continuous window band on the west side; the beam has an overall depth of 1ft 6in (457mm) over most of its length but its depth is increased to 2ft 2¼in (667mm) on the west side, where it cantilevers off the end of each crosswall. These cantilevers form part of the spandrel band, except in the one case where this part of beam is internal; all beams are 9in (225mm) thick and rectangular but change from this shape to the L-shape that is necessary along the spandrel band, in order to support the brickwork. At roof level the cantilever beam is less deep and the beam supporting the parapet, which is faced with a lead-coated copper, is rectangular all along its length. There is good sound insulation across the walls and the floors, because of the mass these elements have, and extra sound insulation is provided on the floors of the six main habitable rooms by a 2½in (64mm) floor screed laid on a layer of glass wool and surfaced with cork tiles. Heating is provided by large low-temperature radiant ceiling panels.

Structural Action

For reasonable economy, it is essential that all the loadbearing walls at each level are in vertical alignment; all such walls are then able to act as shear walls, that is resist horizontal forces in their own plane. Because there are no walls going in a north-south direction on the west side of the building, the shear centre of all loadbearing walls is displaced towards the east elevation; however, in view of the large number of walls going in both directions, this is of no particular significance. The stresses in the walls, even at ground floor level, are moderate compared to the strength of the brickwork.

Close-up on W side of building.

Construction

The total period of construction was 18 months. Concrete floors were poured after completion of each storey height of brickwork. The cantilevered areas on the west side required temporary propping until the concrete had attained full strength and allowance had to be made for the permanent deflection after depropping.

Conclusion

The areas of rooms and the overall scale is generous. The concertina plan allows views out west, as well as views along the face of the building, of the other rooms, thus providing a sense of the relationship of part to whole. The engineering is notable for the way it extends ideas about loadbearing masonry as a method of construction. Materials and detailing are to a high standard in accordance with an ample budget. This is an original interpretation of the requirements.

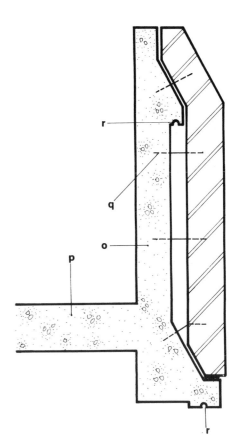

o 4½″ x 3′-8¼″ edge beam; p ⅛″ cork tile on 2½″ screed on ⅜″ glass wool (not shown) on 4½″ concrete slab. q non-ferrous wall ties at 3′ centres; r drip.

Typical vertical section through W wall, between window bands.

Spelman Halls,
Princeton University, New Jersey, USA

Introduction

A consequence of manufacturing elements for an off-the-shelf building system, is that in order to make the system as adaptable as possible, it is necessary to make a large number of different types of element; however, unit costs rise rapidly because many types are only required in small numbers. In precast systems, a result is that few types of element are produced, as few as is necessary for a workable system, and that, consequently, such buildings when erected tend to be monotonous in appearance and, in design terms, ill-suited to their use and setting. This design for student housing adopts a systems-building approach but, in this case, it is a purpose-designed precast concrete system in which the design arises out of particular circumstances and exploits the techniques of production and erection of precast elements, rather than being determined by them. The housing is made up of eight house units, all slightly different and arranged with varying orientations on each side of intersecting pedestrian routes. From the outside the building is seen to be divided up by the windows and the joints between the precast panels. The buildings are crisp and airy, the window arrangements being in marked contrast to the 'punched-hole' windows which are part and parcel of most designs using precast concrete panels. The technical details of the joint both between the interlocking wall panels and between these panels and the floor panels, which are of various shapes, are thoroughly practical and ingeniously avoid congestions of connecting pieces in the corners.

Description

Each house unit is an assembly of precast concrete elements and glazing units, with further internal divisions made by thin but relatively heavy partition walls, generally 3⅜in (80mm) thick. The precast concrete elements, which form the enclosure and structure for each unit, consists of wall and floor panels, parapets, stair flights and long precast beams. Considering the house unit shown bold on the site plan, these 57ft (17.4m) long precast beams run along the south and east sides, the latter being a prestressed post-tensioned

View of houses from NW (photo by George Cserna).

beam which cantilevers 22ft (6.71m) off an internal crosswall and, at the south-east corner, supports the former, which is simply supported at this end. Both beams are 8in (203mm) wide at the top but 11in (279mm) wide at the bottom, thus making a shelf to support the floor panels; the floor panels are attached with galvanized steel angles at 4ft 10in (1.47m) centres using a ¾in (19mm) bolt that fixes to ferrules cast in a recess in the top of the slab and in the sides of the beam. Both beams are supported by the internal crosswall, a ¾in (19mm) thick neoprene pad with a central locating pin being provided here in order to spread the load and obviate cracking. These internal loadbearing walls are 11¼in (286mm) thick. The other loadbearing

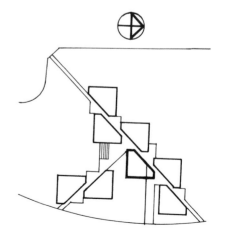

General plan of house units.

SPELMAN HALLS (1974)

Description:
Three or four-storey houses grouped together of precast concrete panel construction
Architects:
I.M. Pei and Partners
Structural engineers:
Le Messurier Associates/SCI

Axonometric
of house unit
from SE:

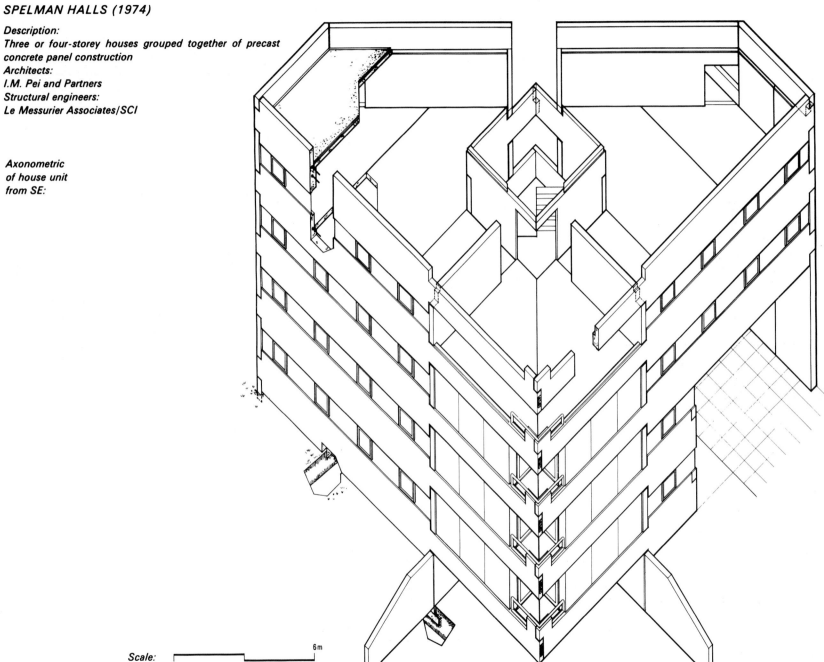

Scale: 6m
20ft

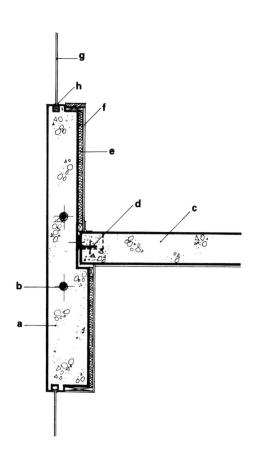

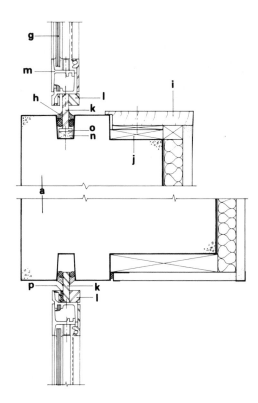

wall panels, including those in the stair core and those supporting the far end of the beams, are 8in (203mm) thick. All the wall panels rest on an upstand wall on a strip footing, both the latter being of cast-in-place concrete construction.

The floor panels are a standard 8in (203mm) thick but have different spans, the different slab strengths, thus required, being conveniently provided by post-tensioning. There is no concrete topping. Most floor panels rest on an indentation at the top of their supporting walls and are attached to the walls by galvanized steel angles at 4ft 10in (1.47m) centres using $\frac{3}{4}$in (19mm) bolts that fix to ferrules cast in the tops of the floor panels and the sides of the wall panels. For the joint between the floor panel and the $11\frac{1}{4}$in (286mm) internal crosswall, these ferrules are cast both in the vertical edge of the floor panel, connecting to bars projecting from the wall panel below, as well as in the top of the floor panel, connecting by means of steel plates to the adjacent floor panel and by means of steel angles to the wall panel above; both types of ferrule are placed at 4ft 10in (1.47m) centres, using $\frac{3}{4}$in (19mm) bolts. The precast floor slabs were prestressed with camber to allow for dead load deflection. As there is no concrete topping, the fine adjustments for level were made by downward tension on the slabs at the connection points on the vertical edge.

There are two types of horizontal joint between the wall panel units. The $11\frac{1}{4}$in (286mm) internal crosswall, which supports floor panels on each side, also supports the wall panel above, initially by bars projecting from the centre of the lower panel, which are joined through a connector allowing adjustment for height. When in the correct position, the gap between the floor and wall panels is filled with mortar or cast-in-place concrete. All the other walls support floor panels only on one side, with a $\frac{1}{2}$in (13mm) joint, on the other side, between it and the panel above; these panels bear onto steel plates with a locating pin using plastic shims to adjust for height. The $\frac{1}{2}$in (13mm) gap between the wall panels is rammed with mortar. For the external wall panels, there is a gasket and sealant on one side of the joint, to provide weatherproofing. In all the horizontal joints, steel angles were bolted to ferrules cast in the top of the floor slab and the sides of the wall

a precast post-tensioned beam; **b** 24/$\frac{1}{4}$" wire prestressing strand; **c** 8" floor panel; **d** steel angle in recess connected by $\frac{3}{4}$" bolts to ferrules in concrete; **e** 1" rigid insulation; **f** $\frac{1}{2}$" gypsum board; **g** $\frac{7}{32}$" plate glass; **h** strip backing and sealant.

Vertical section through cantilevered part of prestressed beam.

i painted sill; **j** blocking piece and shim; **k** $\frac{3}{8}$" steel flat attached to casement; **l** removable steel blocking strip; **m** opening steel frame window; **n** shims; **o** steel flat support; **p** neoprene gasket.

Vertical section through opening windows.

panel, to fix the panel in position. Vertical wall panel joints are also made using steel angles. In all cases where connections are made with steel angles or plates, the connectors have oversize holes to allow a tolerance and are placed in recesses in the panels which are subsequently filled with cast-in-place concrete.

The core walls are neatly planned to provide support to the stairs and floor panels as well as views out over the entrance on the north-east face. The stair core is top lit by $\frac{3}{4}$in (19mm) green-tinted toughened (tempered) glass which also extends down vertically in a strip to the entrance at ground level. Excluding the roof and floor, there were 61 different types of precast element for this house unit, often with only very small differences between the types. At each typical floor, there are nine different types of floor panel; the other floors, or the roof, either repeat exactly or use largely the same floor types. All the panel types in the house unit considered are also used in other units. The inside surface of the external wall panels are fitted with rigid insulation covered by gypsum board but internal wall panels are left as cast. Vertical distribution of services is through small holes in the floor panels that are within the 10$\frac{1}{2}$in (267mm) width of the internal walls to the kitchen and bathrooms.

Structural Action

When all the panel connections are secure, the unit behaves like a box structure with all walls participating in resisting horizontal forces. Good connections are crucial for success. Here the interlocking between the beam and the supporting wall panels allows separate joints for vertical and horizontal load transfer and a separate floor to beam joint thus making the building easier to construct. The post-tensioned beam is stressed, from one end only, by two curved strand cables to a total prestress of about 160 tons (145 tonnes). The tendon anchors are exposed on elevation. Prestressing allows the load applied to be balanced, such that there is no deflection at the end of the cantilever.

Construction

Total construction time including excavation, foundations, erection of the precast elements and finishing of exterior and interior work, was 13

View on corner of house unit (photo © Nathaniel Lieberman).

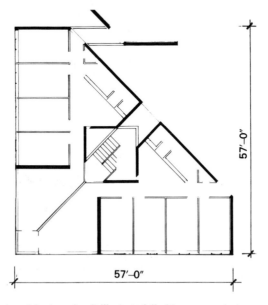

Level 2 plan of unit illustrated (bold on general plan).

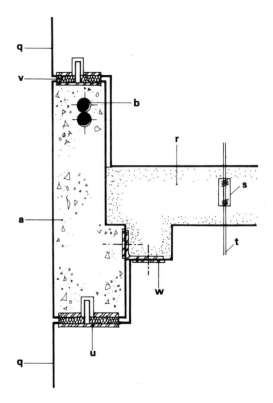

q 11$\frac{1}{4}$" internal wall panel; **r** 8$\frac{1}{2}$" nominal gap between wall panels; **s** adjustable connector attached to ferrule in vertical edge of floor panel; **t** threaded bar from wall panel below joint; **u** $\frac{3}{4}$" neoprene pad with central locating pin on steel plate, with shear studs welded on; **v** compressible filler; **w** 6" x 4" x $\frac{1}{2}$" x 6$\frac{1}{2}$" long steel angle with 2/ $\frac{3}{4}$" and 2/ 1$\frac{1}{2}$" holes taking $\frac{3}{4}$" bolts, fixing to loop ferrules on steel plate cast into concrete.

Vertical section at joint of prestressed beam with interior wall panel.

months. The erection of the 979 precast elements took 8 weeks, the maximum weight of any one element being 19 tons (17 tonnes). Each floor panel was fixed in position before erection of the wall panels above. Only the minimum number of loadbearing walls are provided in order to simplify the scheme and make erection quicker. A smooth, pristine finish was given to the panels by casting against steel moulds or varnished plywood. A special concrete mix was developed with white cement, light brown sand and granite aggregate to match the adjacent buildings of limestone. One disadvantage of the smooth finish is that staining and bumps on the surface are more visible.

Conclusion

Before it was decided to use a precast concrete structure, two other methods of construction were estimated by the general contractor. These were: masonry loadbearing walls with cast-in-place concrete floor slabs and cast-in-place concrete walls and floors. The precast concrete system was found to be the most economical. This is a sophisticated design in which the technical problems have been well solved. The use of post-tensioning is particularly instructive. As in all precast concrete work, much attention has had to be paid to the inaccuracies arising in the manufacture and erection of the elements, in order to arrive at sound joint details. The relatively thick panels used here are necessary both, in the floor, to achieve long spans and in the walls, to achieve simple and workable details. Historically, ambitious detailing of thin panels has often appeared as one of the root causes of subsequent defects. This design is an inspiring one and its quality gives an indication of what the future of panel systems could be.

View from central steps looking SE (photo by George Cserna).

Chapter Nine

Highly Serviced Buildings

Whilst it is true that in almost all kinds of building, there is an increasing amount of money and space devoted to the provision of mechanical and electrical services, and to their efficient operation, some building types have services which account for a particularly large proportion of the total cost. These buildings include hospitals and laboratories, where the cost of services may approach half the total cost and the area occupied by plant up to fifteen per cent of the total floor area. But swimming pools, ice rinks, some kinds of production facilities and any building where internal conditions must be carefully controlled, will also require special provision. A selection of some of the types of highly serviced buildings in use is included in this chapter; some buildings with heavy servicing are also included in other chapters. Many of the buildings in this chapter are small, compared to the largest buildings that are possible in each category, but, in spite of this, the buildings are still of a size and complexity such that ambient energy cannot be used to any significant degree to provide control of the internal

conditions. Reliance is therefore placed on the plant and machinery and on the means of distributing the services required efficiently, throughout the building. Those items of equipment which, in general, occupy most space and thus have a significant influence on the form of the building, particularly the floor system, are the air-conditioning ducts. Bearing in mind that the services have a limited life, typically only a quarter or fifth that of the permanent fabric of the building, the accessibility of services, the provision for new services and the integration of these into the design are major issues. These facts by themselves justify the apparently extravagant provision of space that is sometimes necessary for services. Nevertheless, with advance planning, space can usually be found for all the services required. What is often a more difficult problem is to discover a coordinated pattern of services distribution, in which the services are properly related to the plant rooms and to each other and this may require substantial trial and error during the design process.

Yale Center for British Art, New Haven, Connecticut, USA

Introduction

In the sense that architecture is primarily concerned with reflecting human values in building, many and perhaps most buildings fail as architecture, meeting basic requirements but managing only patchily or by accident to respond to deeper, primordial human aspirations. In this building, by contrast, such ambitions inform every level of the design. Indeed the story of the building would shed an interesting light on the whole scope of architecture as a practical art. It is particularly apt that, in its role as an exemplar, this building uses just a simple concrete frame and that its qualities derive not so much from visual flair, which may not be attached to worthwhile ideas, but from a single-minded concentration on such fundamental issues as proportion, order, light, integration of parts and the sense of place. The four-storey building is for the housing of art and books and contains public galleries, a reference library, a lecture hall, classrooms, offices and a paper conservation laboratory.

Description

The building is entered across a low, square, paved area, open at the sides, at the north-east corner of the building which, on passing through the entrance door, gives onto a quiet, internal court space, 40ft (12.19m) square, which extends the full height of the building and is covered by clear sky lights. Access to other levels is via stairs and elevators in an area to one side of the court. The stair flights follow a square plan but are set inside a round tower with heavy access doors. The tower is made of 8in (203mm) thick cast-in-place concrete for fire resistance. It has a superb sense of weight to go with its strong geometries and is lit artifically by lamps as well as by natural light coming through a grid of glass blocks set in concrete below the roof lights. At level 2 there is another internal court, three storeys high, with a 40 x 60 ft (12.19 x 18.29 m) plan area. This library court is more private than the entrance court, but, like it, uses oak panelling set flush in the concrete frame. The court gives access to three libraries. Level 3 is devoted to library stack space and object storage as well as the display of special

View of building from E (photo by Thomas Brown).

exhibitions. Level 4, the top floor, is mostly set aside for a public art gallery and is lit naturally by means of roof skylights.

The building structure is a cast-in-place concrete frame on a 20ft (6.10m) grid which is fully expressed and used as an ordering principle throughout the building but with variations on this basic theme as necessary: for example, except on the west side, the perimeter columns at street level are at 40ft (12.20m) centres with deep beams above, thereby providing a base to the building and drawing attention to the shop units on the two sides facing the street; perimeter beams are not expressed on elevation at level 2 where the libraries have two storeys. The square spaces between the frame are infilled with various sizes of

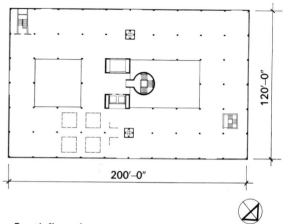

Fourth floor plan.

YALE CENTER FOR BRITISH ART (1976)

Description:
Four-storey building of concrete frame construction with
stainless steel cladding panels
Architects:
Louis I. Kahn/
Pellecchia and Meyers
Structural engineers:
Pfisterer, Tor and Associates

Axonometric
view from NE:

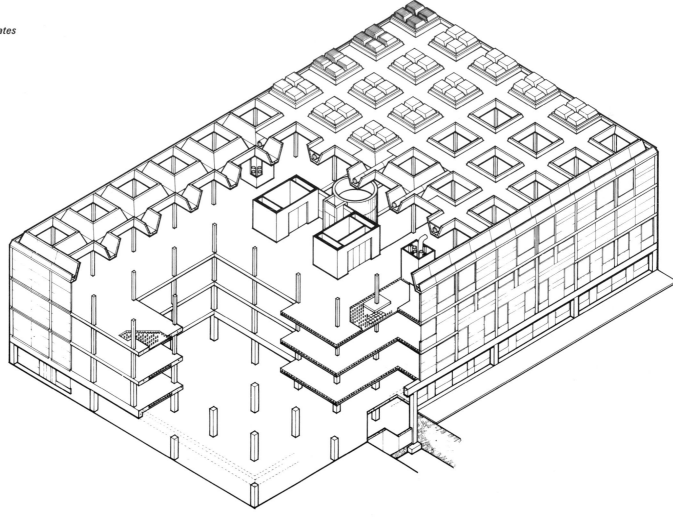

Scale: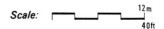

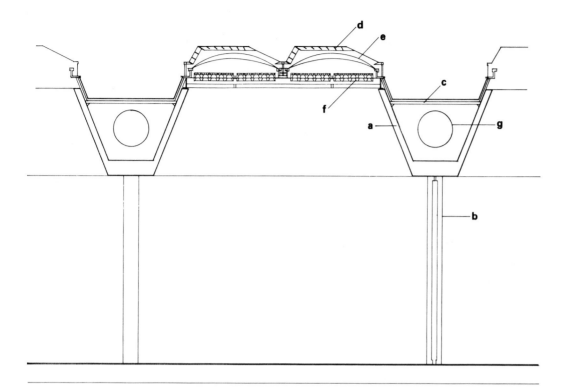

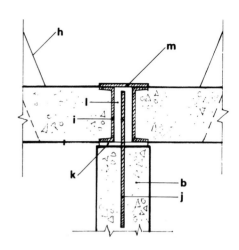

k $\frac{1}{4}$″ steel plate on 11″ x 11″ x $\frac{1}{2}$″ neoprene pad; **l** grout; **m** $\frac{1}{2}$″ steel plate welded to channels.

Vertical section through column at roof.

a 20′ precast concrete units; **b** 1′ square cast-in-place column; **c** 1$\frac{1}{2}$″ metal deck with insulation and waterproofing; **d** aluminium louvres; **e** double skin acrylic skylight; **f** diffuser panel; **g** supply air duct.

Vertical section through roof.

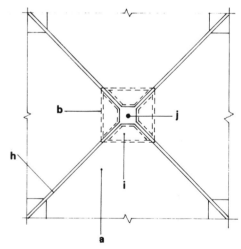

h precast units joined by welding on bent steel plates; **i** 1′ deep steel channels with reinforcement welded on; **j** $\frac{3}{4}$″ dowel bar.

Plan on roof over column.

stainless steel cladding panels and glass. The panels are sandblasted which gives a pewter colour to them but in good light there is a grain and depth to the surface with suffused, banded reflections. This contrasts with the specular reflections off the glass-windows set beside the cladding panels. The frame cladding and glass are set flush so that neither part dominates, giving the elevations a pleasingly spare and disciplined appearance.

Like the structure, the building services are carefully controlled. The main plant is at basement level and vertical distribution of services is via two vertical stainless steel shafts placed near the centre of the long sides which pass upwards through the floors. These shafts contain circular supply ducts and the space in the shaft surrounding the ducts carries the return air. There are no suspended ceilings. The return air from levels 2 and 3 is taken from the perimeter through voids in the middle of the 'air floor' slab, which then feeds into the two vertical service shafts. At both these levels the conditioned air is supplied through eight identical circular overhead ducts with outlets on the underside; each duct is partitioned so that there are, in fact, two separate air supply lines inside. These ducts seem large in some rooms. On the top floor, the roof consists of a deep coffer of V-shaped precast concrete units, four units coming together and getting a 3$\frac{1}{2}$in (89mm) toehold on each column. Supply air ducts and rainwater pipes run inside the units which are also used for return

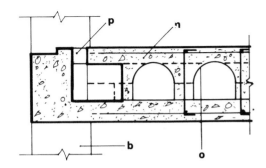

n 1'–2" deep concrete slab with voids; o 7" deep metal domes; p 3" x 12" return air inlets.

Vertical section through outside edge of floor slab at levels 2 and 3.

View of gallery at level 4 (photo by Joseph Szaszfai).

air. The tops of the V-shaped units are covered with sheet metal. Fresh air inlets and exhaust hoods are placed on the roof. The inside air temperature is kept at 74°F (23°C), with the relative humidity varying between 40% in summer and 50% in winter.

The top floor is one of the best gallery spaces built in recent times. It has travertine floor strips running between the columns, on the column grid. The linen-covered panels, for hanging, are placed along the strips so that the gallery is split up into related but separate, almost private, areas. The rooflights placed between the coffer grid give a superb and even natural lighting at all times of the day. The lighting is achieved by a series of aluminium louvres above the skylights which point south and thus reduce the amount of ultraviolet light admitted. They are set at differing angles in order to admit a greater percentage of light when the sun is low than when it is high and overabundant. The skylight itself is acrylic, incorporates an ultraviolet filter and has a double skin for insulation. Diffuser panels are placed below. Internal colours are subdued but warm in tone. Internal finishings look solid and expensive and are in keeping with the design.

Structural Action

Horizontal forces on the building are taken by the stair or elevator cores and by frame action. Except in particular places, the voided floor slab has no beams but works as a two-way spanning flat slab.

Over column positions, the slab is solid to take the shear forces. Columns have pad foundations and basement walls have strip foundations.

Construction

The building was constructed over a period of about 24 months. The voided floor slab was made in two parts. A 4in (102mm) thick bottom layer was poured first, then small 7in (179mm) high interconnected sheet metal domes were placed on top of this forming a voided space. This was then covered with a second concrete pour, connected to the first by vertical steel dowel bars 1ft (300mm) on centre projecting from the bottom layer in the spaces between the metal domes, giving a total slab thickness of 1ft 2in (350mm).

View of reference library (photo by Joseph Szaszfai).

Conclusion

The design of this building not only responds to the most basic component of architecture, function, but captures something of the essence of the activities inside. For example, a subdued atmosphere, protection and quiet are evoked as aspects of study. The many requirements for the building have been organized, boiled down to essentials and then synthesized into distinctive parts of the design. But the parts are reined into a common module and geometry, giving clear physical relationships and a sense of order. The building provides a sense of welcoming niches within a whole master enterprise. Although all parts are expressly and minutely designed, the ideas are always serious, rather than irritating, and seem to go beyond a merely subjective interpretation. This architecture does not insist but appeals in simple and fundamental ways.

Biochemical Sciences Laboratory, Princeton University, New Jersey, USA

Introduction

The uncluttered plan layout for this research laboratory shows how the designers have abstracted the essentials from detailed and highly specific requirements, to produce a clear layout for the laboratories, which is repeated on three floor levels, but with quite individual treatment given to the four elevations and to the office and circulation areas. The clarity and the use of relief and natural light demonstrate bedrock professionalism. A simple building concept, using a cast-in-place concrete frame together with granite panels and glazing are used to produce some strongly modelled elevations.

Description

The major design themes are evident: internally, circulation of people and the efficient distribution of pipes and ductwork in a highly serviced building; externally, the granite panelling and horizontal bands of glazing are matched to the purpose of the rooms, their views out and exposure to the sun. On each of the three laboratory levels a corridor separates a core containing specialised laboratories from the standard laboratories on the east and west sides and the offices to the south. Two foot (600mm) wide granite panels are used throughout, supported by stainless steel angle brackets which bolt to sockets, cast into the reinforced concrete edge beam. The bolt allows adjustment for line and level, so achieving the clean lines and regular width closed joints between the panels. The rounded corners of the building are clad with a series of the standard width panels with a curved exterior face but a flat interior face. At level 4, the floor is set back and the concrete frame is clad with metal panelling. In the laboratory area, the structural frame consists of three bays of portals in the east-west direction of the building, separated by two 8ft (2.44m) wide zones which, not being crossed by a downstand beam, can take the major services, including heating ducts, fume venting and lights. Services are distributed at ceiling level. The frames are at about 20ft (6m) centres with an 8in (200mm) slab spanning between them in the north-south direction. The use of a floor beam,

View of building from SE (photo by Theo Westenberger).

rather than a flat slab, allows holes either side of the column, where they are most useful for vertical distribution of services, and the one-way spanning slab allows a further large service hole between the columns. The outside columns of the portals are set back from the building's edge and thus free the elevation for continuous horizontal glazing. A basement occupies the full area of the plan and contains heavy mechanical plant, storage areas, switchboard equipment, and specialised laboratories. The basement has a 5in (127mm) concrete floor slab on fill with one foot (300mm) thick basement walls on strip footings; the 20 x 20 in (508 x 508 mm) internal columns are founded on individual pad foundations. The one-foot

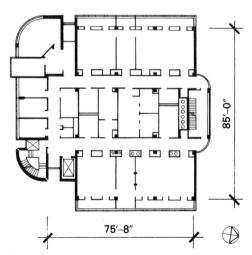

Typical floor plan.

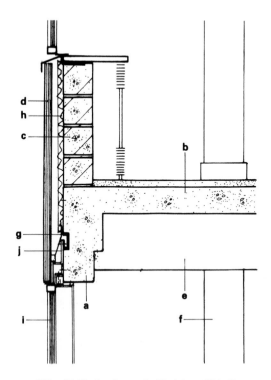

a 10″ x 3′-0″edge beam; b 8″ slab; c 8″ hollow block concrete wall fixed to beam with ½″ steel bar at 1′-4″ centres; d 1″ granite facing; e 1′-8″ x 2′-6″ beam; f 1″-8″ square column; g cast in support for granite facing; h 1″ rigid insulation; i double glazing; j fixing angle for facing using ¼″ shims.

Typical vertical section through wall.

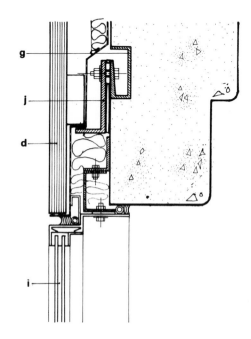

Detail of support to facing panel.

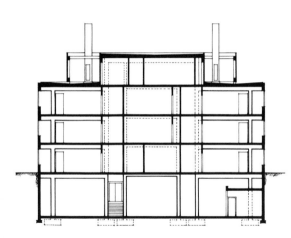

Typical E-W section through building.

(304mm) thickness of the basement walls allows maximum flexibility for openings, recesses and other miscellaneous details or inserts and tolerably reliable water-proof concrete.

Structural Action

Cast-in-place reinforced concrete construction forms rigid joints cheaply and hence lateral stability is conveniently achieved by frame action. The perimeter edge beams not only stiffen the edges of the slab, but support the exterior cladding. At the round corners some torsion is induced in the beams although this is considerably restrained by the action of the slab. Very sensitive instruments are used in this laboratory, needing not only a rigid structure, but one which minimised vibration. Concrete provides reasonably high damping and is therefore suitable for this purpose.

Construction

Contract time was 22 months. Standard beam widths and column sizes helped to reduce shuttering costs.

Conclusion

A reinforced concrete frame has provided a sturdy and economic frame structure which has nevertheless allowed flexibility in the plan shape and in slab thicknesses. With this column arrangement, horizontal runs for services and openings in the slab for staircases and services are easily accommodated. The scope for altering the structure or routes of services at a later date is limited but the replacement of the services themselves is relatively easy. The hard surfaces, with their rough and smooth textures, are made into an incisive, geometrical composition, which is entirely appropriate.

BIOCHEMICAL SCIENCES LABORATORY (1980)

Description:
Four-storey laboratory of concrete frame construction with
granite cladding
Architects:
Davis, Brody and Associates
Structural engineers:
Wiesenfeld and Leon

Axonometric
view from SE:

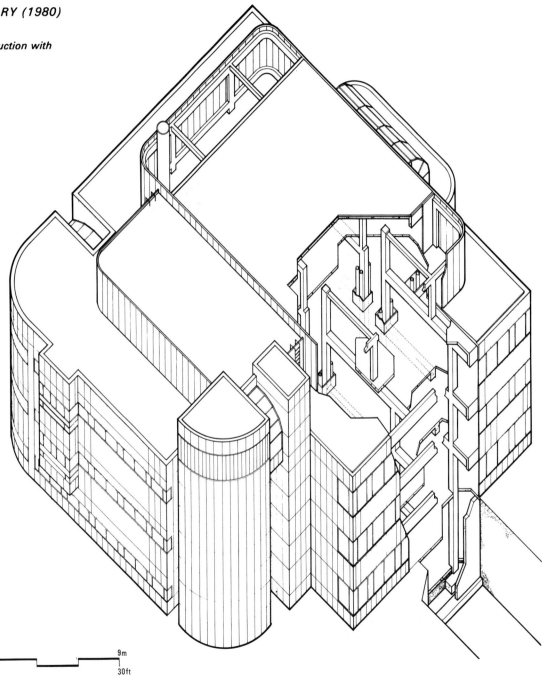

Scale:

9m

30ft

Wellesley College Science Center, Wellesley, Massachusetts, USA

Introduction

There are almost no permanent walls inside this science block, most of the divisions of area being made by a movable, purpose-designed laboratory furniture system. No ceiling soffit is used either. The concrete structure, consisting of deep ribbed slabs resting on flat beams spanning between circular columns, is particularly conspicuous, therefore. The concrete structure is carried through to all elevations, being turned into an architectonic composition to include, as well as the concrete structure itself, circular stainless steel exhaust stacks, exposed steel roof trusses and, on a smaller grid, the external walkways, rails and stairs and the steel tube framing for the windows. The metal elements are painted in bright colours to provide yet another compositional theme. The building successfully establishes itself in an open space as well as providing workable solutions to the problems of service distribution and the reallocation of laboratory space.

Description

There are five floors in the building, the top one, level 4, being set back from the main south-west front and occupying only part of the plan area; it is reserved for mechanical plant, there being no basement structure on account of water-logged ground conditions. Levels 2 and 3 are laboratory levels. The deep ribs of the floor slab at level 2 are at 4ft 3in (1.30m) centres and the overall slab depth is 2ft 4in (710mm); levels 3 and 4 have an alternating grid of 4ft 3in (1.30m) and 8ft 6in (2.59m) and a slab depth of 4ft 4in (1.32m) to allow for the larger number of services required in the ceiling of the laboratory floors. The main beams supporting the ribbed slab are 3ft 6in (1.07m) by 1ft 10½in (572mm) deep and heavily reinforced, to span the required distance between columns. There are four lines of columns in the main body of the building with a series of concrete shear walls in the centre, within which are vertical cores containing services. The columns and shear walls are taken down to pad foundations. The horizontal distribution of services is taken in the space between the ribs. Only glass drains for acid waste need to penetrate the floor slab. The lower

View of building from S (photo by Edward Jacoby/APG).

WELLESLEY COLLEGE SCIENCE CENTER (1978)

Description:
Five-storey science block of cast-in-place concrete with transparent and translucent cladding
Architects:
Perry, Dean, Stahl and Rogers
Structural engineers:
Simpson, Gumpertz and Heger

Axonometric view from NW:

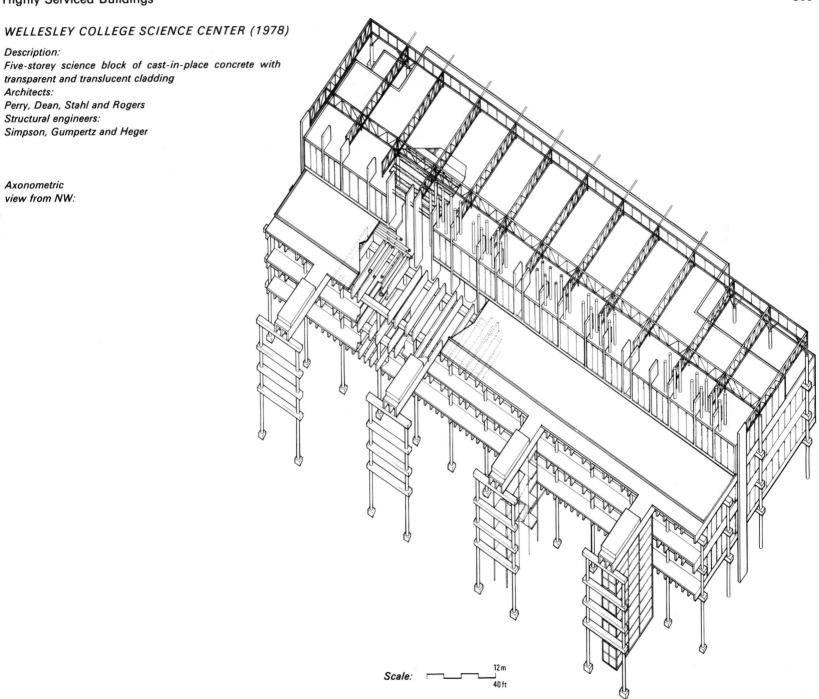

Scale:

12 m
40 ft

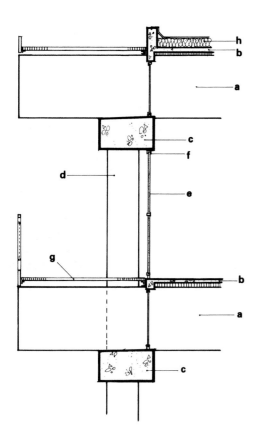

two floors are used mainly for a library but, because of sloping ground, do not occupy the full plan area.

The roof of the plant room is covered by a series of 6ft 6in (1.98m) deep steel tubular trusses, which run across the building and are stabilised by top bracing and by a truss and a frame running at right angles to the trusses. All trusses are painted a light blue. Hangers from the panel points of the main truss support secondary trusses, in turn supporting a 1½in (38mm) deep metal deck with rigid insulation and a built-up roof. On the northern side of the laboratory the roof trusses are continued across to an existing building, forming a large atrium, 60ft (18.29m) high. The four external escape staircases on the south-west side are of painted steel construction and hung from the concrete beams at the top. The cladding of the building is set into the frame and fitted between flush concrete surfaces top and bottom. The windows are heat-reflecting and double-glazed, with a steel surround and supported between rectangular steel tubular mullions. Translucent fibreglass panels alternate with glazing and are supported in a similar way. Conditioned air is supplied to the room terminal units which are positioned in the ceiling between the floor ribs; the units have a hot-water reheat coil and supply air down circular ducts with a maximum diameter of 2ft 2in (660mm). Fume extracts and electricity cables drop down to the rooms from this space. Gas, air, vacuum and hot and cold water are also run in the ceiling and drop to bench level using flexible hoses. Fluorescent strip lighting is fixed to the sides of the floor ribs.

Structural Action

Horizontal forces, including earthquake forces, in the direction across the building are taken by the concrete shear walls and forces at right angles by the frame. Two expansion joints are provided through the concrete structure on lines 70ft (21.34m) and 108ft (32.92m) from each end. The top bracing to the steel roof trusses is discontinued in one of the central bays allowing the two halves to move independently.

Construction

The structure is built in cast-in-place concrete to an extremely high standard of finish. The concrete

floor slab was poured on permanent wood-fibre formwork spanning between the ribs, which in the finished state provided acoustic absorbance. Two holes were left in the slab at each end of the building for tower cranes. The construction of the building took 26 months.

Conclusion

The design provides clear routes for service distribution as well as an open plan to allow flexibility in use. The elevations are expertly handled with interesting detail, although steel parts will require regular maintenance to prevent corrosion and staining of the concrete. About half of the total cost of the building is in the building fabric.

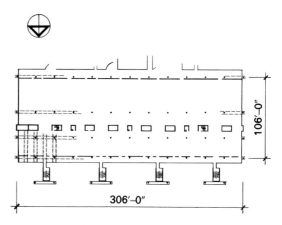

Level 2 floor plan.

a 4'-4" deep concrete floor; b 4" concrete slab on 2" permanent wood-fibre formwork; c 3'-6" x 1'-10½" concrete main beam; d 2'-0"diameter concrete column; e silvered heat-reflecting double-glazed window with galvanized steel surround; f steel surround fixed to floor with polythene block sealed both ends; g metal grille; h rigid insulation with built-up roofing.

Vertical section through top of SW wall.

Sainsbury Centre, Norwich, England

Introduction

Two-thirds of the plan area of this building is taken by an art gallery but the building also houses a school for fine arts, a common room and a restaurant and kitchen. The building has a simple, rectangular shape, with the two gable ends fully glazed, and is detailed with immense care in order to achieve a geometrical purity of line and surface. A scale is provided by box-type panels, outside, and by perforated venetian blinds and the paraphernalia of servicing, inside. Entry of light is moderated by blinds to amounts that impart a certain magic to the space inside. The design is important for the extent to which it treats a building as a high quality product, in which the components are largely shop-fabricated, the materials are expensive and the tolerances very much stricter than those used with traditional building materials.

Description

From inside the usable space in the Centre is seen to be enclosed by wall and roof linings. It is separated from the external cladding on the roof and walls by a buffer zone containing the structure, the services and other utilities. The main internal space contains the art collection. There are two independent mezzanine floors at the north-west end, one housing underneath it offices and study areas, for the fine arts school, and the other a kitchen, for the restaurant next to the glass gable wall at this end of the building. Ground floor and high level access is provided at the south-east end of the building. The structure consists of 37 triangular trusses along the length of the building, which are each about 2.5m deep and 1.8m wide at the top and are supported by lattice columns with a triangular cross-section almost identical to that of the truss. At the ends of the building this balance between the truss and column creates a wide edge around the glass wall. The trusses have a 300mm camber and span 34.40m, with pin joints at one end and sliding joints at the other; there are two joints at each end, these being fixed on the two top diagonal members of the lattice column. Although it creates secondary bending in column members, the joint is set in vertically by 300mm

View of building from S.

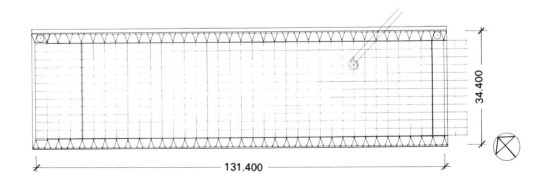

Ground floor plan.

34.400

131.400

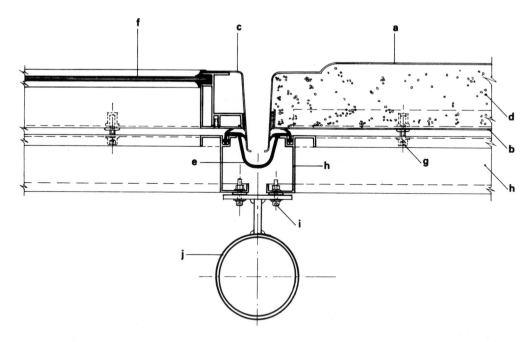

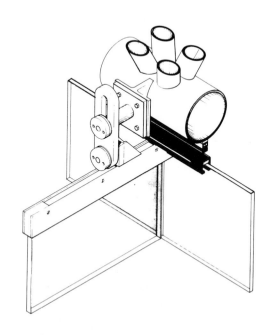

a aluminium outer skin; b aluminium inner skin; c aluminium trim; d insulation; e neoprene gasket; f laminated glass; g stainless steel screws (6 per panel); h enamelled extruded aluminium subframe; i stainless steel nut and bolt; j outer tube of lattice truss/column.

Section on junction between glazed and solid panels.

Junction between truss and glass gable wall (drawn by architect).

from the centre line of the outer tube of the column in order to allow a simple transition of the cladding from the wall to the roof plane. There are two expansion joints down the length of the building, approximately at third points.

The first two rows of truss and columns at each gable end of the building, and those each side of the expansion joints, are crossbraced together on their outer sides to resist horizontal forces. Those at the gable are also crossbraced on their inner side, and have joints on each truss, at the level of the bottom boom of the truss, in order to transfer wind forces from the glass gable wall to ground. The columns cantilever off a concrete strip footing which is integral with the ground floor slab. To allow free passage, the column diagonals are omitted at ground floor level, the column behaving

partly as a frame, partly as a truss. An 8.90m wide basement running the length of the building contains space for a workshop, storage, plant and other utilities and is connected to the ground floor via hydraulic lifts and spiral staircases. Two spiral staircases serve as fire exits to the outside and a ramp on the north-west side allows vehicular access. The basement has its own heating and ventilation system.

The external cladding on the roof and walls consists of solid, grilled or glass panels each being the same size and fitting into a 1.800 x 1.200 m grid of neoprene strips which seal the joint and double up as rainwater channels that discharge into precast concrete channels along the sides of the building. The curved corner panels are either solid or transparent. Solid panels consist of a

vacuum-formed and highly reflective aluminium outer skin and an inner skin, also in aluminium, with phenolic resin foam insulation between, or polystyrene insulation in the case of the curved panels. Each panel is supported by an extruded aluminium Z-section subframe which is bolted to the main structure. The glass gable walls are made of toughened (tempered) glass in panels 2.400 x 7.500 m high and supported by glass fins attached at the floor and ceiling levels. Internal linings consist of perforated and adjustable aluminium louvre strips. In the walls the louvres are in panels and most include a neat row of long-throw air diffusers which are each connected to one of the 40 package heating and ventilation units contained within the buffer zone. The shapes of some of these units are just visible through the

SAINSBURY CENTRE (1978)

Description:
Single-storey art gallery with lattice steel columns and roof
trusses and box-type panel cladding
Architects:
Foster Associates
Structural engineers:
A. Hunt Associates

Axonometric
view from S:

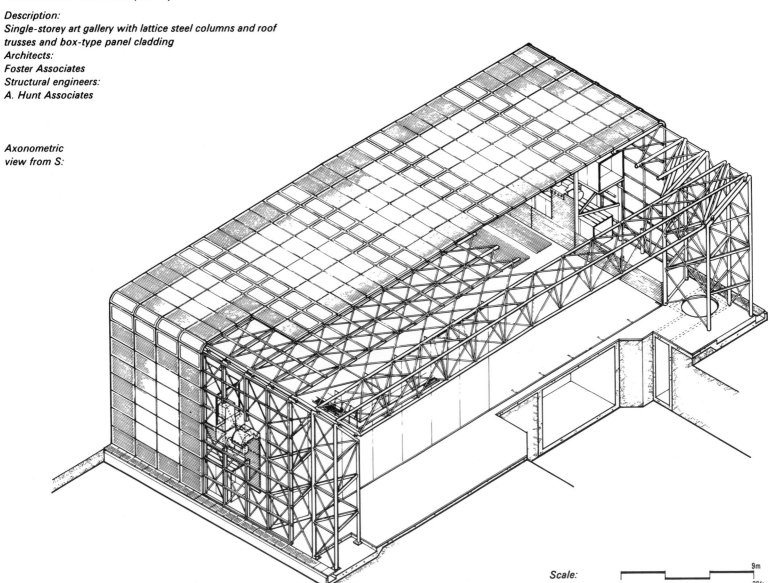

Scale:

9m
30ft

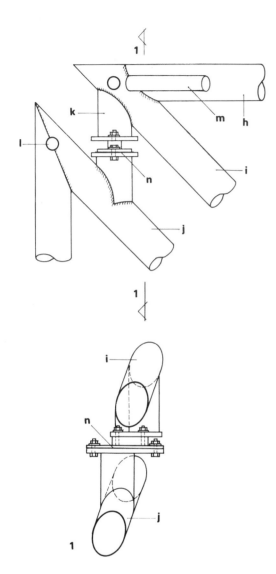

View of entrance on SW side.

h top boom of truss; **i** diagonal member of truss; **j** diagonal member of lattice column; **k** supporting tube; **l** transverse member; **m** diagonal bracing; **n** steel plate with slotted holes resting on ptfe layer.

Sliding joint between truss and column.

louvres. In the roof the louvres are in strips at ceiling level; there are additional louvres underneath the glazed roof strips, at the top of the truss, controlled automatically by light meters. Artificial lighting is provided at ceiling level; access is by catwalks within the depth of the roof trusses. The heating units use fresh and recirculated air; primary heat is supplied by hot water from a central plant. Ventilation is provided but no cooling, hot air being allowed to float up to the ceiling level and solar heat being largely reflected by the external cladding.

Structural Action

The roof truss and lattice columns work like a beam and post system, the columns acting as vertical cantilevers. Wind loads in the longitudinal direction are taken by cross-bracing. The maximum vertical deflection at the centre of the truss is expected to be 84mm and the maximum horizontal sway in either direction at the top of the column is expected to be 25mm. A flexible gasket round the edge of the glass gable wall allows this movement to take place without damage to the glass.

Construction

The lattice columns and truss are of welded construction, the column being brought onto site in one piece and the truss in two pieces. After the columns were erected, the truss was erected on them and on a temporary trestle in the middle; the two pieces were then welded together. Only one crane was needed. Because of the cladding

Inside view looking NW.

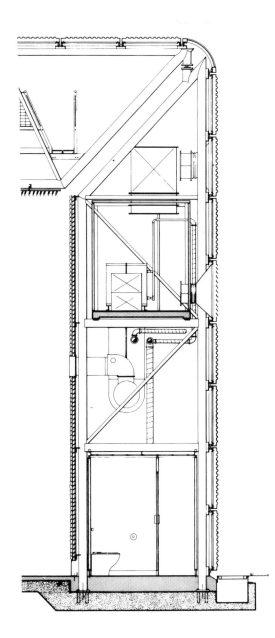

Vertical section through wall (drawn by architect).

system, erection tolerances were extremely tight the tolerance on distances between adjacent columns and trusses being no more than ±3mm, horizontally and vertically, and the absolute positional tolerance on the landing plate lugs, which receive the cladding subframe, being a mere ±1½mm within the plane of the external cladding. This was necessary to achieve a good fit for the neoprene seal but approaches the limits achievable with conventional construction techniques. The total period of construction was 18 months.

Conclusion

The quality of this design is achieved by tenaciously sticking to a few principles concerned with the use of modular panels, open ends, clean edge details and uninterrupted spaces. The control of natural light and the gauze-like effect of the internal linings is particularly successful. In this building the machine aesthetic has been thoroughly tamed, machinery or services having been tidied either to the sides or below in the basement. The result is a piece of almost classic architecture in which, the utilities having been hidden, the visible elements can be elegantly and simply arranged. Even more than most, this building needs materials with good long-term performance so that elements and surfaces continue to exercise their original, and entrancing, effect.

Woodhull Medical and Mental Health Center, Brooklyn, USA

Introduction

Hospital design has been characterised by the extreme complexity of the space planning which arises from several factors: the different, usually increased, demands made on hospital resources; the rapid development and greater use of medical technology; the various, often obscure, functional relationships between departments requiring their close proximity; the numbers of movements of people and of material, such as samples, supplies, refuse or equipment; the need for storage and processing of large amounts of data, partly as a result of more sophisticated medical procedures and fuller patient records; the large number of services required both for the internal spaces and the equipment in it; the need to provide separate plumbing and gas exhausts for risk areas or to prevent cross-infection; the requirements, unusual in most public buildings, that the hospital services be uninterrupted and available at all hours. A consequence of factors such as these is that many existing hospital buildings are obsolete or need modernisation, even soon after completion. The design of this 615-bed hospital meets these problems head on, by providing a generic building arrangement with open spaces that are unplanned, except in a general way, but are adaptable in use and make generous provision for the services. The principle is that detailed planning is separated from the general planning and is not allowed to affect the overall form or future use of the various areas of the hospital. Indeed, in this case, the detailed design for initial fitting out had not been completed by the time the erection of the steel frame started on site and, with half of the steelwork erected, still no final plans or mechanical layouts had been issued to the subcontractors concerned. The freeing of the initial design from all the detailed matters has allowed greater concentration on some of the fundamentals of building design such as circulation patterns and the provision of light. This rugged approach to building is reflected both in plan and on elevation.

Description

The hospital contains 850 000 sq ft (79 000 sq m) of space and is of steel frame construction. On

View of hospital from SE (photo by Henry Wood).

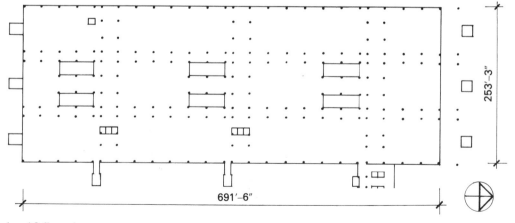

Level 2 floor plan.

253'-3"

691'-6"

WOODHULL MEDICAL AND MENTAL HEALTH CENTRE (1976)

Description:
Ten-storey hospital of steel frame construction using deep interstitial trusses at each floor level
Architects:
Kallmann, Mckinnell and Wood/
Russo and Sonder
Structural engineers:
P. Weidlinger

Axonometric view from SE:

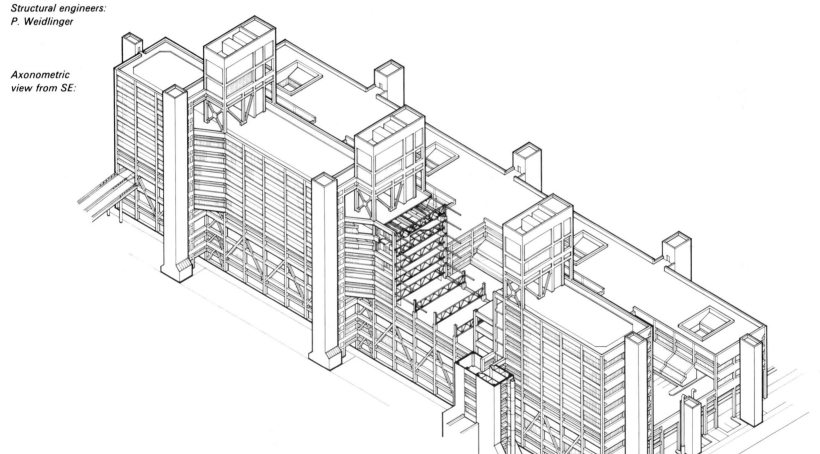

Scale:
12m
40ft

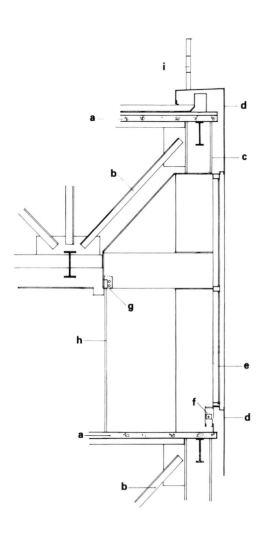

a 4½"concrete slab on metal deck; **b** 8'–0" deep interstitial steel truss; **c** steel column with fireproofing; **d** weathering steel cladding; **e** grey-tinted heat-reflecting glass; **f** fintube radiators; **g** light fixture; **h** sliding glass doors; **i** railing.

Vertical section through wall at top.

elevation, matt, russett-coloured weathering steel surrounds large areas of grey-tinted glazing and direct expression is given of ramps, ward spaces, elevator cores, cross-bracing and the cooling towers. The three lowest levels are reserved for outpatient clinics, these clinics being accommodated in three column-free areas, at each level, with corridors between. The level above this, to which the spiral ramp gives access, is level 4, which is set aside for car parking, both under the two tower blocks and on the roof space between them. Level 5, in the tower blocks, is for mental health care, with the remaining five levels in the tower block on the east side being for inpatient care. The key part of the construction is an interstitial floor system consisting of a nearly 69ft (21m) long truss, 8ft (2.44m) deep at 28ft 6in (8.7m) centres, which is a multiple of the chosen module of 4ft 9in (1.45m). A series of floor beams at 7ft 1½in (2.2m) centres runs between the truss panel points supporting a 4½in (114mm) concrete slab on a metal deck. Light steel trusses run between the bottom chords of the interstitial truss and support the ceiling and catwalks for access within the truss. Within the interstitial truss depth are located the electrical transformer rooms, all the air handling units - thus almost eliminating the need for vertical ducts- as well as horizontal ducts, cables and pipes, including those for domestic, hot and cold water, waste, storm water, acid waste, sprinklers, vacuum cleaning, hospital vacuum, high and low pressure compressed air, oxygen, nitrous oxide, nitrogen, and natural gas, as required. Also included are pneumatic chutes for soiled laundry and refuse and, to deliver packages, self-propelled electric cars moving on tracks within the truss and down vertical shafts. The list indicates the range of services provided and the value of good access for maintenance and renewal without disturbance to patients or staff in the ward levels. The interstitial zone is 10ft (3.05m) deep overall, leaving a clear height of 8ft 4in (2.54m) or 9ft (2.74m) in the wards. The interstitial trusses are used at all levels providing almost 69ft (21.03m) of clear space between the columns. As noted, there are three such zones with approximately 12ft (3.66m) wide corridors between them at the lowest three levels; at higher levels, where the truss spans the full width of the tower block, access corridors are provided on each

side of the wards, acting like buffer zones, with a central corridor for the staff. The north-south orientation of the block and the taper on the ceiling near windows, which are almost 20ft (6.10m) high, allow light through the partly glazed partition wall deep into the wards. Sprinklers are provided in all areas and help to allow increases in the compartmented areas and the distance between stairs. In each tower block the floor is split into four compartment areas with a maximum distance of 214ft (65.23m) between the two-hour fire walls; there are five external staircases, one combined with an elevator core, and three other elevator cores in the body of the building.

Structural Action

Both the top and bottom booms of the interstitial truss have a simple connection to the columns and the truss participates in absorbing horizontal forces in the east-west direction. Forces in the north-south direction are taken by the stair and elevator cores, except below level 5, where cross-bracing is introduced on elevation. The tower blocks contain an expansion joint mid-way down their length.

Construction

The complete separation between the structural and mechanical systems allowed the steelwork contract to be let before the design for mechanical services was complete, thus saving time. The costs of mechanical and electrical services were based on unit prices for estimated quantities, or fixed prices in the case of large items of equipment. Working drawings for each type of work were done in the order the work was started on site. The total period from the start of design until completion of the building was slightly over 5½ years, the construction taking place over a 40 month period.

Conclusion

This building is the result of a search for an architecture suitable for a very large, and utilitarian, building. The 'functional' approach that is adopted directly reflects the need to provide an effective service of health care for very large numbers of people. The building is impersonal in the same way that airport buildings are

Close-up on SE corner of building (photo by David Hirsch).

impersonal, because of the large numbers of people processed. But this is not necessarily unwelcome in this kind of building, where an accent on efficiency and cleanliness can be reassuring. From the outside the building seems enormous, which is not a design choice but the inevitable result of grappling with a large scale problem. Inside, the building is generally light with a nice hum; the ward areas are split up by partitioning. The structural solution adopted for the hospital will allow reorganization without the disproportionately high costs usually associated with this. It also takes due account of the importance of the services which, in this case, amount to more than 40% of total costs, compared to 12% for the structure. The amount of steel used averaged 13 lb per sq ft (64 kg per sq m) of floor area. In spite of the simplifications provided by the use of interstitial trusses, the design is a taxing exercise both in terms of the very complex planning and the external treatment of a large volume, conspicuous even in its urban setting.

Nucleus Hospital, Maidstone, England

Introduction

What are perceived as disorders of the body have created subjects for study as well as important social institutions for their treatment. Treatment, however, does not always bring cure. Of all such institutions the most historic and, based as it is on science, the most successful is the hospital. Nonetheless, for the patient, the great, tangible benefits of hospital treatment have to be set against the disadvantages of bureaucratised care and the passing away of authority from the patients themselves to the medical staff. The layout, modest size and the light touch of the architecture for this hospital do much to dispel these concerns. Indeed the architects manage to suggest that what is offered here is not just efficient treatment but sympathetic handling and care in a modern cottage industry. The hospital has 300 beds which is of a size such that the building contract, including the large number of service installations, can be properly controlled and the planning is known to be workable but which is still of a size that is large enough to support the specialist staff required. The design gives good integration of the building fabric with the services and utilities, making their maintenance and replacement relatively convenient operations.

Description

The design for the hospital was developed from a standard prototype system, known as Nucleus, that has also been used as the basis for other designs. The prototype is a complete but theoretical design consisting, as here, of six two-storey blocks, that are cruciform in plan, a central corridor area, known as the Hospital Street, with plant rooms at roof level, and a supplies and service centre connected to the cruciforms by the central corridor. Only the planning of each cruciform in the prototype needs to be followed in each application of the system, the type of structure, cladding system and choice of materials being decided individually for each case. As hospital planning is notoriously complex, the resolution of the plans and room arrangements in advance saves time. However the design does not allow for future changes of use. The expansion of

View of entrance (photo by P. Lines).

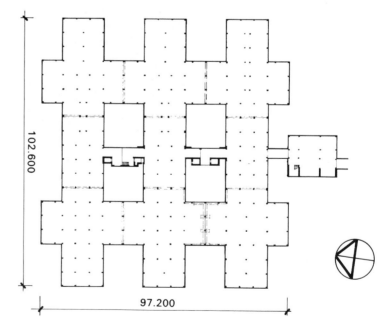

102.600

97.200

Ground floor plan of main block.

MAIDSTONE NUCLEUS HOSPITAL (1983)

Description:
Two-storey hospital with concrete frame, steel roof and metal
cladding
Architects:
Powell Moya and Partners
Structural engineers:
C. Weiss and Partners
Architects for prototype:
DHSS
Structural engineers
for prototype:
Gifford and Partners

Axonometric
view from SW:

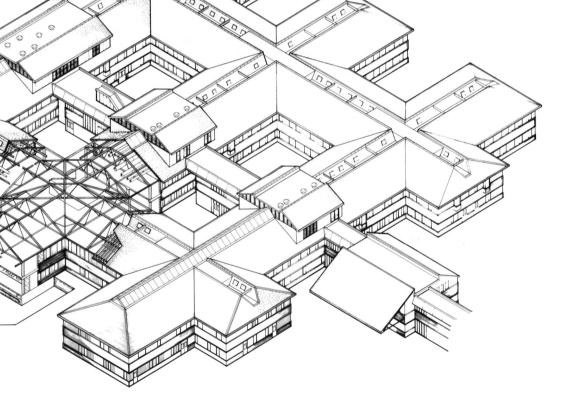

Scale: 12 m
40 ft

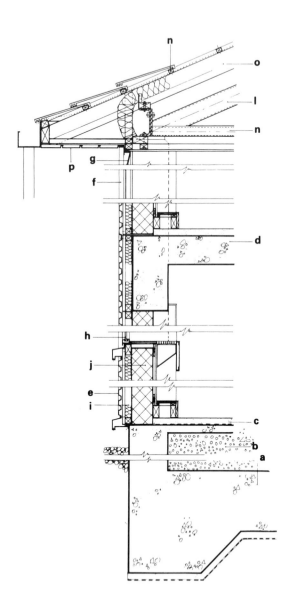

View on cladding (photo by Andrew Clarke).

a 400mm deep concrete raft; **b** 500mm void backfilled after laying of services; **c** 100mm concrete slab on fill with 50mm screed; **d** 175mm concrete slab; **e** white plastic coated galvanised steel sheet attached to softwood vertical battens at 1.8m centres fixed to blockwork; **f** brown plastic coated galvanised steel tray sheets attached to softwood horizontal battens; **g** louvred windows; **h** window; **i** 38mm insulation between battens; **j** 150mm block wall; **k** housing for hot water radiators; **l** 120 x 120 x 5mm square hollow section; **m** 120 x 60 x 3.6mm rectangular hollow section; **n** 25 x 38mm softwood battens on felt; **o** 63 x 150mm softwood rafters; **p** plastic coated steel weatherboarding on 38 x 38mm softwood battens at 600mm centres.

Vertical section through wall of ward units.

the hospitals at any later date occurs simply by addition of more cruciform blocks to those already there.

The construction of this particular hospital consists of a concrete raft foundation, a cast-in-place concrete frame, a steel truss roof with a tiled finish and plastic-coated steel sheet wall cladding. The main building contains the wards and the operating theatres. The supplies and service centre contains a restaurant and kitchen, a pathology laboratory and some other facilities. All the boilers for the hospital are in a separate building on the south side, unlike the prototype where these are dispersed in roof-top plant rooms in an effort to save on distribution. However the three roof-top plant rooms are placed above the central corridor, as in the prototype, at the places where the cruciform blocks join the corridor, with a fourth on the roof of the supplies and service centre. These plant rooms contain air handling units and chiller units and, in one of the three over the main building, there are calorifiers to convert steam from the boiler house to hot water for distribution to radiators around the perimeter of the cruciforms. Heating over most of the ward areas is provided by these perimeter radiators and cooling by natural ventilation. In the core of the cruciform there is full air conditioning, which is automatically controlled, each core being supplied by one dual-duct air-handling unit. Special provision is made for the four operating theatres on the north side which have two separate air-handling units. Distribution pipes run at roof level from the boiler house to the corridor plant rooms and from here through vertical ducts that distribute to horizontal service zones within the steel roof trusses and below the concrete floor structure. From these horizontal zones, services may be dropped down the middle of the interior partitions and behind the dry lining against the exterior walls.

The building structure was almost entirely determined by planning and servicing requirements except that as the ground on this site is subject to swallow holes up to 6m in diameter, a 400mm deep concrete raft foundation was necessary for columns instead of the pad foundations which would have been adequate on good ground. This made it possible to provide a 500mm service zone above the raft for soil and waste pipes which was backfilled and concreted over with a 100mm ground floor slab when the pipes had been installed. The floor above the ground level consists of a 200mm concrete flat slab supported by columns on a 5.4m square grid; at the edges there is a 250 x 500mm perimeter beam; interior columns, which are 250mm square, have pyramid-shaped dropheads. Where the servicing permits, this structure is exchanged for a beam and slab arrangement, the slab being 175mm thick, the beams being 400 x 525mm in section at 5.4m centres and spanning 8m. The overall depth of the floor including the structure and service zones is 1.2m, from finished floor level to the underside of the suspended ceiling.

The top floor is a clear space with only the perimeter columns continuing to eaves level to support the roof trusses, which are 2.6m deep in the middle and made of steel hollow sections. The trusses span 16m across the arms of each cruciform and in the core area two longer trusses placed on the diagonals are connected together to form a space truss. Although the truss arrangement is standard, the roof outline varies; over the wards the roof has a central valley, exposing the top boom of the truss but allowing excellent natural lighting into the middle of the ward; by contrast, over the operating theatres, an extra high ridge is created to enclose the heavy servicing required in the roof there.

The hospital has only two storeys, except where there are corridor plant rooms. The plant rooms need to be at roof level to connect to the main service runs but are slightly too large to be smoothed into the outline of the lower storeys. Nevertheless the scale is kept small, and helped by the sloping tiled roofs, the arms of the cruciform which break up bulk and the bands of cladding seen on elevation with rainwater pipes delicately held in front of them. The cladding is important, given the large wall areas resulting from this plan form, and deftly handled. It consists of brown plastic coated steel planks running vertically, allowing any desired amount of fenestration, and below this, uninterrupted bands of white steel sheets with horizontal ribbing. In general there is copious natural light especially in the corridors creating sharp, 'white' space but the amount of light is always controllable from inside the wards by shutters and blinds. On the inside of the exterior wall there is a 145mm gap for services between the

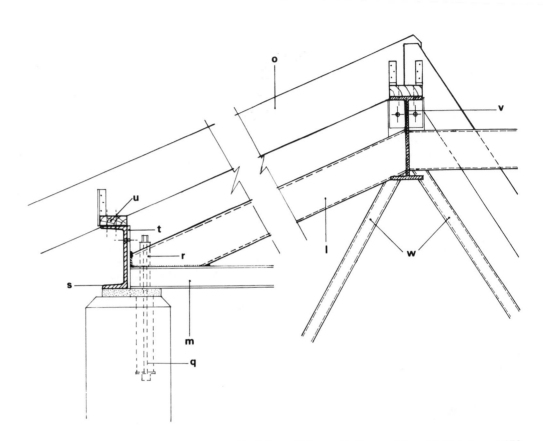

q 20mm bolt 400mm long with 6mm washer; r 48 x 3.2 mm thick round hollow section welded into truss; s 178 x 76 mm steel channel; t 120 x 10 mm steel plate; u 75 x 50 mm softwood attached to rafter by pressed metal clip; v 254 x 102 mm I-section; w 42 x 4 mm thick round hollow section.

Vertical section at eaves and apex of roof.

dry lining and the blockwork behind the metal cladding. The internal partitions are made from metal studs and gypsum board with an overall thickness of 100 or 200 mm providing clear space for services in the middle of 60 or 146 mm respectively. Some interior walls are of blockwork.

Structural Action

Stability against horizontal forces is provided by action of the frame and walls at ground floor level and by cantilever action of the columns on the floor above. Because of the uncertain ground

conditions the building is split by movement joints into separate structural entities: the ancillary buildings to the south are all independent and the main building is split into nine structurally separate units by two north-south joints 27m apart, either side of the corridor, and by two east-west joints 32.4m apart, going through each end of the two central cruciforms.

Construction

The hospital was completed within programme in 37 months. On this open site a single crawler crane

View on courtyard with corridor plant room above (photo by Andrew Clarke).

Construction at corridor plant room showing raft foundation (photo by Andrew Clarke).

was used for lifting instead of a tower crane.

Conclusion

Except at corridor plant rooms, the hospital has appropriately clean shapes, as compared with the ungainly effect of an uncontrolled coalescence of blocks or the austerity and disorientation sometimes produced by an over-simple geometry. The approach is 'cheap and cheerful', almost the only one possible in face of a tight budget, with plenty of light, colour and an explicit discipline at work. The design is strengthened by the formal planning of the buildings and courtyards. The approach to durability, for many components an unknown factor, is 'wait and see' in the knowledge that vulnerable parts, such as the steel cladding, are easy to replace. The building structure is the bare minimum, in deference to the requirements of the services. The cost of the structure is a mere 11% of the total building cost, with a further 5% for the raft foundations, compared with 43% for all the services; external walls, windows and doors amount to 6%, internal walls, partitions and doors to 8%, with site works, finishes and fittings accounting for the remaining building costs. There are equipment costs, too, amounting to almost 25% of the building cost. The running costs in the first year were well over 60% of the building cost and, historically, on a rising trend in real terms; put another way, a fully equipped general hosptial can be paid for by a two-year delay, suggesting that the long-term concerns are not the durability of the building but the resources that must be earned to keep it in existence. This is an inspiring piece of work of obvious value and, in this perspective, of modest cost.

Chapter Ten

Sports and Storage Buildings

The buildings in this chapter are grouped by their type of use but could also be grouped together by the type of space they provide. The basic, common requirement is that the buildings should provide an economic means of covering a large single-storey volume. Scale has an important effect. With buildings of the size of those in this chapter, the structure always has a major influence on the form and appearance of the building and, in general, the structure takes the form of a frame or truss structure. The buildings, here, show some of the infinite number of variations that are possible within these two generic types. They also demonstrate how the architects have been able to exploit the structure in the design and to marry it with other elements. At this scale the movements that occur, for example, those due to temperature variations or accumulations of snow and rainwater, assume great importance in the design of the building. Examples of some other general methods of covering large spaces are given in the next chapter.

Sankey Warehouse,
Epsom, England

Introduction

Only rarely does a utility building receive as much attention at design stage as this. This is a simple rectangular building, crisply detailed and cheaply built, with 2000 sq m of storage space at ground floor level and a further 210 sq m of office space at a mezzanine level. The building throws up general points concerning the factors which affect building costs, and the judgement involved in selecting elements which can be combined into a piece of architecture. Here the internal office walls and the external walls, particularly the well proportioned glass gable wall, constititute the permanent architectural elements; most of the spaces are not consciously ordered and detailed and thus left to develop their own character. This kind of decision, necessary in all design work, can be badly judged or ignored with consequences which may range from awkward-looking lumps or elements in disarray, at one extreme, to fussy detail or irritating irrelevancies at the other. The building structure consists mainly of a series of pitched portal frames but, by an apposite use of hipped ends and a parapet all the way round, the roof is totally separated from the walls to the benefit of the building as a whole.

Description

Immediately behind the glass wall on the south elevation are a small parts store at ground floor level and an office at the mezzanine level, both spaces being separated from the main double-height warehouse space to the north by a 190mm blockwork wall 7.70m behind the glass wall; the gap between the top of the wall and the roof soffit is closed by a plasterboard partition on light metal framework. The building structure consists of 11 portal frames, each with a 5 degree roof pitch, and two rectangular frames at each end of the building with the same height as the eaves of the portal frames. Hip members connect the corners of the building to the ridge of the roof and stabilise it; crossbracing using 25mm tierods and turnbuckles is also provided in the plane of the roof near one end. The roof is covered with steel sheeting on gypsum board with insulation; there are also roof glazing strips in each bay between portal frames.

View of building from E (photo by Jo Reid and John Peck).

Walls are clad in vertically ribbed steel sheet or glass.

The glass wall is made up of standard galvanised steel windows, bolted together and powder-coated in bright green. Two lines of opening lights are incorporated in the glass wall; the frames for these are hardly thicker than those for fixed lights. Temperature movement takes place at each mullion position. A concrete upstand wall around the perimeter of the building is about 1.20m high; it serves both as a retaining wall and as the hard kicker strip at the base of the wall

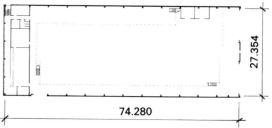

27.354

74.280

Plan at ground floor level.

SANKEY WAREHOUSE (1978)

Description:
Single-storey warehouse of steel portal frame construction
Architects:
Jestico and Whiles
Structural engineer:
Budgen and Partners

Axonometric
view from SE:

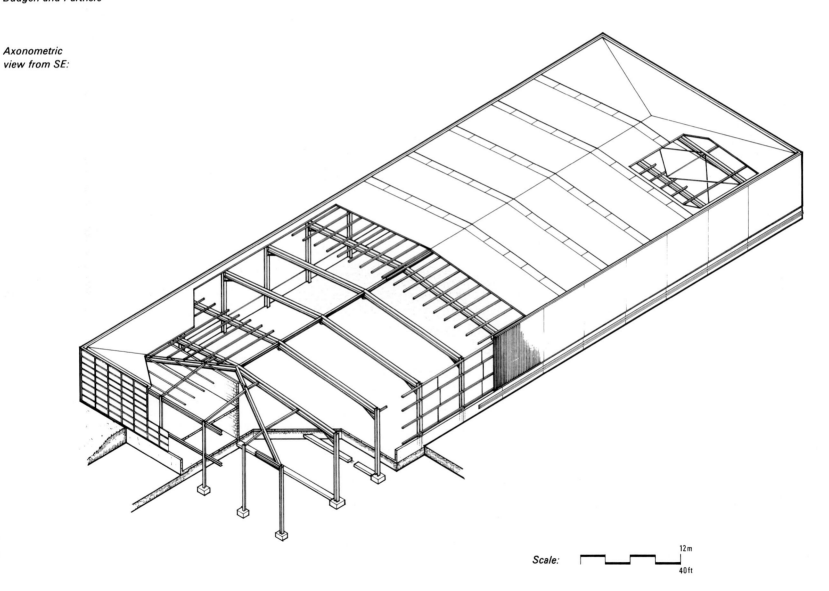

Scale:

12 m

40 ft

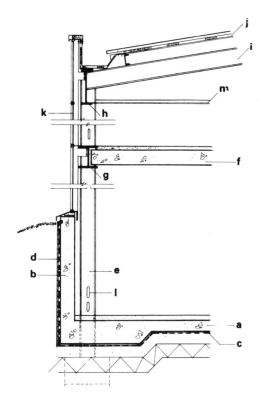

Inside of office looking W (photo by Jo Reid and John Peck).

Interior view of W wall (photo by Jo Reid and John Peck).

a 50mm screed on 150mm concrete slab with top mesh reinforcement; **b** 155mm concrete wall; **c** dpm; **d** fibre board; **e** 203 x 133 x 30 kg/m UB; **f** 200mm precast concrete slab with topping; **g** 254 x 254 x 89 kg/m UC bolted to column web; **h** 406 x 140 x 50 kg/m UB; **i** 203 x 133 x 25 kg/m UB; **j** steel decking on gypsum board with insulation; **k** 100mm deep steel window mullions at 1.856m centres; **l** elongated holes for radiator pipes; **m** suspended ceiling.

Vertical section through S wall.

cladding. Except at the south end, the entire ground floor slab is of unreinforced concrete 200mm thick, 'floating' on hardcore and separated from columns by movement joints. Heating in the offices and small parts store is by hot water radiators fitted directly between the steel columns. Solar gain is controlled by internal blinds and opening lights. A five-level stack in the corner of the main warehouse space contains, a meter, two boiler plants, a calorifier and an expansion tank. The main artificial lighting is by three strips of fluorescent tubes running parallel to the window wall. The staircase leading to the office also provides fire escape access to the outside; it is fabricated in steelwork and all doors leading to it have a half-hour fire resistance. Because it runs near a boundary line, the whole of the west side of the building is given a two-hour fire rating and the columns on this side are encased and designed to remain free-standing after collapse of the rest of the building in a fire.

Structural Action

The single-storey steel portal frame, with columns pinned at the base, is one of the cheapest ways of supplying covered space and rivalled, in terms of cost, only by the steel lattice girder with columns fixed at the base. Ties are needed across the base of each portal frame to restrain side thrusts. The maximum bending moment in the frame occurs at the bolted eaves connection and, under a relatively light roof load, amounts to nearly 440 kilonewton-metres and slightly over a quarter of this in reversed bending. Although the frame is designed as a two pin portal frame, the columns on the west side are given a certain amount of fixity, to enable them to stand in a fire. The portal frame can be thought of as a straight sided arch in which the maximum moments occur at those points, such as the eaves and apex, which are furthest from the thrust line of the arch.

Construction

The total period of construction amounted to 9 months. Each portal frame was brought onto site in four parts and bolted together at eaves and apex joints. The unreinforced concrete ground floor slab was laid in strips about 4.600m wide with 12mm dowel bars 450mm long at 450mm centres across the construction joints.

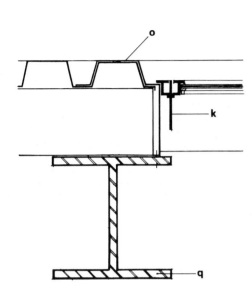

Horizontal section at junction between steel cladding and glass curtain wall.

Conclusion

The low cost of the building is the result of several factors: economy was obtained in the use of the steel window system by selection of standard components and details and by taking proper account of the pricing systems; the steel wall cladding is simple, there being no openings in it apart from doorways and two round holes for the boiler flues. The portal frame at this span and up to about 30m is comparable in cost of steelwork to a truss system but can be lower in height and this tends to save money overall; also the spacing of the portal frames at 5.92m is within the economic range for this span which would extend to about 7.50m, not including cladding costs. Money was also saved by omitting reinforcement in the ground floor slab. The line at which intentional design stops is well drawn and has played its part in reducing cost as well as delivering a robust building.

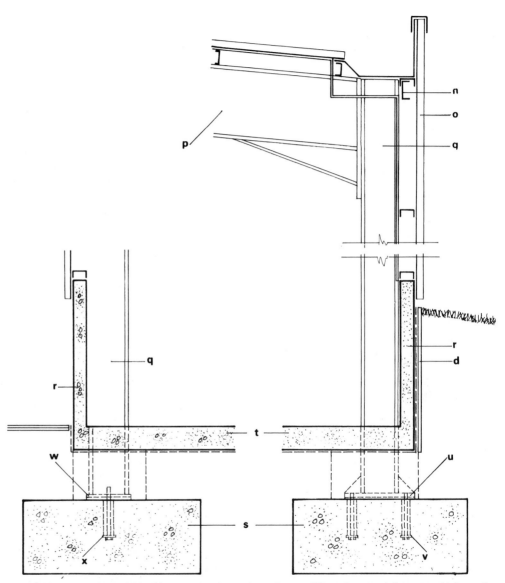

n 152 x 76 channel welded to 203 x 76 channel and bolted to column; o 53mm deep steel sheet on cold-formed steel channel at 1.8m centres with insulation and gypsum board lining; p 610 x 305 x 149 kg/m UB; q 305 x 305 x 198 kg/m UC; r 210mm concrete wall; s 1500 x 1500 x 700 mm deep mass concrete base; t 300mm unreinforced concrete slab on hardcore; u 600 x 600 x 40 mm baseplate with 2/ 40mm plate stiffeners either side of web and 4/ 32 x 600 mm long bolts; v 600mm long anchor plate; w 350 x 350 x 25 mm baseplate with 2/ 25 x 450 mm long bolts; x 350mm long anchor plate.

Typical vertical section through E and W walls.

Penguin Books Warehouse, Harmondsworth, England

Introduction

Warehouses act as the buffer zones between the factories of the manufacturing industries and their markets and are an important class in any typology of buildings. Several general features may be picked out in buildings of this class: large clear areas, small numbers of operating staff, heavy ground floors laid with strict tolerances on level and sophisticated handling systems which help to dictate column arrangements. This building has space for about 38 million books and, more significantly, has a turnover of 65 million books a year with a staff of around four people. The clear height of the building and the distance between adjacent columns is precisely determined by stock widths and the widths required for handling, which in this case is done by a purpose-made fork lift truck system. The building is of precast concrete construction and has a simple form needing only occasional maintenance.

Description

The basic need is to provide large covered areas for metal storage racks. The dimensions of the rack and the fork lift truck operation determined the clear height of the building at 28ft (8.54m) and the column spacing in the east-west direction at 13ft 6in (4.12m). The distance between columns in the north-south direction is 77ft (23.48m) except at the two ends where the roof span goes down to 35ft 1in (10.69m); there is a trade-off here between clear space and structural costs. The roof consists of V-shaped precast reinforced concrete trough units joined together to make a continuous length of 301ft 2in (91.89m), spanning over four internal columns in the north-south direction. An important aspect was the request for a high degree of natural lighting and this together with the desirability of a structure with good fire resistance and bending stiffness led to the choice of concrete in preference to steel. Each line of roof units is structurally independent of the others; a bowed corrugated sheet of clear pvc is put across the 4ft (1.22m) gap between adjacent units and allows in daylight. Apart from very minor differences, each line of units is identical. In each line there are three types of roof unit: the end type, 54ft (16.47m)

View of building from S (photo by Colin Westwood).

long, at the north and south ends of the roof line; the internal type, 35ft 9in (10.90m) with its midpoint over the internal columns; the intermediate type, 12ft 9in (3.89m) long, spanning between the ends of one or other of the first two types. All joints between units occur in the 77ft (23.48m) spans at the ends of the intermediate roof type and are at quarter span positions, which are near the points of contraflexure, those points where there is no bending moment. To limit distortion of the cross-section, diaphragms are cast at both ends of all roof units and over all column positions except, for visual reasons, in the outer end of the end roof type where a diaphragm is placed 14ft (4.27m) from the outer end. There are flange restraints too. The joint consists of a 3in (75mm) nib projecting from the diaphragm of the intermediate type which fits in a recess on the other diaphragm, the two diaphragms then being grouted and bolted together. All columns are precast. The internal columns are 2 x 1 ft (600 x 300mm) in section and the external ones are 2ft (600mm) square but split in two parts to allow room for a drainpipe; columns are attached to roof units by dowel bars cast in the head of the columns. There are a total of 28 controllable ventilators placed in the lighting strips, each with an area of 16.4 sq ft (1.52 sq m); in conjunction with honeycomb brickwork on the

north and south sides they provide natural ventilation and are spring loaded to open up as smoke extracts, in case of fire. Sprinklers are fitted at ceiling level. A rudimentary form of heating is provided by hot water batteries in the roof such that an internal temperature of 50°F (10°C) can be maintained when it is freezing outside.

Structural Action

Without the need for natural light, the roof could have been a folded plate. The V-shaped trough units actually used work independently of each

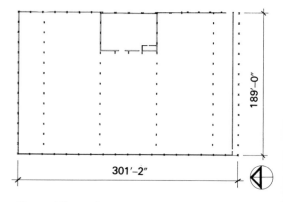

Ground floor plan.

PENGUIN BOOKS WAREHOUSE (1967)

Description:
Single-storey building of precast concrete
construction with trough units for roof
Architects and structural engineers:
Arup Associates

Axonometric
view from NW:

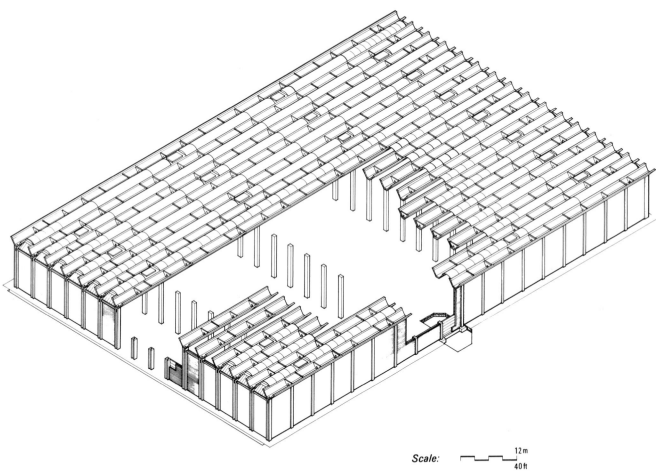

Scale: 12 m
              40 ft

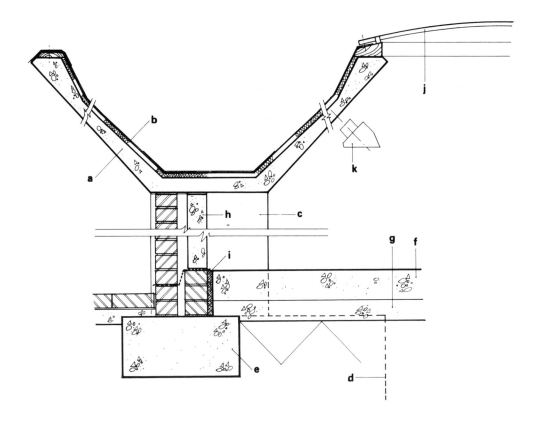

a 9'-6" x 4'-0" deep precast concrete unit with 2½" webs; b 2 layers of roofing felt on ¾" of rigid insulation; c 2'-0" x 1'-0" column of roof unit line; d 4'-0" x 6'-0" x 2'-11" deep base for perimeter columns; e 2'-0" x 1'-0" strip footing; f 6" concrete slab with mesh reinforcement in top; g 4" unreinforced concrete; h 4" precast concrete panels attached to brickwork with cramps; i movement joint; j clear pvc corrugated sheet; k light fitting.

Vertical section through side walls.

other and therefore require greater thickness than a comparable folded plate. The trough units work as beams bending about a neutral axis. The top flanges are in compression and therefore, potentially, are subject to buckling. Buckling is prevented by thickening of the flanges, by flange restraint members and by rigid diaphragms. Some torsion may be present and engenders warping stresses including longitudinal stresses. The roof units are insulated but because there are no expansion joints, the columns are designed to be flexible enough to accept up to ¾in (19mm) movement at their top at the ends of each roof line. Most horizontal forces on the building are taken by the perimeter columns acting as cantilevers and these columns have pad foundations 4 x 6 ft (1.22 x 1.83 m) in plan. The internal columns, although carrying considerably more vertical load, have smaller pad foundations which are 4 x 7 ft (1.22 x 2.13 m) in plan.

Construction

The building was constructed in a period of 10 months. The speed of construction on site was partly due to the extensive use of precast elements. The precast columns were cast into pockets in the pad foundations. The roof units were lifted by crane using a steel lifting beam and lowered onto dowels in the top of the columns. Interior units had to be supported on scaffolding until a complete line had been bolted up.

Conclusion

The cost of the foundations and ground floor slab amounted to 16% of the total, this high proportion being largely due to the cost of the ground floor slab for which some backfilling was necessary from other parts of the site. The building structure and services each amounted to about 27% of the total, the remaining amounts being accounted for by felting of the roof, roof-lights, walls, doors and windows, preliminaries and finishes and fitting. Note that the building is designed for expansion to the west by addition of further lines of structure. The span of the roof units could have been increased by prestressing but the problems of transporting to site would remain. The omission of roof diaphragms on the north and south ends is typical of the artifice needed for such apparently simple solutions.

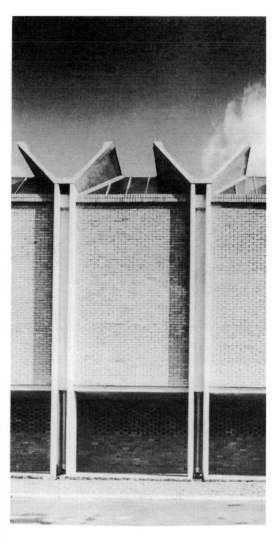

View of S wall of building (photo by Colin Westwood).

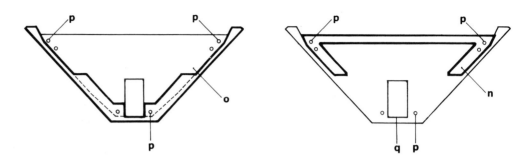

End views each side of roof panel joints.

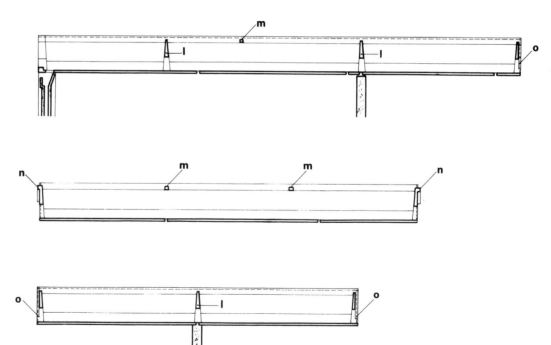

l diaphragm with average thickness of $4\frac{1}{2}''$; **m** 4" square flange restraint; **n** 3" nib at joint; **o** joint recess; **p** 1" holes for $\frac{3}{4}''$ stainless steel bolts; **q** hole for drainage.

Longitudinal section on end, internal and intermediate roof types.

Anacostia Park Pavilion, Washington, D.C., USA

Introduction

This roller rink has been provided in parkland and is covered over by a deep roof structure sitting on smooth round columns. The effect is to give a classic feel and presence to the building. Unusually, but very appropriately in view of its setting, the roof structure is made up of a series of deep trusses, not in steel but in laminated wood.

Description

The two lines of columns are 120ft (36.58m) apart and spanned by the wood trusses with a 13ft 4in (4.06m) overhang beyond the column on each side. The columns are hollow prestressed concrete pipes of 42in (1.07m) diameter with a 5in (125mm) thick wall. They are attached to pad foundations by a plug of reinforced concrete at the bottom and to a 6in (150mm) diameter steel hollow section stub column, which supports the truss, by another plug at the top. The concrete pad foundations rest on strips of fill material which have been compacted to allow a bearing pressure of 1 ton per sq ft (107 kilonewtons per sq m). There are thirteen trusses. They each have an overall depth of almost 14ft (4.27m) in the middle and 12ft 6in (3.81m) at their ends. The bottom chord is designed to retain a 6in (150mm) camber under the dead load. All members of the truss are laminated timber 6¾in (171mm) thick, being 19½, 15 and 10¼in (495, 381 and 260 mm) deep for the top chord, bottom chord and webs respectively. The members are all in one plane and joined by purpose made ½in (12mm) steel plates either side, connected to the members by ⅞in (22mm) bolts using 4in (100mm) shear plates. The protrusions on one side of the shear plate allow the connecting force to bear over a large area of the wood. The maximum working force in the top and bottom booms, at the centre, is 68 tons (62 tonnes). As the truss was made in two halves connected on the centre line, this force has to be transferred by connecting plates on the top and bottom booms. A total of 24 bolts was used for each connection. Purlins, 6 x 14 in (150 x 356 mm) in section are spaced at 6ft 8in (2.32m) centres which is half the truss bay dimension. Transverse bracing to the bottom chord is provided in at least every other bay

View of pavilion from N (photo by architect).

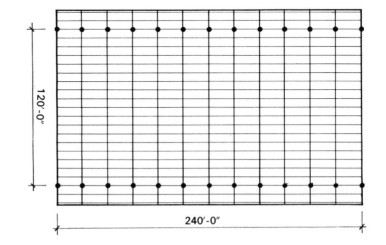

Plan at roof level:

ANACOSTIA PARK PAVILION (1976)

Description:
Single-storey pavilion with precast concrete columns and
timber roof trusses
Architects:
Keyes, Lethbridge and Condon
Structural engineer:
J. M. Cutts

Axonometric
view from E:

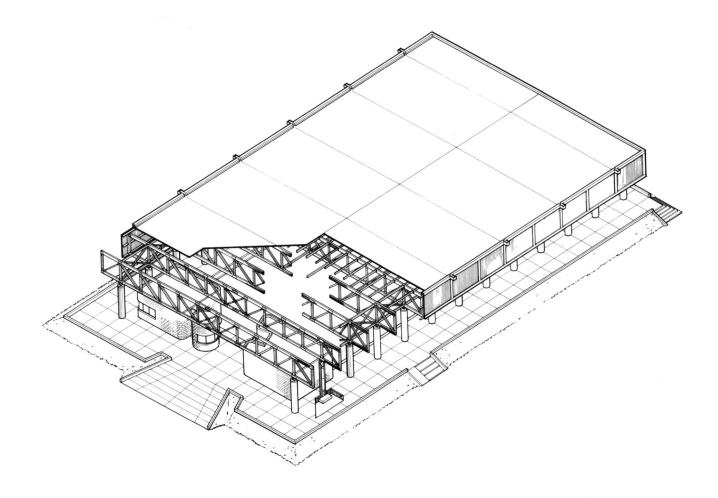

Scale: ⌐‾‾⌐‾‾⌐ 12 m
                    40 ft

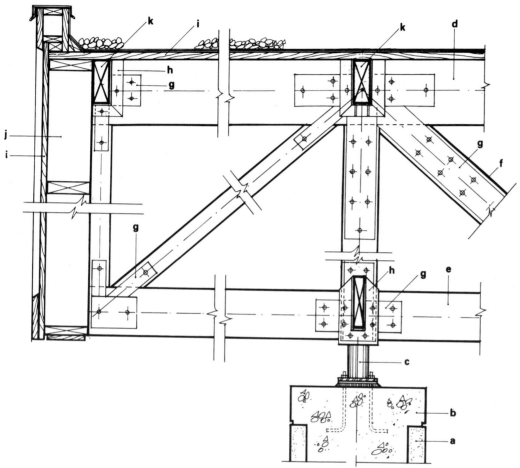

a 5" thick precast prestressed pipe column of 3'-6" diameter; b cast-in-place concrete 'plug' at top; c 6" diameter hollow section stub column; d 6¾" x 19½" laminated timber; e 6¾" x 15" laminated timber; f 6¾" x 12" laminated timber; g purpose made ½" steel plate connector used with 4" shear plates and ⅞" bolts; h seat made from ⅜" steel plate; i 2" thick tongue and groove decking; j vertical blocking piece; k 6" x 14" solid section timber purlins at 6'-8" centres.

Vertical section through SW side.

scuppers protruding from the parapet. The walkway, the low perimeter wall and the steps going down to the skating area are of concrete construction, but the skating area itself is a hard finished asphalt. An office, snack bar, toilets and storage areas are also provided in four free-standing corner blocks in a semi-glazed concrete masonry block. The office has a heating and cooling system in the roof, other areas having electric space heaters only. Lighting in the main areas is provided by four mercury vapour lamps hanging in each bay between the trusses over the skating area. In sunny weather, the pavilion provides shade, while still allowing plenty of light, views out and a gentle breeze to pass through the building.

Structural Action

Although wood has a high strength to weight ratio, similar to that of mild steel, its use in a truss, rather than as a solid section beam, is governed by the efficiency of the joints, especially those joints in tension. In this respect it is at a disadvantage compared to steel which is stronger and therefore easier to join. In small trusses the forces are low. Here a deep truss, to minimise the chord forces, and the use of shear plates are sufficient to solve the problem. The shear plates also greatly reduce the 'give' at joints which can accumulate to produce unwanted deflection. Nevertheless after heavy snow load, the roof will not recover to its original position and proper slope has to be given to the roof to prevent ponding. The total fall on the top surface from the centre to the edge is almost 2ft (600mm).

Construction

The construction was spread over a period of eighteen months.

Conclusion

The building has a simple form which allows contact with the surrounding landscaped area and park. The proportions between column and roof have been carefully chosen and the exposed construction details and the paving patterns are entertaining for the users. The truss with members in one plane provides a pleasingly simple motif for the building.

and, on column lines, the transverse framing is cross-braced. Connections between the trusses and transverse bracing is with joist hangers made from ⅜in (9mm) steel plate. The roof is made of 2 x 8 in (50 x 200 mm) tongue and groove wood planks with built-up roofing on top. The vertical cladding on the long sides of the building consists of light framing attached to the ends of the trusses with 2 x 8 in (50 x 200 mm) wood boarding on the outside framed by larger trim pieces in each bay to give a further scaling effect. Rainwater from the roof is taken clear by metal lined plywood

St. Mary's Athletic Facility, Notre Dame, Indiana, USA

Introduction

Sports buildings require good headroom for ball games. From the surrounding fields, however, this gymnasium is unobtrusive, the headroom being achieved by sinking most of the floor area into the ground. The result is that about 50% of the exterior wall surface is not exposed thus achieving savings in energy use. By surrounding the whole building with a berm of earth about 4ft (1.21m) above the existing ground level, the amount of excavation is reduced and the earth kept drier. The building runs in an east-west line, thus reducing heat gain, and is simply 'chopped' at its ends. Its simple external shape also reduces its prominence. Inside there is good natural light and the detail and geometrical subdivision of the major building elements helps to bring down the scale. Natural light flows inwards, during the day, and artificial light outwards, at night, through high level glass and curved plastic as well as through the translucent double skin fibreglass cladding panels.

Description

The building is entered at the level of the top of the berm. The circulation and standing space for spectators is at this level as is a playing area at the east end. The open high-bay playing area for tennis and basketball, also doubling up as a general assembly area, is 13ft (3.97m) below. There are toilets, showers, storage, plant and electrical equipment rooms at the west end, also at this level, but hidden by the floor slab above. The floors of the two racquetball courts, at the west end, are 21ft (6.4m) below the berm top. Pipes below the floor drain to a sump which can be pumped out. The substructure, the part below the berm top, is of cast-in-place concrete, but not of waterproof construction; the floor slabs are 6in (152mm) thick on a vapour barrier on compacted fill with retaining walls 1ft (305mm) thick damp-proofed and held at their top by the floor at level 1. Blockwork with slotted holes is used inside, to increase sound absorption. The steel trusses supporting the roof span 120ft (36.60m) between circular steel columns which, except at the east end, rest on the two retaining walls going in the east-west direction. The trusses are 5ft 6in

View of building from SW (photo by architect).

(1.68m) deep, relatively shallow, and spaced at 20 ft (6.10m) centres. The top and bottom booms of each truss are braced at the third points, and on the column lines by light steel framing in the longitudinal direction, which has K-bracing every fourth bay. The top booms are further restrained by the 4½in (114mm) deep metal roof decks which are puddle welded to all top booms at 12in (305mm) centres. Light roof loads are hung off the metal deck and heavier ones off the steelwork.

The translucent vertical cladding panels are 2½in (64mm) thick, 12ft (3.66m) high and consist of two sheets of fibreglass with insulation between. Above them are transparent curved acrylic sheets set into extended aluminium sections; acrylic has particularly good weathering properties. At the same level, at the ends of the building, the glazing is ½in (12.7mm) clear floatglass. The plant room in the west end supplies steam and chilled water to eight single zone air conditioning units suspended from the roof. The conditioned air is distributed down short ducts to a

distibutor with five registers (diffusers). The exhaust fans at the centre of each bay, are interlocked with the eight fresh air supply ducts in the roof. If required all supply air may be drawn from the outside. There is plenty of natural light on most days. At night, lighting over the playing areas is provided by sixty-four 400 watt mercury vapour lamps, with fluorescent lights on the bottom chord of the truss, lighting other areas at the upper level. The average power consumption of all the lighting is 1.5 watts per sq ft (16 watts per sq m). The roof and fibreglass cladding have U-values of 0.1 and 0.4 btu per hr sq ft °F (0.6 and 2.3 watts per sq m °C) respectively; the cladding has a shading coefficient of 0.14 further helping to reduce heat losses and gains. The building is completely sprinklered. The roof decking acts with the insulation to make an acoustic absorbent.

Structural Action

Lateral forces in the north-south direction are taken by the truss and circular columns acting as a

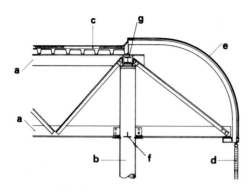

a 5'–6" deep truss with WT9 x 35 lb/ft booms top and bottom (WT9 x 42.5 lb/ft top boom in middle); **b** 12¾" diameter x ½" thick circular column; **c** 4½" acoustic deck; **d** 2½" insulated fibre glass panels on aluminium subframe; **e** ¼" clear acrylic high level glazing on aluminium profiles; **f** bottom boom of bracing framework; **g** top boom of bracing.

Section through S side at top.

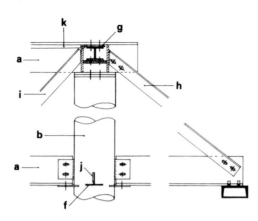

h 2/ 3½" x 3½" x ¼" angles with slotted holes; **i** 2/ 3½" x 3½" x ⁵⁄₁₆" angles; **j** ⅜" steel plate welded to column; **k** 1" steel rod for temporary diagonal bracing.

Details of steelwork at end of truss.

View at SE corner (photo by architect).

frame with pinned feet. The columns have a wall thickness of ½in (12mm) and are very strong. Lateral forces in the east-west direction are transferred through the roof decking to the column lines. The columns and longitudinal framing take the forces, again by frame action. All the trusses have an initial camber of 7in (178mm). However the two end trusses each have two 1in (25mm) tie rods near their centres which are tensioned to reduce the camber to 3¼in (83mm) under dead load thus making their movement compatible with that of the cladding. The gymnasium can be extended at either end by removing the tie rods and the truss can then work as a normal intermediate truss.

Construction

The total construction time was eleven months. Each truss was brought to site in three parts which were welded together. All welds were tested. All bolted connections use friction grip bolts. Plan cross bracing was used in every fourth bay but removed after the welding of the roof deck to the trusses was completed. The truss bottom chord to column connection was only made after the roofing was in position, thus ensuring that dead loads do not transfer bending moment into the column.

Conclusion

In spite of all the different activities in it, this design is brought into a strong and unified whole. The structural and cladding elements have been well used to this end. It is a brilliant demonstration of a building conceived only in terms of the basic and fundamental characteristics of architecture: geometry, function and the available construction techniques.

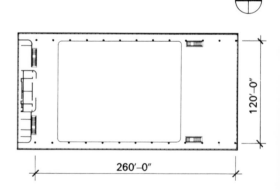

Upper level plan.

ST MARY'S ATHLETIC FACILITY (1977)

Description:
Multipurpose facility with concrete substructure and steel
columns and trusses on upper level
Architects and structural engineers:
C.F. Murphy Associates

Axonometric
view from SW:

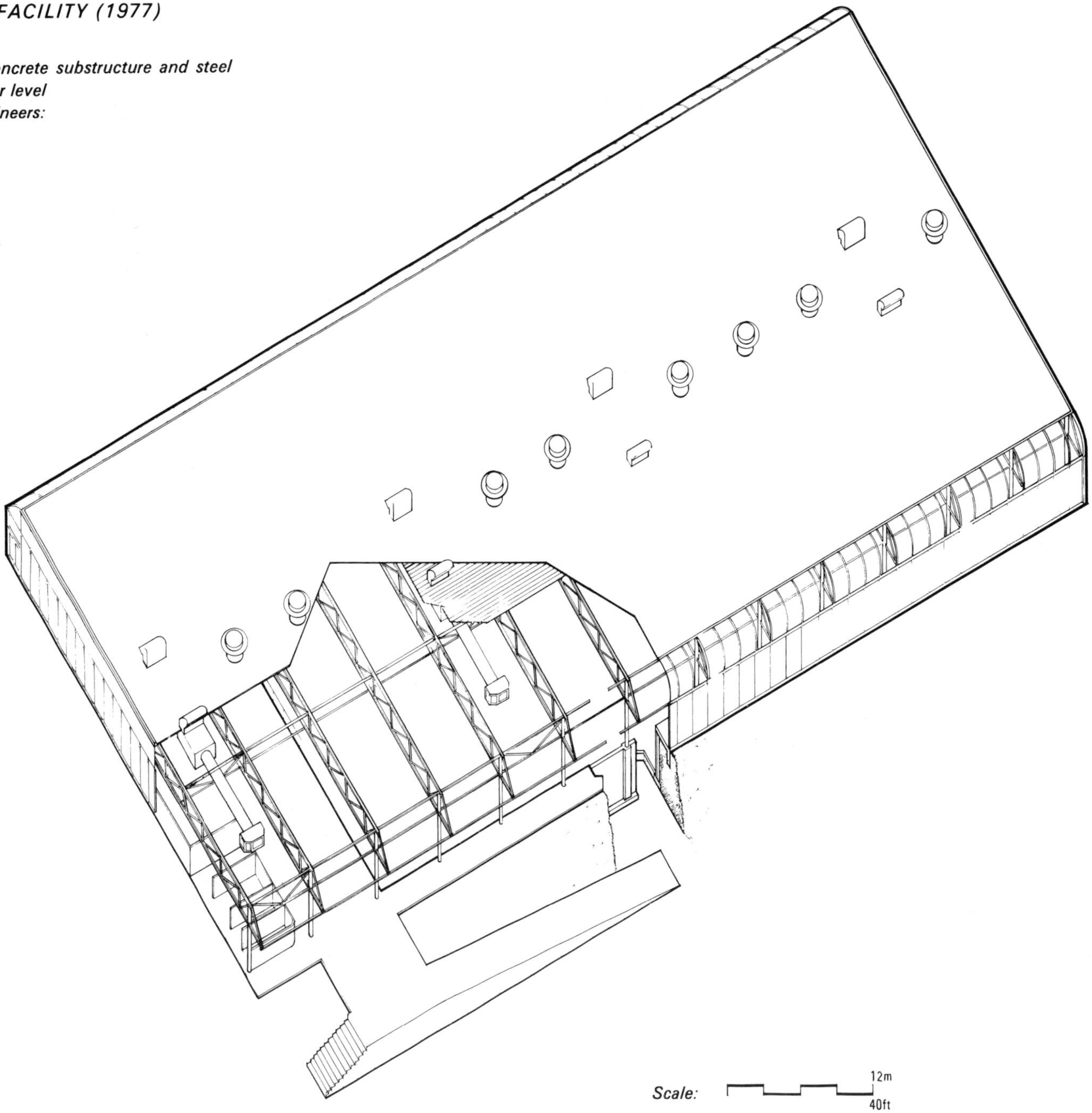

Scale: 12m
40ft

Sports Hall for School of Gymnastics and Sport, Magglingen, Switzerland

Introduction

Whilst not apparent from outside, this sports hall has a space inside with a clear height of nearly twelve metres and a clear floor area measuring 84 x 44.5 m, which practically qualifies it as a stadium; however the height of the building is disguised both by the length of the building and the way it has been lowered into the ground. The sports hall has a simple, geometrical shape divided up like a rule, with metric precision, nicely contrasting with the rugged and wooded landscape area in which it is set. A novel aspect of this design is the use of a prestressed steel roof truss.

Description

The lowest four metres of the building, which mostly are hidden below ground, are of concrete construction. The floor of the main space is at this bottom level, as are the entrance halls, plantrooms, changing facilities and other ancillary rooms on the north-east side. On the south-east side are tiers of seating leading up a gallery walkway which goes round the perimeter of the building. The structure above this level is entirely of steel. The roof consists of seven trussed beams which are prestressed and have a span to depth ratio of 24, which is double that of a standard simply supported plane truss. Each of the seven trusses consists of five longitudinal members, connected by diagonal and transverse members to form a stable space truss. The truss is able to accept load from any direction so that horizontal plan bracing between the trusses, in the plane of the roof, is unnecessary. At each end, the truss is supported by two 406mm diameter by 25mm thick round steel tubular columns and, at the end of the three upper members which overhang the columns, a vertical prestressing cable is attached, the three cables being prestressed to a combined force of 300 tonnes and anchored to bedrock. The upper members that connect adjacent trusses together are round steel tubes 82.5mm in diameter and 3.2mm thick, as are the top and bottom members that run parallel to the long sides of the building in each truss. Large-section steel sheets span between the longitudinal members of the truss and at the gable ends, where there are secondary steel

View of sports hall from N (photo by Christian Moser Fotograf).

columns, the sheets span the 4.20m distance between the truss and the colunmns and are flexible enough to accept the differential movement between the two. All columns are fixed at the base either by extending the column downards from the gallery to the main floor level or by using a very large foundation.

A secondary framework of steel on a 4.20 x 2.25 m grid is provided around the perimeter of the building to support a glass curtain wall. The secondary columns are supported at the top and bottom only; on the long facades, the top connection to the space truss slides to allow for temperature movements. The main area has good natural lighting and, at night, 230 mercury lamps provide about 300 lux of vertical illumination

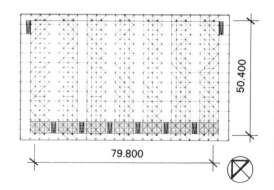

Roof plan.

SPORTS HALL MAGGLINGEN (1976)

Description:
Sports hall with steel frame and concrete substructure
Architects:
M. Schlup
Structural engineers:
Schaffner and Dr. Mathys

Axonometric
view from W:

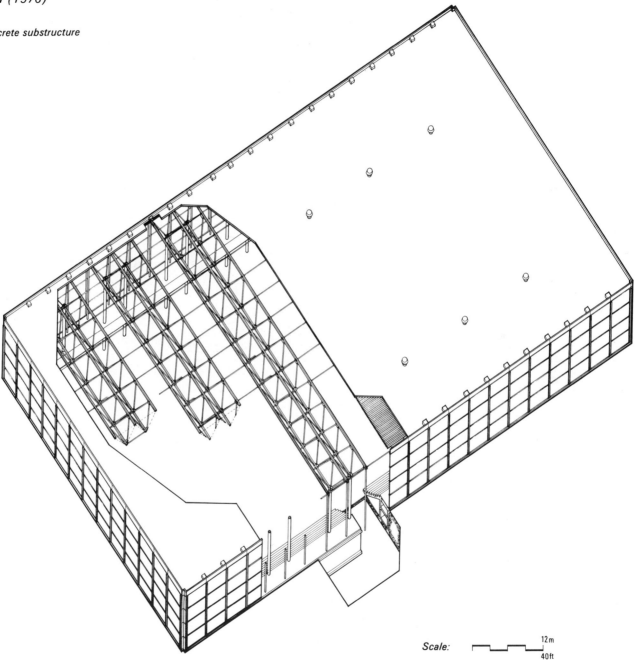

Scale: 12 m
        40 ft

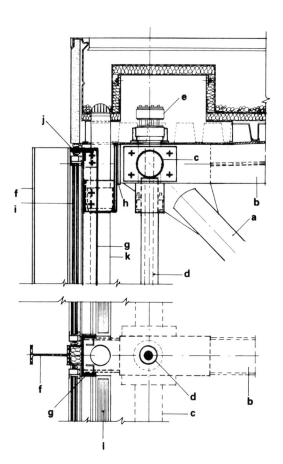

View of NE side of building (photo by Beno A. Dermond).

which, for TV transmission, can be increased to 750 lux by 42 spotlights.

Structural Action

The prestressing cables introduce additional tension in the upper members and compression in the diagonal overhanging members of the truss, which however reduces bending and deflection in the middle of the span. The trusses then behave somewhat as if they were continous constructions. They are designed to take snow loads of 300 kg per sq metre. Complete failure of the ties was also considered and was the critical factor in sizing many members.

Construction

Each space truss was erected in three sections, each of these sections in turn being made up by bolting together transverse members and plane trusses, which were shop fabricated in approximately 18m lengths; the plane trusses are the four containing the diagonal members of the finished space truss. The three sections were lifted by crawler cranes and placed on the columns and two temporary trestles before bolting up. Care was needed to ensure that the longitudinal members were properly aligned. The building was constructed in a period of 24 months.

Conclusion

Apart from the prestressing used, this steel frame is also unusual in having no vertical bracing and no plan bracing in the roof, the one allowed by the fixity of columns at their base, the other by the diagonal members of the space truss. This produces a clean and elegant design for the price of a small amount of extra steel. Altogether 420 tonnes of steel were used, averaging 83kg per sq metre over the plan area.

a diagonal member; **b** upper member; **c** transverse member; **d** prestressing cable with 95mm steel tube surround; **e** cable anchorage; **f** 200mm deep I-section column; **g** 200mm deep channel section column; **h** sliding connection between channel column and truss; **i** 4.20 x 2.25 m double glazing units with 8mm glass; **j** T-section transom; **k** rainwater pipe; **l** heating grille.

Vertical section, top, and horizontal section, bottom, through facade where rainwater pipe is present.

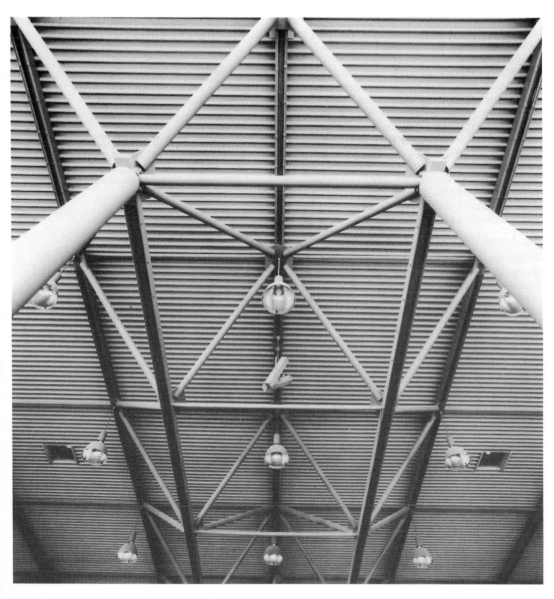

View of space truss (photo by Beno A. Dermond).

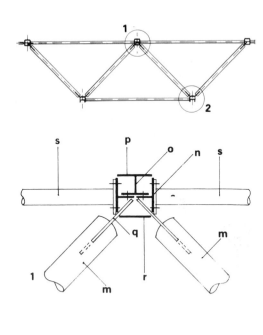

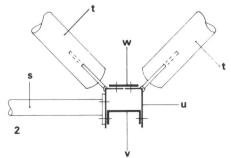

m 140 x 40 mm round steel tube diagonal; **n** end plate for diagonal; **o** half of 200mm deep narrow I-section; **p** 180 x 14 mm continuous top plate welded on to half of 200mm deep I-section; **q** 150 x 104 x 10 mm plates each side of transverse member; **r** 170 x 620 x 10 mm bottom reinforcing plate welded on; **s** 82.5 x 3.2 mm round steel tube transverse member; **t** 139.7 x 7.1 mm round steel tube diagonal; **u** 2/ 200 x 100 x 10 mm angle sections; **v** 180mm deep channel section; **w** 150 x 12 mm continuous plate.

Vertical section through 8.40m wide by 2.10m deep space truss showing typical connection details.

Sports Centre, Sokoto, Nigeria

Introduction

At spans exceeding about 50 metres cable trusses can be competitive with the standard rigid plane truss and have a practical span limit of up to about 150 metres, well beyond that of the rigid truss. Because cable steel has about five times the strength of normal structural steel and because the cable truss does not suffer from instability all members being prestressed in tension, the cross-sectional areas of the cable truss are very much less than those of the equivalent rigid truss. This being so the cables are light but still look strong, an impression reinforced by their curving lines. In fact their flexibility gives them a considerable reserve loadcarrying capacity over the equivalent rigid structure. One drawback to cables is the cost of anchorages. This design for a sports centre properly addresses these two issues: while the inherent advantages of the cable truss have been fully exploited, the cost of providing anchorages has been overcome by attaching the cables to the high concrete structure used for the grandstand. The design gives a clear visual expression to the forces in play.

Description

The sports centre can hold 4000 spectators and has a surface area of 3900 sq m. It contains a 40 x 20 m pitch which is set 4.3m below ground level and orientated with its long axis in the north-south direction. Either side is concrete seating, that nearest being cast directly on the ground and that furthest away being precast and supported by a cast-in-place concrete grand stand structure. The cable roof has a clear span of 71m across this, the cables running in the long east-west direction of the total plan area covered. This arrangement lets in natural light at either end of the pitch and allows the use of the grandstand as a supporting element for the roof. Underneath the grandstand seating are ancillary rooms for changing and refreshment. Emergency stairs are provided at the four corners of the building. The cable roof has eleven cable trusses spaced 5m apart which are attached to the uprights of the grandstand and tensioned from the outside. The cables are of high-tensile pre-stretched steel wire rope and terminate in a cast

steel hammer head at the 'dead' end and a cast steel cap with a threaded rod at the 'live' end, from which the cable is pretensioned. The threaded rod at the 'live' end is tensioned by a hydraulic jack, against a steel plate set in the concrete and locked in position by a large nut. A spherical washer is used which allows the rods to take their correct orientation. The cables are covered by an insulated sheet metal roof. The roof has a slight parabolic curve in the short direction, as well as in the long direction, to allow run-off of rainwater. The resulting saddle shape also prevents sound focusing. The seating of the grandstand is supported by a series of three-pin concrete frames stabilised in the short direction by nearly vertical concrete walls cast between them.

Structural Action

In the sense that this roof is shaped only by the loads on it, the roof can be classified as a lightweight structure. The supporting cable is steadied by the lower stabilising cable against static and dynamic forces. The sag of the supporting cable is just over 5% and the rise of the stabilising just under 5% of the span, figures which are typical. Smaller sag ratios lead to soft structures whose maximum deflections may easily exceed 1% of the span. High pretension, as well as curvature, will stiffen the truss, as do diagonal compared to vertical connectors. The natural frequency of the cable truss increases with the pretension but decreases with increasing span and load. Under dead load the intermediate cable trusses in this roof have forces of 49 and 26 tonnes in their supporting and stabilising cables respectively and the truss has a natural frequency of the order of 3Hz. Under live and dead load, the respective forces are 72 and 19 tonnes and, with wind uplift and dead load, these practically reverse becoming 20 and 71 tonnes. The basic wind pressure is 80 kg per sq m and suction over the roof is estimated to be some 20% greater than this. Working stresses in the cables are of the order of 600 newtons per sq mm, about half the ultimate strength. In spite of a certain elasticity of the concrete upstands, the extreme changes in temperature cause considerable variations in stress in the cables. The pretension in the cables is set to avoid any cable going slack even under the most extreme conditions.

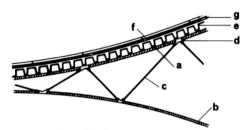

a supporting cable; b stabilising cable; c diagonal connector cables; d cast steel connectors with bolted friction joint; e deep galvanised steel sheet; f 40mm rigid insulation; g external roofing sheet.

Vertical section through roof.

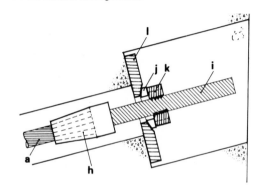

h cast steel cap; i threaded rod; j spherical washer; k nut; l steel plate.

Connection of cable to concrete.

Construction

Although substantially complete as a design, this sports centre was not built. It was intended that the cables be brought to site in coils, assembled on the ground and lifted into position by two cranes before anchoring and tensioning.

Conclusion

This is a good example of an economic use of the cable truss. The uprights in the grandstand structure have been restricted in height and tension in the cables balanced against the dead load of the grandstand so as to keep bending within reasonable bounds. The building has a pleasing openness and simplicity and provides a shelter, which though rudimentary, serves to moderate the fierce heat of this climate.

SPORTS CENTRE SOKOTO

Description:
Grandstand using steel cable truss roof
Structural engineer:
V.Mosco

Axonometric
view from N:

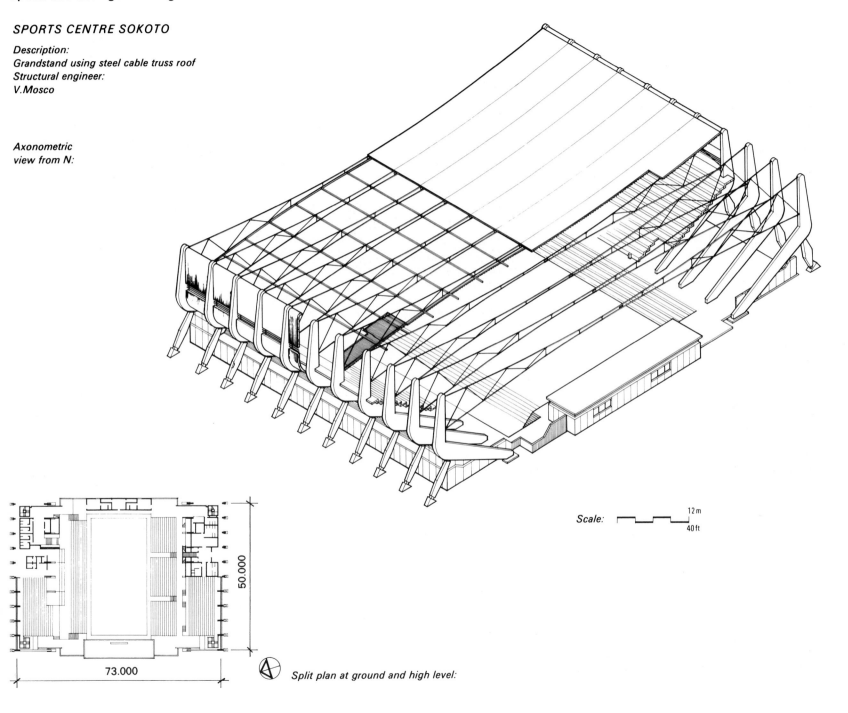

Scale:

12 m
40 ft

50.000

73.000

Split plan at ground and high level:

Eisstadion,
Braunlage, West Germany

Introduction

An assymmetrical but balanced-looking arrangement of masts and cables that cover this ice-
skating stadium are visible from a long way away.
The structure is deliberately distinct and takes the
form of a cable-stayed frame, which in fact is
covering a very large area. However, as the
building is almost completely open on all sides
with the roof split into four sloping planes the
stadium sheds any impression of bulk. This is an
excellent example of a first stage in the use of
tension cables, in which the cables vastly increase
the span but the frame still retains the advantages
of a rigid structure. The cables are tidily brought
back to the feet of the piers, thus avoiding the need
for the ground anchorages often associated with
the use of tension cables.

Description

The principal cable-supported frame has two steel
masts of rectangular section, each leaning slightly
outwards and supporting twin box-section ridge
beams passing either side of it. The span is 82
metres. The ridge beams have an apex which is
nine metres nearer to the smaller mast on the south
side. There are two cables at each suspension
point except the two central points which have
four to compensate for the shallower cable angle
there; the cables pass in the gap between the twin
beams and are attached to 1.60m diameter steel
cylinders which are cut in and welded to the
beams. The cylinders are subsequently filled with
concrete in order to ensure that the cables are
properly anchored to them. Twin 200 x 1650 mm
laminated timber beams span 24m between the
ridge beams and slender steel columns set in from
the perimeter; the columns have pinned
connections top and bottom to eliminate any
bending moment, which would increase their size.
Timber purlins at 3.75m centres span between the
laminated beams and prevent buckling or twisting;
steel angles, in turn, span between the third points
of the purlins and brace them. Each 9m bay of the
roof is cross-braced with steel flats. Galvanised
steel sheet, with a plastic coating is attached to the
purlins. Timber secondary roof members were
chosen in preference to steel as this was thought

View of stadium from E (photo by FotoLange).

to be more suitable for a building in a holiday area.

Two transverse frames, one at each end, are
connected to four sturdy concrete columns at the
corners of the building. These columns absorb all
torsion on the building as well as the wind forces
in the east-west direction transferred to it by the
roof. The bearings on the columns allow
movement in the north-south direction so that
wind force in this direction is transferred through
the horizontal, triangular-shaped trusses of the
transverse frames to the main cable-stayed frame.
The foundations of the two masts are connected
by a prestressed concrete tie. Advantage has been
taken of a sloping site to house a ticket office and
other facilities in a two-storey concrete structure
by the entrance on the south side. The spectator
stands and back walls are built of cast-in-place
concrete but with precast seating units.

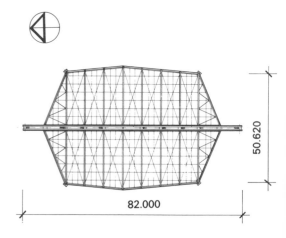

82.000 · 50.620

Roof plan.

EISSTADION BRAUNLAGE (1974)

Description:
Cable-stayed steel frame with steel and laminated timber roof
and concrete substructure
Architects:
Architektengruppe Westermann
Structural engineers:
Von Hirschhausen, Klingenberg und Partner

Axonometric
view from NW:

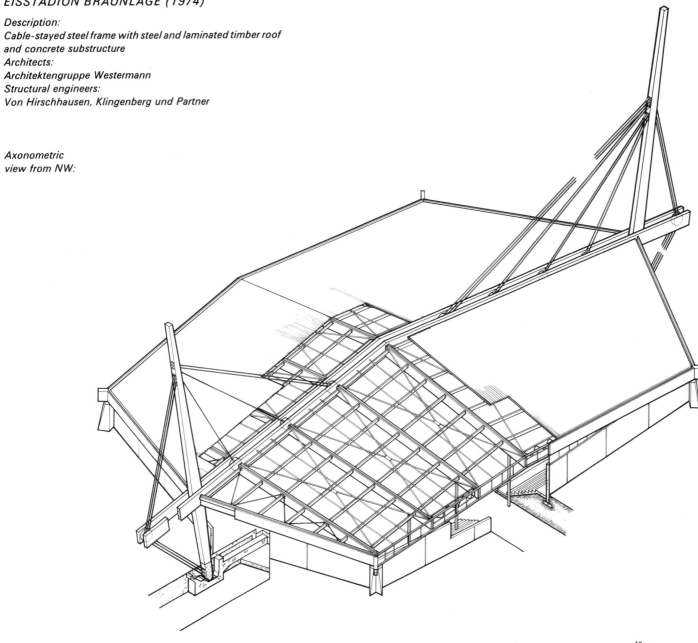

Scale: ⌐_⌐_⌐ 12 m
40 ft

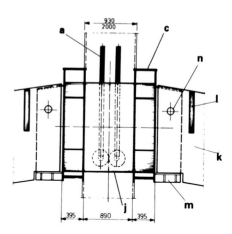

k 2/ 200 x 1650 mm laminated timber beams; l 100 x 750 mm timber purlin; m steel bracket; n 108mm steel bolt.

Vertical section through ridge of roof.

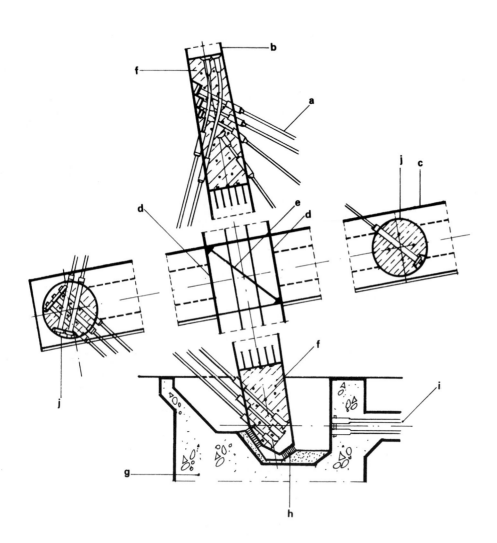

a prestressing strand in polyethylene tube filled with cement grout; b box section mast with internal stiffener plates; c one of two 395 x 2020 mm deep box section ridge beams with internal stiffener plates; d vertical diaphragm in column and ridge beams; e inclined diaphragm in ridge beams only; f reinforced concrete; g mast foundation; h renewable neoprene pads; i prestressed concrete tie; j 1.60m diameter steel drum filled with concrete.

Vertical section through middle of column and one of twin ridge beams.

Structural Action

The effect of the masts and cables is to more than double the span of this same frame without cables. The shape of the cable-stayed frame follows the general pattern of the bending movement in a portal frame with pinned feet and deep haunches. The snow load of 410 kg per sq m is taken by axial forces in the cables and bending of the ridge beam and, if the load is asymmetric, causes some cables to go slack. Load effects then become non-linear, that is deflections are not proportional to applied loads so that the effects of different load cases may not be simply added together. Linear analysis is sufficiently good for the analysis of dead load effects however. The cables used are low-stretch prestressing strand cables. The masts receive compression forces of up to 1100 tonnes from the cables. With wind forces acting at right angles to the main axis of the building, the lateral stabilising system allows the cable anchorage points to move up to 226mm in the east-west direction from the equilibrium position. As in any large structure, the build-up of forces due to temperature variations is released as far as possible, in this case by pinned connections and sliding joints. However the main cable-stayed frame is internally indeterminate and

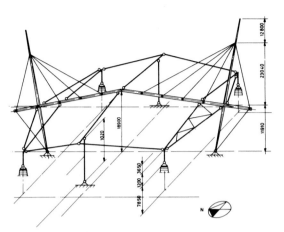

Structural model of building (drawn by engineer).

has to absorb these forces; the transverse frames are flexible and bend under temperature stresses so that the concrete corner supports do not receive excessive horizontal force.

Construction

The total period of construction was 24 months. Steelwork was brought onto site in large sections and welded up in position using temporary trestles.

Conclusion

With heavy snow loading a structure of strength and rigidity was required. However reasonable economy has been achieved by the elimination of ground anchors, the use of a continuous ridge member and the careful selection of angles and prestressing force in the cables. Higher prestressing forces would have increased the size of the ridge beam. This building is an interesting alternative to a series of trusses across the shorter dimension on plan. It is estimated that with laminated timber replaced by steelwork, which would normally be desirable, the weight of steelwork including masts and cables would average 35 kg per sq m, a figure that demonstrates the potential of this type of construction.

View of pylon at construction (photo by FotoLange).

Crosby Kemper Arena, Kansas City, Missouri, USA

Introduction

When large column free spaces are required, inevitably the structure of the building is a major element in the design and, most often, largely responsible for its final form. A good illustration is provided by this arena which has a roof supported by three goliath triangular space trusses. The three space trusses span 324ft (99m), are completely self-supporting with elegant joints which allowed the structure to be joined on site almost entirely by bolting. The building is a reminder of the range and versatility of the truss. The enclosure is set within the space truss structures and is made up of metal panels which are separated by wide joints. Inside, the area seating accomodates as many as 18 000 people, which is partly achieved by sinking the playing surface in the arena almost 30ft (9.14m) below the level at which the spectators enter the building.

Description

There are two distinct parts to the arena, the triangular space trusses, the roof substructure hung off it and the light framework for the cladding, all in steel, and the seating, walkways and support rooms in concrete. The upper tier of seating, taking about half the total number of people, is made of L-shaped precast prestressed concrete units which are supported by raking beams and columns, both cast in place. In general the lower tier of seating is concrete, simply cast against fill made up to the correct level. The building is entered at concourse level which separates the two tiers. In plan the seating has an approximately oval shape which gave more seats close to the playing area and a shorter roof span compared to a circular shape. The support rooms are situated below concourse level and are out of sight of the spectators. In each corner, at the same level as the highest seats, there are plant rooms fitted between the curved line of the seating and the rectangular lines of the cladding. These plant rooms, containing the air-conditioning equipment, are hung off the roof structure.

The space trusses are 27ft (8.23m) high and made of mild steel tubes of 48in (1.22m) diameter and up to 1¼in (32mm) thick for the top chords,

View of building before modifications from W (photo by architect).

36in (914mm) and up to 1in (25mm) thick for the bottom chords and 30in (762mm) and up to 1⅝in (41mm) thick for the web members. Tubes have good buckling resistance and a small surface area to save painting work. The top chord carries a maximum working load of approximately 2500 tons (2260 tonnes). This huge compressive member is restrained against buckling by the inclined web members. At bottom chord level, cross bracing is provided in each bay by two steel rods of 3in (76mm) diameter. The space truss has great rigidity and strength against vertical, horizontal or twisting forces. Suspended below the space trusses by hangers, are secondary roof trusses, generally at 54ft (16.46m) centres, the space truss panel length. They are 9ft (2.74m) deep, decreasing to 4ft 6in (1.37m) deep over the 45ft (13.7m) central portions between trusses. The space trusses are positioned so that they all have approximately equal loads on them from each side. For the two end trusses, the load from one side includes the weight of the wall cladding, it being partly supported by the roof, as well as the roof weight itself. Joists 4ft 5in (1.35m) deep at

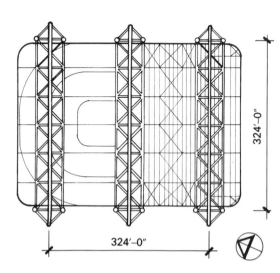

Split plan on main level and roof.

CROSBY KEMPER ARENA (1974)

Description:
Single-storey arena with steel space truss roof
Architects:
C.F. Murphy Associates
Structural engineers:
C.F. Murphy Associates/
Bob D. Campbell and Co.

Axonometric
view from W:

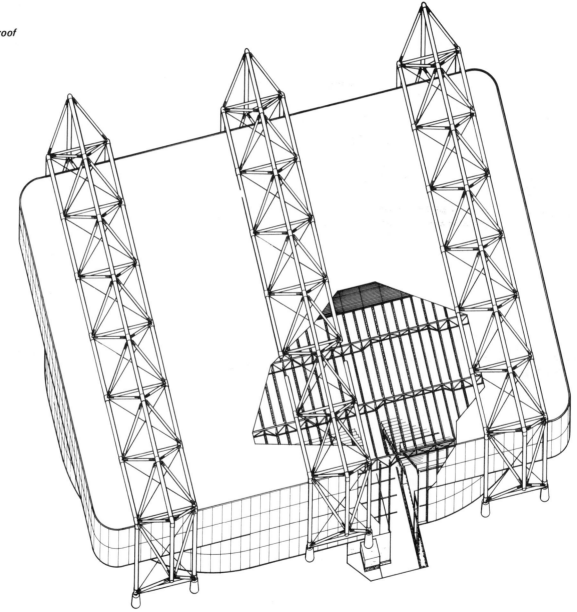

Scale: 12m
40ft

9ft (2.74m) centres span the 54ft (16.46m) between the roof trusses and in turn, support the roof decking. To give the roof surface a certain amount of stiffness in its own plane, bands of cross-bracing are provided over the 45 ft (13.7m) central portions between the trusses, going in an east-west direction, and on the east and west sides of the building, going in a north-south direction. The wall cladding panels are generally 15ft 6in by 9ft (4.72 x 2.74 m) and supported by mullions at 15ft 6in (4.72m) centres, in turn supported by cross beams and then by columns at 18ft (5.49m) centres. The columns are suspended from the perimeter roof beams so that the cladding panels move with the roof, except the lower band of panels at the four corners whose mullions are supported on the ground. Lateral forces on the cladding are taken to the seating structure and either the roof or floor respectively. A wide joint between panels takes up thermal movement.

Structural Action

The triangular trusses work like a two pin portal frame. However at this scale many effects which would not be significant in a smaller span structure must be considered. A prime consideration is that temperature movements be allowed to take place without this causing damage. The three space trusses are independent of each other by virtue of movement allowed by the roof hanger detail and some flexibility of the roof surface in its own plane. A revised hanger detail consists of a $2\frac{1}{4}$ x $6\frac{1}{2}$ in (57 x 165 mm) steel hollow section connected to a pin joint below the space truss and connected to the top chord of the secondary roof truss. The hanger detail allows relative movement of the secondary truss in the north-south direction.

Another important problem is ponding of water. With interior drains, 4in (100mm) of rainwater was shown by calculation to produce 7in (178mm) deflection. Therefore a 2ft 6in (760mm) camber was put in the roof at midspan. The upper half of the wall cladding is hung off the roof and moves with it, because of these movements of the roof. A very important feature in the triangular trusses is the use of internal tube stiffeners which, in principle, lie in the plane of the tube members being joined. It is important that the plate connector at the end of each tube does not weaken its capacity in compression. The joint also

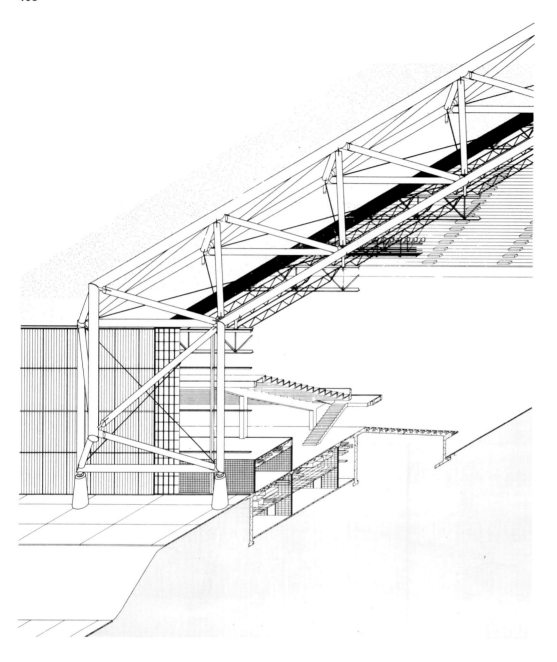

View at end of space truss (drawn by architect).

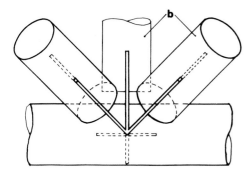

Plan view on joint at bottom boom of space truss.

has to be quick to erect, allow for tolerance and yet be waterproof enough to prevent corrosion developing. The joint satisfies these criteria and nicely articulates the members too. The feet of the space truss are supported on spherical bearings, on pile caps in turn resting on nine $10\frac{3}{4}$in (273mm) diameter piles taken about 75ft to bedrock and slightly inclined each side of the vertical to resist side thrust.

Construction

The total construction time was 19 months with design running parallel with site work. Top and bottom chord members were brought to site in long lengths and welded up on site. Otherwise all steel connections were bolted. The envelope was completed quickly to allow finishing work and services to be done under cover.

Conclusion

This building is a reminder of the range and versatility of the truss structure as well as a good illustration of the extra difficulties and sometimes fine judgements required. The roof allows movement while still retaining its structural integrity. The truss joints are worth further application. The building was constructed economically and fast. The weight of steel framing used averages 24 lb per sq ft (1.17 kg per sq m).

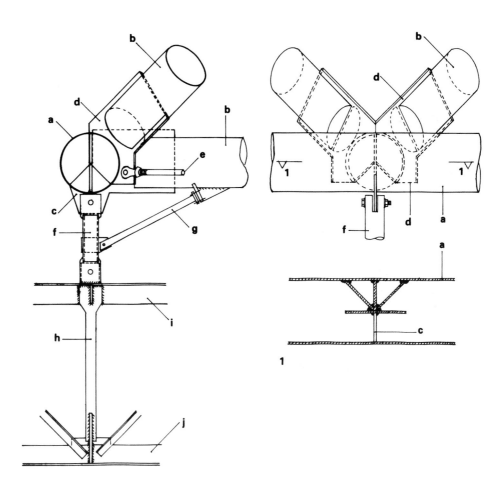

a 3'–0" tube; b 2'–6" tube; c $\frac{3}{4}$" hanger plate; d diagonal member plate; e bracing rod; f 10" tubular hanger with fork ends and $3\frac{1}{2}$" pin at both ends; g 4" tubular brace at 4 points in span, on one side of each space truss only; h $6\frac{1}{2}$" x $2\frac{1}{4}$" steel flat hanger; i top boom of secondary truss; j bottom boom of secondary truss.

Joint of secondary truss to space truss showing N-S section, left, E-W section, right.

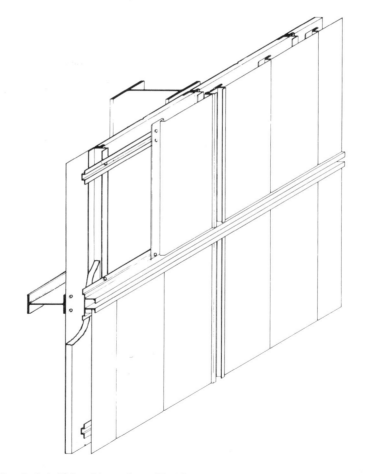

Horizontal section through cladding (drawn by architect).

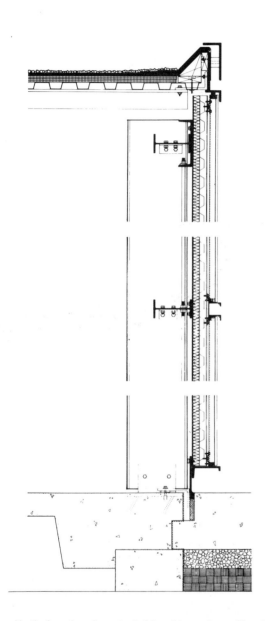

Vertical section through cladding (drawn by architect).   *Detail of claddding (drawn by architect).*

Chapter Eleven

Space Structure Buildings

The buildings in this chapter are all assembly or sports buildings, and thus overlap in type with those in the preceding chapter but are grouped together because of the type of roof structure they use. These structures are non-planar and are referred to as space structures, meaning not ony that, like all objects, they exist in space but that they can only be conveniently seen by using three-dimensional drawings and, in particular, that their structural action can only be understood by considering a spatial or three-dimensional model of the action. In most buildings, by contrast, it is possible to analyse the structural system by splitting it up into independent planar systems loaded in their own plane. A space structure cannot be simplified in this way and must be thought of as a structure whose basic mode of action involves three dimensions. In most cases, the space structures have been chosen because of their structural efficiency and this is particularly so in the case of large span buildings. But a space structure is a legitimate choice where its lightness, in appearance or in fact, are desirable qualities. Although space structures represent only a fraction of the building structures in existence, they are an important class because of their efficiency in terms of the amount of material used. Hence the designation of some types of space structure buildings as lightweight structures. Essentially this efficiency derives from the elimination of bending, either by membrane action within the surface or direct axial forces in individual members. In many cases the structures have non-developable shapes, but, in all cases, their strength and stiffness derive from their resistance to changes of shape as a result of the membrane action or axial forces which develop within the structure.

Liverpool Garden Festival Theatre, Liverpool, England

Introduction

The theatre is an outdoor one, semicircular in plan, and based on the classical greek form to which there are numerous allusions. However unlike the original, this theatre is entirely covered by a canopy, designed to be in place six months, which is, in fact, a coated polyester fabric prestressed by tension into a three-dimensional surface shape; the complex geometry, which is part and parcel of what may be called an architecture of pure force associated with the prestressed tent, contrasts with the simple geometry of the theatre itself. The original associations of these Neo-classical geometries with perfection and order are reinforced rather than counteracted by the tent structure. The tent is symmetrical but its low profile and large overhangs are apt. The tent is an unusual one: over most of its surface it has a large radius of curvature, and in places is almost flat, to be compared to the tight curves that are normal in tent structures. As a consequence the clear span across the theatre, between the raking steel columns on each side, is 50m, considerably more than is normal for a tent of this size, and there is seating in the interior space for 1500 people. The columns are the compression structure, the necessary counterpart to the tension structure, but far from being a necessary evil these have been made into a significant part of the design.

Description

The entrance to the theatre is from the east side leading to the concourse from where the tiered semicircular seating falls away towards the stage. The seats are timber baulks set on a sand bed. Running in a semicircle behind the seating is a pergola having smooth 650mm diameter concrete pipes for columns, the enlarged faucet ends becoming a doric capital, and the same timber baulks making a suitably weighty entablature. The pipes also form a backdrop to the stage, these pipes being up to 6m in height; some are used as part of the roof structure and are filled with concrete and reinforcing bars, so enabling them to cantilever from the floor slab which is 350mm thick over the backstage area. The whitepainted steel columns supporting the tent from inside have

View on stage looking N (photo by Judy Cass).

a diameter of only 140mm, by contrast. There are seven supports on each side, each having a broom shape. The 'broomheads' at the top have a pin connection with the straight column enabling them to swivel about it and are set out, on plan, to a 22m radius curve; the 'broomheads' lie as a series of straights along this radius, end members being kinked in the middle. This curve ensures that the north and south sides of the tent can take on a double-curvature shape. The 'broomheads' are loosely connected to each other by a 25mm bolt which allows adjustment on site. On elevation the row of 'broomheads' make a hump shape, each column being made to a different length with a final adjustment of this length made possible by an adjustable telescoping section at the foot of the

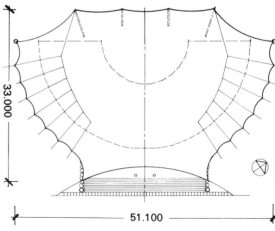

Plan on roof.

33.000

51.100

LIVERPOOL GARDEN FESTIVAL THEATRE (1984)

Description:
Coated polyester fabric tent covering theatre space
Architects:
Cass Associates
Structural engineers
for tent:
Gifford and Partners

Axonometric
view from N:

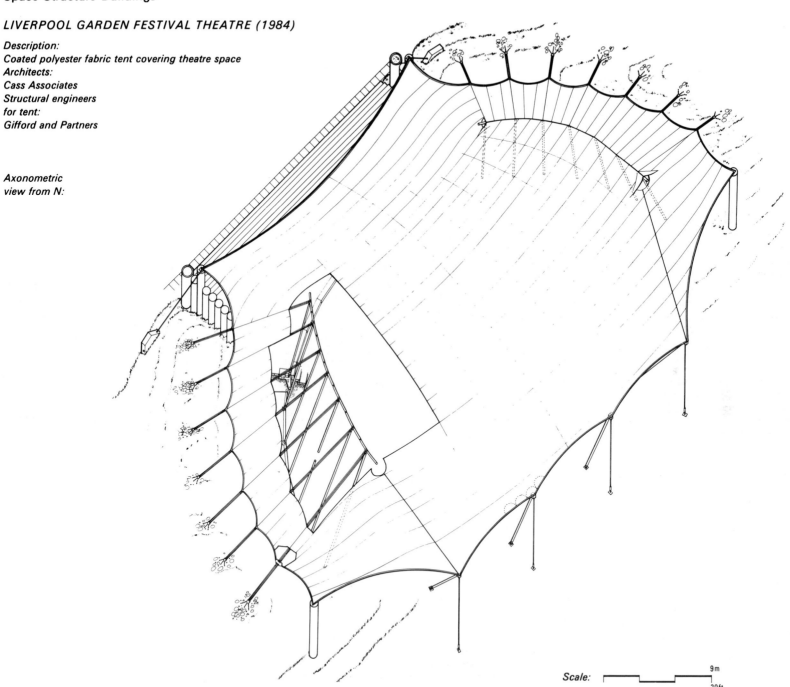

Scale:
9m
30ft

View on internal columns and edge of tent on S side (photo by Judy Cass).

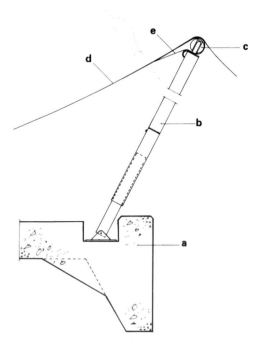

a concrete foundation; **b** 140 x 5 mm thick round tubular column with telescoping base using sand jack; **c** 140 x 6 mm thick round tubular 'broomhead'; **d** 1.5mm thick coated polyester fabric; **e** webbing straps.

Side elevation on internal column.

column, operated as a sand jack; the foot has a pinned connection to the floor. The columns lean in towards the stage, in a somewhat ceremonious fashion, and are restrained by webbing straps which loop round the 'broomheads' but, elsewhere, are sewn into the fabric and connected by other webbing straps to ground anchors; the columns are held by the webbing and by the fabric, which must be stressed in order to retain its shape. There are vent holes in the fabric at either end of the row of columns.

The remaining supports for the tent fabric, are those at the perimeter. At the front and back, the east and west sides respectively, the edges of the fabric are held by 18mm plastic-coated prestressing strand which has a breaking force of 38 tonnes. The attachment is by steel twist connectors which loop round the cable and connect to reinforcing strips, which are in the form of a series of semicircles, bordering these two edges of the tent. At the front, there are two strand cables in parallel, because of the shallowness and lack of stiffness of the arc; the two anchorage points at either end which are bolted to the top of an infilled concrete pipe, are held in balance by a 32mm high strength bar, itself attached to a

View showing the struts and semicircular reinforcing strips at NW corner.

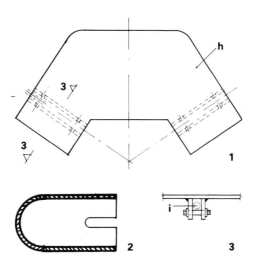

Details at top of central strut.

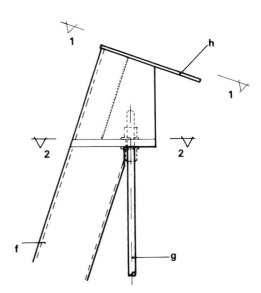

concrete foundation weighted down with backfill. At the back, the cable is held by four intermediate inclined struts as well as the two corner anchor points which bolt to another infilled concrete pipe. The inclined struts of the back cable have adjustable feet and also use a 32mm bar this time as a vertical tie; the back cable is supplied in five lengths joined on a plate at the top of each strut. Tensioning of the cable length takes place by tensioning of the whole fabric canopy. On the north and south sides, where there are frequent tie-downs, the edges of the fabric are sewn between top and bottom webbing strips; the strips in each perimeter arc pass round the steel edge plate, which is at the point where the webbing straps tie down the tent to the ground anchors. The tie-downs are a pair of webbing straps with a roller ratchet and connect to chains and then to a ground anchor.

Structural Action

The tent maintains its shape by double curvature. Under dead load, which is negligible, the main stress lines at right angles to each other have opposing but equal curvture. The critical load is

wind which, in this case, at a high enough speed, causes a slight but soundless movement, of the order of 150mm, near the centre, controlled by the tension in the surface; tent structures absorb such imposed loads by gross deformation to a new shape. Although the tent has a lower natural frequency than most, it is still high enough for it not to be affected by wind buffeting. The tent was analysed by computer as a series of triangular finite elements with one side of each element lying along seam lines. First a surface geometry was found that was in equilibrium with tensile stresses at all points in all directions on the fabric; next a check was made that the fabric could be put into a proper state of stress by the adjustments available at the columns and around the perimeter; with this complete the stresses under wind load were checked and cutting patterns plotted. During analysis horizontal movements of the nodes of the finite elements were suppressed, this being one way of ensuring that the cutting patterns have smoothly curving edges so that they may be easily cut from flat pieces of cloth. Polyester fabric with a pvc coating has a low modulus of elasticity and can easily stretch into position so that great

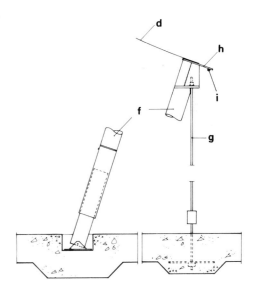

f 219 x 6.3 mm thick round hollow section strut with telescoping base using sand jack; g 32mm high strength tie; h 12mm steel anchor plate; i 18mm plastic coated edge cable held at anchor plate.

Side elevation on one of central struts on W edge of tent.

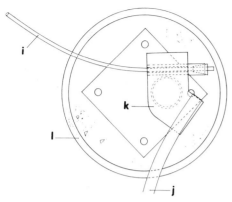

j 50mm wide webbing strip to edge of fabric; k 12mm steel anchor plate on round tube on baseplate bolted to concrete column; l 650mm diameter infilled concrete pipe.

Plan on corner anchor plate at end of W edge.

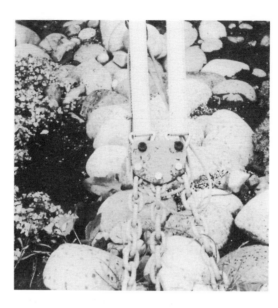

Connection of webbing straps to ground anchor chains.

Connection of tent to webbing straps from inside.

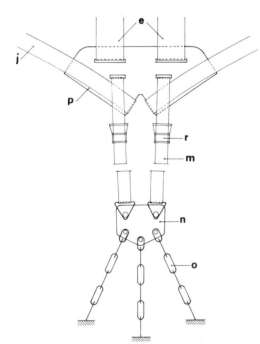

m webbing tie-down strap; n anchor chain connection plate; o chains to duck bill ground anchors; p 12mm steel edge plate; r roller ratchet.

Connection of tent to ground anchors on N and S sides.

accuracy in cutting pattern shapes is not required. In spite of this elasticity, the material can still be difficult to put up and into tension such that there are no creases, if the curvature is not reasonably uniform over its surface and this was found to be the case for a small area each side of the entrance. In its final state the design managed to have directions of principal stress which lined up, or very nearly so, with the warp and weft (fill) directions of the fabric threads.

Construction

Unlike most buildings, the tent is not properly stabilised until completely tied into position. As an adjustment of one part of the tent affects other parts, erection requires skill and accuracy in positioning of foundations and the fabric supports. The tent was erected by laying out the raking columns level, with the fabric in place over them, and then raising both rows of columns incrementally until the corner points and side anchors could be attached. The design provided many ways of tensioning the fabric, both at the rigid supports, that is the columns, and at the flexible edge supports. Although the edges take a

shape depending on the ratio of the principal stresses, the four corner anchor points, the tie-downs and the vertical ties of the raking struts all allow adjustment. Erection was very rapid taking one day with a further three days for adjustment.

Conclusion

The tent makes a most excellent temporary building providing cover, light and good acoustics; the curved surfaces act as ideal reflectors for high frequency notes; lower frequencies may be reinforced electronically. The shape of the theatre also gives good contact with the stage. In this case the tent was provided to give protection against rain but the idea is equally valid in hot climates, where it provides cool naturally ventilated spaces. The theatre is rich in detail and full of allusions, ancient and modern. This is a piece of architecture which, like our perception of the present, usefully incorporates the past.

La Lumiere Gymnasium
La Porte, Indiana, USA

Introduction

Traditionally, shell constructions of anything more than moderate span have been built of reinforced concretes, or reinforced cement pastes, with thicknesses varying from about a quarter to three-quarters of an inch (6mm to 19mm). However even with small thicknesses the dead weight of the shell forms a major part of the total design load. A much lighter material such as plastic suffers from its relatively high cost, with somewhat random variations in dimension with temperature changes, and its lack of strength especially at joints. A logical alternative, which is not only lighter than a concrete shell but much cheaper to erect, is steel sheet. In this school gymnasium, just two types of standard curved corrugated steel panels are used to form the complete outer shell of a 100ft (30m) wide building, one panel being half the length of the other. There is an inner shell perforated for acoustic absorption, but otherwise of similar construction, with insulation provided between the two shells. All panels are simply bolted together, a 2in (50mm) spacer being used between the inner and outer shell. The end walls are glass which establishes contact with the outside, reduces the bulk of the building and, most importantly, allows the circular arch to read clearly as a distinct element.

Description

All arch panels are cold-formed galvanized steel just over 2ft (600mm) wide and curved to a 70ft (21.35m) radius along their length, with drilled holes around the perimeter to receive $\frac{3}{8}$in (9.5mm) bolts for connection to the adjacent panels. There is a double row of holes for the joint connecting the panel to those above and below it. In the outer shell this joint is staggered with reference to those in the panels either side, but is lined up in the inner shell. In section the panels are 9$\frac{1}{4}$in (235mm) deep which gives them considerable effective bending strength. Between the outer and inner shell there is a 2in (50mm) thick blanket of fibreglass. This acts not only as thermal insulation, but, with the perforated holes on the inner sheet, as a broad band Helmholtz resonator for absorbing sound. A problem with shell structures is the difficulty of

View of gymnasium from NW (photo by architect).

attaching equipment loads and the relative weakness of the shell under point loads. Here heaters and equipment loads are hung off the roof by means of a shallow steel beam on the underside of the shells, which is attached to the shell by a longer bolt but otherwise uses the normal panel bolting detail; on each beam, two of these longer bolts support a $\frac{1}{2}$in (50mm) steel plate which is welded to the top flange of the beam at several places. The shells are supported at ground level by concreting into a lightly reinforced edge beam resting on a shallow strip footing. There is a 5 or 6 in (127 or 152 mm) mesh reinforced concrete floor slab which steps down more than 4 ft (1.22m) below ground level to give enough headroom in the main playing area. The floor absorbs the side thrust from the shells. However, where the floor is below ground (grade), special tie bars at 12ft (3.66m) centres are cranked down from the arch springing points and taken to the middle of the floor for concreting in.

Plenty of natural light is let in at each end of the gymnasium. The building lines up in an east-west direction so that blinds are not needed against glare for most of the day. However, a strip light, going across and set between the corrugations of the steel panels, is provided at 12ft (3.66m) intervals down the length of the building; this helps to eliminate glare and allows night-time use. Gas-fired unit heaters are provided at each end as well as standing cores containing lockers, showers

and toilets. Holes are required in the shell surface for flues and ventilators. A large exhaust fan sits on the top in the middle of the gymnasium and can pull in fresh air through casement windows in the glass curtain walls at each end of the gymnasium. The curtain wall is supported off a light steel framework which also provides lateral stiffness at each end of the building. This framework is set in 2ft (600mm) from the end of the shells and bolted up against them using the modified standard panel bolting detail.

Structural Action

Slightly less than thirteen standard full length steel panels, bolted end to end, are needed to span the width of the gymnasium. For the outer shell, full or half length panels, alternately, start the arch on one side and, on the other side, panels are cropped to suit the exact span dimension. Fundamentally, the shell works by mobilising axial and shear forces in the plane of the shells but some bending usually occurs in the steel sheet too. However, although the bolted connections can transfer the in-plane forces, a single line of bolts does not efficiently transfer bending moment so that the bending at right angles to the lines of the corrugations is small. Both shells are load-bearing. The critical uniformly distributed load is with snow on one side of the arch only. The effect of the steel framework at each end is to greatly reduce the in-plane stresses under such asymmetric loads.

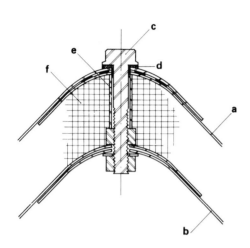

a cold-formed corrugated galvanized steel panel; **b** perforated inner shell; **c** $\frac{3}{8}'' \times 2\frac{1}{2}''$ flange bolt; **d** neoprene washer; **e** $\frac{9}{16}''$ steel sleeve with nut; **f** fibreglass insulation.

Connection between inner and outer shells.

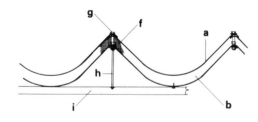

g $\frac{3}{8}'' \times 12''$ flange bolt; **h** $\frac{9}{16}'' \times 7\frac{7}{8}''$ steel sleeve; **i** steel beam with $\frac{1}{2}''$ plate welded on top.

Section through shell of gymnasium showing steel spreader beam.

Detail at springing of shell (photo by architect).

View of W end of gymnasium (photo by architect).

Construction

The outer shell panels were bolted together on site to make complete arch segments 10ft (3.05m) wide. These segments were hoisted into position by crane and bolted to each other. Support was provided by lines of scaffolding in the centre of the arch. With the feet of the outer shell temporarily fixed in position, the central scaffolding was adjusted to allow the insulation, inner shell, spreader and end frameworks to be bolted up. The feet of the two shells were then concreted into position and, after setting, all scaffolding was removed. Total construction time was 6 months.

Conclusion

The gymnasium is a good example of a simple and economic building given shape by its structure, which also doubles up as the enclosure. It can easily be extended in length. The equipment, flues and vents puncturing the shell tend to mar its shape from the outside but are difficult to reduce in size. However from ground level they are not particularly apparent. The span achieved here is close to the limit of what may be achieved with thin gauge steel sheet although larger buildings could use the sheet as permanent formwork for a reinforced concrete shell.

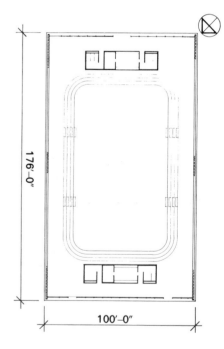

Ground floor plan.

LA LUMIERE GYMNASIUM (1979)

Description:
Single-storey gymnasium with double skin of corrugated
steel panels
Architects and structural engineers:
C.F. Murphy Associates

Axonometric
view from   W:

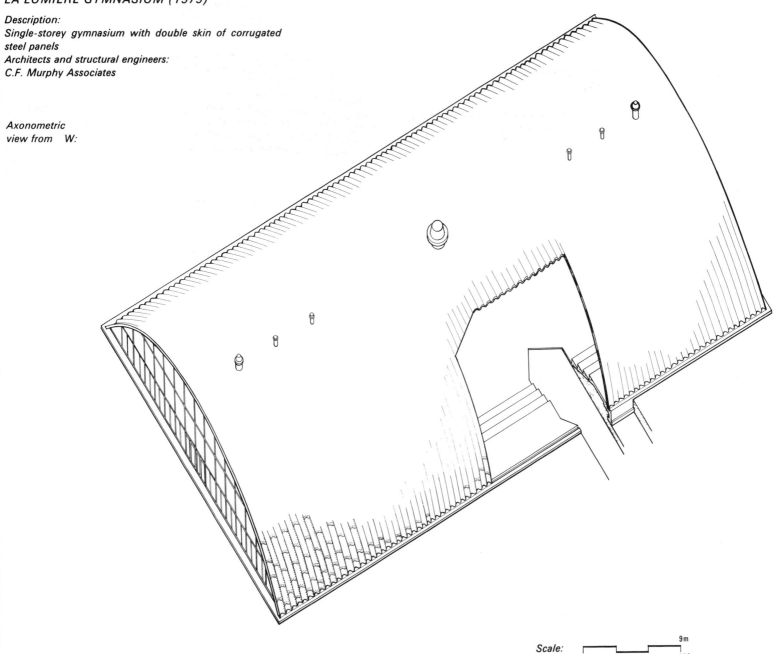

Scale: 9m
30ft

Wayland School Field House, Wayland, Massachusetts, USA

Introduction

Assuming the shape to be suitable, one economic way of covering a large area is to build a dome. This field house uses a reticulated timber dome, 209ft (64m) in diameter, for sports or large assemblies of people and includes a running track and a grandstand. The dome makes excellent use of the timber material and was erected with great economy of means, using only six wooden gin poles.

Description

The field house is designed for a high school with 850 pupils. Inside there is space for a 750-seat grandstand, by the running track, as well as basketball courts and general games areas. In the spaces between the outside of the track and the building's perimeter are housed exercise areas, to the west, and showers, locker rooms and offices, to the east. To the south is the entrance, through a concrete frame building, and to the north a heating building, which supplies warm air to the dome through a 5 x 9 ft (1.52 x 2.74 m) wide duct; the return duct to the building runs below, at floor level. The dome rests on a circular steel ring beam and is supported by 48 regularly-spaced circular steel tube stub columns, at the points where the members spring off the ring beam. The stub columns rest on an 11in (279mm) thick concrete retaining wall with strip foundations and allow a continuous window band to be inserted between the wall and the ring beam. The floor of the building is some 10ft (3.05m) below the springing level of the dome. The dome is part of a spherical surface with a radius of 173ft 6in (53m) and has a diameter of 209ft (64m) at the springing level, with the apex 35ft (10.67m) above this level. The dome consists of six identical segments, each with one corner at the apex of the dome and two corners at the springing level. The detailed geometry of the segment was established by projecting the three corner points of the segment onto a plane at the springing level, joining the points to form an equilateral triangle at this level and then subdividing this large triangle into 49 smaller, identical equilateral triangles. The lines of these triangles are then projected onto the

View of dome from S during construction (photo by engineer).

spherical surfaces by lines radiating from the centre of the sphere. The area between the ring beam and the bottom of the large triangle was subdivided by simply joining points to the stub column positions. The projection chosen gives a slightly greater density of members at the bottom of the dome where stresses are greatest.

All members of the reticulated dome structure, placed along these grid lines, are 3 x 13 in (75 x 330 mm) laminated douglas fir beams, which are jointed at the intersections of the lines. The members are all curved to the same radius, equal to the radius of the sphere, all grid lines being great circles. Each segment of the dome is symmetrical about its centre line but otherwise the lengths of members are all different and make different angles with each other. Purlins placed between the main members are 3 x 8 in (76 x 203 mm) sawn solid section members; they support 2in (50mm) thick tongue and groove wood planks and also help to brace the main members. Built-up roofing is applied in strips to the six segments and then, to take care of the curve, the dome is covered by asphalt shingles which are coloured white. The pipe joint between the main members is crucial to success. It consists of a circular steel tube at the hub with three separate steel flats, top and bottom, which bolt to the wood members and are held in the tube by means of a central bolt, thus making a

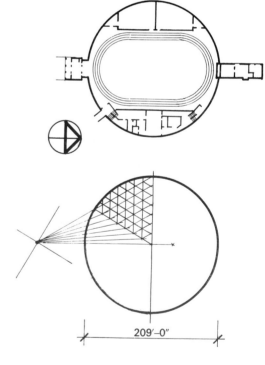

Ground floor plan and one segment of roof plan.

WAYLAND SCHOOL FIELD HOUSE (1960)

Description:
Sports building with dome roof of timber lattice construction
Architects:
The Architects Collaborative
Structural engineers:
Souza and True

Axonometric
view from NE:

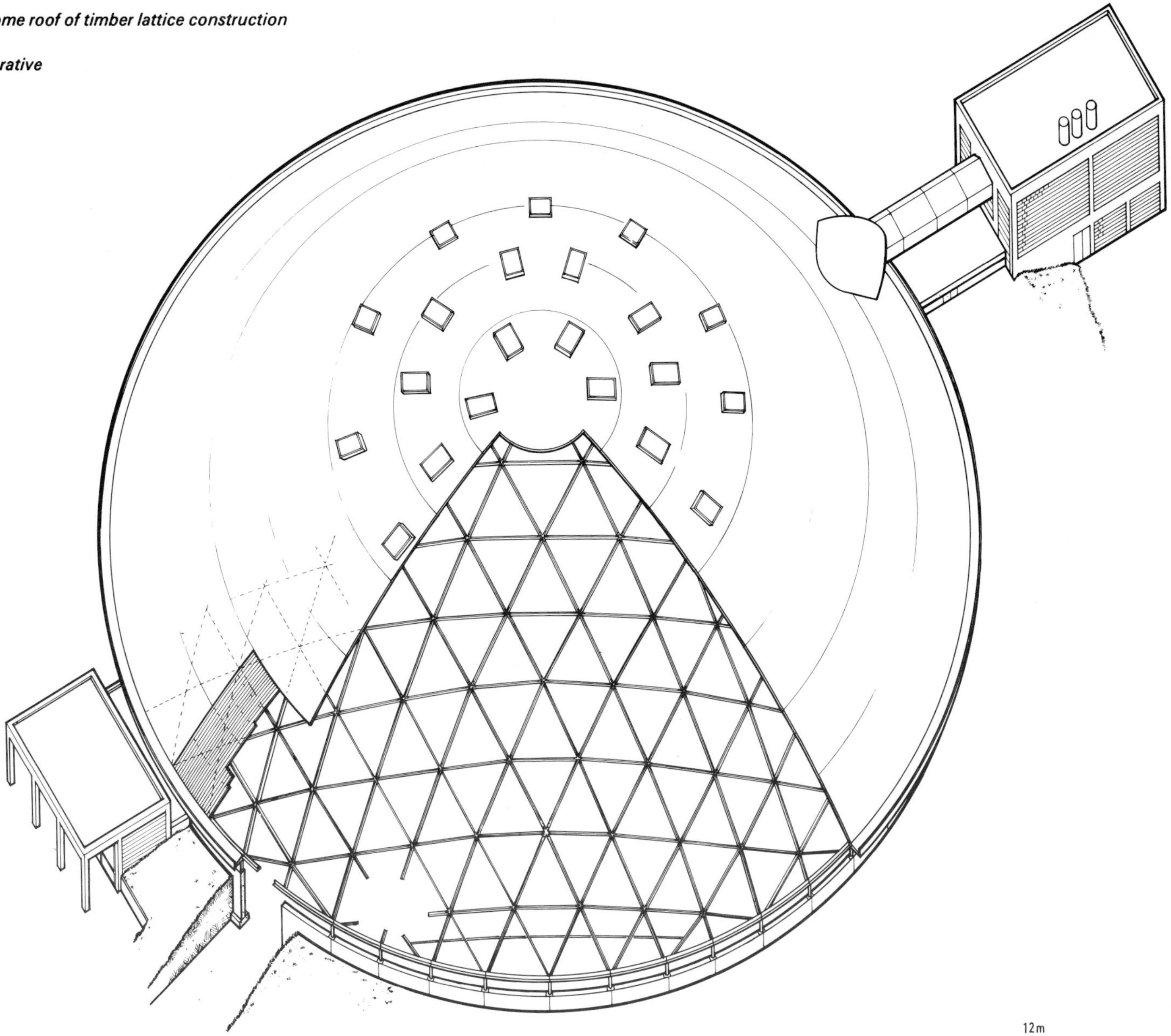

Scale: 12 m
40 ft

six-way joint. This detail allows for errors in the length of members and also allows any angle between the three grid lines to be accommodated.

Structural Action

The main members of this reticulated dome are set out on a three-way grid so that all members are triangulated and the dome has stiffness against shear in the plane of the surface of the dome. Because of this, such reticulated domes can be analysed as thin shells. Under symmetrical load the dome is in compression everywhere, largely as a result of its small plan diameter compared to that of the sphere from which it is formed. Under asymmetrical load from snow, some members develop sufficient bending moment to make the top or bottom of some connectors go into tension. However, the shear stiffness of the surface also helps the dome to absorb unsymmetrical snow and wind loads. Domes need to be checked against buckling which may be of three types: general buckling, local or snap-through buckling and member buckling. Member buckling is the same type of buckling that occurs in columns. Snap-through buckling may occur as a result of a point load applied at a connector; snap-through occurs when the loaded point passes downwards through the plane of the dome surface causing tension in the members surrounding the connector and can lead to general buckling of a large area of the dome. Surfaces without much curvature are more prone to general and snap-through buckling. Deviations of the surface from the geometry assumed in the design, for example because of play in connectors accumulating to cause depressions in some parts of the surface, are also important. However the dome, being non-developable, has good resistance to changes of shape and therefore to buckling, if there is reasonable curvature in it. For example, its buckling resistance is orders of magnitude higher than similarly sized developable surfaces, such as cylindrical shells. In this dome the span is still moderate and the depth of the members is such that buckling problems are easily resolved. The wood plank decking does not have a structural role except that of stabilising members under asymmetric loads. The connection detail adopted has some fixity, assumed to be about 25% of that of a fully continuous member. However the fixity

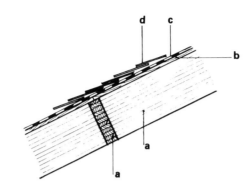

a $3\frac{1}{4}''$ x 13" laminated Douglas Fir member; b 2" thick t and g wood planks; c built-up roofing; d asphalt shingles;

Vertical section through dome.

Three-way grid of dome (photo by engineer).

View before erection by gin poles (photo by engineer).

Pipe joint of dome (photo by engineer).

of the joint is not relied on in the calculation to allow for eccentric or concentrated loads, the joint being taken as pinned.

Construction

The dome was erected using only six timber ginpoles, one placed in the middle of each dome segment. The top of each pole was stabilised by three guys; winch cables, attached to each segment at two points, were used to lift the dome to its correct height. The winches were operated by engine units outside the perimeter of the building. The dome was assembled at ground level beforehand, only the edge members between the dome and the ring beam being fitted after lifting of the dome. The inner part of the steel ring beam was brought to site as 24 individual pieces, straight except for a kink in the middle, which were then welded together. The outer part is connected to the inner part of the ring beam and was constructed in a similar way, the welded joints being staggered against the inner ones. The field house took fourteen months to construct, of which the grid of the dome took only two weeks, with another two weeks for laying of the planking.

Conclusion

This dome was found to be considerably cheaper to build than a concrete dome or a steel radial dome. Since this dome was built, other domes using similar geometry and with more than twice the span have been erected, indicating the general validity of the method. In climates with heavy snowfalls, these domes are economic compared to air-supported structures which require heating to disperse the snow and high inflation pressures to carry the load. In general the wooden domes are competitive with steel domes in spans up to about 500ft (150m). The domes may conveniently be given very high thermal insulation and provided with an abosrbent inner layer to diminish the effects of sound focusing. A possible difficulty with closed domes is their flying-saucer shape, which, as shapes, may be too strong to fit in comfortably with adjacent buildings. Here the dome has been separated from other school buildings as a way round this difficulty but there seems no doubt that the dome looked best during construction when a proper scale was provided by the members of the dome.

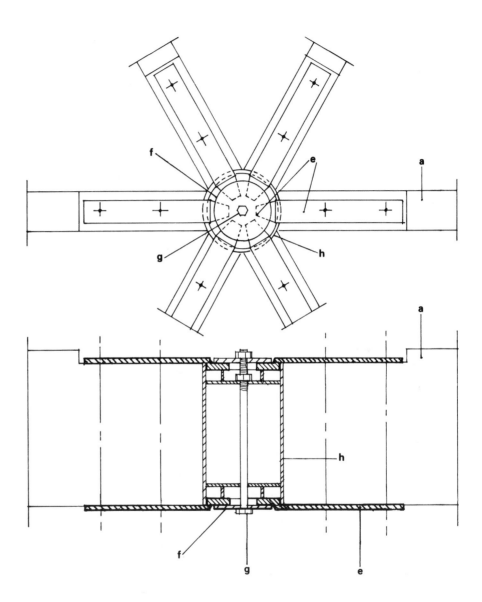

e $\frac{1}{4}$" steel flat bolted to laminated member with 2/ $\frac{1}{2}$" bolts and having radiused lug piece welded to end for keying into tube; **f** $\frac{3}{8}$" round steel washer to hold lug ends; **g** 13$\frac{1}{2}$" x $\frac{3}{4}$" steel bolt with 3" thread at one end; **h** 6$\frac{5}{8}$" x $\frac{1}{4}$" thick steel tube with $\frac{1}{4}$" diaphragm plates.

Plan and section on type of connection between members.

Oasis Swimming Pool, Swindon, England

Introduction

All that separates an unreliable climate from the make-believe tropical paradise inside this dome is a single layer of plastic. The dome contains a swimming pool with a free-form shape, as well as beaches, slides, ramps and thickets of green plants, and the only view out is upwards, to the sky. From outside the quilted bubble shape of the roof surface is visible above the earth berm surrounding the building but gives no clue as to the activities inside. The dome structure itself is made of aluminium alloy and is extremely light and notable for its ease of erection.

Description

The dome uses rolled aluminium alloy sections with cast aluminium alloy connectors; it is part of a spherical surface with a radius of 32.42m and has a diameter at its base of 45.13m and a height above its base of 9.14m. There are 48 meridional ribs and 7 horizontal loop rings, both types having 203 x 114 mm wide elliptical sections with an average wall thickness of 7.5mm. The meridional ribs spring off a ring beam, which is in concrete, half of them framing into a 3.05m compression ring at the apex of the dome, the other half framing into the hoop ring next to this compression ring.

The compression ring is made of a 305 x 80 mm deep aluminium channel section. Because of the sizes of the roof panels that were available, eight additional rings of hollow section secondary purlins were necessary; they are placed midway between the principal hoop elements. Straight diagonal members are provided across each main panel up to about half the height of the dome; these are 101mm diameter round tubular sections. The joint between meridional and hoop members uses a cast aluminium connector piece that is bolted to the meridional rib; as this prevents the diagonal members from being connected into the centre of the joint, some eccentricity arises. Horizontal and vertical thrusts from the dome are absorbed by the concrete ring beam which can be considered to be rigid; it is supported by 16 slender columns spaced at equal intervals round the circumference and integral with the perimeter retaining wall.

View of complex from N side (photo by David Wrightson).

The dome is covered by shaped sheets of a clear pvc plastic, sealed by butyl tape and neoprene gaskets, two separate sheets covering each main panel area; the hoop and meridional glazing bars incorporate a channel to carry away condensation. Extractor fans are provided at the apex of the dome, within the compression ring. Supply air is provided by a duct which runs around the base of the dome. As a form of lighting, a glazed dome has the advantage of providing good natural light without glare during daylight hours. To the west of the swimming pool dome is a sports centre linked to the pool by floors at two levels.

Structural Action

The dome works almost entirely by membrane action, which causes axial forces in the members, although some bending is caused by restraints on meridional members at the base and apex of the dome and by the weight of the fan units at the apex. The bending moment and axial forces in the members were found by treating the dome as a continuous thin shell of spherical shape, for which standard solutions exist, and summing the stresses over a panel width. The main axial forces are found by considering membrane action in the shell and bending moments by assuming the shell to be fixed at its base but to have a pinned connection

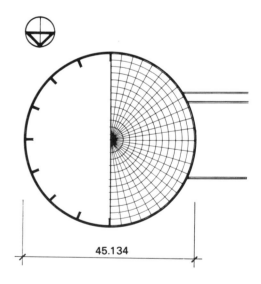

45.134

Split plan on roof and substructure.

OASIS SWIMMING POOL (1976)

Description:
Swimming pool with aluminium dome and concrete
substructure
Architects and structural engineers:
Gillinson Barnett and Partners
Structural engineers for roof:
Roper IBG/
P.E. Mast

Axonometric
view from SW:

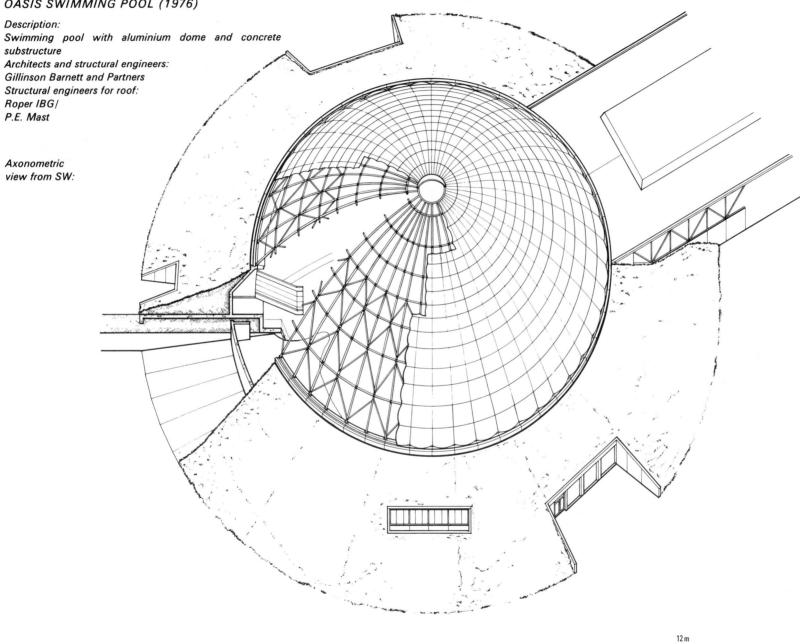

Scale: 12 m
                              40 ft

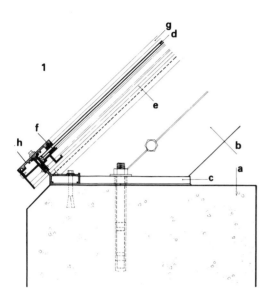

a 1500 x 900 mm concrete ring beam; b 203 x 114
x 7.5 mm elliptical aluminium tube; c baseplate
with 2 drilled bolts having stainless steel collars
and washers; d clear pvc roof panel shaped by
thermoforming; e condensate tray; f butyl tape; g
clamping bar with neoprene gaskets; h clamping
bar in hoop direction.

Vertical section near base of meridional rib.

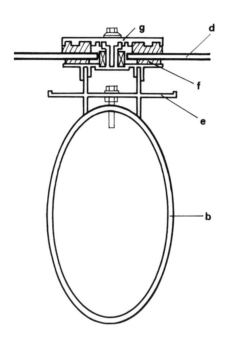

Section through meridional rib.

*Apex of dome during construction (Photo by O.F.
Clarke).*

with the compression ring at the apex; bending
moments decrease rapidly, away from the apex
and base. Asymmetric loads, whether point loads
or distributed loads, cause shear in the plane of the
surface of the shell which is resisted by the
diagonal members or, where there are none, by the
frame action of the panels. Twisting about a
vertical axis through the apex, which can lead to
instability, also causes shear forces which are
resisted in the same way. For light domes, it is the
asymmetric loading which is most critical; in this
case the peak value of the asymmetric, distributed
load is three times the dead load. Buckling
required careful consideration especially in

aluminium domes which tend to be slender.
General, snap-through and member buckling
were all investigated; the critical load which
causes general buckling is proportional to the
elastic modulus of the shell material and to the
square of the ratio of the thickness to the radius of
the spherical surface. A calculated factor of safety
of critical over working loads of at least two was
specified to prevent general buckling. For snap-
through buckling, where the methods of analysis
are not conclusive, a calculated factor of safety of
five was required; testing of part assemblies,
however, showed the actual safety factor to be just
in excess of two.

Construction

The total period of construction of the whole
complex, including the sports centre to the west of
the dome, amounted to 23 months. The erection of
the aluminium dome took only 2½ months and the
fixing of the pvc glazing panels a further 3 months.
For the purposes of erection, the dome was split
into 'ladder' segments which were bolted up on
the ground and lifted into place by crane; each
segment of the dome was supported by
scaffolding at the apex and by the concrete ring
beam. Opposite pairs of 'ladders' were erected
together and the compression ring was

Interior view looking E (photo by JBW Photography).

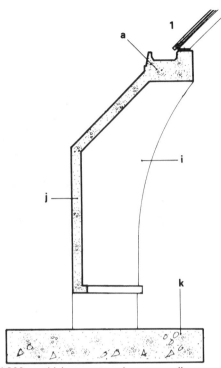

i 300mm thick concrete columns, equally spaced round perimeter; **j** concrete retaining wall; **k** 6 x 1 m concrete strip foundation.

Typical vertical section through substructure below dome.

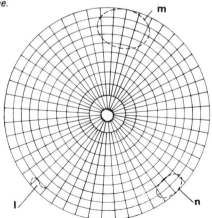

l member buckling; **m** general buckling; **n** snap-through buckling.

Dome buckling modes.

temporarily braced internally to prevent distortion. The pvc roof panels were fixed in quadrants using scaffolding, the scaffolding being rotated one quadrant at a time. Cadmium plated bolts 16mm in diameter were used for the assembly of the dome.

Conclusion

This dome can be classified as a single layer ribbed dome, although it has some crossbracing. It is less efficient, structurally, than the other popular single layer type, the three-way grid dome, which has more load paths and is triangulated over its whole surface. However the ribbed dome has relatively few members, is very easy to erect and, as this

dome shows, at moderate spans is still very light, having a weight of only 0.43 kilonewtons per sq m, including the glazing; this suggests that the already considerable efficiency of this type of dome with a span to rise ratio of about five is sufficient at this scale. Acrylic roof panels would have remained clearer than the pvc panels chosen but the latter were preferred on the grounds of their better fire performance. However there is good daylighting in all weathers. The dome creates a lively space and, with its spatial bubble looking on the stars above, also succeeds with its intended touch of fantasy. In general, the artifice is lavish enough to succeed.

Faulerbad,
Freiburg, West Germany

Introduction

Shell structures, especially those of a non-developable shape, achieve strength, stiffness and resistance to buckling by their curvature. With such shaping, the shell can work as a membrane and be very thin but still lightly stressed. Concrete or ferro-cement shells require a large amount of labour and a skilled labour force, for their construction, whether precast or cast-in-place. In addition, they are heavy, require a minimum thickness to protect the reinforcement and need a period for curing. The elegant hyperbolic paraboloid (hp) timber shells covering this swimming pool suffer none of these disadvantages. They have been constructed on site by nailing the different layers of the shell together, fixing edge beams and lifting each completed shell into its final position.

Description

There are three floor levels in the building containing the swimming pool. At the entrance level there are changing rooms, showers, a snack bar, sitting space and rooms for the staff. One level below this gives access to the swimming pool, learner's pool and seats for spectators and below this are the plant rooms and utility rooms including service tunnels running around the sides of the swimming pool. The floor slab at this level also serves as a foundation raft and is generally 400mm thick. Coming off this raft are the four 600mm diameter main concrete columns on each side of the pool that support the timber hp shells. Outside, beyond these supports, there are two triangular concrete slabs, on both the north and south sides, which have beams, 600 x 600 mm in section, along the inside edges. These slabs act as horizontal diaphragms and, combined with the steel roof tie bars, take all horizontal thrust from the shells, so that, except at the top, none of the eight columns takes anything but vertical load. The roof itself is composed of three types of shell, one, approximately square in plan, on the north side spanning in the east-west direction, another with a kite shape on plan, on the south side spanning in the same direction, while the largest one spans 21m across the pool in the north-south direction.

Inside view of swimming pool looking E (photo by Bruno Krupp).

Each shell is separate from the adjacent shells except for a connection at third points of opposing edge beams. A shell requires only two points of support to take the sidethrusts but needs connecting at some other point to prevent rotation about the line joining the supports. To this end, the edge beams of each shell are connected to each other at the three ridge points over the pool, these edge beams in effect forming three pyramid structures spanning between the main columns. The horizontal sidethrusts on each column from the edge beams of the shells are large and are taken by 70mm solid steel tie bars in a cross shape connected to the column tops. The connection of

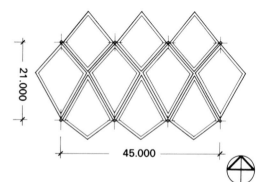

Roof plan.

FAULERBAD, FREIBURG (1984)

Description:
Swimming pool with concrete substructure and 3 layer
hyperbolic paraboloid timber shell roofs
Architect:
H-D. Hecker
Structural engineer:
Max Sherberger

Axonometric
view from SE:

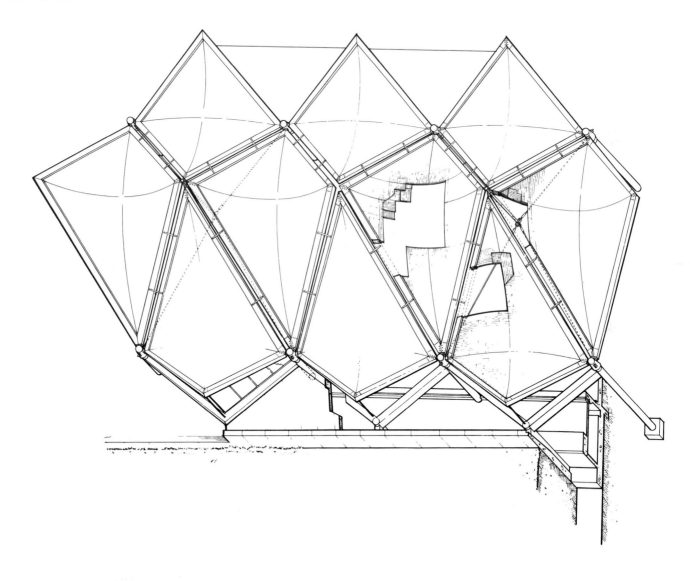

Scale: 9m

                                                                          30 ft

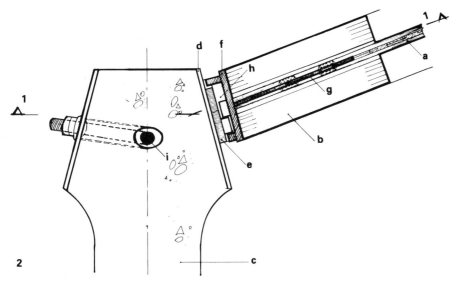

Top of column at SW corner (photo by engineer).

a 3 layers of softwood 22mm thick; **b** 400 x 700mm edge beam; **c** 600mm diameter concrete column; **d** 20mm thick steel cone; **e** 40mm steel support plate with lugs; **f** steel corner plate with lugs; **g** 20mm steel connecting plate dowelled to edge beams; **h** 50mm elastomeric bearing pad (not drawn); **i** 70mm steel tie.

Vertical section through column at NE corner looking W.

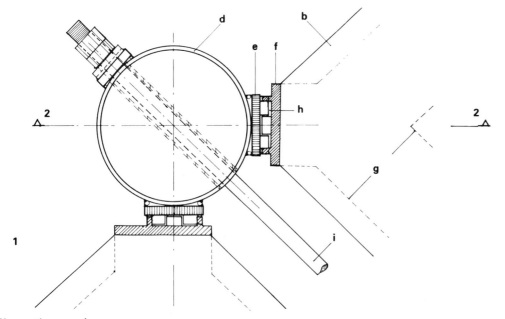

Plan section on column.

the ties and the shells to the column is made via a 20mm thick steel cone cast into the top of the column. A 40mm support plate with steel lugs is welded to the cone, these lugs supporting others welded to the steel plate at the corners of the shell. Other lugs prevent sideways movement. The thrust from the shell to the top of the column is taken through a 50mm thick elastomeric bearing pad. The ties go through the cone and are bolted up on the far side. The three shells on the south side, because they are unbalanced with respect to the supporting columns, have steel tie-down bars anchored to the wall on their south corner. Each shell is 66mm thick and has 400 x 700 mm edge beams, the longer dimension being in the plane of the shell. The shell is waterproofed with several layers of felt.

Structural Action

There are three 22mm layers of pine planking in each shell. The top and bottom layers are parallel to each other and run in the direction of the column supports while the middle layer is at right angles. The top and bottom planks may be thought of as compression 'arches' with the middle planks as 'cables' in tension, the two systems causing nearly axial compression in the edge beams which is tranferred via steel plates to the columns. In the three kite-shaped shells on the south side, forces also arise vertically to the axis of the edge members, because of the eccentricity of these shells with respect to their line of support; these forces were the critical ones in determining the dimensions of the edge beams. For construction reasons, all edge beams have the same dimensions. For the final analysis, each shell is split into 64 discrete areas by the straight lines generatrices in the two directions; the stresses in the shell, the membrane stresses, and the stresses in the edge members were then calculated, to a large extent by hand. Membrane action, which occurs when stresses act in the plane of the shell, is present over the whole area of the shell, bending being neglected in the calculations.

Construction

The shells were constructed next to the building on the ground. First the lower halves of the edge beams were put in position, then the planks, 120mm wide, were nailed to this and to each other, three nails connecting layers one and two at each crossover area and with a further four nails connecting all three layers. Screw nails were used. There was no glueing. Finally, the top halves of the edge beams were presented and dowelled to the lower halves. A difficulty is that the edge beams, while straight, have a twist along their length corresponding with that at the edge of the shell. Only two straight temporary beams, placed under a generatrix, were needed to support the planks during construction. The two high points of each shell were held at the correct distance by an assembly tie; another tie connected the two low points to take up the sidethrust. Each shell was then lifted into position by a tower crane.

Conclusion

This is an excellent example of the use of timber shells and one with a significant span. The shell is made without glue and any swelling or movements of the timber planks can take place without having any significant effect on stresses in the shell.

View of swimming pool from SE (photo by Bruno Krupp).

Swimming pool at construction looking W (photo by Bruno Krupp).

Florida Festival,
Orlando, Florida, USA

Introduction

The arrival of strong, durable non-combustible fabric materials directly led to the introduction of several completely new building types and marks one of the most significant recent innovations in construction techniques and form. More than most building types, fabric structures depend for their basic analysis, and their final shape, on the power of computers to do large amounts of calculation quickly. This tent structure is a superb example of the possibilities of building with fabrics both in terms of its striking form and its light interior spaces which result from the translucency of the fabric. The roof of the building is constructed entirely of a single layer of fabric and could properly be called a prestressed tent, in that the whole fabric surface is curved and prestressed in tension so that it does not crease or flutter in the wind. The building contains entertainments, shops, restaurants as well as many kinds of subtropical plants under a fabric that behaves somewhat like an artificial sky.

View of tent from NE (photo supplied by roof designer).

Description

Apart from a concrete floor and a 16ft (4.88 m) high earth berm around most of the perimeter, the building enclosure consists almost entirely of the fabric. This fabric is stressed between linear supports at the level of the top of the berm, and point supports above and below the berm. The upward supports consist of four steel masts. The edge supports are concrete beams on top of the berms and catenary cables over the entrances. The downwards support is a system of holddown cables, at the centre, forming a reversed tent shape. The tent is symmetrical about the diagonal line running north-south. About 90 000 sq ft (8360 sq m) of fabric was needed to cover a plan area of nearly 70 000 sq ft (6500 sq m), indicating the height needed at the four peaks in order to introduce sufficient curvature into the fabric surface. A 106ft (32.31m) high lattice steel mast supports the fabric over the largest square area with three smaller and identical 62ft (18.90m) high tubular steel masts supporting the fabric over other areas.

From the top of the high mast 24 $\frac{5}{8}$in (16mm)

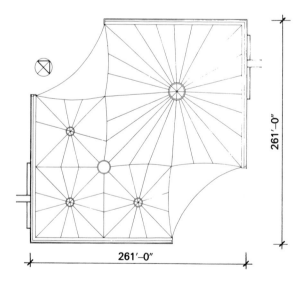

261'-0"

261'-0"

Plan on tent.

FLORIDA FESTIVAL (1980)

Description:
Prestressed tent structure using PTFE coated glass fabric
Architects:
R.L.Hart
Roof design and
structural engineers:
Geiger Berger Associates

Axonometric
view from E:

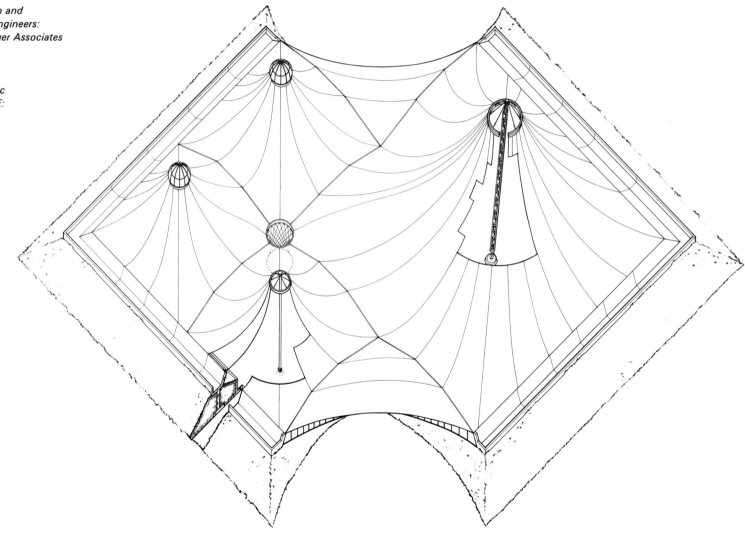

Scale: 12 m
         40 ft

cables radiate outwards pretensioned to a maximum of 12 tons (11 tonnes); 12 $\frac{5}{8}$in (16mm) cables radiate from each of the smaller masts pretensioned to a maximum of 6 tons (5.5 tonnes). There are enough radial cables to keep the stress in the fabric to manageable levels under wind loads and to allow the tent to read as a relatively smooth surface with panel divisions. There are two cutting pattern strips between each pair of adjacent cables. The valley cables, joined to the radial cables, and the catenary cables, above the entrances, are 1in (25mm) or 1$\frac{5}{8}$in (41mm) in diameter and pretensioned to a maximum of 34 tons (31 tonnes). At each peak, the fabric is clamped to a steel ring which, in turn, is attached via adjustable open clamps to short cables going to the top of each mast. A steel ring is also used at the single tie down position, the ring being anchored to foundations by 32 straight cables criss-crossing to make a hyperbolic paraboloid shape. Rainwater runs down the roof and through drainage holes at this tie down position. The rings at the peak and tie down positions are covered by acrylic plastic domes. The perimeter edge beams act as drainage channels for the roof. At the two entrances, glazing is held between a series of steel A-frames, the gap between the top of the frame and the fabric roof which overhangs the glass line, being made by a flat piece of fabric.

The fabric used for the tent is a ptfe coated glass cloth weighing 45 oz per sq yd (15 newtons per sq m) with a relatively open weave to give high light transmission. In this case 18% of natural light was transmitted with nearly 70% being reflected on the outer surface. Most of the natural light transmitted consists of visible or infrared radiation but there is a small proportion of uv light which allows the growth of some plants. The natural light level varies between about 15 and 70 lux, depending on the weather, and gives a uniform light with little directional quality. However some areas are covered with an interior fabric layer to provide a change in light levels.

Structural Action

Prestressed tents are self-supporting and at every point the surface must be anticlastic, that is the principal directions of curvature of the surface must have opposite sign. Consequently the forces along the edge of any small element on the surface

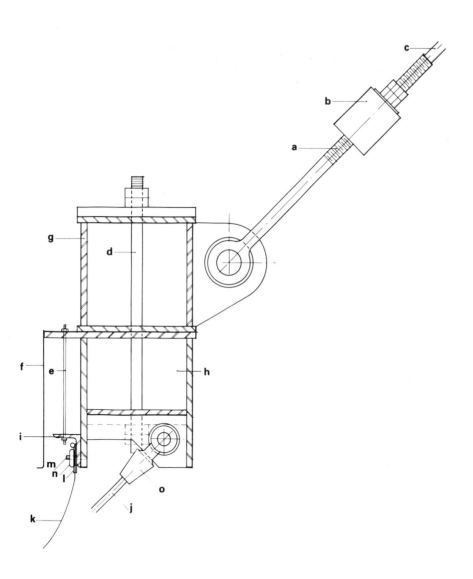

a open socket with 9″ take up; **b** socket block; **c** 1$\frac{1}{2}$″ strand cable connected to socket block and suspension bracket on mast; **d** 1$\frac{3}{8}$″ steel bar; **e** $\frac{1}{2}$″ steel bar; **f** cover ring; **g** upper steel ring; **h** lower steel ring; **i** adjustable fabric ring; **j** $\frac{3}{4}$″ strand radial cable; **k** fabric.

Vertical section through ring at top of high mast.

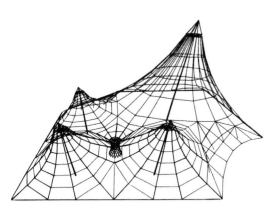

Computer model of tent.

pulling it outwards are balanced by other forces pulling it inwards. Here, forces in the radial cables are balanced by circumferential stresses in the fabric. The maximum and minimum stresses in the fabric are those due to the pretensioning and the superimposed loads. In this case the wind load is the only important superimposed load causing uplift over most of the area of the surface. The pretensioning is set by the need to keep minimum tensile stresses above zero, although some slackening of the fabric in extreme winds is permissible in one direction, as long as the overall stability of the system is guaranteed. The greater the curvature in the surface, the lower are stresses due to wind and the lower the pretensioning required. Fabric structures carry loads not only by increases of stress but also by gross, non-linear deformations in which the structure adapts to a shape that is more efficient for carrying the load. Such non-linear behaviour gives hidden strength to flexible structures. More than half of the wind load on this tent is carried by such changes of shape, rather than increases in stress. To avoid loss of prestress due to creep, the pretension in the fabric must be low and less than a fifth of its tensile stress. In addition the maximum stress in a glass fabric must be kept less than about an eighth of its tensile strength to prevent stress concentrations

Top of small mast (photo supplied by roof designer).

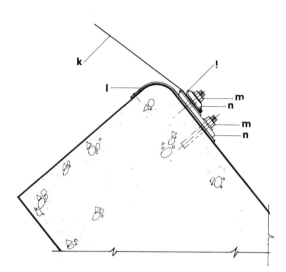

l neoprene layer; **m** $\frac{1}{2}$" stainless steel bolt at 8" centres; **n** aluminium plate.

Typical fabric connection to concrete edge.

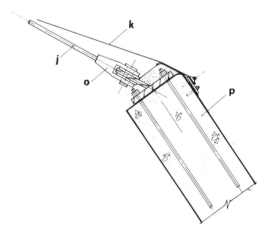

o open socket; **p** 1'–6" wide concrete edge beam.

Vertical section at bottom of radial cable on high mast.

causing fracture of the glass filaments; this requirement is usually determinant.

The basic shape of the roof was developed with the help of a stretch fabric study model. After determining the plan configuration of the cable net, the shape of the membrane system was arrived at by a computer process representing the fabric as a two-way system of linear strips, in which the fabric stress was kept uniform in both directions, throughout the system. This iterative process starts with entering approximate lengths and stresses in each component ending up with final lengths, final stresses and the coordinates of every node point of the system in perfect equilibrium. The shape is thus created as a response to a given stress pattern. Desired adjustments to the shape are achieved by adjusting the stress pattern and re-running the shape program. The stresses for this shape were analysed using a non-linear analysis program. The cutting pattern is derived directly from the shape program.

Construction

In the construction of prestressed tents it is vital both that the surface can be pushed from a limp fabric into a taut surface and that the method chosen to do this will give the correct prestress in all parts of the fabric. The displacements intended to pretension the fabric can be applied to a computer model of the unstressed fabric to check how much prestress is introduced. In general a strain between 2% and 6% is required along the weft (fill) direction; the warp direction will generally have no strain, or a slightly negative strain, during prestressing. In this case the tent is prestressed by adjustment of the heights of the suspension point on each mast. The straight edges of the fabric need to be tensioned along their edge line before they are clamped to the edge beams. The fabric attached to the steel rings at the peaks and tie down position also needs stretching circumferentially before clamping in position. Edge beams with some curvature would have allowed the fabric to be tensioned more conveniently but was not possible in this case. On the small masts, the height of the suspension point is adjustable by a small steel ring which slides on the very top section of the mast; the same thing is accomplished on the high mast by a telescopic section, at the bottom, which can be moved by

three jacks. On the cable clamping ring, at the top of both types of mast, the fabric is attached to a separate adjustable ring to make sure that the cables are receiving the load and that the fabric is not overstressed locally. A further adjustment is provided, in both types of mast, by the open clamps above the cable clamping ring. The whole tent fabric was made in six pieces which were joined by bolting between aluminium strips along the valleys and attached to the valley cables. Fabric was lowered over the small masts after they had been stabilised in an upright position. The erection of the high mast and its fabric was done together, a crane outside hoisting the top steel ring with a smaller crane under the fabric moving the foot of the mast horizontally to its correct position. The building took 13 months to construct of which only 3 months was needed to erect the fabric roof.

Conclusion

This is a highly accomplished design of a tent which not only provides good clear space but fully encloses it, with neat details between the fabric and perimeter supports. The fabric is well suited to the purpose of covering indoor recreation areas and, in this climate, the translucency and high reflectivity of the fabric saves energy, by allowing both good daylighting and rejection of a large part of the solar heat. In colder climates the low thermal insulation could give rise to large heat losses. Bearing in mind that this is a hurricane area, this tent, which only has radial cables, operates near the limit of the working strength of the fabric. Tents with larger spans would need a two-way grid of cables to support the fabric or a yet stronger fabric. The method of tensioning the fabric by jacking up the mast suspension points conveniently allows the fabric to be retensioned if necessary.

Baxter Laboratories Dining Hall, Deerfield, Illinois, USA

Introduction

This dining hall building set in a complex of laboratories and offices, provides a focal point for the whole site. The building is distinguished, from a distance, by its suspension roof structure and, closer to, by glass walls on all four sides made of well-proportioned rectangular sheets set into aluminium mullions and crosspieces. There are no vertical supports in the wall, apart from rods for tying the roof down. The roof has a very thin edge to complement an extremely light, patterned wall.

Description

The dining hall floor seats 1000 people, has only two columns in it, to support the roof, which are symmetrically placed to balance the loads, and is open on all four sides. There are two floor levels below the dining hall. The retaining wall and basement floor in these levels are of concrete construction. The dining hall floor, and the floor below it, are of steel and concrete construction supported by steel columns on a 24ft (7.32m) grid. Below the dining hall level, the two columns which go up to support the roof are 6ft (1.83m) diameter concrete columns, laterally supported by the floor and resting on 80ft (24m) deep caissons; above this level the two columns are tapered steel tubes filled with concrete . The columns rise 32ft (9.75m) above the roof level, this giving a large enough angle to the cables to allow them to act as vertical supports for gravity load, even at the perimeter. The roof is made up of 1ft 6in (450mm) deep steel beams on a 24ft (7.32m) grid with diagonal beams and a 4½in (112mm) metal acoustic deck, also on a diagonal to increase the in-plane stiffness of the roof. The metal deck is welded at each intersection of its lower flute with the roof beams below. At each grid intersection point there is a 1¾in (35mm) diameter supporting cable and, except at the five intermediate grid points on the east-west centre line, a ¾in (19mm) diameter stabiliser cable underneath to limit wind oscillations. At the perimeter these stabiliser cables are ⅜in (15mm) diameter thick and run inside every fourth mullion; the steel perimeter columns supporting the dining hall floor are hollow over the depth of the floor and contain a

View of Dining Hall from SE (photo by Howard N. Kaplan © HNK Architectural Photography).

2in (50mm) thick plate inside them to which the stabiliser cables are attached. The stabiliser cables serve to limit deflections from wind or unequal snow loads to an amount that can be accommodated by a vertical slip joint between the

roof and curtain wall; the joint also contains a fluorocarbon pad to allow small horizontal movements to take place. The roof is pitched towards the masts and four pipes inside each column provide for drainage. The roof is topped

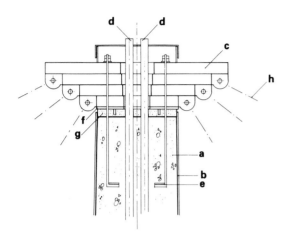

a reinforced concrete; b $\frac{1}{2}''$ thick steel jacket with 3'–9" diameter at top; c Steel masthead made from 6" plates of 42 ksi yield strength stress relieved after fabrication; d cast iron vent pipes; e anchor bolts torqued to 6 tons in tension; f 1" setting plate; g high strength non-shrink grout; h line of $1\frac{3}{8}''$ bridge strand cable.

Vertical section through masthead.

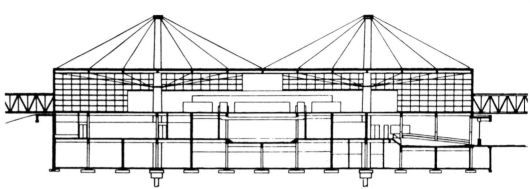

E-W section through building (drawn by architect).

with tar and gravel.

Structural Action

With uniform gravity load the roof structure is able to behave as a balanced cantilever. It is a fully triangulated space truss and designed to accept the resulting tension and compression forces. Unequal gravity loads, for example those due to snow drifts, as well as horizontal loads, cause deflections at the perimeter and some bending in the columns and this accounts for the large diameter of the columns. However, stiff cables help to limit these deflections. An important objective is to ensure that no cable can go slack.

Construction

A problem with cable construction is to ensure that the tension forces in the cables assumed in the design are achieved on site. Here at each grid intersection point, the roof structure was supported at its correct height by a scaffold column. First the supporting cables were stressed to overcome dead load. The stabilising cables were stressed to their design load, and then the supporting cables were restressed to their design load or until the node just lifted off its scaffold. Opposite pairs of cables were stressed together. In this condition the maximum cable loads are in the supporting cables at the perimeter near the north-south centre line and are equal to about 25 tons (23 tonnes).

Conclusion

There is no fat whatever in this design, all elements being properly exploited so that the original design aim for a light-looking wall and a thin, plate-like roof have been fully achieved and perhaps surpassed. At the perimeter there are only cable supports where many other designers may have been tempted to use rigid columns instead. In the event the roof framing weighs only $6\frac{1}{2}$ lb per sq ft (31.8 kg per sq m).

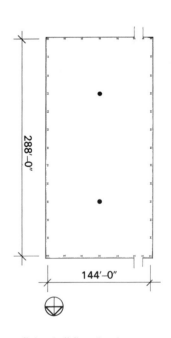

Plan at dining hall floor level.

BAXTER LABORATORIES DINING HALL (1975)

Description:
Three-storey building of composite construction with cable-supported roof system
Architects and structural engineers:
Skidmore, Owings and Merrill

*Axonometric
view from SE:*

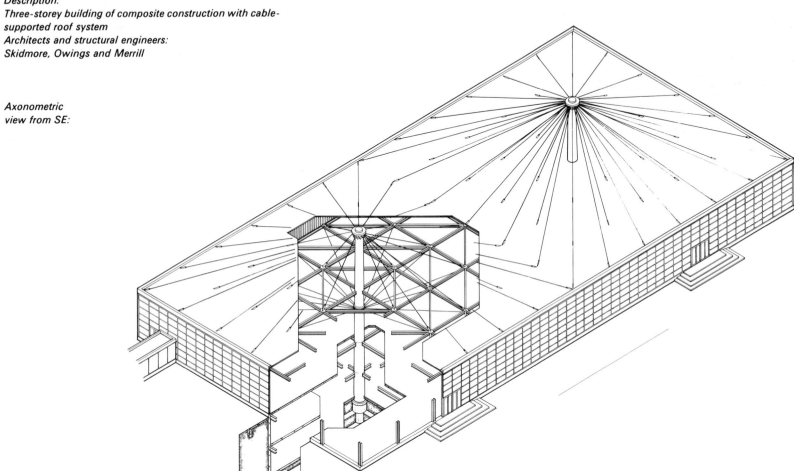

Scale:

Bundesgartenschau Lattice Shell, Mannheim, West Germany

Introduction

A grid shell is a lattice having a convex and double-curved surface shape which is funicular for an important load case. This shell roof for the Bundesgartenschau is one such. It consists of light timber laths running in two directions and is designed to be funicular, that is to have no bending moment in it, under dead load or any similar uniform load distribution. In spite of its lightness, the shell spans across a main hall with plan dimensions of about 60m in the longitudinal and transverse directions. The most interesting aspect of the grid shell is its ability both to take a free form shape over almost any plan arrangement and yet to be lifted into this final shape, on site, from a flat grid of plain, straight strips. In this case the timber laths were pushed into position from below using scaffolding towers, hydraulic jacks and fork lift trucks, one of the cheapest possible ways of bringing a large shell structure into existence. This erection procedure was possible because of the flexibility of the laths in bending and because of the pin joint between the laths going in the two different directions, allowing them to rotate relative to each other in their own plane; in this way each initially square mesh could lozenge slightly, by varying amounts, into the parallelograms that can be seen on the doubly-curved surface of the completed structure.

Description

The complex consists of a multi-purpose hall on the west side, with a transverse span in the east-west direction of about 60m, and a restaurant to the east with a span, in the same direction of about 50m. The two main spaces although separate are linked by a central corridor which has three spurs off it, leading to the outside. The plan provides through routes for large numbers of people. On the west side of the hall, under a crescent-shaped roof, is an indoor terrace. An outdoor terrace is provided on the west side of the restaurant containing storage plant and ancillary equipment. Below the main floor level is an extensive concrete substructure containing storage, plant and ancillary rooms. The plan depicts all these spaces individually but the building is brought into a unity by the over-arching lattice shell. The shell consists of 50 x 50 mm timber laths of Western Hemlock set out on a 500mm grid. A single lattice construction consists of two layers of laths, at an angle to each other, one crossing over the other at the node points which are at a uniform spacing of 500mm in the two directions. Before erection, the roof is in the form of a flat, square grid. A single lattice is used for the crescent-shaped roof, which has only a modest span, but over almost all the remainder of the roof a double lattice was necessary to give the roof sufficient bending stiffness; over parts of the restaurant roof, where it lacked curvature and therefore took high axial loads, a triple lattice was needed to provide the required bending stiffness.

Along most of its perimeter the shell springs off a plywood edge board resting on steel stubs at 1.25m centres which are bolted down to a low concrete boundary wall. In other parts of the boundary the shell is supported by 60mm thick deep laminated timber beams fixed to each side of the lattice shell, which span between steel columns; the columns incline inwards in the direction of the forces from the shell; a similar system using circular laminated beams is used in the valley between the crescent-shaped terrace and the rest of the main hall. Over part of the boundary to the restaurant, near the outdoor terrace, a cable boundary was used. There are two cables each tensioned to over 6 tonnes; they are in a parabolic profile that implies the forces from the laths are reasonably uniform, although a plywood edge does supply some bending stiffness. Support to the shell is also provided by laminated timber arches: there are two in the central corridor and one at each end of the three spurs that lead from this corridor; the latter are made, like the beam edges, of timber pieces sandwiching the lattice construction. An important decision was to put the grid of laths at an angle to the longitudinal axes of the corridors and the main spaces; this helps to ensure that the laths in both directions will carry load. In general the laths are at about 45 degrees to the principal radial of curvature of the shell surface which minimises their curvature, an important consideration with laths which are relatively easy to break.

Once in position and attached to its boundary supports, the shell can be self-supporting but the lattice roof requires bending stiffness to prevent dimpling of the surface by non-uniform snow loads. Deformation caused by lozenging of lattices under asymmetric load must also be prevented; pairs of 6mm 19-wire strand cable ties were run right across the roof surface in the two directions parallel to the lattice diagonals and attached to every sixth node, which are at about 4.5m centres in this direction; any in-place deformation of the lattice puts one of these two sets of ties into tension. The use of a double lattice required special attention to the node joints: for the two laths which are in line with each other to work together properly in bending, no slippage can be allowed between laths at the node joint; during erection, however, the two laths must be able to slip over each other to allow the shell to be put into shape. The detail adopted, to meet these requirements, has slotted holes in the laths of the top lattice and an 8mm bolt through the joint which is tightened after erection and supplies a clamping force of 800 kg to prevent slippage; four disc springs, placed under the nuts and working in series, keep the clamping force reasonably constant in spite of shrinkage and expansion of the timber under changing conditions. Although there is no slippage at the nodes, in those parts of the roof with high axial load in the laths, deformation in shear of the lath at right angles to, and between, the loaded members would be excessive; wedge blocking pieces were inserted to reduce this movement between laths, thus increasing the bending stiffness of that part of the roof. Timber nailing strips for the roofing fabric are placed parallel to the top lath of the grid shell and attached to it through spacer blocks that lift the strips clear of the fixing bolts.

The roofing fabric is a pvc-coated polyester grid, supplied in rolls, and is attached to the timber nailing strips by 26mm long galvanised steel staples. At the edges, galvanised flat steel strips and screws are used to secure the fabric. Where the fabric is punctured, it is immediately sealed by a soft pvc film that is applied as a liquid. Welding between the fabric strips was by means of a hot-air gun to plasticize the pvc coating. To install the roof skin, the fabric was first prestretched in the warp and weft (fill) directions to about 10% of its tear strength, welded to the fabric already in place and then nailed down. A clear fabric with 30% light transmittance was used but, because of cracking,

View of main hall partially erected with restaurant grid in foreground (photo supplied by Ove Arup and Partners).

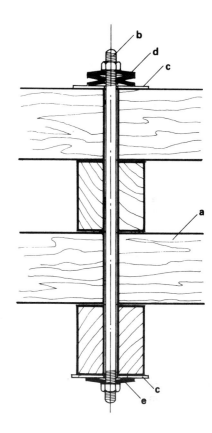

a 50 x 50 mm timber lath; b 8mm diameter threaded bar; c 55mm washer; d 3/ 35mm diameter disc springs; e 1/ 35mm diameter disc spring.

Standard node detail.

this was replaced after five years with a white pvc fabric which is expected to last in excess of ten years. Heating and ventilation systems were installed for ancillary rooms, toilet areas as well as the kitchen and restaurant areas. In the main hall, full air conditioning was required, because of the need to provide cooling for events held in the summer. A low-pressure all-air system was used here to provide four air changes per hour of which at least a third must be outside air, in order to provide 20 cu m of fresh air per person per hour.

Two air handling units are placed in the substructure below the hall terraces and distribute, via concrete underfloor ducts and conspicuous, large steel ducts above the floor, to high-level supply air grilles. In winter the system is able to protect against frost and to thaw very heavy snowfalls on the roof to prevent overloading.

Structural Action

The genesis of this building was a small experimental model; calculations based on this,

using the principle of equilibrium, gave an exact geometrical definition of the roof's funicular shape under dead load; another physical model was made, properly scaled to reproduce important structural characteristics, and in parallel with this, a mathematical model was built up to reproduce as far as possible the behaviour of the actual lattice shell in all its detail aspects under any kind of load; finally a load test was conducted on the finished structure, serving to check the validity of this mathematical model. The first experimental model,

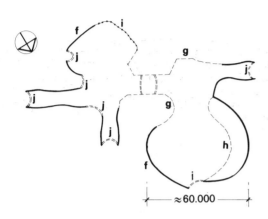

f concrete boundary (full lines); g deep laminated timber beams sandwiching lattice and spanning to steel columns; h 500mm diameter circular laminated timber valley beams spanning to steel columns (dashed line); i cable boundary (dotted line); j laminated timber arches.

Plan on shell showing boundary and intermediate supports.

Aerial view of building from N (photo supplied by Ove Arup and Partners).

for finding the roof shape, consisted of hanging chains at a scale of 1:100, with every three laths in the real structure represented by a single element in the model. The shape required was one given by the dead load of a uniformly spaced two-way grid of chains, all chain elements being in pure tension. The upturned shape of this was the required shape, although modifications had to be made to this shape near some supports. Without the diagonal steel ties, the roof is a pure grid shell with a shape that is funicular for dead load. In this state the loads on the shell can be divided into the funicular loads, producing axial compression, and unbalanced loads, giving rise to bending and deflection; any bending and deflection would be increased by increased funicular loads and, if these are high enough, they can cause denting of the surface leading to collapse even under the smallest disturbance or geometrical imperfection. This behaviour may be summed up as that of a series of interconnected flexible arches which get their stability from arch action. In the real structure, with

diagonal cables attached, the roof behaviour is improved and is slightly more like that of a continuous shell.

The roof was calculated as a series of discrete elements with up to 12 laths in the real structure being represented by a single element in the mathematical model. The calculations showed the roof of the main hall would collapse with a total uniform load of 88 kg per sq m, over the heated part of the shell, giving a factor of safety of 2.5 on the assumed maximum load. An indication of the importance both of preventing in-plane shear deformation and of forcing the two lattices of the shell to work together in bending is provided by another calculation on the hall: this showed that after fixing the shell to the boundaries, in its unbolted condition without diagonal ties, the collapse load of the lattice shell would be slightly less than its self-weight of 20 kg per sq m. The assumptions used in the computer calculations concerning the stiffness of the shell were based on tests on individual elements and connections. The

calculations for buckling of the surface uniform load were checked by hand by the proofing engineer; this calculation was done in the hall and restaurant where the radii of curvature are largest and the roof surface nearly spherical and assumed the buckling to be similar to that of a spherical shell but making some allowance for the low shear resistance of the grid shell. A full scale load test of the completed roof of the hall, with a 500 sq m area loaded at 1.7 times the design load, that is 40 kg per sq m, gave a pattern of deflections that corresponded closely with those calculated by computer and provided further, direct verification of the assumptions made about stiffnesses. The measured deflection at the centre point of the roof was 77mm. Except at the arch and cable boundaries, the boundary supports to the shells were assumed in calculations to be pinned supports. The maximum force in any set of laths at the edge of the roof is 0.75 tonnes and this is transferred to the boundary by bolts acting in shear.

BUNDESGARTENSCHAU LATTICE ROOF (1975)

Description:
Timber lattice shell roof with concrete substructure originally
designed for garden show
Architects:
C. Mutschler and Partner
Roof consultant:
Frei Otto
Structural engineers for roof:
Ove Arup and Partners
Structural engineers for
substructure:
H. Spah

k blocking pieces; **l** 2/ 6mm diameter 19-wire strand ties at 4.5m centres on lattice diagonals; **m** wedge blocking pieces secured by 3/ 8mm bolts as standard node detail; **n** thick plywood board bolted to steel bracket by 8/ 16mm bolts; **o** steel stubs at 1.25m centres; **p** lattice bolted to edge board by 10mm bolts; **q** nailing strip for fabric.

Detail on concrete boundary.

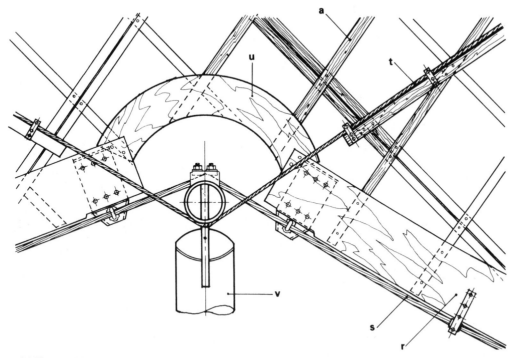

r 2/ 36mm thick plywood edges sandwiching lattice; s 2/ 30mm diameter boundary cables; t 15mm diameter tie-down cable; u plywood trimmer; v 300mm diameter round steel tubular column.

Cable boundary for restaurant building.

Interior view of corridor looking NW by entrance to restaurant (photo supplied by Ove Arup and Partners).

Construction

The boundaries of the lattice shell were set in their correct position and all node points were put at their correct height. It was assumed that this would ensure that the node points were in their correct plan position too and only a few nodes had their plan position checked. With the boundary supports substantially complete, the timber laths were laid on roughly boarded scaffolding which was reasonably flat, although not necessarily level, and set well above the floor. The timber laths were brought to site with maximum lengths of just over 30m, jointing of lengths in the fabricating shop being done by glued finger joints. Site joints between laths were done with 50 x 25 mm lapping pieces nailed on each side of the laths. Instead of a toothed plate, spring washers were used to generate friction between the laths and lapping pieces; this was sufficient to prevent slippage and therefore loss of bending stiffness in the roof. Breakages of laths were repaired in the same fashion. Cranes were not used to lift the roof into position because of the very long reach, up to 40m, that would have been required. Lifting of the lattice shell was therefore done from underneath by means of scaffolding towers, at 9m centres, which were attached to 3.5m long H-shaped timber spreaders, under the shell, through a swivelling ball joint. The towers were lifted by jacks or by fork lift trucks which had the advantage over static jacks of being able to move horizontally with the spreader as the shell took shape. With all the towers near their correct height it was possible to start bolting up. In the Hall two strips running parallel to each other in the east-west direction were bolted up first, starting from the centre of the shell and finishing with the boundary connections. A line of towers, which was on the strip between these two, was then lowered, to remove bumps, and bolted up; the whole of this bolted up area could then be adjusted for height. This procedure was repeated for strips running in the north-south direction and then for the remaining parts of the shell. At arch and beam boundaries, the laths were lightly attached to the inner member and bolt holes drilled; the outer member was then put in position and drilled through from inside so that the bolts could then be fitted.

A 1:60 scale model of the Hall was made representing its state at erection before bolting up; this was used to check lifting loads by scaling up the readings from a spring balance used on the model. In many areas the laths had to be bent to a

View of building from E (photo by Robert Hausser).

very small radius of curvature, as low as 10m and sometimes down to 6m; this causes significant bending stress which, however, reduces with time because of creep. In spite of the preliminary work needed to establish values for calculations, the complete roof was designed and built within a period of eighteen months. The total period of construction, including building of the substructure, was sixteen months; the lattice shell roofs were laid out on the scaffolding, erected and covered in just over seven months.

Conclusion

This grid shell construction used is a pioneering effort in terms of the cost of providing a free-form shell at a large scale. However the boundary supports were expensive to design and fabricate as each support had to be in the same plane as the shell surface it was connected to; in the case of the beam and arch supports this meant they had to be twisted along their length. The decision to make the shell funicular for uniformly distributed loads meant that, in spite of the ties, non-uniform loads caused bending in the laths. An important aim in the design of shells is, as far as possible, to take loads by membrane action, that is with axial forces in the laths; as the load of the lattice is only a moderate proportion of the total, unlike a masonry shell for example, this suggests that it would be worthwhile to find other shapes for the lattice in which a greater proportion of the non-uniform load could be taken by membrane action. This could lead to lighter construction and further reductions in dead load. The method of constructing a grid shell by pulling up an initially flat, regular grid is only possible with rectangular, triangular or hexagonal grid shapes, these being the only polygons that fill a plane in a completely regular way. Of these the rectangular grid, especially the square grid, appears most convenient; the use of a triangular grid looks particularly difficult but diagonal laths could be added to a rectangular grid, after erection, in the manner of the steel ties used here. The grid shell method of construction can be seen as requiring a careful balance in those properties of the lath, such as its flexibility and creep deflection, that are advantageous at erection, but generally disadvantageous in the finished state. This lattice shell creates its own kind of space. It can be used in a span range of up to about 60m; lath sizes would go up more or less in proportion to the span. As a piece of structural engineering, these are interesting forms of shell construction that were done at moderate cost and in minimum time.

Fleetguard Factory, Quimper, France

Introduction

The use of cables as structural supports has traditionally been confined to long span elements such as bridges where there are few connections and the very high tensile strength of bridge cable allows large loads to be carried. This factory and office building, at the opposite end of the scale range, demonstrates the use of cable for supporting roofs, nicely overcoming possible disadvantages by having square bays and by tie rods in a 'cat's cradle' arrangement between the columns. Good proportions on the external beam and column elements and well-crafted roof connection details give a spare and disciplined appearance to the factory that still holds as different elements take on significance, in moving the vantage point from far away to close to. The cable-stayed roof reduces the depth of the roof beams, making service distribution easier, and in spite of the very large number of connection details and inevitably stricter construction procedures, this building came well within the economic range.

Description

The building consists of a steel frame having columns spaced on an 18m square grid, to suit racking and machine layouts, with insulated profile steel sheet cladding and a composite flat panel roof on I-beams. The principal steel roof beams, 330mm deep, are supported at their third points by tubular steel hangers which puncture the roof membrane and connect to the steel rods, between 26mm and 40mm in diameter, which make up the roof suspension system in each bay. The secondary roof beams are 160mm deep. Strip glazing above the cladding separates the roof from the rest of the building. The cladding spans horizontally between light vertical steel trusses which connect into a horizontal truss around the perimeter which in turn carry wind loads to the external columns. On two sides of the building these external columns are braced by a raking 244mm diameter steel tube. Any thermal expansion of the roof takes place on the opposite sides. There are no expansion joints. The building may be extended on these sides and, indeed, new

View of NW side of building (photo by engineer).

bays of steelwork can be added even before cladding needs to be removed.

Independent of the main sructure is a mezzanine floor supported by columns on a 6m grid. The ground floor is a continuous 150mm thick concrete slab reinforced top and bottom to take wheel loads. All the foundations are on or near to granite and are conventional pad footings. Services runs are exposed on the inside and are organized by the structural grid; from the plant room at ground floor level, the services are led up and run at roof level down the length of the factory branching off at every other bay; low-pressure hot water for heater units, compressed air, water, gas and electricity are carried. Each area is ventilated and heated separately and, inevitably, a large number of extracts and pipes from the units, on or below the roof, need to cross the roof membrane. The bulkiness of those units on the roof is obscured to some extent by the cradlework of steel rods.

Structural Action

The most interesting part of the structural system is that of the roof. The roof structure works by simultaneous action in all three spatial dimensions; it is complex to analyse because

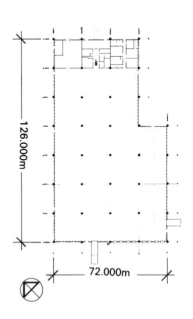

Ground floor plan.

FLEETGUARD FACTORY (1981)

Description:
Single-storey factory with steel frame and suspended roof
structure
Architects:
R. Rogers and Partners
Structural engineers:
Ove Arup and Partners

Axonometric
of N corner
of building:

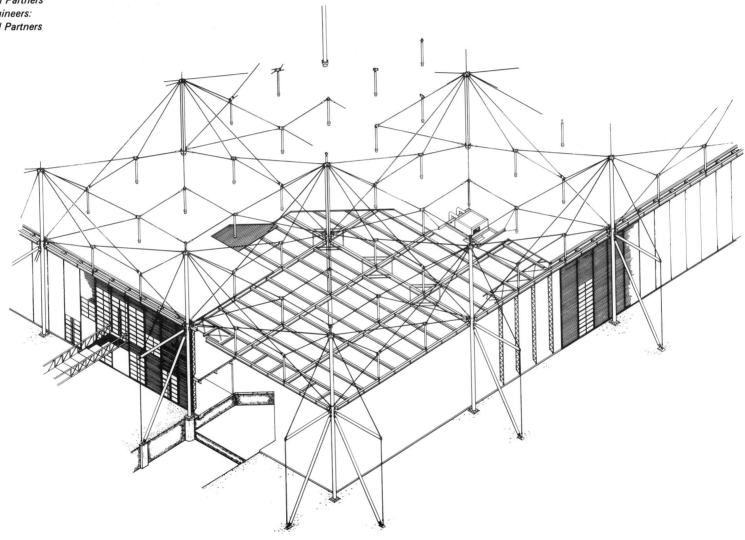

Scale: 9m / 30ft

under some loads the tension rods go slack, effectively changing the load-carrying system, and because loads and combinations of loads, in very many different places, affect the design of each individual member, that is, the effects of loads are highly interactive. Nevertheless separate load-carrying systems can be distinguished as being active within the overall roof structure depending on what loads are present. The three primary load conditions are those due to uniform gravity load, those due to wind uplift and those due to unbalanced point loads. The arrangement of rods connects the tops of columns to the adjacent columns at roof level and ingeniously prevents the deflections due to the point loads causing significant bending in the columns or upward movement of the roof beams in adjacent bays. The degree to which this does happen depends on the amount of stretch in the rods so that the sizing of rods depends on their stiffness rather than their strength. The arrangement of rods described also provides a means of coping with uplift forces. Rods were chosen in preference to cables, being three to four times stiffer than cable of the same diameter and easier to protect from corrosion. The rods were made taut but not pretensioned at the time of construction. The primary roof beams on the column grid carry a significant axial load from any temperature differences which may occur in the roof as well as from the horizontal outrigger booms which frame into the perimeter columns and are in compression. However the pinned connections prevent bending moments being transferred into the column and, very logically, allow the strength of the roof system to be fully used in carrying vertical load under all conditions.

Construction

For convenience, site connections were bolted or pinned. Connections between rods are pinned. The forks for the pinned connection were made by cutting and shaping from steel blocks and were then welded to the steel rods. Columns were made in two pieces and joined, by welding, just above the roof level. Most rods were provided with threaded adjusters which were altered until the columns were plumb and the beams level. An indication of the force in any tie rod was obtained by measuring its deflection in the middle against a taut string line. The roof beams were levelled with

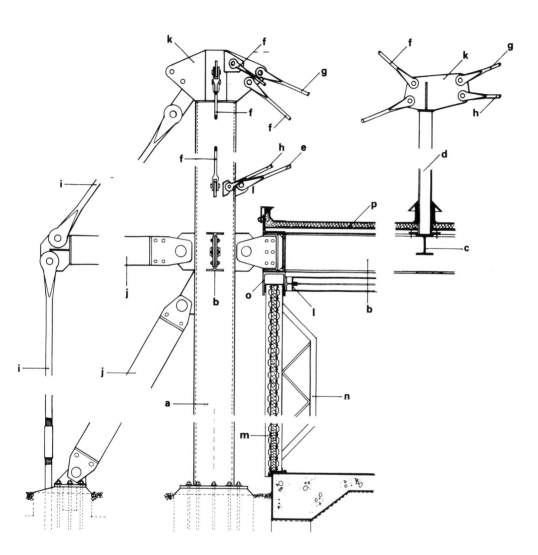

a 550mm diameter hollow steel column; b IPE 330 main steel beam; c HEA 160 secondary steel beam; d 114mm diameter tube hanger; e 40mm rod; f 32mm rod; g 36mm rod; h 26.5mm rod; i 55mm rod; j 244mm diameter tube restraints; k 20mm steel plate; l horizontal wind bracing; m double skin cladding with 50mm insulation; n 350mm deep steel truss at 2m centres; o Channel section at movement joint; p built-up roofing on insulation on metal deck.

Vertical section through NE wall, omitting mezzanine floor.

View of top of side column (photo by engineer).

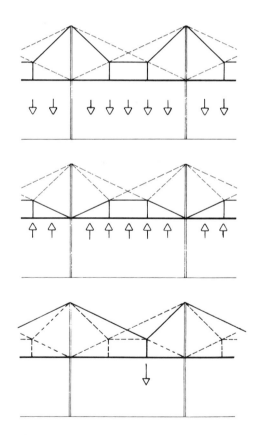

adjusters in the tubular hanging rod. Construction was completed within 20 months.

Conclusion

Out of a plain brief, a very elegant building has been made. The facade is broken up and a good scale is provided either by the corrugations of the wall panels, close to, or, from further away, by the repetition of column and beam elements in the bays. The roof system is a fully fledged tensile design in the sense that supporting cables make large angles with the horizontal, giving effective vertical support for loads, and in that the roof system is fully stabilised against load from any direction, by rods put into tension, similar, in this respect, to the way a saddle shaped net works. The weight of steelwork used in the building averages 46 kg per sq m of floor area, said to be 17% less than that using beams only but, even so, it is more expensive than a conventional beam system. The elements and connection pieces, in all their different sizes and shapes, are well orchestrated into a whole structural system that is a delicate piece of work and entirely in keeping with the clean, rectilinear lines in the other parts of this building.

Diagram showing loadcarrying systems for uniform load, wind uplift and point load.

View at bottom of side columns (photo by Ken Kirkwood).

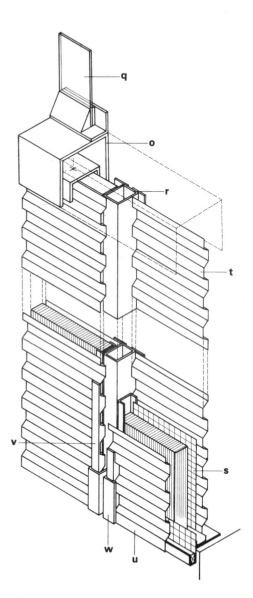

q clerestory glazing; **r** post of steel truss; **s** vapour barrier; **t** perforated acrylic coated steel internal sheet; **u** silver pvf2 coated external steel sheet; **v** cellular plastic filler piece; **w** aluminium cover strip screwed to **r**.

View on cladding at steel truss support.

Augusta Civic Center, Augusta, Georgia, USA

Introduction

Notwithstanding the large number of joints and members, two-layer space frames can be a suitable and nicely comprehensive solution for long-span roofs, especially those of an approximately square shape. Popular geometrical arrangements for the members of space frames on a square grid are those with the top and bottom chord members parallel to one another, both chords being either parallel or skewed at 45 degrees to the edge of the roof structure. Another popular arrangement is to have one layer of the space frame at 45 degrees to the edge, with a smaller grid modulus on the top layer, which generally is in compression, than in the bottom layer, which is generally in tension. Space frames spanning distances up to about 100ft (30m) may use proprietary joints which are easy to fix and of proven ability. For this arena the space frame has purpose designed joints and grids parallel to the edges. It spans a 300ft (91.44m) square space and is turned down at the edges into four load-bearing walls, making a 'squared off' dome which significantly reduces the roof weight and depth.

Description

The chord members of both layers of the space frame roof are placed on a 13ft 6in (4.11m) square grid with the top layer offset from the bottom layer. The roof has a depth of 12ft (3.66m), giving a relatively high span to depth ratio of 25 and showing the beneficial effect of the continuity and regular support provided by the walls. It has a 1ft 6in (457mm) high ridge along the east-west centre line to help drainage. The space frame walls have the same offset grids but a reduced depth, equal to half the grid dimension. The members of the space frame are made up of double or triple angle sections placed back to back, giving the roof an average weight of 14 lb per sq ft (68.5 kg per sq m). Excluding the weight of connections, the total weight of the roof is about 550 tons (500 tonnes); the weight of steel in the walls is about half this figure.

On the north-east and south-west faces the space frame rests on 6¾in (169mm) diameter

View of Arena from N (photo © Nathaniel Lieberman).

concrete-filled steel pipe columns supported by concrete beams, in turn supported by concrete columns or walls on footings. By rotating slightly out-of-plumb, the pipe (tubular) columns allow temperature movements to occur. Glass panels, 8ft (2.44m) high by 6ft (1.83m) wide, are placed immediately in front of the pipe columns and below the space frame. All lateral forces are taken by the walls on the north-west and south-east faces which together act like shear walls or like a large portal frame, as the lateral force is parallel or perpendicular to them respectively. On these faces the space frame rests on a sliding joint on a steel I-section stub column which is cast into a concrete upstand beam. The space frame is completely exposed from the inside having circular service ducts, with up to 3ft 6in (1.05m) diameter, within its depth. The cladding on it consists of a 3in (75mm) metal deck with cement plaster backing as an inner skin, and a 2in (50mm) insulated aluminium panel system, as an outer skin. The aluminium cladding panels are shaped and,

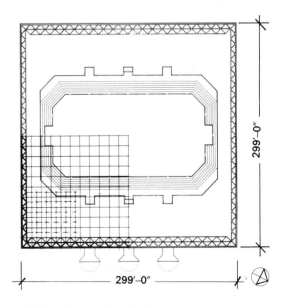

High level plan and roof grid.

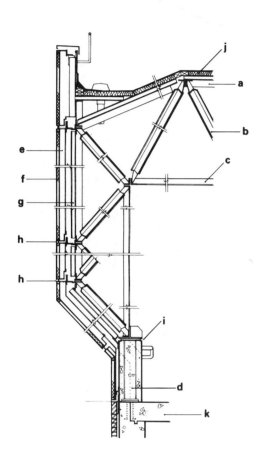

a top chord 2/ 7″ × 4″ × ½″ angles; **b** diagonal member 2/ 4″ × 3″ × ¼″angles; **c** bottom chord 2/ 6″ × 4″ × ⅝″angles; **d** W8 x 40 lb/ft stub column; **e** vertical support to cladding panels; **f** 2″ insulated aluminium panel with pvdf coating; **g** 1″ cement plaster on lath on 3″ metal deck; **h** movement joint; **i** sliding joint; **j** built-up roofing on rigid insulation on vapour barrier on 3″ metal deck; **k** lobby level slab.

Vertical section through middle of SE wall.

View of top chord of space frame (photo by Stanley Goldstein).

typically, are in the form of 13ft 6in square (4.11 x 4.11 m) panels made from eight triangular panels, with sliding horizontal and vertical joists between the panels. The panels have a surface area of 85 000 sq ft (7900 sq m); their cost, after erection, is about double that of the steelwork. The floor of the arena is set 9ft (2.74m) into the ground to reduce the areas of cladding and eliminate the need for escalators.

Structural Action

For preliminary design a space frame may be analysed as a flat plate. The analogy is valid because the space frame has torsional stiffness and strength, like a slab, by virtue of the diagonals collecting the chord intersection points in each layer. This contrasts with a grid of vertical trusses which has very little torsional rigidity. The heart of the space frame is the connection system which determines both the strength of the joint and the allowable geometry of the space frame. In this case the maximum chord forces exceed 100 tons (92 tonnes) and are outside the range of most proprietary joint systems. With angle sections as chord members, connection plates may be introduced right into the centre of each joint and this makes it easier to arrange for the centroids of the eight members in a typical joint to meet in the point and thus avoid bending in the joint. With connections behaving like pinned joints, it would

View of construction showing erection towers on inside (photo by Stanley Goldstein).

be possible to completely eliminate bending movement in the members too, which would be advantageous, although in practice some bending is almost unavoidable.

Construction

The space frame was erected piece by piece using steel beams on trestles as temporary supports. Total construction time was 24 months.

Conclusion

Because the cost of space frames depends primarily on the number of joints and therefore the number of members to bolt up, it is important to use a large grid module, typically about one and a half times the space frame depth and between a tenth and a twentieth of the span. A disadvantage is that large grids increase the connection forces. This design uses a relatively small grid but keeps a simple geometry suitable both for the roof and the walls. The erected cost of space frames is high, higher per ton than for conventional frames, partly because the space frame has the same density of members where the forces are low as where they are high, for example at supports and near the middle of the span. Nevertheless the space frame, with its standard module, can be a unifying element in the design. In this arena with a square plan and full continuity at the edges, its use appears to be entirely appropriate.

AUGUSTA CIVIC CENTER (1980)

Description:
Arena with concrete grandstand and steel space truss roof
and walls
Architects:
I.M.Pei and Partners
Structural engineers:
Le Messurier/SCI

Axonometric
view from E:

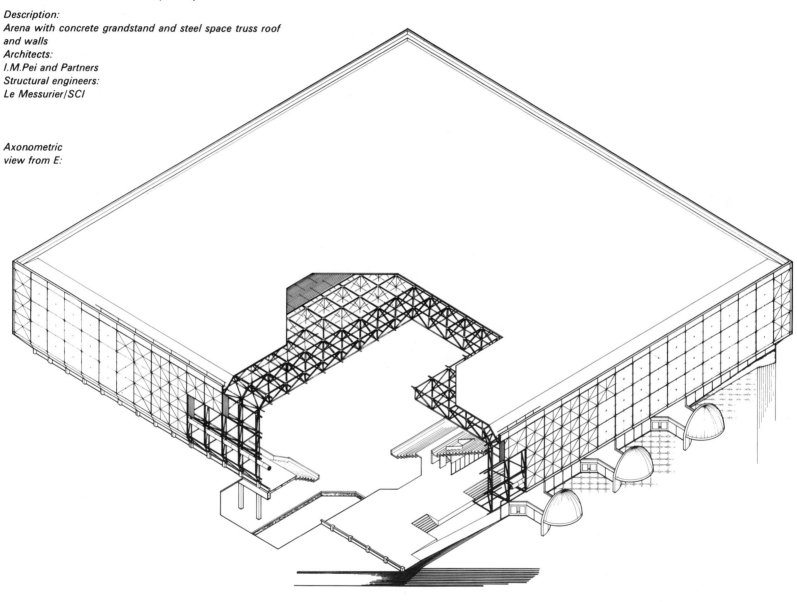

Scale: 12 m
40 ft

Leavey Activities Center,
Santa Clara, California, USA

Introduction

Inside an air supported structure, the atmosphere is not just for breathing but is also the medium of support for the roof. Because air is the supporting medium, the potential span of these structures is enormous. The idea of inflating the inside of a building in order to support the roof is not new but has awaited suitable materials and forms. This facility consists of a swimming pool using a pvc coated polyester fabric roof and a main building using a ptfe coated glass fabric roof, both roofs being air supported and reinforced by cables. These are typical applications of the low profile air supported roofs which, although vulnerable to damage, have made dramatic reductions possible in the cost of enclosing large areas. The swimming pool roof is removable and made of a material that can flex without damage.

Description

The main building has two levels. The entrance level contains two small playing areas and circulation space around the perimeter of the building which gives access to the swimming pool. The main arena level is 13ft below this, down the steps of the concrete bleachers, as are utility rooms. The substructure is of concrete construction. Four steel lattice towers spring 35ft from this level to support a steel lattice lighting gantry which goes round the four sides of the main arena. At night the lights reflect off the fabric roof, no artificial lighting being required during the day because of the translucency of this fabric. The fabric roof in the main building spans between six steel cables at 40ft (12m) centres and a concrete compression ring that runs around the periphery. Below the compression ring is an earth berm that serves as an outside wall for the building. The fabric weighs 37.5 oz per sq yard (12.5 newtons per sq m) but the total weight of the roof including cables and fittings is about 0.90 lb per sq ft (0.43 kilonewtons per sq m) so that the air inside must be at least this amount above atmospheric pressure for the roof to stay up. The normal operating pressure is 5 lb per sq ft (2.39 kilonewtons per sq m), maintained by four fans each capable of handling 40 000 cu ft per minute

View of arena and pool from SW (photo by Julius Shulman).

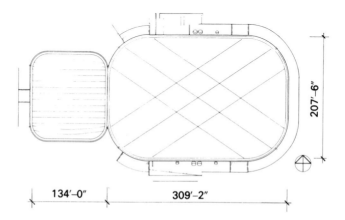

Roof plan.

LEAVEY ACTIVITIES CENTER (1975)

Description:
Air supported fabric roofs over sports arena and swimming
pool with concrete substructure
Architects:
Caudill, Rowlett, Scott/
A.A. Hoover and Associates
Structural engineers:
Geiger Berger Associates/
Pregnoff, Matheu, Kellam, Beebe

Axonometric
view from S:

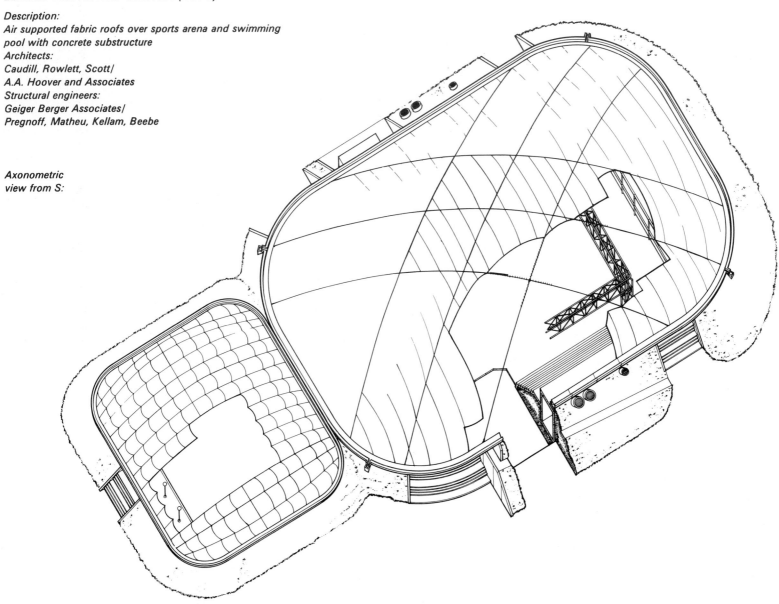

Scale: ⌐⌐⌐⌐ 12m / 40ft

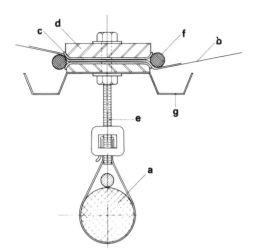

a 1⅞″ strand cable; **b** fabric; **c** neoprene layer; **d** aluminium strip; **e** ⅜″ cadmium plated steel bolt at 12″ centres; **f** rope edge to fabric; **g** condensation channel.

Vertical section through fabric panel joint.

View of arena from pool (photo by Balthazar Korab).

(1132 cu m per minute). These fans are located in fan rooms immediately below the compression ring on the long sides of the building. The same fans are also used for distributing heated or conditioned air. With this climate, the requirement during the day is mostly for air conditioning or the direct intake and circulation of outside air. An exhaust fan is also located in the fan rooms. The necessary cooling capacity for the air conditioning system is provided by a 406 ton (1427 megawatts) chiller unit. In addition to this, three fans operate in the area of the utility rooms. There are also four standby fans for use with the other fans, in the event of the fabric roof developing a large tear, say of area greater than about six foot square (3.34 sq m), or in the event of the emergency exits, which are not air locked, having to be kept open. Such extra fan capacity constitutes the real safety factor in air supported structures. With holes in the fabric and no fan power, the fabric would still be able to come to rest on the lighting gantry and hand rails, or without these, on the cables in their hanging position.

The swimming pool roof is supported by ten ⅝in (16mm) cables and two ¾in (19mm). The cables are sewn into the polyester fabric. A bleed off from the exhaust air of the main building provides the inflation pressure. The roof can be retracted over the summer months; this is effected by wrapping the cables round a long drum which can roll along two suspended cables running in the north-south direction.

Structural Action

The internal pressure in these air supported roofs is that necessary to keep the roofs stable under snow or fluctuating wind loads. The rise in the middle of the roof is 24ft (7.32 m) and, with such a low profile, wind creates suction over most of the area of the roof and tends to keep the roof fabric in shape. The slope of the fabric at the perimeter is similar to that of the earth berm and this helps to prevent slackening of the fabric at this point in high winds. A suitable shape for such air-supported roofs is essential to prevent wind buffeting, especially as the frequencies of the buffeting are often close to the natural frequency of the roof. However changes in internal pressure can be made to alter the natural frequency, if this were to become necessary. While wind loads increase the tension in the cables, snow loads cause a decrease. Since the internal pressure is

limited by the capacity of doors, windows and other components, in areas of more than nominal snow loads, these roofs must install melting equipment to remove the snow load. If the loads from snow or melted water are high enough, they may cause individual fabric panels to sag downwards and, in this event, flap valves in the middle of each panel can open to release water and prevent damage to the roof. The roof is given a reasonably high profile to help prevent this happening and to reduce the fabric stress under wind suction. The design wind suction is 12 lb per sq ft (5.74 kilonewtons per sq m) and, for the given fabric strength, largely determines the cable spacing. The forces in the cables depend both on cable spacing and the rise of the roof but, unlike prestressed tents, do not depend on the curvature given to the adjacent fabric. The cable profiles were determined by finding the shape under constant internal pressure for which the cable net is in equilibrium; if the cable forces in the two directions were equal, the tent would have a spherical shape, a condition which is approached near the centre of the roof.

Unlike prestressed tents, errors in dimensioning of the cables or fabric are unimportant as they can

Inside view of arena from E side (photo by Balthazar Korab).

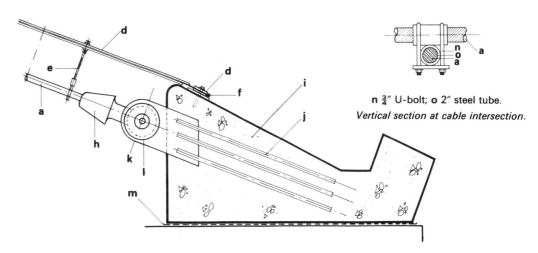

n ¾″ U-bolt; **o** 2″ steel tube.
Vertical section at cable intersection.

h open strand socket; **i** 6′ wide concrete compression ring; **j** steel reinforcement; **k** 1½″ steel plate; **l** spacers; **m** ptfe layer.

Vertical section through perimeter compression ring.

be taken out by a slight change in the general shape, although local errors in fabric panels will still cause creasing; some creases can be seen near the perimeter support. At the design internal pressure, the stresses in the fabric are low. The most likely cause of failure of the fabric is tearing from an existing tear due to snagging, construction damage or other factors not connected with the normal service loads. Cable forces are absorbed by the concrete compression ring which is given a plan shape such that horizontal components of the cable forces, under design conditions, only cause pure compression in the ring, that is, the shape is funicular. All cables are laid parallel to the diagonals of the rectangle which just circumscribes the ring. However, the ring still requires bending strength to cope with non-uniform snow and wind loads, with the roof in its inflated or deflated state. At the design internal pressure, more than 150 tons of upward lift is transferred to the ring by the cables and fabric. The compression ring is designed as a flexible beam and is placed on a sliding ptfe layer which allows it to move horizontally, independently of the concrete strip on top of the berm on which it rests.

Construction

The roof is divided into sixteen panel sections which span between the cables and the compression ring. As the material is vulnerable to damage by creasing, each panel section was brought onto site on a 40ft (12.19 m) long, 8in (200mm) roller from which the fabric could be unrolled and attached to the cables and compression ring. The joints are made with neoprene gaskets and aluminium strips.

Conclusion

The fabric over the main arena is just the soft top of a huge air bubble, casting a neutral, directionless light over the inside. The curving roof, so close to the floor level and only lightly marked by cables and fabric seams, creates a sense of vast space. In spite of the need for large mechanical systems, and other special facilities to keep the roof up, the design gives an economic way of covering large areas, especially this area where the ground is waterlogged, of poor bearing capacity and subject to earthquakes. At this scale, which is modest compared to some other air-supported roofs, the roof fabric is not vulnerable to damage from wind or snow loads. As this is a warm climate, the heat loss through the roof is mainly beneficial. Heat gain through the roof during the day can be partly offset against heat losses from the thermal mass during the night. The provision of two layers of fabric with insulation or ventilation between them could have reduced the air conditioning loads but at the cost of reducing the daylighting available. This is not necessarily a problem with those newer fabrics which have higher translucency than ptfe coated fibreglass. Air-supported structures generally have poor acoustics because of their low mass, causing high transmission, their large volume causing overlong reverberation times and their very large concave surfaces causing reflections and high sound levels in spite of the low reflectivity of the fabric. In this case the berm provides good protection from noise in the neighbouring areas and the large radius of curvature of the roof prevents the sound being focussed at floor levels. Some absorption is already provided and, if necessary, could be greatly increased by an acoustically absorbent inner fabric layer, although, for a sports area, the existing sound level is not excessive.

Oakland Alameda County Coliseum Arena, Oakland, California, USA

Introduction

The Arena is circular on plan, with a 420ft (128m) diameter roof supported by hanging cables, and is skilfully proportioned and shaped, and manages to achieve a proper integration of the different parts of the design. Of particular note is the dramatic use made of the roof structure. The building is designed for basketball, ice hockey and large gatherings and has seating for up to 15 000 people.

Description

The cable-suspended roof comprises an outer concrete compression ring of 420ft (128m) diameter and an inner steel tension ring of 45ft (14m) diameter, at the centre of the roof. Radial ribs of precast concrete are supported on 96 galvanised steel bridge strand cables, 2$\frac{3}{16}$" (56mm) in diameter, which hang between the compression and tension rings. The compression ring has a trapezoidal section with a maximum height and width of 6ft (1.82m). The tension ring is a welded steel box member 3ft 7in x 2ft 11in (1.04 x 0.89 m) high. Each of the radial ribs going between the tension and compression rings was precast in two 90ft (27.43m) length sections with projecting diaphragms for making a cast-in-place connection to the adjacent ribs. The ribs have an I-section shape, with a web thickness of 2$\frac{1}{2}$in (64mm), a flange width varying from 10in (250mm) to 1ft 2in (356mm) and a maximum depth of 8ft (2.44m) in the middle, decreasing to 4ft 6in (1.37m) and 2ft 6in (0.76m) at the compression and tension ring respectively. Each rib has a continuous slot in the centre of the bottom flange. Semicircular steel shoes are fitted into the slot at 9ft (2.74m) intervals and ride on 6in (150mm) length ptfe tubes $\frac{1}{4}$in (6mm) thick wrapped round the cables.

In the centre of the roof is a 260ft (79m) diameter penthouse of steel frame construction supported off the ribs with inclined steel tubes in the middle echoing the arrangement of the main columns. The penthouse contains plant including pumps to transfer rainwater to a drainline at the compression ring. In case of pump failure any excess rainwater, over the 160 000 gallons (605 000 litres) that can be stored, will be

View of Arena from NW (photo by Ezra Stoller © ESTO).

dumped onto the arena floor. Except in the penthouse area, the roof is formed with small precast concrete purlins at 2ft (600mm) centres spanning between the tops of the ribs and supporting form boards for cast-in-place gypsum that is poured round the top flange of each purlin. The roof is then waterproofed.

The compression ring of the roof is supported by inclined cast-in-place perimeter columns which run in straight lines from the compression ring to another ring beam just above promenade level, the effect being to give a taut, waisted appearance to this circular band of perimeter columns. The ring beam at promenade level is supported by 8ft (2.44m) high concrete columns that transmit the load to a 30ft (9.14m) high basement wall which, in turn, is supported by 80 ton (72 tonne) piles. The grandstand inside the building is completely separate from the roof structure and consists of cast-in-place concrete raker beams on columns, with precast seating units spanning between. An important part of the design is a glass wall inside the column band which allows the roof and the huge sweep of the

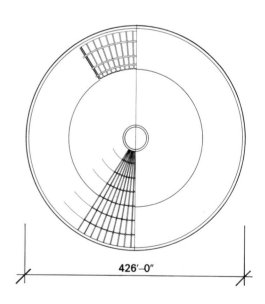

426'-0"

Roof plan.

OAKLAND ALAMEDA COUNTY COLISEUM ARENA (1966)

Description:
Arena of cast-in-place concrete construction with hanging
cable roof
Architects and
structural engineers:
Skidmore, Owings and Merrill
Structural engineer
for roof:
Ammann and Whitney

Axonometric
view from NW:

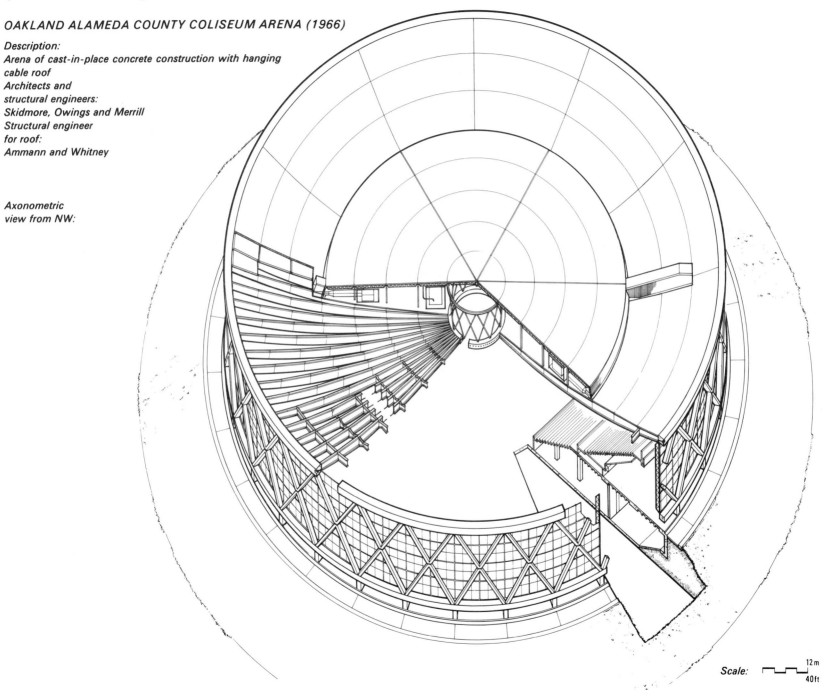

Scale: 12 m
40 ft

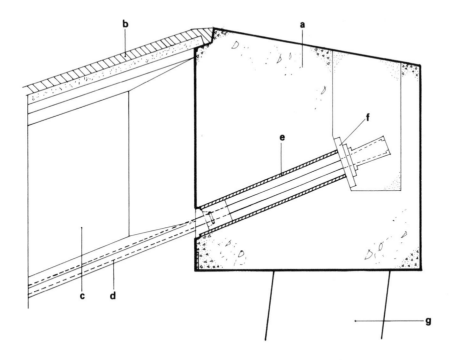

a 6'–0" x 6'–0" concrete compression ring; b cast-in-place gypsum; c precast concrete rib; d 2$\frac{3}{16}$" strand cable; e 8" tube; f 10" slotted anchor plate; g 1'–6" x 3'–6" concrete column.

Vertical section through compression ring.

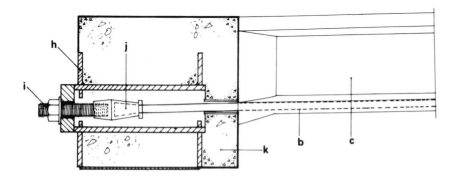

h 3'–5" x 2'–11" steel tension ring; i 4" x 1'–3" threaded rod with 3" adjustment; j socket; k infill concrete; l 2$\frac{1}{2}$" thick concrete diaphragm.

Vertical section through tension ring.

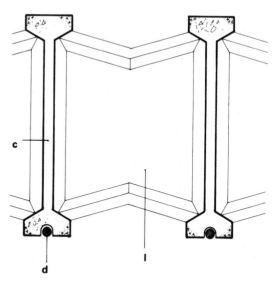

Vertical section through rib.

grandstand to be seen from the outside. It is supported by vertical open-web joists at 6ft 10in (2.08m) centres hanging from the roof with plan bracing at midheight. The glass wall has aluminium mullions and transoms with the vertical expansion joints at the joist positions and a horizontal expansion joint at midheight.

Structural Action

The connections between roof ribs and between every other joint in the annular rings of diaphragms, as well as those between the ribs and the tension and compression rings, were not made until all the dead load was in place, so allowing all this load to be carried by the cables. With all the structural connections made, the roof acts as an inverted dome for carrying live load. Dead loads are symmetrical, causing a uniform tension in the inner ring of 2250 tons (2040 tonnes) and a uniform compression in the outer ring of 2400 tons (2175 tonnes). Because of the large force present, the compression ring was required to be built with an error of less than $\frac{1}{2}$in (12mm) both in the level of its base and in the radius of its inner face; the cable

Inside view of Arena (photo by Ezra Stoller © ESTO).

anchor points were required to be placed with an error of less than ¼in (6mm) relative to these two positions. Columns below are inclined in order to take vertical loads and any horizontal loads due to earthquake forces. The cross-joint in the inclined column is of welded steel construction to ensure its integrity in the event of an earthquake.

Construction

First the inclined columns were poured. Then the compression ring was concreted in eleven separate sections, with the intermediate section done at least a week later to allow shrinkage to have taken place. The tension ring was made in four pieces and bolted together, with 1¼in (32mm) high-strength bolts, on scaffolding set slightly higher than the final position. The cables were then attached to the two rings. Two opposing cables, and an adjacent cable to each of these, were strung first and then two more pairs at right angles to the first ones. With the loads balanced in this way, the remaining cables could be strung working clockwise round the circle. With all cables strung, the central scaffolding was

lowered and adjustments made to the cable drape by adjusting nuts inside the tension ring. A crane, placed inside the tension ring erected the inner ring of radial ribs and was then moved outside the building to erect the outer ring. On completion the cables had a nearly parabolic shape. Final adjustment to the cable drape was made before erection of the steelwork penthouse and before pouring of the gypsum roof. Only on completion of this latter stage were the connections between the ribs made by welding reinforcement bars together and infilling with concrete.

Conclusion

The dish shape of the roof prevents focussing of sound and gives an intimate feel to the space while reinforcing the interest of the large space. The use of deep ribs and the inclined columns and glass wall involve extra construction costs which, however, seem entirely justified by the results. This is a robust and durable building, rationally conceived, boldly handled at the large scale and excellently marries the structure with the rest of the design.

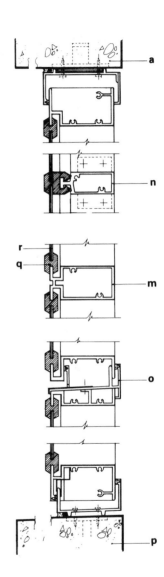

m typical aluminium transom; **n** penultimate transom; **o** horizontal joint at midheight; **p** ring beam at promenade level; **q** structural gasket; **r** grey glass.

Vertical section through glass wall.

Calgary Saddledome,
Calgary, Alberta, Canada

Introduction

The galloping edge and taut, curving surface of
this stadium roof could serve as a metaphor of
force and balance. The saddle surface is, in fact, a
hyperbolic paraboloid with an edge defined by
intersection with the spherical surface of the walls.
The roof consists of a concrete ring beam with a
network of steel cables carrying precast concrete
panels whose action as a net can be compared to a
tennis racket pushed out of shape. The pure
geometrical shapes of the external surfaces have
geometrical regularity and symmetry but are
selected not for their formal properties but because
of the structural logic and the way they are able to
control the flow of forces down to the supports.
The roof has a maximum span of 135 metres and,
having a suitable form at this scale, provides solid
economic benefits.

Description

The Saddledome has five independent structural
units: two two-tier grandstands, two three-tier
grandstands and the roof which floats on top of
these grandstands. The rectangular playing area is
below flooding level so that a heavy cast-in-place
concrete retaining wall has been placed around
the perimeter; it is trenched 3m into the ground
and at the top is level with the entrance which is
9m above ground level. The retaining wall was
cast in four segments, with expansion joints
between and therefore is unable to act as a
compression ring, each frame being designed to
be stable in its own plane. In extreme flood
conditions, water can percolate through holes in
the slab around the main playing area and thus
prevent uplift. The retaining wall and grandstand
columns have pile foundations. The grandstands
are made from precast concrete elements; they
consist, typically, of precast H-frames, for double-
T floor units, and raking beams, for the bleacher
seating; the H-frames and raking beams stack on
top of each other and are connected by welding at
a steel shoe joint. At the perimeter, below entrance
level, the frames attach to the cast-in-place
retaining wall and, above this level, to one of the
32 curving perimeter columns that are visible on
elevation.

*View of completed building from SE (photo by Angus of
Calgary).*

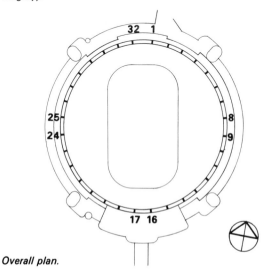

Overall plan.

CALGARY SADDLEDOME (1983)

Description:
Sports stadium with precast, prestressed concrete
grandstands and hyperbolic paraboloid lightweight concrete
roof
Architects:
G. McCourt
Structural engineers:
Jan Bobrowski and Partners

Axonometric
view from SW:

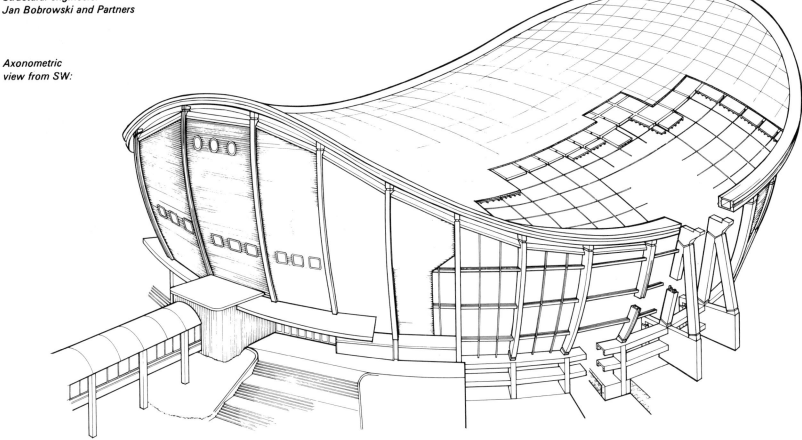

Scale: 12m
40ft

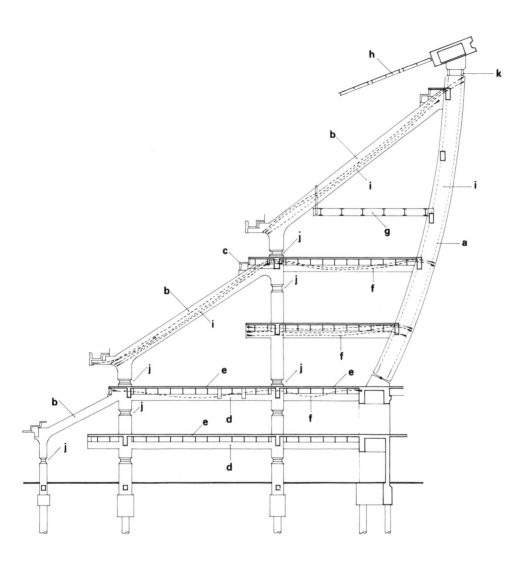

The perimeter columns are hollow precast post-tensioned lightweight concrete elements, pinned at their base; they all have identical shape, being meridians of the same sphere, and were made, in various lengths, from the same mould. Adjacent lines of H-frames are joined to each other by precast prestressed U-beams; these are subsequently filled with cast-in-place concrete and post-tensioned to provide lateral stability to the frames. The floors are precast double-T units spanning up to 13m between the H-frames. Bleacher seats are L-shaped units which interlock and span the same distances between rakers. Extensive use is made of prestressing strand which is post-tensioned both to provide the required strength and as a convenient means of connecting elements together. Elements with steel shoe joints are match cast to each other providing a virtually perfect fit on site. In most cases prestressing cables pass through the middle of the steel shoe joints, to accommodate the uplift forces from the overturning effect which the roof has on the frames.

Separating joints between the two-tier and three-tier grandstand structures are on radial setting-out lines 29, 4, 13 and 20. The centre lines of the perimeter columns are set out on a sphere with a radius of 67.65m, the centre of the sphere being level with the highest point of the centre of the soffit of the ring beam. The lowest point of the roof is 20m below this and the sag of the roof, the height from the high point to the central point, is 14m so that the rise, from the low point to the central point, is 6m; of the two sets of roof cables at right angles to each other, the sagging cables, therefore, have a greater proportion of their prestress in the vertical direction and it is this component which carries gravity loads on the roof.

The main structural component of the roof is the ring beam; this is supported at the two low points, vertically, and in any horizontal direction by a shear wall, with an A-frame at each end of the wall, and elsewhere, by the perimeter columns, which, however, only provide vertical support to the ring beam; a bearing at the top of each column allows free horizontal movement up to ±150mm radially, ±75mm tangentially with rotation in the vertical plane of up to 4 degrees. The roof is a near-perfect hyperbolic paraboloid so that the sagging and hogging cables have parabolic vertical traces.

a 900 x 1800 mm deep prestressed, precast hollow perimeter column; **b** 750 x 1300 mm deep prestressed raker beam with step supports for seating units; **c** precast L-shaped seating units; **d** precast unit with 750 x 1220 mm deep precast beam supporting floor units ; **e** 2400 x 610 mm precast double-T floor unit with 100mm cast-in-place topping; **f** 750 x 1200 mm deep precast beam joined at ends by welded connection and by prestressing; **g** steel beam; **h** 5670 x 5670 x 350 mm deep precast roof unit; **i** prestressing cable pair; **j** shoe joint designed to take tension; **k** roof sliding bearing.

Vertical section through structure at roof high point, near radial lines 8, 9, 24 and 25.

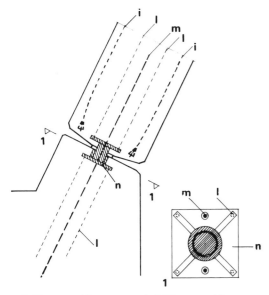

l 45mm steel bar; m coupled 36mm steel bar; n 75mm steel plate.

Vertical section and plan detail at column base on radial lines 7, 10, 23 and 26.

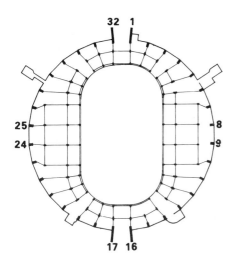

Plan at base level.

Erection of perimeter column (photo by Matthews Photo Lab. Ltd.).

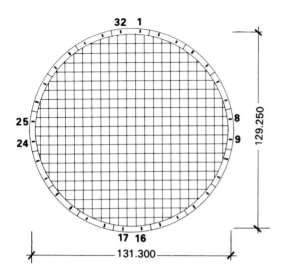

Plan on roof showing cables.

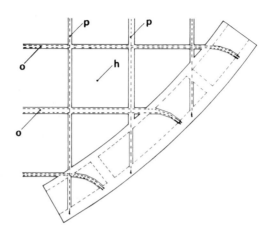

o 2 hanging cables of 12/15mm strand together with 6 unbonded tendons; **p** 1 stabilising cable of 19/15mm strand with 6 unbonded tendons.

Detail plan at edge of roof on lines 12 and 13.

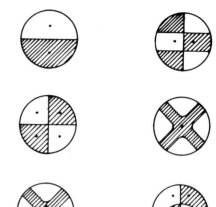

First six fundamental modes of vibration of roof with lines showing stationary points and dots points of maximum amplitude.

Cables are set out on a 6m grid in true space, sagging cable positions consisting, generally, of two cables each having twelve 15mm diameter prestressing strands, and hogging cable positions consisting of a single cable of nineteen 15mm strands; the total tensile strengh of the sagging and hogging cables at each position, 6m apart, is 735 and 582 tonnes respectively. The four sagging cables nearest the centre, however, have to support an extra 50 tonnes from a scoreboard and other hanging loads and here the two cables contain 15 strands each.

Extra-lightweight precast concrete panels, 5.67 x 5.67 m on plan and 350mm deep, are placed between the cables but are only supported by the hanging cables; the average weight of the panels is low, only 180 kg per sq m. The gap between the panels which is about 330mm wide is filled with a lightweight cast-in-place concrete; the lines of infill in both directions each contain, as well as the main cables, three 15mm diameter unbonded tendons which were post-tensioned after the infilling had been completed; at this stage the roof

has the action of a shell and the unbonded tendons control cracking. With the structure complete the roof then received an asphalt layer, an insulation layer, contact cement and finally a single-ply roofing membrane. Insulated aluminium wall cladding is used between the curving perimeter columns over most of their height. However at the top, the external surface is indented inwards so that the bearings for the ring beam are visible from outside. An L-shaped steel truss spans between the columns, below the ring beam, and provides the top support to L-shaped precast mullions; the mullions run vertically and support the cladding.

Structural Action

The roof reacts to load in two ways, working either as a cable net or as a shell structure. During construction the roof is a flexible cable net which is supported by the ring beam; almost all dead load is carried by this action. On completion, the roof reacts to further load as a rigid shell that is reinforced by cables and prestressed by unbonded tendons, the ring beam serving to collect load and

stiffen the edge; all live load is carried by this action. In all cases the design aims to minimise bending moment and torsion in the ring beam. If the ring beam has a circular projection on plan, which is nearly true for the Saddledome, this can be achieved by making the horizontal components of the forces in all the cables equal. The action is similar to that of a planar ring and cable net, in which the cables on any small segment of the ring apply approximately radial forces which are balanced by uniform compression in the ring. In a cable net, because the cables within each set have the same parabolic shape, the horizontal component of the cable forces must be the same, for the same distributed loading, in spite of the variation in lengths of the cables. In its completed state, under dead load, the maximum moment in the ring beam is only 433 tonne-metres with axial compression of 5000 tonnes; with a uniform snow load as well these figures become 2152 tonne-metres and 6250 tonnes respectively.

The action of the roof as a shell is somewhat similar to that of a square hyperbolic paraboloid

Connections for raker and T-beam units (photo by Matthews Photo Lab.).

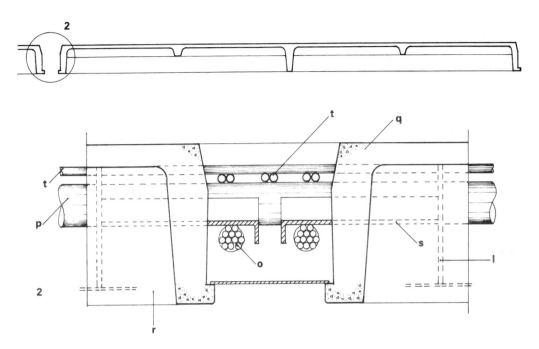

q 50mm slab; r 350mm deep ribs; s hangers; t 15mm unbonded tendon.
Vertical section through 5.670m square roof panel and cast-in-place joint.

shell in which straight edge beams collect load by shear between the edge beam and the shell, causing an axial force in the edge beam which increases linearly towards the supports at the two low points; unlike the cable net, the sagging and hogging curvatures of the shell combine so that, with the central area loaded, the low points tend to spread apart and the high points to lift. In the Saddledome, the four roof bearings near each high point can cater for uplift forces of 180 tonnes each and the first two bearings on each side of them 44 tonnes.

The two A-frames at each main support point provide lateral restraint by a spring action in order to control horizontal movement and bending moment in the ring, particularly during construction when the ring beam is very sensitive to the forces in the cables. In the completed state, the A-frames give a good compromise between the large tensile stresses that would arise in the

shell without any such horizontal support and the high compressive stresses in the shell and the very large horizontal forces collected by the support if it were not to move at all. In fact the A-frames take less than half the horizontal load they would have taken if completely fixed in position. Their average stiffness is equal to 22 tonnes for each millimetre of horizontal movement at the top of the frame. The stiffness is less than this under high horizontal load. The inner leg of the A-frame consists of a central core of steel tubes filled with high strength concrete, the tubes being covered by six layers of bitumen and surrounded by a casing of lightweight concrete. Initially there is a gap at one end of the casing which is then closed by vertical prestressing. If the tension in the leg exceeds that of the prestress then the stiffness is only that provided by the prestressing cables and the surrounding concrete instead of that of the whole construction, so that with a high force, pushing

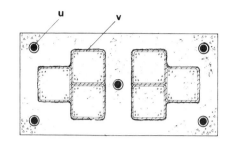

Horizontal section through tension leg of A-frame.

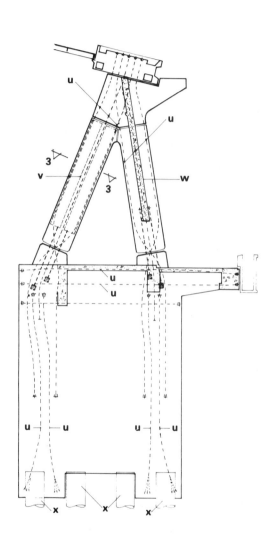

u 19/15mm strand cable; **v** core of 3 square tubular steel pipes infilled with high-strength concrete and coated on the outer surface with 6 layers of bitumen; **w** 200mm concrete shear wall **x** 1300mm diameter piles, six in all.

Vertical section through A-frame at roof low point.

outwards on the supports, the shell carries a greater proportion of the total load than it would with a low force on the supports. Under dead load there is a horizontal force, outwards, of 273 tonnes with a corresponding movement of 12mm but, under snow and temperature effects as well, this increases to 910 tonnes and 40mm.

Temperature effects were investigated as well as dead, live and wind load and, in combination with other effects, gave some of the most severe conditions. Uniform temperature changes between 4 and 33 °C were investigated, without serious effect as the roof is free to move, as well as temperature differences across the ring beam of 58°C which, however, gave rise to the worst bending moment in the ring beam equal to 3510 tonne-metres coexisting with a more moderate axial force of 6000 tonnes. Lightweight concrete was used exclusively in the roof and having a lower elastic modulus than normalweight concrete considerably reduces the parasitic stresses engendered due to these temperature effects. The creep of lightweight concrete is also greater than normalweight concrete and the effect of this has to be considered too; the high creep leads to greater readjustments of stresses and loads over time than with normalweight concrete but the effect can be beneficial in shedding load from highly stressed parts to less highly stressed parts. Creep of the ring beam with time causes it to shorten and transfer compressive stress into the rest of the shell surface.

The effect of wind on the roof is complex. Wind pressures and suctions at any point on the roof vary with time and also from point to point. The calculations assumed likely patterns for these wind loads and the magnitudes of these loads were then determined by wind tunnel tests. The main concern is to check that the frequencies of the wind buffeting do not coincide with the natural frequencies of the roof as determined by a dynamic analysis of a finite element model. Each natural frequency has a certain mode of vibration associated with it. Stresses and deflections, however, were not found to be large.

Construction

On completion of the substructure, the first precast elements erected were those for the A-frames and the inside frame of the lower two tiers of the three-tier grandstands. The curved perimeter columns for the grandstands were erected using two cranes. After the pin at the base of the column had been fitted into the socket at the playing level, one crane held the top of the column while the other crane was free to lift a raker beam for the third tier and, subsequent to that, horizontal beams too; these beams and rakers were used to connect the perimeter column to the rest of the grandstand. Because the perimeter columns lean outwards some welded shoe joints in the grandstand structure are designed to take tension. All temporary connections to the perimeter columns use welded or bolted connections to give immediate strength; the columns are then post-tensioned against the adjacent beams and rakers. The two-tier grandstand is simpler than the three-tier one but is erected in a similar way. The ring beam is then placed in sections; it was precast in 16 segments, each 27m long and, at 88 tonnes, the heaviest of all the precast elements. The neutral surface of the ring beam is tangential with the roof surface, which practically eliminates all torsion in it but means that it has to continuously change in shape, having a radius of curvature of 67m and a twist of 22 degrees downwards at the high points and a radius of curvature of 63m and a twist of 13 degrees upwards at the low points. Although there were five different types of precast ring segments, they were all able to be precast in one adjustable steel form. Each ring beam segment was placed by two cranes, the detail for the bearing on top of the column giving a tolerance for final positioning. Once in position cast-in-place concrete is used for increasing the thickness of the ring beam flanges, for the connection between adjacent segments as well as for the whole top surface of the ring beam, the latter requiring permanent steel shuttering.

There were a number of separate stages in the construction of the rest of the roof: first, cables were pulled across the stadium using winches, the sagging cables being placed first and then the hogging cables; cables were tightened so as to give an initial roof geometry with a sag of 12.5m in the hanging cables; first stage stressing of cables took place, balanced so that only moderate bending developed in the ring beam; placing of precast panels followed; there was a second stage of stressing of the hogging cables, to re-establish the geometry so that on completion there was only moderate bending in the ring beam, although the axial force was higher than in the first stage stressing; placing of unbonded tendons followed this; then cast-in-place joints between panels were poured in one ten-hour operation; finally, the unbonded tendons were stressed. During construction the ring beam was given far greater bending moments than are present in the final condition. No falsework was needed to place the panels. The sagging cables were placed parallel to each other and automatically assume a catenary, near parabolic, shape under the uniform load from the panels; hogging cables followed geodesic lines, the shortest distance across the surface, assuming there is no frictional restraint from the sagging cables. This means that the joints between the panels on hogging lines increase slightly in width towards the ring beam and all roof panels can be identical.

Stressing of both sets of cables was effected by stressing of hogging cables only. Hogging cables were stressed to 40% of their minimum tensile strength for first stage stressing, sagging cables in this way being stressed up to 20% of their minimum tensile strength; for the second stage stressing these figures were 70% and 50% respectively. Roof panels were lifted by cranes outside the building except for the 12 central ones which were lifted through the cables from the inside. The weight of the roof and the central hanging loads amounts to some 2500 tonnes which, as noted, is almost exactly balanced, in their bending effect on the ring beam, by the second stage stressing of cables. All unbonded tendons were nearly uniformly stressed around the perimeter to eliminate any significant tensile stress

A-frames at construction (photo by Matthews Photo Lab. Ltd.).

in the shell. The extra-lightweight concrete used for the precast roof panels has a dry density of 1630 kg per cu m and a strength of 30 newtons per sq mm; the cast-in-place concrete had similar strength but was a little lighter; the semi-lightweight concrete, for columns and rakers, had 50% more strength than the extra-lightweight concrete but only 10% more weight.

Conclusion

The shape of the roof for the stadium encloses very much less volume than a dome with the same number of seats, thus saving on heating and air conditioning; it also gives good sound dispersion.

The ring beam, bearings and curving columns are used to good effect on elevation, although the stairs and walkways outside the building lack a satisfactory visual discipline and the aluminium cladding, by spanning horizontally rather than vertically, detracts from rather than adds to the power of the structural form. The building is a most instructive example in the use of large precast elements with post-tensioning. Erection was tricky in some places: the rectangular-shaped playing area means that rakers make awkward angles with the curving perimeter columns; and a small number of temporary steel props were required for purposes of erection; also the ring

View of building at consruction from SE (photo by Angus of Calgary).

beam with its twisting shape was awkward to construct, especially at high level. Precast elements are mass produced, the only way to achieve economy. For example all 391 roof panels are identical and most of the bleacher seats, of which a 1000 were required, were made from one mould.

The stadium is a prestressed rather than a reinforced concrete structure, and is a reminder that prestressing is a wholly different concept from reinforcement, allowing the designer control of the stresses in the structure, particularly the elimination of tensile stresses, rather than passive acceptance of them. It is worth noting that the prestressing of the roof by the unbonded tendons does not increase its susceptibility to buckling failure as the tendons also supply a stabilising force. In fact the hyperbolic paraboloid shape of this roof is intrinsically safe and, unlike a dome, the main roof area cannot fail by buckling. The main drawback of the roof acting as a cable net is the slackening of the hogging cables under load, with a consequent increase in bending of the ring beam; this is largely overcome by converting the roof to a shell. The dimensions of the ring beam are set by the need to achieve economy, to limit movement of the ring beam and to ensure that, as far as possible, the cables remain in tension under asymmetrical load. When it is flexible, the ring beam is lighter, and therefore cheaper to build, and tends to deform so as to keep the cables in tension but these advantages have to be balanced against an acceptable horizontal movement of the ring beam. In the Saddledome the horizontal movement is restrained both by the stiffness of the ring beam and the spring stiffness of the A-frames. This roof form is suitable for larger span roofs although movements of the ring beam would be larger and would probably need to be accommodated in a different way than by the movement of bearings. Unlike a dome, the main compression element of the roof is the ring beam and the size of this may be increased without penalty because of frequent support from the perimeter columns. This building is an exemplary work of structural engineering whose economy is a direct result of imaginative and clear thinking from first principles.

Chapter Twelve

High Rise Buildings

Of all building types, the high rise is the most spectacular and the most disconcerting. High rise buildings are particularly, but not exclusively, associated with cities and would exemplify G.K. Chesterton's view of the modern city as 'anarchic and surging with selfish and materialistic energies'. The New York skyscrapers were referred to by Henry James as 'expensively provisional', but built with the future of the city in mind or not, the high rise building nevertheless seems to carry a message about the future. Although their effect on the urban fabric is drastic, their vast and sometimes threatening scale is, in its origins, only a reflection of economic progress and the shortage of space within cities. Technically the high-rise building can be characterised as one that is at least twenty storeys in height and has a ratio of height to least width that exceeds five; with this size, at these proportions, the effects of wind have a critical influence on the structural design of the building. The principal requirements are for stiffness against horizontal load and, allied with this, a means of reducing perceptible vibrations in the building. All the buildings in this chapter are office buildings and therefore complement those in the preceding chapter on office buildings, but there is no overriding reason for the high rise structure to be confined to office use. And indeed it is not. Such is its overwhelming size and radical nature that the high rise may not be categorized by type of use at all.

Knights of Columbus Building, New Haven, Connecticut, USA

Introduction

This building has a height of 23 storeys, and provides 30ft (9.14m) of column free space around a central core, which is a normal enough arrangement for offices. However, here, the central core of the building is only 30 x 30 ft (9.14 x 9.14 m) in plan. There are, generally, no column supports, the steelwork is not painted or protected against fire and there is no false ceiling inside. An ambitious decision to expose the structural elements is justified by clear, ordered detailing. This design is distinctive without being forced and its eccentricity as an office building raises several points of interest.

Description

Except at the four lowest levels there are no columns in this building, five slipformed shaft structures taking not only the wind forces but all the gravity loads. The shafts are cantilevered off a 5ft (1.52m) thick concrete slab, 20ft (6.10m) below ground level. Of the four circular shafts at the corners of the building, two are used for escape stairs going directly to the outside, because the lowest part of the building is recessed; one of these shafts accommodates a smoke vent. The other two shafts take air conditioning ducts and services fed directly from the plantroom on the top level of the building, one of these shafts containing wash rooms. The space provided for services is possibly extravagant but also exemplary in that it would allow a refit of the mechanical systems with relative ease. The square central core shaft has only to accommodate the elevators. The main girders of weathering steel are simply slung between the shafts and support secondary beams and a 5½in (139mm) concrete floor slab which acts compositely with the secondary beams. The peripheral beams are exposed, and set 5ft 3in (1.60m) in front of the glass line so that they do not need fire protection. Sun shades are placed between the peripheral beams and the glass lines. The beams are attached at their centre to secondary beams and therefore tied into the floor slab but have sliding connections with the other secondary beams and a sliding connection at both

shaft supports to allow for temperature movement. By contrast, the main beams, between the circular corner shafts and the square core shaft, have fixed connections at each end. All steelwork on the inside is also exposed to view, as well as the channel shaped tracks at the level of the bottom flange of the secondary beams which carry lighting and sprinkler pipes. Sprinklers are provided but otherwise there is no fire protection. The building was treated for the purposes of the fire regulations as 23 separate one-storey buildings that are stacked up on each other. In this arrangement there is easy access to the shafts which are almost invulnerable to fire, do not conduct heat and thus provide reliable supports to all the main floor beams. Smoke control is a more significant problem, however.

Structural Action

The plan form of this office is not ideal as a structural arrangement but there are no major cost penalties for a building up to this height and this width. The five shafts act as linked shear walls, that is, they bend as five separate cantilevers which nevertheless have the same horizontal sway because they are connected by the floor slabs at each level. These corner shafts have been considerably thickened either side of the opening in them because of the weakening effect of openings and because both the vertical floor loads and the horizontal wind forces are applied on this side. These forces tend to make the shaft bend and twist. The shaft is prestressed on the side opposite the opening, reaching a maximum prestress force of 655 tons (595 tonnes) at the bottom, which increases the bending strength and also the stiffness of the shaft. The building has more total core area than a conventional frame building with one large central concrete core carrying the same total load. However the building saves on columns and, importantly, the number of connections required.

Construction

The four corner shafts and central core were slipformed in parallel rising continously at the rate of 10ft (3.05m) per day. Subsequently the steelwork was placed between the shafts. The four corner shafts were clad in brown tile, the work being done from platforms suspended from the top

View of building from SW (photo by architect).

KNIGHTS OF COLUMBUS BUILDING (1969)

Description:
Twenty-three storey office block with steel beams supported
on five concrete shafts
Architects:
Roche, Dinkeloo and Associates
Structural engineers:
Pfisterer, Tor and Associates

Axonometric
view from SE:

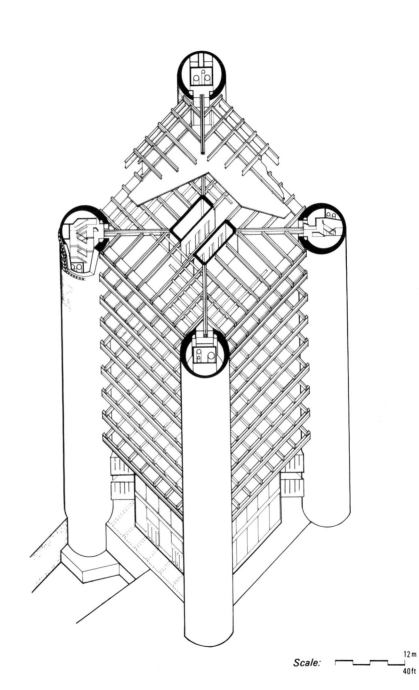

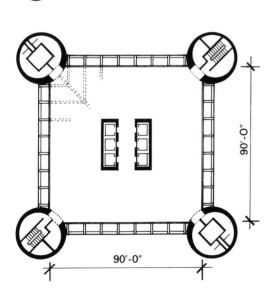

90'-0"

90'-0"

Upper level floor plan.

Scale:

12 m

40 ft

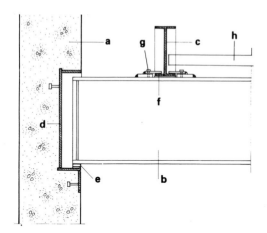

a walls of shaft; **b** W36 x 194 lb/ft main peripheral beam; **c** W21 x 55 lb/ft secondary beams; **d** steel box; **e** 4" x 18" bearing plate with 2 layers of teflon under; **f** 2 layers of teflon; **g** erection bolt; **h** sun shades.

Elevation on sliding support of peripheral beam on shaft.

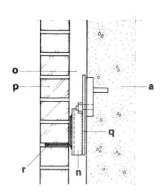

n spacer welded to plate; **o** $2\frac{1}{4}$" gap; **p** $3\frac{3}{4}$" brickwork; **q** 8" x 10" x $\frac{1}{3}$" steel plate bolted to adjustable inserts; **r** $3\frac{1}{2}$" x $3\frac{1}{2}$" x $\frac{5}{16}$" curved angle at 27' vertical spacing.

Vertical section through supporting bracket for brickwork tiles.

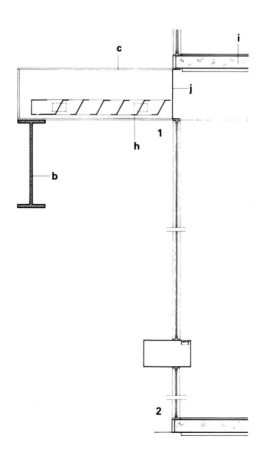

i $5\frac{1}{2}$" concrete slab; **j** $\frac{3}{16}$" weathering steel.

Vertical section through wall.

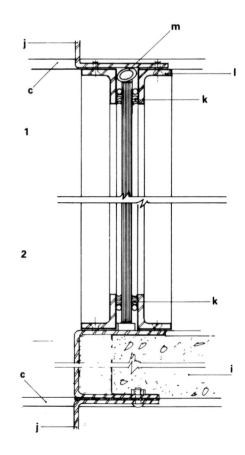

k neoprene rope with sealant; **l** $\frac{1}{4}$" thick angle in weathering steel; **m** neoprene tube.

Detail vertical sections at window.

of each shaft. The total period of construction was about 24 months.

Conclusion

The Knights of Columbus building demonstrates in an original design the use of slipformed shafts to take both horizontal and vertical loads. From the outside the building makes a nice contrast between its strongly shaped corner shafts and the glass and exposed steel. The detailing, both inside and outside, is particularly well done, giving clear expression to each part.

Mercantile Tower,
St. Louis, Missouri, USA

Introduction

This 35-storey office building uses classic K-braced shear trusses but, here, expressed on elevation instead of wrapped around the elevator shafts. The saving in weight of structural steel over the more conventional solution is of the order of 14%. The framing is just adequate for the building's height and proportion and shows the possible economy of material by the choice of a structural scheme suited to its scale.

Description

The building has its four corners on 45 degree diagonal lines which allows more light into the interiors and reduces wind load in the east-west direction on the broad face. The two shear trusses at each end are welded to a rigid centre bay on the short side and the first 30ft (9.14m) bay, which is also rigid, on the long side, this forming a large five-sided channel shape. These channel shapes at each end resist all the wind forces. All the other columns, including those in the middle of the long sides, are designed to take gravity loadings only. The floor uses concrete on a metal deck supported by a stub girder system. This girder system comprises a W14 steel beam spanning 38ft (11.58m) between the core and external columns with secondary beams at right angles at about 10ft (3.05m) centres on top but also, either side of each secondary beam, stub lengths of I-section in line with the beam are welded to its top flange. Spaces between the secondary beams and stubs are used for duct runs. Metal deck is placed across the secondary beams and shear studs are then welded through the deck on to the secondary beams and stub lengths to connect them to the concrete slab. This forms a kind of vierendeel beam which is easier to fireproof than the alternative, a steel truss.

The depth of the floor zone, between top of slab and ceiling soffit, is only 3ft 6in (1.06m). At the diagonal faces of the building the floor slab has a zig-zag edge. Because the diagonal in the K-bracing needs to be three storeys high in order to make a good angle with the horizontal, the corners of the slab at the two intermediate levels, which have no spandrel beam, are supported by hangers from the spandrel above. The K-bracing to the

View of tower from NW (photo by Barbara Martin).

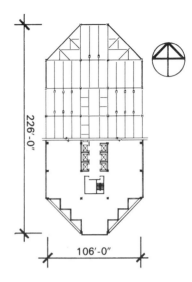

Typical floor framing plan.

shear truss is a convenient framing system which provides support to the midpoint of the spandrel and has shorter diagonal lengths than cross-bracing. Any truss with large members tends to develop secondary bending movements at its joints; this truss uses a pure pin connection at the bottom end of the diagonal and web plate connections elsewhere to eliminate or greatly reduce this bending moment. The connection, by avoiding flange gusset plates, is also easier to clad. The shear pin at the bottom of the building has a 5½in (138mm) diameter and takes an axial force of 300 tons (272 tonnes). At the floor level below each spandrel beam, the diagonal is tied into the floor structure thus reducing its unbraced length. All exposed steelwork is insulated and clad in anodised aluminium. The insulation is designed to limit the change of temperature to within 10°F (5.5°C) in any eight hour period.

Structural Action

The shear trusses being put at 45 degree angles in plan can take wind forces from any direction. Being placed on the outside they also give the building good torsional rigidity. The floor slab is of crucial importance in transforming the wind forces over long distances, by diaphragm action, to the frames at each end of the building. The frames, with three-storey high bays, then transfer these forces to the shear trusses on either side. An analysis of the column stresses, with wind on the broad face, shows that, while the two shear trusses at each end are to some extent coupled together, they do not exhibit so-called partial tube action, that is the channel shape at each end does not bend as one complete unit, because of the relative flexibility of the frame at each end of the building. With wind on the broad face the maximum deflection at the top of the building is less than 10in (250mm).

Construction

The total period of construction was 23 months. Steelwork erection proceeded several floors above the casting of the concrete slab and its stability in this temporary state, without a concrete slab, depended on the diaphragm action of the metal deck alone.

Conclusion

Wind bracing is logically expressed on elevation and by setting back the glass line and restricting the amount of diagonal bracing no extra costs on cladding have been incurred. The structural scheme and sensible floor spans have kept the weight of steel down to an average 16lb per sq ft (78 kg per sq m) of floor area.

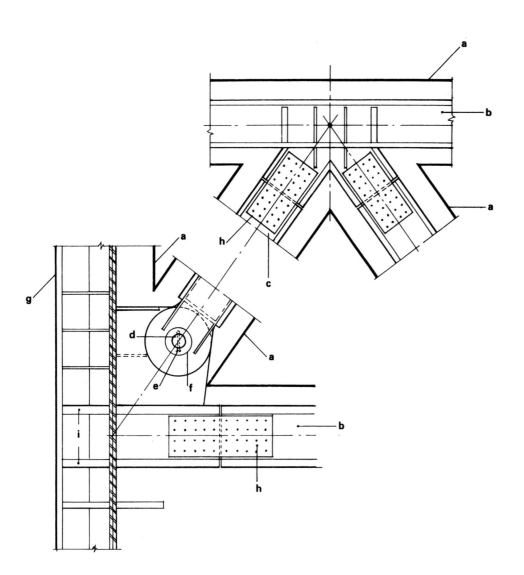

a line of cladding with insulation under; **b** built-up steel spandrel I-beam; **c** W14 x 198 lb/ft steel diagonal; **d** 5½" steel pin set in hole ½" larger; **e** cotter pin; **f** ⅜" steel washer; **g** built-up steel I-section column at 45° to plane of shear truss; **h** web connector plate; **i** stiffener plates.

Detail of shear truss at levels 3 and 6.

MERCANTILE TOWER ST LOUIS (1976)

Description:
Thirty-five storey office block of steel construction with exposed shear trusses
Architects:
Thompson, Ventulett and Stainback/
Sverdrup and Parcel and Associates
Structural engineers:
Ellisor Engineers

Axonometric
view from NW:

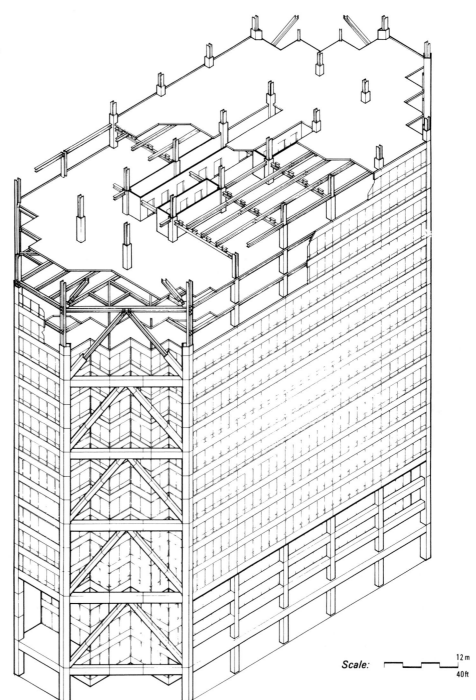

Scale: 12 m
40 ft

Sabah Foundation Headquarters, Kota Kinabalu, Sabah, Malaysia

Introduction

Suspended by umbrella trusses at two levels from a circular core, this 32-storey building is superbly logical and achieves simplicity in its shape, in its structural system but above all, and most significantly, in its construction procedure. In general the building extracts all possible advantages from the concept of the suspended frame building.

Description

The floors are circular in plan, the usable office space surrounding a reinforced concrete core which consists of two connected concentric circular walls, approximately 1ft (300mm) thick between which the lifts and air conditioning ducts are housed. In the centre of the core are the washrooms and escape stairs. Thirteen floors are hung off each of the two umbrella structures, each floor being supported at 24 points around its perimeter by hanging bars which reduce in size or number at each floor level going down. The floors are straight-forward reinforced concrete slabs using 24 radial beams supported by the hanging bars at one end and the core at the other end. Each umbrella structure consists of 24 steel triangular trusses attached to a post-tensioned concrete tension ring at the top, balancing the tension in the raking arms, and a concrete compression ring at the bottom, balancing compression in the horizontal arms. Both rings are eventually prestressed against the core. The core is supported by a concrete raft 9ft 3in (2.82m) deep and 68ft (20.72m) across resting on 232 steel piles. The hanging structure, like any other structure, is more economic where soil conditions are good, as the loads that are gathered into the core do not need to be distributed back over a large ground area. However in poor ground, with high capacity piles, such concentration of load is just as economic as other foundation solutions. The building is clad in a reflective glass. Plant room space is provided at the ground floor and levels 16 and 30, at which the umbrella structures are situated. A central plant supplies chilled air to two air handling units on each floor of the tower. The air distribution system on each floor comprises a central zone with a constant cooling load and six perimeter zones controlled by variable air volume (VAV) systems.

Structural Action

Half the floor load at each level is supported by the hanging bars, taken up to the umbrella and there transferred to ground down the core. With two umbrellas, instead of one, this load path is relatively short but still longer than in conventional column construction and hence more material is used. However costs do not increase proportionally, the material accounting for only a minor part of total construction cost. All the wind loads, as well as the gravity loads, are taken by the core acting as a cantilever. The gravity load in effect prestresses the core, making it more resistant to wind forces. Compared to a conventional arrangement, where outside columns taken to ground would be used in place of the hanging bars, the gravity load in the core of the hanging building is doubled and either the vertical prestress doubles or, if the wall thickness is doubled, the section modulus doubles. In either case the core is able to take twice the overturning moment and, for a typical distribution of wind forces, this means the building could be about 35 per cent taller. In a conventionally framed building, the core would attract all the wind shear and moment anyway, so that the proportion of axial to shear load in the columns is very different from that in the core. It can be shown that it is most efficient for this proportion to be equal for all the loadcarrying elements, a condition automatically fulfilled by the single core element of the hanging building. The circular shape of this building helps to cut down wind load and provides another bonus in the design against horizontal forces.

Construction

The construction procedure was slick and well organized. After construction of the mat foundation, the slipforming of the 376ft (115m) high core walls started; this was completed in eight months. The top umbrella was constructed at ground level and raised by twelve 150 ton (138 tonne) jacks placed at the top of the core. The 24 hanging rods were attached to the umbrella at one end and to the pre-assembled nineteenth floor, the lowest floor supported by the top umbrella, at the other end. After raising to the top, the umbrella

View of completed building from S (photo by architect).

Typical office floor at construction (photo by architect).

SABAH FOUNDATION HEADQUARTERS (1983)

Description:
Thirty-two storey office tower of concrete construction
hanging from 'umbrella' supports at two levels
Architects:
J.Ferrie and Partners/
Wisma Akitek
Structural engineers:
Ove Arup/
Rakan Rakan

Axonometric
view from S:

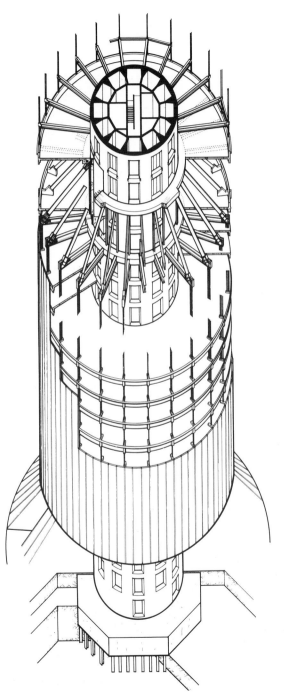

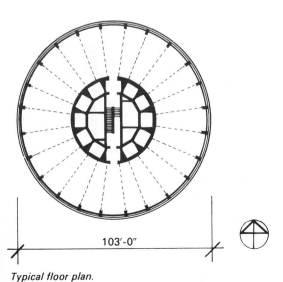

103'-0"

Typical floor plan.

Scale: 12 m
40 ft

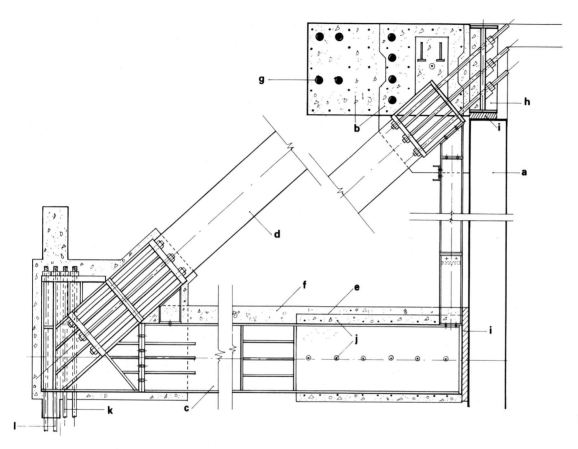

a concrete core; b tension ring, first and second pour; c W24 x 120 lb/ft steel beam; d 2″ x 17″ high yield steel raking arm; e compression ring; f concrete floor slab; g prestressing cable; h 10″ x 30″ x 3′-9″ long built-up steel beam supporting one raking arm at each end; i dry pack mortar; j longitudinal reinforcing bars; k 2/ 32mm high strength bars; l 2/ 36mm high strength bars.

Vertical section through umbrella support.

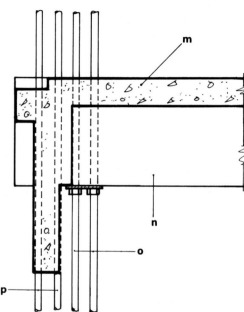

m 5″ concrete floor slab; n 1′-1″ x 1′-10″ concrete beam; o 2/ 23mm to 32mm high strength bars supporting floor; p 2/ 36mm high strength bars passing through ducting.

Typical detail at edge of floor slab in upper levels of each half.

was fixed in position and the construction of floors proceeded upwards from the nineteenth floor, with traditional formwork. The procedure was repeated for the lower half of the building. The prestressed concrete tension ring of the umbrella was poured in two parts: the first part was cast at ground level; the second outer part of the ring was cast in place at the top, after adjacent pairs of the raking arms in the umbrella were each connected

to short lengths of steel beam, 10 x 30 in (250 x 750 mm) deep, set into slots around the core. After casting of the outer part, the whole ring was then prestressed around its circumference and radially against the core. Floors are built up to 1¾in (44mm) high at the perimeter to allow for elastic extension of the hanging rods and the shortening of the core, these two deformations being additive.

Conclusion

Hanging buildings off a core is easier to do than it may once have seemed because of the speed of core slipforming techniques and the support available from the core and rods to support the floors during construction. Nevertheless hanging buildings are of limited application, because it is only possible to support small plan areas economically.

Xerox Center,
Chicago, Illinois, USA

Introduction

In spite of its opulent looks, this building has been designed and built with economy in mind. A speculative office block with 40 storeys and a gross floor area of 880 000 sq ft (81 750 sq m), it occupies an important corner site in the city. The style of the building is set by its pristine surface and the distorted reflections in it and the full rounded corner, while making a continuous facade of the two sides facing the street, helps to create the glossy, confident character of the building. At street level a curving clear glass 'stops' the building at this level, by indenting inwards, thereby breaking the standard wall pattern and providing a change of scale. This also provides a smooth lead-in for the two entrances. The design is daringly done. As usual in buildings built to a tight budget, underlying the attention to the facade and entrance areas is an obvious concern for simple solutions for the building structure, the enclosure and the detailing of the enclosure.

Description

Except at the rounded corner, the column grid in both the east-west and north-south directions is 22ft 6in (6.86m) in each end bay and 20ft (6.10m) in the intermediate bays. An 8in (200mm) thick reinforced concrete flat slab spans between the columns at each floor level. However there is a 2ft (0.60m) deep beam connecting the perimeter columns and at the top of all the interior columns, the floor slab is thickened by 4in (100mm) drops to limit stress due to punching shear. Interior columns are square and perimeter columns are circular, to reduce their apparent bulk, both increasing in size down the building. At street level the interior columns are 3 x 3 ft (0.91 x 0.91 m) and are made with 6000 psi (42 newtons per sq mm) strength concrete. Lateral stability is provided by core walls which increase in thickness down the building and, to some extent, interact with the perimeter frames. The core walls are all about one foot thick at mid-height.

The key feature of this design is the enclosure. There are horizontal bands of double glazing, of a sea green colour from the outside, alternating with insulated aluminium panels coated with a fluoropolymer which is off-white. The aluminium panels have a matt finish and properly contrast with the distorted mirror images in the glass panels. Transom and mullion pieces are in the same aluminium. The outer skin of the double glazing has a reflective silver coat while the inner one is clear glass. Overall the double glazing gives a light transmission of 30% and a radiant heat transmission of 30%. Glazing occupies 50% of the facade except on the north face and the rounded corner, where there is little or no solar gain. Here it occupies 75% of the facade area and gives a better view of the square to the north side. A further level of control of the light and direct radiated heat is given by venetian blinds. At seven different levels on the outside of each face of the building, except the north face, there are two temperature sensors, one dry bulb and one wet bulb, and a solar gain sensor. On the north face just one dry bulb temperature sensor is provided at each level. These sensors feed back information to the air conditioning control system. At level 3 and at roof level, there are double height floors for mechanical equipment. Ducts for vertical distribution of services are provided at each end of the core structure, a duct from the plantroom at level 3 serving the bottom twenty-one floors and another duct from the roof serving the remaining floors.

Of the sixteen elevators at street level, half serve the lower levels up to the 21st floor and the other half, the levels above this. Between the lifts are stairs, toilets and rooms for electrical, transformer and telephone equipment. Air conditioning is by a variable air volume system with supplementary baseboard heating at the perimeter, just above floor level. There are two main supply and two main return air ducts at each floor level with branches off that can be independently controlled. There is a suspended ceiling to allow horizontal distribution of services including electric power lines. The notable feature of the cladding is that it does read as a skin with the glazing and aluminium panel in the same plane and no shadow lines from mullions or horizontal rails. The cladding all comes as pre-assembled panels 5ft (1.52m) wide by 11ft (3.53m) high whatever the amount of glazing. The horizontal joint between each panel is put above the glazing. The left hand mullion of each panel slots into the right hand mullion of the adjacent panel which is already fitted. Both mullions are

View of office block from N (photo by architect).

View of top of office block from E (photo by architect).

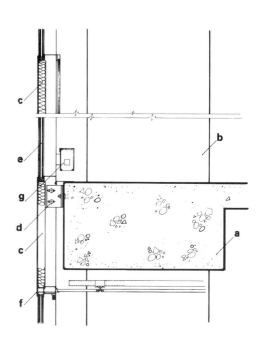

a 2'–0" deep concrete edge beam; **b** concrete column; **c** insulated aluminium panel; **d** angle for fixing each mullion on panel to cast in slot; **e** double glazing unit; **f** horizontal joint between panels; **g** baseboard heating.

Vertical section through outside wall.

attached by angles to the perimeter edge beam and to a horizontal rail at the head of the window which, in turn, is attached to the edge beam of the floor above. The wind pressure on the cladding at the top of the building, where it is not protected by the surrounding buildings, is expected to reach up to 60 lb per sq ft (294 kg per sq m). In general each column is founded on a caisson and the core walls on a series of caissons. The caissons have a diameter of 4ft 6in (1.37m) and extend some 50 or 70 ft (15 or 20 m) to the bedrock.

Structural Action

The flat slab floor has relatively small depth allowing room for horizontal service runs. It is a two-way system, the principal reinforcement being provided along column lines. Because the slab is relatively flexible compared to the perimeter beam, that part of the lateral load not taken by the core structure is taken by the perimeter frames rather than the internal construction. The action of the perimeter frame is most effective near the top of the building. There is a basement which is used to transfer horizontal load on the building into the silty clay nearer the ground surface.

Construction

The total construction time from foundations to topping out was 24 months. The floor slab at each level, on average, took one week to complete. Two tower cranes, taken through the north and south parts of the building, were used to deliver material and equipment.

Conclusion

Bearing in mind a tight budget and the need to maximise the useful internal space, it is a tribute to the professionals involved that the building does make something of this corner site. The building more than competes with its neighbours, as it was meant to, under the transforming effect of the skin wall. The horizontal banding, and the alternating of matt and mirror surfaces, successfully emphasises the corner curve.

483

XEROX CENTRE OFFICES (1979)

Description:
40 storey office block of concrete flat slab construction with
panel cladding
Architects:
C.F. Murphy Associates
Structural engineers:
Cohen Baretto Marchertas

Axonometric
view from NE:

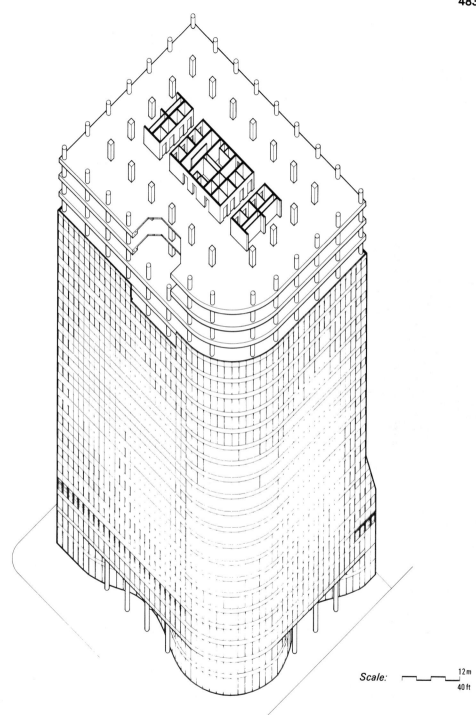

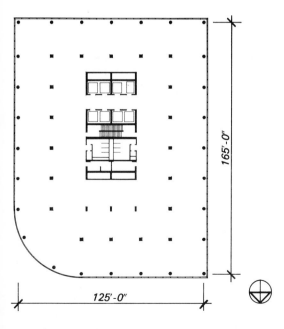

Typical upper floor plan.

165'-0"

125'-0"

Scale: 12 m / 40 ft

First International Building, Dallas, Texas, USA

Introduction

This is a fifty-six storey tower for offices using the most simple and efficient form for resisting wind forces on high rise buildings - the trussed tube.

Description

The central core of the building contains the elevators and all services including plant rooms, vertical ducts for pipes and cables, wash rooms and emergency stairs. Between the core and the outside, a clear 40ft (12.20m) wide space is available for office use. Because of a relatively restricted plan area, use is made of 'piggyback' elevators, consisting of a two level elevator cab serving odd and even floors at the same time. The twenty-four elevators are grouped into four banks of six, each bank finishing at quarter, mid, three-quarter and full height. The exterior skin is a double-glazed curtainwall set in a grid of anodised aluminium mullions and spandrel frames. The inside surface of the outside heat-reflecting glass layer has a silver film to reflect infra-red rays; the glass has a shading coefficient of 0.22. The heat-reflecting glass also reflects back interior heat, which is helpful in winter but not in summer. Of the total energy requirements, approximately 50% goes to lighting, 30% to cooling, 6% to heating, the remaining 14% being used for fans, elevators and other equipment. In summer, an all-air air-conditioning system is used. In winter, a waste-heat recovery system transfers heat from the interior, which is warm, to the periphery, which is cooler; this is done by means of hot water which is fed to peripheral air-handling units. The water is heated either by two double-bundle condensers in the 6000 ton (21 megawatts) central refrigerating plant, using the extracted interior heat, or, if the temperature falls below about 30°F (-1°C), by electric heaters.

The building structure consists of columns on the external wall at 25ft (7.62m) centres with spandrel beams at a floor to floor height of 12ft 6in (3.81m). Diagonal members are incorporated into the wall and intersect with the columns every four floors. There is a large horizontal bracing member connecting the two diagonals at these levels; under gravity load the member acts as a tie,

helping to distribute the gravity load evenly between all the columns and the diagonals. This in turn means that the external columns can all be of a similar size. Under wind load the diagonal members are, in general, prevented from going into tension by the gravity load on them. A stub girder floor system is used which provides a large effective lever arm for the main floor beams by separating the concrete slab and metal deck from the bottom girder with stub pieces. The resulting voids are used for air conditioning ducts. The stubs have shear connectors on their top to ensure composite action with the slab.

Structural Action

To provide a high rise structure with the necessary stiffness and strength the efficient solution is to make the outside surface into a closed section tube without any openings at all; the floors help to prevent distortion of the cross-section of the building. The practical alternative, as used here, is a trussed tube, that is to say a properly triangulated space truss where each member is braced and works principally in axial load, instead of bending. The trussed tube uses very much less material for example than a framed tube, which has to work in bending, but in both cases, the object is to approach the performance of a perfect tube, that is to say the solid cantilever rather than the frame. Both these systems have their cantilever action spoiled by shear lag, the framed tube being the less efficient, structurally, of the two. Shear lag is the result of the flexibility in shear of the surface of the tube, preventing the full development of axial forces in the 'flange' part of the tube. Here the diagonal elements, which increase in size towards the bottom of the building, control the effects of shear lag. All the wind forces are taken by the exterior framing with the interior columns only having to take gravity loads, thus giving greater freedom in positioning of these columns.

Construction

Members in the primary external frame were standard section shapes, except at the bottom where built-up members were made by welding together 5 or 6 in (125 or 150 mm) thick steel plates. Plates were welded by the electroslag process and subsequently stress relieved. Diagonal pieces were fabricated four storeys high

View of building from SW (photo by Barbara Martin).

FIRST INTERNATIONAL BUILDING (1975)

Description:
Fifty-six storey office block of steel trussed tube construction
Architects:
Hellmuth, Obata and Kassabaum/
Harwood K. Smith and Partners
Structural engineers:
Ellisor and Tanner

Axonometric view
of lower half
from SW:

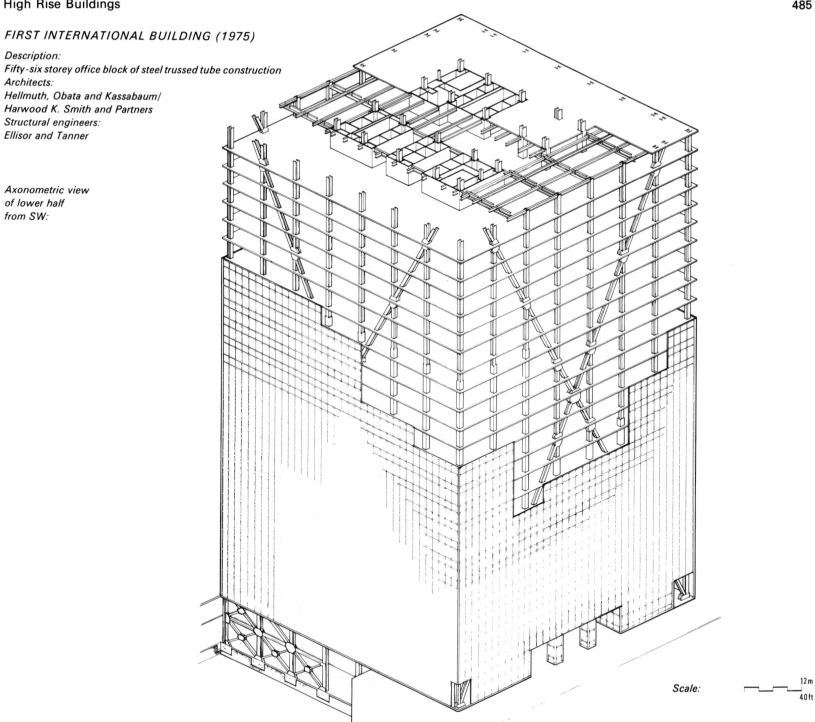

Scale: 12m
                  40ft

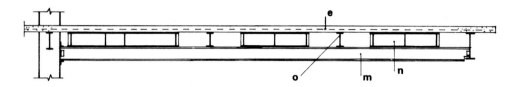

Elevation on stub girder floor system.

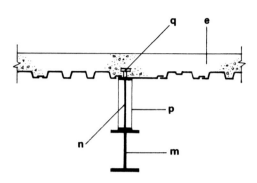

m W14 x 68 lb/ft beam; n W16 x 31 lb/ft stub beam; o continuous floor beam; p $\frac{1}{4}$" stiffener plate on stub beam; q shear connector.

Section on stub girder floor system.

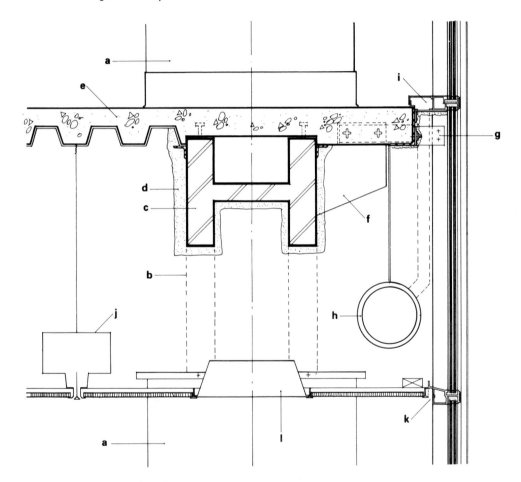

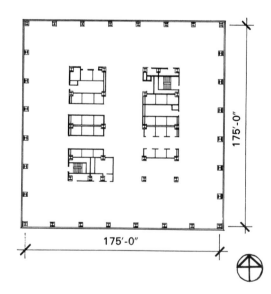

Typical mid-height plan.

a drywall column enclosure; b column; c horizontal bracing member; d fireproofing; e $6\frac{1}{4}$" concrete slab on metal deck; f outrigger; g aluminium support for glass curtain wall; h insulated duct; i perforated duct; j supply air; k return air slot; l light fixture.

Vertical section through facade at level of horizontal bracing member.

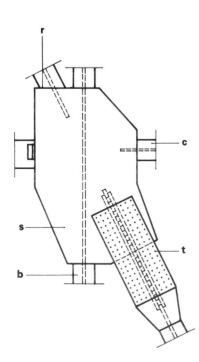

r full penetration weld done on site; s 2/ 6" thick connection plates; t high strength bolts.

Elevation on connection between horizontal bracing and diagonal members.

being welded to a 6in (150mm) thick gusset connection plate at one end, to save material, and being bolted through a splice plate at the other end, to provide the erection tolerances needed for correct positioning and alignment. Steelwork erection took ten months, the whole building taking 40 months to complete.

Conclusion

In this building considerations of economy have come uppermost. The floor system, framing and heat recovery systems partly associated with this economy are of continuing interest.

View of corner connection below street level (photo supplied by engineer).

Texas Commerce Tower, Houston, Texas, USA

Introduction

Composite construction of steel and concrete, in whatever form, is an attempt to make optimum use of two different materials. This seventy-five storey office tower is an example of composite construction applied to a building of extreme height, where the advantages of concrete combine with the flexibility and speed of construction of steelwork. The building uses an architecture of pure geometry and surface which conveniently accepts the idea of the repetition of elements that is essential for economy.

Description

The form of the building is of a square tube with one corner chamfered and clad in glass and stainless steel over its full height. This provides good views out and allows a contrast with the granite panel cladding on all other faces of the building. At the entrance is a five-storey glass wall supported by a stainless steel space frame. Inside, there is a clear space of the same height in front of banks of elevators and, one level down, a concourse area, seen beyond the circular edge of the ground floor slab to one side of these elevators. There are four levels of basement. The tower is supported by a 9ft 9in (2.97m) thick concrete mat foundation, containing 1700 tons (1569 tonnes) of reinforcement, which rests on a stiff clay 63ft (19.20m) below street level. All the interior columns, which are steel, are positioned in the core area and provide 40ft (12.20m) of clear space around the core at all floor levels. All the exterior faces of the building, except the chamfered corner, are made up of steel columns and spandrels which are subsequently encased in concrete. The steel columns are at 10ft (3.05m) centres. The chamfered corner has no columns, a steel girder spanning the 85ft (25.90m) clear distance across its face at each level above the sixth floor. A channel-shaped shear wall of composite steel and concrete construction is set back 40ft (12.20m) from the chamfered face of the building but is attached to the exterior columns and spandrels by two 3ft 6in (1.05m) deep steel girders at each floor level. These span from each end of the shear wall and, by linking the exterior walls with the shear

wall, form, in effect, the enclosed if irregular shape that gives the building tube action against wind forces.

The floors are also of composite construction, being 2ft 2in (650mm) deep overall. The interior columns are plain steel and, in the bottom half of the building are purpose made using plates up to 6in (150mm) thick. The composite exterior columns are generally 3ft 10in (1.17m) wide; their depth is the same as the width of the spandrel beams, which varies in five stages from 1ft 6in (450mm) at the top to 2ft 6in (750mm) at the bottom; the depth of the spandrel is a constant 4ft (1.22m). The faces of the columns and spandrels take the granite panels, the exterior glazing fitting between them without the need for intermediate mullions. There are seventeen different heating and cooling zones in each floor.

Structural Action

Without the significant connections between the channel shaped interior shear wall and the exterior walls, this building would have worked as an open-section thin-walled tube. In such a case the building would have poor torsional rigidity, even though the floors would prevent the building going out of shape in plan. A corollary is that longitudinal warping forces would develop, that is to say axial tension and compression forces would occur in the columns. This particularly affects forces in the triangular columns either side of the chamfered face which could almost double. Advantage has therefore been taken to transfer these potential axial forces to the shear wall, via the rigidly connected link girders acting in vertical shear. This effectively restores tube action, although because this is a relatively flexible or 'soft' link, the tube action is imperfect. The steel girders spanning across the chamfered face also help to limit movement between the triangular-shaped columns on each side. The resultant action is that of a framed tube with some warping. Structurally the framed tube has both frame and cantilever action.

It is necessary in framed tube construction for spandrel stiffnesses to increase towards the bottom of the building, as is the case here, in line with the increase in wind shear. This indicates that frame action is significant. However, it is interesting to note that the two link girders

View of Tower from NW (photo © Richard Payne AIA 1985).

TEXAS COMMERCE TOWER (1982)

Description:
Seventy-five storey office block of steel and concrete composite construction
Architects:
I.M. Pei and Partners/
3D International
Structural engineers:
Colaco Engineers
Cladding contractor:
Cupples Products

Axonometric view from SW:

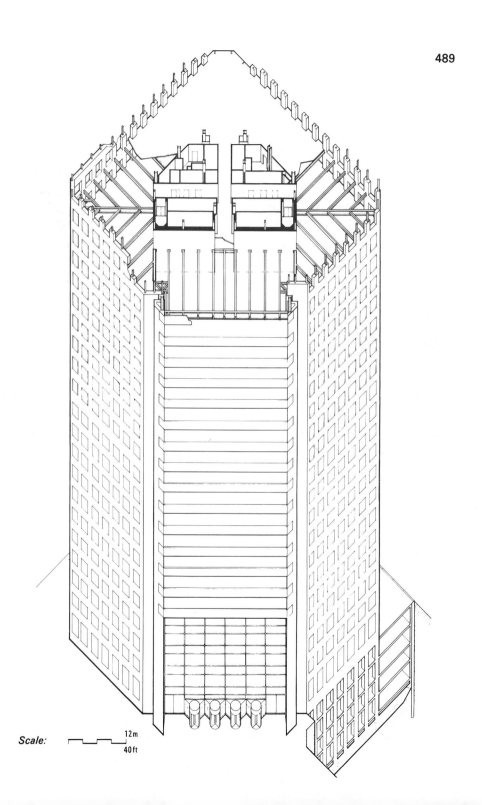

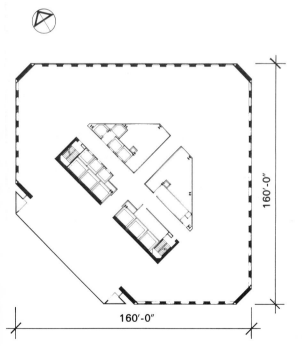

160'-0"

160'-0"

Upper level floor plan.

Scale: ⊢——⊣ 12m
        40 ft

increase in stiffness towards the top of the building, indicating their role in promoting cantilever action, that is to say forcing the shear and exterior walls into tube action. The interior steel beams and columns are designed simply for gravity loads and this allows small sizes to be used and greater flexibility in planning. Allowance has to be made at construction for the changes in length of the columns due to elastic shortening and, for the composite elements, shrinkage and creep of the concrete. Generally the steel columns are built slightly high because they shorten more than the composite exterior columns.

Construction

Composite high rise building is fundamentally an innovation in construction method; the finished composite elements behave almost precisely like a reinforced concrete structure would. First the steelwork was erected with only small section columns on the periphery which, however, are strong enough to take the construction loads from up to twelve floors above. Six levels below the steel erection level the concrete floor slab was poured, two or three levels below that the shear wall and two or three levels below that, the exterior wall of the building using custom made steel panel forms. Concrete was pumped, to heights of over 1000ft (305m). The rate of construction was one floor every three days, achieved by strict coordination of work. The total period of construction was 42 months.

Conclusion

Steel construction provides long spans, small columns, free planning of space, flexibility in use and fast construction. In the comparison, concrete construction provides a free choice of element shapes, fire resistance, some insulation, savings in material costs and, significantly for the high rise building, cheap rigid joints, stiffness and good damping of vibrations. This building shows that enough of the advantages of each material can be achieved in practice. In particular the rate of construction is more than double that of an all-concrete structure. The encased steel may be thought of as a permanent scaffolding for the concrete work. Hence this method is unlikely to be economic where material costs are high relative to labour. However, trends are in the opposite

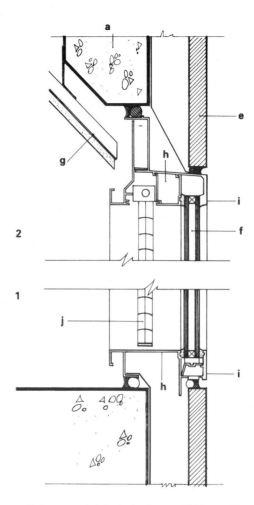

a 4' deep spandrel; b steel column; c 5" floor with lightweight concrete on metal deck; d steel floor beam; e 1¼" granite panel attached to concrete face with aluminium angles; f 1" double glazing; g false ceiling.

Typical vertical section through wall at lower levels.

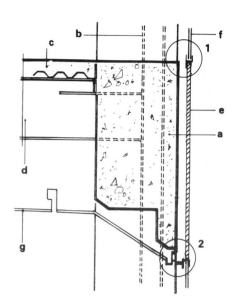

h extruded aluminium rail; i stainless steel snap-on cover; j blind.

Detail vertical section through wall.

direction and composite construction is likely to become more common. This is a spectacular example of its use.

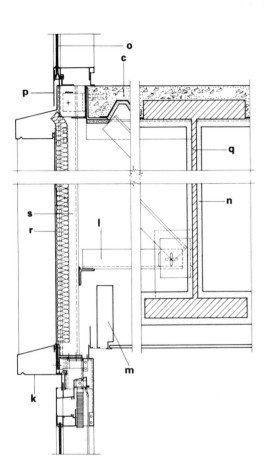

k $\frac{1}{16}''$ stainless steel cill; **l** $2\frac{1}{2}''$ x $2\frac{1}{2}''$ x $\frac{1}{4}''$ steel angle site welded to steel tube and bolted to girder; **m** air diffuser; **n** fireproofing; **o** glazing with neoprene gaskets and continuous silicon seal; **p** $\frac{1}{16}''$ stainless steel cover on extruded aluminium rail with weep hole below glazing; **q** steel girder spanning chamfered corner of building; **r** $\frac{1}{8}''$ stainless steel cladding with $2''$ insulation behind; **s** steel tube at $5'-3''$ centres.

Vertical section through wall on chamfered corner.

View of main entrance from W (photo © Richard Payne AIA 1985).

Metro Dade Center, Miami, Florida, USA

Introduction

Space at ground level for use by pedestrians is at a premium, especially in city centres. However it is precisely at the bottom of buildings that the column loads are high and where it is most expensive to provide clear space. In this thirty storey office building, for the County Administration, the columns at the base of the tower go through an 80ft (24.38m) high open space provided at the base of the tower for the use of the public. Within this open space are retail shops, terraces and paved routes which are devoted to public use as well as the mayor and commissioners' offices. Although pedestrians at the base of tall buildings are often exposed to high wind forces due to downdrafts, especially at the corners, here, the public space below the offices is completely enclosed; to prevent funnelling of the wind, the entrance doors are recessed and the building is bevelled at the corners thus allowing some of the downdraft to 'spill' past the buildings. The building shape also allows a significant reduction in general wind pressure compared to that with a rectangular shape; this is an important consideration in an area with hurricane force winds. The building structure is of concrete construction and is notable for use of a 60ft (18.29m) deep spandrel girder above the public open space which is designed to mobilise just sufficient dead load to prevent uplift on the foundations in anything but extreme conditions.

Description

The building is entirely of cast-in-place concrete with shear walls, at the east and west ends of the building, next to the elevators and services, these being connected into the floor structure. On the outside the concrete surfaces are clad with limestone panels. The floor has main and secondary beams: the main beams in the floor go in the north-south direction spanning up to 40ft 6in (12.34m) between the columns and 44ft (13.41m) at the ends, adjacent to the elevators; it is haunched, with a depth of 45in (1125mm) in the 10ft (3.05m) either side of the column and a depth of 27in (675mm) over the middle portion; the secondary beams in the east-west direction

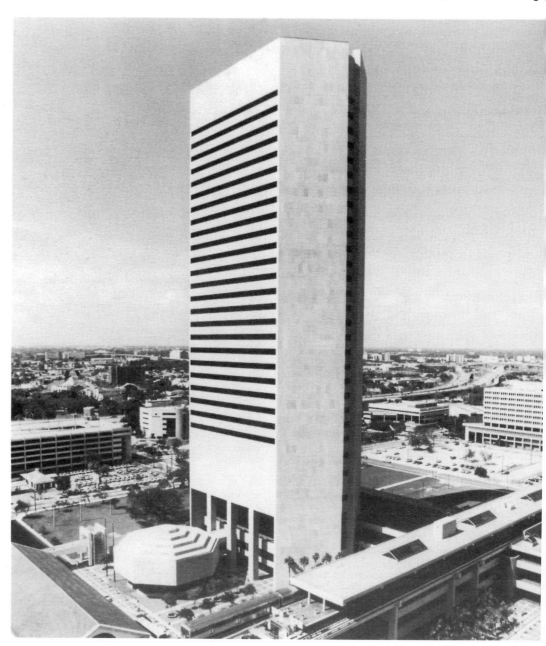

View of building from SE (photo by Metro Dade County).

METRO DADE CENTER (1983)

Description:
30 storey office building with concrete frame and shear walls
Architects:
Hugh Stubbins and Associates
Structural engineers:
Le Messurier Associates/SCI

Axonometric
view from SW:

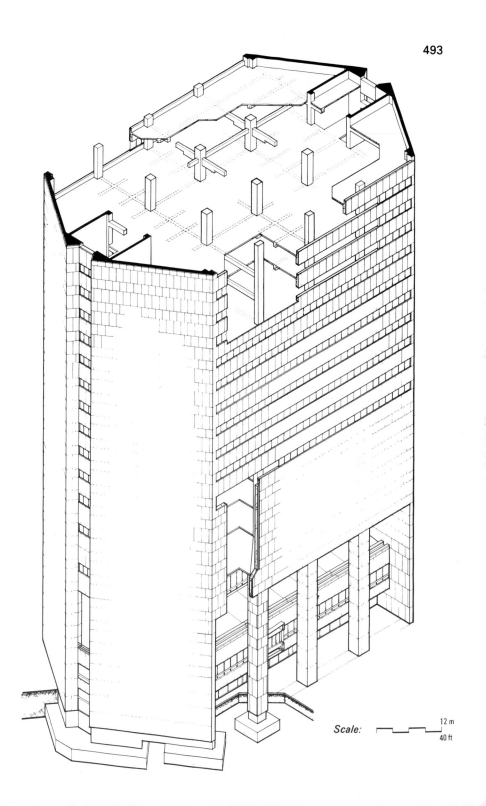

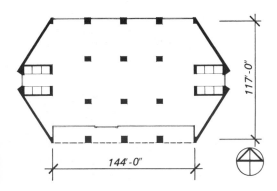

117'-0"

144'-0"

Ground floor plan.

Scale: 12 m / 40 ft

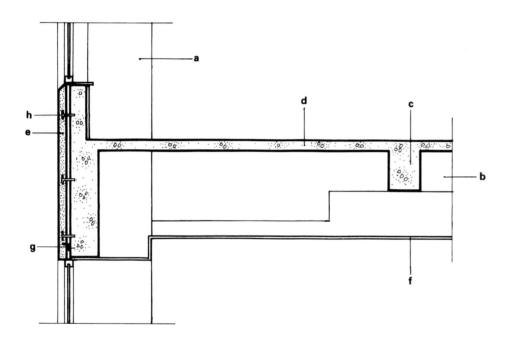

a concrete column; **b** 24″ × 27″/45″ haunched beam; **c** 18″ × 27″ secondary beam; **d** 5½″ slab; **e** 4″ limestone panel with 3 disc restraints and support angle at each vertical joint; **f** suspended ceiling; **g** 3″ x 6″ x ½″ stainless steel support angle at each vertical joint between panels; **h** 3″ x 3/16″ disc restraint in vertical joints.

Typical vertical section through wall in upper storeys.

spaced about 13ft (3.96m) on centre are also 27in (675mm) deep and support a 5½in (138mm) slab. The arrangement allows service ducts to run uninterrupted below secondary beams. The interior concrete columns are 30 x 30 in (750 x 750 mm) at the top increasing in stages to 54 x 76 in

(1350 x 1900 mm) at the ground floor. At this level these columns are carrying up to about 4000 tons (3500 tonnes) of gravity load. On the north and south faces the spandrel beams are 62in (1550mm) deep and form a rigid frame with the exterior columns. Shear walls increase in thickness

by stages being 1ft (300mm) thick at the top. Below level 6 they are 2ft (600mm) thick and are joined to the 60ft (18.29m) deep spandrel girders, which are also 2ft (600mm) thick. Shear walls and columns are supported on piles, through pile caps, the piles resting on a sandstone stratum and having a working load capacity of 600 tons (550 tonnes). Floor to floor height is generally 13ft 6in (4.11m) but is about double this in the plant room floors at levels 3 and 30. A suspended ceiling is provided in the office spaces. Windows on the north and south faces are continuous double glazed aluminium strip windows with a bronze tinted outer glass to reflect back radiant heat.

The cladding to the building is done with limestone panels which are 4in (100mm) thick and have a 2in (50mm) clearance space behind them. The standard panel is 8ft (2.44m) high by 4ft 6in (1.37m) wide and is set between window strips. Each panel is supported by a stainless steel angle at the two bottom corners and restrained by three disc anchors set into grooves cut in each vertical edge of the panel. Each angle and each anchor also supports the adjacent panel. A half-inch horizontal relieving joint is provided every storey height, below the support angles, and vertical joints between panels also allow movement. Where there are no windows a panel of the same height replaces them. It is supported on the standard panel below and the three disc anchors on each side. Three floors within the height of the 60ft (18.29m) deep spandrel beams have no natural light, consisting of plant and control rooms, and are cheaper to cool and heat than the other floors. Some areas may require staircases at a later date and, here, use is made of precast concrete floor planks which are removable.

Structural Action

The building is 500ft (152m) high, 120ft (37m) across and, at the top, has a general wind pressure going up to 105 lb per sq ft (514 kg per sq m). Therefore an efficient method of resisting wind forces had to be found. Wind forces on the broad face of the building are resisted above level 6, the top of the 60ft (18.29m) girder, by the shear walls acting like cantilevers. At each end, the two shear walls are coupled together, and stiffened, by 8ft (2.44m) deep, 11ft (3.35m) long beams at each floor level; however the coupled shear walls do go into tension on the windward side above level 6. Below level 6 the building behaves more like a tube structure, the 60ft (18.29m) girder transferring loads, by shear, to the north and south faces. Under normal wind loads, because of the tremendous gravity load acting downwards, and mobilised into service by the girder, no tension is developed in any columns or foundations on the windward side. Wind on the narrow face above level 6 is also resisted by the shear walls which cantilever and act in concert with the exterior frames on the north and south faces; below level 6, in spite of the depth of the girder, tube action cannot be properly developed because the exterior frames above the girder are insufficiently stiff. The girder and shear walls at each end act like a huge portal frame. No less than thirty-four $1\frac{3}{8}$in (34mm) bars are placed both at the top and bottom of the girder with sixty bars at the same levels in the shear walls to resist bending moments imposed by the cantilevers above level 6. These two sets of bars and a third set in the north-south direction are joined via a connection made of heavy steel beam section. The girder and shear wall being non-planar, the third set of bars serves to triangulate the joint in plan. Again the design ensures that no uplift occurs on foundations under normal wind loads.

Construction

The tower block took 36 months to build from the start of foundation work.

Conclusion

The designers have provided a high and 'clean' looking building which, from a distance, is a landmark in the urban sprawl but, near to, it is, to some extent, broken down in scale for the benefit of pedestrians near ground level. The haunched floor beam system is similar in concept to the flat slab with a hammer head column used at smaller spans. The placing of services at either end of the building and the bevelling of the corners on plan has given a high ratio of usable floor area to perimeter length. This should be a low maintenance building.

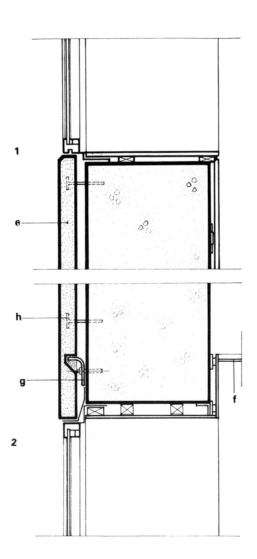

Vertical section through wall in lower levels.

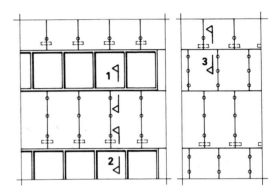

Elevations on limestone panels.

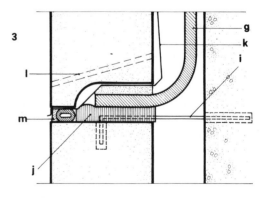

i restraining strap; j compressible filler; k stainless steel flashing; l weep holes at vertical joints; m sealant and backing strip.

Vertical section at horizontal joint between panels.

First Winconsin Center, Milwaukee, Wisconsin, USA

Introduction

This 42 storey bank and office tower shows a classic application of a belt truss and outrigger system, at the 15th and 41st floor levels, with a transfer truss at the 3rd level. These trusses are fully expressed on elevation.

Description

The tower building has a light open frame with large windows, rising from a two-storey glazed podium building containing shops and other facilities. The tower building has exterior columns at 20ft (6.10m) centres and interior columns on a 40ft (12.20m) grid, column depths ranging from 14in (350mm) at the top to 36in (900mm) at the base. The spandrel beams range from 21in (525mm) to 36in (900mm) deep. The beams and columns are standard or built-up sections and are clad with aluminium plate painted white. The floor to floor height is 13ft (3.96m) but this is doubled at levels 3, 15 and 41. At level 3 there are transfer trusses on all four sides allowing the column spacing below to be increased to 40ft (12.20m). Levels 15 and 41 contain the plant rooms (mechanical rooms) and also, on the outside, on all four sides, belt trusses which are connected to the central core by four outrigger trusses of the same height running in the north-south direction at 40ft (12.20m) centres. The core, which runs the full height of the building, consists of four K-braced shear trusses, in the same plane as the outriggers, to which they are interconnected. Typical floors consist of a 5¼in (131mm) lightweight concrete slab composite with a 2in (50mm) metal deck in turn supported by secondary beams at 10ft (3.05m) centres. At foundation level the columns are on a 40ft (12.20m) grid, the loads on the core columns being in excess of 6000 tons (5540 tonnes). Steel piles, taking working loads of 250 tons (230 tonnes) each, were taken through soft glacially deposited silts and clay to depths of up to 160ft (48.77m); a cluster of piles supported each column through a pilecap.

Structural Action

Gravity loads either travel down the core columns

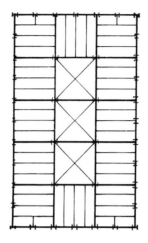

Typical floor framing plan.

at 40ft (12.20m) centres or down the outside columns which are at 20ft (6.10m) centres, or 40ft (12.20m) centres below level 3. Under wind load and without the belt or outrigger trusses the building would deflect as a frame with some shear truss interaction; the spandrel beams are not short enough or deep enough to provide significant tube action. With the belt trusses, however, the frame is stiff enough to behave as a partial tube, inducing tension and compression into the exterior columns. With the outrigger trusses, as well, acting in vertical shear, shear lag is reduced and the tube action greatly improved. The structural action may be summarised as that of a partial tube with shear truss interaction, somewhat similar to tube in tube action. With wind in the north-south direction this is how the building takes the horizontal load; the lateral drift was calculated to be 30% less than that without a belt truss-outrigger system. With one belt truss-outrigger system at the top, the second may be placed anywhere between one and two-thirds of the height and still give a near optimum effect. Wind in the east-west direction is taken by frame action, there being no outriggers in this direction. To this end all exterior frames are moment connected, beam-column junctions being welded

View of tower from NE (photo by Ezra Stoller © ESTO).

FIRST WISCONSIN CENTER (1974)

Description:
Forty-two storey office tower of steel construction using belt truss-outrigger system
Architects and structural engineers:
Skidmore, Owings and Merrill

Axonometric view
of lower part
from NE:

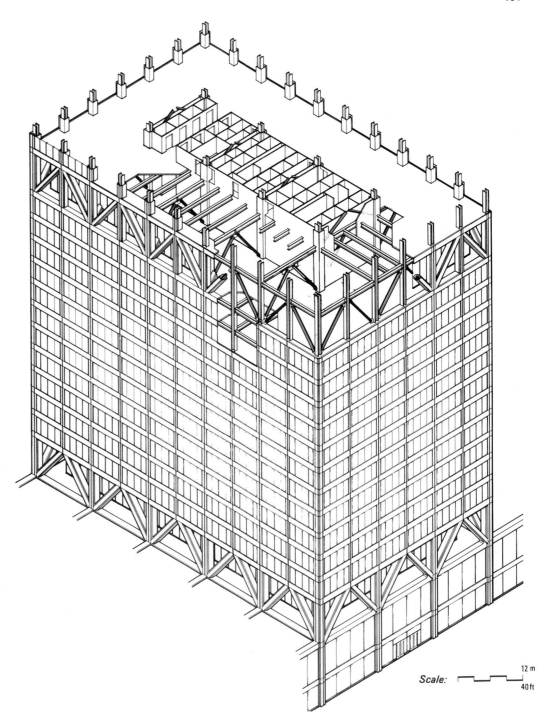

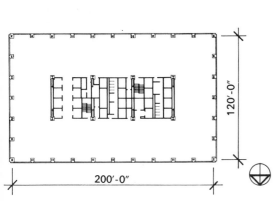

120'-0"

200'-0"

Typical floor plan.

Scale:

12 m

40 ft

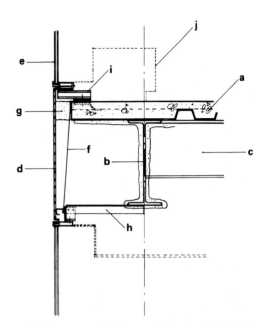

a $5\frac{1}{2}''$ concrete slab; b spandrel beam; c W21 x 44 lb/ft secondary beam; d $\frac{1}{4}''$ aluminium plate 3'-4" deep; e reflective double glazing; f aluminium sheet flashing; g sound absorbent fire-stop; h window wall restraint with fixing allowing vertical movement; i sill fixing to window; j induction unit enclosure.

Vertical section through N wall.

or with beam flanges bolted to horizontal plates which are welded to the columns. However, all interior frames are simply supported.

Construction

The total period of construction was 36 months.

Conclusion

The belt truss-outrigger systems seems to have further application for buildings of regular or irregular shape. Above about 40 storeys high it starts to become less economic than diagonally braced or framed tubes but allows greater freedom in treatment of the elevations. This building used only 24 lb per sq ft (117 kg per sq m) of floor area and is an outstanding example of its application.

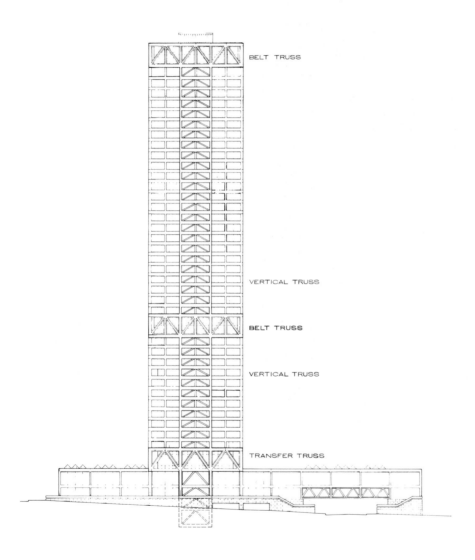

Vertical section in E-W direction (drawn by engineer).

One Shell Plaza,
Houston, Texas, USA

Introduction

This is a classic structure, still one of the tallest concrete buildings in the world, and a paradigm of the art of structural engineering, what may be called the resolution of structural design by research and ingenuity. In a building of such scale and proportions, subject to hurricane wind forces, it is not surprising, but rare in practice, that the ideas of the structural engineer have had such a visible influence on the building form. The key structural elements are seen, on plan, to be the core and the exterior walls. The system has been referred to as a 'tube in tube' system.

Description

Being in an area where there is no hard bearing stratum the only practical foundation is a floating-type mat foundation, and the maximum height of the building depends primarily on the amount of soil excavated in the basement and the building's weight. The object is to minimise soil bearing pressures. Lightweight concrete weighing 115 lb per cu ft (1850 kg per cu m) was specified for the entire building. It was found possible to excavate down to 60ft (18.29m). The mat is 8ft 3in (2.51m) thick and uses 80lb of steel reinforcement per sq ft (391 kg per sq m) area of the mat. The core wall 'tubes' and the external wall 'tube' then climb off this mat to a height of 52 storeys above ground level. There are four basement and fifty office levels. The core walls are 2ft (600mm) thick at the bottom reducing to 10in (250mm) thick at the top. The clear floor space between the core and outside wall is 36ft (9.14m), which is sufficient for office use. The floor consists of one-way spanning joists 2ft (600mm) deep at 6ft (1.83m) centres with a $3\frac{1}{2}$in (88mm) slab on top, all in lightweight concrete. At the corners a waffle slab was used and analysed as a two-way spanning grid. The columns are 2ft (600mm) wide and also at 6ft (1.83m) centres so that each joist is supported at a perimeter column. Near the corners the column depth is increased to compensate for the heavier load from the waffle slab. A 9ft 6in (2.89m) deep transfer truss at level 2 creates larger openings in the external wall at street level. The columns are clad in $1\frac{1}{4}$in (31mm) thick travertine marble but are

not insulated. In order to restrict column movement, it was decided to limit the average temperature in the external columns on the coldest days to 50°F (10°C) and, the columns being of different depth, it was necessary to set the glass line, which controls this average temperature, in

View of building from SE (photo by Ezra Stoller © ESTO).

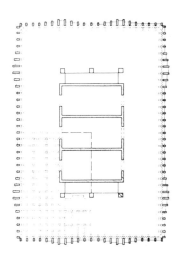

Plan showing glass line and part of floor structure.

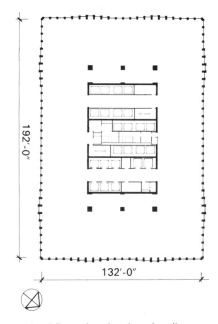

Lower level floor plan showing glass line.

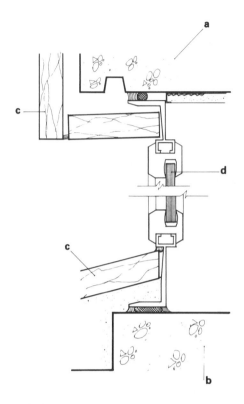

a 5'–0" deep spandrel beam; b top of 9'–6" deep transfer truss; c 1¼" marble facing; d ½" thick bronze-tinted glass.

Vertical section through window above transfer truss.

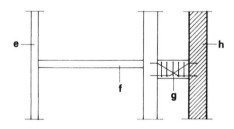

e perimeter column; f floor slab; g connecting beam; h wall of core.

Vertical section through floor on SW and NE sides.

different positions. The glass amounts to only about 45 per cent of the total exterior surface area. This was decided on an overall or systems approach. The advantages include very simple window details, easy positioning of the windows in different planes, reduced heat loss and heat gain and a chunky exterior framed tube which, structurally, behaves in a similar way to the true cantilever, that is to say, successfully limits the effects of shear lag.

Structural Action

Compared to a steel building which would require rigid joints and whose costs rise more or less in proportion to the number of joints, the concrete structure achieves closely spaced rigid joints with impunity. Under simple wind load the framed tube has both tube action, causing axial tension or compression in all the outer columns, and frame action, which causes bending moments on the two sides of the building parallel to the wind, the 'web' sides. For example the total deflection could be obtained by adding together that from tube and frame action. The efficiency of the framed tube, as a cantilever, depends on the shear stiffness of the spandrel beams and columns relative to the axial stiffness of the columns. The column stiffness is relatively constant while the spandrel shear stiffness is sensitive to changes in its dimensions and especially the ratio of its depth to its effective span. This ratio should be not less than about a quarter for efficient tube action. At One Shell Plaza this ratio is about one and a quarter, and gives good tube action, the horizontal deflection due to frame action accounting for less than a fifth of the total deflection. This framed tube interacts with the concrete shear walls of the inner core, which contains lifts and services. This core, or inner tube, acts principally to restrain the frame action on the 'web' sides of the framed tube. In such frame-shear wall interaction almost all shear at the base, in this case amounting to some 2750 tons (2540 tonnes), is transferred to ground via the shear walls. The internal columns adjacent to the core are made to act with the core by deep connecting beams, and this action is intensified by creep: the cores, having lower percentages of vertical reinforcement, creep more than the columns and therefore progressively shed load to the columns as creep takes place.

With a building of this height, account had to be taken of the movement between the inner core and the external columns due to elastic shortening of the columns, temperature, shrinkage and creep, and in this case, also from differential settlement between the middle and the edge of the foundation mat, although some of this potential movement can be absorbed by the floor joists. The foundation mat settles to a dish shape and has the least effect on the higher floors which are built after a large proportion of the differential movement has occurred. However, temperature movements, being cumulative upwards, have most effect on these higher floors. The temperature movement between core and outside columns is under ½in (12mm) at the top, a limit of ¾in (19mm) being set as just tolerable for structural and partition design. The vertical movement from floor to floor due to elastic shortening of the columns under wind load is also less than ½in (12mm). Horizontal drift between floors under wind load is less than ¼in (6mm) at all levels. Total horizontal deflection at the top is less than 7in (177mm) under hurricane wind loads.

Construction

The total period of construction was 34 months. Emphasis was placed on strict quality control of the lightweight concrete, in order to achieve the values assumed in design.

Conclusion

This building makes a good case for concrete as the natural material for high rise building. Concrete is well suited for high compressive stress and provides stable, if large, columns. It also has fire resistance, a natural rigidity and good internal damping. In this way the extra cost of incorporating material to supply stiffness and suppress the awkward dynamic responses of structures in a buffeting wind can be avoided. In this respect it compares favourably with a steel building. The unit price of this building is said to be no more than a 35 storey concrete shear wall building. As in all good designs, of this sort, gravity loads rather than wind forces control the sizes of the elements. The small window areas and high thermal mass have considerably reduced the air-conditioning loads.

ONE SHELL PLAZA (1971)

Description:
Fifty-two storey office block of lightweight concrete
construction using tube-in-tube system
Architects and structural engineers:
Skidmore, Owings and Merrill

Axonometric view
of lower part
from S:

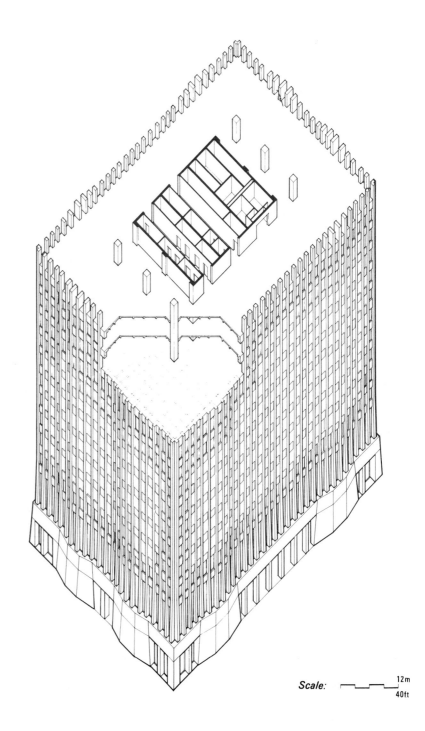

Scale: 12m
40ft

One Mellon Bank Center,
Pittsburgh, Pennsylvania, USA

Introduction

This tower building has 55 storeys with a 17-storey office block appended to it on its south side. The development is indicative of the still continuing movement towards the concentration of office facilities in the city centres. The goliath scale associated with this elevation and massing are partly relieved by tapering the tops of the two buildings. The chief interest of the tower is in its use of purpose-made painted steel cladding panels which are also used as part of the structure to limit wind drift. This idea of using a 'stressed skin tube' is, potentially, of wide application.

Description

The building is of steel frame construction, with a core structure, occupying an area of about 112 x 36 ft (34.14 x 10.97 m) at level 20 , and having a clear span from the core to an exterior framed tube, this span being about 47ft (14.32m) on the long side. The column spacing in the core is, in general, nearly 20ft (6.10m) while that on the exterior tube is 10ft (3.05m). The core columns only take gravity load, while perimeter columns, in the exterior tube, take gravity and wind loads. Except at the eight corner positions at lower levels, all columns are standard rolled sections. In the tube the columns vary in size from W14 x 76 lb/ft, at the top, to W14 x 550 lb/ft, at the bottom, and the corner built-up columns are 21 x 21 in (533 x 533 mm) square sections made of 3 in (75mm) thick plates. Spandrel beams typically are 2ft 6in (750mm) deep standard rolled sections, except at the eight corner positions on plan, where a 2ft 10in (864mm) deep beam is provided across the corner bay. In general the floor structure consists of W24 x 55 or 68 lb/ft beams, on the long sides, and W16 x 26 or 50 lb/ft, on the short sides. These floor beams are composite with a 2in (50mm) cellular deck, blended with a non-cellular deck, and a $2\frac{1}{2}$in (63mm) normal weight concrete topping. Holes, up to 20 x 10 in (500 x 250 mm), are provided through these beams for ducts.

There are double-height plantrooms (mechanical rooms) at levels 2, 17, 35 and 55 . In the middle two plantrooms cross-bracing is placed round the perimeter, to stiffen the tube, but with $1\frac{1}{2}$in

View of tower at construction from NE (photo supplied by engineer).

(38mm) plate across the eight corner bays.

The steel cladding for the building is $\frac{1}{4}$in (6mm) thick, or $\frac{5}{16}$in (8mm) thick below level 24 , and is supplied in panels one-bay wide and three-storeys high which weigh about 3 tons (2.7 tonnes).

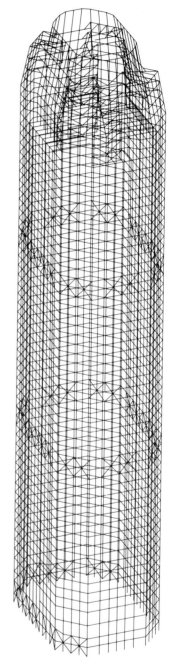

Computer model of exterior tube.

ONE MELLON BANK CENTER (1982)

Description:
55-storey office tower having external steel framed tube with steel cladding acting as shear membrane
Architects:
Welton Becket Associates
Structural engineers:
Lev Zetlin Associates

Axonometric view from NE:

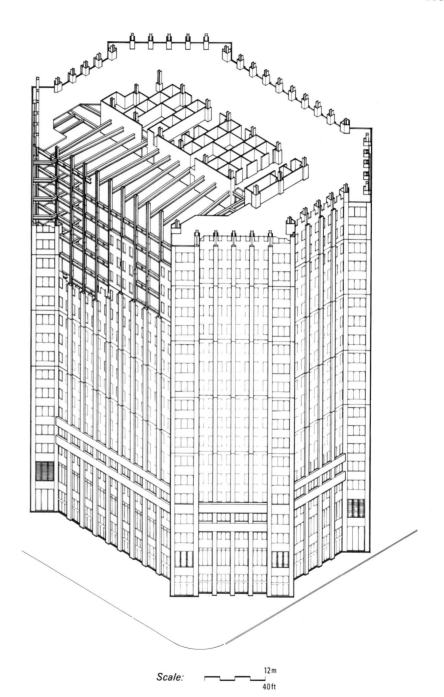

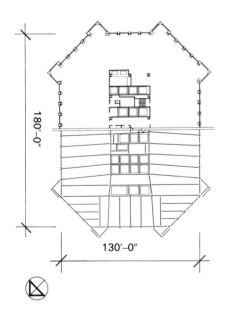

180'-0"

130'-0"

Typical floor plan.

Scale:
12m
40ft

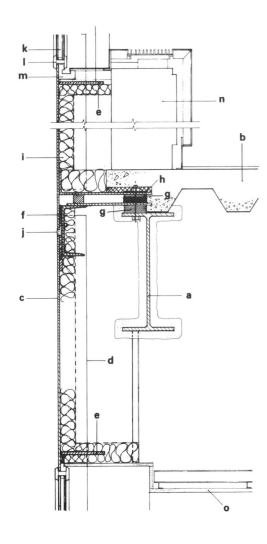

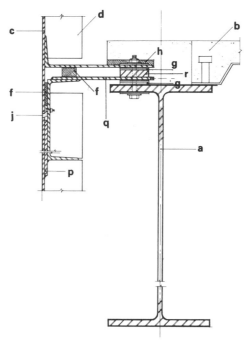

p $\frac{1}{4}$" spacer plate; q $\frac{1}{4}$" plate; r $\frac{3}{4}$" x $3\frac{1}{2}$" plate welded to q.

Detail section through wall at panel joint.

a spandrel beam with slotted holes for cladding bolts; b $4\frac{1}{2}$" concrete slab with 2" metal deck; c $\frac{1}{4}$" to $\frac{5}{16}$" steel sheet; d 4" x $\frac{1}{2}$" stiffeners; e 6" x $\frac{1}{3}$" horizontal stiffener; f neoprene gasket; g compressible shims; h $\frac{1}{2}$" compressible filler; i semi-rigid insulation with vapour barrier; j $\frac{5}{8}$" joint at erection with sealant; k 1" double glazing; l neoprene window gasket; m pvc channel on pvc shims; n fan-coil unit; o suspended ceiling.

Typical vertical section through wall.

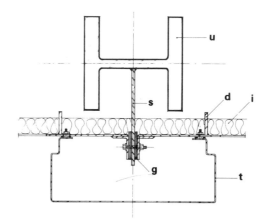

s connection plate; t $\frac{1}{8}$" steel column cover; u column.

Horizontal section at panel joint.

There are 16 panel types. Under horizontal forces, the panels, being part of the structure, are put into shear. However at the eight corner positions, where there are right-angled corners, the wall panels are flexible and not used as part of the structure; here, shear stiffness is provided by the 2ft 10in (864mm) deep spandrel beam in the corner bay, which is in line with the long facade. In a typical case, four wall panels are erected in a row. The panels are bolted to each other over their height but only attached to the supporting columns at their mid-points; the main connections to the columns are the two end ones in the row of panels. This arrangement prevents the panels picking up compressive stresses as the columns shorten, as well as allowing relief of thermal stresses. The connections at the top and bottom of the panel to the spandrel beams allow vertical movement, as do the horizontal tie connections which are installed to prevent outward movement of the panels under wind pressure or suction. Windows occupy about 25% of the wall area and are cut out of the panels with a plasma torch. The windows are frameless and supported by H-shaped neoprene gaskets with a zipper strip pressed on to the window edges. Stress concentrations at the corners of the windows are reduced by providing a corner radius, cut automatically during fabrication. Stiffeners are welded to the inside of the panel on lines above and below and each side of the window openings. All panels were blast cleaned on both sides. The inside surface was painted with a 2-3 mil coat of zinc-rich primer; the outer surface had the same primer, followed by a 0-5 mil zinc chromate wash primer, followed by two 2-3 mil coats of acrylic urethane. Horizontal joints between panels are waterproofed by neoprene gaskets and sealant and vertical joints by column covers which are sealed at the ends and sides. Perimeter offices are air conditioned by four-pipe fan coil units at 10ft (3.05m) centres; interior spaces have a central station VAV air-conditioning system.

Structural Action

The exterior framed steel tube is designed to resist all the horizontal loads on the building without exceeding the allowable material stresses but, by itself, would give a horizontal sway at the top of the building of about height divided by 290, compared to an allowable sway of height divided by 500 . The horizontal sway coupled with torsional movements are generally the controlling factors in high-rise buildings. In this building, the stiffness is increased not by increasing frame member sizes but by connecting the exterior framed tube with the cladding. The structure is analysed as a framed tube with a shear membrane to represent the cladding. The cladding and connections are designed to resist in-plane shear forces, wind forces perpendicular to the face, residual stresses due to the window openings, thermal stresses and to resist overall and local shear buckling. This arrangement gave savings not only in the frame but in the cladding as well. As the cladding is not necessary for structural safety it is not fireproofed. The 17-storey office block attached to the tower is 'tuned' to deflect in ways more or less compatible with those of the tower. The axial stresses in the perimeter columns were designed to be within 10% of each other under dead and live loads to minimise unintended redistributions of stress.

Construction

The total period of construction was 42 months. Erection of the steelwork took 12 months. All steelwork in the tower was erected by two climbing cranes inside the tower. Cladding panels were lifted by a crane at ground level and fixed from the inside. To allow for elastic shortening, the columns in the core were made longer than those at the perimeter, the core columns being more highly stressed under dead and live load.

Conclusion

The use of a 'surface active' skin to control stiffness is logical, especially in high-rise buildings where accelerations and the drift, between storeys and over the full height, are controlling factors in the design. Cladding used in this way is reminiscent of traditional masonry cladding which, consciously or not, provided great reserves of stiffness and strength to a building. A total of 21 000 tons (19 050 tonnes) of structural steel was used in the frame, representing 28 lb per sq ft (135 kg per sq m) of gross floor area. A total of 6200 tons (5735 tonnes) of steel was used for the cladding.

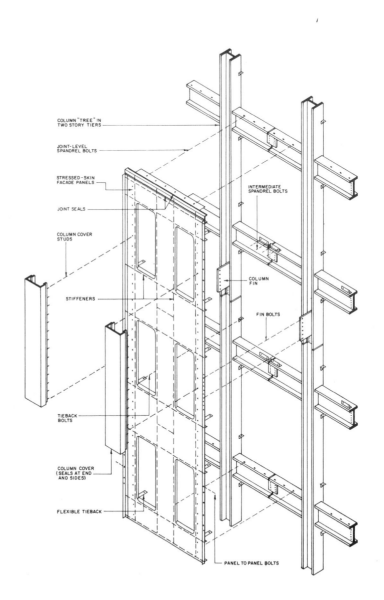

Steel 'tree' subassembly and steel cladding panel (drawn by engineer).

The Sears Tower, Chicago, Illinois, USA

Introduction

This office block is important not for its extreme height but for the original and simple method by which it resists the huge wind loads on it. The building is 1450ft (442m) high, with 109 storeys above ground, and has a gross floor area of 4.4 million sq ft (408 760 sq m), housing more than 16 000 office workers. In spite of its vast size, only a modest number of design drawings were done. The building was designed to have maximum repetition of elements and building methods and this was a major factor in successfully achieving the required cost and speed of construction.

Description

From street level up to level 50, the building is made up of nine 75ft (22.86m) square area modules which combine to form a larger square with sides having an overall dimension of 225ft (68.58m). Below, occupying a larger plan area than the office tower, are three basement floors formed inside 2ft 6in (750mm) thick concrete slurry (diaphragm) walls in a nearly square shape; these walls support the basement floors and are braced by them. At level 50 the building is stepped back, two of the corner area modules being 'dropped off'. The other two corner area modules are 'dropped off' at level 66, leaving five area modules in a cruciform plan shape, and another three area modules at level 90, leaving only two going to the full height. The arrangement allows variations in plan area while not significantly effecting the structural action, each area module being enclosed by a 'framed tube' of steelwork. The complete building is said to have a 'bundled tube' structural system. The framed tube of each modular area consists of deep built-up columns at 15ft (4.57m) centres welded to deep built-up beams at the floor to floor distances, typically 12ft 10in (3.91m). Typical column and beam depths were 3ft 3in (1.00m) and 3ft 6in (1.06m) respectively. Major columns, those on grid line intersections, have flanges varying in area from 24 x $\frac{3}{4}$ in (600 x 19 mm) at the top to 24 x 4 in (600 x 100 mm) in the box sections at the bottom; other columns, the minor columns, are generally smaller; beam flanges vary from 10 x 1 in (250 x 25 mm) to

View of Tower from SW (photo by Ezra Stoller © ESTO).

SEARS TOWER (1974)

Description:
109-storey office tower with bundled tubes of steel construction
Architects and structural engineers:
Skidmore, Owings and Merrill

Axonometric view from NW:

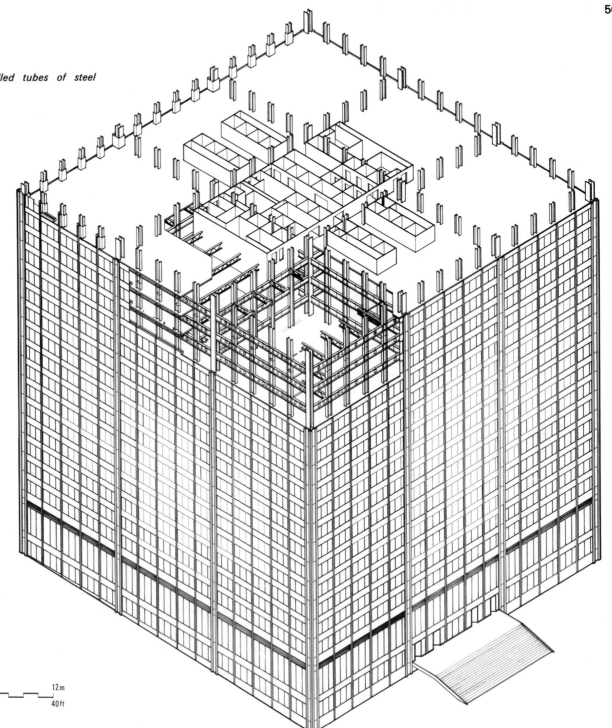

Scale:
12 m
40 ft

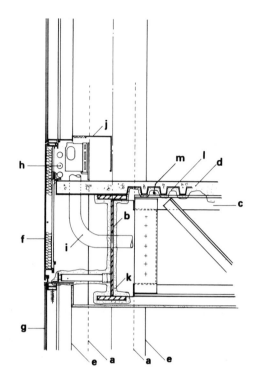

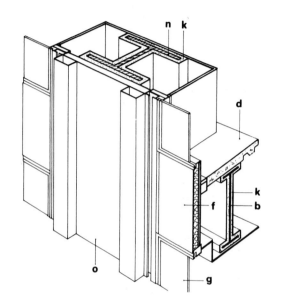

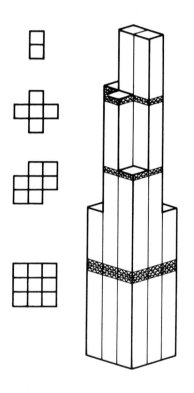

a edge of minor column typically 3'–3" deep; **b** built-up beam typically 3'–6" deep; **c** 3'–4" deep truss; **d** 5½" concrete slab with 3" metal deck; **e** column casing; **f** aluminium cover with rigid insulation; **g** bronze-tinted glazing; **h** water supply and return to induction unit; **i** air supply to induction unit; **j** induction unit; **k** 3 hr fireproofing; **l** 2 hr fireproofing; **m** electric, telephone and telecommunication cables.

Vertical section through wall.

n major column; **o** 4'–7" wide aluminium column cover.

View on major column.

Typical floor plans at lower, sky lobby, intermediate and upper levels.

16 x 2¾ in (400 x 69 mm). Two adjacent framed tubes share one set of beams and columns.

Two-level high belt trusses are provided on grid lines below levels 66 and 90, which are set-back levels; four-level belt trusses are provided below level 33 and at the very top of the building. There are plant rooms (mechanical rooms) in all these positions so that the diagonal members of the trusses do not interfere with the movements of the office users. The trusses serve to spread out the concentrations of gravity force that occur in members at set-backs, to reduce the dishing effect due to differential column shortening under the wind and gravity loads and to increase the overall lateral stiffness of the building by some 15%. The floor in each modular area consists of 3ft 4in (1.02m) deep trusses at 15ft (4.57m) centres, spanning between the beams on the grid lines, with a composite cellular metal deck and lightweight concrete floor supported on the trusses. The floor is made composite with the truss by shear studs. Every six floors the span direction of the trusses is altered by 90 degrees to equalize loading on the columns. Circular holes in the beams and the spaces between diagonals in the trusses allow room for mechanical services. Cabling passes underneath the metal deck. Each column on the grid lines is supported by a caisson of about 7 to 10 ft (2.13 to 3.05 m) in diameter and 120ft (36.58m) length cored into rock. The tops of the caisson are tied together by a 5ft (1.52m) deep concrete mat which also serves to transfer a design horizontal wind force of 4500 tons (4080 tonnes) to a substratum of clay with a cohesive capacity of 500 lb per sq ft (2441 kg per sq m). For vertical transportation the building is divided into three zones, each 30 to 40 storeys high, separated by sky lobbies. Double deck elevators serve these lobby floors from which 'local' elevators depart, stopping at each floor in the zone. Two express elevators, with travel speeds of 30 ft per second (9.14m/s) serve the top of the building. The steelwork structure is clad with a black aluminium skin and has bronze-tinted glass.

Structural Action

Under wind loads, the structure works in a similar manner to a tube without openings cantilevering from ground level. The bundled tube system provides two internal 'web' frames in each grid direction, in addition to those on the outside. The effect is to reduce 'shear lag' on the 'flange' frames, that is there is a more uniform distribution of axial load among those columns on lines perpendicular to the wind force. An even distribution indicates good cantilever efficiency. The bundled tube system makes good use of the internal columns to increase the building's stiffness. The wind sway is about 0.3 in (7.5mm) per storey, the design wind pressure being 65 lb per sq ft (317 kg per sq m) at the top. The fundamental natural period was calculated to be 7.6 seconds. The exterior columns were clad with 4in (100mm) of insulation and had gravity circulation of inside air around them in order that at a design temperature of -20°F (-29°C) outside, the column was within 7°F (3.8°C) of the inside temperature of 75° F (24°C).

Construction

The steelwork was brought on to site as shop-welded 'tree' sub-assemblies consisting of a two-storey column and half-length beams on either side. The 'trees' weigh 15 tons (13.84 tonnes) and are bolted together at beam mid-points, these connections being designed for shear only. The column connections above and below are welded and are mid-height between the floors. A quarter

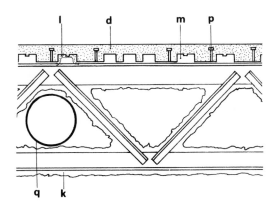

p shear studs; **q** 1'–9" duct.
Vertical section through floor structure.

of these column splice welds were tested ultrasonically. All on-site full penetration welds between beams and columns, where lamellar tearing can occur, were also tested. Almost all the welding necessary was done at the fabrication plant and these welds were extensively tested too. Structural steel was erected by four stiffleg derricks, and one guy derrick above level 90. The derricks were lifted, after each four storeys were erected, by electric winches on cathead beams supported on the steel just erected. The steelwork was erected in a 15 month period. The total period of construction was 44 months.

Conclusion

The bundled tube system is applicable to very high buildings which can be split into tubes. The tubes may have different areas or shapes in plan. Of the completely regular ways of subdividing a plan shape into identical area modules, apart from the square, only hexagonal and triangular modules are possible. The concept has given good economy here, the total weight of steel used being 76 000 tons (70 148 tonnes), averaging out at 33 lb per sq ft (161 kg per sq m).

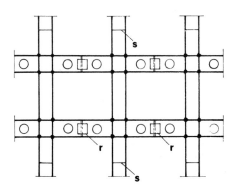

r 15' between bolted beam connections; **s** 25'–8" between column site welded joints.
Typical prefabricated beam-column 'tree' subassembly.

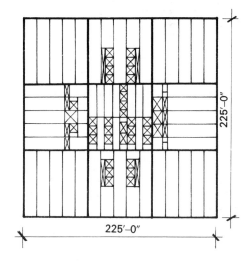

Typical floor framing plan.

The Hongkong and Shanghai Banking Corporation Headquarters, Hong Kong

Introduction

The cost of any product reflects the costs of the men, machines and materials involved but buildings, not generally being made in series, have costs that particularly depend on the first two factors so that their costs broadly correlate with the number of operations necessary on the basic materials and the number of these operations that are different. This logic usually leads to simple shaped buildings, flat facades and undifferentiated spaces, leaving the designer to concentrate on the regular pattern of elements, detailing and swift execution. This 45-storey office tower was conceived with a generous limit on its costs but an emphasis on design standards which is unique in a building at this scale. The two most costly parts of the building, the structure and the cladding, have their form determined by, and completely linked in with the overall concept rather than by their intrinsic minimum costs. The building that results has many qualities: flexible internal planning but with a variety of light, open spaces, including a spectacular atrium space at street level; good, and sometimes dramatic, use of natural light; a successful expression of the titanic scale of its structure giving relief to the elevations and an exciting clash of scales inside. The superstructure is largely factory-built, with many large items having alarmingly strict tolerances, and contains many still novel features. An idea of the complexity, and cost, of the project is given by the numbers of drawings issued: more than 50 000 drawings were necessary for this building to be completed. These included those from design consultants as well as subcontractors, of which there are more than 80 with some 12 principal subcontractors. However, in spite of its complexity and novelty, the building was designed and built, with backbreaking effort and an unrelenting insistence on quality, in a period of six years.

Description

The building has four basement levels and 43 storeys above ground to the top of the highest steel masts, with a helipad structure rising above this, giving the building an overall height of 179m. Going up the building, there is a slow gradation in

View of building from N   (photo by Foster Associates).

the type of space provided from a public plaza at ground floor level to a banking hall at level 3, reached by long escalators from the plaza, to local offices, to executive offices, to headquarter offices and finally to the board rooms and chairman's apartment at the top. Generally, access is by high-speed lifts to one of five double-storey height spaces from where escalators serve each floor in the zone above. The lift cars are translucent and some run within transparent shafts. The main feature at the plaza level is a central atrium space twelve storeys high, lit by glass windows at either end and also by a curved reflector at the top which passes light down the centre of the atrium from another reflector on the outside of the building,

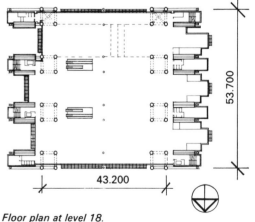

Floor plan at level 18.

THE HONGKONG BANK HEADQUARTERS (1975)

Description:
44-storey office tower of steel frame construction with aluminium and glass curtain wall cladding
Architects:
Foster Associates
Structural engineers:
Ove Arup and Partners
Services engineers:
J. Roger Preston and Partners
Steelwork contractor:
BSC/Dorman Long
Cladding contractor:
Cupples Products

Axonometric view of first 12 levels from NE:

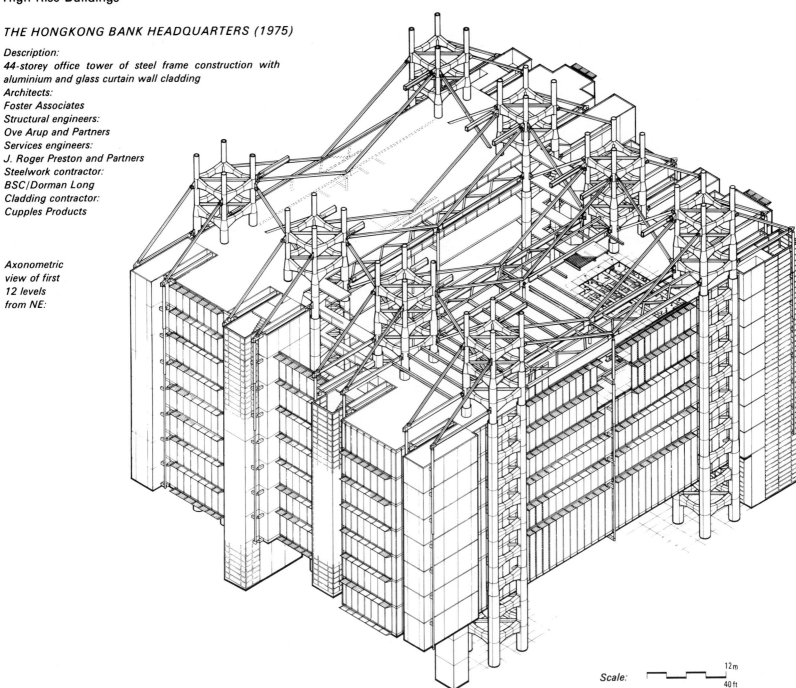

Scale:

12 m
40 ft

Close-up on E side showing four principal types of cladding (photo by Foster Associates).

which tracks the movement of the sun. The plaza is separated from the banking hall above by two layers of glazing supported by steel ropes within a catenary-shaped box section across the width of the atrium. An important planning concept is that there be a maximum of clear space in the centre of the floor areas, the services, plant, lifts and stairways, being pulled to the east and west sides. The structure consists of only eight masts, some of which are visible on elevation. The masts consist of four round vertical tubes with horizontal bow-tie-shaped box sections and plan crossbracing connecting them together at the storey-height intervals of 3.90m. Each mast acts like a vierendeel truss. There are four lines of masts running in the east-west direction, the two masts on each line

supporting, at intervals in the building's height, a pair of double-storey height suspension trusses which span 33.60m between the masts and cantilever 10.80m beyond them. In the three bay areas between the outer column lines, the floors terminate at levels 30, 37 and 43 in the south, north and central bays respectively. There are suspension trusses at all these three levels, as well as further down at levels 11 and 20. The trusses effectively divide the building over its height into five independent structures.

The floors in each of these five horizontal zones are supported by vertical hangers attached to the suspension trusses above. All the trusses have a similar form except that the trusses on the exposed north and south faces do not have the top boom in

the central span that is included in the others. At the suspension truss levels, the masts are also connected in the north-south direction, at each side of the building by cross-bracing two-storeys high running on the inner line of the masts tubes only. Three-storey high cross-bracing, in the same plan position, is provided across the two central columns of the atrium between levels 5 and 8 and is of a spectacular size. The floor structure consists of 900mm deep plate girder primary beams in the east-west direction running along the mast tube lines, supported between the masts and the hangers. These support secondary beams at 2.40m centres which support 54mm deep metal decks with 100mm of concrete topping. Each mast is taken down to the lowest basement level where it is supported, vertically, by four 3m diameter caissons taken to rock, one under each leg. Horizontal support is provided principally by the basement floor structure one level below ground. The masts, suspension trusses, hangers and any other exposed or important elements are given corrosion protection by a 12mm thick sprayed cement barrier coat containing a polymer additive and 5% by weight of stainless steel fibres. It is designed to provide the impermeability of a traditional 50mm covering of dense concrete. All the main elements of steelwork are given two hours' fire protection by a 30mm blanket of ceramic fibre which is applied over the cement barrier coat and protected, during construction, by a silver foil. Fire proofing to the primary and secondary floor beams is by board boxed round the rolled sections with fibre spray to the underside of the floor metal deck.

The external skin of the building consists of aluminium cladding and mainly glass curtain walls and is unusually complex. All visible structural elements are clad. In addition, although all eight masts continue at least to level 30, the full floor area, as noted, is progressively reduced, going upwards from level 13, and the step-backs create a large number of different panel and joint types. Some 2000 working drawings of the cladding and curtain walling and more than 50 000 parts drawings were required to define the cladding scheme. There are four main types of cladding. The first type, for office areas, is a glass curtain wall, seen particularly on the north and south elevations. It comprises extruded aluminium

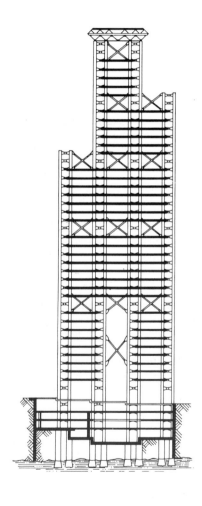

N-S section through building (drawn by engineer).

View of atrium from level 6 looking E (photo by Foster Associates).

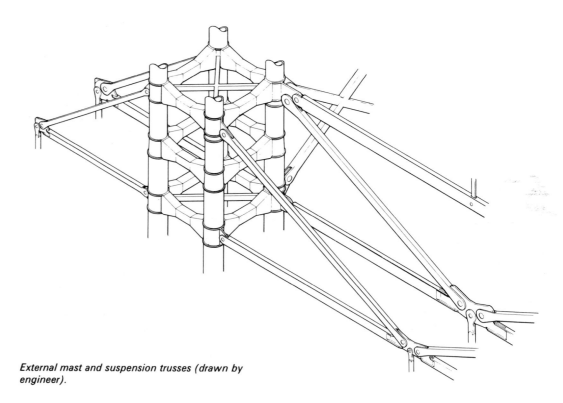

External mast and suspension trusses (drawn by engineer).

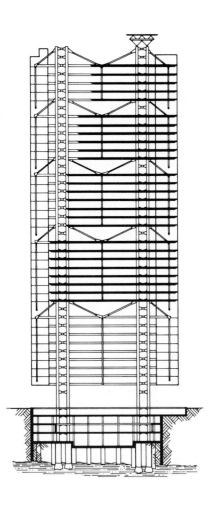

E-W section through building (drawn by engineer).

mullions at 1.20m centres with cill rails at storey heights into which are fixed 12mm thick toughened (tempered) clear glass sheets. A steel T-section anchor, attached to the floor through vertically slotted holes and to an aluminium bracket with horizontally slotted holes, allows the aluminium bracket, which supports the cill and mullions to be precisely positioned. The glazing therefore only needs to allow for small tolerances. Extruded aluminium sunscreen blades fixed back to the mullions are provided at each level to prevent direct solar gain.

An inner wall of lightly tinted glass is provided inside the external glazing with reflective perforated venetian blinds between. This lowers the cooling load to acceptable levels although, thermally, the tinted glass is best in the external layer. A horizontal joint at each storey allows for floor deflections and thermal movements. The second type of cladding consists of glass panels in a metal grid cladding the stairs on the east and west sides. The panel size is 2.40m wide by a storey height consisting of four panes of 12mm toughened (tempered) glass attached to the aluminium subframe by a structural silicone sealant. Adjacent panels interlock at the subframe. The third type consists of laminated panels of the same size, for the service modules and 'risers' on the east and west sides. The panel is 25mm thick and consists of aluminium face sheets between which is an aluminium honeycomb. The panel is glued and riveted to an aluminium sub-frame which interlocks with adjacent panels. The fourth type consists of the curved and flat sheet metal panels which clad the structure; they are 6mm thick aluminium sheets plug welded to extruded aluminium edge sections which form the pressure-equalized joints. The cladding is bolted through an L-shaped aluminium anchor to a stainless steel channel section that is attached to the structural members by threaded stainless steel studs welded to the structure. There is a separating layer between the carbon steel structure and the stainless steel channel to prevent bimetallic corrosion. The aluminium anchor has slotted holes and serrated edges allowing positional adjustments in all three directions and wedge shims also allow the anchor to be slightly rotated.

To speed up the fit-out time and to ensure good quality, service modules containing toilets and mechanical plant were prefabricated under factory conditions. They are independent structural units supported by hangers and the floor structure. There are 139 of these modules, being 9.60 or 12.00m long by 3.60m wide by 3.90m high, with a typical weight of 30 tonnes and a maximum weight of 55 tonnes. Also on the east and west sides are 160 stair assemblies made off-site complete with landing and stair flights. The service modules and stair assemblies are positioned between the two supporting primary beams which cantilever beyond each mast and stack to form complete towers. The service modules occupy the two central positions on the west side and the two extremities on the east side, the stair assemblies occupying the other four positions. The 'risers', clusters of finished vertical piping, are installed beside the stairs and modules. There is a raised floor with a 600mm deep void for the horizontal distribution of flattened ducts to distribute CAV and VAV primary air as well as cabling and sprinkler pipework. Floor mounted outlets supply conditioned air, while sealing between the floor panels is sufficiently good for the void to be used for most, about 80%, of the return air. The remaining 20% is extracted through the ceiling lighting fixtures. The main air-conditioning system is a constant temperature VAV system which supplies an upward-moving curtain of air near the windows as well as conditioned air for the main parts. The climate is hot and humid with temperatures up to 30°C in summer, imposing heavy air-conditioning loads. Two air-conditioning plants are installed at each typical floor level. Heavy plant is located in the basement, the chiller units being cooled by sea water. A

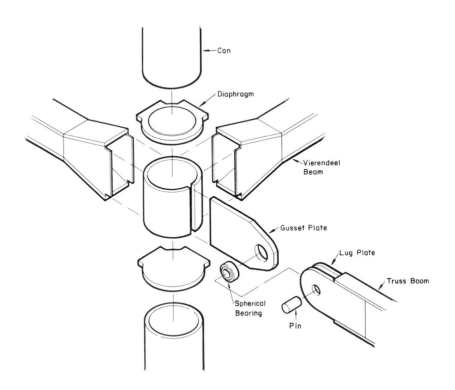

Constituent parts of joint between mast and bottom boom of truss (drawn by engineer).

ceiling is suspended from dovetail slots in the floor metal deck and is taken round the floor beams, thus showing the grid pattern of the floor beams. Fluorescent light panels and adjustable tungsten-halogen light fittings are set within this grid.

Structural Action

Gravity loads are taken from the floor structure directly to the masts or indirectly via the vertical hangers and double-storey height suspension trusses. Loads on the central span of the suspension trusses, as they are not balanced by loads on the cantilevers, cause bending in the masts in a similar manner to loading on a portal frame. Under horizontal load from either the north-south or east-west directions, the building deflects in a similar manner to a five-storey portal frame, the horizontal element of the portal being provided by the suspension trusses and by the cross-bracing at right angles. Floor slabs act as diaphragms. Horizontal deflections are due principally to the forces in the masts which, although stocky, are framed rather than trussed elements and relatively flexible. Dynamic analysis indicated the lateral deflections to be coupled with torsional movements, because of the increasing distance between the centre of mass and the shear centre at the top of the building where there are 'set-backs'. The fundamental natural period is 4.4 seconds, with movement in the east-west direction; the second and third modes have greater torsional coupling, with a more tightly curved movement, mostly in the north-south direction, and periods of 3.7 and 3.1 seconds. The total weight of steelwork used amounts to 27 500 tonnes, averaging 280 kg per sq m of floor area, allowed for at installation is +50mm to −10mm. The interlocking extrusions form pressure-equalized joints and have weepholes to the outside. The cladding was designed for a wind pressure or suction, of 4.8 kilonewtons per sq m.

Construction

The particular features in the construction of this building are the high degree of prefabrication of elements, in the interests of speed, and the large number of purpose-made pieces of equipment, many being developed after the start of construction. The largest contract was for the structural steelwork, there being some 4000 fabrication drawings. The most important steel elements are the masts, over half the total weight of steel being in these units, and the double-storey height suspension trusses. The trusses are made of built-up box sections, the diagonal elements being about 600mm deep and the booms about 900mm deep. All connections made on site between the masts and the truss or the north-south cross-bracing were made by passing pins through two wing plates at the ends of the members and through a central gusset plate projecting from the mast in the thickness of which is a large spherical bearing. This detail makes insertion of the pin easier and reduces the amount of bolting. Similar details are used at the centre and ends of the truss. The wing and gusset plates have thicknesses of up to 175mm at lower levels and the bearings have diameters of between 150 and 600 mm. More minor connections, for example between primary floor beams and the hangers, consist of machined pins passing through 1.5mm oversize holes in the wing and gusset plates. The pins have diameters of between 110mm and 150mm and are held in position by side plates. The tubular legs of the masts vary progressively in diameter from 1400mm, with wall thicknesses of 90 or 100 mm, at the bottom to 800mm with thicknesses of 40mm at the top. The masts are brought on to site as corner subassemblies two or three storeys high, four such units being placed in sequence and then welded together at the beam midpoints and to the mast below.

Hangers were temporarily converted to struts to support the trusses above while they were being built. Six self-climbing luffing jib cranes were installed on the mast structures, most cranes

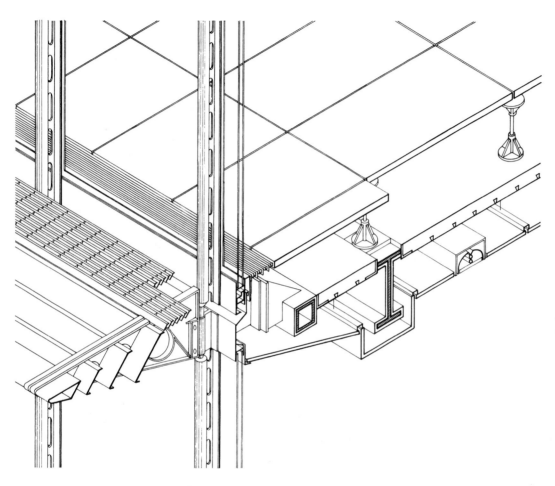

View on a glass curtain wall from above floor.

indicating the relative inefficiency of such a portal frame structure for a high-rise building. Among other items, detail analysis was done of the twisting of the masts and high local loading on mast connections. The maximum design load through the bearing of a pin connection was taken by 380mm diameter bearings in the suspension arm and amounted to almost 2000 tonnes. Horizontal sway of the building, as well as thermal movements and column shortening, cause vertical

and racking movements to occur between the interlocking extrusions or slip systems around the edges of all the cladding and curtain wall units. A typical horizontal joint between the panels at each floor level allows movement of ±30mm. At suspension truss levels the joint allows for movement between any of the five structural 'zones', a large part of which is closing of the joint due to erection of steelwork following the installation of the cladding; the joint movement

View of building from NE (photo by Foster Associates).

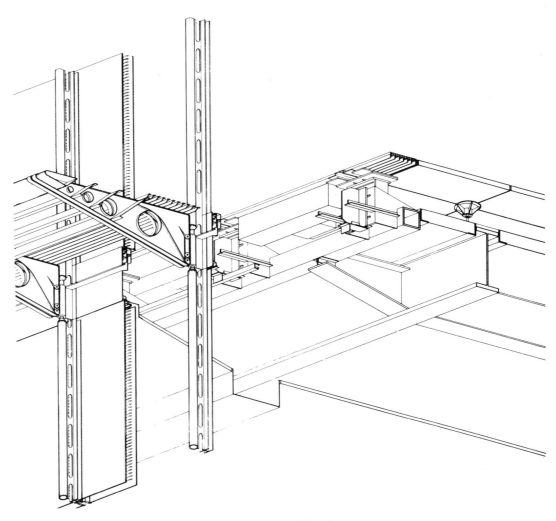

View on a glass curtain wall from below floor (drawn by architect).

having a capacity of 50 tonnes at 13m radius. The tolerances specified for the fabrication and erection of steelwork were extremely exacting. Mast sub-assemblies were machined to within 0.5mm of the specified length, and beam ends were within 2mm of the true plan positions after welding had been completed in the shop. Observance of specified tolerances on site had to take account of deflections subsequent to the erection of the elements. Concrete floors levels were placed within a tolerance of +10mm and and −25mm elements being positioned to take account of the calculated floor deflections, larger movements, column shortening and 'play' in connections. The welding of thick plates brings an increased risk of cracking along the fusion line.

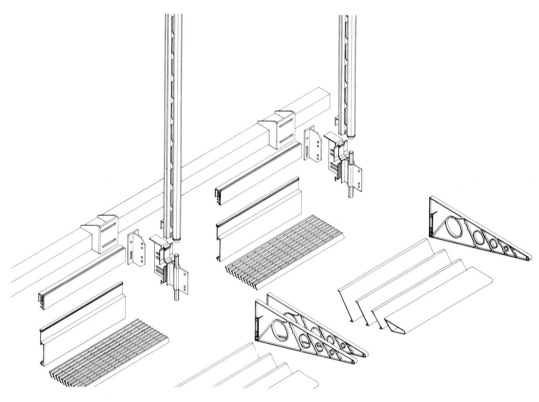

Metal parts of glass curtain wall (drawn by architect).

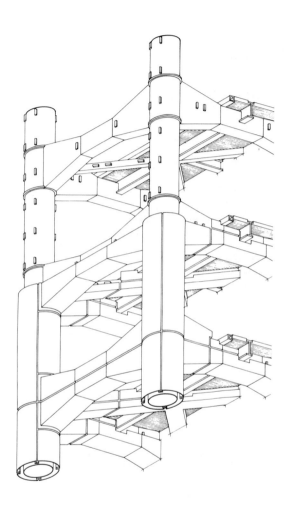

Axonometric of mast with anchor slots for attachment of rounded and flat sheet metal cladding panels, showing joint lines.

The welding procedures and chemical composition of the steels required strict selection and control. A programme of weld testing was put into effect. Steelwork erection took place over a period of 17 months, fabrication having started nearly 12 months previously. Erection of steelwork took place simultaneously with construction of the basement from the top down, a slurry perimeter wall having first been taken down to rock. The total period of construction was 48 months.

Conclusion

This building has been a pace-setter both in terms of the design standards set and achieved and the development of a large number of items and sub-assemblies, specifically for this building, in an impressively short time. Most items need to be made to a tough specification; the long-term performance of cladding and joints, for example, being of crucial importance, and in the case of the cladding, being to some extent unknown. Fundamental design concepts have been adhered to in spite of some, mainly moderate, losses in technical performance, for example the heat transfer across large areas of glazing. Extremely good use has been made of the available plan area, the usable floor space amounting to 73% of the gross area. As far as possible, walls, partitions and other obstructions have been eliminated or reduced in size. There are excellent provision for natural light, good views with interesting interconnections and variations of space. Except at suspension truss levels, the building structure provides minimal interference but is everywhere apparent. The structure frames the spaces with further divisions given by secondary elements

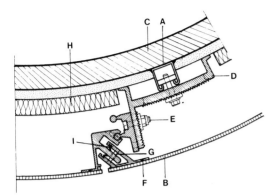

A fixing channel welded to structure; B 4.5mm aluminium cladding panel; C steel structure; D aluminium anchor; E ⅜" bolt with serrated washer and lock washer; F plug weld; G stainless steel pin; H insulation on corrosion protection layer; I neoprene gasket.

Typical horizontal section at joint for curved sheet metal panel cladding to masts.

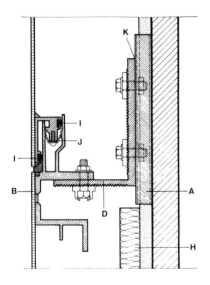

J stainless steel spring clip; K wedge shim inserted behind anchor to correct for out of plumb.

Typical vertical section at joint for flat sheet metal cladding to mast and suspension truss.

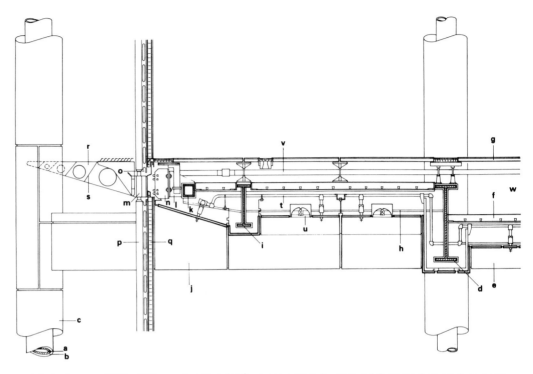

a tubular hangers (250 - 400 mm diameter); b 12mm cement barrier coat; c 4.5mm thick aluminium cladding panel; d 900mm deep primary beam; e 410 x 180 mm I-section secondary beam; f 100mm concrete floor slab with 54mm metal deck; g 1200 x 1200 mm floor panel with aluminium honeycomb and face panels; h 356 x 171 mm I-section beam supporting slab; i 500mm outer trim beam; j 360mm deep beams between hangers; k 150mm square tube edging; l steel bracket with horizontal slots welded to tube; m aluminium anchor with horizontal slots retaining stainless steel centre tube of mullion; n steel T-section anchor with vertical slots; o horizontal joint with interlocking extrusions; p extruded aluminium mullion; q double glazing with 9mm thick clear outer glass and 5mm thick green-grey inner glass and blinds; r cast aluminium bracket; s aluminium blades; t sprinklers; u fluorescent light panel; v air-conditioning duct to perimeter; w 600mm void for services.

Typical vertical section through walls on N and S sides near hangers.

such as the aluminium sunscreens, floor panels, light reflectors and air supply and power outlets in the raised floor system, all items worth further study. A notable aspect of the design is the simple repetition of the internal arrangement on the outside, a device which gives the building a certain integrity. Although clad, the building structure is strongly projected on elevation; analogies have been drawn with building kits and mechanical objects. The building creates a suavely futuristic, but altogether likeable, version of the working place, which is delicately scaled, and, if this symbolises anything, it is a technology which is cleaner, more refined and better adapted to use than anything seen previously. But beyond echoing the appearance of machinery in its composition, the building's aspect also reveals an interest for buildings seen in cross-section where, somewhat like a doll's house when opened up, it may be imagined that all activities are revealed, not only the workings of lifts, structure or plant but teeming, random human activity too.

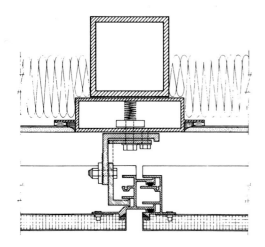

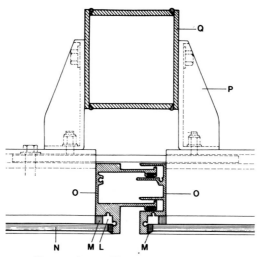

Vertical section at joint between laminated aluminium panels.

L silicon gasket; M silicon bonding strip; N 9.5mm toughened (tempered) glass; O aluminium rail; P cast aluminium anchor; Q 120 x 120 mm steel tube.

Horizontal section through glass grid panel joint.

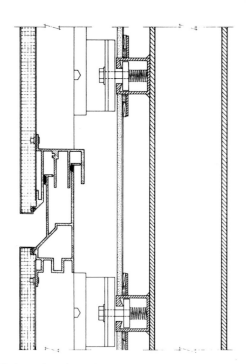

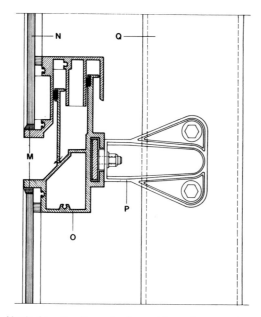

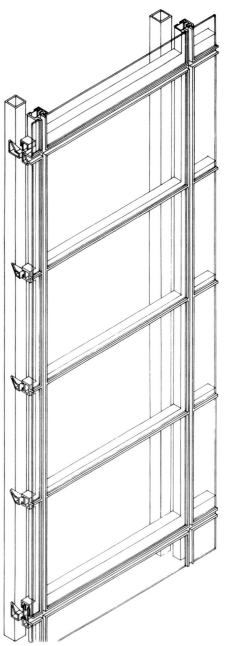

Horizontal section at joint between laminated aluminium panels.

Vertical section through glass grid panel near mullion, showing structural silicon sealants.

Axonometric on 2.40m wide by 3.85m deep unit panel of glass grid wall, showing vertical and horizontal joints.

Appendix

Metric and Imperial Units

Table A1   SI Metric System and Conversion Factors

Quantity	Metric Unit	Abbreviation	Conversion Factors (Imperial to Metric Units or other Imperial Units)			
Length	kilometre	km	1 mile	= 1.609 km	inch (in)	= 25.40 mm
	metre [1]	m	1 yard	= 0.9144m		
	millimetre	mm	1 foot (ft)	= 0.3048 m		
Area	square kilometre	km^2	1 sq mile	= 2.590 km^2	1 sq yd	= 0.836 m^2
	hectare (= 10 000 m^2)	ha		= 259 ha	1 sq ft	= 0.0929 m^2
	square metre	m^2	1 acre	= 0.405 ha	1 sq in	= 645.16 mm^2
	square millimetre	mm^2		= 4047 m^2		
Volume	cubic metre (= 1000 litres)	m^3	1 cu yd	= 0.765 m^3	1 cu in	= 16 390 mm^3
	cubic millimetre	mm^3	1 cu ft	= 0.0283 m^3		= 16.39 ml (millilitres)
Capacity	litre	l (L)	1 UK gallon	= 4.546 L	1 pt	= 0.568 L
			1 US gallon	= 3.785L	1 ft oz	= 28.413 ml
Mass	kilogramme	kg	1 UK ton	= 2240 lb	1 US ton	= 2000 lb
	tonne (= 1000 kg)	t		= 1.016 t		= 0.907 t
	gramme	g (gm)	1 lb	= 0.454 kg	1 oz	= 28.35 g
Time	hours	h (hr)	1 hr	= 60 mins		
	seconds	s		= 3600s		
Density	kilogramme per cu m	kg/m^3	1 lb/ft^3	= 16.018 kg/m^3	ρ_w (water)	= 62.42 lb/ft^3
				= 0.1571 kN/m^3		= 999.84 kg/m^3
			1 lb/yd^3	= 0.593 kg/m^2		($\approx$ 10 kN/m^3)
Mass per unit length	kilogramme per metre	kg/m	1 lb/ft	= 1.488 kg/m	1 oz/in	= 1.116 kg.m
Mass per unit area	kilogramme per sq m	kg/m^2	1 lb/ft^2	= 4.882 kg/m^2	1 oz/ft^2	= 0.305 kg/m^2
Velocity	metre per second	m/s	1 mph	= 1.609 km/hr		
				= 0.447 m/s		
Acceleration	metre per s per s	m/s^2	g (gravity)	$\approx$ 32.2 ft/s^2		
				$\approx$ 9.81 m/s^2		
Frequency	cycles per second	Hz	1 cycle/s	= 1 Hz		
Force	newton	N	1 oz(f)	= 0.278 N	1 US ton(f)	= 8.896 kN
	kilonewton (= 1000 N)	kN	1 lb(f)	= 4.448 N	1 lb(f)/ft	= 14.59 N/m
			1 kip(f)	= 4.448 kN	1 ton(f)/ft	= 32.69 kN/m
			1 UK ton(f)	= 9.964 kN	1 kip(f)/ft	= 14.59 kN/m

Table A1 continued   SI Metric System and Conversion Factors

Quantity	Metric Unit	Abbreviation	Conversion Factors (Imperial to Metric Units or other Imperial Units)			
Pressure/ Stress	newtons per sq m (pascals) newtons per sq mm millibar (= 100 Pa)	N/m^2 (Pa) N/mm^2 (MPa) mb	1 ton(f)/ft^2 1 ton(f)/in^2 1 lb(f)/ft^2 1 lb(f)/in^2 (psi)	= 107 kN/m^2 = 15.44 N/mm^2 = 0.04788 kN/m^2 = 0.006895 N/mm^2	1 ksi(= 1000 psi) 1 atmosphere 1 oz/yd^2	= 6.895 N/mm^2 = 14.696 psi = 101.325 kPa = 0.3325 N/m^2
Bending moment/ Torsional moment	kilonewton metre	kN m	1 inch kip(f) 1 ft kip(f)	= 0.113 kN m = 1.356 kN m	1 ft ton(f) (US)	= 3.037 kN m
Section modulus	millimetre^3	mm^3	1 in^3	= 16 390 mm^3	1 in	= 16.39 cm^3
Second moment of area	millimetre^4	mm^4	1 in^4	= 416 200 mm^4	1 in^4	= 41.62 cm^4
Modulus of elasticity	gigapascals (= 10^9Pa) kilonewtons per sq mm	GPa kN/mm^2	1 ksi 1 ksi	= 6.895 x 10^{-3}GPa = 6.895 N/mm^2		
Toughness	joules per sq m	J/m^2	1 lb(f) in/in^2	= 0.175 kJ/m^2		
Fracture toughness	meganewton metre$^{-\frac{3}{2}}$	MN/m$^{\frac{3}{2}}$	1 ksi $\sqrt{\text{in}}$	= 1.10 MN/m$^{\frac{3}{2}}$ = 1.10 MPa m$^{\frac{1}{2}}$		
Temperature	degree Kelvin degree Celsius (= $^\circ$K$-$273)	$^\circ$K $^\circ$C	$^\circ$C	= 5($^\circ$F$-$32)/9	$^\circ$F	= $^\circ$R$-$460
Work/ Energy/ Heat	joule (=1 N m) kilowatt hour (= 3.6MJ)	J kW hr (kWh)	1 ft lb(f) 1 btu	= 1.356 J = 1.054 kJ	1 therm 1 kilocalorie [3]	= 106 MJ = 4.184 kJ
Power	watt (= 1 joule/second)	W	1 btu/hr 1 hp	= 0.293 W = 2545 btu/hr = 0.746 kW	1 ton of refrigeration	= 12 000 btu/hr = 3.516 kW
Thermal conductivity	watts per m deg C	W/ m $^\circ$C (W/ m K)	1 btu in/ hr ft^2 $^\circ$F = 0.1441 W/ m $^\circ$ C			
Thermal transmittance/ Thermal admittance	watts per sq m deg C	W/ m^2 $^\circ$C (W/m^2 K)	1 btu/ hr ft^2 $^\circ$F	= 5.674 W/ m^2 $^\circ$C		
Thermal diffusivity	sq metres per s (= 10^6 mm^2/s)	m^2/s	1 ft^2/hr	= 25.8 x 10^{-6} mm^2/s		
Thermal absorption	watts^2 sec per m^4 $^\circ$C^2	W^2 s/ m^4 $^\circ$C^2	1 btu^2/ hr ft^4 $^\circ$F^2	= 115 920 W^2 s/ m^4 $^\circ$C^2		
Thermal capacity/ Entropy	kilojoules per kg deg C	kJ/ kg $^\circ$C (J/ gm $^\circ$F)	1 btu/ lb $^\circ$F	= 4.184 kJ/ kg $^\circ$C		

Table A1 continued — SI Metric System and Conversion Factors

Quantity	Metric Unit	Abbreviation	Conversion Factors (Imperial to Metric Units or other Imperial Units)			
Enthalpy/ Internal energy	kilojoules per kg	kJ/kg (J/gm)	1 btu/lb	= 2.324 kJ/kg		
Vapour permeance	grammes per newton second	gm/ N s	1 perm	= $2.02 \times 10^-$ lb/hr lb(f) = 5.71×10^{-8} gm/ N s		
Vapour permeability	gm mm per newton second	gm mm/ N s	1 perm in	= 145×10^{-8} gm mm/ N s		
Moisture content	grammes per kilogramme	gm/kg (g/kg)	1 lb	= 7000 grains	1 grain/lb	= 0.1429 gm/kg
Illuminance	lumens per sq m(= lux)	lux (lx)	1 lumen/ft²	= 1 ft candle	1 ft candle	= 10.764 lux
Luminance	lumens per sq m (=apostilb) candelas per sq m (= π apostilbs)	asb cd/m²	1 footlambert (fL)	= 1 lumen/ft² = 10.764 asb	1 cd/ft²	= 10.764 cd/m²
Sound absorption	square metres times α	m²	α ft²	= 0.0929α m²	α	= absorption coefficient

Notes:

1. Multiples and sub-multiples of units used in the metric system are given below. Choice of the multiple or sub-multiple will depend on convention; there is generally a factor of 10^3 between each entry in this list:

Factor		Name	Symbol
one million million	10^{12}	tera	T
one thousand million	10^9	giga	G
one million	10^6	mega	M
one thousand	10^3	kilo	K
unity	10^0		
one tenth	10^{-1}	deci	d
one thousandth	10^{-3}	milli	m
one millionth	10^{-6}	micro	μ
one thousand millionth	10^{-9}	nano	n
one million millionth	10^{-12}	pico	p

e.g. 1 km, 1 mm, 1 μm, 1 nm (= 1 angstrom unit)

2. The weight of an object is the force the object exerts on its support when at rest in a gravitational field; the weight is equal to the mass of the object in pounds (lb) or kilogrammes (kg) multiplied by the acceleration due to gravity at the place considered. The acceleration due to gravity is approximately 9.80665 m/s² on the earth's surface so that one kilogramme weighs 1 kgf $=9.80665$ kg m/s² $=9.80665$ N (1 newton = 1 kg m/s²)
In imperial or old metric systems, the weight of a pound or kilogramme in a gravity field is known as the pound-force (lbf) or the kilogramme-force (kgf), although the word 'force' (f) is often omitted, especially in units derived from force units.

3. Thermal conversion factors are based on the thermochemical definitions of 1 btu = 1054.350 J and 1 kcal = 4184 J.

References

References

Figures given are reference numbers

Chapter 2

1. AISC 1980 *Manual of steel construction: eighth edition.* American Institute of Steel Construction

2. Haussler R W 1962 *Roof deflections caused by rainwater pools.* Civil Engineering (USA) October 1962

3. Macleod I A 1970 *Shear wall frame interaction* Portland Cement Association

4. Cheong-Siat-Moy F 1974 *Control of deflections in unbraced steel frames* Proc. part 2: December 1974. Institution of Civil Engineers (UK)

5. Rush R 1980 *Structure and circumstance* Progressive Architecture december 1980. Reinhold Publishing

Chapter 3

1. Billington N S 1967 *Building Physics: heat.* Pergamon Press

2. Reid D A G 1973 *Construction principles: function.* George Godwin, London

3. Milbank N O, Harrington-Lynn J 1974 *Thermal response and the admittance procedure* Building Research Establishment CP 61/74. HMSO

4. Building Research Establishment 1986 *Digest 310 Estimating daylight in buildings: part 2.* HMSO

5. CIBS 1984 *Code for interior lighting.* Chartered Institution of Building Services, London

6. Building Research Establishment 1976 *Digest 143 Sound insulation: basic principles.* HMSO

7. TRADA 1983 *Timber frame separating walls* Section 1 sheet 19. Timber Research and Development Association

Chapter 4

1 AISI 1979 *Fire-safe structural steel: a design guide* American Iron and Steel Institute

2 Butcher E G, Parnell A C 1983 *Designing for fire safety.* John Wiley

3 Hinkley P L 1971 *Some notes on the control of smoke in enclosed shopping centres. Fire Research Note 875* Fire Research Station (UK)

4 Butcher E G 1975 *Plastics and fire: an increasing risk.* Fire Engineers Journal (UK) **35**, 1975

5 Building Research Establishment 1985 *Digest 300 Toxic effects of fires.* HMSO

Chapter 5

1 Keldy Castle Forest Cabins: *Building* (UK) 14 September 1979

2 IBM Exhibition Pavilion: *Architectural Review* November 1984; *Architects' Journal* 24 October 1984

3 South Poplar Health Centre: *Building* (UK) 10 April 1981; *Architects' Journal* 18 February 1981

4 Schulitz House: *Progressive Architecture* October 1977; *Bauen + Wohnen* February 1978; *Deutsche Bauzeitung* November 1976

5 Marin Tennis Club: *Architectural Record* February 1977

6 Dune Houses: *AIA Journal* April 1978; *Architectural Record* mid-August 1977

7 Beach Bathhouse: *Concrete International* April 1979

Chapter 6

1 TRADA Offices: *Architects' Journal* 10 November 1976

2 Chloride Technical Offices and Workshop: *Acier Stahl Steel* 1-1980

3 Havas Conseil Offices: *Acier Stahl Steel* November 1973

4 Slough Estates House: *L'Industria Italiana del Cemento* April 1979; *Building* (UK) 23 July 1976

5 Mercartile Bank Tower, Kansas City: *USS Building Report* August 1976; *Civil Engineering* (US) January 1976

6 Federal Reserve Bank: *Acier Stahl Steel* June 1973; *Architectural Record* November 1973; *Bauen + Wohnen* April 1975

7 Gateway House: *Architects' Journal* 24 August 1977

8 Centraal Beheer Offices: *Domus 522* 5-1973; *Architects' Journal* 29 October 1979; *Werk* 1-1976; *Designers' Journal* October 1985

9 One Finsbury Avenue: *Architectural Review* May 1985; *Architects' Journal* 24 and 31 August 1983; *BSC Framed in Steel* 14 September 1984

Chapter 7

1 South Holland Centre: *Brick Bulletin* (UK) March 1975; *Concrete* February 1975

2 St Antony's College: *Architectural Review* February 1971; *Asian Architect and Builder* August and September 1978

3 Guilford County Courthouse: *Concrete International* January 1979; *L'Industria Italiana del Cemento* November 1978

4 Design Research Building: *Architectural Record* May 1970; *Contract* July 1970

5 Centre Georges Pompidou: *Acier Stahl Steel* September 1975; *Constrado/BFS/OTUA Steel and Form* 1980; *Centre Pompidou* Proc. part1: November 1979. Institution of Civil Engineers (UK)

6 Boston City Hall: *Architectural Record* February 1969; *Architectural Forum* January/February 1969

Chapter 8

1 Boulton House: *Concrete Quarterly* (UK) July/September 1975; *Architectural Review* August 1969

2 Harewood Hotel: *Brick Bulletin* (UK) January 1974

3 Hyatt Regency Hotel: *USS Building Report* September 1977; *Building Design and Construction* December 1978

4 William Stone Building: *Architectural Review* September 1965

5 Spelman Halls: *A + U 61* 1-1976

Chapter 9

1 Yale Center for British Art: *The Architecture of the Yale Center for British Art* J D Prown Yale Univ. 1977; *Architectural Record* mid-August 1974; *AIA Journal* mid-May 1978

2 Biochemical Sciences Laboratory: *Architectural Record* March 1980

3 Wellesley College Science Center: *Architectural Review* September 1977; *Progressive Architecture* March 1978

4 Sainsbury Centre: *Architectural Review* December 1978

5 Woodhull Medical and Mental Health Center: *Contract* February 1978; *Architectural Record* November 1975

6 Nucleus Hospital: *Building* (UK) 9 July 1982; *Architects' Journal* 21 September 1983

Chapter 10

1 Penguin Books Warehouse: *Architects' Journal* 20 November 1968

2   Anacostia Park Pavilion: *Architectural Design Cost and Data* (US) June/July 1978

3   St Mary's Athletic Facility: *Detail* 4-1979; *Progressive Architecture* July 1978

4   Sports Hall for School of Gymnastics: *Bauen in Stahl 25* SZS 1976; *Bauen + Wohnen* April 1977

5   Eisstadion: *Acier Stahl Steel* November 1974; *Der Bauingenieur 49* 1974

6   Crosby Kemper Arena: *Architectural Record* March 1976; *Detail SS9* 1979; *ENR* 16 August 1979, 13 March 1980

Chapter 11

1   Liverpool Garden Festival Theatre *Architects' Journal* 25 July 1984

2   La Lumiere Gymnasium: *Architectural Record* July 1979

3   Wayland School Field House: *Architectural Forum* November 1960

4   Oasis Swimming Pool: *Proc. 2nd Int. Conf. on Space Strutures Univ. of Surrey* 1975

5   Florida Festival: *Architectural Record* May 1980

6   Baxter Laboratories Dining Hall: *IABSE Structures C 23/82* November 1982

7   Bundesgartenschau Lattice Shell: *Insititute for Lightweight Structure IL 13* August 1978

8   Fleetguard Factory: *Architectural Review* February 1982; *Structural Engineer* (UK) September 1984

9   Leavey Activities Center: *Progressive Architecture* May 1976; *Acier Stahl Steel* September 1977

10   Oakland Almeda County Coliseum: *Civil Engineering* (US) January 1967; *ENR* 14 July 1966

11   Calgary Saddledome: *L'Industria Italiana del Cemento* May 1984; *Proc. Canadian Soc. for Civ. Eng. Annual Conf.* May 1985; *ENR* 22 December 1983

Chapter 12

1   Knights of Columbus Building: *Architectural Record* August 1970; *Building Design and Construction* (US) August 1970

2   Xerox Center: *L'Industria Italiana del Cemento* June 1985

3   First International Building: *Acier Stahl Steel* March 1976

4   Texas Commerce Tower: *Concrete International* July 1981; *ENR* 5 March 1981; *Proc. Int. Conf. on Tall Buildings Singapore* October 1984

5   First Wisconsin Center: *IABSE Structures C 23/82* November 1982

6   One Shell Plaza: *Architectural Forum* April 1972

7   *One Mellon Bank Center: USS Building Report* July 1984

8   The Sears Tower: *Architectural Forum* January/Feburary 1974; *Civil Engineering* (US) November 1972; Acier Stahl Steel July/August 1973

9   Hongkong and Shanghai Bank Headquarters: *Architectural Review* April 1986; *Structural Engineer* (UK) September 1985

Bibliography

Bibliography

Chapter 1

Ashby M F, Jones D R H 1980 and 1986 *Engineering Materials 1 and 2.* Pergamon

Herubin C A, Marotta T W 1981 *Basic construction materials* 2nd edition. Reston Publishing

Everett A 1978 *Materials.* B T Batsford

Faupel J H, Fisher F E 1981 *Engineering design: a synthesis of stress analysis and materials engineering* 2nd edition. John Wiley

Chapter 2

Torroja E 1962 *Philosophy of structures* (translation of *Razón y ser de los tipos estructurales*). University of California Press

Lin T Y, Stotesbury S D 1981 *Structural concepts and systems for architects and engineers.* John Wiley

Benjamin B S 1984 *Structures for Architects* 2nd edition. Van Nostrand Reinhold

Gaylord E H, Gaylord C N (eds) 1979 *Structural engineering handbook* 2nd edition. McGraw-Hill

Calladine C R 1983 *Theory of Shell Structures* Cambridge University Press

Schodek D L 1980 *Structures.* Prentice Hall

Chapter 3

Cowan H J, Smith P R 1983 *Environmental systems* Van Nostrand Reinhold

Billington N S 1967 *Building physics: heat.* Pergamon Press

Van Straaten J F 1967 *Thermal performance of buildings.* Elsevier Publishing

Reid D A G 1973 *Construction principles: function.* George Godwin, London

Griffin C W 1982 *Manual of built-up roof systems.* McGraw-Hill

Stevens W R 1969 *Building physics: lighting.* Pergamon Press

Egan M D 1983 *Concepts in architectural lighting.* McGraw-Hill

Lam W M C 1986 *Sunlighting as formgiver for architecture.* Van Nostrand Reinhold

Egan M D 1972 *Concepts in architectural acoustics.* McGraw-Hill

Moore J E 1978 *Design for good acoustics and noise control.* Macmillan

Bovay H E (ed) 1981 *Handbook of mechanical and electrical systems for buildings.* McGraw-Hill

McGuiness W J, Stein B, Reynolds J S 1980 *Mechanical and electrical equipment for buidlings* 6th edition. John Wiley

Chapter 4

Butcher E G, Parnell A C 1983 *Designing for fire safety* John Wiley

Anchor R D, Malhotra H L, Purkiss J A (eds) 1986 *Design of structures against fire.* Elsevier